FIFTY ENGLISH STEEPLES

FIFTY ENGLISH STEEPLES

The Finest Medieval Parish Church Towers and Spires in England

JULIAN FLANNERY

Thames & Hudson

To Julia

Page 2: The tower at Redenhall, Norfolk,
is a masterpiece of flushwork decoration.

Opposite: The spire of St Mary Redcliffe, Bristol
soars above the pinnacles of the north porch.

First published in the United Kingdom in 2016 by
Thames & Hudson Ltd, 181A High Holborn, London WC1V 7QX

Fifty English Steeples © 2016 Julian Flannery
Text, drawings and photographs © 2016 Julian Flannery
Design and layouts © 2016 Thames & Hudson Ltd

Jacket and book design: Peter Dawson, Namkwan Cho, www.gradedesign.com

British Library Cataloguing-in-Publication Data
A catalogue record for this book is available from the British Library

ISBN 978-0-500-34314-2

Printed and bound in China by C & C Offset Printing Co. Ltd

To find out about all our publications, please visit
www.thamesandhudson.com.
There you can subscribe to our e-newsletter, browse or download
our current catalogue, and buy any titles that are in print.

Contents

Introduction 8

1. Earls Barton 52
NORTHAMPTONSHIRE

2. Forncett St Peter 58
NORFOLK

3. Barnack 64
HUNTINGDONSHIRE

4. Castor 70
HUNTINGDONSHIRE

5. North Rauceby 78
LINCOLNSHIRE

6. Witney 84
OXFORDSHIRE

7. West Walton 90
NORFOLK

8. Long Sutton 98
LINCOLNSHIRE

9. Raunds 106
NORTHAMPTONSHIRE

10. St Mary,
Oxford 114
OXFORDSHIRE

11. Adderbury 124
OXFORDSHIRE

12. Grantham 130
LINCOLNSHIRE

13. Newark-on-Trent 142
NOTTINGHAMSHIRE

14. Ketton 152
RUTLAND

15. St Mary,
Stamford 160
LINCOLNSHIRE

16. St Mary Redcliffe 170
BRISTOL

17. Ewerby 182
LINCOLNSHIRE

18. Brant Broughton 192
LINCOLNSHIRE

19. Heckington 198
LINCOLNSHIRE

20. Higham Ferrers 206
NORTHAMPTONSHIRE

21. Patrington 218
YORKSHIRE, EAST RIDING

22. Moulton 228
LINCOLNSHIRE

23. St Cuthbert,
Wells 238
SOMERSET

24. Tickhill 246
YORKSHIRE, WEST RIDING

25. Laughton-en-
le-Morthen 254
YORKSHIRE, WEST RIDING

26. St Michael, Coventry 262
WARWICKSHIRE

27. Fotheringhay 274
NORTHAMPTONSHIRE

28. Salle 286
NORFOLK

29. Stoke-by-Nayland 294
SUFFOLK

30. Southwold 302
SUFFOLK

31. Eye 310
SUFFOLK

32. Redenhall 316
NORFOLK

33. Chipping Campden 322
GLOUCESTERSHIRE

34. Ludlow 330
SHROPSHIRE

35. Kettering 338
NORTHAMPTONSHIRE

36. Whittlesey 344
CAMBRIDGESHIRE

37. Wilby 352
NORTHAMPTONSHIRE

38. Lowick 358
NORTHAMPTONSHIRE

39. Titchmarsh 364
NORTHAMPTONSHIRE

40. Evercreech 370
SOMERSET

41. Leigh-on-Mendip 378
SOMERSET

42. Kingston St Mary 386
SOMERSET

43. St Mary Magdalene, Taunton 392
SOMERSET

44. North Petherton 402
SOMERSET

45. Lavenham 412
SUFFOLK

46. Dedham 420
ESSEX

47. Ingatestone 428
ESSEX

48. St Nicholas, Newcastle-upon-Tyne...... 434
NORTHUMBERLAND

49. Boston 444
LINCOLNSHIRE

50. Louth 458
LINCOLNSHIRE

Supplementary 472
Information

APPENDIX 1 479
The Contract for Fotheringhay Church

APPENDIX 2 481
The First Churchwardens' Book of Louth, 1500–24

APPENDIX 3 485
The Distribution of Spires and Lanterns

Glossary 486

Bibliography 489

Index 492

Acknowledgments 496

Introduction

Unsurpassed in height and faultless in execution, Louth is the apotheosis of English steeple-building.

Five hundred years ago, on 13 September 1515, the weathercock was raised over the spire of St James's Church in LOUTH. The churchwardens' accounts record a day of singing, celebration and feasting to mark the completion of fifteen long years of toil and expense. In retrospect this event takes on a poignant significance, for it marks an important watershed in English cultural achievement. LOUTH, the tallest and most perfect of all parish spires, represents the culmination of five centuries of development in the art of steeple-building. It also stands perilously close to the end of medieval civilization and the Age of the Mason.

England was never more beautiful than in the two brief decades between the completion of LOUTH and the arrival of the English Reformation. The pre-industrial landscape was dominated by the steeples of 17 cathedrals, 900 monasteries and 9,000 churches. The spire of Lincoln Cathedral was the highest man-made structure the world had ever seen, and the construction of the great chapels at Westminster, Windsor and Cambridge had reached its magnificent conclusion. Within a generation the monasteries had been dissolved, church-building had ceased, Lincoln spire had fallen, and medieval England had passed into history. Five hundred years or more after their creation, across all but the densest of urban settlements church steeples remain the most visible manifestation of the medieval world.

In architecture the Middle Ages can be characterized as the Age of the Mason, for the architect was a master mason, a trained craftsman with an extraordinary ability to unlock the latent potential of stone through the application of pure geometry and a chisel. His *modus operandi* was, therefore, fundamentally different from that of the self-conscious gentleman architect of the seventeenth century or the academically trained professional of the modern age. The intimate connection between man and material is one of the distinguishing features of medieval architecture, and at its best it leads to an architecture of great individuality and great humanity.

Architecture is the art of building, and in the church steeple the artistic impulse is dramatically concentrated, for the brief is simple and the symbolic value is high. So long as the bells were audible across the parish, the Saxon church tower served its purpose, but as a work of architecture it was naive and primitive. This volume traces the development of the church steeple from such humble beginnings to consummate work of art. Fifty steeples measured and drawn by the author are arranged in a loose chronological order to illustrate a journey that extends from the final flowering of Anglo-Saxon culture to the break with Rome in 1534.

First and foremost, this is a book about architecture written by an architect. It does not pretend to be a general history of medieval church architecture, for the reader is already well served by an extensive literature. Francis Bond's *Gothic Architecture in England* (1905) remains the definitive guide to the subject. Unlike most historians, Bond presents architecture not as a closed catalogue of self-contained styles but as a continuing process of transition. This approach is more enlightening, more challenging and more honest than conventional stylistic pigeon-holing, and it is the approach adopted in the current work.

Every major advance in steeple design, such as the invention of the broach spire, occurred independently of changes in tracery design upon which traditional classifications are based. Such classifications provide a useful means of signposting the meandering path of history, but they can also become inflexible compartments that conceal more than they illuminate. Thomas Rickman's division of Gothic architecture into Early English, Decorated and Perpendicular styles is too crude for anything but a cursory study. Here Edmund Sharpe's more useful division into Lancet, Early Geometrical, Late Geometrical and Curvilinear styles of tracery is employed, and a necessary distinction is made between Perpendicular and Tudor architecture.

THE STEEPLES

No apologies are offered for the strong geographical bias of this selection, for most of the country played only a minor role in the evolution of the English steeple. Today transport is cheap and labour is expensive, but in pre-industrial times the situation was reversed. Skilled masons were plentiful, but transporting stone by water, and particularly by land, was costly and hazardous. The best building stones, which combine workability with durability, are to be found along the Great Limestone Belt running diagonally from Somerset through the Cotswolds and the East Midlands to Yorkshire. Three limestone-rich counties dominate the history of the English steeple: Lincolnshire is famous for its spires, Somerset for its towers, and Northamptonshire for its sheer inventiveness.

The great majority of the fifty steeples are of national significance, and without them a study of this nature would be incomplete.

Others are included to illustrate important historical developments or as the representative of an outstanding type. FORNCETT ST PETER is of this second category, being one of the best-preserved of many similar Saxon round towers to be found across East Anglia. By contrast EARLS BARTON is unquestionably the finest work of Anglo-Saxon architecture, and it sets a benchmark for judging all subsequent development. Similarly, despite its modest size, CASTOR is the best Norman tower in the country.

In the early Gothic period WEST WALTON is exceptional not only for its sturdy beauty and its free-standing isolation, but also for its cathedral-like construction. ADDERBURY tower illustrates the emergence of the diagonal buttress in the early fourteenth century, but it is the rapid development of the spire that dominates the story of the English steeple during this period.

Spires are surprisingly rare, appearing on only one out of every fifteen medieval towers. They are, nevertheless, one of the most successful and original achievements of English medieval architecture, and they are represented here in no fewer than half the surveys. LONG SUTTON is the finest medieval timber spire still standing, for this once common form proved extremely susceptible to decay, destruction or replacement. The chronology of stone spires starts at the end of the first quarter of the thirteenth century and divides neatly into three centuries of evolution. Each century is marked by the completion of a great masterwork reaching close to 300 feet in height: GRANTHAM around 1320, ST MICHAEL, COVENTRY a century later, and LOUTH in 1515.

These are all recessed spires, but the first century of development was dominated by the oversailing form of stone spire. WITNEY is the finest achievement of the short-lived Oxfordshire school of pinnacled broach spires, while modest NORTH RAUCEBY represents the first generation of pure broach spires in the East Midlands. BARNACK is a highly idiosyncratic early design combining octagonal upper tower and spire for the first time. The technical

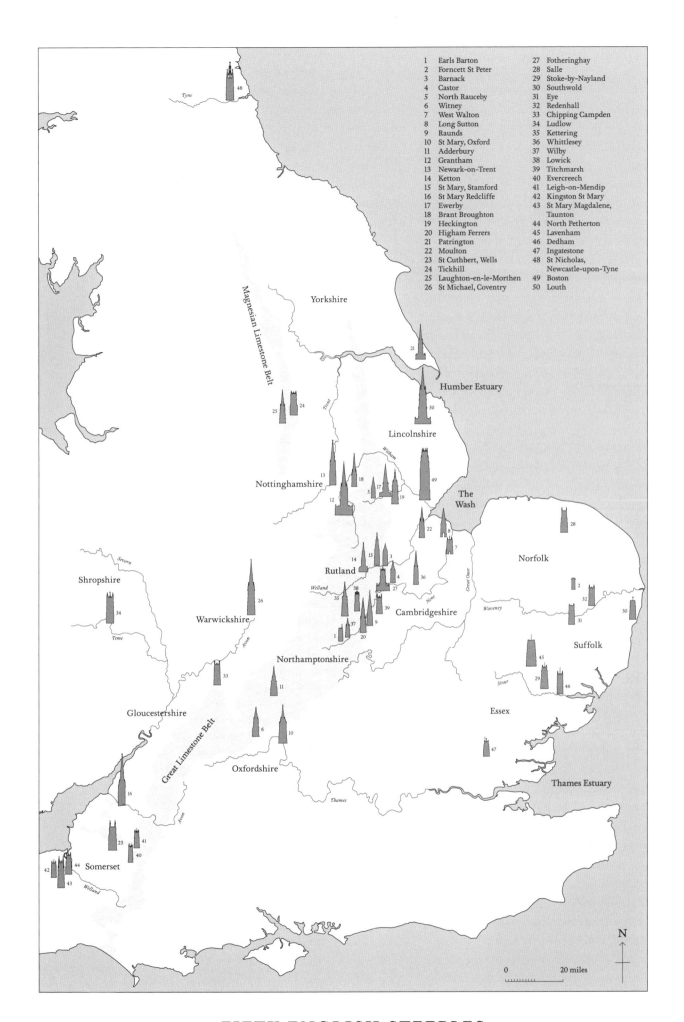

1	Earls Barton	27	Fotheringhay
2	Forncett St Peter	28	Salle
3	Barnack	29	Stoke-by-Nayland
4	Castor	30	Southwold
5	North Rauceby	31	Eye
6	Witney	32	Redenhall
7	West Walton	33	Chipping Campden
8	Long Sutton	34	Ludlow
9	Raunds	35	Kettering
10	St Mary, Oxford	36	Whittlesey
11	Adderbury	37	Wilby
12	Grantham	38	Lowick
13	Newark-on-Trent	39	Titchmarsh
14	Ketton	40	Evercreech
15	St Mary, Stamford	41	Leigh-on-Mendip
16	St Mary Redcliffe	42	Kingston St Mary
17	Ewerby	43	St Mary Magdalene, Taunton
18	Brant Broughton	44	North Petherton
19	Heckington	45	Lavenham
20	Higham Ferrers	46	Dedham
21	Patrington	47	Ingatestone
22	Moulton	48	St Nicholas, Newcastle-upon-Tyne
23	St Cuthbert, Wells	49	Boston
24	Tickhill	50	Louth
25	Laughton-en-le-Morthen		
26	St Michael, Coventry		

FIFTY ENGLISH STEEPLES

development of the tall broach spire is complete at RAUNDS as early as 1250. Aesthetic maturity was achieved later in the sumptuous enrichment of KETTON and ST MARY, STAMFORD, and in the sophisticated austerity of EWERBY.

Three early recessed spires are contemporary with GRANTHAM and share the same intensity of expression. ST MARY, OXFORD is on a grand scale and surrounded by the finest cluster of pinnacles in the land, while NEWARK, with its high broaches, has the most romantic of silhouettes. The spire of ST MARY REDCLIFFE owes a good deal to Salisbury Cathedral and the Victorian imagination, but the composition is memorable and the richly decorated tower is magnificent. HECKINGTON is unmatched as an exercise in raw sculptural power, while the closely related tower at BRANT BROUGHTON is transformed by a needle spire into a composition of exquisitely sharp verticality. In Northamptonshire the middle of the fourteenth century is marked by the arrival of perforated flying buttresses around the spire of HIGHAM FERRERS.

The universal adoption of the Perpendicular style in the late fourteenth century led to both improved technical efficiency and a renewed spirit of inventiveness. MOULTON is a highly sophisticated experiment in the control of perspective. The octagonal spire is combined with octagonal arcading at PATRINGTON, an octagonal parapet at LAUGHTON-EN-LE-MORTHEN and an octagonal drum at WILBY. WHITTLESEY is the classic mature Perpendicular spire of the mid-fifteenth century, and at KETTERING a near-identical design is transformed by a theatrical parade of military fortifications. Finally, there is the spectacular flying spire of ST NICHOLAS, NEWCASTLE, an over-ambitious flight of the imagination held together by industrial quantities of post-medieval metalwork.

Returning to the late fourteenth century, ST CUTHBERT, WELLS may be the most influential unspired tower design in English history. This phenomenally powerful composition, from around 1385, rendered the spire obsolete in Somerset and optional across the rest of the country. TICKHILL illustrates the rapid spread of this revolutionary concept and its successful adaptation to awkward circumstances.

Two regions in particular are celebrated for their late medieval towers. Somerset is pre-eminent, with at least fifteen towers of the first rank. ST CUTHBERT, WELLS, LEIGH-ON-MENDIP and NORTH PETHERTON are arguably the three finest church towers in England, while EVERCREECH, KINGSTON ST MARY and ST MARY MAGDALENE, TAUNTON are only slightly inferior. The towers of East Anglia are architecturally less sophisticated and more reliant upon surface patterning and volume, but STOKE-BY-NAYLAND, SALLE, SOUTHWOLD, EYE, REDENHALL, LAVENHAM and DEDHAM are all worthy of their inclusion. INGATESTONE is geographically and physically distinct, for it illustrates the emergence of brick construction as a rival to natural stone at the end of the medieval period.

Gloucestershire rarely matches the brilliance of her southern neighbour, but CHIPPING CAMPDEN is a unique and exceptionally beautiful invention. The tall crossing tower of LUDLOW is equally unusual, with a fortress-like exterior that is intended to impress rather than delight. Northamptonshire continued to the end of the Middle Ages as a centre of innovation and excellence, and TITCHMARSH is the equal of all but the finest Somerset towers. Experimentation with octagonal lanterns at FOTHERINGHAY and LOWICK led to the gargantuan but flawed masterpiece at BOSTON affectionately known as 'the Stump'.

Inevitably this selection reflects the author's preferences, but care has been taken to ensure a balance between different periods and styles. Except in the very earliest works, architectural quality rather than archaeological or historical interest has been the overriding concern. It is, nevertheless, a matter of regret that no space can be found for such exquisite works as Huish Episcopi (Som), Silk Willoughby (Lincs) and Snettisham (Norfolk), to name just a few.

There is no better way to appreciate a church steeple than by climbing to the parapet. At the time of writing the towers of LOUTH, BOSTON,

LUDLOW, ST MARY, OXFORD and ST MICHAEL, COVENTRY can be climbed by visitors on most days of the year, while DEDHAM, LAVENHAM, NEWARK, ST MARY MAGDALENE, TAUNTON and ST NICHOLAS, NEWCASTLE-UPON-TYNE hold occasional tower open days.

THE DRAWINGS

It is surprising to discover that, in the five hundred years since the completion of LOUTH, there has been no systematic survey of the major English steeples. Even the most reputable reference books confidently repeat heights that have no firmer basis than local tradition or an anonymous entry in *Kelly's Directory*. Every steeple in this survey was measured by the author with tape, laser and theodolite, and at least four readings were taken to establish each of the critical vertical dimensions. Written dimensions on the drawings are rounded to the nearest inch, for any greater level of detail suggests a precision that does not exist in the masonry itself.

Historical measured drawings exist for around one-quarter of the surveyed buildings, but in most cases detailed examination revealed some significant errors. It was, therefore, decided at an early stage to disregard existing measured information and consult such drawings only as a record of historical change.

A schedule of measured heights, along with previously published figures for comparison, appears overleaf. Only one previously recorded height was found to be precisely in accordance with the new survey. Unfortunately, Thomas Wallis's theodolite survey of LOUTH (287' 6"), recorded in 1884, has been overlooked in every subsequent publication. The widespread tendency towards exaggeration and guesswork is best illustrated by BRANT BROUGHTON and ST MARY REDCLIFFE, both of which were found to be thirty feet lower than previously claimed. In the case of REDCLIFFE, documentary evidence has been uncovered to explain the origin of this startling anomaly.

Some discrepancies are only to be expected, for the height of a steeple is not a quantity that is fixed in perpetuity. Ground levels may be reduced to improve drainage, as at STOKE-BY-NAYLAND, or to suit the gradient of an adjacent road, as at ST MARY, STAMFORD. Conversely, churchyards tend to rise over the centuries as burials disturb the ground as, for example, at FOTHERINGHAY and TICKHILL. At MOULTON the original bases were submerged when the ground level was raised to reduce the risk of flooding.

At the other extremity, spires and pinnacles have frequently been rebuilt. The vast majority of capstones have been replaced over the centuries, usually in a harder stone, and it is impossible to know how accurately the masons replicated the original design. At BRANT BROUGHTON, for example, it is known that the architect George Bodley added seven feet during the restoration of 1897, but this may have been in an attempt to correct a previous anomaly.

The situation is further complicated by the lack of consistency in measurement, for sometimes weathervanes and flagpoles are included within the previously published heights, and sometimes they are not. The fibreglass flagpole at DEDHAM adds 21' 0" to the true height of the structure, and even a medieval weathervane can be seven or eight feet tall. Such impermanent fixtures are not an integral part of the building fabric, and only the top of the masonry can be considered to be the true summit. This is the only meaningful figure to be used when comparing buildings, and it is the figure that is used consistently throughout this volume. For the day-tripper or the proud parishioner, the height to uppermost piece of metalwork, timber or twenty-first-century fibreglass may be of passing interest, and so both figures are provided on the drawings.

Plans and sections are drawn at a consistent scale of 1:210. Primary elevations have been scaled to suit the space available on the page, and range from 1:150 for the smallest towers to 1:210, 1:240, 1:300 and 1:350 for the tallest spired steeples. Dimensions are in feet and inches, since most steeples were designed and set out using this system of measurement. Historical county names are used throughout.

STEEPLE HEIGHTS

SURVEYED	HEIGHT	PREVIOUSLY PUBLISHED HEIGHTS
Louth†	287' 6"	287' 6" T. Wallis (1884); 294' Kelly; 300' Bond; 295' BoE, Guide
St Michael, Coventry	284' 4"	303' Kelly; 295' BoE
Grantham	274' 0"	280' Kelly (1885); 279' Kelly (1909); 282' BoE; 282' 10" Guide
Boston‡	266' 9"	300' Kelly (1885); 272½' Kelly (1919); 288' Allen; 272' BoE
St Mary Redcliffe	261' 11"	292' Godwin* (Kelly, BoE, Guide)
Newark-on-Trent	231' 11"	252' BoE; 236' Guide
St Nicholas, Newcastle	194' 2"	196' Kelly; 193½' BoE
St Mary, Oxford	191' 4"	188' 6" Ferrier (Case, Bond)**
Kettering	178' 6"	178' 11" VCH; 179' Lee (BoE)
Heckington	176' 2'	175' BF; 185' BoE
Raunds	175' 8"	186' Kelly (Guide); 180' VCH; c. 190' Lee
Patrington	174' 10"	189' Kelly (Guide)
Higham Ferrers	173' 11"	170' Kelly (Guide); 175' Lee
Whittlesey	171' 3"	[not recorded]
St Mary, Stamford	168' 1"	163' Kelly; 162' BoE
Laughton-en-le-Morthen	167' 10"	185' Kelly (Guide)
Ewerby	166' 9"	172' Kelly (BoE, Guide)
Brant Broughton	166' 8"	198' BoE (SL)
St Mary Magdalene, Taunton	157' 9"	163' Kelly; 163' 6" Allen/Brereton (BoE)
Moulton	157' 6"	165' BoE
Ludlow	157' 0"	166' Kelly; 135' Guide
Witney	153' 9"	165' or 157' [not referenced]
St Cuthbert, Wells	150' 6"	142' 7" Allen/Brereton; 122' BoE
Long Sutton	148' 11"	162' BoE
Adderbury	148' 0"	[not recorded]
Ketton	144' 2"	150' Kelly; c. 145' VCH; 148' Guide
Lavenham	137' 8"	141' Kelly(Allen/T. H. Bryant, BoE, Guide)
Salle	130' 5"	111' Guide
Tickhill	127' 6"	124' Allen/Revd H. E. Booty (BoE)
Stoke-by-Nayland	126' 4"	120' Allen/T. H. Bryant (BoE, Guide)
Chipping Campden	119' 4"	over 120' Allen/Dr Cox; 120' Guide
Dedham	117' 7"	131' Kelly; c. 130' Allen/Dr Cox (BoE)
Fotheringhay	115' 8"	103' 4" Allen/Revd C. N. Croyden-Burton
Castor	115' 3"	[not recorded]
Barnack	113' 11"	[not recorded]
North Petherton	111' 5"	108' 8" Allen/Brereton; 109' BoE
North Rauceby	107' 3"	[not recorded]
Eye	107' 3"	101' Kelly (BoE, Guide)
Redenhall	106' 2"	c. 110' Guide
Wilby	104' 8"	[not recorded]
Titchmarsh	102' 8"	99' Allen/Canon A. M. Luckock
Southwold	96' 2"	100' Kelly (Allen/T. H. Bryant, BoE, Guide)
Lowick	95' 10"	95' 3" Allen/D. H. McMorran

STEEPLE HEIGHTS *cont.*

SURVEYED	HEIGHT	PREVIOUSLY PUBLISHED HEIGHTS
Evercreech	93' 10"	92' 7" Allen/Brereton
Leigh-on-Mendip	93' 8"	91' 6" Allen/Brereton (BoE)
West Walton	90' 3"	[not recorded]
Kingston St Mary	88' 6"	90' Kelly; 85' 8" Allen/Brereton
Ingatestone	82' 9"	[not recorded]
Earls Barton	68' 7"	68' 8" VCH
Forncett St Peter	60' 10"	[not recorded]

NOTES

†   Only two medieval cathedral spires are recorded as being higher than Louth: Salisbury 404' and Norwich 320' (JH). The spires of Chichester (rebuilt) and Lichfield are around 277' and 258' respectively (JH).

‡   The tower of Boston may just be surpassed by the central tower of Lincoln at 271' (JH).

*   Survey by George Godwin, in Revd J. P. Norris, 'Notes on the Church of St. Mary Redcliffe'.

**   Survey by Captain R. E. Ferrier, 1875, noted by Thomas Case, repeated by T. G. Jackson and Francis Bond.

SOURCES FOR PREVIOUSLY PUBLISHED HEIGHTS

The earliest known sources are listed, with later repetitions shown in parentheses.

Allen	Frank J. Allen, *The Great Church Towers of England* (1932); other sources quoted by Allen are noted.
BF	Sir Banister Fletcher, *A History of Architecture on the Comparative Method*, 17th edn (1961)
BoE	Sir Nikolaus Pevsner et al., *The Buildings of England* (1951–74)
Bond	Francis Bond, *Gothic Architecture in England* (1905)
Guide	church guidebook
JH	John Harvey, various publications
Kelly	*Kelly's Directory* (1881–1919), editions as noted
Lee	L. G. H. Lee, *The Church Spires of Northamptonshire* (1946)
SL	Statutory Listing: Historic England, *The National Heritage List for England* (c. 1947–70)
VCH	Victoria County History

Church towers have their earliest origins in Italy. Spreading gradually across north-west Europe, they reached France some time before the year 600, but in England they appear only during the late Anglo-Saxon period. The hundred or so Saxon towers that still remain are but a tiny fraction of those that once existed, for in 1086 the Domesday Book recorded over 1,400 churches in just nine English counties.

Prior to the Norman invasion there was considerable variety of tower form, function and location. Of the surviving Saxon towers, twenty-one are round west towers, sixty-two are square west towers, and the remainder are predominantly square towers placed centrally over the body of the church. Two of the most famous constructions of the period, EARLS BARTON and Barton-on-Humber (Lincs), were built as turriform or tower churches, in which the lowest level of the tower formed the body of the church. Ranging from thirty-five to seventy feet in height, the uppermost storey of these early towers was always designed for the ringing of bells. Speculation that the structures were intended as watchtowers and places of refuge has no basis in fact, for they all post-date the end of the Viking raids.

In Normandy the cruciform church with a central crossing tower had become the standard type well before 1066, and it was introduced to England with great enthusiasm. The central tower is eminently suited to the cruciform plan, for the walls of the tower provide a flat abutment to terminate the roofs of the nave, chancel and transepts, which may be of different heights and pitches and constructed at different times. Moreover, the tower walls could be perforated by high level windows to form a lantern to illuminate the central crossing of the church. Unfortunately, this fine feature rarely remains intact, for it was frequently rendered invisible by the addition of later medieval vaults and ceilings.

The external composition of the Norman great churches was significantly enhanced by the central tower, which provided a welcome vertical counterpoint to the relentless horizontality of the main volumes. This contrasts with the high and compact French cathedral, which required no emphatic external gesture to mark the focal point of the plan. It was principally for their effectiveness in unifying large, sprawling compositions that central towers were accepted and retained in English cathedrals long after they were rejected in the more compact parish church.

The main objection to the central tower is that four massive supporting piers are required, which dominate the centre of the church interior, restricting both movement and views. In the parish church there was the equally pressing problem of arranging access to the ringing chamber. The cathedral was extensive enough to allow the bells to be hung in a separate belfry, as at Salisbury and Chichester, or in one of the western towers, as at Lincoln. Alternatively, a passage might be devised to reach the central tower through the tribune or up a spiral staircase concealed within a crossing pier, as at LUDLOW. For most parish churches, however, such extravagant solutions were impractical.

That few Norman central towers remain is due not only to their inconvenience, but also to their poor quality, for Norman construction was notoriously unreliable. The fine ashlar face of the thick walls, piers and arches concealed a mass of loose, uncoursed rubble and mortar. If the mortar was poor, then the core might crumble and settle, concentrating all the load of the wall on the thin outer skins. Winchester Cathedral was the most prominent of many towers that fell for precisely this reason. Some were demolished in anticipation of their collapse, while others were simply encased, propped and sandwiched by later construction, as, for example, at Canterbury Cathedral. CASTOR is the finest Norman central tower remaining over an English parish church. When a later tower is centrally located, at KETTON and PATRINGTON (p. 17 (a)), for example, its position is invariably inherited from an earlier Norman cruciform plan.

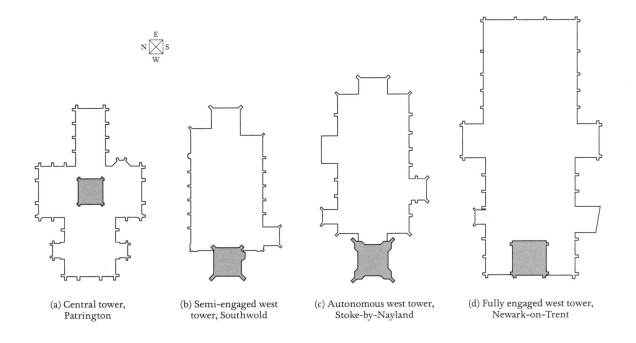

N
E ⊠ S
W

(a) Central tower,
Patrington

(b) Semi-engaged west
tower, Southwold

(c) Autonomous west tower,
Stoke-by-Nayland

(d) Fully engaged west tower,
Newark-on-Trent

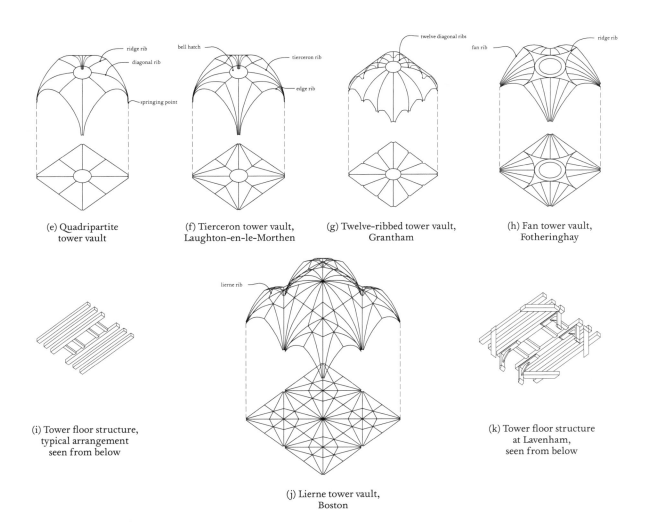

ridge rib
diagonal rib
springing point

(e) Quadripartite
tower vault

bell hatch
tierceron rib
edge rib

(f) Tierceron tower vault,
Laughton-en-le-Morthen

twelve diagonal ribs

(g) Twelve-ribbed tower vault,
Grantham

fan rib
ridge rib

(h) Fan tower vault,
Fotheringhay

(i) Tower floor structure,
typical arrangement
seen from below

lierne rib

(j) Lierne tower vault,
Boston

(k) Tower floor structure
at Lavenham,
seen from below

TOWER LOCATION AND FORMS OF VAULTING

THE WEST TOWER

Despite their preference for centrally positioned towers, the Normans continued to follow Saxon precedent on many smaller parish churches and to build western towers. As the Norman Romanesque transformed into the first flowering of Gothic architecture, the parish tower moved decisively to the western position, where it mostly remained. In the Fens, where ground conditions were invariably suspect, free-standing belfries were built to reduce the potential impact of a tower collapse on the body of the church. The towers of WEST WALTON, LONG SUTTON, Terrington St Clement (Norfolk), and Fleet and Whaplode (Lincs) were originally detached, while those of Donington (Lincs) and Wisbech (Cambs) were set adjacent to the aisles and used as porches. On good ground, however, the western bell tower had become the dominant form before the end of the twelfth century.

The ideal tower plan was compact and symmetrical in the two cardinal directions. In areas of good stone, this led to the near-universal adoption of the square plan. In areas of flint, such as East Anglia, the round tower prevailed until transport links were sufficiently good for rectangular stone quoins to be imported from outside the region. After the Norman period the circular form was decisively rejected, no doubt because of its association with inferior building materials. A third alternative, investigated in a fascinating series of interrelated projects such as Ely Cathedral, Coxwold and Sancton in Yorkshire, and FOTHERINGHAY and LOWICK in Northamptonshire, was the octagon.

The rectangular tower appears only when forced by circumstances, most commonly when nave and transepts of unequal widths meet at a crossing, at Melton Mowbray (Leics) and Bath Abbey (Som), for example. The only triangular tower in England is to be found at Maldon (Essex), a peculiar response to an awkward site.

Autonomous west towers standing forward of the body of the church, such as STOKE-BY-NAYLAND (p. 17 (c)), are rare in medieval times. Far more common is the semi-engaged tower, in which the eastern buttresses of the tower merge with the western elevation of the church, as at SOUTHWOLD (p. 17 (b)). A more problematic, though on occasion highly successful, arrangement is the fully engaged tower, in which the aisles are extended to embrace the two side elevations of the tower. Such an arrangement is rarely encountered south of Lincolnshire. TICKHILL is the first significant example. It directly inspired NEWARK (p. 17 (d)) and GRANTHAM, and indirectly EWERBY, LAUGHTON-EN-LE-MORTHEN, NEWCASTLE and LOUTH. The engaged west tower shares some of the characteristics of the central tower, with massive arches carrying the weight of the tower to huge free-standing piers, opening vistas across the church and bringing the presence of the tower dramatically into the interior. For this arrangement to succeed externally, the western elevation of aisles and tower must form one seamless composition, as they do at EWERBY but not, unfortunately, at NEWARK.

In the western tower the desire for complete symmetry in the two cardinal directions had to be modified, at least in the lower stages. The introduction of the stone staircase and the proximity of the church on one side of the base led to a more sophisticated aesthetic in which studied asymmetry and the concentration of detail on the west façade became accepted principles. The lowest stage of the tower remained symmetrical only around the east–west axis of the ceremonial route passing from the west door through the tower arch and up the nave to the high altar. The contrast between the strong directionality at the base and the self-contained symmetry of the upper tower was found to be highly desirable, and was the model for most English steeples.

Symmetry can be severely compromised on north and south side elevations even in work of the highest quality. Buttresses do not necessarily sit directly on the corner of the tower, and the implied centre of the composition may therefore not be the true geometrical centre. Disturbing asymmetries deriving from this problem are illustrated on the south elevations of BRANT BROUGHTON and BOSTON.

VERTICAL ORGANIZATION OF THE TOWER

All but the most modest towers have at least three principal stages: the ground level, open to the body of the church through a tower arch or arches; the ringing chamber; and the bell chamber. These three stages form the principal articulation of the elevations, for they are delineated externally by horizontal string courses. These may line through with the floors precisely, as at WEST WALTON, but more usually they are adjusted up or down to suit the fenestration or arcading. Taller towers may be subdivided by additional floors, but these serve little purpose other than to accommodate a clock mechanism or provide a baffle chamber to reduce the volume of bells in the ringing chamber below.

Towers were, as a general rule, raised by no more than ten feet per year to allow any settlement of the foundations to take place gradually. Stones would be cut in the masons' workshop during the winter and laid only during the warmer months, with the strings providing convenient breaks between the work of one year and the next. Additional string courses were regularly included at the springing of the west window or the upper windows, but when taken to excess, as at Great Ponton (Lincs), the effect could become decidedly ponderous. Strings either run unbroken around buttresses or they are cut by them. Continuous strings, which emphasize the continuity of form, are standard across all regions. The discontinuous string, seen at MOULTON and LOUTH, is a rare and sophisticated solution that can significantly increase the vertical momentum of the composition.

A typical upper-floor structure in a tower consists of three oak beams, between eight

and twelve inches square, either side of a bell hatch five feet square (p. 17 (i)). To reduce the risk of timber decay, beams are frequently supported on individual corbels projecting from the internal face of the tower wall, as at PATRINGTON, or by a continuous running corbel, as at BRANT BROUGHTON. In East Anglia the thick flint wall construction was stepped internally to provide a continuous ledge for each floor structure. Typically, floors alternate in the direction of span, so that a clock chamber floor spanning from east to west is followed by a bell chamber floor spanning from north to south.

At 23' 2" the bell chamber floor at LAVENHAM (p. 17 (k)) is the widest original floor structure in this survey and incorporates diagonal braces back to vertical wall posts supported by stone corbels. Braced floor beams also appear at FOTHERINGHAY, TICKHILL, PATRINGTON, and ST MARY, STAMFORD. Numerous medieval floor structures have been lost to over-zealous architects in the nineteenth century and campanologists in the twentieth century. Tragically, this vandalism continues today, for hidden tower chambers are an under-appreciated historical asset and do not receive the same level of protection as more visible areas of the fabric.

Continuous running corbels, individual stone corbels and beams spanning empty space may originally have supported floors, or they may have been provided to support lifting beams to assist with construction or the installation of bells. Free-spanning beams found at the base of the spire at WHITTLESEY may have supported lifting machinery similar to the 'Wild Mare' that remains in situ at LOUTH.

Medieval tower galleries, open to the body of the church, are rare outside East Anglia and the West of England. Galleries at DEDHAM, REDENHALL and KINGSTON ST MARY all support monstrous organs that block the tower arch. Even the most successful medieval galleries, such as SALLE, are essentially detrimental to the architecture of the church interior. Although the Georgians derived great pleasure from disfiguring tower

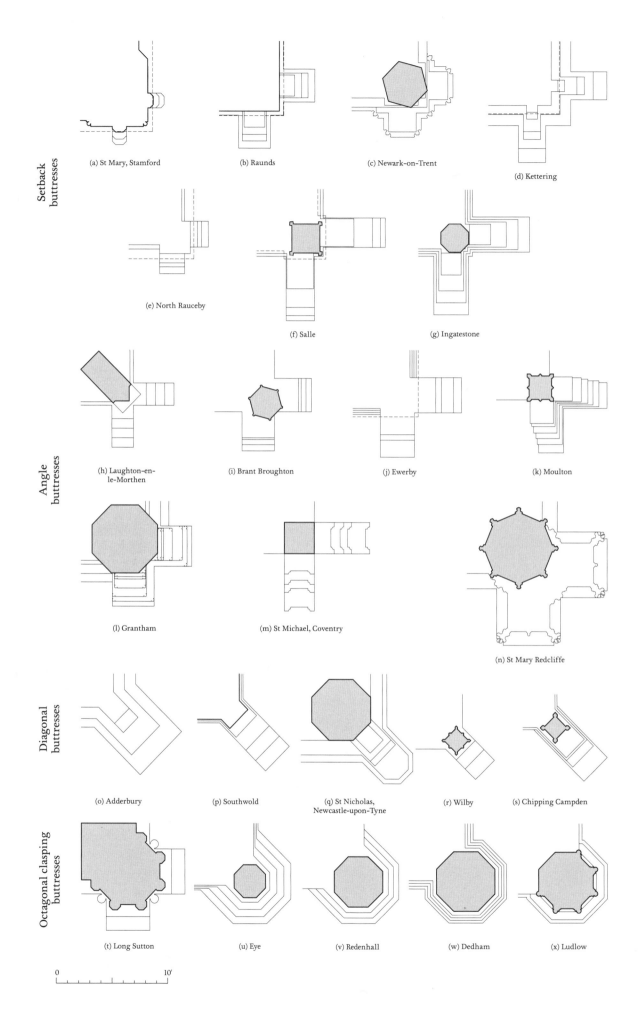

Setback buttresses

(a) St Mary, Stamford   (b) Raunds   (c) Newark-on-Trent

(d) Kettering

(e) North Rauceby   (f) Salle   (g) Ingatestone

Angle buttresses

(h) Laughton-en-le-Morthen   (i) Brant Broughton   (j) Ewerby   (k) Moulton

(l) Grantham   (m) St Michael, Coventry

(n) St Mary Redcliffe

Diagonal buttresses

(o) Adderbury   (p) Southwold   (q) St Nicholas, Newcastle-upon-Tyne   (r) Wilby   (s) Chipping Campden

Octagonal clasping buttresses

(t) Long Sutton   (u) Eye   (v) Redenhall   (w) Dedham   (x) Ludlow

0   10'

PRIMARY FORMS OF TOWER BUTTRESS

interiors with musicians' galleries and organ lofts, most, such as the gallery at TICKHILL, were removed during the Gothic Revival.

TOWER BUTTRESSES: PRIMARY FORMS

Saxon and Norman architecture relied upon the sheer mass of masonry in a wall to maintain its stability. By contrast, the defining feature of Gothic architecture is buttresses construction, which allows the thickness of a wall to be reduced while its strength is increased. It significantly improves the efficiency of the construction and reduces the volume of stone required to enclose a given space.

Buttresses are normally set perpendicular to the plane of the wall that they support, but where two walls meet at a corner a variety of arrangements are possible. This is of particular importance in the design of towers where the four external corners take on enormous prominence. Indeed, in later towers such as KINGSTON ST MARY (p. 22 (nn)) and LEIGH-ON-MENDIP (p. 22 (mm)), the corner becomes the single most important element of the design. Tower buttresses are of five primary types, and these forms may be combined together to create a variety of composite forms.

Setback buttresses (p. 20) are set perpendicular to each other and to the adjacent faces of the tower wall, but they are also set back to expose the corner of the tower. Early setback buttresses, from around 1220, at ST MARY, STAMFORD (a) are too shallow to provide any real structural benefit. The contemporary tower at RAUNDS (b) is more convincing, and the two major aesthetic benefits of buttresses – to frame the elevations and to provide the edge profile of the tower – are immediately apparent. The lower stages of NEWARK (c) illustrate a typical motif of early Gothic towers: setback buttresses with corner shafts used to provide vertical emphasis.

The setback buttress allows the corners of the tower volume to remain visible, so

that at KETTERING (d) the tapering form of the tower is readily appreciated between the attenuated corner buttresses. The early tower at NORTH RAUCEBY (e) is more complex than it at first appears, for the setback buttress projects from a square clasping mass rather than the true corner of the tower; it is therefore an early example of composite form. Inferior flint walling necessitates larger, simpler buttresses, as at SALLE (f), another composite example terminated by a clasping square. At INGATESTONE (g), precisely modulated set-offs derive from the standardized dimensions of bricks.

Angle buttresses (p. 20) are also set in perpendicular pairs, but they tightly abut and conceal the corner. The buttresses at LAUGHTON-EN-LE-MORTHEN (h) and BRANT BROUGHTON (i) meet precisely on the corner of the tower, but this is not always the case. At EWERBY (j), MOULTON (k) and ST MARY REDCLIFFE (n) the buttresses meet beyond the geometrical corner of the plan, whereas at GRANTHAM (l) they meet further in. The buttresses at GRANTHAM and at Oakham (Rutland) are very unsatisfactory, for they have an excessive number of shallow set-offs arranged with no discernable logic. By contrast, the angle buttresses at ST MICHAEL, COVENTRY (m) are a model of clarity. The remarkable angle buttresses at MOULTON may be unique, for they lean in towards the centre of each elevation with a pronounced entasis, which is so unexpected that it remained unnoticed until the current measured survey.

Diagonal buttresses (p. 20) are single buttresses bisecting the external angle between adjacent wall faces. Appearing from the early fourteenth century at ADDERBURY (o) and elsewhere, this structurally efficient form has two significant disadvantages. First, the proportions of the tower are changed for the worse, for the elevation is not tightly confined into a vertical strip but merges with the splayed side faces of the buttresses. Second, without sharp square corners the modelling of the façade by sunlight is too soft. At SOUTHWOLD (p) and other flushwork towers, these limitations are turned to

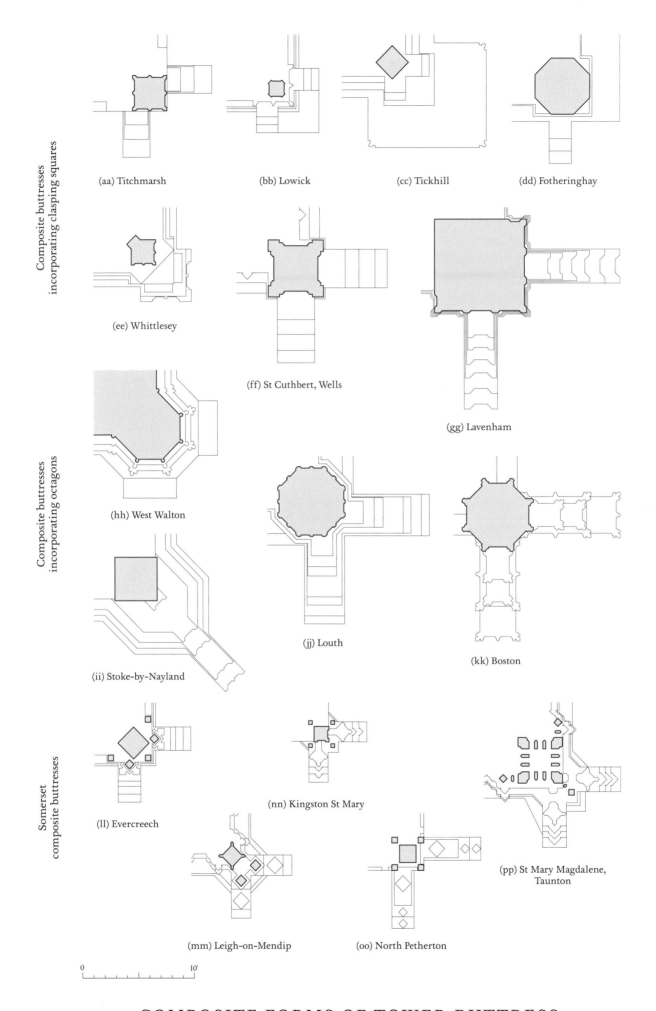

Composite buttresses incorporating clasping squares

(aa) Titchmarsh   (bb) Lowick   (cc) Tickhill   (dd) Fotheringhay

(ee) Whittlesey

(ff) St Cuthbert, Wells

(gg) Lavenham

Composite buttresses incorporating octagons

(hh) West Walton

(jj) Louth

(kk) Boston

(ii) Stoke-by-Nayland

Somerset composite buttresses

(ll) Evercreech

(nn) Kingston St Mary

(mm) Leigh-on-Mendip

(oo) North Petherton

(pp) St Mary Magdalene, Taunton

0   10'

COMPOSITE FORMS OF TOWER BUTTRESS

advantage, for the absence of shadow and the open aspect are ideal for the display of flat surface decoration. Diagonal buttresses can be very successful when used in combination with an octagonal drum, as at WILBY (r), or an octagonal parapet, as at West Retford (Notts). This form prevailed across Gloucestershire, CHIPPING CAMPDEN (s) being a fine example; but for a tower on the scale of NEWCASTLE (q) they are a disappointing choice.

Square clasping buttresses enclose the corner of the square tower in a solid block of masonry with no re-entrant corner. They occur occasionally in most counties outside East Anglia and are a particular feature of late towers in the Stamford region. Usually they form part of a composite buttress, but at Elton (Hunts) and All Saints, Aldwinkle (Northants) they appear in isolation.

Octagonal clasping buttresses (p. 20) follow the same principle but in octagonal form. They briefly flourished in Fenland churches of the mid-thirteenth century, such as the upper stages of LONG SUTTON (t), decorated with octagonal corner shafts. After an absence of two centuries the type reappears in some of the finest flushwork towers of East Anglia, at EYE (u), REDENHALL (v), DEDHAM (w), Bungay and Laxfield (Suffolk). Like the diagonal buttresses at SOUTHWOLD, the soft transitions in vertical plane were ideal for displaying rich surface decoration. Elsewhere, octagonal buttresses appear on the ashlar towers of Thornbury (Glos) and Bath Abbey (Som), Newbury and Reading (Berks), Marlborough and Mere (Wilts), and LUDLOW (x). Usually only five of the eight potential faces of the octagon are visible, but at DEDHAM seven faces are articulated, significantly increasing the visual autonomy and verticality of the buttress.

TOWER BUTTRESSES: COMPOSITE FORMS

The first loose classification of composite buttresses (p. 22) includes forms incorporating a clasping square. ST CUTHBERT, WELLS (ff) demonstrates the combination of setback and clasping square buttresses to perfection. St Martin, Stamford, St John, Stamford (both Lincs) and Easton-on-the Hill (Northants) use clasping buttresses for the lowest stage, with pairs of setback buttresses above. The opposite approach is adopted at TITCHMARSH (aa), where setback buttresses rise to the bell stage of the tower, at which point the centre of the façade drops back to leave clasping buttresses around the corners. At LOWICK (bb), setback buttresses rise from a clasping base, an unusual and very satisfying feature. The colossal early clasping buttresses with angle shafts at TICKHILL (cc) were ingeniously transformed into bases for angle buttresses on the upper stages, but this is essentially two superimposed ideas rather than one composite entity. The same criticism can be levelled at FOTHERINGHAY (dd), but not at WHITTLESEY (ee), where the complexity of form is unmatched outside Somerset. The final word in this line of development is the sumptuous composite buttress with a nine-foot-square clasping core at LAVENHAM (gg).

The second grouping of composite buttress is those incorporating octagonal forms (p. 22). WEST WALTON (hh) shows a tentative exploration of this idea, which was subsequently ignored until the mid-fifteenth century. At Brightlingsea (Essex) and STOKE-BY-NAYLAND (ii), octagonal core and diagonal buttress are combined in designs of exceptional power. At LOUTH (jj) and BOSTON (kk), the full potential of buttressed skeleton construction in tower design was realized for the first time. Both combine massive angle buttresses in the lower stages with octagons above. The primary purpose of these huge buttresses is to resist the outward thrust of giant internal relieving arches that allow the tower walls to be reduced to the slenderest of screens. BOSTON is by far the largest medieval structure within this survey, and yet remarkably, at just 3' 1" wide, its walls are the thinnest.

The third group of composite buttresses, developed in Somerset in the fifteenth and early sixteenth centuries, is characterized by extreme inventiveness and delicacy (p. 22). A profusion of rotated and orthogonal pinnacles rise from setback buttress surrounding a variety of clasping cores at EVERCREECH (ll), LEIGH-ON-MENDIP (mm), KINGSTON ST MARY (nn), NORTH PETHERTON (oo) and ST MARY MAGDALENE, TAUNTON (pp).

Gables had been applied to the buttresses at WEST WALTON and RAUNDS. From around 1320 they were used with great effect around the base of some fine spires across Lincolnshire and at NEWARK, Empingham (Rutland) and WHITTLESEY. Gabled buttresses are also characteristic of the grandest spireless towers of Huntingdonshire and Yorkshire, including TICKHILL.

TOWER PARAPETS

From the start of the medieval period it became accepted practice for the roof of the tower to be enclosed by a parapet, of which there were two principal types: horizontal and crenellated. A plain horizontal parapet has little to recommend it but when pierced by quatrefoils, trefoils or arcading, it can combine simplicity with delicacy. Such is the case in Somerset, where Shepton Mallet and the West Mendip Group favour the quatrefoil motif, while the North Somerset Group prefers the perforated arcade. Outside the West Country, pierced horizontal tower parapets are associated with some outstanding spires: rounded trefoil perforations at Ashbourne (Derbyshire), ADDERBURY and ST MARY, OXFORD, pointed trefoils at Caythorpe and Silk Willoughby (Lincs), and quatrefoils at HIGHAM FERRERS, WILBY, Rushden and Easton Maudit (Northants). The horizontal parapet does not lend itself naturally to subdivision by pinnacles, and where they do appear – centrally at Weare, Blagdon, Lympsham and Wrington, or as a pair at Winscombe (all Somerset) – they lack conviction.

The crenellated parapet, or battlement, is one of the most familiar features of medieval England. These mock fortifications were never intended to have any defensive purpose on churches, and there was no official control on their use. Of the 5,800 licences to crenellate issued before 1622, only 127 were for ecclesiastical purposes, principally for the fortification of abbeys or cathedral precincts.

The battlement was adopted both as a display of prestige and to enliven the silhouette of the wall. On the aisles and nave of the church this became increasingly necessary in the late Middle Ages, when low-pitched lead roofs disappeared out of sight behind parapets. From the fourteenth century crenellations became universal on spireless towers of any importance, and where they are absent, at LAVENHAM, SOUTHWOLD, Ruishton (Somerset), and Trunch and Cawston (Norfolk), the assumption must be that the tower was never completed. Battlements were also added to protect the walls of many earlier towers such as EARLS BARTON and FORNCETT ST PETER.

Battlements are most satisfying when framed between corner pinnacles. A straight battlement running between square pinnacles is common in Northamptonshire and in East Anglia, even in grand towers such as SALLE, DEDHAM, Laxfield (Suffolk) and Blakeney (Norfolk), which rely on fine decoration and simplicity for their effect. In Somerset straight battlements are more usually framed by rotated corner pinnacles, such as at Bruton, Mells and Cranmore. The straight pierced battlement with pinnacles underwent a fascinating process of transformation at the hands of Somerset masons. In the most sophisticated examples, such as Huish Episcopi, parapet and pinnacles become fully integrated into one seamless design.

One further variation on the crenellated parapet is the stepped battlement, constructed in flint at EYE, Great Bromley (Essex) and East Harling (Norfolk), and in brick at INGATESTONE and Freyerning (Essex). This form is strongly suggestive of Flanders and Holland, close trading partners of the wool-producing regions of eastern England at this time. A further elaboration of the stepped battlement is the addition of a centre pinnacle, in flint at REDENHALL, Soham (Cambs) and Garboldisham (Norfolk), or in stone at Wisbech (Cambs).

Parapets in eastern England rarely approach the delicacy and magnificence achieved by the masons of Somerset, but two of the best are at Great Ponton (Lincs) and TITCHMARSH. Both have beautifully decorated pierced battlements with descending rotated centre pinnacles, a detail that appears only in towers of exceptional quality. The gabled and perforated merlons at TITCHMARSH are reminiscent of the perforated parapets of Yorkshire such as TICKHILL, Beeford, Holme-on-Spalding-Moor, Skirlaugh and Blyth (just over the Nottinghamshire border). TICKHILL, the best of the group, is also marked by the descending rotated centre pinnacle. Yorkshire parapets with regular screen-like perforations occur at Holy Trinity, Hull and Hedon.

TOWER PINNACLES

In about 1330 the hexagonal pinnacle was briefly in vogue on spired towers such as NEWARK, BRANT BROUGHTON, HECKINGTON and Caythorpe (Lincs), but the intersection of a hexagonal pinnacle with a straight parapet is awkward, and the idea was soon dropped in favour of the octagon.

Octagonal pinnacles were used to terminate octagonal buttresses or to complement octagonal spires or lanterns but rarely in other circumstances, Colne Engaine (Essex), Easton-on-the-Hill and All Saints, Aldwinckle (Northants) being the most notable exceptions. Where the military-looking crenellated octagonal turret without pinnacle occurs at FOTHERINGHAY, Deopham (Norfolk), Haslingfield and Elm (Cambs), it was, no doubt, inspired by the west front of Ely Cathedral or the Cambridge colleges.

Apart from these exceptions, tower pinnacles were square, either set orthogonally to the tower or rotated on the diagonal.

The possibilities inherent in combining square with rotated square formed a major preoccupation of the Somerset masons, particularly in the Quantock Group, which includes several of the most beautiful towers in England. At NORTH PETHERTON, KINGSTON ST MARY, Bishops Lydeard, St James in Taunton, Staple Fitzpaine, Isle Abbots and Huish Episcopi, the primary corner pinnacles are encircled by clusters of exceptionally slender secondary pinnacles. For vertical intensity, however, nothing rivals the twenty closely packed pinnacles of LEIGH-ON-MENDIP from the East Mendip Group.

The greatest elaboration of all is to be found in the so-called 'Gloucestershire crowns', where not only the parapet, but also the pinnacles are perforated and hollow, creating a brilliant, fragile, lattice-like silhouette. The parapet at Gloucester Cathedral, completed around 1460, provided the model for nine designs distributed either side of the Severn Estuary, of which St Stephen, Bristol and ST MARY MAGDALENE, TAUNTON are the pre-eminent examples.

SOMERSET TOWERS

The art of tower-building reached its zenith in Somerset during the fifteenth and early sixteenth centuries. The fame of the region rests on the reputation of fifteen towers of the very first rank.[1] Apart from ST MARY MAGDALENE, TAUNTON and ST CUTHBERT, WELLS, the towers are modest in height, but this is no disadvantage, for their authority derives from their sophisticated composition, exquisite detailing and immaculate execution.

The urge to classify this fascinating family of interrelated masterpieces is irresistible but has led to some questionable history.[2] Pevsner's proposed grouping is too generalized to be of much assistance, and major towers such as Ilminster and Chewton Mendip fail to be captured by the alternative systems of ordering. The most convincing

SOMERSET TOWERS AND GLOUCESTERSHIRE CROWNS

classification proposed to date is that of Frank Allen in his 1932 work *The Great Church Towers of England*, and this is repeated, with some limited amendment, here and in the evolutionary chart on pp. 28–29. The fifteen masterworks are associated with just four interrelated tower groups.

The Wells Group (Allen's 'Cathedral Group') is centred on the cathedral but finds its purest expression at ST CUTHBERT's church in the city. The pronounced verticality of this group inspired the distinctive but geographically dispersed Long-Panel Group of EVERCREECH and Wrington, and, indirectly, Batcombe and the crossing tower of Illminster.

The East Mendip Group of triple-windowed towers includes Mells, Bruton and the most exquisite of all Somerset designs, LEIGH-ON-MENDIP. Within the more extensive double-windowed Quantock Group are six outstanding works, at Isle Abbots, Staple Fitzpaine, KINGSTON ST MARY, NORTH PETHERTON, Huish Episcopi and ST MARY MAGDALENE, TAUNTON. Chewton Mendip combines elements from all of the preceding groups and extends the timeline beyond the English Reformation.

TOWER VAULTS

Stone tower vaults were first introduced in an attempt to increase strength, and only later for decorative effect. Timber vaults, such as LUDLOW, are a rare extravagance, for they offer no structural benefit. Medieval tower vaults are distinguished by the provision of a central circular timber bell hatch. Early vaults invariably suffer from poor illumination, and the introduction of substantial side windows at Clifton Campville (Staffs), WHITTLESEY and MOULTON in the fourteenth century was a welcome development. This was perfected a century later at LOUTH, where the ultimate parochial tower vault is brilliantly lit by pairs of great windows on all four elevations.

The simplest form of vault is the quadripartite vault (p. 17 (e)), of four arched bays separated by four diagonal ribs. At BARNACK, CASTOR and ST MARY, STAMFORD this form of vault was added to strengthen existing towers receiving the additional weight of a spire, whereas at CHIPPING CAMPDEN and EWERBY they are fully integrated into the design. BRANT BROUGHTON is sexpartite, having six diagonal ribs, while GRANTHAM may be unique in having twelve bays separated by twelve diagonal ribs (p. 17 (g)).

The tierceron vault, with secondary ribs rising directly to a ridge rib, is suited to spans of less than twenty feet. It appears at WHITTLESEY, LAUGHTON-EN-LE-MORTHEN (p. 17 (f)), RAUNDS, MOULTON, Holbeach and Sleaford, and most spectacularly in the vault at ST MICHAEL, COVENTRY set ninety-six feet above the pavement.

Lierne vaulting, in which tertiary ribs connect primary or secondary ribs, is appropriate only for the most substantial parish church. ST CUTHBERT, WELLS (17' 9" square), NEWCASTLE (23' 2" square), ST MARY REDCLIFFE (21' 11" square) and the high vault at LOUTH (20' 10" square) are all fine designs. With a span of 26' 6" and forty-one bosses, the Victorian vault at BOSTON (p. 17 (j)) is a magnificent achievement. There are fine examples of fan vaults at FOTHERINGHAY (p. 17 (h)), NORTH PETHERTON and ST MARY MAGDALENE, TAUNTON, and one modest effort forming the porch roof at EYE.

CHURCH BELLS

The primary purpose of the church tower is to raise bells high enough to ring clearly across the parish. Bells were an essential piece of ecclesiastical equipment from the eighth century, and medieval canon law assumed that all parish churches had at least two bells. They were rung for numerous reasons: to announce Mass, Matins or Vespers; the curfew at the end of the day; the death of a parishioner; or a funeral. The

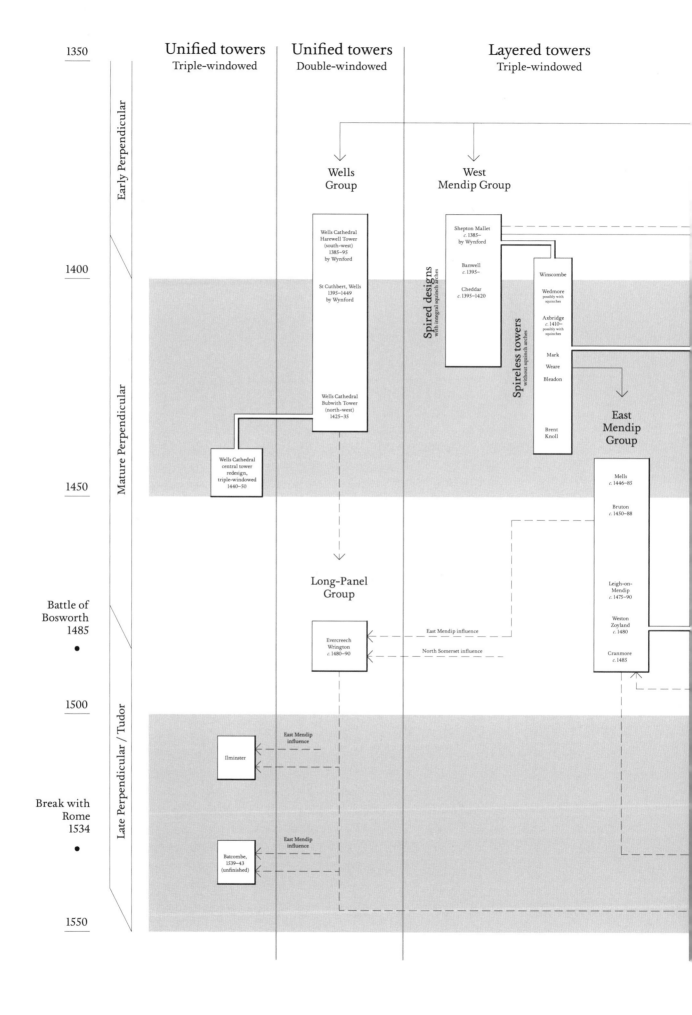

1350

Early Perpendicular

1400

Mature Perpendicular

1450

Battle of
Bosworth
1485

•

1500

Late Perpendicular / Tudor

Break with
Rome
1534

•

1550

Unified towers
Triple-windowed

Unified towers
Double-windowed

Layered towers
Triple-windowed

Wells
Group

West
Mendip Group

East
Mendip
Group

Long-Panel
Group

Wells Cathedral
Harewell Tower
(south-west)
1385–95
by Wynford

St Cuthbert, Wells
1395–1449
by Wynford

Wells Cathedral
Bubwith Tower
(north-west)
1425–35

Wells Cathedral
central tower
redesign,
triple-windowed
1440–50

Shepton Mallet
c. 1385–
by Wynford

Barnwell
c. 1395–

Cheddar
c. 1395–1420

Spired designs
with integral squinch arches

Winscombe

Wedmore
possibly with
squinches

Axbridge
c. 1410–
possibly with
squinches

Mark

Weare

Bleadon

Brent
Knoll

Spireless towers
without squinch arches

Mells
c. 1446–85

Bruton
c. 1450–88

Leigh-on-
Mendip
c. 1475–90

Weston
Zoyland
c. 1480

Cranmore
c. 1485

Evercreech
Wrington
c. 1480–90

East Mendip influence

North Somerset influence

Ilminster

East Mendip
influence

Batcombe,
1539–43
(unfinished)

East Mendip
influence

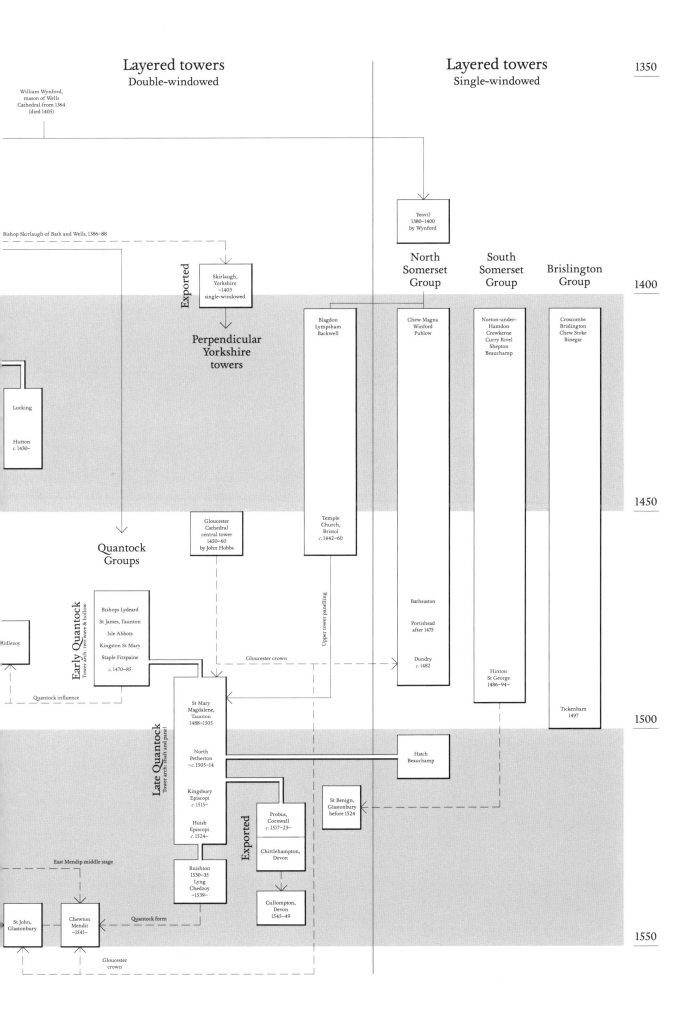

William Wynford,
mason of Wells
Cathedral from 1364
(died 1405)

Bishop Skirlaugh of Bath and Wells, 1386–88

Yeovil
1380–1400
by Wynford

Exported

Skirlaugh,
Yorkshire
–1403
single-windowed

North
Somerset
Group

South
Somerset
Group

Brislington
Group

1400

Perpendicular
Yorkshire
towers

Blagdon
Lympsham
Backwell

Chew Magna
Winford
Publow

Norton-under-
Hamdon
Crewkerne
Curry Rivel
Shepton
Beauchamp

Croscombe
Brislington
Chew Stoke
Binegar

Locking

Hutton
c. 1430–

Quantock
Groups

Gloucester
Cathedral
central tower
1450–60
by John Hobbs

Temple
Church,
Bristol
c. 1442–60

1450

Early Quantock
Tower arch: two wave & hollow

Bishops Lydeard
St James, Taunton
Isle Abbots
Kingston St Mary
Staple Fitzpaine
c. 1470–85

Gloucester crown

Upper tower panelling

Batheaston

Portishead
after 1475

Dundry
c. 1482

Hinton
St George
1486–94–

Tickenham
1497

Midlezoy

Quantock influence

Late Quantock
Tower arch: shaft and panel

St Mary
Magdalene,
Taunton
1488–1505

North
Petherton
–c. 1505–14

Kingsbury
Episcopi
c. 1515–

Huish
Episcopi
c. 1524–

Exported

Probus,
Cornwall
c. 1517–23–

Chittlehampton,
Devon

Hatch
Beauchamp

St Benign,
Glastonbury
before 1524

1500

East Mendip middle stage

St John,
Glastonbury

Chewton
Mendit
–1541–

Quantock form

Ruishton
1530–35
Lyng
Chedzoy
–1539–

Cullompton,
Devon
1545–49

1550

Gloucester
crown

EVOLUTION OF THE SOMERSET TOWER

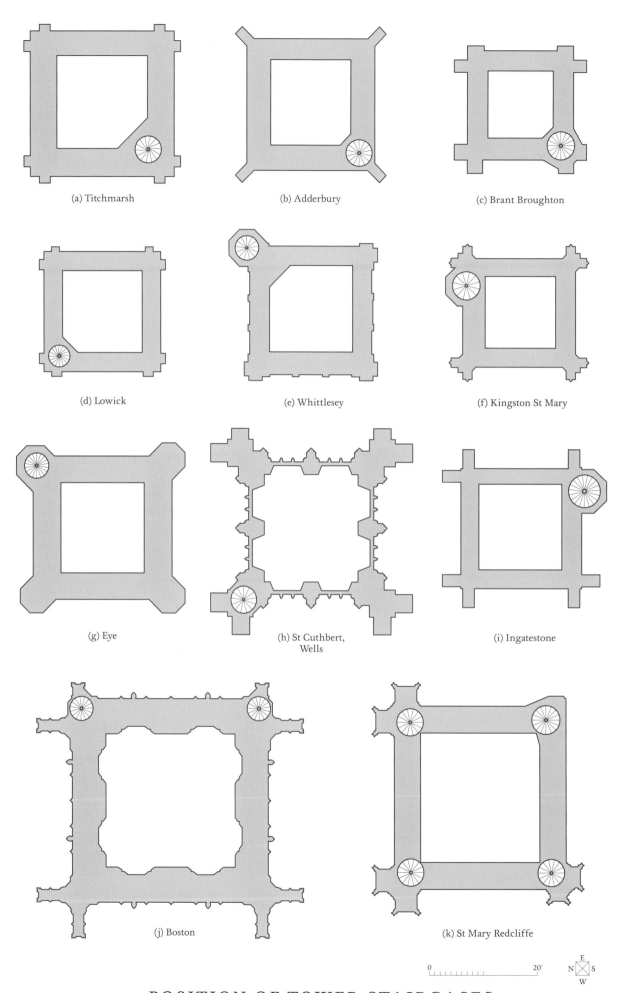

(a) Titchmarsh

(b) Adderbury

(c) Brant Broughton

(d) Lowick

(e) Whittlesey

(f) Kingston St Mary

(g) Eye

(h) St Cuthbert,
Wells

(i) Ingatestone

(j) Boston

(k) St Mary Redcliffe

0   20'

N E S W

POSITION OF TOWER STAIRCASES

churchwardens' accounts for LOUTH reveal that the ringing of the great bells for the dead at 8*d.* or 20*d.* per day provided a significant and reliable source of revenue for the church.

The chronology of bells is well documented, for inscriptions are frequently dated and carry the name of the bell-founder. The oldest bell within this survey, at SALLE, was cast by Edmund de Lynn of Kings Lynn around 1353. Change ringing – the art of ringing a set of tuned bells to follow a mathematical sequence – was developed in England in the seventeenth century. It required the bells to be swung through 370 degrees by means of a large wheel on each headstock, with bell ropes arranged in a circle of descending order of pitch. Such specific requirements led to the wholesale replacement of medieval bell frames, and the only frame predating the nineteenth century in this survey is at WEST WALTON.

Frames are usually square to the tower, but at TICKHILL and the circular tower at FORNCETT ST PETER they are set diagonally. Oak frames were gradually superseded by cast-iron side frames then full frames during the nineteenth century, and by steel in the twentieth century. One unwelcome development in recent years has been the introduction of massively oversized concrete padstones within medieval wall constructions to support steel bell frames.

The load that bells impose on the tower is inconsequential compared with the weight of the masonry itself; however, the vibration from sustained bell ringing may open up cracks through existing lines of weakness in the structure. Consequently the bells at DEDHAM, WEST WALTON and ST MARY, STAMFORD have been permanently disabled, and change ringing is prohibited at KETTON.

THE TOWER STAIRCASE

In Saxon times access to the upper stages of a tower was by ladder, and ancient examples, made from long, split logs, are still in use at EARLS BARTON and FORNCETT ST PETER. It was during this early period that primitive forms of spiral stair first appear, at Brixworth (Northants), Broughton-by-Brigg and Hough-on-the-Hill (both Lincs).

The Normans introduced the true newel stair, in which the step and the newel post are cut from one stone. This significant technical advance changed little throughout the medieval period. The newel stair was of limited use as long as towers continued to be placed over central crossings, for only churches on the scale of LUDLOW could accommodate a stair in one of the free-standing tower piers. In most parish churches alternative access routes had to be devised such as the cantilevered stair over the chancel arch at KETTON and the crawlway at PATRINGTON.

Once the west tower became the dominant form, the spiral stair (or helical stair, as it is more correctly known) was employed as a matter of course (p. 30). Of the four potential locations, north-east and south-east corners were potentially in conflict with the tower arch, while the north-west and south-west corners might impact on the principal west elevation.

In spire-building regions there was a consistent preference to conceal the stair in the south-west corner, as at TITCHMARSH (a). Twenty-one west towers in the survey follow this principle. Five towers including LOWICK (d) and ST CUTHBERT, WELLS (h) have stairs in the north-west corner, WHITTLESEY (e) and KINGSTON ST MARY (f) are reached by north-east stair turrets, and ST MICHAEL, COVENTRY by a south-east stair turret. BOSTON (j) enjoys the luxury of two pre-existing stair turrets that sit comfortably either side of the tower arch. Where a south-west stair projects internally, it may impact on the elevation. At TITCHMARSH and Oakham (Rutland), west windows are pushed completely off centre, and at NEWARK the stair shaft can be seen cutting across the bell stage window on the west elevation.

A more sophisticated south-west stair design evolved in fourteenth-century

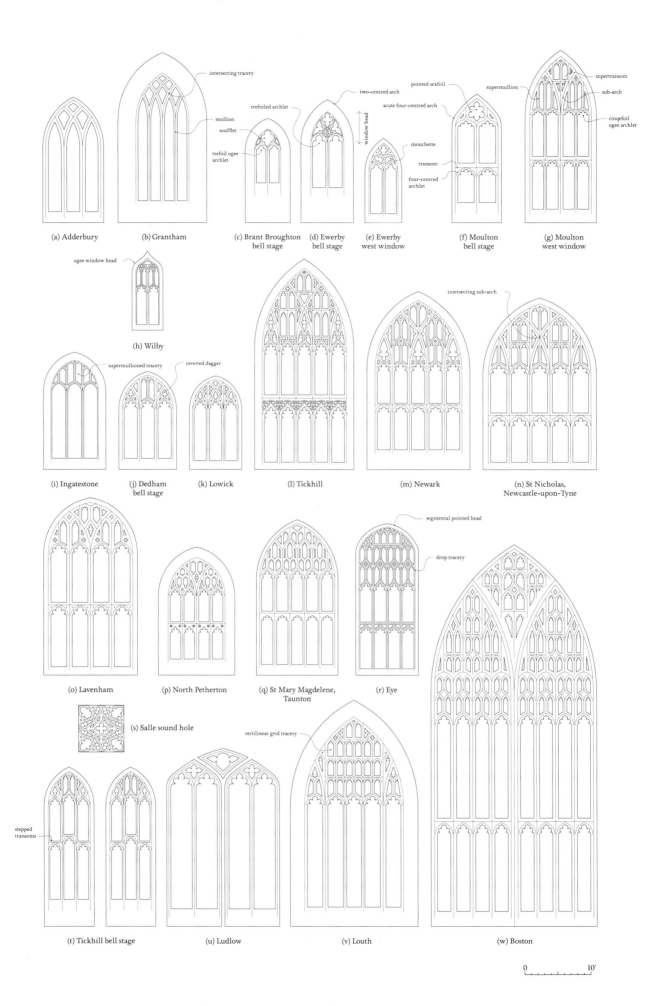

intersecting tracery

mullion

soufflet

trefoil ogee
archlet

trefoiled archlet

two-centred arch

window head

pointed sexfoil

acute four-centred arch

mouchette

transom

four-centred
archlet

supermullion

supertransom

sub-arch

cinqefoil
ogee archlet

(a) Adderbury

(b) Grantham

(c) Brant Broughton
bell stage

(d) Ewerby
bell stage

(e) Ewerby
west window

(f) Moulton
bell stage

(g) Moulton
west window

ogee window head

(h) Wilby

supermullioned tracery

inverted dagger

intersecting sub-arch

(i) Ingatestone

(j) Dedham
bell stage

(k) Lowick

(l) Tickhill

(m) Newark

(n) St Nicholas,
Newcastle-upon-Tyne

segmental pointed head

drop tracery

(o) Lavenham

(p) North Petherton

(q) St Mary Magdelene,
Taunton

(r) Eye

(s) Salle sound hole

rectilinear grid tracery

stepped
transoms

(t) Tickhill bell stage

(u) Ludlow

(v) Louth

(w) Boston

0   10'

TOWER WINDOW TRACERY

Lincolnshire. The magnificent but flawed steeple at GRANTHAM had placed the stair too far from the corner of the tower, allowing the staircase turret to unbalance the whole composition. Such awkward asymmetry was resolved on subsequent designs by moving the stair further in, towards the corner of the tower, keeping it subservient to the overall composition while adding a degree of asymmetry and restless tension. Three very beautiful examples are illustrated, at HECKINGTON, EWERBY and BRANT BROUGHTON (c).

In late medieval spireless towers, the usual preference was for a north-east staircase. In East Anglia the octagonal or square clasping buttresses of major flint towers such as EYE (g) and LAVENHAM are big enough to fully conceal such a north-east stair, although at REDENHALL the alternative south-east location is preferred. In the brick tower at INGATESTONE (i) a south-east location was chosen to avoid the north and west elevations, which face the main street. From around 1400 the north-east stair turret became a significant feature of many fine Somerset towers, including LEIGH-ON-MENDIP and KINGSTON ST MARY.

Stairs follow the military convention of turning anticlockwise as they rise, with only four exceptions in the survey: WHITTLESEY (e), INGATESTONE (i), GRANTHAM and LUDLOW. The two stairs at BOSTON and the four at ST MARY REDCLIFFE (k) all turn in the same clockwise direction. Sizes vary considerably, from 3' 10" diameter at WILBY to a palatial 6' 5" at TICKHILL. Stairs became tighter over the generations as the skill of the mason increased and smooth ashlar wall surfaces replaced rough rubble. Within the survey the average diameter reduces from 5' 6" in early work to 4' 9" in late work, although East Anglian flint construction maintains a more relaxed 5' 7". Stairs frequently reduce in size and quality as they pass the ringing chamber or bell chamber, and even the grandest stair can become very constricted as it makes its final turn to reach the roof.

TOWER WINDOWS

The single most recognizable feature of the Anglo-Saxon bell tower is the double opening for the bells, as seen at FORNCETT ST PETER. In Norman times this motif continued to be used for window openings within the arcading of the bell stage, for example at CASTOR, Great Tey (Essex) and Southwell Minster (Notts). With the advent of the pointed lancet window, the twin bell opening fell out of fashion but later re-emerged as a recognizably English feature.

The first clearly defined style of Gothic window is the Lancet (c. 1190–1245),[3] in which openings were limited to the width of a single undivided arch. One or two tall lancets sufficed for the west window of a tower, such as the tall single light of Warboys (Hunts). Masons at this time were obsessed with shafts and whenever resources permitted would run continuous arcades of richly shafted lancet openings around each stage of the tower. The bell stage at KETTON is surrounded by no fewer than eighty-eight detached and engaged shafts. Plate tracery developed when lancets were combined under a single dripstone, creating a spandrel that could be perforated by small decorative openings including circles at WEST WALTON, and quatrefoils and more complex forms at NORTH RAUCEBY.

The stone mullion was introduced from France shortly before 1245. Early Geometrical window design (c. 1245–90) in the body of the church was dominated by the use of nested plain or foliated circles. Tower openings, however, never progressed beyond simple two-bay 'Y' tracery as, for example, at LONG SUTTON.

In Late Geometrical work (c. 1290–1315) the principles of 'Y' tracery extend across three or more bays of intersecting tracery (p. 32). This is perfectly illustrated in its simplest form at ADDERBURY (a) and with sumptuous ballflower decoration at GRANTHAM (b). The parallel development of complex geometrical tracery had little impact on tower design, for modest two-bay openings surrounded by plain expanses of masonry were standard even for the west window.

Curvilinear tracery (c. 1315–60) introduced the ogee curve into work of extraordinary inventiveness and craftsmanship. In the body of the church, windows of five, seven or even nine bays dissolved the space between buttresses, but tower windows remained remarkably small, deep set and uniform in design (p. 32). The bell chamber window at BRANT BROUGHTON (c) illustrates the standard two-bay type found across the East Midlands, with trefoil ogee archlets supporting a soufflet in the head. The ogee arch encircling the soufflet runs smoothly into the main arch, creating a simplified form of reticulated tracery. The shaft capital reduces in importance and is entirely omitted in the west window at EWERBY (e). The unusually adventurous bell stage window at the same church (d) contains pointed trefoils framed by swinging tracery.

Perpendicular tracery (c. 1360–1550) first appeared at Gloucester and Old St Paul's Cathedral in the 1330s, when the mullion was allowed run straight into the window arch. This innovation dramatically increased the structural capacity of tracery, allowing tower windows to reach an unprecedented scale (p. 32). MOULTON (f, g) illustrates the transition to this new style. The bell opening (f) includes flat cinquefoil arches, supermullions rising vertically from the archlets and a horizontal transom.

The ogee arch continues to appear in early Perpendicular work such as MOULTON (f, g), WILBY (h) and TICKHILL (l) but then fell out of fashion. It subsequently reappears around 1440 in Somerset, for example at KINGSTON ST MARY, in Gloucestershire at CHIPPING CAMPDEN, and in East Anglia at EYE (r) and SALLE. WILBY is one unusual instance of the structurally weak ogee form being used for the main arch, albeit over a very short span. Crocketed ogee hood-moulds are used to great effect over each window on the bell stage at TICKHILL (t) without influencing the form of the

windows below. This idea was successfully revisited at LOUTH (v), BOSTON (w) and Great Driffield (Yorks).

During this period supermullioned tracery, seen in three bays of brick tracery at INGATESTONE (i), dominated in the east of England and as far west as Oxfordshire. Alternating tracery, in which the lower mullions do not continue above the archlets, as at NORTH PETHERTON (p), was the preserve of the west of England. One hefty exception to this rule is the bell stage at BOSTON.

MOULTON (g) illustrates the use of subarcuated tracery, in which secondary arches divide the primary arch. Four bay examples can be seen in many late towers in Somerset and East Anglia, including LAVENHAM (o) and NORTH PETHERTON (p). In windows of four, six or eight bays – at BOSTON (w), for example – the sub-arches sit neatly adjacent to each other. With an odd number of bays, sub-arches may be restricted to the outermost bays, which is satisfactory over three bays at DEDHAM (j) but weak over five bays at LOUTH (v). Alternatively, wide sub-arches may cross to form subarcuated intersecting tracery, a preferable arrangement seen over five bays at TICKHILL (l), NEWARK (m) and NEWCASTLE (n), and three bays at LOWICK (k).

Only occasional use is made of flat arches, for the obvious reason that they contradict the verticality of the tower. They work best near the base of a broad tower, such as TITCHMARSH, or on flushwork towers where the emphasis is on decorative texture, such as EYE (r). Flat window heads are detrimental to the major towers of Holy Trinity, Hull, Howden and LUDLOW (u). Windows of exceptional verticality, such as at LOUTH, continued to be employed in the upper tower long after they were discarded elsewhere.

Air holes (or sound holes) are a speciality of Norfolk. Large, square openings filled with delicate, feminine tracery are positioned at the centre of gravity of weighty masculine compositions such as Foulsham, South Repps, North Repps, Cromer and SALLE (s).

The motif occasionally appears outside Norfolk, on the west elevation of WILBY, for example, but only on a modest scale.

ARCHES AND DOORWAYS

Anglo-Saxon round towers were invariably accessed from the church through an eastern doorway or a tower arch. FORNCETT ST PETER is one of only two round towers with west doors, although externally the details are not original. Half of the surviving square west towers from this early period have external doors, usually on the west, as at EARLS BARTON, but sometimes on the north or the south, as at BARNACK.

Throughout the Gothic period the west door was almost, but not quite, de rigueur on major towers, irrespective of the geography of the site. At LAVENHAM the door faces a quiet country lane, and only a minority of churches, such as GRANTHAM, use their tower doors at the main entrance. During the fourteenth century there was a welcome trend to omit unnecessary west doors, for example at BRANT BROUGHTON, EWERBY and LAUGHTON-EN-LE-MORTHEN.

In the Lancet period doors were deeply recessed, with sumptuous displays of shafts and dogtooth ornament, such as at Warmington (Northants). In the same county HIGHAM FERRERS is distinguished by a deeply recessed double doorway, a feature more commonly associated with the cathedral chapter house.

The two most common means of finishing the west door in late towers are illustrated by the rectangular hood-mould over the door arch at FOTHERINGHAY and the crocketed ogee hood-mould at STOKE-BY-NAYLAND. Cromer and BOSTON were wealthy enough to afford projecting door surrounds complete with panelled battlements. The English were nevertheless content that the west doorway should always retain a human scale. Steps were provided only where essential, to address variations in ground level, and never to impress or intimidate.

Even in early Gothic towers such as NORTH RAUCEBY and RAUNDS, the tower arch was made as wide as possible, with the responds being kept tight against the side walls of the tower. Tower arches range from five-and-a-half feet wide at FORNCETT ST PETER to twenty-two feet wide at BOSTON. They were rarely rebuilt, and the profile of the responds and the arch can provide invaluable evidence for the early history of a tower.

ORIGINS OF THE SPIRE

The spire is one of the most powerful architectural forms ever devised. Combining strength with grace, it provides the most natural and beautiful conclusion to the heavenward thrust of the tower. In medieval times the spire carried such symbolic resonance that it was reserved exclusively for sacred purposes.

The principal division of English spires is into oversailing and recessed forms. The oversailing spire is wider than the tower on which it sits to ensure that rainwater is thrown clear of the walls, whereas the recessed spire is set behind a parapet, with a continuous path around its base acting as a gutter. In medieval England, there was always a clear distinction between spire and tower, and the articulation of the junction between the two forms became a major preoccupation in steeple design. Apart from the hexagonal spire over the triangular tower of Maldon (Essex), medieval English spires are always octagonal in form, and they are constructed of either stone or timber.[4]

Stone spires first appeared in France, on a vastly ambitious scale, towards the end of the twelfth century. The south-west spire at Chartres Cathedral, finished in 1170, reached an astonishing 349 feet, and across northern France spires were raised to a prodigious height at a very early date. The influence of the French masons is seen most directly in Oxfordshire, where a short-lived school of pinnacled spires developed from the early thirteenth century at St Frideswide, Oxford and WITNEY (p. 39 (d)). These oversailing spires, with their dominant corner pinnacles and large dormer windows, had no lasting influence. Around the same time the masons of the East Midlands developed a purer form of broach spire that became the dominant form for over a century.

One common characteristic of English spires is that they are frequently much younger than the towers on which they sit. Only ten of the twenty-six spires featured in this survey were built concurrently with their towers. Across the remainder, the average delay in construction is sixty years, the most extreme instance being CASTOR (p. 39 (b)), with a delay of over three centuries.

THE TIMBER SPIRE

The earliest English spires were of timber, but few have survived, and those that have are not easy to date without the use of dendrochronology. LONG SUTTON is the tallest early timber spire still in existence, but originally it would have been unremarkable, for great timber spires crowned the cathedrals of England. At 524' the wooden spire at Lincoln was the tallest man-made structure on earth until it fell in a storm in 1548. The spire of Old St Paul's Cathedral in London was said to have been four feet lower and lasted only thirteen years longer.

Timber spires had many weaknesses. They relied for their longevity upon the quality of the oak, the geometry of the framing, the construction of the joints and the condition of the cladding. Most were replaced by stone, which is inherently durable, stable and fireproof, during the medieval period except in counties lacking good stone, such as Essex and Suffolk. Tall lead-covered spires, such as Wickham Market, are usually octagonal from the base, but many humble shingle-covered spires have splayed bases, which inspired one of the earliest forms of English stone spire.

THE SPLAY-FOOTED STONE SPIRE

In the splay-footed spire, simple chamfered corners form the transition from square base to octagonal upper spire. It is easily recognized since it has a single triangular face on each corner, compared with two triangular faces on a broach spire – a basic distinction that is frequently overlooked in even the most authoritative sources, including Pevsner and the Statutory Listings.

The earliest splay-footed spires are to be found in humble form at Burton-le-Coggles (Lincs) and more assertively at Etton (Hunts). Bythorn (Hunts) was needlessly reduced to a stump within living memory, while Clipsham (Rutland) and Piddington (Northants) are wonderfully inventive small spires from the fourteenth century. The splay foot was never very popular, for it looks weaker than the broach spire, with its cardinal faces being cut into the awkward shape of an inverted 'Y'. Although CASTOR (p. 39 (b)) is a recessed spire, it illustrates well the principle of the splay-footed form.

THE BROACH SPIRE

The broach spire is octagonal and rises from a square base, with small hipped roofs, or broaches, covering the four corners of the tower. It is a uniquely English phenomenon that appeared around the year 1220, flourished for 130 years and then fell into disuse. Early specimens are distinguished by tall broaches and large lucarnes profusely decorated with dogtooth. The earliest broach spires at NORTH RAUCEBY (p. 39 (c)) and Sleaford (Lincs) are remarkably mature designs set just three miles apart. Their spire lights have plate tracery that predates the 'Y' tracery of early spires such as Frampton (Lincs) and Warboys (Hunts).

Squinches are arches or corbels spanning the internal corners of a square tower to support the diagonal face of a spire; they turn a square plan into an octagon. In the broach spire, squinches are constructed

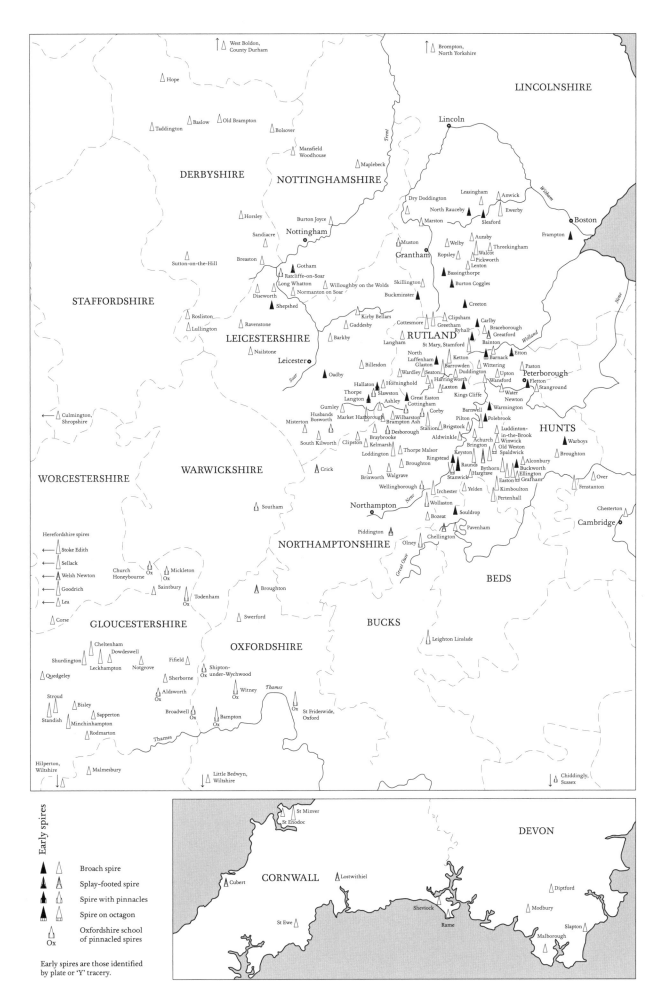

DISTRIBUTION OF OVERSAILING SPIRES

entirely within the height of the spire, which makes the form ideal for adding to a pre-existing tower. Early spires such as NORTH RAUCEBY have high broaches not for aesthetic reasons but because the design of the squinches was cautious.

In the early thirteenth century churches were, by later standards, very low. Even great cathedrals had only the humblest of crossing towers. The tallest masonry structures in England were the west tower at Ely and the central tower at Norwich, neither rising more than 150 feet from the ground. Around 1250 both were surpassed by a modest parish church in a quiet corner of Northamptonshire. The magnificent spire at RAUNDS (p. 39 (g)) represents a second, and more ambitious, generation of broach spires and set the benchmark for future development. Soaring broach spires followed in the immediate area, at Keyston, Brington, Spaldwick, Easton, Ellington, Kimboulton (all Hunts) and Pertenhall (Beds).

The richest period of broach spire design coincided with the flourishing of Curvilinear tracery in the first half of the fourteenth century. The incomparable roll-edged spires of KETTON (p. 39 (f)) and ST MARY, STAMFORD (p. 39 (h)) are only four miles apart, and almost certainly from the hand of one mason. Both have highly ornamented, alternating lucarnes, a profusion of ballflower decoration, broaches crowned with canopied statues, and projecting heads to the base of the rolls. They are vigorous, sculptural and intensely romantic. KETTON is more elegant, STAMFORD more luxuriant.

Three things are required for a successful broach spire: well-proportioned broaches, fine lucarnes, and a crisp square base with a deep overhang to cast a good shadow. A well-proportioned broach spire gives the impression of two pyramids intersecting: a lower square pyramid and a taller octagonal pyramid. The octagon provides height, the square solidity, and together they give the impression of great strength, weight and permanence.

A broach spire does not necessarily need to be tall, for a modest spire on an unpretentious rural church can still be immensely satisfying. Smaller spires appear comfortably proportioned if they are at least twice as high as they are wide – that is to say, if they have an apex angle of twenty-eight degrees. The elegant design at NORTH RAUCEBY (p. 39 (c)) has an apex angle of twenty-one degrees, where the sumptuous small spire at Warmington (Northants) has an angle of twenty-four degrees. Tall broach spires, such as KETTON (p. 39 (f)) and EWERBY (p. 39 (e)), maintained the ideal apex angle of fourteen degrees established by RAUNDS.

In the Sleaford district of Lincolnshire there are several examples of spires with convex entasis, such as Welbourn, Walcot and EWERBY (p. 39 (e)). Entasis is the application of a subtle curve to the profile of a building element to create the illusion of greater solidity, height or strength. EWERBY is also notable for the way in which spire tower and aisles were conceived as one unified pyramidal composition.

Crocketed edges are only found on broach spires at Walcot, a gloriously fruity variation of the EWERBY design, and at Market Harborough (Leics). The broach spire fell into decline after the middle of the fourteenth century, although impressive individual designs were occasionally realized, such as Olney (Bucks), a very tall design with pronounced entasis, four orthogonal tiers of lucarnes and roll edges.

THE OVERSAILING OCTAGONAL SPIRE

An oversailing octagonal spire rises directly from the eight walls of an octagonal tower or tower stage and therefore requires no broaches. Examples are scarce and very individual. BARNACK is famous both for its early medieval quarry and for having one of the oldest spires in England (p. 39 (a)). This excessively broad spire is a strangely elemental design, appearing almost as a catalogue of unresolved components.

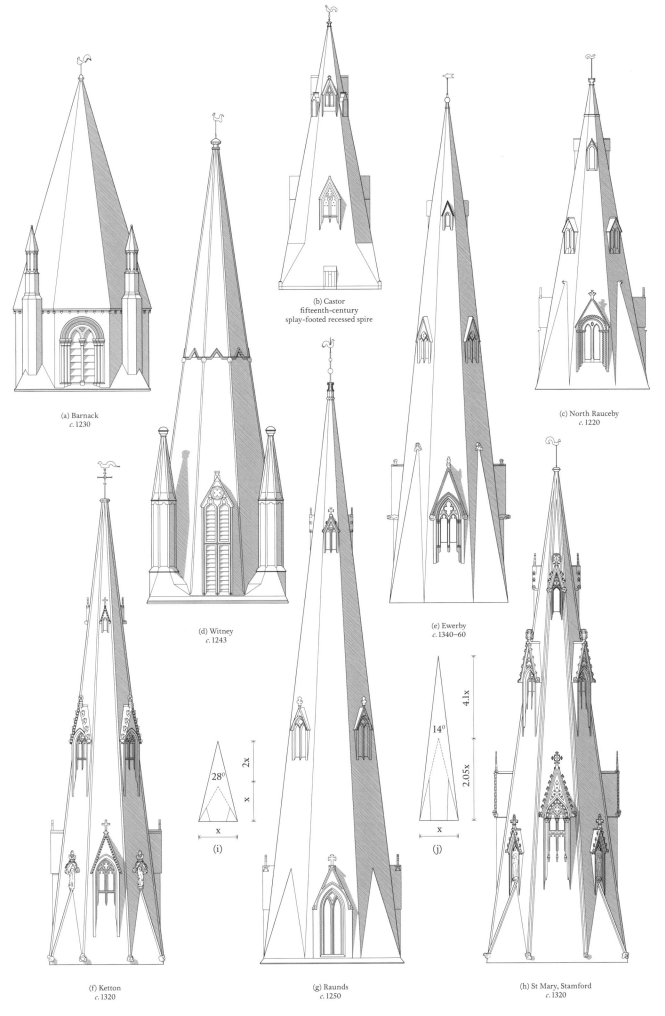

(a) Barnack
c. 1230

(b) Castor
fifteenth-century
splay-footed recessed spire

(c) North Rauceby
c. 1220

(d) Witney
c. 1243

(e) Ewerby
c. 1340–60

28°

2x

x

x

(i)

14°

4.1x

2.05x

x

(j)

(f) Ketton
c. 1320

(g) Raunds
c. 1250

(h) St Mary, Stamford
c. 1320

OVERSAILING SPIRES

20'

Grafham and Old Weston (Hunts) follow similar principles, but with very different proportions. All three rise from octagonal top stages on square towers, but at Stanwick (Northants) the tower is octagonal from the base. The appealing conceptual logic of this proposition is not matched by the reality, for the smooth continuity of form lacks the characteristic sculptural vigour of the traditional English steeple.

THE RECESSED SPIRE

In the early 1300s the broach spire was reaching maturity at ST MARY, STAMFORD, KETTON and Market Harborough (Leics); however, the masons were working comfortably within the technological limits set at RAUNDS three generations earlier. Change was overdue, and around this time recessed spires started to appear across eastern and central England. Initially they were modest and, unsurprisingly, very similar to the oversailing spires on which they were modelled. Deene and Denford (Northants) are of the splay-footed variety, while Bingham (Notts) has broaches. It was, however, at Lichfield Cathedral and particularly at GRANTHAM (p. 42 (k)) that the real revolution in spire design took place.

A precise chronology is difficult to establish, but there is documentary evidence to suggest that the three spires at Lichfield were complete by 1323, and stylistically GRANTHAM appears to be slightly earlier. GRANTHAM was altogether on a different scale from any stone spire that had been built before and, until the completion of Salisbury Cathedral in the second half of the fourteenth century it was the tallest stone structure in England. It was a leap of faith, showing astonishing confidence in the mason's intuition. Vastly ambitious, the steeple of ST WULFRAM set the standard for the following 200 years.

The impact of GRANTHAM was immediate. Across the country great towers were crowned with magnificent recessed spires.

Ashbourne (Derbys), ST MARY, OXFORD and NEWARK (p. 42 (m)) are from this period. In the west of England work commenced on the great spire at ST MARY REDCLIFFE (p. 42 (l)) and restarted on the crossing tower at Salisbury. GRANTHAM was, however, far from perfect, and a period of refinement was required until the vocabulary of the recessed English spire was fully established around 1350 and the broach spire fell into terminal decline.

A recessed spire has a continuous path, protected by a parapet, running around the base of the spire. The path is typically between 1' 6" and 2' 6" wide, with the parapet supported beyond the face of the tower by a corbel table or cornice. The path acts as a gutter for rainwater running off the spire, which is discharged through gargoyles, and it provides permanent and convenient access for structural maintenance.

The recessed spire is significantly more efficient than the broach spire, requiring far less material to reach a specific height. The tall broach spire at RAUNDS (p. 39 (g)) is constructed from over 610 tons of limestone, whereas the recessed spire at LOUTH (p. 43 (r)), which is one-third higher, weighs only 200 tons. This represents an astonishing fourfold increase in efficiency. For a particular tower, the base of a recessed spire is four or five feet narrower than the base of an oversailing spire. In the most efficient spires, such as MOULTON (p. 43 (n)), the squinch is set entirely within the uppermost stage of the tower, so that the spire is thin-walled right from the base.

Even the slenderest broach spires, such as KETTON (p. 39 (f)), achieve an apex angle of only fourteen degrees, but recessed spires are far more slender, ranging from twelve degrees at KETTERING (p. 43 (o)) to a razor-sharp nine degrees at LOUTH. The true needle spire, which developed in the fifteenth century, is no wider than ten degrees; BRANT BROUGHTON (p. 43 (q)) is one example.

Compared with the tower on which it sits, the recessed spire is an exceptionally thin and efficient form of construction, and it was, therefore, relatively inexpensive to

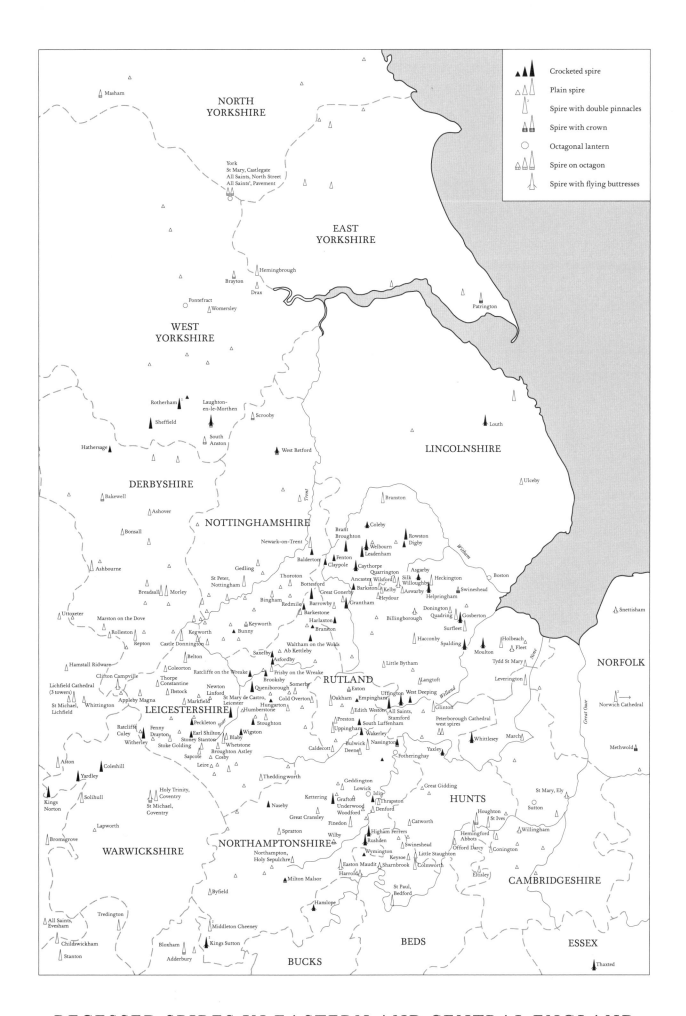

Legend

	Crocketed spire
	Plain spire
	Spire with double pinnacles
	Spire with crown
	Octagonal lantern
	Spire on octagon
	Spire with flying buttresses

NORTH YORKSHIRE

Masham

EAST YORKSHIRE

York
St Mary, Castlegate
All Saints, North Street
All Saints', Pavement

Hemingbrough
Brayton
Drax

Pontefract
Womersley

WEST YORKSHIRE

Patrington

Rotherham
Laughton-en-le-Morthen
Sheffield
South Anston
Scrooby

Louth

Hathersage
West Retford

LINCOLNSHIRE

DERBYSHIRE

Ulceby

Bakewell
Ashover

Branston

Bonsall

NOTTINGHAMSHIRE

Coleby

Brant Broughton
Rowston
Welbourn Digby
Leadenham

Ashbourne

Newark-on-Trent

Balderton
Fenton
Claypole
Caythorpe
Quarrington

Gedling

Thoroton

Ancaster Wilsford
Barkston
Kelby
Silk Willoughby
Aswarby
Asgarby
Heckington

Breadsall Morley

St Peter, Nottingham
Bottesford
Great Gonerby
Heydour
Helpringham

Swineshead

Uttoxeter

Bingham
Redmile
Barrowby
Grantham
Boston

Marston on the Dove
Rolleston
Repton

Keyworth
Barkestone
Harlaxton
Branston

Donington
Quadring
Gosberton
Surfleet

Billingborough

Hacconby

Kegworth
Bunny
Castle Donnington

Waltham on the Wolds
Ab Kettleby

Hamstall Ridware

Belton

Saxelby
Asfordby
Frisby on the Wreake
Brooksby
Somerby

Little Bytham

Holbeach
Spalding
Fleet
Moulton

Clifton Campville
Coleorton
Thorpe Constantine
Ibstock
Ratcliffe on the Wreake
Newton Linford
Queniborough

RUTLAND

Langtoft

Tydd St Mary
Leverington

NORFOLK

Lichfield Cathedral (3 towers)
St Michael, Lichfield
Appleby Magna
Whittington
Markfield
St Mary de Castro, Leicester
Hungarton
Cold Overton

Exton

Snettisham

Little Bytham

Oakham
Empingham

Uffington West Deeping

Edith Weston
All Saints, Stamford
Glinton

LEICESTERSHIRE

Peckleton
Humberstone
Stoughton

Preston
South Luffenham

Peterborough Cathedral west spires

Ratcliffe Culey
Fenny Drayton
Witherley

Earl Shilton
Stoney Stanton
Stoke Golding
Sapcote
Broughton Astley
Cosby

Blaby
Wigston
Whetstone

Uppington
Wakerley

Whittlesey

March

Methwold

Aston
Coleshill
Yardley

Leire

Caldecott
Bulwick
Deene
Nassington

Fotheringhay
Yaxley

Kings Norton
Solihull

Theddingworth

HUNTS

St Mary, Ely

Holy Trinity, Coventry
Naseby

Geddington
Lowick
Islip
Grafton Underwood
Woodford
Thrapston
Denford

Great Gidding

Houghton
St Ives

Sutton

Lapworth
St Michael, Coventry

Kettering

Catworth

Willingham

Bromsgrove

Great Cransley
Finedon
Spratton

Wilby
Rushden

Higham Ferrers

Swineshead

Hemingford Abbots
Offord Darcy
Conington

WARWICKSHIRE

NORTHAMPTONSHIRE

Northampton, Holy Sepulchre

Wymington
Keysoe
Easton Maudit Sharnbrook
Harrold

Little Staughton
Colmworth

Eltisley

CAMBRIDGESHIRE

All Saints, Evesham
Tredington

Byfield

Milton Malsor

St Paul, Bedford

Childswickham

Middleton Cheeney

Hanslope

Bloxham
Kings Sutton
Adderbury

BEDS

ESSEX

Stanton

BUCKS

Thaxted

RECESSED SPIRES IN EASTERN AND CENTRAL ENGLAND

(i) Patrington
c. 1368–71

(j) Higham Ferrers
c. 1340

(k) Grantham
c. 1300–1320

(l) St Mary Redcliffe
early fourteenth century (rebuilt 1872)

(m) Newark-on-Trent
c. 1315–38

EARLY RECESSED SPIRES

0   20'

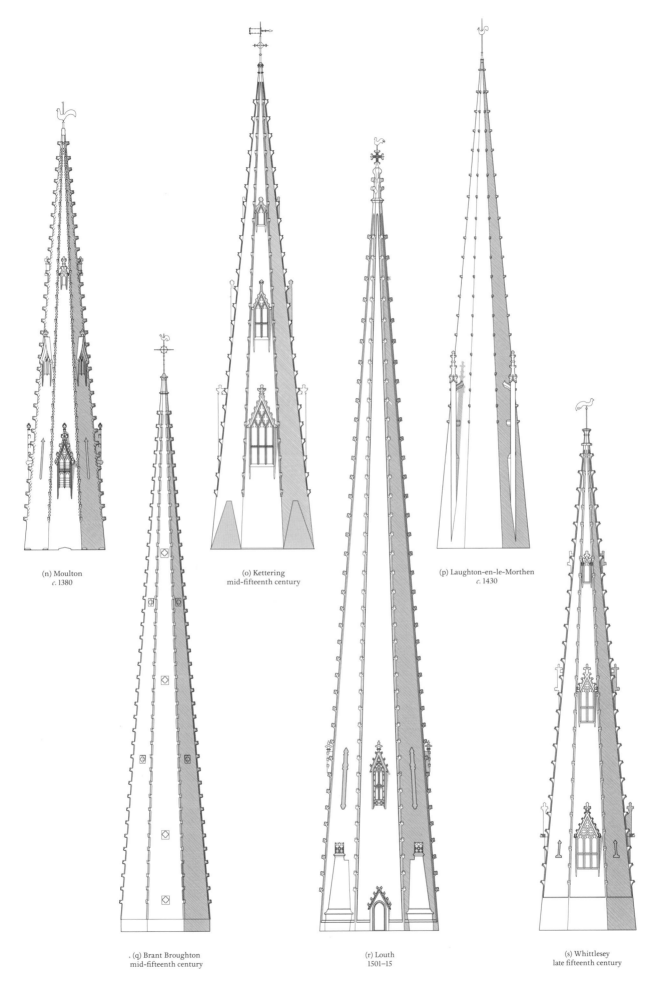

(n) Moulton
c. 1380

(o) Kettering
mid-fifteenth century

(p) Laughton-en-le-Morthen
c. 1430

. (q) Brant Broughton
mid-fifteenth century

(r) Louth
1501–15

(s) Whittlesey
late fifteenth century

MATURE RECESSED SPIRES

0   20'

construct. The basic form never varied, but when funds permitted attention was lavished on spire edges, lucarnes and supporting pinnacles. It has been suggested that lucarnes were added by the medieval mason for structural reasons, to allow wind to pass through the spire rather than press upon it. This is, however, contradicted by the evidence, for solid spires are concentrated in the more exposed but poorer northern counties of England, and lucarnes in the more sheltered but affluent regions.

For broach spires, corner pinnacles are, with few exceptions, an unnecessary irritation, but for recessed spires they are an essential part of the design. The drawings show how naked and unfinished a recessed spire appears when presented in isolation. The principal failing of Queniborough and several other tall spires in Leicestershire is that they lack the visual support of strong framing pinnacles. By contrast, the great spire at LOUTH (p. 43 (r)) is designed with restraint compared with the magnificent pinnacles and flying buttresses encircling its base.

Masonry joints were set horizontally rather than perpendicular to the sloping face of the spire, to prevent moisture from draining down the joints to the interior. The wall of the spire was kept in place principally by the weight of stone above, and so the capstone at the summit had to be as large and heavy as practicable. Capstones were subject to the most severe exposure and in most cases have been replaced during restorations by harder and darker stone. The top of the spire may be tied together by a metal holding-down rod fixed to a pair of cross trees built into the upper masonry. With the notable exception of the great spire at Salisbury Cathedral, the centre of stone spires were constructed hollow and empty, the timber structure at LOUTH being a later addition.

Broaches and splays are frequently visible above the parapet at the foot of a recessed spire, and this has led to much confusion. The distinction between the broach spire and the recessed spire with broaches is straightforward but often overlooked, for a recessed spire has a parapet, while a broach spire does not.[5] Prominent broaches on a recessed spire are usually an indication of high squinches and an early date. NEWARK has very high immature squinches and prominent broaches, but many recessed spires have low squinches and small broaches concealed behind the parapet and all but invisible from the ground.

LUCARNES

The development of the lucarne, or spire light, closely followed that of smaller twin-light and single-light tower windows. The evolution of plate, Geometrical, intersecting and Curvilinear tracery is condensed and framed by an enclosing miniature gable to form a concise synopsis of the mason's art. Lucarnes either follow the same orientation as the tower walls in an orthogonal arrangement, or they are rotated diagonally at each level in an alternating arrangement.

Across England 180 of the almost 200 medieval oversailing spires have lucarnes. Three of these – Sleaford, Olney and Buckminster (Leics) – are decorated by four tiers of lucarnes. Of the remaining spires, one-quarter have three tiers, half have two tiers, and one-quarter have a single tier. There is a pronounced regional variation in the number and orientation of oversailing spire lucarnes.[6] Extravagant alternating arrangements dominate in Lincolnshire, while less extensive orthogonal arrangements are preferred in Northamptonshire and Leicestershire. In peripheral counties alternating lucarnes are entirely absent, and openings can be reduced to the meanest of proportions.

The transition from oversailing to recessed spire had no immediate impact on the evolution of spire-light design, and regional variations continued much as before.[7] One peculiar development of the late Perpendicular lucarne is diamond tracery, in which the tracery bars run parallel to the gable roof slope and consequently cross each other at an acute angle. In two-light windows the difference is subtle, but over three lights the effect is pronounced. At WHITTLESEY (p. 43 (s)), KETTERING (p. 43 (o)), Easton Maudit (Northants), Helpringham (Lincs), St Mary-de-Castro, Leicester (currently dismantled), Queniborough (Leics) and Thaxted (Essex), the tiers follow the eminently satisfying sequence of three lights, two lights and one light.

FLYING BUTTRESSES AND SPIRES

At GRANTHAM the parapet path cuts awkwardly through the huge corner pinnacles, which as a consequence have to be propped off the spire with strange wedges of masonry. The same awkwardness occurred at Oakham (Rutland) and HECKINGTON before the masons realized that the pinnacles should either be set further out or reduced in size. A more articulate means of providing a visual connection between pinnacle and spire was soon found in the flying buttress.

The flying buttress evolved in England and France during the twelfth century to transfer the lateral thrust of high stone vaults to perimeter buttresses. By contrast, flying buttresses adorning English medieval spires are, with few exceptions, of no structural significance. Spires are inherently stable thin-walled structures. Buttressing works through the concentration of loads down lines of structure, but in a spire the loads are not concentrated, and placing a flying buttress on the centre of a thin wall serves little functional purpose. The enormous flying buttresses at LOUTH are supposedly resisting the outward thrust of a spire wall that is no more than ten inches thick. BOSTON and NEWCASTLE are rare examples of flying buttresses that do perform essential structural functions, because they span to the stiff corners of substantial octagonal lanterns rather than the weak centres of their walls.

The flying buttress was limited to areas where the finest materials were available to the most skilful masons. Across England only thirty-two spires and three octagons employ flying buttresses, and only three of these – ST MICHAEL, COVENTRY, Weobley (Shrops) and Clifton Campville (Staffs) – are outside eastern England. The best designs may conveniently be divided into two distinct types.

The Lincolnshire form of flying buttress appears in its purest form at Billingborough, Silk Willoughby and, remarkably, at Thaxted in Essex. It consists of two slender members, the upper straight and the lower arched, joined only where they spring from the corner pinnacle. More elaborate versions occur at Caythorpe and Welbourn (Lincs), where quatrefoils and mouchettes are introduced between the members, and at Fleet and MOULTON, where pointed trefoils are formed. Crockets adorn the flying buttresses at Asgarby, Coleby, Gosberton, Spalding (Lincs) and MOULTON, and in the latter two examples the upper members follow gentle ogee curves and terminate with finials. The slenderest flying masonry, seen at MOULTON and elsewhere, was achieved only by combining the separate structural member and coping stone into a single piece of masonry.

Several flying buttresses in Lincolnshire make no pretence of being structural members. At Asgarby the flying buttresses are so flat and so slender that the only surprise is that they are strong enough to support their own weight. However, at LOUTH, WHITTLESEY, Yaxley (Hunts) and Thaxted (Essex), the flying buttress provides the most refined, delicate and satisfying aesthetic device for leading the eye from the tower to the spire.

In Northamptonshire an alternative form was favoured, with upper and lower members connected by a solid web perforated by quatrefoils. When used in combination with a perforated quatrefoil parapet, this created a wonderfully integrated solution and achieved a perfect balance between delicacy and strength. Four closely grouped spires followed this principle in fourteenth-century Northamptonshire: Rushden, Easton Maudit, WILBY and, earliest and noblest of all, HIGHAM FERRERS. WHITTLESEY, Hanslope (Bucks) and Yaxley (Hunts), just beyond the county boundary, only lack the perforated parapet.

There is considerable variety beyond these two main schools. Flying buttresses at West Retford (Notts) and LAUGHTON-EN-LE-MORTHEN lead to the slenderest of spire pinnacles. The plain, smooth ogee curves of ST MICHAEL, COVENTRY contrast with the delicate prickliness of Kings Sutton (Northants). Development concludes with the great flying buttresses of BOSTON and LOUTH, both highly original compositions that combine the best features of the Lincolnshire and Northamptonshire schools.

TYPES OF RECESSED SPIRE

Recessed spires do not readily lend themselves to classification. However, the following loosely defined groupings illustrate significant shared characteristics and themes. Except where specifically stated, these groupings should not be taken to infer any suggestion of a common authorship by either a single master mason or a group of masons.

EARLY ROLL-EDGED SPIRES
A group of modest roll-edged spires from around 1300, all located within a five-mile radius. Two or three tiers of lucarnes with Geometrical tracery, gable crosses and prominent broaches or splays visible above a plain parapet, giving a characteristic tapering profile when viewed on the diagonal: Deene, Denford, Grafton Underwood, Woodford (Northants).

TRANSITIONAL SPIRES
Large, profusely decorated early fourteenth-century spires, with up to five alternating tiers of Curvilinear lucarnes; spire edges

decorated with rolls, crockets or ballflower ribs; prominent broaches occasionally surmounted by finials or canopied figures: GRANTHAM, NEWARK, ST MARY REDCLIFFE, Gedling (Notts) and Ashbourne (Derbys).

PLAIN CURVILINEAR SPIRES
This small group, from the early to mid-fourteenth century, displays considerable vigour and individuality. Surrounded by hexagonal flat-faced pinnacles except at Billingborough (square) and Oakham (octagonal). Sculptural, plain-edged spires with two or three tiers of alternating Curvilinear lucarnes and extremely prominent finials and carving, resulting in a characteristic knobbly silhouette at HECKINGTON, Billingborough, Silk Willoughby, Donington (all Lincs), Snettisham (Norfolk) and Oakham (Rutland).

CLUSTERED PINNACLE SPIRES
Geographically dispersed spires with pinnacles set either side of the parapet path, both on the corner of the tower and on the corner of the spire. Well suited to the scale of Salisbury Cathedral and ST MARY, OXFORD, also appearing at Kings Sutton, Middleton Cheeney (Northants) and Rotherham (Yorks West).

FORTIFIED SPIRES
Conventional spires surrounded by castellated corner turrets, occasionally incorporating loopholes, appearing first at Leverington (Cambs), where the turrets sit on the base of the spire. Subsequently at KETTERING and All Saints, Stamford (Lincs), turrets are set on the corners of the tower to achieve greater prominence. Oundle (Northants) and Exton (Rutland) appear to date from the seventeenth and nineteenth centuries respectively.

MATURE LINCOLNSHIRE SPIRES
Classic crocketed spires, with alternating lucarnes of Perpendicular tracery, carrying prominent finials and projecting carving, giving a characteristic frilly silhouette.

Flying buttresses, usually crocketed, spring from panelled and crocketed pinnacles, which are square except for the early spire at Welbourn (hexagonal) and the late spire at Louth (octagonal). Early spires are distinguished by full-bodied sculptural crockets and conventional tracery; later spires have flat-sided angular crockets combined with diamond tracery in the lucarnes. Appearing at Asgarby, Coleby, Gosberton, Helpringham, LOUTH, MOULTON, Spalding and Welbourn (Lincs), and at Thaxted (Essex). Uffington (Lincs) dates from 1639.

Modest spires lacking flying buttresses but only slightly inferior in quality appear at Barkston, Claypole, Digby, Fenton, Leadenham and West Deeping (Lincs), and at Empingham and South Luffenham (Rutland).

QUATREFOIL PERFORATED SPIRES

Modest, plain spires with up to three orthogonal tiers of small quatrefoil perforations at Ab Kettleby, Humberstone, Ibstock, Markfield, Newton Linford, Radcliffe Culey, Broughton Astley, Fenny Drayton, Leire, Stoke Golding (Leics) and Ulceby (Lincs). Associated tall Lincolnshire spires with alternating perforated quatrefoils appear close to the county border at BRANT BROUGHTON (five tiers) and Caythorpe (six tiers), and more remotely at Fleet (three tiers). Solihull (Warks), geographically isolated and with abnormally large quatrefoils, is probably from a reconstruction of 1757.

QUATREFOIL FLYING BUTTRESS SPIRES

Spires with prominent flying buttresses of the Northamptonshire form perforated by quatrefoils to be found at HIGHAM FERRERS (p. 42 (j)), Rushden, Easton Maudit, WILBY (Northants) and Hanslope (Bucks), WHITTLESEY (Cambs) and Yaxley (Hunts). The four spires in the county, all within a five-mile radius, have matching perforated parapets. The standard three tiers of orthogonal lucarnes are reduced to two on the smaller spires of Wilby and Yaxley.

ARCADED SPIRES

Spires encircled at the base by a continuous arcade of sixteen bays at PATRINGTON (p. 42 (i)) and Swineshead (Lincs) or twenty-four bays at Methwold (Norfolk). Wide differences in treatment and location suggest only the loosest of connections.

SPIRES RISING FROM OCTAGONAL DRUMS

Recessed spires arising from octagonal drums on square towers appearing after 1380 to be found in two distinct locations. The northern type of solid roll-edged spire, with the octagon surrounded by diagonal buttresses, appears at St Mary Castlegate and All Saints North Street in York, Masham and Brayton (Yorks West), and Chester-le-Street (Durham). The southern form of spire has two orthogonal tiers of lucarnes at Houghton (Hunts) and WILBY. Simpler variations exist at Tong (Shrops), Halsall (Lancs) and Bakewell (Derbys). Nassington (Northants) is from the seventeenth century.

OCTAGONAL PARAPET GROUP

A closely related group of four imperforate northern spires from the early fifteenth century, rising from octagonal parapets surrounded by diagonal buttresses at LAUGHTON-EN-LE-MORTHEN (p. 43 (p)), South Anston (Yorks West), and West Retford and Scrooby (Notts).

COLESHILL GROUP SPIRES

Four late medieval spires, each with three tiers of twin-light lucarnes appearing on all eight faces of the spire. The geographical arrangement is striking, for the spires follow a straight line running twenty miles from Kings Norton (Worcs) to Yardley (Worcs), Coleshill (Warks) and Witherley (Leics). By a strange coincidence this line leads directly to GRANTHAM, which provided the only significant precedent for an eight-lucarne design.

OCTAGONAL LANTERNS

A logical development of the steeple at
BARNACK and the west tower at Ely Cathedral
was to terminate the tower not with a
recessed spire but with an octagonal lantern
(p. 49). Where the octagon remains solid
and heavy, as at Pontefract (Yorks West),
and Sutton-in-the-Isle (Cambs), the result
is ponderous, but where full advantage is
made of the strength of Perpendicular
tracery open lanterns can be as light and
elegant as any spire.

The term 'lantern' for such windowed
octagons is a misnomer for, contrary to
local legends, there was never any intention
of providing illumination to the church
below or a beacon for travellers. Fine lanterns
exist at All Saints', Pavement, York, LOWICK
(t), FOTHERINGHAY (w) and supporting the
spire of ST MICHAEL, COVENTRY (x), but
none surpasses the scale and refinement
of the monumental unglazed lantern of
BOSTON (v).

THE FLYING SPIRE

In the flying spire, giant flying buttresses
provide the sole means of support for
a lantern and centre pinnacle raised
high above the roof of the tower. This
form is essentially alien to England for,
apart from NEWCASTLE (p. 49 (u)), it appears
only north of the border, at King's College,
Aberdeen, Cross Steeple, Glasgow and
St Giles's Cathedral, Edinburgh. The eight
flying buttresses employed at Edinburgh
appear heavy and congested when compared
with the four buttresses used elsewhere.

NOTES

1   The author concurs with Alec Clifton-Taylor's list
    published in *Buildings of Delight* (1986); Bruton and
    Taunton were excluded from his earlier list in *English
    Parish Churches as Works of Art* (1st edn 1974).
2   In *The Parish Church Towers of Somerset* (1981), Peter
    Poyntz Wright attempted the impossible task of dating
    seventy-two towers, each within an accuracy of seven
    years, using thirty-seven variables, a set of punch cards
    and a Fortran computer program. Despite John
    Harvey's comprehensive critique in 'The Church
    Towers of Somerset', *Ancient Monuments Society's
    Transactions*, vol. 27 (1983), the results of this flawed
    methodology have gained a wide currency, including,
    at the time of writing, Wikipedia.
3   Edmund Sharpe's classification of tracery proposed
    in *The Seven Periods of English Architecture* (1888) is
    used throughout.
4   The Statutory Listings incorrectly identify hexagonal
    spires at Walsoken (Norfolk) and Yardley (Worcs).
    The square pyramidal spire is a Victorian invention.
5   See, for instance, Pevsner's description of Grantham
    in *Buildings of England: Lincolnshire.*
6   See Appendix 3, Table 1.
7   See Appendix 3, Table 2.

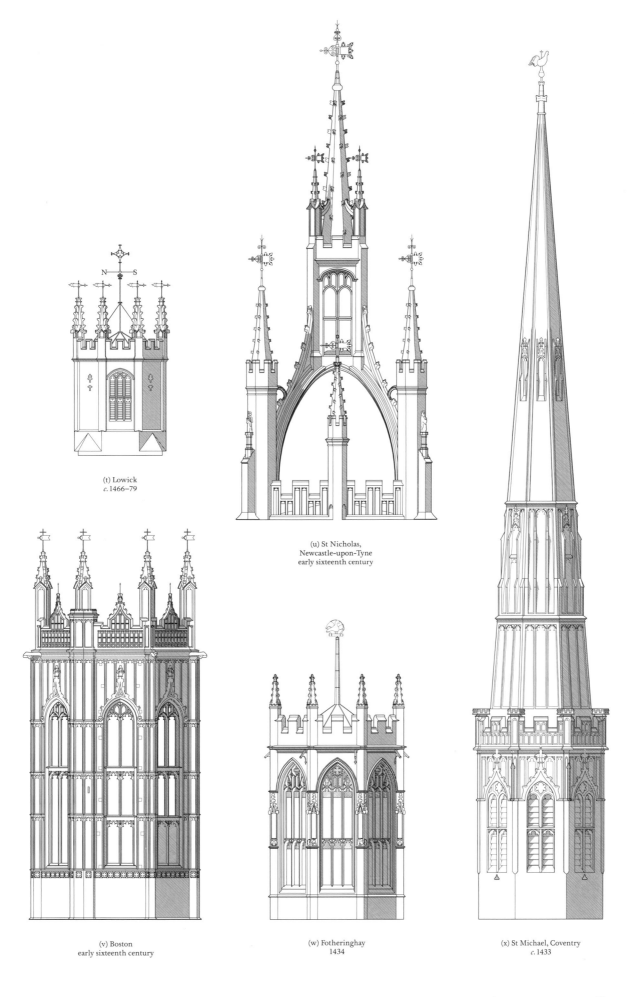

(t) Lowick
c. 1466–79

(u) St Nicholas,
Newcastle-upon-Tyne
early sixteenth century

(v) Boston
early sixteenth century

(w) Fotheringhay
1434

(x) St Michael, Coventry
c. 1433

OCTAGONS AND FLYING SPIRES

0   20'

The Fifty Steeples

Earls
Barton

Forncett
St Peter

Barnack

Castor

North
Rauceby

Witney

West
Walton

Long
Sutton

Raunds

St Mary,
Oxford

Ewerby

Brant
Broughton

Heckington

Higham
Ferrers

Patrington

Moulton

St Cuthbert,
Wells

Tickhill

Laughton-en-
le-Morthen

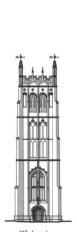

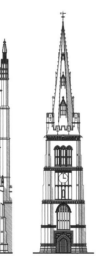

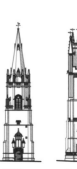

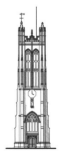

Chipping
Campden

Ludlow

Kettering

Whittlesey

Wilby

Lowick

Titchmarsh

Evercreech

Leigh-on-
Mendip

Kingston
St Mary

Adderbury

Grantham

Newark-on-Trent

Ketton

St Mary, Stamford

St Mary Redcliffe

St Michael, Coventry

Fotheringhay

Salle

Stoke-by-Nayland

Southwold

Eye

Redenhall

St Mary Magdalene, Taunton

North Petherton

Lavenham

Dedham

Ingatestone

Newcastle-upon-Tyne

Boston

Louth

I

Earls Barton

NORTHAMPTONSHIRE

EARLS BARTON is by far the most impressive monument of Anglo-Saxon architecture. It is one of the few buildings of the period that is of aesthetic as well as archaeological interest for, as a general principle, the Saxons were far more accomplished at metalwork, jewelry and manuscript illumination than they were at building. The magnificently preserved west tower is a dignified early attempt at creating art from roughly hewn stone. Indeed, the very primitiveness of the carving makes the great labour involved in cutting stone from the ground, squaring it, raising it high up a scaffold and setting it upright all the more palpable. Saxon architecture makes the craft of the mason look relentless and backbreaking.

Saxon towers are concentrated in the eastern half of England and along the South Coast. Lincolnshire towers are gaunt and tall, reaching up to seventy-five feet high at St Peter-at-Gowts, Lincoln. Northumbrian towers are plain but lower, with modest decoration around the bell openings. In the East Midlands, however, there is a small but celebrated class of sturdily proportioned towers that employ elaborate pilaster decoration: BARNACK, Barton-on-Humber (Lincs), Stow-Nine-Churches (Northants) and EARLS BARTON.

The Domesday Book reveals that the settlement of *Bartone*, as it was then known, was held by a court official called Bondi. This official also owned the settlement of BARNACK, and it was from the great quarry

there that the stone for EARLS BARTON was obtained. The church of All Saints stands on a prominent spur overlooking the north-west bank of the Nene as it meanders down to Wellingborough. Immediately to the north of the church is a broad ditch and mound, but the view from this direction is blocked by an unwelcome wall of twentieth-century yew trees.

EARLS BARTON is impressive not only for its height, almost sixty feet to the top of the Saxon work, but also for its breadth. The composition is more convincing than the detail, and it illustrates several important characteristics that would persist in English tower-building. The four stages become progressively shorter and narrower, and they are emphatically divided by prominent string courses. There are sound construction reasons for a tapered profile, but there are also aesthetic benefits, for it emphasizes the solidity of the base and the height of the crown. The horizontality of the stacked independent stages is countered by the forceful verticality of the decoration. This was to become a recurring principle of English tower design, particularly where the buttress was at its least assertive, for example at ST MARY, STAMFORD or EYE.

The setting-out of the tower is careless, with the east wall significantly skewed on plan. Rendered limestone-rubble walls are remarkably slender, being just 3' 11" thick at the base. The Saxons may have been unskilled at cutting stone but they built with great diligence, and their mortar was excellent.

Despite a thousand years of bell ringing, the tower has never required strengthening.

The wall surface is articulated by pilaster strips, or lesenes, four inches wide, of alternately long and short stones. The effectiveness of this 'long and short' work is hard to determine, for it is unclear how far the stones extend into the body of the wall. More certain is the structural significance of the 'upright and flat' construction of the corners, in which flat, square horizontal slabs alternate with thin vertical stones. The lowest string course corresponds closely to the level of the first floor, but there is no evidence to suggest that any of the upper strings were aligned in the same way.

On the first stage, five long and short pilasters, rising from small, square plinth blocks, divide each elevation. To the west is an imposing ceremonial door opening formed of colossal upright and flat through-stones enclosed within an arched pilaster strip. The interior has been difficult to appreciate since the introduction of a vestry screen that blocked the tower arch in the 1930s. The original Saxon arch was rebuilt after little more than a century, for the scalloped and moulded imposts on the responds (a) and the double row of billet moulding on the arch are unmistakably Norman. These have been crudely altered by later Gothic masons, with two inner chamfered orders of ironstone lifting the arch into a point high above its original position.

Another Norman addition is the internally splayed window over the west door, which disrupts the original Saxon paired openings. These are better preserved on the south elevation (b), where deep external reveals are framed by banded balusters sitting on square corbel blocks and carrying shallow monolithic arches decorated with crosses. Set centrally within the depth of the wall are transennae, or vertical slabs, perforated by the silhouette of an open cross.

Second and third stages follow the same six-bay organization but with less convincing results. The second stage is decorated with an arcade of sorts, but with the arches dropped to the floor, while the third stage reads to modern eyes as nothing so much as a house of cards rising in two precarious tiers. No fewer than six doorways are cut into these stages apparently at random – Baldwin Brown's 'enigmatical doorways apparently leading no wither'.[1] The single door to the east (c), which now gives access to the nave roof, may originally have led to a chamber in the roof space of the early church, but there is no apparent explanation for the other five openings (d). The theory that they were used for the periodic display of relics is unconvincing.[2]

EARLS BARTON's arcaded bell stage is unique among surviving Saxon towers. Six baluster shafts running across each elevation vary comically in their proportions. Capitals are square blocks with soft edges and the semicircular arches above are framed by two shallow radiused bands. Saxon masons took great delight in turning balusters on the

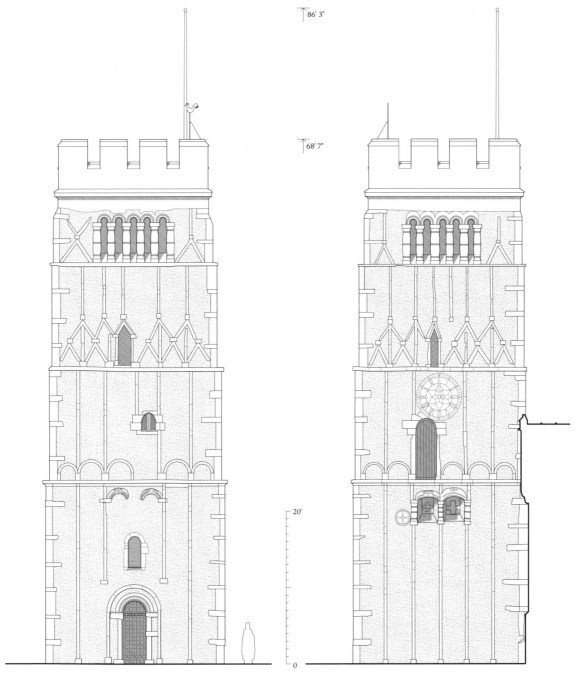

86' 3"

68' 7"

20'

0

West elevation

South elevation

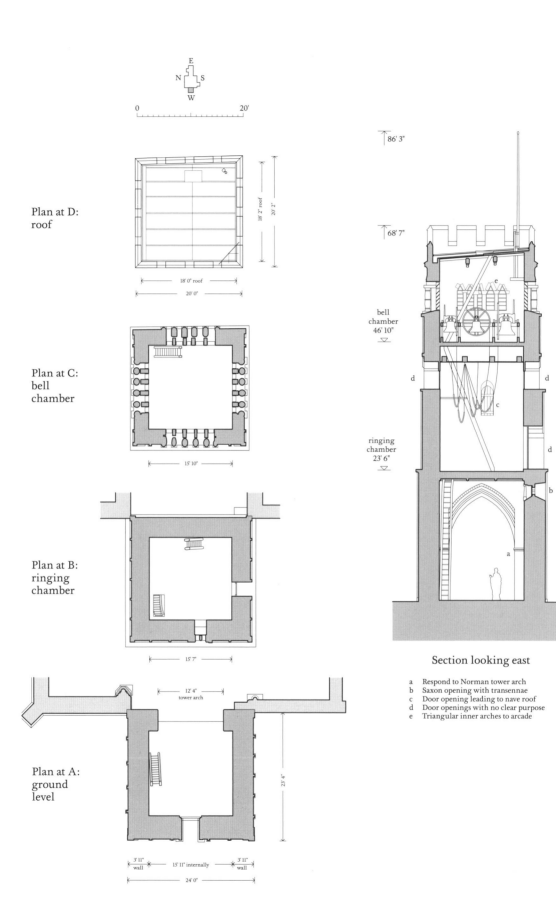

Plan at D:
roof

Plan at C:
bell
chamber

Plan at B:
ringing
chamber

Plan at A:
ground
level

0   20'

18' 2" roof
20' 2"

18' 0" roof
20' 0"

15' 10"

15' 7"

12' 4"
tower arch

23' 4"

3' 11"
wall

15' 11" internally

3' 11"
wall

24' 0"

86' 3"

68' 7"

bell
chamber
46' 10"

ringing
chamber
23' 6"

D

C

B

A

d   d

c

d

b

a

e

Section looking east

a Respond to Norman tower arch
b Saxon opening with transennae
c Door opening leading to nave roof
d Door openings with no clear purpose
e Triangular inner arches to arcade

lathe, but here they were clumsily carved by mallet and chisel. Shafts are placed according to their quality, with smoothly rounded shafts to the north and south, elliptical shafts to the west, and the poorest work consigned to the east. These shafts carry only the outer half of the wall, the inner half being borne by triangular arches on simple rectangular piers (e). Pilaster strips fill between the arcades and the corners. The original upper termination has been lost to two levelling courses and a plain parapet of orange fifteenth-century ironstone.

The present appearance of the tower as the western termination of the body of the church may be deceptive. There is strong evidence that the tower was originally a turriform church, in which the tower itself formed the body of the church. The upright and flat quoins framing the east elevation continue within the body of the church, suggesting that the original annex in this direction must have been narrower than the tower and subservient to it. This hypothesis is reinforced by a steeply pitched roof line visible above the present nave. It may seem extraordinary that a church only sixteen feet square within its walls should have been raised four stories above the ground, but examples of this arrangement exist at Broughton-by-Brigg and Barton-on-Humber (Lincs) and at Eastdean (Sussex).

The great Saxon tower at EARLS BARTON is an archaeological site of national importance and a poignant reminder of a native Romanesque building tradition lost to an aggressive foreign invader. Nonetheless, it contains many of the central themes of English tower design: the tapering profile, the stack of independent stages separated by horizontal strings, the concentration of effort on the top stage, and the prominent ceremonial west door. In the history of the English steeple EARLS BARTON is the starting point against which all subsequent developments can be measured and judged.

NOTES

1   Quoted from the first authoritative study of Saxon architecture: G. Baldwin Brown, *The Arts in Early England*, vol. 2: *Ecclesiastical Architecture in England* (1903), p. 188.

2   For an exhaustive examination of this issue and all aspects of Saxon architecture see H. M. and J. Taylor's *Anglo-Saxon Architecture* (1964).

2

Forncett St Peter

Round towers have such a loyal following that they have their own fan club. Since 1973 the Round Tower Churches Society has supported conservation projects to safeguard the majority of the 185 or so towers still standing. In the society's estimation there are 126 towers in Norfolk, 42 in Suffolk, 7 in Essex, 2 in Cambridgeshire and 8 in Surrey, Sussex and Berkshire. They are all constructed of flint-rubble walling, for they are found only in areas where the lack of good building stone prevented the construction of square corners. These survivors may represent just a small proportion of the original numbers, and their current distribution reflects the relative poverty of their particular neighbourhoods during the later Middle Ages.

The round tower is a Saxon form that lingered long after the Norman Conquest. English round towers were universally designed for the ringing of bells, which was becoming an essential part of church and community life by the start of the tenth century. They were not, as is sometimes suggested, defensive structures like the round towers of Scotland and Ireland, for they appeared only when the prolonged period of Viking raids was at an end. Around twenty-four towers, almost all in Norfolk, are recognizably Saxon, for they incorporate double bell openings with straight reveals, double-splayed windows and oculi (small circular windows). The vast majority of towers with dateable features are Norman, but there is also frequent evidence of a

transition between the two styles. This is only to be expected, for although the government of England underwent a fundamental change in 1066 the imported style of building was assimilated by the rural mason only gradually.

Invariably, the summit of an English round tower is protected by later medieval work, whether in the form of a simple stone coping to throw off the rain, a tall parapet to conceal a lead roof, or a complete bell stage. Some towers are celebrated for these distinctive later additions, such as the chequerboard flushwork parapet at Haddiscoe (Norfolk). Such idiosyncratic terminations may be entertaining, but for the purist they are also a distraction. Not only is FORNCETT ST PETER one of the best-preserved and most imaginatively designed of the Saxon towers, but it is also finished by a satisfyingly restrained parapet.

The Domesday Book records four settlements and two churches in the area between the Roman road from Norwich to Ipswich and the River Tas. The 'honour of Forncett' became a property of the Norman nobleman Roger Bigot before drifting into bucolic obscurity, to the great benefit of the church tower. For the first 500 years of its existence ST PETER'S was merely a chapel of ease serving the neighbouring church of St Mary, but from 1496 the positions were reversed. During the fourteenth and fifteenth centuries the body of the church was rebuilt over Saxon foundations, and extended with aisles of three bays and a north porch. The tower, however, remained untouched apart from the addition of a plain battlement, five feet high, faced with knapped flint.

The Saxon tower is fifty-six feet of neatly coursed flint in random shades of brown, grey, black and white, tending towards the herringbone patterning of the eleventh century. The form is slightly conical, for the external diameter reduces with remarkable regularity from 18' 8" at the base to 17' 3" immediately below the parapet. The diminution of width with increasing height would become a recognizable characteristic of the best English medieval towers, but it is a surprisingly sophisticated feature for such an early date. Not only does this convey a sense of stability and permanence, but it also counters the optical illusion that a truly vertical tower may appear to splay outwards at the top. The tower walls, 3' 10" thick at the base, are set out with three-quarters of the circular plan exposed and one-quarter overlapping the west wall of the church – the ideal balance between autonomy and connection.

Flint-rubble construction placed severe limitations on the size of penetrations through the wall, but there is still a conscious attempt to develop a cohesive composition within a restricted vocabulary. Just below the summit, a row of eight regularly spaced oculi is rotated off the main axis of the plan (d; Plan at D). These are constructed of double-splayed flint-work conoids, the splays being intended to reflect light through

the tiny circular apertures, though with limited success.

Beneath the oculi are the four double openings to the bell chamber set squarely on the principal axis (Plan at C). The stonework may be restored, but the form is immediately recognizable as late Saxon work, with lathe-turned cylindrical mid-wall shafts each supporting a single through-stone running the entire depth of the wall. These shafts are relatively sophisticated for Saxon work, having cushion capitals and bases delineated by small semicircular astragals. Such masonry was an extravagance in Norfolk, and even the narrow arches that spring from the through-stone are constructed of flint rubble. Triangular arches are used to north and south, and semicircular arches to east and west. The western opening is an effective nineteenth-century reconstruction, indistinguishable now from the original work, and the openings are filled with delightful Arts and Crafts-inspired louvre boards.[1]

Below are four narrow, round-headed slit windows, splayed internally and set on the diagonal (Plan at B), followed by an orthogonal tier of four oculi, regrettably blocked in recent years (c).[2] Finally, the slit-window motif reappears in the centre of the west face, where it allows the merest glimmer of illumination to fall within the ground floor of the tower. The Saxon west portal has been lost to an anachronistic nineteenth-century Norman Revival design; however, the authenticity of the

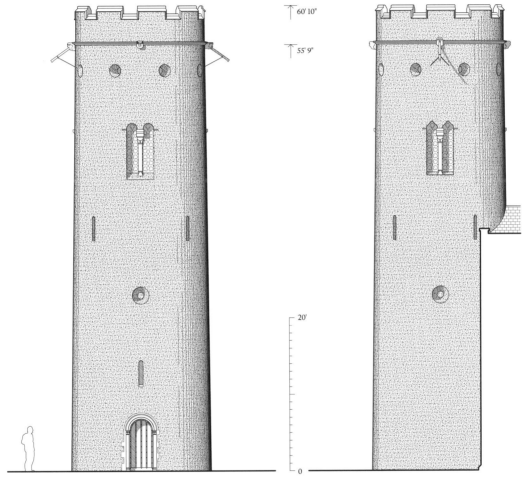

60' 10"

55' 9"

20'

0

West elevation   South elevation

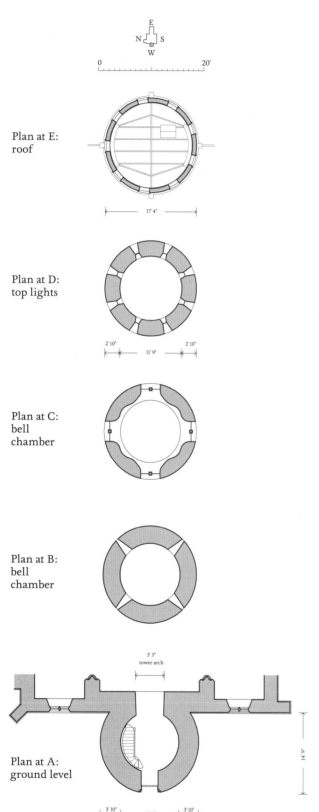

E
N—S
W

0 ————————— 20'

Plan at E:
roof

17' 4"

Plan at D:
top lights

2' 10"   11' 9"   2' 10"

Plan at C:
bell
chamber

Plan at B:
bell
chamber

5' 5"
tower arch

Plan at A:
ground level

3' 10"   11' 0"   3' 10"
wall   wall
18' 8"

14' 9"

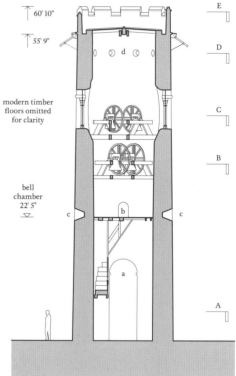

60' 10"

55' 9"

E

D

modern timber
floors omitted
for clarity

C

B

bell
chamber
22' 5"

c   b   c

a

A

Section looking east

a   Semicircular Saxon tower arch
b   Small arched door opening
c   Oculi blocked in twentieth century
d   Oculi splayed inside and out

location is confirmed internally by a deep, round-headed flint reveal.

The tower arch that leads to the nave is of a similar form but considerably larger, reaching almost fifteen feet in height (a). Internally, the tower is a straightforward tubular shaft, except around the bell openings, where the walls bulge erratically in and out to an extent that is only hinted at by the plan (Plan at C). The floor and roof structures are partly modern, but original beams have been preserved wherever possible. The access up to the first floor is precarious and ancient, with oak steps strung between twisting strings and the radiused face of the tower wall. High-level doorways are a common feature of Saxon towers, and here a small arched opening (b) would originally have led to an upper chamber within the roof space of the church. The bell frame is double stacked and set diagonally, to rest within the reveals of the narrow slit windows. It is unclear how the tower was originally roofed for the flat lead roof, draining to side-facing gargoyles, is contemporary with the parapet.

That the tower of FORNCETT ST PETER, and many like it, should be capable of withstanding storms and bell ringing for over a thousand years is a wonderful testament to the foresight and skill of the ancient builders. It is easy to disregard the round tower as a primitive form forced upon unsophisticated builders by poor materials, but this is to misunderstand a pragmatic and inherently satisfying invention. What is remarkable is not that the circular form was retained by the Normans, but that it was so definitively rejected by the Gothic mason. The circular form was a significant loss from the vocabulary of the medieval steeple-builder, for not only is it inherently satisfying and beautiful, but it is also exceptionally strong. Surprisingly, the slender proportions achieved in the flint tower of FORNCETT ST PETER at the end of the first millennium would not be improved upon at EYE or REDENHALL, despite four centuries of technological development.

NOTES

1   A drawing of the church from 1823, published in R. Ladbrooke, *Views of Churches in Norfolk* (1821–34), shows late medieval work to the western bell chamber window and the west door opening. The louvres were replaced in 2007 to an existing design.

2   Recorded as being open in H. M. and J. Taylor's monumental *Anglo-Saxon Architecture* (1964).

3

Barnack

BARNACK is of particular importance in the early history of English architecture, not only for being the site of the greatest medieval quarry, but also for the steeple of St John's Church, which combines one of the finest Saxon towers with one of the earliest stone spires.

In AD 664 King Wulfhere of Mercia granted Barnack to the nearby abbey of Peterborough, and so it is probable that a church existed on the site long before the tower was added in around 1020. The obvious similarities to the great tower at EARLS BARTON would have been stronger before the loss of the original bell chamber, which must have risen above the present second stage. BARNACK is larger, more efficient and, by implication, slightly later than EARLS BARTON. It is sixteen feet higher to the top of the second stage and two feet wider at the base, and yet at 3' 5" the walls are six inches narrower. This construction is astonishingly slender and, although strengthening has been necessary, it is still a fine testament to the dedication of the Saxon masons and the quality of their mortar. Despite the technological advances of the Gothic period, only one medieval tower in this survey approaches such slenderness and that is the great tower at BOSTON built 450 years later.

At BARNACK the division between stages is more pronounced than at EARLS BARTON, with two square strings separated by a recessed band dividing the levels. The second stage steps back noticeably, as no doubt the following stages would also have done. The walls are of small blocks of Barnack ragstone, now exposed but originally rendered. The varied treatment of the corners on the two stages suggests a break during construction. On the first stage the quoins are little more than a stack of large, square stones set in alternating directions. There does not appear to have been any attempt to hide this irregularity behind the render, for the quoins are set proud of the stone walling. The second stage is more sophisticated, for it uses so-called 'pseudo-long and short' work. Constructionally, this is 'upright and flat' work; however, the extending faces of the flat, horizontal stones are dressed back and concealed beneath the finishing render, giving the appearance of genuine long and short work. The walls of both stages are consistently decorated with three lines of tapering long and short pilasters to each face. To the first stage these sit on conventional square block bases, but on the second stage quirky half-round ribbed bases project beyond the face of the string.

Bursts of decoration are spread inconsistently across this grid. The severity of the quoins on the first stage is replicated around the openings, particularly the round-headed south doorway. Constructed entirely of massive through-stones, this is framed by hefty stripwork up the vertical jambs and around the arch, and thumping corbel blocks that carry the outer arch. Three high-level windows, small, round arches to north and south, and a larger, triangular-headed opening to the west provide

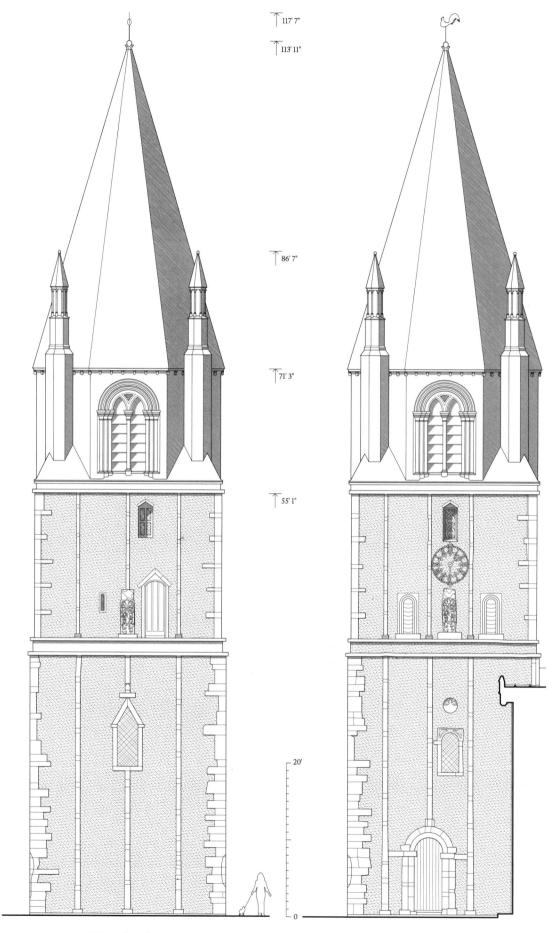

117' 7"

113' 11"

86' 7"

71' 3"

55' 1"

20'

0

West elevation

South elevation

inadequate illumination within the tower. As before, construction is of heavy through-stones and chunky imposts. Shallow carvings of birds stretch across the south window spandrels, and leaf motifs are cut into the face of a circular Saxon sundial above.

The quality of work improves on the second stage. To the centre of each of the main elevations are richly carved monoliths six feet high. Abstract fields of spiralling stems and foliage support proud cockerels in a variety of poses. This work is reminiscent of the planar art of Saxon metalwork, and by later standards it is remarkable for its lack of integration into the fabric of the building.

In this respect the perforated stone mid-wall slabs, set within the small triangular-headed openings that follow, are more satisfactory. These are similar in construction to the 'transennare' slabs at EARLS BARTON, East Lexham (Norfolk) and Langford (Oxon). Simple slots to east and west are replaced by elaborate patterns of interlaced circles to north and south. To the west, there are two apparently random openings: a triangular-headed doorway to the right of centre and a tiny slit window to the left. The reinstatement of these blocked openings in 1936 is one of several questionable decisions made during a deeply intrusive restoration.[1]

The interior is dominated by two periods of alteration: strengthening works undertaken around 1230 in preparation for the spire, and the restoration of 1934–36 funded by Canon Henry Fry. There are two fine pieces of original Saxon work to enjoy: a triangular-headed seat recess in the west wall, and the tower arch (a). Originally the recess was accompanied by a range of timber seats to either side, leading to theories that the ground floor may have been used for legal proceedings or as a western sanctuary for the church. The round-headed tower arch is impressive for its date. Arch and responds are of two primitive square-edged orders, the outer order rising from a crude square base. Horizontal striations on the imposts imitate the pattern formed by superimposed Roman tiles seen not far away at Brixworth (Northants).

The early thirteenth-century quadripartite vault with plain chamfered diagonal ribs and a small, circular bell hatch (b) may have been intended to strengthen the tower, but it is unlikely to have produced any significant benefit. It is supported off 'L'-shaped square-edged responds added to three internal corners of the tower, and by the wall of a spiral stair built at the same time in the south-west angle. This stair reaches only to the flat upper surface of the vault, which may once have formed a ringing chamber floor. Unfortunately, the interiors of the upper tower suffered irreparable damage during the ill-conceived 1934–36 restoration when a deeply intrusive concrete frame was used to reinforce the structure (c).

Although BARNACK is not, as is sometimes claimed, the earliest stone spire in England, it is certainly from the first, experimental generation of spires, of which there are now few survivors. The composition is simple to the point of severity. The plain, widely spreading spire is raised over an octagonal bell stage, with paired openings on the cardinal faces. Corner broaches surmounted by octagonal pinnacles cover the transition from square to octagonal plan, much as they do at contemporary spires in Oxfordshire. Regular notch heads decorate the spire overhang, but the colonnaded pinnacle caps from the 1930s introduce an inappropriate note of fussiness and verticality. The arches spanning these openings are typical of the transition from round Romanesque to pointed Gothic forms that was nearing completion in the early thirteenth century. NORTH RAUCEBY and Etton (Hunts) have a similar arrangement of round-headed arches enclosing pairs of pointed lights and plate tracery, while at Sleaford, Burton-le-Coggles and Frampton (Lincs), the main arch is just developing a point. The detailing at BARNACK

is consistent with the best of these examples, showing three detached shafts to either side and one dividing the lights, all finished with tall, well-moulded ring capitals and bases. Squinch arches (d) and tracery are more developed than at NORTH RAUCEBY, suggesting a slightly later date.

As a composition the steeple at BARNACK is far from perfect, for the divergent styles of the eleventh and thirteenth centuries sit uneasily together. The tower is an object of exceptional archaeological interest rather than great beauty, but the spire and octagonal bell stage are an elegant and robust design full of promise. Its influence can be seen initially in the octagonal drum steeples of Huntingdonshire, at Grafham and Old Weston, and later in a number of exceptionally inventive designs such as Masham (Yorks North), Bloxham (Oxon), WILBY and the great steeple of ST MICHAEL, COVENTRY.

NOTE

1   Illustrated by a photograph taken prior to the restoration by Francis Bond in *Gothic Architecture in England* (1905), p. 613, and by a perspective view by J. Johnson in Edmund Sharpe, J. Johnson and A. H. Kersey, *Churches of the Nene Valley* (1880), p. 97.

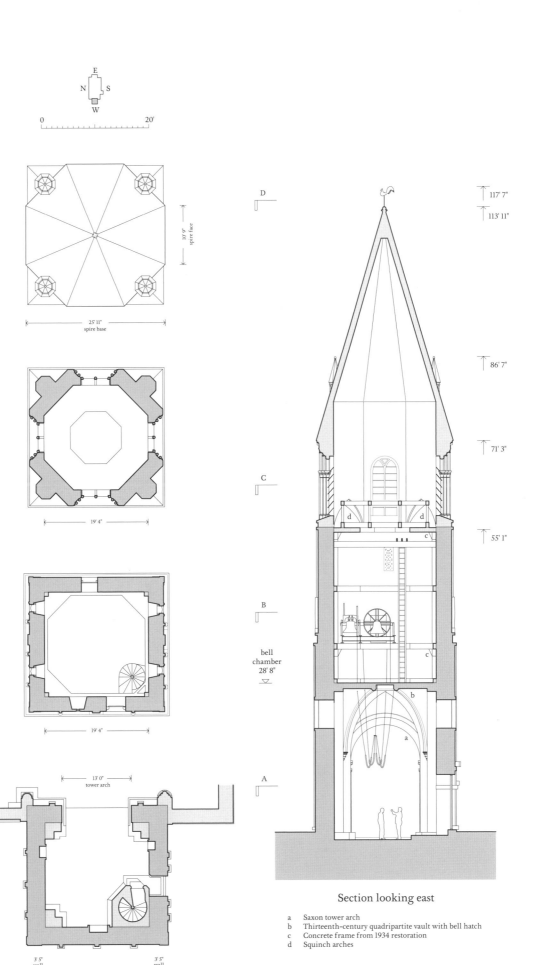

Plan at D:
spire

10' 9"
spire face

25' 11"
spire base

Plan at C:
spire base

19' 4"

Plan at B:
modern bell
chamber

19' 4"

Plan at A:
ground
level

13' 0"
tower arch

3' 5"
wall

19' 4"

3' 5"
wall

26' 2"

D

C

B

bell
chamber
28' 8"

A

117' 7"

113' 11"

86' 7"

71' 3"

55' 1"

d   d

c

c

b

a

Section looking east

a   Saxon tower arch
b   Thirteenth-century quadripartite vault with bell hatch
c   Concrete frame from 1934 restoration
d   Squinch arches

0   20'

E
N   S
W

4

Castor

HUNTINGDONSHIRE

The Normans built as they governed, with great ambition and rough impatience. At its worst, their style of architecture is as oppressive as the political system that it represents. Unlike Gothic architecture, it was not the creative expression of free and skilled men, but the imposed style of an elite core of masons controlling a large workforce of semi-skilled native labour. Norman architecture is dominated by massive rubble-filled walls, round arches and huge cylindrical columns. Shallow buttresses, little more than thickenings of the wall, start to articulate the body of the church, but they have little structural significance.

In the first major church tower built under the new regime, at St Albans (*c.* 1077), shallow corner and central buttresses create an effective composition with a degree of vertical emphasis. In the flurry of great towers constructed in the first half of the following century, a different and ultimately less successful approach was adopted, with shallow, arcaded clasping buttresses articulating the corners. This feature is prominent in the twin towers of Exeter Cathedral (*c.* 1133) and the central tower at Norwich Cathedral (from *c.* 1121 in the upper stages), more subdued at Tewkesbury Abbey (*c.* 1150) and Southwell Minster (*c.* 1108), and altogether absent at CASTOR (*c.* 1124). Without strong buttresses, English tower design continued to employ the same mode of composition that was evident at EARLS BARTON, of piling one independent square

stage upon another and relying on a mass of small scale articulation for vertical emphasis.

The dominant motif that would provide such articulation is present in unrefined form at St Albans, where pairs of narrow, round-arched openings, supported on circular shafts, are enclosed below a single, broad semicircular arch. The extent to which this became the dominant obsession of tower designers can be seen in the escalating number of shafts, from 64 in three tiers at St Albans, to 134 in two tiers at Southwell, 284 in three tiers at Tewkesbury, and 296 in four tiers at Norwich. CASTOR is tame by comparison, for it only employs 100 shafts in two tiers, and yet it is, without doubt, the most satisfying of all the Norman towers of England.

CASTOR is a site of exceptional historical interest. A major Roman settlement existed near the strategic crossing of Ermine Street over the River Nene until around AD 450. Excavations have revealed a *praetorium* or palace below the churchyard, one of the largest Roman buildings in England. It is thought that Christian worship started here as long ago as the fourth century. In Saxon times the princesses Kyneburgha and Kyneswitha founded a convent on the site of the Roman ruins, and this in turn was destroyed by Vikings. The Normans rebuilt on the sacred site using a good deal of material salvaged from the two previous structures. A dedication stone inscribed in Latin, now set above the south chancel priest's door, reads: 'The dedication of this church was on 17 April AD 1124.' CASTOR drifted into obscurity in later medieval times owing to its proximity to Peterborough, which prevented it from expanding into a market town. As a result there was little pressure to enlarge the ancient structure, and St Kyneburgha's remains one of the least-altered Norman parish churches in the country.

Even from a distance, the cruciform plan that was so dear to the Normans is immediately apparent. The effect would have been far more powerful when the four limbs abutting the tower, and not just the south transept, were covered by steeply pitched roofs. Externally, the tower is of three stages: a solid plinth to receive the ridge of the adjacent roofs, followed by two highly decorated stages. The uppermost stage, with the widest openings, was naturally for the bells, but without the original floor structure in place it is unclear if the stage below was floored, or whether it formed a clerestory to illuminate what is now the ringing chamber. The later addition of the spire is not unwelcome, but for the first 300 years of its existence the tower would have been terminated by an overhanging pyramidal roof, possibly of local Collyweston slate.

Together the two decorated stages of the tower approximate a cube twenty-four feet across, and on elevation each stage forms a double square. This is a considerable improvement on the leaden proportions of Southwell, Tewkesbury and most other Norman towers, and this is at the heart of CASTOR's appeal. The main features of the

design are prominent corbel tables, arcades of paired openings and lashings of surface decoration. With internal access restricted to ladders, there are no staircase windows to disrupt the symmetry of the four identically organized faces.

The lower stage is of three unequal bays. Blind outer bays are of two narrow, round-headed openings set beneath one semicircular arch carrying two rows of billet, a Norman favourite of alternating, offset half-cylinders. The plain tympanum is carried by the square cushion capitals of three slender detached shafts. Matching shafts on the exposed outer corners of the tower provide a seamless continuity to the encircling arcade.

Unfortunately, the weak central bay fails to command the composition, for the arch is so broad that it can be accommodated only by dropping the springing line and squashing the shafts into stubby submission. An outer arch of billet running down to the base is followed by a sausage-like inner arch rising from shafts. The paired window lights are finished with oriental-looking cusped arches, and the central shaft is divided into two and raised on a high base in a misjudged attempt at increasing its status. A continuous hood, cut with a fine (if indistinct) chevron pattern, separates plain walling below from a delirious chevron grid above.

There is more regularity in the five regular bays of the upper stage, which present an intense display of seventeen detached shafts across each elevation. The

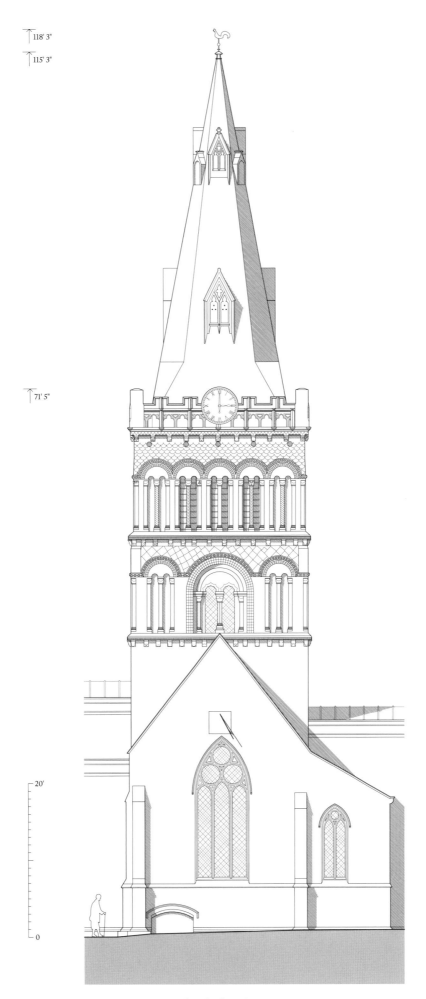

118' 3"

115' 3"

71' 5"

20'

0

South elevation

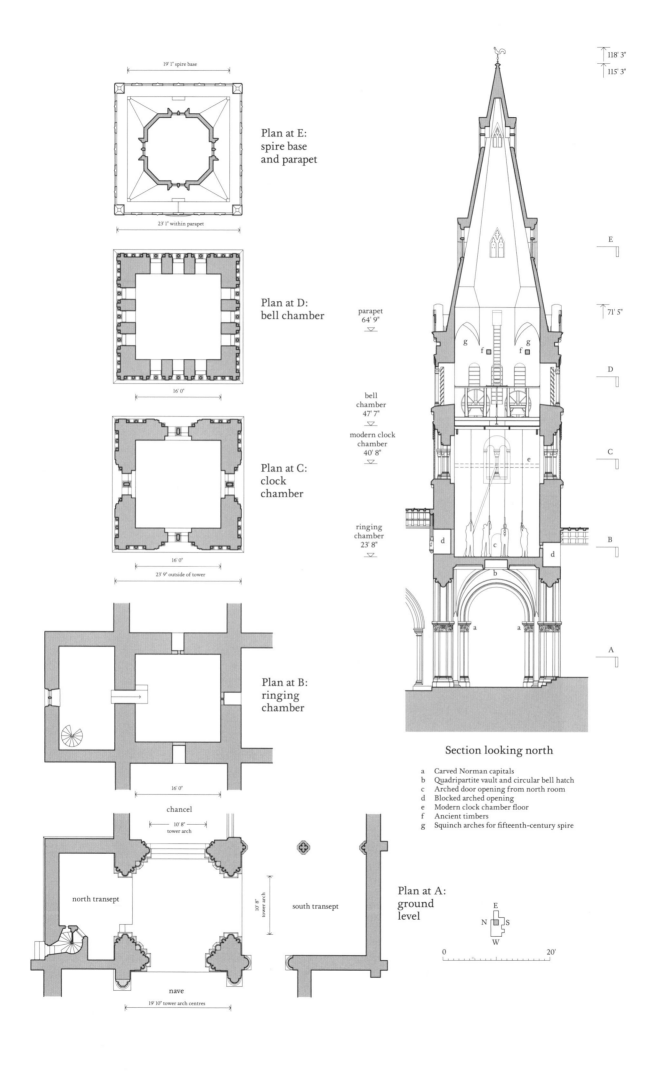

Plan at E:
spire base
and parapet

19' 1" spire base

23' 1" within parapet

Plan at D:
bell chamber

16' 0"

Plan at C:
clock
chamber

16' 0"

23' 9" outside of tower

Plan at B:
ringing
chamber

16' 0"

parapet
64' 9"

bell
chamber
47' 7"

modern clock
chamber
40' 8"

ringing
chamber
23' 8"

118' 3"

115' 3"

71' 5"

E

D

C

B

A

g   f   f   g

e

d   c   d

b

a   a

Section looking north

a   Carved Norman capitals
b   Quadripartite vault and circular bell hatch
c   Arched door opening from north room
d   Blocked arched opening
e   Modern clock chamber floor
f   Ancient timbers
g   Squinch arches for fifteenth-century spire

chancel

10' 8"
tower arch

10' 8"
tower arch

north transept

south transept

nave

19' 10" tower arch centres

Plan at A:
ground
level

E
N   S
W

0   20'

three centre bays are louvered for the bells, while the outer bays are blind. Here and there, with no discernible logic, capitals break out into a rash of foliage, and shafts into spirals and chevrons. Above the billet arches and the chevron hood-mould, the wall surface dissolves into crazy fish-scale patterning, with small, circular holes bored above every arch, like the oculi of a Saxon bell stage. The finest carving is reserved for the three tiers of corbels, where the faces of humans, animals and mythical creatures stare incredulously at the twenty-first-century visitor.

The perforated arcaded parapet is unworthy of what has gone before; indeed, it would be unworthy of any medieval tower. The chubby splay-footed spire is later than the guides suggest, for the splays are not the sign of an early date but are necessitated by the lack of squinch arches within the Norman construction (a). The diamond tracery in the two tiers of orthogonal lucarnes is a clear sign that the fifteenth century has arrived. Unusually, the spire is not a true octagon but a chamfered square pyramid, for the splays finish too soon, and consequently the diagonal faces are noticeably narrower than those in the cardinal directions. This may be intentional, for it allows room for twin upper lights with gabled niches on the diagonal, very close to the apex.

At CASTOR the interior is every bit as good as the exterior. Despite the insertion of a later vault, the original Norman crossing supporting the tower is preserved in its entirety. The capitals on the responds, carved with religious, mythological and secular scenes, are superbly executed and in near-perfect condition (a). To the north-east there are Sampson and the Lion, a boar hunt and a harvest, and to the south-west two men fighting over a lady. Green men, an elephant with cloven feet, a pelican and a palm tree can be seen to the north-west, and two dragons and a man picking grapes to the south-east. These are set between twisting rope astragals and chamfered square abaci.

Sculpted chevrons run around the circular bases, matching those of the external arcades. The powerful responds and tower arches are almost identical in profile, with three-quarter shafts either side of a half-round inner order. Some clarity has been lost by the later insertion of additional corner shafts on octagonal bases, to support the pointed quadripartite vault and circular bell hatch (b), but this still remains a superb ensemble.

The upper floors within the tower are less memorable. Access is a perennial problem in the central tower over a parish church. Here there is no record of the original route, and a sloping passage passes beneath a low, arched opening to reach a room added above the north transept (c). Similar arches on the other three sides of the ringing chamber (d) may have led to voids within the original steeply pitched roofs. The clock room floor (e), which cuts across the lower arcade windows, is a modern insertion, as is the bell chamber floor, and the only ancient timbers are two beams at the base of the spire (f).

CASTOR is a wonderful and precious survivor, for Norman towers of quality are rare on parish churches. Of the many hundreds that were built, some collapsed from poor workmanship and others were encased within later remodelling, but many more were removed by choice, to be replaced by less intrusive western towers. It is, therefore, difficult to judge whether CASTOR was originally as exceptional as it now appears, or whether it was one of many equally sumptuous creations. Certainly, it is as well crafted as any of the towers that remain on the great churches, but it is also a great deal more intimate and concise. Romanesque steeple design was never going to progress far above the elementary level, for it lacked the commanding vertical line of the projecting buttress. Nevertheless, there is much to commend the cheerful, life-affirming exuberance of CASTOR. Here, at last, the tower is becoming transformed into a work of art.

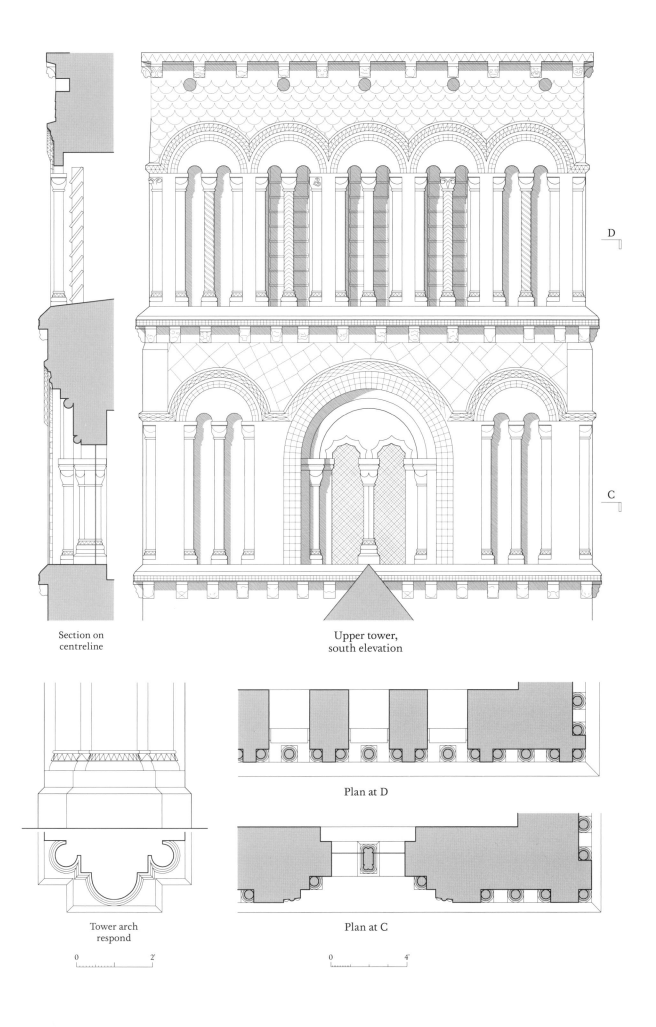

Section on
centreline

Upper tower,
south elevation

Tower arch
respond

Plan at D

Plan at C

D

C

0   2'

0   4'

5

North Raceby

LINCOLNSHIRE

St Peter's Church at NORTH RAUCEBY represents the first generation of English stone spires. Spires from the first half of the thirteenth century, before the introduction of bar tracery, are exceedingly rare. Broach spires from this period are to be found at NORTH RAUCEBY, Sleaford (Lincs) and Kings Cliffe (Northants), and splay-footed spires at Burton-le-Coggles (Lincs) and Etton (Hunts). In distant Oxfordshire an alternative form of broach spire carrying large corner pinnacles developed concurrently, starting around 1230 with St Frideswide's Church, now Oxford Cathedral. The steeple at Sleaford, overlooking a busy marketplace, suffers from an intrusive Victorian restoration and is crowded by embracing aisles. By contrast, NORTH RAUCEBY, just three miles away, has a calm air of mellow antiquity, and it is a joy to visit.

Nowhere in England is quite as well endowed with spectacular spires as the district of south Lincolnshire within easy reach of the Ancaster quarries. In the face of such splendid competition as Silk Willoughby, Caythorpe and BRANT BROUGHTON, the more subtle and ancient pleasures of St Peter's Church are easily overlooked. The parish church is shared between the carefully manicured estate villages of North Rauceby and South Rauceby, which command the high ground between the roads leaving Sleaford for Newark to the north-west and Grantham to the south-west. The young Pugin knew this charming church well, for his uncle Adlard

Welby, commemorated in a window in the north aisle, managed the Rauceby estates.[1]

The tower at St Peter's was built during the transition from the Norman Romanesque to the early Gothic, when the pointed arch was replacing the round-headed arch, and the projecting west tower was replacing the central tower. West towers are easier to build than central towers, for they require only one arch at ground level rather than four, and they do not congest the centre of the church with large masses of intrusive masonry. The west tower at NORTH RAUCEBY is of two distinct phases, with the smooth ashlar work of the upper stage wrapping around an earlier tower of roughly coursed rubble. This early rubble tower is exceedingly plain. Two stages are separated by a simple semi-hexagonal Norman string course. In the second stage are three original openings: a round-headed doorway through the east wall that opens into in space over the nave (a), and small, pointed windows with deep splays to north and south (b). This combination of late Norman and early Gothic work is characteristic of the Transitional period around 1180.

The second phase of work is of smooth ashlar throughout and consists of the third stage of the tower: the buttresses, the tower arch, the staircase and the spire. This construction is of the early thirteenth century, and the arrival of the first vicar, William de Lexington, in 1229 may have coincided with the completion of the steeple. The corners of the original rubble tower

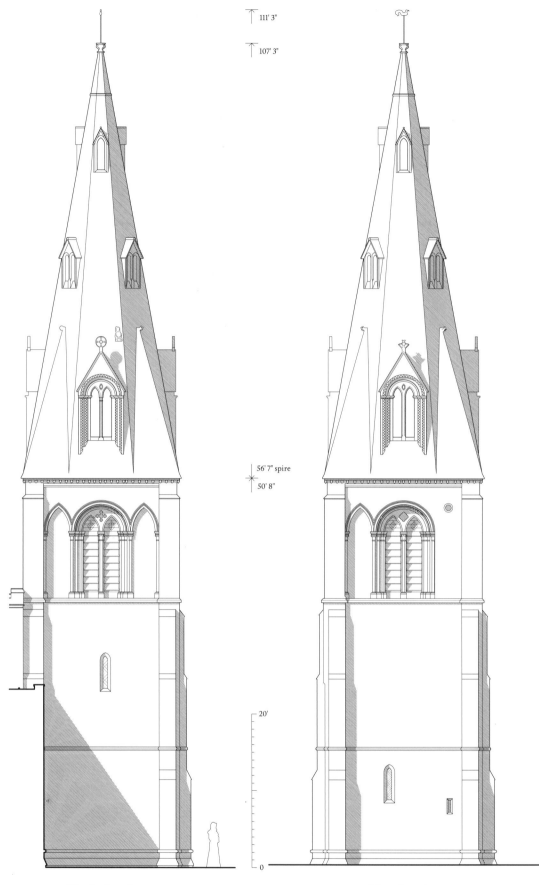

111' 3"

107' 3"

56' 7" spire
50' 8"

20'

0

North elevation

West elevation

Late medieval west window
omitted for clarity

were encased and strengthened by clasping buttresses, seven inches deep, from which simple setback buttresses project. Unusually, the masons copied the profile of the earlier basement and string courses to run them around the buttresses.

A new west window was introduced at ground level at this time, for parts of a string course suggest the level of a cill. Unfortunately, the existing west window is an unsympathetic late medieval replacement. Another addition of around 1220 is the double-chamfered tower arch with a simple hood-mould (c) that rises from capitals decorated with the nailhead pattern, typical of the early thirteenth century. The responds are of one major and four minor shafts.

The bell stage was intended to make a show of arcading, but this was frustrated first by the intrusive presence of the south-west staircase and, later, by the raising of a clerestory above the nave. As a result, the elevation is now much finer on the concealed north elevation than on the other three faces. An arcade of three bays runs between clasping buttresses rising from below. A central semicircular arched bay frames twin lancet openings to the bell chamber, either side of which are blind bays with pointed arches. The same arrangement occurs at the contemporary towers at Sleaford and twenty miles away at Frampton. One disadvantage of the semicircular arch is that settlement is far move visible than with the pointed arch, and here the arches on all faces are noticeably elliptical.

The twenty-one detached and four engaged shafts that originally decorated the bell stage at NORTH RAUCEBY are a foretaste of the mania for shafting that would come to dominate tower design in the second half of the thirteenth century. Detached, four-inch-diameter shafts double up around the central opening and carry capitals carved with nailhead or stiff-leaf decoration in the centre. Spandrels between the bell chamber lancets are perforated by plate tracery of several different motifs composed of overlapping arcs. The south-west stone staircase, which was to be become standard in Lincolnshire, seriously disrupts the arcading on both west and south elevations. The tower concludes with a corbel table of irregular notch heads, and the clasping buttresses are gathered in just below the spire.

Internally, the tower, along with the rest of the church, suffered the indignity of being scraped during the restoration of 1853. The removal of medieval plaster was the most objectionable of Victorian habits, and at NORTH RAUCEBY irreplaceable wall paintings in the north aisle were wantonly destroyed. There is no evidence of any original floor structures within the tower. During the 1907 restoration iron tie-rods (d) were added in the ringing chamber, to prevent the walls from spreading, and a timber-joisted floor was constructed over ancient beams found high within the spire (e).

The main attraction at NORTH RAUCEBY is the early broach spire. When one considers that this is one of the first spires to be built in England, it is a remarkably accomplished design. Proportions are excellent, for spire and tower are equal in height and the broaches are tall and steep. The three tiers of alternating lucarnes were to become a Lincolnshire trademark. Round-headed dogtooth arches on the principal lucarnes are the clearest indication of an early date, and keeled jambs and two rows of matching vertical dogtooth frame the openings. Twin pointed lights are separated by an octagonal mullion, and a chamfered vesica perforates the spandrel above. Plain gabled roofs carry variations on the theme of a cross carved within a circle. Each broach carries a figure at its apex, worn into anonymity by 800 years of wind and rain. The upper tiers of lucarnes are small and plain. A narrow band encircles the apex of the spire, which concludes with a decorative finial that

no doubt has been replaced on more than one occasion.

High broaches are a feature of early spires, but they were a constructional necessity rather than a fashionable extravagance. The cross section reveals very high and very narrow squinch arches (f) topped by an amorphous, tapering mass of masonry that gradually achieves the required form of a thin-walled octagon. As the mason's confidence grew, squinch arches would became wider and the transition to the octagon much sharper, but here the broaches rise high to cover an immature mode of construction. NORTH RAUCEBY may lack the finesse of RAUNDS and Warmington later in the thirteenth century, but all the constituent parts of the mature broach spire are present and correct. Here and at Sleaford, that most original of English inventions, the stone broach spire, makes its brilliant debut.

NOTE

1   See Rosemary Hill, *God's Architect: Pugin and the Building of Romantic Britain* (2007), pp. 29, 49.

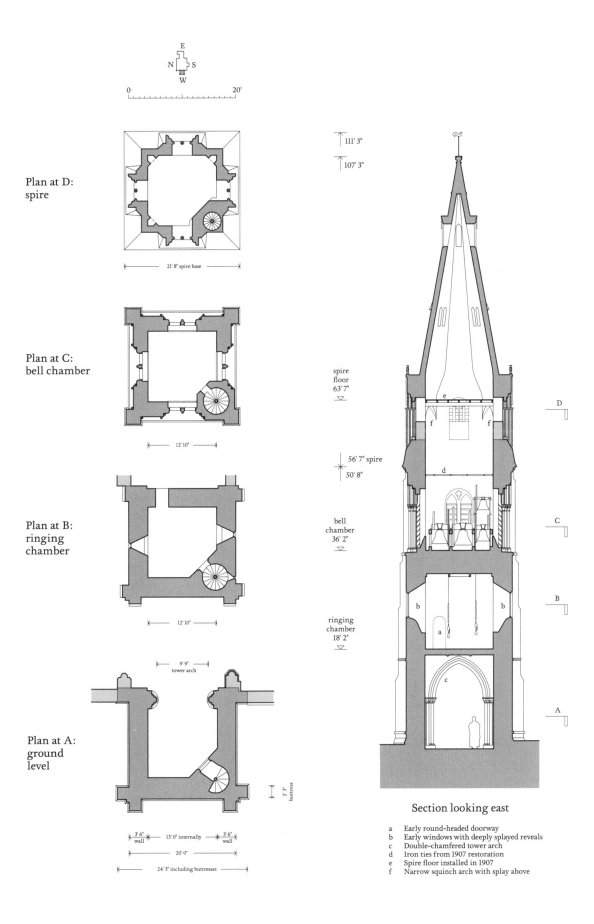

E
N S
W

0   20'

Plan at D:
spire

21' 8" spire base

Plan at C:
bell chamber

12' 10"

Plan at B:
ringing
chamber

12' 10"

Plan at A:
ground
level

9' 9"
tower arch

2' 3"
buttress

3' 6"
wall   13' 0" internally   3' 6"
wall

20' 0"

24' 3" including buttresses

111' 3"

107' 3"

spire
floor
63' 7"

56' 7" spire
50' 8"

bell
chamber
36' 2"

ringing
chamber
18' 2"

D

C

B

A

Section looking east

a   Early round-headed doorway
b   Early windows with deeply splayed reveals
c   Double-chamfered tower arch
d   Iron ties from 1907 restoration
e   Spire floor installed in 1907
f   Narrow squinch arch with splay above

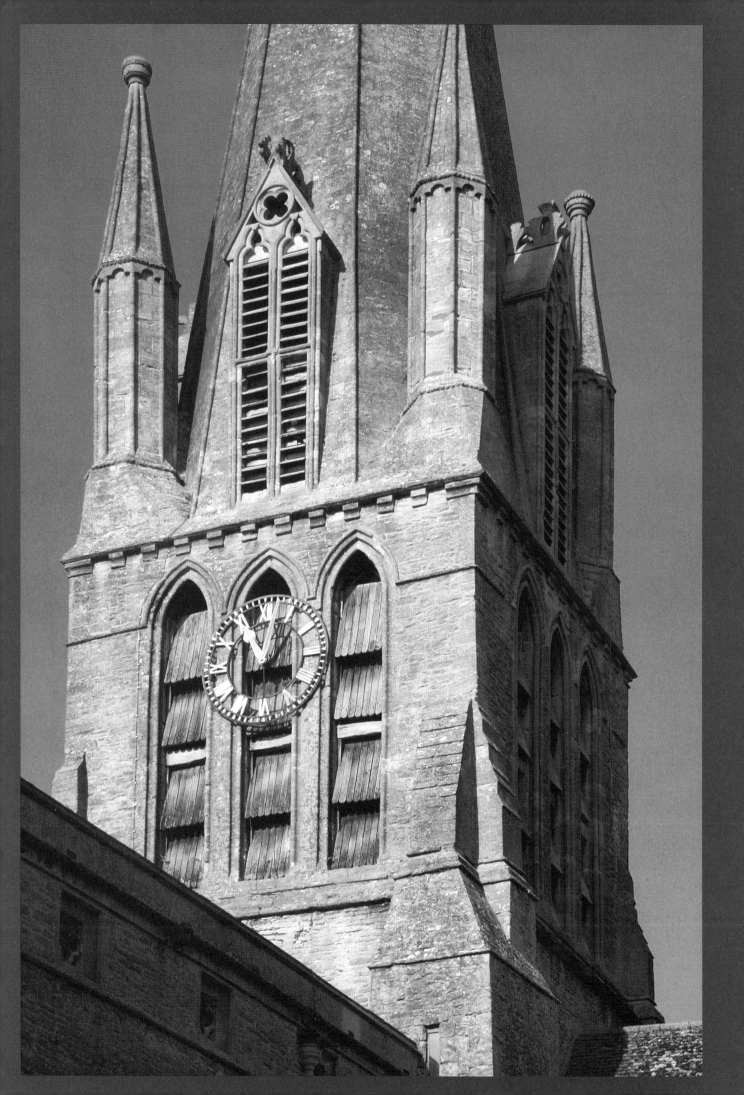

6

Witney

OXFORDSHIRE

Francis Bond identified four characteristics shared by what he considered to be the earliest form of stone spire: the early thirteenth-century pinnacled spires of Normandy and Oxfordshire:

> The chief characteristics of this spire are that it has dripping eaves, and therefore is without a parapet; secondly, that its angles are weighted with tall massive pinnacles, which in Normandy are highly elaborated; thirdly, that it has no spire lights; fourthly, that it has large dormer windows on the cardinal sides, the object of which is mainly decorative, but which are also of value in lightening the load on the belfry windows below.[1]

In Normandy, the spires of Caen, Bretteville and Bernières are on a huge scale and with great elaboration of detail. The Oxfordshire group are more pragmatic and closer to the ground, but in their own way they are no less effective. The earliest of the group is assumed to be Oxford Cathedral, originally the priory of St Frideswide. WITNEY, Bampton and Shipton-under-Wychwood form a compact group ten to fifteen miles further west. Its most powerful and refined member is WITNEY, which is thought to have been completed in 1243 prior to a reconsecration service in the same year.

WITNEY church is a fascinating but amorphous mass of building that succeeds externally only because of the unifying effect of the central steeple. This is not,

as might be expected, the location of a Norman crossing tower, for transepts, chancel, nave arcades and tower arches are all of the thirteenth century. Evidence suggests that the original Norman church was much smaller, the aisleless nave terminating at the edge of, or just within, the line of the later tower.

The interest of the interior is more archaeological than architectural, for much of the character was lost during Street's 1869 restoration. Within the crossing, whitewashed walls, a carpeted, raised floor and a varnished pine soffit – set so low that it crashes thoughtlessly into the tower arches – seem calculated to dull the spirits. Strong and simple tower arch responds are of three plain chamfered orders to the north and south, with the addition of semicircular shafts to the east and west supporting a fourth chamfered order in the arch. The chamfered responds are finished by nothing more than the narrow chamfered abacus of the simple shaft capitals. With bases lost beneath dull grey carpet, the only other point of interest is the small blocked doorway in the corner of the south transept that once gave access to the tower staircase.

Access to this stair is now up a straight external flight into the base of a large rectangular clasping buttress supporting the south-east corner of the tower below the ringing chamber. Immature angle buttresses prop the corners of the tower in a lazy, matter-of-fact sort of way, petering out part way up the bell stage. The tower itself could not be simpler, for it is nothing but a pure cube with three lancet openings cut into each face. Around these bell chamber openings runs nothing but a filleted roll. There are no bases, no capitals, and only the plainest of hood-moulds and mid-height transoms. The undecorated corbel table supporting the base of the spire follows the same muscular aesthetic.

Internally, the design is unexpectedly complex. A mid-wall passage runs continuously through the construction more or less at roof level, connecting the main south-east stair to a north-west stair that continues upwards. The passage steps up in a clockwise direction (a) and connects to the central chamber through pairs of triangular-headed openings. This is more reminiscent of the contemporary mid-wall gallery concealed at RAUNDS than the structurally significant twin-wall construction of WEST WALTON. One explanation for this unusual arrangement, bearing in mind that the current ringing chamber floor is self-evidently at the wrong level, is that the passage openings originally looked down upon the central crossing of the church. Bell openings are more complex than they appear externally, for their inner faces are supported by semicircular arches (c). The clock room floor is another modern insertion (b).

At almost eighty-five feet in height, the roll-edged spire must have been the tallest stone spire in the country when first completed. The main interest on the spire

itself occurs just above the half-way point: a string course decorated with corner heads and snaking up and down over tiny triangular openings, too small to be called lucarnes. Apart from this, all the interest is concentrated around the base. The octagonal pinnacles are massive and very tall. The most convincing details are at the top, in the form of roll edges leading to a bulbous circular finial, recalling the design of the main spire. Less well resolved are the crude panels on the pinnacle shaft and the large chamfered pyramid formed around the base.

Francis Bond was correct to refer to the tall spire windows as dormers rather than lucarnes, for they rise straight from the plane of the tower wall. The filleted roll motif of the previous stage appears again but at a smaller scale. It runs around twin lights, finished with non-structural trefoiled heads, and encircles the quatrefoil plate tracery in the spandrel. Weather-beaten carvings sitting astride the gables are hard to interpret, for unlike most of the masonry at this level they do not appear to have been restored. As before, transoms are necessitated by the height of the openings, and the internal construction is unexpectedly complex.

The outer dormer opening is revealed to be a thin line of structure separated by a void from an inner line of support headed by a triangular arch (d). Such simple twin-wall construction is not uncommon in this period and appears in a more sophisticated form within the spire at Oxford Cathedral.[2] There are no squinch arches, the diagonal

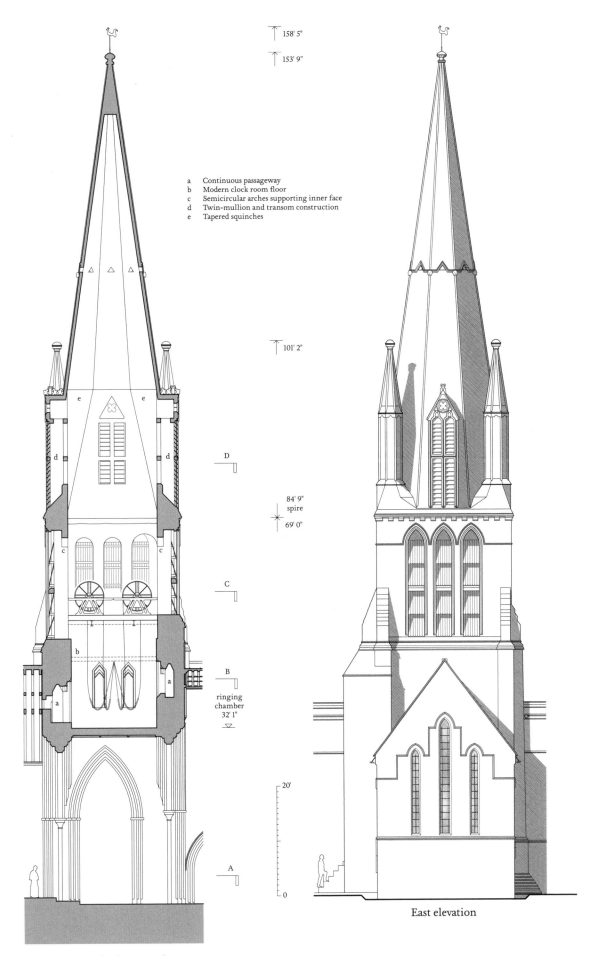

a   Continuous passageway
b   Modern clock room floor
c   Semicircular arches supporting inner face
d   Twin-mullion and transom construction
e   Tapered squinches

158' 5"

153' 9"

101' 2"

D

84' 9"
spire

69' 0"

C

B

ringing
chamber
32' 1"

20'

A

0

Section looking south

East elevation

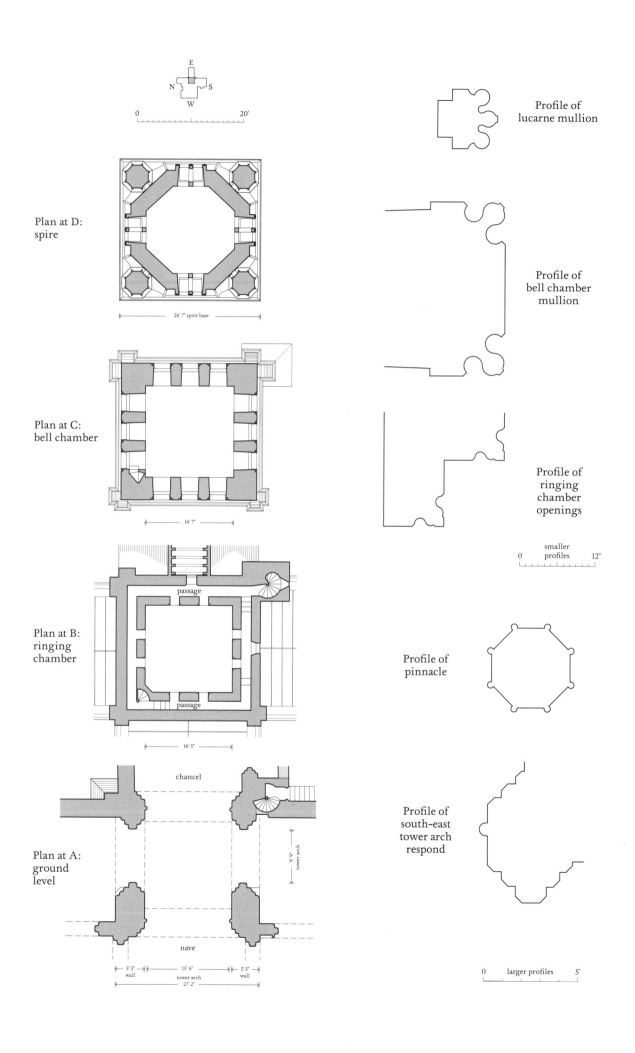

E
N   S
W

0   20'

Profile of
lucarne mullion

Plan at D:
spire

26' 7" spire base

Profile of
bell chamber
mullion

Plan at C:
bell chamber

16' 7"

Profile of
ringing
chamber
openings

smaller
profiles
0   12"

passage

Plan at B:
ringing
chamber

passage

Profile of
pinnacle

16' 5"

chancel

Profile of
south-east
tower arch
respond

9' 9"
tower arch

Plan at A:
ground
level

nave

5' 5"
wall

15' 6"
tower arch

5' 5"
wall

27' 2"

0   larger profiles   5'

spire faces being supported by tapering masses of masonry rising to almost one-third of the height of the spire, an easy but inefficient solution (e).

A comparison with the other spires in the Oxfordshire group is instructive. All are finished with roll edges, all rise with an apex angle in the order of sixteen degrees, and all have tall twin-light dormers. Bampton shares with WITNEY the dormer transom and strings decorating the upper spire. At Shipton there is similar plate tracery to WITNEY, but this time in the form of a trefoil; there is carving on the gable; and the octagonal pinnacles are finished with circular finials. Bampton and Oxford are connected by strong clusters of pinnacle shafts, although those at Bampton support sculptures and are connected to the spire by elementary flying buttresses. The spire finial at Oxford must be the result of over-imaginative restoration, but elsewhere the circular, ball-like forms have strong similarities.

Unless further documentary evidence comes to light, it is impossible to know whether the Oxfordshire group predates the first generation of broach spires in the East Midlands, which includes Sleaford and NORTH RAUCEBY. WITNEY's pioneering achievement may have been short-lived, for technical advances in the east saw the spire at RAUNDS passing the 100-foot mark within just a few years. Nevertheless, the tall corner pinnacles and prominent dormers of this early group created a regional precedent followed later by fine oversailing pinnacled spires at Broadwell (Oxon), Church Honeybourne (Worcs), Mickleton and Todenham (Glos), and by the wonderful recessed Oxfordshire spires of ST MARY, OXFORD, Bloxham and ADDERBURY.

NOTES

1   Francis Bond, *An Introduction to English Church Architecture*, vol. 2 (1913), p. 927.
2   See an illustration in J. H. Parker, *Glossary of Gothic Architecture* (1850), reprinted in Francis Bond, *Gothic Architecture in England* (1905), p. 512.

7

West Walton

NORFOLK

The free-standing belfry is an eminently satisfying concept, for it allows the sculptural form of a building to be appreciated in the round.[1] In medieval times separate bell towers served many great churches, including Salisbury, Worcester and Chichester cathedrals. Most of these are lost, but they must have formed a picturesque counterpoint to huge centralized compositions. Free-standing towers on the scale of the parish church are rare outside Gloucestershire, Herefordshire and the Fens. On soft Fenland ground, the masons were nervous about the stability of heavy stone towers and placed them safely away from the body of the church. Wisbech (Cambs), Whaplode, LONG SUTTON and Donington (Lincs) were all constructed as free-standing towers but are now, to varying degrees, attached to their churches. Fleet (Lincs) and Terrington St Clement (Norfolk) are set slightly apart from their churches, and at WEST WALTON the separation is complete, for the tower is placed sixty feet away from the church and acts as a lichgate between the street and the churchyard.

Like many well-preserved ancient structures, WEST WALTON is the result of early prosperity followed by centuries of stagnation. In this case the village's wealth resulted from its proximity to the mouth of the River Nene, and it was the river that allowed Barnack ragstone to be obtained easily and economically. Dating from around 1240–50, this is one of the finest early Gothic parish churches in England. The foliate capitals of the nave arcades are outstanding, as are the Purbeck marble shafts clustered around the circular piers, a rare luxury outside a cathedral.

WEST WALTON tower is famous not for its height, which is unremarkable, nor for its proportions, which are robust, but for the sophisticated articulation of every part of its structure. The composition represents a fundamental shift away from the stack of independent stages, familiar from EARLS BARTON and CASTOR, to an integrated composition of strong verticals and subservient horizontals. Huge octagonal corner buttresses, telescoping as they rise, dominate the design. The octagonal buttress was a passing and very localized fashion during the mid-thirteenth century, for it is found only at LONG SUTTON, Leverington (Cambs), Walsoken and Elm (Norfolk), all within seven miles of WEST WALTON. The inspiration may have come from the earlier west front of Ely Cathedral and from Lincoln Cathedral, where the central tower was raised with octagonal corners by Master Alexander between 1238 and 1250. In the most extravagant of the Fenland towers, the octagonal buttresses and adjacent elevations are wrapped by a continuous arcade. This is carried on circular shafts at WEST WALTON, octagonal shafts at LONG SUTTON, and by a combination of the two at Walsoken. After this brief burst of experimentation the octagonal form of buttresses fell out of use on parish church towers for two centuries.

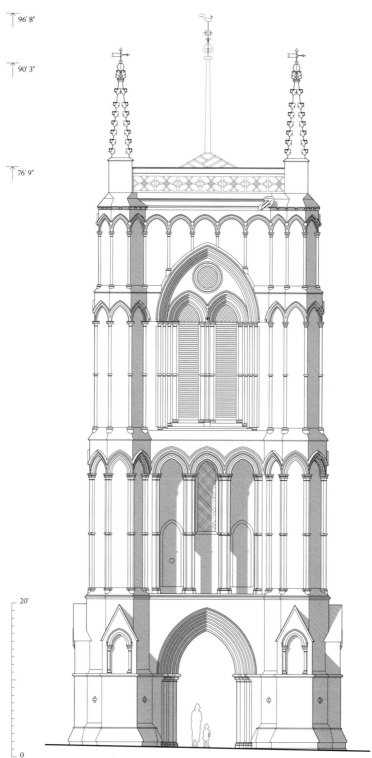

96' 8"

90' 3"

76' 9"

20'

0

West elevation

The bell tower at WEST WALTON is of four stages finished by a later parapet and pinnacles. Three arcaded upper stages reduce in height and complexity as they rise. The base is of plain ashlar with pairs of low setback buttresses, decorated with empty niches and carved heads projecting from each corner. Broad arches penetrate through the centre of each elevation, adding great depth to the composition. The rich ornamentation of keeled rolls and dogtooth to the north and south arches contrasts with plain diagonal chamfers to east and west. These dissimilar elevations are tied together by the continuous upper moulding of the shaft capitals, which forms the cill to the niches.

The space beneath the tower is noble and well illuminated by the four great arches. Apart from the sea of utilitarian tarmac spread liberally around its base, the tower is a textbook example of good conservation practice. Overhead is an oak floor from the 1985 restoration (a), and on each of the diagonal corner faces is a low segmental-arched doorway (b). Three doors lead to empty, conically vaulted octagonal chambers illuminated by small quatrefoils punching through the diagonals. The fourth door, to the south-east, leads to the spiral stair. The large octagonal buttress comfortably conceals the corner staircase within its bulk, the only external indication of its presence being a discreet sprinkling of inconspicuous quatrefoil and slit windows. One unusual subtlety in the staircase is a gentle incline away from the vertical, so that it moves closer to the centre of the tower as it rises.

Arcading commences on the second stage, with triplet clusters of engaged shafts carrying annulets, reducing to single shafts carrying annulets on the third stage, and single plain shafts on the fourth. The use of annulets on engaged shafts formed within the profile of the wall stones is illogical, for shaft rings were devised to connect free-standing stone shafts together. Keeled arches, adding a subtle vertical emphasis, are used throughout, with the deeply profiled hood-moulds rippling like waves across the elevations. Arcade spacing is set by the face width of the octagonal buttress, which reduces at each level. Consequently, three bays on the second stage become five narrow bays on the final stage.

In an audacious and highly effective move the second stage arcade is left open across the elevations, separated from the solid face of the tower wall by a continuous passage over two feet deep. Such substantial twin-wall construction is uncommon outside cathedral crossing towers, and in this instance there is an obvious parallel with the structure of the central tower at Lincoln Cathedral, rebuilt after the collapse of 1237. The intriguing possibility that Alexander of Lincoln may have been involved at WEST WALTON cannot be ruled out.

The astonishing slenderness of the construction, particularly apparent on the cross section, is in part achieved through perpendicular stiffening walls (c) connecting

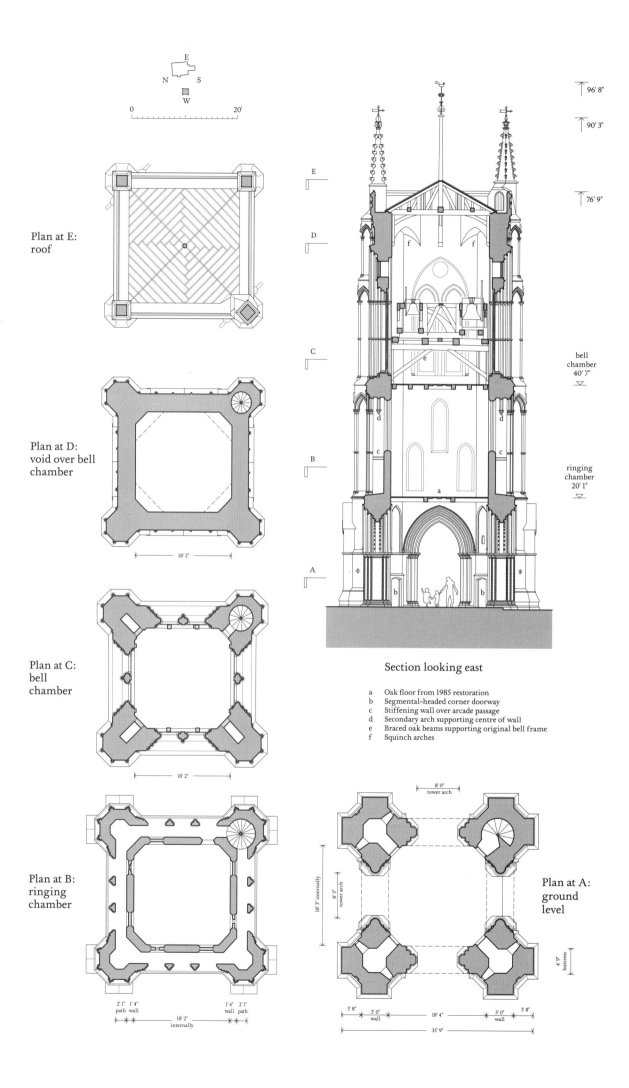

Plan at E:
roof

Plan at D:
void over bell
chamber

Plan at C:
bell
chamber

Plan at B:
ringing
chamber

Plan at A:
ground
level

E

D

C

B

A

96' 8"

90' 3"

76' 9"

bell
chamber
40' 7"

ringing
chamber
20' 1"

f   f

e

d   d

c   c

a

b   b

Section looking east

a   Oak floor from 1985 restoration
b   Segmental-headed corner doorway
c   Stiffening wall over arcade passage
d   Secondary arch supporting centre of wall
e   Braced oak beams supporting original bell frame
f   Squinch arches

E
N — S
W

0   20'

18' 2"

18' 2"

18' 2"
internally

2' 1" 1' 4"   1' 4" 2' 1"
path   wall   wall   path

8' 0"
tower arch

18' 3" internally

8' 3"
tower arch

4' 9"
buttress

3' 8"   5' 0"   18' 4"   5' 0"   3' 8"
        wall   wall

35' 9"

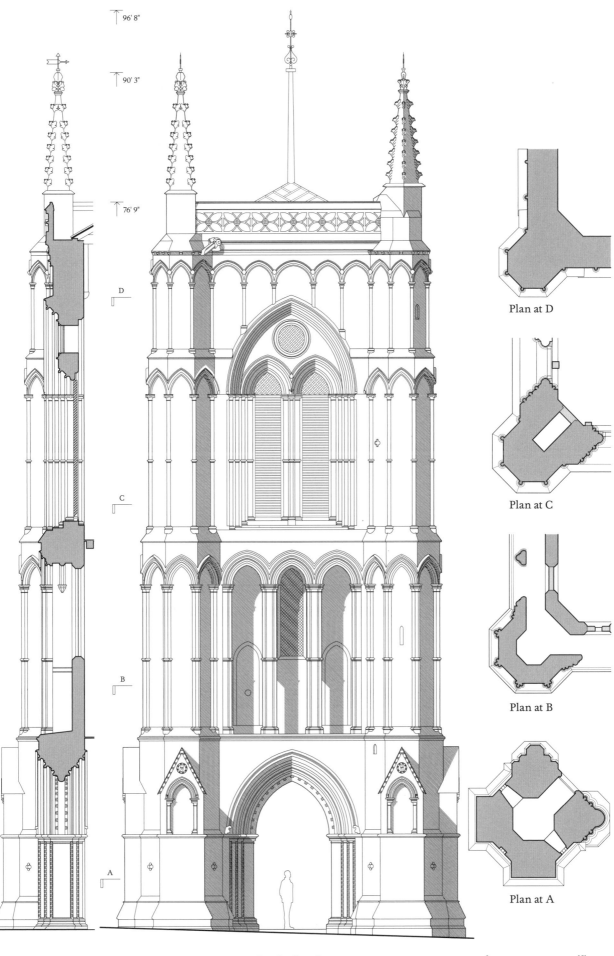

96' 8"

90' 3"

76' 9"

D

C

B

A

Section on
centreline

South elevation

Plan at D

Plan at C

Plan at B

Plan at A

0   10'

the arcade piers to the inner wall. Small secondary arches spring from corbels on these stiffening walls to support the centre of the main tower wall (d). On each face of the inner wall are three stepped lancet openings that may originally have been left open. Within is one large, empty volume, for all the accoutrements of the ringing chamber are long gone. Both of the modern oak upper floors correspond to the level of the external string courses: a logical arrangement that is surprisingly rare in medieval work.

The bell chamber is spectacular within and without. Within is one of the most ancient bell frames in England, a congested mass of beams, struts, posts and braces. Much of this confusing structure, including the lowest tier of deep-braced beams (e), represents the work of several generations of restorers. Despite all the valiant strengthening work, the bells wheels have been smashed and the ropes removed to protect the ancient structure from vibration.

No other medieval English tower has such dominant bell openings. These huge, deep recesses, formed of tall paired lancets below a containing arch, take over the third stage in its entirety and cut through the fourth stage arcade. The plate tracery may be elementary but the detailing is sumptuous, with four orders of shafts, dogtooth and keeled rolls to the arches. This is yet another example of cathedral-like construction, for even the greatest parish steeples such as GRANTHAM boast only three orders around their deepest arches.

The thirteenth-century work terminates with a line of small notch heads around the buttresses. The under-nourished square pinnacles that follow after some severe contortions are a poor substitute for the octagonal terminations so clearly intended by the original mason. The rotation of the enlarged south-east pinnacle over the staircase unnecessarily disrupts the carefully controlled symmetry. Rectangular parapet panels, of four mouchettes radiating from a five-petal flower, and rippling pinnacle crockets suggest that this is work of the late fourteenth century.

It is unclear how the tower was intended to be finished, for perfectly formed squinch arches (f) transform the plan into a pure octagon before the summit is reached. At this time squinches were usually set much higher to form an integral part of a broach spire, as at RAUNDS. The obvious parallel is with the contemporary steeple of LONG SUTTON just seven miles to the north-west. This has integral tower squinches that do not provide any direct benefit to the timber spire that follows. The squinches at WEST WALTON may have been added simply to stiffen and strengthen the top of the structure, but it is, perhaps, more likely that they were intended to receive a tall stone spire that never materialized.

It is hardly necessary to state that the tower at WEST WALTON is exceptionally beautiful. It is a prime example of a tower that achieves greatness not through height, but through robust sculptural massing articulated with great precision. St Mary's tower is now in the expert care of the Churches Conservation Trust, an under-appreciated organization that performs a vital role in preserving redundant church buildings across England for the enjoyment of future generations.

NOTE

1   The term 'belfry' is used throughout the current work to describe a free-standing church tower. The word is commonly assumed to mean 'bell chamber'; however, its derivation is not from the English *bell*, but from the Old French *belfrei*, meaning a 'mobile watch tower'.

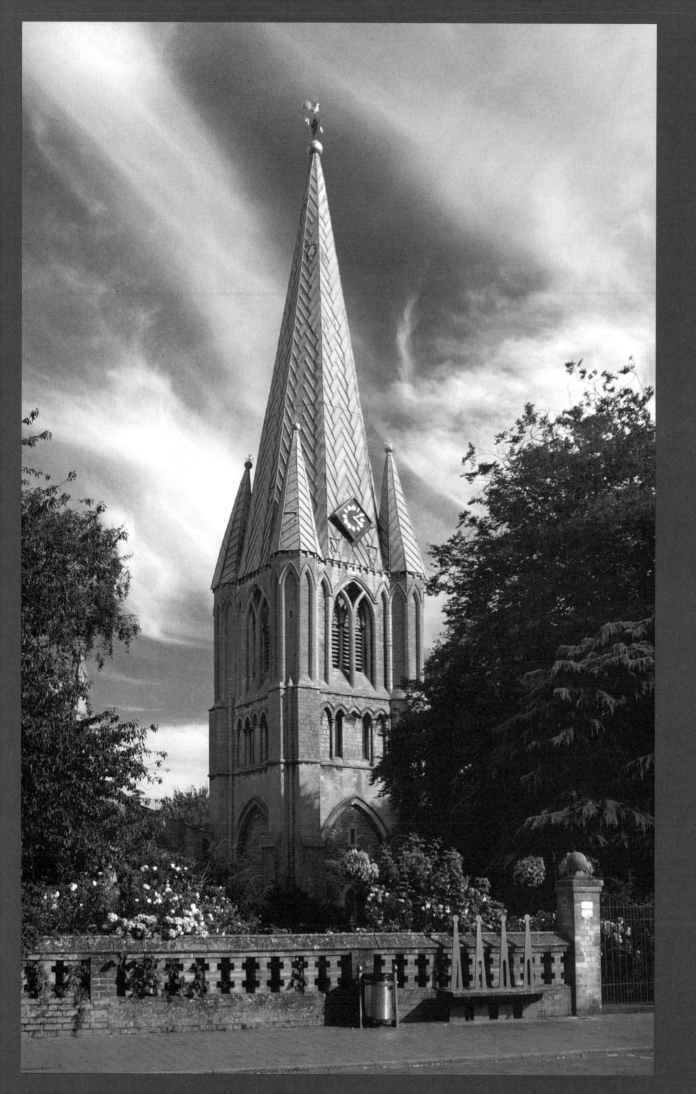

8

Long Sutton

LINCOLNSHIRE

Timber spires were once commonplace in England. Cathedral towers were finished with spires as a matter of course, and when stone was unaffordable, or too heavy for the structure to bear, lead-clad timber sufficed. The central timber spire at Lincoln was the first construction in the world to rise higher than the Great Pyramid of Giza, and from Canterbury to Durham wooden spires once adorned most of the great churches across the kingdom. Unfortunately, this form of construction proved far less durable than stone. Lincoln blew down in 1548, and Old St Paul's fell 'due to the carelessness of a Plumber'[1] in June 1561. During the following two and a half centuries, the majority of timber spires were lost to lightning, wind and decay. Most of the prime examples that remain, such as Hadleigh (Suffolk) and Hemel Hempstead (Herts), date from at least the fourteenth century and are found in areas where good building stone remained unaffordable throughout the Middle Ages. In this context, the tall spire at LONG SUTTON is a remarkable early survivor.

St Mary's is one of several churches built, or rebuilt, to express the prestige of the great monastic houses surrounding the Fens. The town owes its fine church not to the competing Lincolnshire abbeys of Crowland and Spalding, but to Castle Acre Priory, just across the Norfolk border. In a charter written around 1180, William, son of Erneis, granted three acres of 'the old fen-land' inherited by his wife to Castle Acre for the construction of a new church. The old wooden church was demolished, the graveyard emptied, and the bodies of the deceased reinterred at the new site. The arcades and clerestory of this first structure are still preserved at St Mary's within a cocoon of later medieval extensions. This work is surprisingly retrograde for the date, for the cylindrical piers and semicircular arches are late Norman Romanesque rather than early Gothic in style.

LONG SUTTON is one of several Fenland towers originally constructed as free-standing belfries. The thirteenth-century masons were wary of the soft reclaimed marshland and wished to avoid damaging the body of the church should the tower fall. Originally a comfortable space was left around the tower base, and the main path to the church no doubt passed beneath its arches. When the south aisle was extended during the fourteenth century the separation was lost, but the church and tower remain structurally independent. The steeple conforms to the early medieval ideal of symmetry around both orthogonal axes, so that the four elevations are almost identical. This scheme suffers only minor disruption from the staircase on the south-west corner, a sundial and mass dial on the south elevation, and clock faces to east and west.

The age of the steeple at LONG SUTTON is a conundrum. While most authorities state that the steeple was built in its entirety around 1200, this is hardly credible.[2] There are substantial reasons to believe that construction occurred in three distinct phases. The first two stages of the tower, dominated by heavy buttresses, were indeed constructed around the year 1200, but the third stage, with its continuous arcade, is unlikely to have been started much before 1260, and the spire did not immediately follow.

The angle buttresses of the first two stages of the tower are heavy, being precisely the same width as the walls to which they lend support. The bases are little more than chamfered plinths, and the buttresses have but a single plain set-off. Nine-inch-diameter nook shafts (a) surround each corner of the tower both externally and internally except on the south-west, where they are replaced by the bulging circular form of the staircase. The buttresses needed to be substantial, for the entire weight of the tower walls is supported by four hefty pointed arches. Their profile indicates an early date for, as the cross section reveals, they are little more than three recessed orders of plain rectangular blocks with plain chamfered hood-moulds. This Norman Romanesque construction in early Gothic form must be slightly later than the round-headed arches of the nave, constructed during the 1180s. The muscular responds, of two quadrant shafts either side of one semicircular shaft, have robust ring capitals and simple water-holding bases. Above an expanse of plain walling runs a plain chamfered string course of Norman profile supporting a five-bay arcade on each elevation. Shafts are detached and circular in the centre, engaged and keeled to either end, with lancet windows in the second and fourth bays set close to the face of the wall with deep internal splays. All of this is consistent with a date of around 1200.

The third stage is dramatically different from everything that has gone before. The figure of the octagon suddenly dominates both in plan and in detail. A deeply splayed base cleverly facilitates the transformation of the corners into octagonal clasping buttress, and a noble arcade of thirty-six bays encircles the tower. Engaged octagonal shafts are austerely detailed, having neither capitals nor bases. Above the continuous arcade hood-mould, a regular band of notch heads marks the completion of the tower.

There are at least three reasons to suspect that this third stage is substantially later than the preceding work. First, the preceding nook shafts, which were clearly intended to support concentrated loads, are terminated abruptly by insubstantial conical finials reminiscent of candle snuffers. Second, the central openings to the bell chamber are much later in style than the preceding work. These beautiful openings are divided by octagonal mullions diverging to form simple 'Y' bar tracery in the head, a detail that is unlikely to have appeared before 1240. The inner face of the wall is carried by a broad arch, but the centre of the wall is carried by a delightful mid-wall arcade of three bays (b). In a design of remarkable sophistication, the two outer bays and three inner bays deliberately contradict each other. Such a wilful arrangement has no obvious precedent, the complex offset tracery at Melrose Abbey being considerably later.

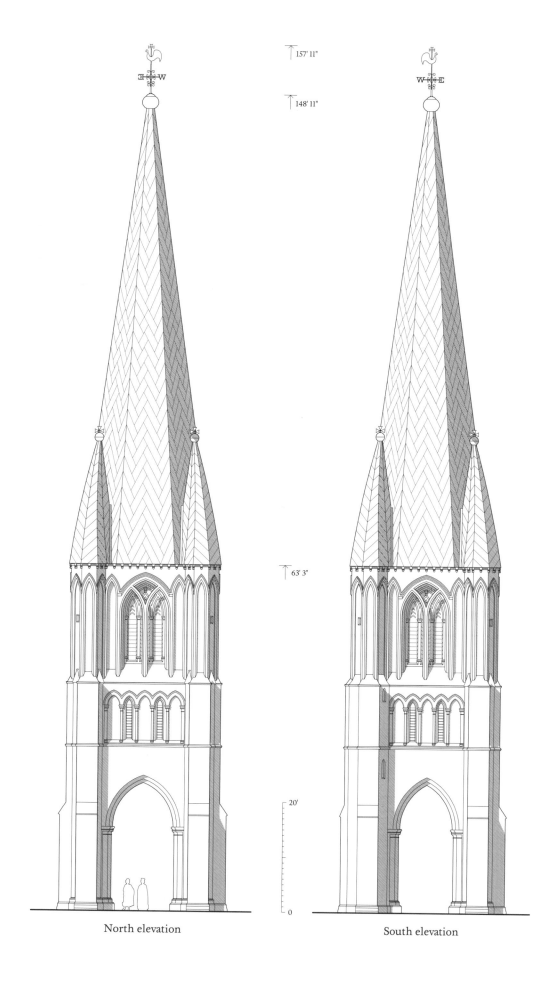

157' 11"

148' 11"

63' 3"

20'

0

North elevation

South elevation

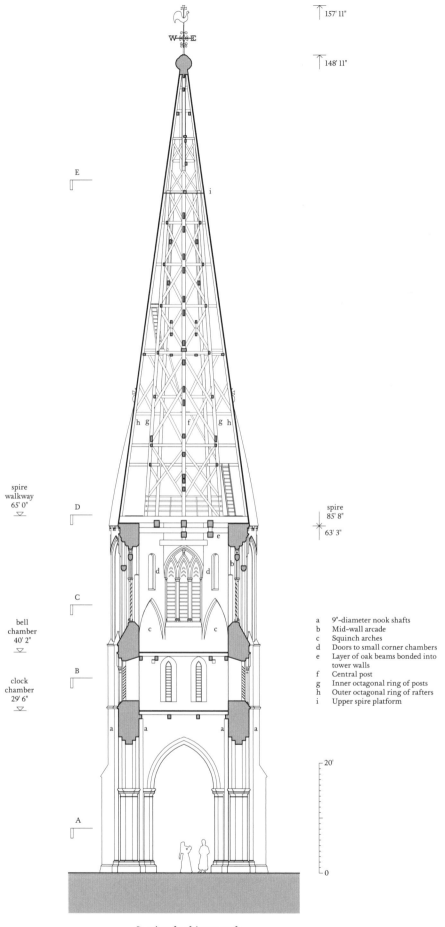

157' 11"

148' 11"

E

spire
walkway
65' 0"

D

spire
85' 8"

63' 3"

C

bell
chamber
40' 2"

B

clock
chamber
29' 6"

20'

A

0

a   9"-diameter nook shafts
b   Mid-wall arcade
c   Squinch arches
d   Doors to small corner chambers
e   Layer of oak beams bonded into
     tower walls
f   Central post
g   Inner octagonal ring of posts
h   Outer octagonal ring of rafters
i   Upper spire platform

Section looking north
Modern walls and ground floor omitted

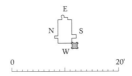

0   20'

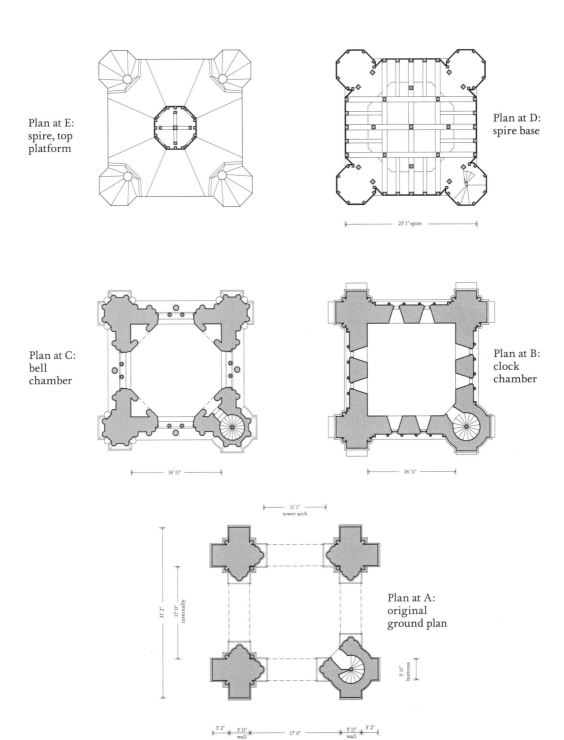

Plan at E:
spire, top
platform

Plan at D:
spire base

25' 1" spire

Plan at C:
bell
chamber

Plan at B:
clock
chamber

16' 11"

16' 11"

11' 1"
tower arch

Plan at A:
original
ground plan

31' 2"

17' 0"
internally

3' 11"
buttress

3' 2"   3' 11"
        wall

17' 0"

3' 11"   3' 2"
wall

31' 2"

Further evidence for a later date appears on the cross section. Towers built before 1240, such as NORTH RAUCEBY, ST MARY, STAMFORD, RAUNDS and KETTON, have no squinch arches. It is only at WEST WALTON that the squinch finally descends into the tower. The finely crafted squinch arches at LONG SUTTON (c) are far more confident and mature than those of her Norfolk neighbour, with small, windowed chambers cut into the masonry above (d). The purpose of these chambers is unclear, for there is no evidence that a floor was ever installed at this level. The implication of such substantial squinch arches is that the tower at LONG SUTTON was always intended to receive a spire.

Before proceeding to the spire, it is necessary to explain the tragic misfortune that still blights this outstanding monument. Some time in the eighteenth or early nineteenth century, the churchwardens in their wisdom decided to enclose the base of the tower to form a ringing chamber.[3] To add insult to injury they employed utilitarian rubble walling that carelessly submerged the arches and responds. Beneath campanologists' clutter and peeling paint, the medieval masonry within the tower still appears remarkably complete, and it is entirely conceivable that in the future the arches could be reopened and the tower returned to its former glory.

The heavy squinches strongly suggest that the tower was designed to support a stone spire. The plan at the base of the spire (Plan at D) shows how little benefit the timber

structure gains from the internal corners of the tower being chamfered off. The change from stone to timber may have resulted from shortage of funds, but this seems unlikely, for its extravagant height is hardly the sign of economy. A more convincing explanation is that there were lingering concerns about overloading the foundations on the soft reclaimed ground. A broach spire eighty-five feet high would have added some 500 tons to the structure, but the lead-clad timber spire weighs little more than 50 tons.[4]

Stone and timber spires work in very different ways. A stone spire relies upon its own weight for stability, and the most vulnerable part in high winds is the apex, which is consequently finished with one very heavy capstone. By contrast, the timber spire is light and relies upon the stiffness of its framing. Its weakest point is at the base, for it must be soundly anchored to the masonry tower if it is not to be blown away in high winds. Here, three of the four perpendicular layers of oak beams that support the spire are firmly bonded into the tower walls (e).

The spire is tall and plain. At first sight the structure is overwhelming in its complexity, but the essential components are a central post (f), an inner octagonal pyramid of eight posts (g), and an outer octagonal pyramid of rafters (h) to which the roof boarding is fixed. The principal members are around eight inches square, the rafters slightly shallower, and the other timbers are considerably smaller. The inner pyramid is stiffened by a confusing mass of diagonal and horizontal struts, with inner and outer pyramids connected at regular intervals by further horizontal struts. Wooden ladders spiralling around this ever-reducing structure lead to a tiny platform near the apex (i).

Over the course of seven centuries of neglect and repair a good deal of ancient timber has been replaced, but sufficient remains to suggest that the design is original. The four corner spirelets lean significantly inward, to the extent that they merge into the profile of the spire. Both Charles Wickes's engraving of 1853 and an image from the eighteenth century show the spirelets rising vertically, but by 1905 they had adopted their current posture. While it is possible that both artists corrected what they considered to be an anomaly, it is more probable that the architect William Smith streamlined the profile during the restoration of 1873. The spirelets are finished with orbs carrying crosses, and the central spire with an orb carrying a weathervane. No doubt the uppermost orb originally contained a small relic to ward off peril, the only protection available before the invention of the lightning conductor in the eighteenth century.

Lead roofing, which appears in England as early as the seventh century, would come to dominate church roofing in the late Middle Ages owing to its durability and relative affordability. On a steeply pitched spire, lead is used only in small sheets laid diagonally to minimize the risk of creep. At LONG SUTTON the sheets, which are no more than fifteen inches wide and seven feet long, overlap in a regular herringbone pattern.

The timber spire at St Mary's is not the tallest in the land, and it is hard to say with any confidence that it is the oldest, but it is most certainly the finest. The tower on which it sits is robust, vigorous and highly original. Marred only by the blocking of the great arches at its base, the steeple at LONG SUTTON is one of the great monuments recording the birth of Gothic architecture in England.

NOTES

1   Revd Benjamin Street, *Historical Notes on Grantham and Grantham Church* (1852), p. 79.
2   The usually dependable architect Edmund Sharpe may be responsible for this confusion, for W. E. Foster in 'Some South Lincolnshire Churches', *Memorials of Old Lincolnshire* (1911), quotes him as saying that the tower and spire were erected at the very commencement of the Lancet period, which, according to his own classification, would mean around 1190. Francis Bond, Pevsner and the Statutory Listings all accept his verdict and describe the steeple as early thirteenth-century in its entirety, while Norman T. Wills,

The History of the Parish and Church of Long Sutton (1986), confidently asserts that the spire was built around 1200. An archaeological survey using dendrochronology would be extremely useful here.
3   The tower arches remain open in an unsigned eighteenth-century illustration in the care of the church. By 1853, when Charles Wickes prepared his fine engraving of the tower, the arches had been blocked.
4   A notice in the spire records that 27 tons of lead were used during the 1972 restoration, at a cost of £300 per ton. The oak structure would weigh in the order of 25 tons.

9

Raunds

NORTHAMPTONSHIRE

Between the Saxon tower at EARLS BARTON and the Norman tower at CASTOR, the River Nene flows past the richest unbroken sequence of fine steeples in England. From the Middle Ages on, the Nene Valley was celebrated for both its spires and its shoe-making. The small market town of RAUNDS once specialized in the manufacture of military boots, but its only claim to fame is now the magnificent church of St Peter, which contains medieval wall paintings of national significance.

RAUNDS church is also graced by one of the finest thirteenth-century steeples in England. The proportions are startling, for the spire is far taller than the tower from which it rises. The ratio of spire to tower, which approaches 3:2, is far from the commonly stated ideal of 1:1, and yet the composition is still extremely satisfying.

The tower was started around the year 1230, to the west of a small cruciform church built during the previous century. It is a four-square and sturdy design that overflows with naive enthusiasm. It is one of the first early Gothic towers to face emphatically to the west, and in this respect it provided an important model for subsequent development.

The north and south elevations of the tower are articulated by three arcaded stages that correspond closely to the internal levels. On the first stage a tall plinth supports a richly decorated arcade with natural leaf capitals and fine sculptures of musicians in the spandrels. The four bays are subdivided by delicate archlets springing from corbel heads.

Concave chamfered arches and triplet clusters of shafts repeat on the offset five-bay second stage. Twin-light ringing chamber windows predate the arrival of bar tracery, for the central mullions prop flat tympana decorated with non-structural trefoiled arches.

No fewer than seventy-six engaged shafts encircle the third and final stage, bringing a restless intensity to the composition. Blind outer bays frame the two subdivided openings to the bell chamber. Plain buttress gables and a modest corbel table, supported by widely spaced notch heads, terminate the tower.

Across the west elevation is a sumptuous layer of decoration supported at its base by the west door arch and secondary arches to either side. The same motif is awkwardly handled at NEWARK, but at RAUNDS continuous square jambs are introduced to separate the three arched openings. The ceremonial west door is deeply recessed to form a shallow porch with benches against the side walls, an idea repeated in Northamptonshire at HIGHAM FERRERS, Rushden and Oundle. Capricious, irregular, deeply undercut forms in the door arch demonstrate the extraordinary skill of the mason. The outer arch is supported by a triplet of five-inch engaged shafts, with tall, plain ring capitals and water-holding bases that have weathered to a nothingness.

The west front is dominated by the strikingly abstract composition of the middle stage, best described as a central gable surrounded by two half-gables. No doubt this highly original feature was initially finished with a cross or finial, but this has been lost,

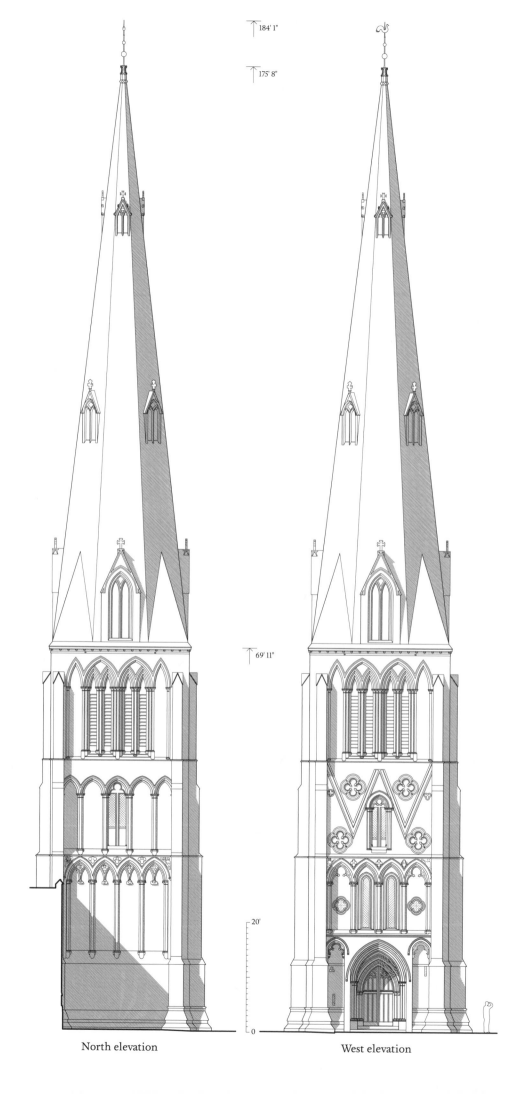

184' 1"

175' 8"

69' 11"

20'

0

North elevation

West elevation

so that the crudely truncated form suggests nothing so much as a large letter 'W'. The triangular expanses of wall remaining around this figure are perforated by quatrefoils, trefoils and the ringing chamber window. All this might be dismissed as nothing more than a random sprinkling of unsophisticated motifs, and yet the disarming inventiveness of the masons sweeps away any reservations.

Internally, the tower is intriguing but badly compromised. The space beneath the tower arch is confused by the addition of a shallow fifteenth-century tierceron vault (a) that destroyed what must have once been a very beautiful space. The arches carrying the edge of the vault crash chaotically into the tower arch just above the main responds (b). The awkward spandrel panel formed between the vault and the tower arch is filled by a painted 24-hour clock facing the nave. The original chamfered tower arch (c), springing from a cluster of five shafts, spans the full width of the tower.

Both western corners within the tower are chamfered, the north-east chamfer concealing a small, triangular room, the south-west chamfer the staircase. The spiral stair leads to a gallery formed within the depth of the west wall, running directly over the porch, which can be seen on the clock chamber plan (Plan at B). The greatest surprise at RAUNDS is to find the original gallery arcade concealed but intact above the fifteenth-century vault. This is the single most beautiful feature of the tower, even though it can be seen only in segments. Its original

appearance was painstakingly reconstructed by Orlando Jewitt in an engraving for later editions of Rickman's *Architecture of England* (see p. 112), where it is described as:

> a very rich window of two lights, which are simple lancets externally, but in the interior they are splayed out to wider arches, with trefoil heads, richly ornamented with foliage, and in the space formed by a bold moulding springing from the point of each arch, and meeting in a pointed arch, is introduced a sunk circular quatrefoil panel, with the points of the cusps ornamented with foliage.[1]

In the centre of the clock chamber floor, the bell hatch has been replaced by a peculiar octagonal lantern (d). The bell chamber above appears unchanged since the 1898 rehanging of the peal of eight in a cast-iron frame.

Construction must have stopped for several years at the top of the tower, for by the time work started on the spire the masons had been educated in the use of bar tracery. The date is therefore unlikely to be earlier than 1250. The spire, like the tower, is built from fine limestone quarried within the town, or Raunds marble, as it is known locally. At 105' 9" in height it represented a phenomenal achievement; indeed, it is possible that when completed it was the tallest masonry structure in England. Lofty broach spires continued to be built for at least sixty years after RAUNDS, but the slender proportions achieved here were never improved upon.

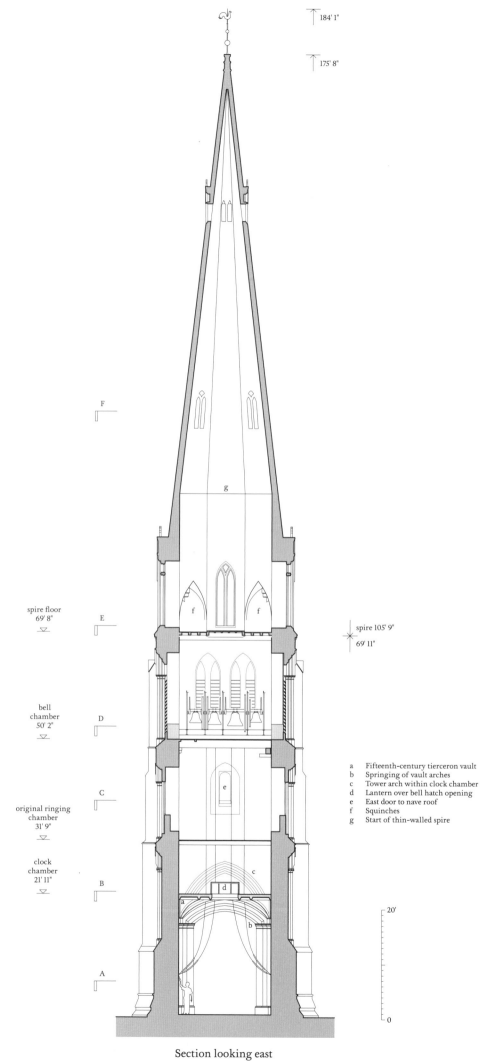

184' 1"

175' 8"

F

spire floor
69' 8"

E

spire 105' 9"
69' 11"

bell
chamber
50' 2"

D

original ringing
chamber
31' 9"

C

e

a   Fifteenth-century tierceron vault
b   Springing of vault arches
c   Tower arch within clock chamber
d   Lantern over bell hatch opening
e   East door to nave roof
f   Squinches
g   Start of thin-walled spire

clock
chamber
21' 11"

B

c

d

a

b

A

20'

0

Section looking east

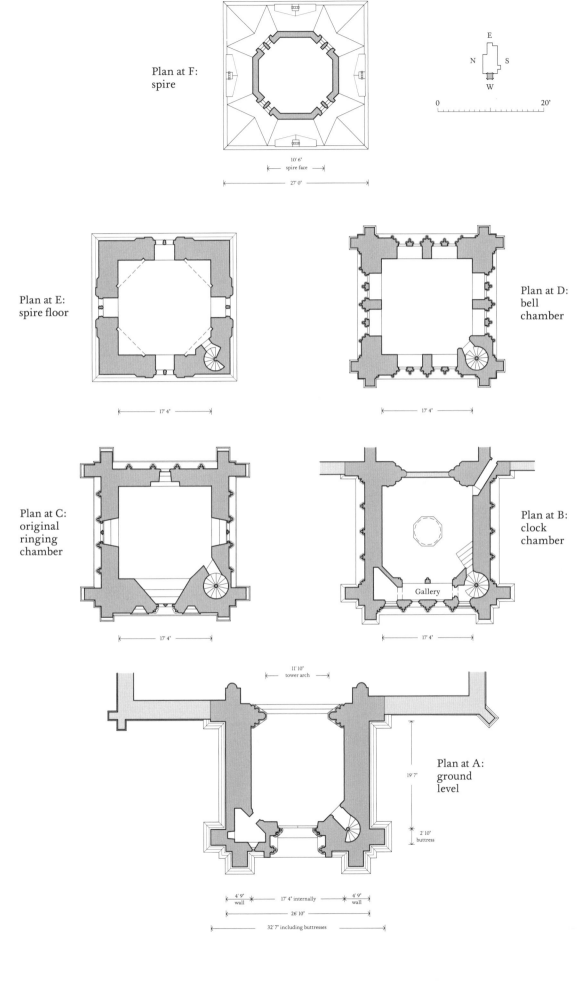

Plan at F: spire

10' 6"
spire face

27' 0"

E
N   S
W

0   20'

Plan at E: spire floor

17' 4"

Plan at D: bell chamber

17' 4"

Plan at C: original ringing chamber

17' 4"

Plan at B: clock chamber

Gallery

17' 4"

11' 10"
tower arch

Plan at A: ground level

19' 7"

2' 10"
buttress

4' 9"
wall

17' 4" internally

4' 9"
wall

26' 10"

32' 7" including buttresses

The soaring plain-edged spire has three alternating tiers of modest lucarnes separated by great heights of smooth ashlar. It commences with two masonry courses of a shallow pitch concealing the tower floor structure. This construction may be continuous with the tower below and represent the start of an initial, less ambitious design that was immediately abandoned. The octagonal pyramid, the broaches, the squinch arches and the lucarnes all start together from the top of this masonry. The spire floor provides a perfect platform for enjoying fine views from the lucarnes and for inspecting the arched and corbelled squinches at close quarters (f). Internally, the lowest quarter of the spire is a regular octagonal shaft of coursed rubble. Up to this point the structure of the spire is essentially a continuation of the tower walls. Above this level (g) the spire becomes a thin, pyramidal shell of ashlar.

Externally, the modest, unadorned broaches closely match the height of the lucarne gables. The first two tiers of spire lights are of divergent 'Y' tracery, with wide filleted rolls beneath a chamfered outer arch. Hood-moulds, gable roofs and crosses are all simply detailed, and the cheeks of the lowest tier are exceptionally wide. An inconsistency arises with the top tier of lucarnes, for their twin-light cusped diamond tracery is unlikely to have been constructed before 1400. The capstone, which reaches to 175′ 8″, also has a Perpendicular feel, suggesting that the top was rebuilt following storm damage during the later Middle Ages. It is known that Charles Squirhill rebuilt the uppermost thirty feet of the spire, including the lucarnes, following a lightning strike in 1826, but a reconstruction at this date is unlikely to have introduced inconsistent late Gothic detailing without any justification.

The main lucarnes, which appear to extend directly up from the face of the tower, visually lock the composition of the steeple together. The reason that the unequal division between spire and tower does not appear top heavy now becomes apparent, for there are not two but three vertical zones in the design. Between the square tower and the pure octagonal spire there is an intensive zone of intersection where the broaches and lucarnes rise from the tower and appear to clasp the base of the spire. This central zone, dominated by the tall lucarnes, forms the centre of gravity of a beautifully balanced composition.

Orlando Jewitt illustrated the original appearance of the gallery arcade at Raunds for Thomas Rickman's formative work An Attempt to Discriminate the Styles of Architecture in England, *first published in 1817.*

NOTE

1   Thomas Rickman, *An Attempt to Discriminate the Styles of Architecture in England from the Conquest to the Reformation*, 5th edn (1868), p. xxv.

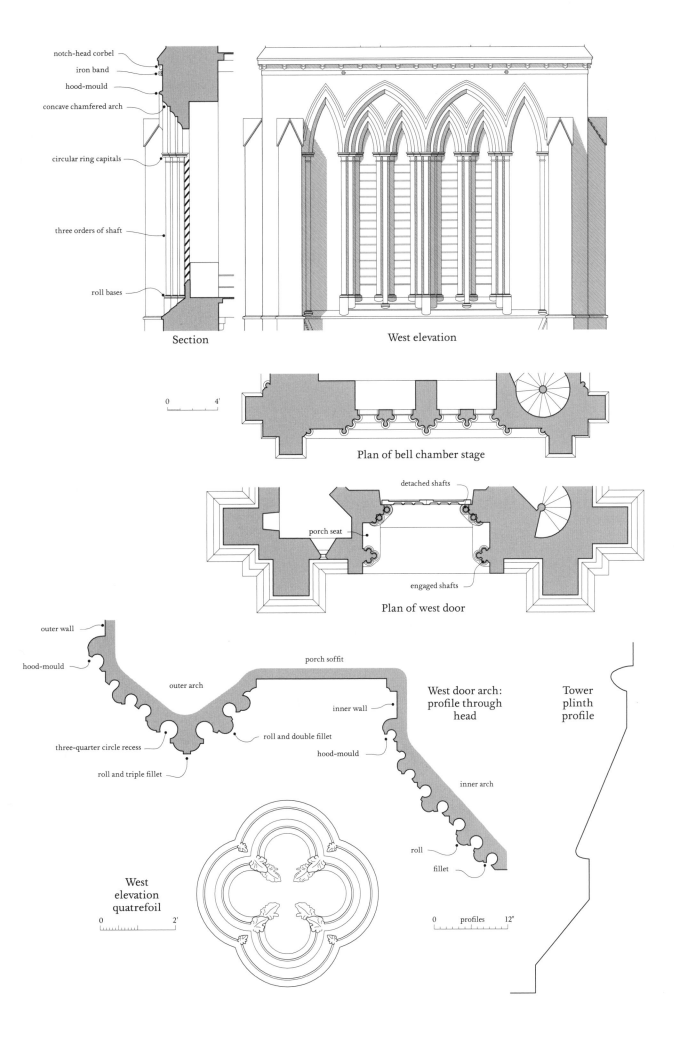

notch-head corbel
iron band
hood-mould
concave chamfered arch

circular ring capitals

three orders of shaft

roll bases

Section

West elevation

0   4'

Plan of bell chamber stage

detached shafts

porch seat

engaged shafts

Plan of west door

outer wall

hood-mould

outer arch

porch soffit

inner wall

roll and double fillet

three-quarter circle recess

roll and triple fillet

hood-mould

West door arch:
profile through
head

Tower
plinth
profile

inner arch

roll

fillet

West
elevation
quatrefoil

0   2'

0   profiles   12"

10

St Mary, Oxford

OXFORDSHIRE

S T MARY, OXFORD demands superlatives. After the three great masterworks of GRANTHAM, COVENTRY and LOUTH, it ranks as one of the finest parochial steeples in England. It is climbed by more visitors than any other steeple in this survey and it boasts the finest ensemble of clustered pinnacles in the land.

There have been three churches on the tight urban site sandwiched between the High Street and Radcliffe Square, the heart of the university. Nothing remains of the Saxon church inferred by the Domesday survey. The second church has also been swept away, except for the north-facing tower and spire, and the Old Congregation House abutting its eastern wall. The unusual positioning of the tower implies that this second church filled the available width between St Mary's Passage to the west and Catte Street to the east. The third church is essentially the late fifteenth-century Perpendicular structure the visitor sees today, with a six-bay aisled nave, an elongated choir and a Lady Chapel abutting the west face of the tower.

The principle of composition employed in the steeple can be seen as a development not only from WITNEY, but also from RAUNDS, half a century earlier. At both churches the zone of intersection between a square tower and an octagonal spire was becoming the focus of the design. At ST MARY's this concept is relentlessly pursued, for all the energy is concentrated in one brilliantly intense zone of intersection. Whether or not this was the intention of Richard de Abingdon, the master

mason known to be responsible for the tower in 1275,[1] is unclear, for there is an important stylistic break at the base of the parapet. However, as T. G. Jackson observed, the substantial buttress depth maintained at the top of the tower implies a pre-existing notion of great pinnacles on the corners, whatever their final form.[2]

Massive angle buttresses 4' 9" deep and 7' 7" wide dominate the tower to the extent that the flat elevation between occupies less than half of the overall width. The articulation of these great flat-sided slabs by five simple set-offs could not be simpler. A rather amorphous basement course serves to spread the structural and visual load into the ground. Only one string course, that of the north window hood, is taken around the buttresses. In some respects, therefore, the treatment is even more austere than the closely related design of ADDERBURY.

The similarities to the tower at ADDERBURY would have been even stronger before the unnecessary introduction of a north door and 'Decorated' tracery in 1852. According to an 1812 engraving, north window and bell chamber openings originally shared the same late thirteenth-century intersecting tracery, albeit with additional trilobe figures at the upper level. This is the putative original design reconstructed on p. 118.

After the bold simplicity of the exterior, the confusing clutter within is a disappointment. Even before the arrival of gift-shop fixtures, the space had been compromised by medieval alterations and strengthening works. The primary arch to the south must have been noble when it opened into the north transept, but this was lost to a fifteenth-century aisle extension and a mezzanine floor (c). The head of the arch still reads externally above the aisle roof (d). The east window has been blocked except for a remnant of head tracery above a high splayed cill. The Old Congregation House, built shortly after the tower, abuts on this side with a remarkable lack of coordination. A crudely cut passageway (b) leads visitors on a contorted ramble up the steeple, for both of the original spiral staircases were lost in the nineteenth-century restoration. To the west a combination of high-level frameless glass and low-level classicism leaves the original opening visible but extremely confused.

Once the visitor has clambered across the aisle roof, the ringing chamber is reached and the north-west stair restarts. The bell chamber is reached only by a stepladder (f) passing through a shallow baffle chamber (g). Three concentric chamfered squinch arches prepare for the great sculptural tour de force that is to follow (h).

The noble roll-edged spire and the twin-light lucarnes thirty-five feet high at its base follow the Oxfordshire tradition established a century before at the priory of St Frideswide (Oxford Cathedral). The sumptuous ballflower decoration of the spire lights, with their richly crocketed gables, shows the design moving confidently into the fourteenth century. The perforated trefoil balustrade is consistent with the contemporary towers of Ashbourne (Derbys) and ADDERBURY; however, the extraordinary complexity that develops between these elements is unprecedented.

The pyramidal massing around the spire is perfectly judged. The lower layer consists of eight outward-facing niches, finished with acutely pointed and crocketed gables that terminate each of the eight buttresses. Ballflower fills the mouldings, and grotesques spring from every gable base. The two return faces of each buttress are treated in a similar but more constricted fashion, and a plain mass of masonry returns on the diagonal to the face of the spire. The parapet path slices through these masses except on the north-west corner, where the staircase arrives. Of the twenty-four niches created by this arrangement twelve were filled with statues before Jackson's restoration of 1897. Three of these figures had been replaced in 1850, and all but one of the remaining nine statues were discovered to be so fragile and patched that they were replaced; the originals now stand in New College cloister.

Two tiers of inner pinnacles set close to the spire follow. The lowest of these tiers follows the original design up to the springing at the top of the twin panels on each face. Above this, the original arrangement had been lost even before 1610. Jackson's well-considered design retains twin arches and gables to each face of the main square shaft. Above rises a second and narrower shaft, panelled as before, but finished with a single gable to each face and a tall, crocketed finial.

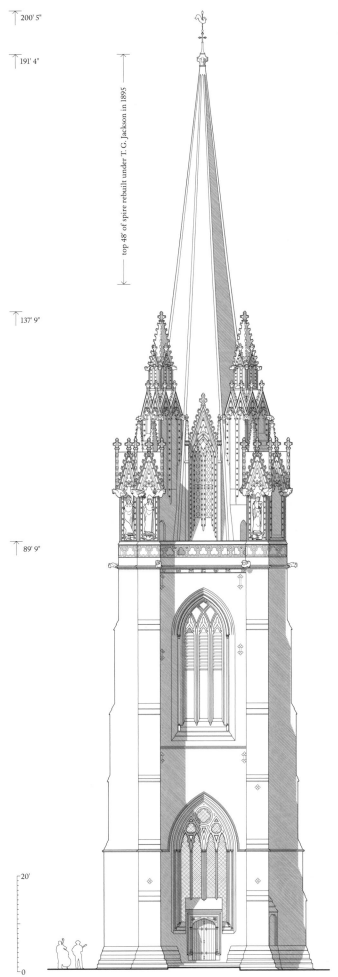

200' 5"

191' 4"

top 48' of spire rebuilt under T. G. Jackson in 1895

137' 9"

89' 9"

20'

0

North elevation

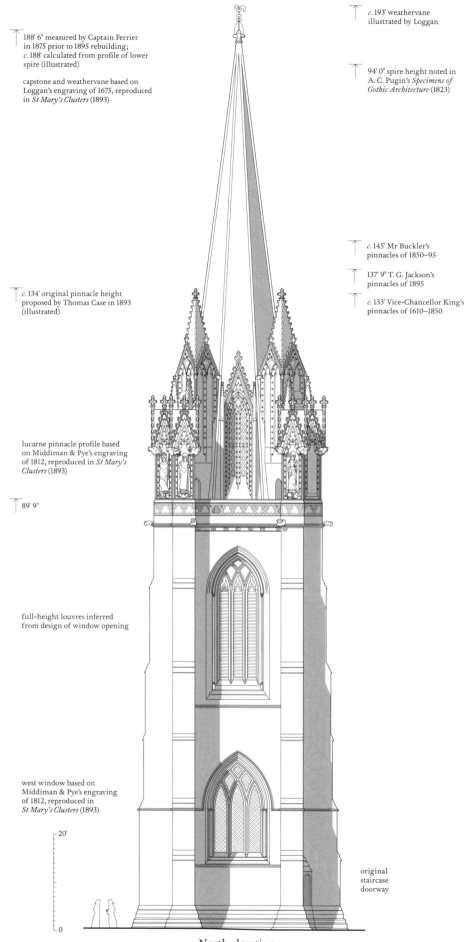

c. 193' weathervane
illustrated by Loggan

94' 0" spire height noted in
A. C. Pugin's *Specimens of
Gothic Architecture* (1823)

188' 6" measured by Captain Ferrier
in 1875 prior to 1895 rebuilding;
c. 188' calculated from profile of lower
spire (illustrated)

capstone and weathervane based on
Loggan's engraving of 1675, reproduced
in *St Mary's Clusters* (1893)

c. 145' Mr Buckler's
pinnacles of 1850–95

137' 9" T. G. Jackson's
pinnacles of 1895

c. 133' Vice-Chancellor King's
pinnacles of 1610–1850

c. 134' original pinnacle height
proposed by Thomas Case in 1893
(illustrated)

lucarne pinnacle profile based
on Middiman & Pye's engraving
of 1812, reproduced in *St Mary's
Clusters* (1893)

89' 9"

full-height louvres inferred
from design of window opening

west window based on
Middiman & Pye's engraving
of 1812, reproduced in
St Mary's Clusters (1893)

20'

0

original
staircase
doorway

North elevation
Hypothetical original design

Rising, as it does, from the parish church of the oldest university in England, ST MARY's steeple has generated more acrimonious academic debate and ill-informed interference than any other steeple in the country. The nadir of bungling amateurism was reached during the restorations that started in 1848 and dragged on for nine long years.

The *Oxford University Herald* reported on 29 April that 'at length a contract has been entered into for the repair of the beautiful tower and spire belonging to this handsome church'.[3] The vicar and churchwardens had been unable to raise sufficient funds for the long-anticipated restoration from within the Parish and turned to the university for assistance, with near-disastrous consequences. The supervising architect, Edward Blore, was under instruction to repair all the defective ornamental work with Tainton stone 'in strict accordance with their original designs'. By June 1848 the Oxford Architectural Society was concerned by Blore's efforts on the south-east pinnacle and urged that nothing further be done without 'careful consideration'.

In December the university took full control of the project, and the Vice-Chancellor established a delegation of ten academics to superintend the works. All expenses incurred over and above the £50 raised by the parish would come from the university's General Fund, which effectively handed the delegation an open cheque. From its inception the objective of the delegation – to restore the 'original design' of the steeple – was compromised by ignorance and vanity.

By August 1849 Mr Blore was being asked to advise on his own replacement. In December Mr Orlando Jewitt[4] presented a beautifully illustrated report proposing a limited restoration of the inner pinnacles to reflect the 'Decorated' style of the surrounding work. Mr Jewitt never received payment for his services, and in April 1850, two years after the work had commenced, J. C. & C. Buckler, Architects, were appointed to complete the restoration of the spire. In June a prominent member of the delegation, Dr Harrington, confidently informed the Archaeological Institute that 'it is to be hoped that in a few months the whole will be completed'.[5]

Debate raged around the appropriate strategy for restoring the 'debased' inner pinnacles installed in 1610 under Vice-Chancellor King. Buckler, and Jewitt before him, had suggested embellishing the existing form in 'Decorated' dress, but a more radical alternative was also proposed in which the pinnacle was substantially enlarged and raised in height. The indecision was broadcast across the city in June 1850 when two pinnacles were completed to competing designs. Predictably, the faction supporting the large pinnacle fifty-eight feet high won the argument, and Buckler was duly instructed to proceed. This illiterate fantasy proved an immediate success, and E. A. Freeman, writing just six years later, was gushing in his enthusiasm:

Neither the Tower nor the spire, taken alone, is worthy of the connection between the two. Both tower and spire are rather bare, while the pinnacles which unite them are of the most elaborate richness ... The spire ... without even an upper range of spire-lights, rises in painful bareness from amid the grand array of pinnacles.[6]

The Vice-Chancellor's accounts reveal that extraordinary expenditure for the restoration of ST MARY's amounted to £3,904 15s., with just £50 being contributed by the parish. In addition to the work on the pinnacles, the original intersecting tracery to the north window had been replaced by new 'Decorated' work, pairs of incongruous un-Decorated castellated pinnacles were added to the lucarnes, the spire capstone was replaced, and a general repointing was carried out with the newly popular, but intrinsically damaging, Portland cement. Throughout this meddling beautification the integrity of the structure was ignored.

As soon as January 1856, the pre-eminent church architect of the time, George Gilbert Scott, was reporting to the Vice-Chancellor on large settlement cracks that had developed on the north, west and east faces of the tower. Removal of the internal plaster revealed large areas of previously undetected ancient cracking that had been exacerbated by the additional weight and disturbance of the restoration. Of greatest concern was the tendency of the northern buttresses to sink 'and to cause the external ashlar to bulge outwards and crack'.[7]

In Scott's view the main defect was the isolation of the north-east and north-west corners resulting from the spiral staircases concealed within their cores. The solution was massive temporary shoring, walling-up of doorways, the moving of the ringing chamber, the filling of the staircases, the insertion of strong cast-iron ties at three levels (e) and an investigation of the foundations. The parish was not impressed by the university's request for further financial assistance to meet the final bill of £1,089 2s. 11½d., reporting in their minute book:

> In the works lately executed the Parish was not allowed to take any part whatever ... the Parishioners cannot but think that such has been caused from want of due precaution on the part of the Architect employed by the University in his not having first examined the sub-structure and thereby satisfied himself that it was in a sufficiently substantial state of repair to bear the additional weight he was about to place upon it.

The impact of this tragic debacle on the young undergraduate William Morris, who arrived at Exeter College in the summer of 1852 and who would in due course revolutionize the philosophy of building conservation, is not directly recorded. It may have influenced his view that:

> The city of Oxford, has been ravaged for many years past, not only by ignorant tradesmen, but by the University and college authorities ... a lamentable example

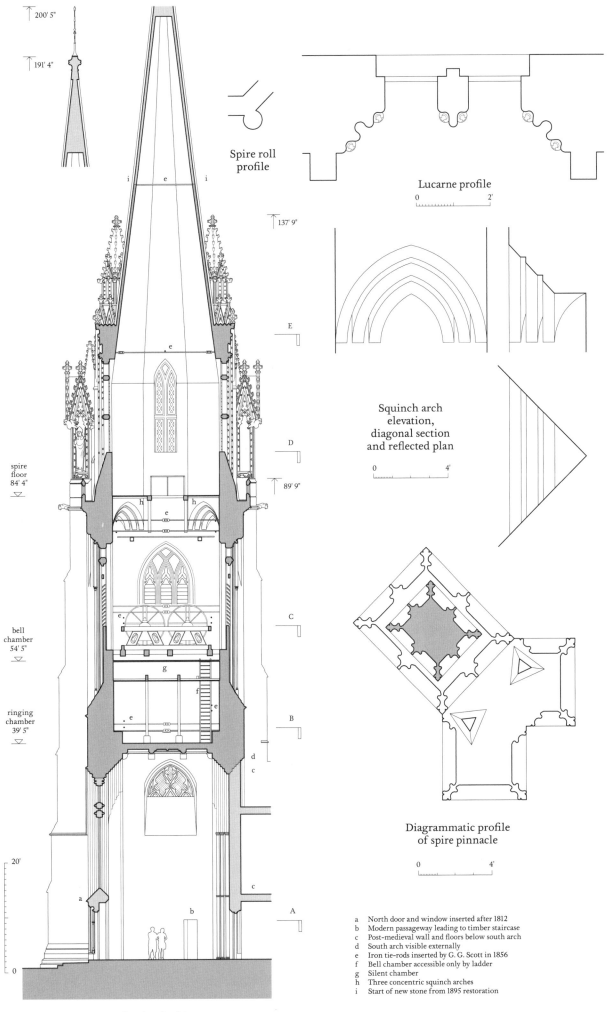

200' 5"

191' 4"

Spire roll
profile

Lucarne profile

0   2'

137' 9"

E

D

89' 9"

spire
floor
84' 4"

Squinch arch
elevation,
diagonal section
and reflected plan

0   4'

C

bell
chamber
54' 5"

Diagrammatic profile
of spire pinnacle

0   4'

ringing
chamber
39' 5"

B

d
c

c

20'

A

0

a   North door and window inserted after 1812
b   Modern passageway leading to timber staircase
c   Post-medieval wall and floors below south arch
d   South arch visible externally
e   Iron tie-rods inserted by G. G. Scott in 1856
f   Bell chamber accessible only by ladder
g   Silent chamber
h   Three concentric squinch arches
i   Start of new stone from 1895 restoration

Section looking east

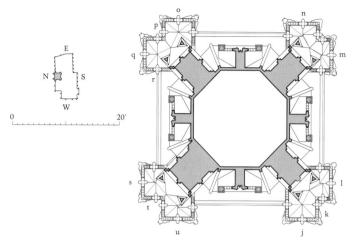

Plan at E: spire

Location of original sculptures identified by T.G. Jackson in 1897:

j   St Mary the Virgin
k   St John the Evangelist
l   Bishop (replaced by a modern figure of Walter de Merton)
m   St John the Baptist
n   Archbishop, possibly St Thomas of Canterbury
o   King Edward II
p   St Hugh of Avalon, Bishop of Lincoln
q   Bishop, possibly St William of York
r   Archbishop
s   St Cuthbert, Bishop of Durham
t   Archbishop
u   Bishop, possibly Richard of Chichester

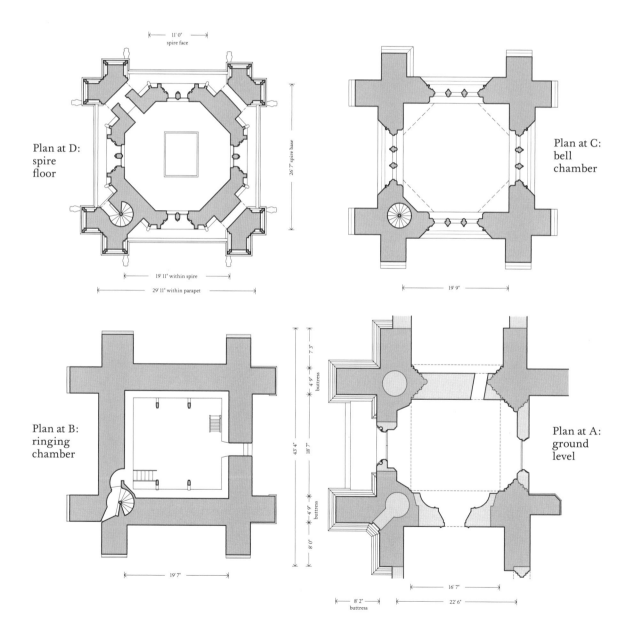

Plan at D: spire floor

Plan at C: bell chamber

Plan at B: ringing chamber

Plan at A: ground level

of all kinds of architectural errors and mistakes, and crimes.'[8]

This unhappy saga was recounted in great detail by another professionally unqualified academic. Thomas Case was Professor of Moral and Metaphysical Philosophy at Magdalen College, but no architect. Of all the learned works contained within the bibliography of the present book, none comes close to Case's *St Mary's Clusters: An Historical Enquiry* in filling so many pages with so narrow an argument. The author's purpose, which is repeated ad nauseam and justified through a forensic analysis of town maps, historical illustrations and documentary evidence, is to ascertain the original design of the inner pinnacles. On page 101 he finally proposes a design informed by Lichfield and Salisbury cathedrals in which the inner pinnacles are finished with a single gable to each face and a single spirelet rising forty-seven feet from the base of the spire. Case's argument is

weakened by inaccurate survey information, a misunderstanding of structural principles and a bizarre ignorance of A. C. Pugin's widely published 1823 survey drawings.[9] Despite these shortcomings, the result is a surprisingly convincing proposition that is incorporated here within the design on p. 118.

In their current form, T. G. Jackson's inner pinnacles are an acceptable and carefully considered compromise. More questionable is Jackson's rebuilding of the top forty-eight feet of the spire, which appears to have raised the top of the finial by almost three feet. This unnecessary accentuation of the proportions is achieved by a tapering of the roll edges that merge into the surface of the upper spire. The 'hypothetical original design' corrects this anomaly and reproduces the profile of weathervane and capstone illustrated in Loggan's engraving of 1675. The proposed height of 188' 6" is derived from Captain Ferrier's theodolite survey made exactly two centuries later.[10]

NOTES

1   John Harvey, *English Medieval Architects* (1984), p. 1.
2   T. G. Jackson, *The Church of St Mary the Virgin, Oxford* (1897), p. 83.
3   Thomas Case, *St Mary's Clusters: An Historical Enquiry* (1893), pp. 44ff.
4   Orlando Jewitt was also responsible for the engraving included within the chapter on RAUNDS.
5   *St Mary's Clusters*, p. 48.
6   Introduction by E. A. Freeman to Charles Wickes, *Illustrations of the Spires and Towers of the Medieval Churches of England*, vol. II (1858–59), p. 11.

7   Letter from George Gilbert Scott to the Vice-Chancellor of the University of Oxford, 18 January 1856, cited in *St Mary's Clusters*, pp. 73–74.
8   William Morris quoted in Aymer Vallance, *The Life and Work of William Morris* (1897).
9   A. C. Pugin's *Specimens of Gothic Architecture; Selected from Various Antient Edifices in England*, vol. II (1823) would have been known to every student of architecture, but Case admits that he first became aware of its existence on the day after completing his text.
10 *St Mary's Clusters*, p. 1.

II

Adderbury

OXFORDSHIRE

ADDERBURY church is celebrated for an exquisite chancel, completed to the design of Richard of Winchcombe in 1419, and for the finest collection of medieval carvings in the county of Oxford. A total of 317 carvings have been catalogued by the local historian Nicholas Allen, including the superb 'bestiary' frieze on the corbel table of the south aisle, constructed around 1325–30, and the musicians' frieze on the north aisle that immediately followed.[1] On the slightly earlier west tower there are six gargoyles, all in very good condition, and four badly weathered friezes. Of the forty-three frieze carvings, only fourteen remain intelligible, including six ballflowers, three animals, two grotesques suffering with toothache, a knight and a lady. The upper gargoyles take the form of winged beasts, probably griffins, traditional symbols of strength. Allen assumes a date of *c.* 1315 for the carvings, which is not unreasonable given the stylistic evidence of the architecture.

This is a heavyweight design, but it is by no means unsophisticated. The structurally efficient diagonal buttress appeared occasionally in the twelfth century, for example to lend support to the tower of Polebrook (Northants), but it came into its own as a generator of architectural form only after 1300. The diagonal buttress was to become almost de rigueur throughout Gloucestershire and in Oxfordshire, outside the county town, but it was never more emphatically used than at ADDERBURY. At 5' 3" wide and 5' 10" deep, the buttresses start on a

colossal scale. Diagonal buttresses emphasize the width of a tower, and at ADDERBURY this is given further accentuation by three continuous strings that appear even before the bell stage is reached. The proportions are, however, very appealing, for the ratio between the second stage and the equal stages above and below closely approximates the golden ratio.

As at STOKE-BY-NAYLAND in the following century, the diagonal line generates the entire composition, so that tower arch, window openings and door openings consist of little more than diagonal chamfers. Nothing could be simpler than the near-equilateral tower arch, of four plain chamfers. The screen, part Gothic Revival and part twentieth-century frameless glass, is an unfortunate intrusion. Similarly, the west door arch is formed of nothing but three diagonal chamfers. In profile, however, they are not flat but swollen by ogee curves to form characteristic early fourteenth-century wave mouldings. This illustrates how the Curvilinear spirit, appearing in England around 1315, takes on a subtle and undemonstrative form in less expensive work. The failure of Rickman's 'Decorated' nomenclature to embrace all the diverse work of this period is well illustrated at ADDERBURY, for although the decoration may be of high quality it is very limited in extent and has no influence on the architectural form. Even more than at EWERBY and HECKINGTON, this early fourteenth-century aesthetic is one where powerful sculptural

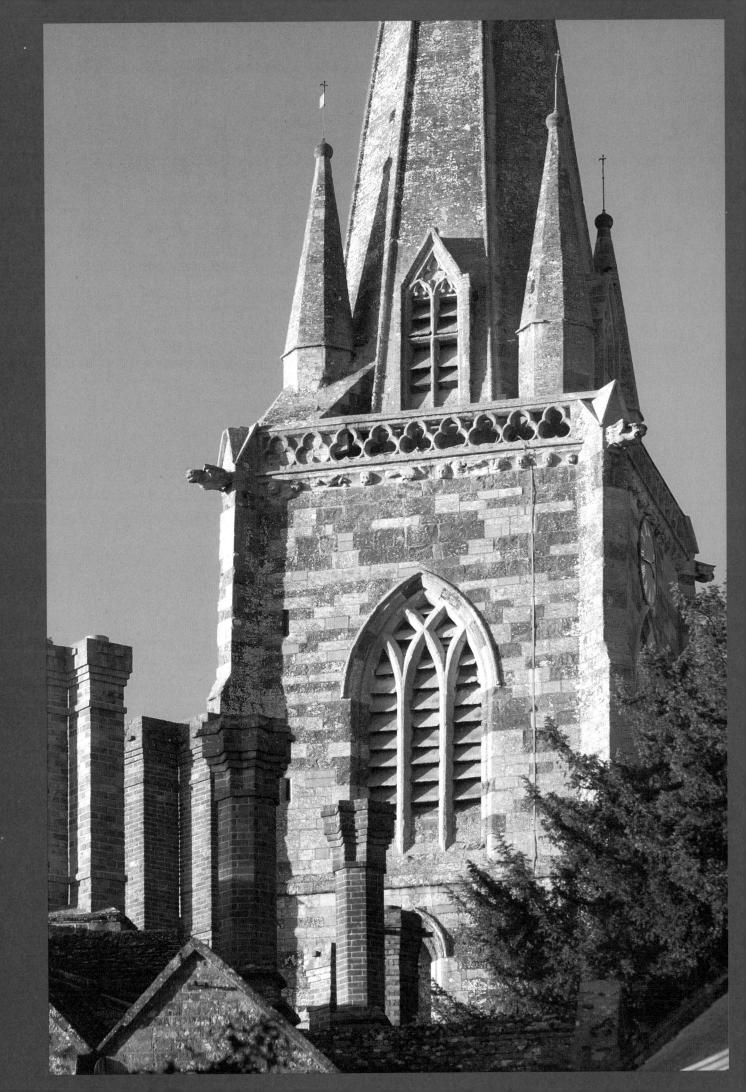

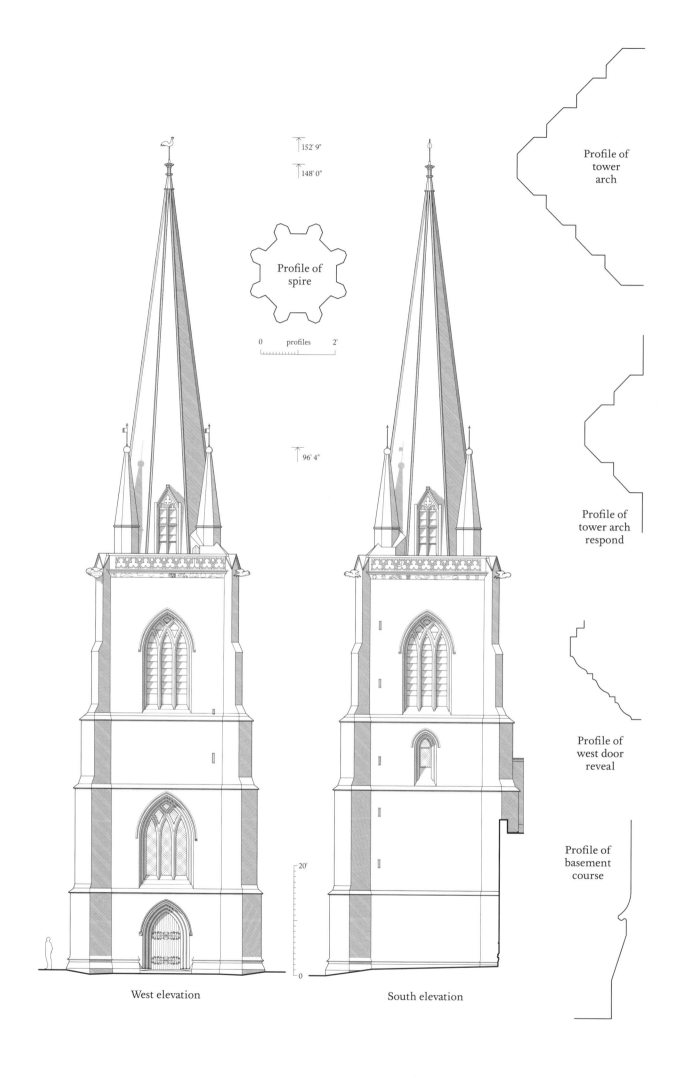

Profile of spire

0   profiles   2'

152' 9"

148' 0"

96' 4"

Profile of tower arch

Profile of tower arch respond

Profile of west door reveal

Profile of basement course

20'

0

West elevation

South elevation

massing takes precedence and decoration becomes secondary.

Geometrical rigour continues unabated in the three-bay intersecting tracery of the west window and the four bell-stage openings above. Even the plain stone louvres follow the same incisive forty-five-degree cut line (b). The interior of the tower reveals the structure of the bell openings to be split between two arches, the inner set slightly lower than the outer. A small door opening (a) leads to the nave roof space, a common feature of the period shared with HECKINGTON, EWERBY and BRANT BROUGHTON. Single squinch arches (c) are set low, resulting in a considerable expanse of masonry between the bell chamber openings and the parapet.

All of the fine-scale interest is concentrated at the summit of the tower, in a narrow band of frieze, gargoyles and parapet. The perforated rounded-trefoil parapet is a rare form shared with two contemporary towers of the highest quality: Ashbourne (Derbys) and the sumptuous ST MARY, OXFORD.[2] Ashbourne may have fourteen trefoils to each face, compared with ADDERBURY's nine (or ten on the east), but it lacks any corner emphasis. At ADDERBURY the abrupt termination of the diagonal buttresses, with plain low gables, is only slightly better. A visit to the parapet reveals that both the pinnacles and the associated south-west staircase roof are independent of the tower parapet, indicating a pause in construction. Further

supporting evidence is to be found within the steeple, where there is a significant step in the inner wall face (e).

One of the pleasures in surveying ancient buildings is the occasional discovery of the unexpected. ADDERBURY is included within this volume not because it is a steeple of the very first rank, but because it provides an eloquent illustration of an important stage in steeple evolution. ADDERBURY perfectly encapsulates a number of major preoccupations of early fourteenth-century steeple-building, including intersecting tracery, the diagonal buttress and pyramidal composition.[3] This last point is shown to perfection by the tapering silhouette that starts in the buttresses and continues through the large inset corner pinnacles to the moderately inclined spire. This at least was the expectation.

From a distance, the spire fits comfortably within the Oxfordshire tradition inherited from WITNEY and the first generation of oversailing spires in the early thirteenth century. There are tall twin-light dormer windows with mid-height transoms and ascending soufflets in the heads. Making allowances for the later date, the principle of this tracery is not unlike that of WITNEY, with its non-structural trefoil heads, or Bampton. The plain octagonal corner pinnacles finished with ball finials only differ from Shipton-under-Wychwood in the elongation of the proportions. There is, however, one jarring inconsistency that places ADDERBURY well into the fifteenth century, for it is finished not with rolls, but with a sharp, angular spire edge.

This form of angular spire edge is almost always employed in conjunction with a matching angular form of crocket. Around fourteen spires of this type exist across the East Midlands and, apart from its appearance on the late broach spire of Walcot (Lincs), it is an emphatically fifteenth-century motif.[4] Research has revealed only two uncrocketed examples of the angular edge: ADDERBURY and Middleton Cheney (Northants). These two ironstone villages are less than five miles apart, suggesting that any similarities are more than a coincidence. Middleton Cheney tower is a thoroughly Perpendicular fifteenth-century affair, with strongly regimented arcading in the parapet and supermullions in the bell chamber lights. The spire is later still, for the inner group of castellated spire pinnacles is unrelated to the design of the outer tower pinnacles. It is, therefore, not unreasonable to assume a date no earlier than 1450 for Middleton Cheney and, by implication, the spire of ADDERBURY.

Such a substantial break in construction also explains the unusual inboard positioning of the pinnacles at ADDERBURY. It appears that the masons took great care to follow the established tradition of the Oxfordshire pinnacled steeple without compromising the parapet inherited from the previous century. The fine pyramidal silhouette of ADDERBURY appears to have been achieved more through happy accident than by design.

NOTES

1   Nicholas J. Allen, 'The Medieval Stone Carvings of the Church of St Mary's, Adderbury', *Cake and Cockhorse*, Banbury Historical Society, vol. 15, nos. 4–5 (2001–02).

2   The Ashbourne parapet may derive from Lichfield Cathedral Lady Chapel (*c.* 1315–36), the church falling within the Lichfield Diocese; parapets with rounded trefoils set within triangular bays appear in the same period, for example at ST MARY REDCLIFFE.

3   In *The Buildings of England: Oxfordshire* (1974), Pevsner considers that tower and spire were completed by 1350.

4   This excludes two post-medieval instances of crocketed angular spire edge at Uffington (Lincs, 1639) and Nassington (Northants, 1640). A slightly different form of crocketed edge with a concave face appears in the West Midlands.

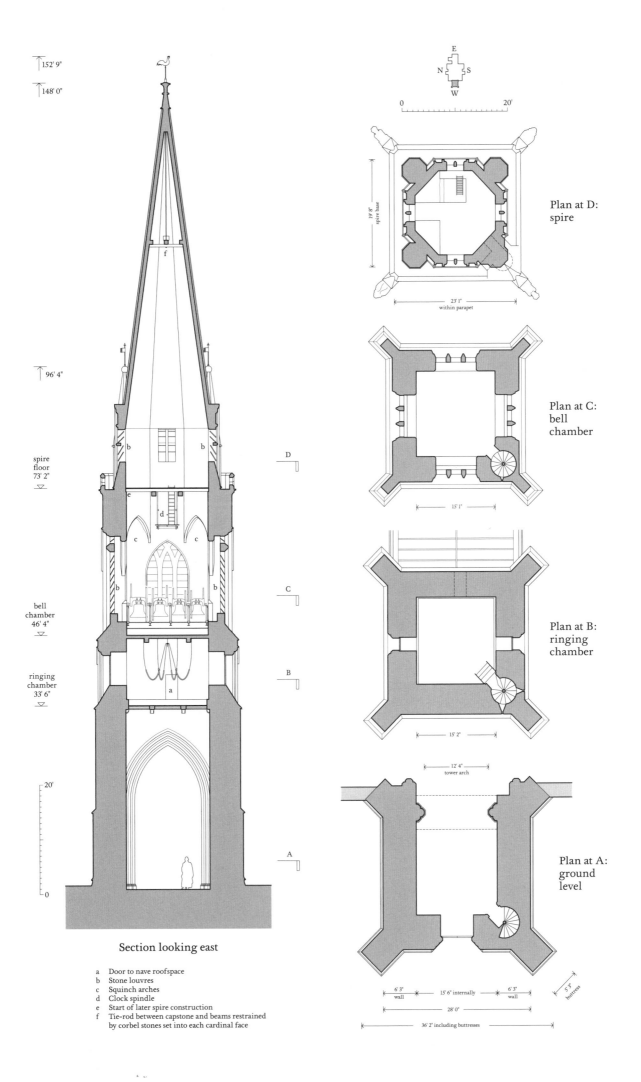

152' 9"

148' 0"

E
N S
W

0   20'

Plan at D:
spire

19' 8"
spire base

23' 1"
within parapet

96' 4"

Plan at C:
bell
chamber

D

b   b

spire
floor
73' 2"

e

d

c   c

C

15' 1"

bell
chamber
46' 4"

b   b

Plan at B:
ringing
chamber

ringing
chamber
33' 6"

C

B

a

15' 2"

20'

B

12' 4"
tower arch

A

Plan at A:
ground
level

0

Section looking east

a   Door to nave roofspace
b   Stone louvres
c   Squinch arches
d   Clock spindle
e   Start of later spire construction
f   Tie-rod between capstone and beams restrained
     by corbel stones set into each cardinal face

6' 3"
wall

15' 6" internally

6' 3"
wall

5' 5"
buttress

28' 0"

36' 2" including buttresses

12

Grantham

LINCOLNSHIRE

GRANTHAM has a phenomenal reputation. Ruskin is reported to have swooned when he first laid eyes upon the steeple; Pevsner considered it to be perfect;[1] and, for Sir George Gilbert Scott, it was second only to Salisbury.[2] The architectural historian Francis Bond was more circumspect, expressing disquiet about the cluttered base of the spire and the encroachment of the aisles upon the tower.[3] In truth, GRANTHAM is a brilliant but flawed experiment. It is spectacularly ambitious, but it is also frustratingly compromised.

The story of its creation starts around the year 1280 when a vast scheme of rebuilding commenced. Salisbury Cathedral had been responsible for St Wulfram's Church since 1091, but it was local wealth, particularly from the wool trade, that funded the work. A Norman church with crossing tower, built on the site of a Saxon predecessor, had been badly damaged by fire in 1222. More space was required not only for the growing congregation, but also for numerous guild chapels and for the relics of Saints Symphorian, Etritha and Wulfram. The aisles were to be rebuilt to match the scale of the nave, and the west end was to be extended over sixty feet into what was then the marketplace.

Two sources are readily identifiable in the initial design: the plan of NEWARK and the elevations of the Angel Choir at Lincoln Cathedral. Fifty years earlier, NEWARK had adopted the innovative plan of TICKHILL church, in which the west tower was

embraced by the aisles. The tower had been opened up with broad arches on three sides, providing a processional route around the west end of the church. At NEWARK this design had been an afterthought, but at GRANTHAM it was intended from the first. The eastern corners of the embraced tower are supported by two huge square piers, each carrying twenty engaged shafts, set diagonally like the crossing piers of a cathedral.

The other source of inspiration was the Angel Choir at Lincoln, built between 1256 and 1280. This employed some of the finest Early Geometrical tracery in England, and the windows of its east elevation were copied almost directly at GRANTHAM. Work started first on the north elevation of the north aisle, where the three-light windows are borrowed directly from Lincoln. Turning the corner, the north aisle west window, adjacent to the tower, is a six-bay version of the eight-bay east window of Lincoln Angel Choir, at that time the largest window in England. GRANTHAM may not be quite on this scale, but the magnificent design, of fourteen circles of three interlocking sizes, is still of national importance. The stone cusps were added only in the twentieth century, replacing earlier Victorian cast-iron cusps, but they do not look out of place.[4]

The fine south aisle window, copied from the gable of the Angel Choir, is noticeably smaller, leaving the west elevation in a state of restless imbalance. These disparate parts are tied together by a continuous basement course and a continuous horizontal string at the top. The ends of the aisle roofs are masked by minor gables projecting above the parapet, both disconcertingly offset from the window arches below.

The fame of St Wulfram's steeple depends primarily upon its exceptionally slender proportions, which set the benchmark for all future development. The ratio of height to width is 13:2, a figure matched later at NEWARK and WHITTLESEY, but exceeded only at ST MICHAEL, COVENTRY. However, GRANTHAM appears even more attenuated than COVENTRY, for whereas ST MICHAEL stands exposed on three sides, GRANTHAM is flush with the aisles. Consequently the eye reads the projecting western buttresses as representing the full width of the tower at the base. This is a clever optical trick, for read in this way the steeple appears to achieve the supremely slender ratio of 8:1. The tower is of four principal stages, most of which are subdivided by decoration.

The first main stage is contiguous with the west ends of the aisles, and together they form part of one expansive composition, framed by large corner buttresses and square pinnacles. This is very much in the tradition of the screen wall that finishes the west front of many of the great cathedrals, most particularly Salisbury, which had been finished only in 1266. The west door is exceedingly rich, with five engaged shafts alternating with filleted rolls and a steeply pointed arch of sumptuous profile. The crispness of the detail suggests that this

can only be work from Scott's restoration of 1866–68. Ballflower make its first appearance in the outer recess of the door arch and then swarms across the noble intersecting tracery of the four-light west window above, both inside and out. In the west of England ballflowers were occasionally carved from the solid stone of the tracery bars, but here the majority of the 1,148 flowers were cut separately and then dowelled into place.[5] Three tiers of trefoiled niches, on the buttresses and to either side of the west door and window, are occupied by a congregation of life-size twentieth-century statues. Work stopped at this level for several years.

Within the tower, north and south tower arches are of three chamfered orders rising from a corresponding number of stubby shafts on each respond (a). To the east, the major arch is of four orders of intricate filleted rolls entirely unrelated to the supporting responds (b), suggesting a significant break in construction at this point. The void beneath the tower (c) is impressive but underwhelming, for it is poorly lit through the heavy Victorian glass of the west window. The unusual stone vault is of twelve regular bays with an amorphous infilling between the ribs.

As the west front rises clear of the aisles, two tiers of steeply gabled blind arcading zigzag across the elevation. Below the ringing chamber windows is the first of three strings at which the tower wall reduces in depth. This stepped wall profile is significant, for until this date, with few

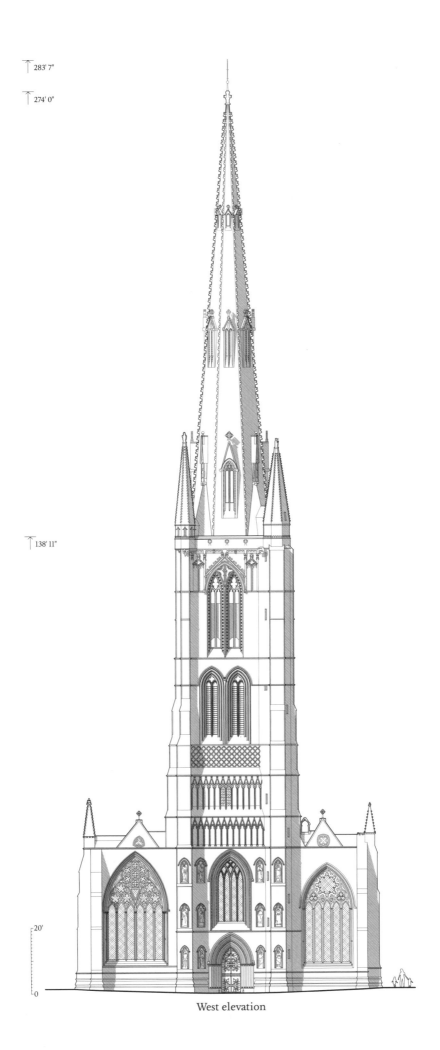

283' 7"

274' 0"

138' 11"

20'

0

West elevation

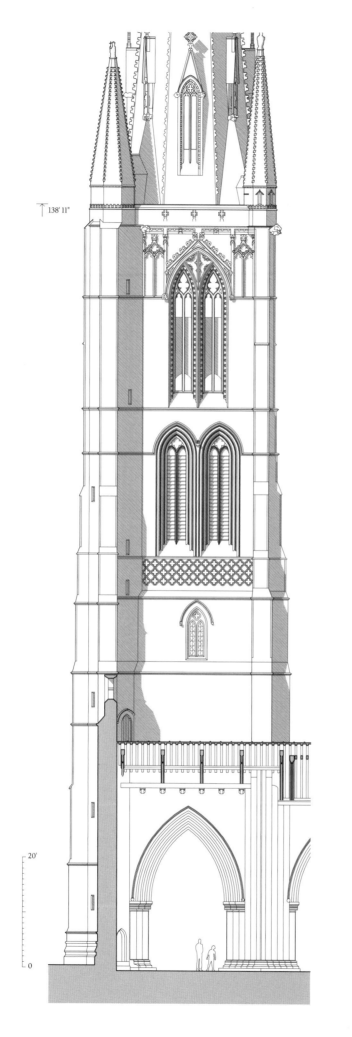

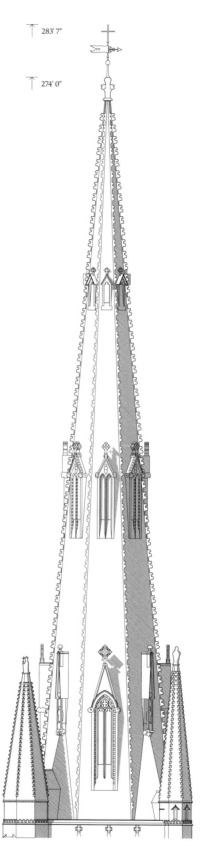

283' 7"

274' 0"

138' 11"

20'

0

South elevation
with section
through south
aisle

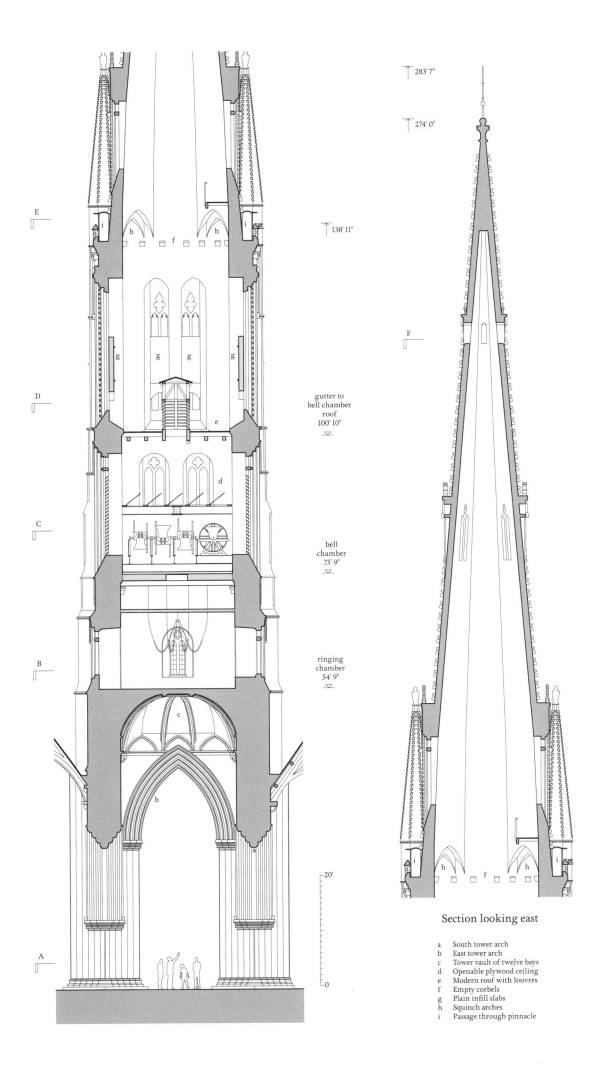

E

D

C

B

A

138' 11"

gutter to
bell chamber
roof
100' 10"

bell
chamber
75' 9"

ringing
chamber
54' 9"

20'

0

283' 7"

274' 0"

F

Section looking east

a   South tower arch
b   East tower arch
c   Tower vault of twelve bays
d   Openable plywood ceiling
e   Modern roof with louvres
f   Empty corbels
g   Plain infill slabs
h   Squinch arches
i   Passage through pinnacle

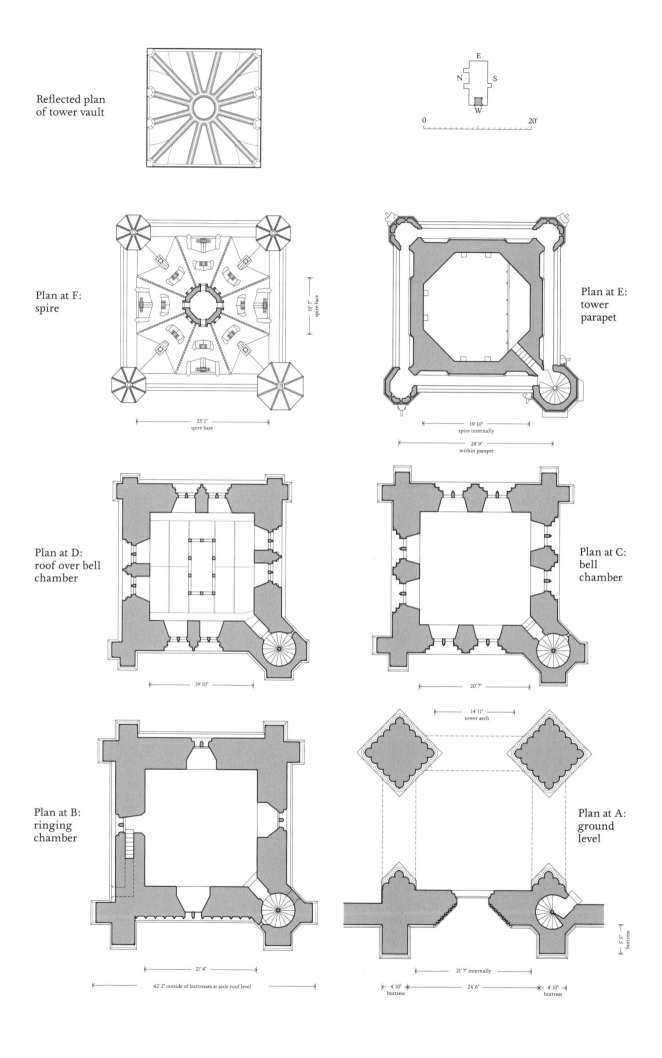

Reflected plan
of tower vault

Plan at F:
spire

10' 5"
spire face

25' 1"
spire base

Plan at E:
tower
parapet

19' 10"
spire internally

28' 9"
within parapet

Plan at D:
roof over bell
chamber

19' 10"

Plan at C:
bell
chamber

20' 7"

Plan at B:
ringing
chamber

21' 4"

42' 2" outside of buttresses at aisle roof level

14' 11"
tower arch

Plan at A:
ground
level

5' 5"
buttress

21' 7" internally

4' 10"
buttress

24' 6"

4' 10"
buttress

E

N   S

W

0   20'

exceptions, tower walls were more or less vertical for their entire height. The stepped wall profile was essential for the efficiency and stability of the exceptionally tall tower at GRANTHAM. Surprisingly, this important technical innovation was entirely overlooked by the early fourteenth-century masons who continued to pursue the sculptural possibilities of inefficient thick-walled structures.

On the third stage pairs of tall lights, framed by keeled shafts, rise from an expansive field of regular quatrefoils. These openings conceal the bell chamber, with its modern cast-iron and steel bell frame. Enclosing this chamber is a lid formed of electronically controlled plywood flaps that can modify the volume of the bells to suit the ringers below (d). The bells are kept dry by a modern flat roof with a central louvre, constructed over old floor beams (e).

In the normal course of events this stage would mark the termination of the tower, but the masons at GRANTHAM added one further, exceptionally tall stage entirely for show. It is primarily to this additional stage that the steeple owes its fine proportions. Although it is occasionally referred to in guidebooks as the belfry, there is no evidence that bells were ever hung at this level. The original spire floor is missing, leaving only empty corbels (f) and an awe-inspiring void that soars 150 feet into the tapering darkness beneath the apex of the spire.

The ballflower-encrusted paired openings of this fourth stage are tight and slender. The central mullion splits three ways in the head,

and the main arch is contained by the outline of a crocketed gable, a device that reappears directly at NEWARK. Additional framing of the arch is provided by blind trefoiled niches carrying crocketed gables, all rather dainty but unnecessary. Ineffectual loopholes shelter beneath the straight parapet coping.

Two criticisms can reasonably be levelled at the final stage. First, the window openings are crudely stiffened by massive slabs of plain masonry (g) that could easily be concealed behind louvres. Second, and more significantly, the openings are shallow and lack modelling as a direct consequence of the use of a thin-walled upper tower.

This fine work is marred by one unfortunate decision made in the initial setting-out and never rectified: the south-west staircase is far too prominent and throws the south and west elevations completely off-balance. The stair itself is exceedingly wide and thick-walled, and ignores convention by turning anticlockwise as it rises. No attempt is made to restrain this mighty shaft as it soars relentlessly upwards, and what starts as a minor irritation at the base becomes a major defect by the time the parapet is reached. The south-west corner is the worst possible position for such an error of judgment, for deep shadows are cast across the principal west façade in the early afternoon. It is no coincidence that the steeple is at its best when viewed from the north-east, with the protruding stair tower obscured.

The angle buttresses are shallow on plan and conservative in detail. Above the first string course the corners are softened by engaged shafts in the manner of ST MARY, STAMFORD half a century before. There is a wearisome lack of logic in the twelve buttress set-offs, but the octagonal pinnacles are a considerable improvement. Little widowed turrets, spanning the angle between the buttresses, carry tall spirelets, with twenty-nine miniature crockets running up each edge. Four ancient and indistinct statues adorning the pinnacles are believed to represent Saints Wulfram, Hugh of Lincoln, Thomas of Canterbury and Symphorian.[6]

The spire is unique and exceedingly beautiful. GRANTHAM was considerably higher than any stone spire previously attempted in England, either recessed or broached. The proportions were as slender as the masons dared to go, and it remained the tallest masonry structure in the country until it was overtaken by the colossal spire of Salisbury Cathedral. It remains the third-highest steeple built for a medieval parish church after LOUTH and ST MICHAEL, COVENTRY.[7]

The silhouette is busy but never excessively so, for the continuous crocketing and tall lucarnes are perfectly judged. This is the first time that crockets were used to decorate the edges of a spire and, rather surprisingly, they would not be widely adopted for a further half a century. By later standards the form is experimental, for each stone is carved into an unequal pair of crockets that, when joined together, form one continuous rippling edge.

The three tiers of lucarnes are exceptional, for they decorate all eight faces of the spire. These continuous rings of spire lights are a delightful conceit but they are not quite as they appear, for four lights in each tier are open and four are blind. A similar treatment was tried on the contemporary western spires at Lichfield Cathedral, with rather less success, and then in the fifteenth century in a handful of spires in central England.[8] On the diagonal faces of the lowest tier there is insufficient room for full lucarnes, so exceedingly narrow gabled niches, housing stone figures, adorn the top of the broaches. Open lucarnes on the lowest two tiers are identified by ballflower decoration, and gable crosses appear at every opportunity. As with all early recessed spires, the squinch arches are set high, making prominent broaches a constructional necessity (h).

The beauty of the spire is marred only by the confusion around its base. This is the fault of the pinnacles rather than the spire, for they are so large that they block the parapet path. The rather makeshift solution is to cut a passageway through the base of each pinnacle (i) and to prop the unsupported corner back to the spire with a solid wedge of masonry. This clumsy solution appeared again at Oakham and at HECKINGTON, but was then avoided by either reducing the size of the pinnacles or setting them further away from the spire.

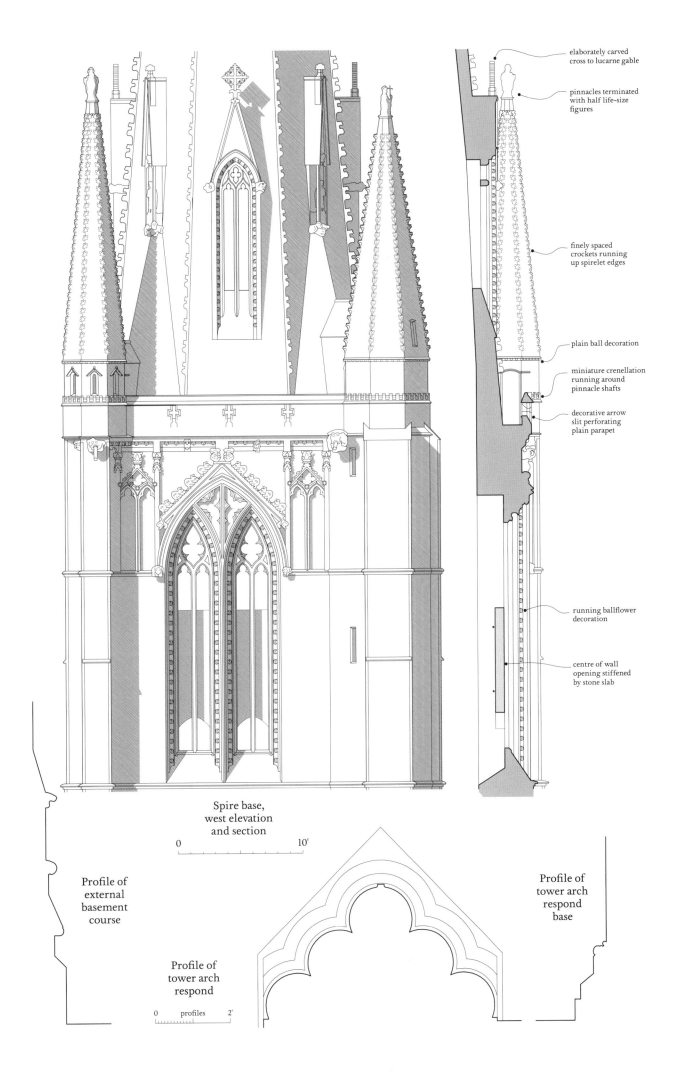

elaborately carved
cross to lucarne gable

pinnacles terminated
with half life-size
figures

finely spaced
crockets running
up spirelet edges

plain ball decoration

miniature crenellation
running around
pinnacle shafts

decorative arrow
slit perforating
plain parapet

running ballflower
decoration

centre of wall
opening stiffened
by stone slab

Spire base,
west elevation
and section

0   10'

Profile of
external
basement
course

Profile of
tower arch
respond base

Profile of
tower arch
respond

0   profiles   2'

GRANTHAM has suffered badly from storm damage. In 1628 the churchwardens reported 'the steeple ... being in notorious decay and like to fall into utter ruin without speedy reparation'.[9] When the top of the spire shattered during a lightning storm in 1652 repairs were delayed by the Civil War, and the bell frame was damaged by rain cascading through the apex. Matters were little better in 1797, when a large millstone was used to cap the top of the spire following another lightning strike. George Gilbert Scott was preoccupied with re-roofing, stripping out box pews and scraping medieval plaster from the walls during his restoration of 1866–68. The spire was restored to its original glory only in 1884, when his son, John Oldrid Scott, reinstated its original height. The most noticeable twentieth-century addition is the unworthy glass lobby inside the west door. In 2014–15 the final forty feet of the spire was rebuilt at a cost of over £600,000 under the supervision of the church's architect, Graham Cook.

St Wulfram's was to dominate steeple design in the two centuries following its completion. The achievements, and also the mistakes, made at GRANTHAM in the early years of the fourteenth century formed a constant point of reference for masons throughout the late Middle Ages, and nowhere is its influence more strongly felt than at the final great masterwork of LOUTH.

NOTES

1   Sir Nikolaus Pevsner and John Harris, *The Buildings of England: Lincolnshire* (1964).

2   Sir George Gilbert Scott, 'The Architectural History of St Wolfran's Church, Grantham', *Reports and Papers of the Architectural and Archaeological Societies of the counties of Lincoln and Northampton*, vol. 13 (1875). Scott was far from being an impartial critic, for he enjoyed a lucrative career re-creating the 'Middle Pointed' style of GRANTHAM.

3   Francis Bond, *Gothic Architecture in England* (1905), pp. 596, 623.

4   Edmund Sharpe, *A Treatise on the Rise and Progress of Decorated Window Tracery of England* (1849), p. 63, refers to cast-iron cusps installed 'during a recent restoration'. Francis Bond, *An Introduction to English Church Architecture* (1913), states that cast-iron cusps had been removed but not yet replaced in stone.

5   Bond, *English Church Architecture*, vol. 2 (1913), p. 584, note by A. Hamilton Thompson.

6   Ven. Edward Trollope, 'Notes on the Churches visited by the Society, June 19th and 20th 1867', *Reports and Papers of the Architectural and Archaeological Societies of the counties of Lincoln and Northampton*, vol. 9 (1867), p. 9.

7   ST MICHAEL, COVENTRY was elevated to cathedral status only in 1918.

8   The spires are at Coleshill (Warks), Witherley (Leics), and Kings Norton and Yardley (Worcs).

9   Michael Pointer, *The Glory of Grantham* (1978), unattributed quotation.

13

Newark-on-Trent

NOTTINGHAMSHIRE

For generations of travellers, the glorious spire at NEWARK marked the gateway between the north and the south of England. In the Middle Ages the Trent, running from the Humber Estuary to the foothills of the Pennines, formed a major barrier across the east of England. NEWARK was founded in the tenth century as the 'new work', guarding a vital ford over the Trent immediately west of the Fosse Way. Following the construction of a permanent stone bridge and the diversion of the Great North Road through the town, NEWARK become one of the twenty largest settlements in England. Until the Reformation it was a possession of the bishops of Lincoln, who gifted the church to the Gilbertine Priory of St Katherine in Lincoln. This close association with Lincoln proved critical to the development of the splendid church of St Mary Magdalene, for it has little in common with the pedestrian work of the Nottinghamshire masons west of the Trent. Like most of the great steeples of the period, NEWARK is the result of two quite distinct phases of construction. Unusually, the break occurs not at the base of the spire but at the base of the bell stage.

The original Saxon church at NEWARK was rebuilt around 1190, but all that remains of the second church is the crypt and four piers of a central crossing. George Gilbert Scott, architect of the nineteenth-century restoration, considered that these piers were too small to have supported a central tower.[1] Between around 1230 and 1245 a four-stage tower was constructed to the west of the

church, and this remains substantially intact except for internal alterations and the insertion of a later west window. The original design was remarkably close to RAUNDS: despite the fact that NEWARK is eight feet taller, the sturdy proportions of the two towers are almost identical.

Even by the standards of the early thirteenth century the west door is impressively framed, with four detached shafts, 4½ inches in diameter, alternating with filleted engaged shafts. Fine dogtooth ornament races along the circular ring capitals, across the deep door arch, below the intrados and around the hood-mould. Compared with RAUNDS, the arch is awkwardly framed, the two adjacent niches being uncomfortably close, so that their shafts disappear behind the central hood-mould. The high basement course is an awkward sequence of steep chamfers. Setback buttresses project from square clasping masses encasing each corner – a complex arrangement resulting in seven external angles, each finished with a slender filleted shaft. On the cardinal faces these shafts carry lancet arches framing narrow dogtooth-ornamented niches. Intriguingly, these shafts and niches continue around the north and south sides of the buttresses, and reappear internally within the church. To understand why this might be, it is necessary to consider the development of the ground-level plan.

The tower at NEWARK stands on one solid wall and three arches, but originally it was intended to stand on three solid walls and

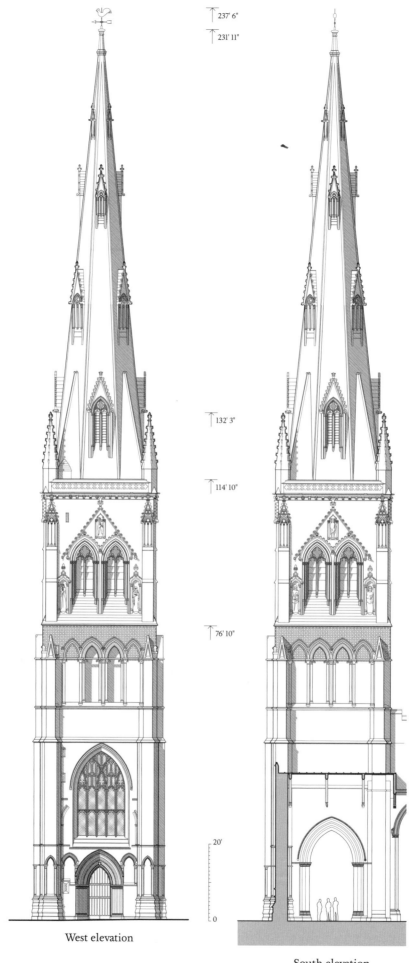

237' 6"

231' 11"

132' 3"

114' 10"

76' 10"

20'

0

West elevation

South elevation
with section through south aisle

one arch. When construction started, the design was for a conventional west tower projecting from the west end of the church (see Plan at A: ground level, original design). Early in the construction, possibly in the second or third year, when the walls had risen no more than twelve feet from the ground, the masons had a sudden change of plan. At TICKHILL, thirty miles to the north, a revolutionary new design was under way in which the aisles embraced the side faces of the tower. This had allowed north and south arches to be introduced, opening vistas across the church and offering greater scope for ritual processions within the church. The masons of NEWARK were impressed. They cut wide openings through previously finished masonry and bonded in new responds to allow the construction of additional tower arches to north and south.

The tower arch responds are a robust cluster of five shafts with dogtooth running around the capitals. The openings vary in size, the northern arch being constrained by the north-west corner staircase and the responds of the primary eastern arch rising to twice the height of its neighbours (a). Plain chamfered tower arches, of three recessed orders, are framed by dogtooth hood-moulds. All of this is in fine condition. Weathering courses, still visible within the church (b), indicate where the aisle roofs were originally intended to hit the tower, but there is no evidence that they were ever used. The aisles that exist today are much later in date and follow very different profiles. Externally, the gabled termination of the south aisle, with six fine bays of flowing tracery, is sympathetic to the steeple, but the shallow castellated parapet to the north fatally unbalances the composition of the west front.

The original second and third stages are indicated by broken string courses either side of the west window. These segments suggest a second-stage arcade of four bays of lancet arches carrying dogtooth ornament, but the design of the third storey is lost. The Perpendicular west window, framed by a wide casement, was inserted over a century later. Inverted daggers alternate with supermullions in five cinquefoiled bays of subarcuated intersecting tracery with a mid-height transom. This architectural vocabulary may be alien to the original design, but the improved illumination would have been very beneficial to the interior, at least before the arrival of gloomy Victorian glass.

The tower was originally intended to be vaulted, for internally, above the north and south tower arches, are scars in the masonry left by two broad arches springing from empty corbels. Above the apex of these arches a horizontal line in the masonry probably marks the level of the original ringing chamber floor (c). Vault and floor were later removed to make way for the west window, at which time a new ringing chamber floor was inserted at a higher level, supported by decorated corbels (d).

The top stage of the original tower can be confidently dated to the 1240s, for the diagonal trelliswork derives directly from the rebuilding of the crossing tower at Lincoln Cathedral after 1237. Indeed, the stylistic evidence is strong enough to suggest that this may be the work of the same master mason, Alexander of Lincoln. It starts with a deep string course drawing in all the faces of the tower and improving the proportions of the buttresses. The stage is divided into three horizontal bands following the ratio of 2:3:2. The upper band is uniformly decorated with trelliswork, while the lowest band forms a blank plinth to a beautifully proportioned four-bay arcade. Single shafts with foliate capitals are doubled around centre bays that were originally left open to the bell chamber. A chamfered step in the tower wall neatly coinciding with the base of the arcade openings (e) indicates the probable level of the original bell chamber floor. The square tower plan is far from symmetrical, for the eastern buttresses are either omitted or set far away from the corners.

For sixty years or so the tower at NEWARK remained in this unexceptional form. In the normal course of events a fine stone broach spire would have been added, as it was at RAUNDS, KETTON and many other towers. However, NEWARK in the early fourteenth century must have been exceedingly wealthy, for what happened next was quite extraordinary. The rebuilding of the south aisle to the nave from 1313 marked the start of a wholesale reconstruction that would transform NEWARK into one of the finest parish churches in England.

Work on the steeple followed immediately after the south aisle and was probably completed before the arrival of the Black Death in 1348. In a design of astonishing imagination, the masons at NEWARK proposed to triple the height of the original steeple. The beautiful trelliswork arcade provided a perfect square plinth for a sumptuous new bell stage carrying an exceptionally tall recessed spire of unparalleled grace. The arcade openings to the redundant bell chamber were blocked to strengthen the tower (f). On the inconspicuous east elevation small Curvilinear windows were introduced to illuminate the new ringing chamber, and the heads of the north and south arches were glazed for the same purpose (g).

The start of the new bell stage is inspired. Paired windows are set high and deep, with steeply inclined cills extending thirteen courses from the drip.[2] On each face the plane of the cill extends to the corners of the tower so that, seen in perspective, the elevation appears to rise from a substantial square-based pyramid. This tremendous design has, unfortunately, been compromised by four skeleton clock faces cut into the drip, but this woeful insensitivity has been corrected on the drawings.

Flat angle buttresses, carrying crocketed gables and finials, rise the full height of the new bell stage. Plain sloping drips divide the buttresses into thirds, the upper third containing two bays of blind tracery beneath an ogee head and canopy. Paired twin-light

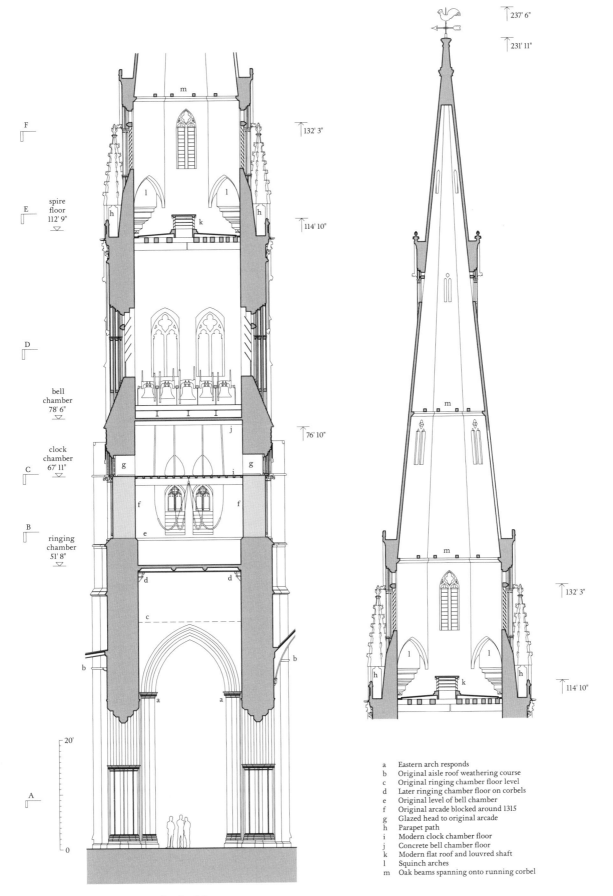

F

E spire
   floor
   112' 9"

D

bell
chamber
78' 6"

clock
chamber
67' 11"
C

B

ringing
chamber
51' 8"

A

20'

0

132' 3"

114' 10"

76' 10"

m

l   l

h   h

k

j

g   i   g

f   f

e

d   d

c

b   b

b

a   a

237' 6"

231' 11"

m

l   l

h   h

k

132' 3"

114' 10"

Section looking east

a   Eastern arch responds
b   Original aisle roof weathering course
c   Original ringing chamber floor level
d   Later ringing chamber floor on corbels
e   Original level of bell chamber
f   Original arcade blocked around 1315
g   Glazed head to original arcade
h   Parapet path
i   Modern clock chamber floor
j   Concrete bell chamber floor
k   Modern flat roof and louvred shaft
l   Squinch arches
m   Oak beams spanning onto running corbel

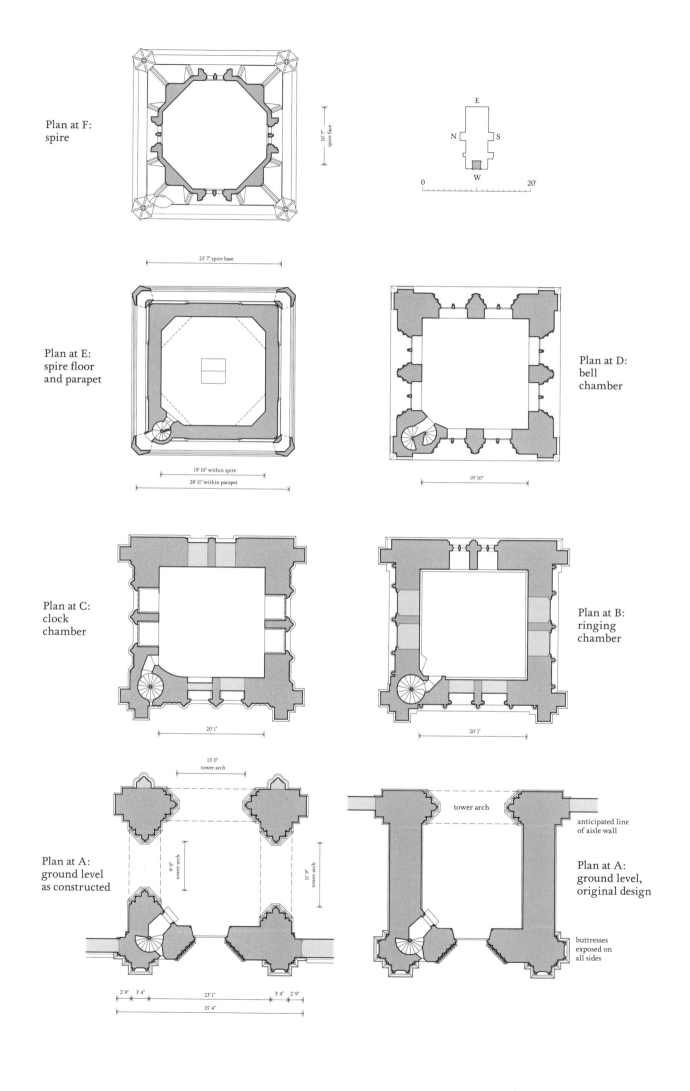

Plan at F: spire

10' 7" spire face

E

N   S

W

0   20'

25' 7" spire base

Plan at E: spire floor and parapet

Plan at D: bell chamber

19' 10" within spire

28' 11" within parapet

19' 10"

Plan at C: clock chamber

Plan at B: ringing chamber

20' 1"

20' 1"

13' 0" tower arch

tower arch

anticipated line of aisle wall

Plan at A: ground level as constructed

9' 0" tower arch

11' 9" tower arch

Plan at A: ground level, original design

buttresses exposed on all sides

2' 9" 3' 4"   23' 1"   3' 4" 2' 9"

35' 4"

openings are sumptuously decorated by filleted shafts carrying compact natural-leaf capitals. Openings employ the most popular Curvilinear tracery motif of the period, of two lights carrying trefoil ogee archlets beneath a broad soufflet.

A sprinkling of ballflower on the crocketed hood-moulds reappears along the wide triangular hood-mould that embraces the paired openings. The composition is completed by ogee-headed niches framed by engaged shafts. The statues populating the niches are part Victorian and part original. Everything is well considered and nothing feels cramped, with the exception of the north-west stair shaft that subtly intrudes into the openings of the principal elevation. The finest carving is reserved for the sixty corbel heads that carry the shallow cornice. A plain parapet is decorated by sixteen bays of quatrefoil carved in situ across stones of varying widths.

In the early fourteenth century there was a brief vogue for hexagonal pinnacles. The form appeared at BRANT BROUGHTON, HECKINGTON, Welbourn and Caythorpe in Lincolnshire before being decisively dropped in favour of the octagon. The principal disadvantage is well illustrated at NEWARK, for if one face of the hexagon is set diagonally on the corner of the tower the parapets hit the adjacent faces at a soft glancing angle. By contrast, octagonal pinnacles provide a more emphatic termination to the parapet. The parapet path tunnels neatly through the centre of the plain pinnacle shafts (h),

avoiding the complexity that had marred GRANTHAM but still leaving awkward voids in the silhouette when viewed from certain angles. The heads of the pinnacles, their crockets and their finials are modestly in scale with the adjacent lucarne gables. Writing in 1817, the architect Thomas Rickman described the pinnacles as finishing with statues, but either he was mistaken or they have been subsequently replaced.[3]

Alterations to the tower since medieval times have been modest. In 1842 NEWARK received the first peal of ten ever installed by John Taylor & Co. of Loughborough, now the world's largest bell-founder. George Gilbert Scott restored the steeple in 1869 and was probably responsible for removing a gallery below the tower, the position of which is indicated by a blocked staircase doorway visible adjacent to the west window. The clock chamber floor (i) may be from this date or from 1898, when a new clock mechanism was installed. A beamed concrete slab replaced the bell chamber floor (j), possibly in 1954 when the bells were rehung on a cast-iron and steel frame. Finally, during the late twentieth century the original structure at the base of the spire was covered by a flat roof with a central ventilation shaft to keep the bells dry (k).

The spire at NEWARK is hard to fault. It was built at the most fortuitous time of transition, for no other spire in England combines the restlessly romantic profile of the broach spire and the slender proportions of the recessed spire with such panache.

After NEWARK, spires became more efficient and broaches were lowered or omitted altogether. The most graceful broach spires, such as KETTON, were never less than fourteen degrees wide at the apex, but the recessed spire at NEWARK was able to reach an even more satisfying angle of twelve degrees. The proportions of spire to tower are perfect, for the tower parapet is set precisely at the midpoint of the composition.

The spire has exceptionally tall broaches and carries four tiers of slender, alternating Curvilinear lucarnes beneath crocketed gables. Sophisticated recessed roll edges, similar to those of ST MARY, STAMFORD, emphasize the verticality of the spire without disrupting its profile. Within the spire the squinches are set very high (l), and two running corbels carry oak beams left from the original construction (m). The tall broaches are finished with carved finials, now rather indistinct, at more or less the same level as the lucarne gables.

The spacing and the scale of the lucarnes are perfectly judged. The lower three tiers of lucarnes employ twin-light tracery following the pattern established by the bell stage windows, but with increasing vertical emphasis. Gables are decorated with rich, bulbous crockets and emaciated finials on the lower tier, and relaxed crockets and luxuriant finials above, suggesting a change of mason. The weathervane, which was lying in the crypt at the time of the author's original survey, was regilded and reinstalled in 2014 following a £100,000 restoration of the spire.

The final height of the spire, at 231' 11" to the top of the masonry, is unusual, for apart from the three giants of GRANTHAM, BOSTON and LOUTH few parish steeples in the east of England rise above 180 feet. This is an eminently satisfying height for, while the Ancaster stone steeple dominates the fine marketplace and all of the approaches to the town, it never appears overbearing. Thomas Rickman singled out the steeple of NEWARK for praise. In his view 'there are no specimens superior in composition and execution, and few equal.'[4] The wonderfully romantic, tapering silhouette of NEWARK has never been bettered.

NOTES

1   George Gilbert Scott, 'Newark Church: its Architectural History', *Reports and Papers of the Architectural and Archaeological Societies of the counties of Lincoln and Northampton* (1856).

2   The final stage of Lincoln Cathedral tower (1307–11) by Richard of Stow has a similar twelve-course cill and other similarities of detail, although not enough to provide a conclusive link between the designs.

3   Thomas Rickman, *An Attempt to Discriminate the Styles of Architecture in England*, 5th edn (1848), p. 176.

4   Ibid., p. 177.

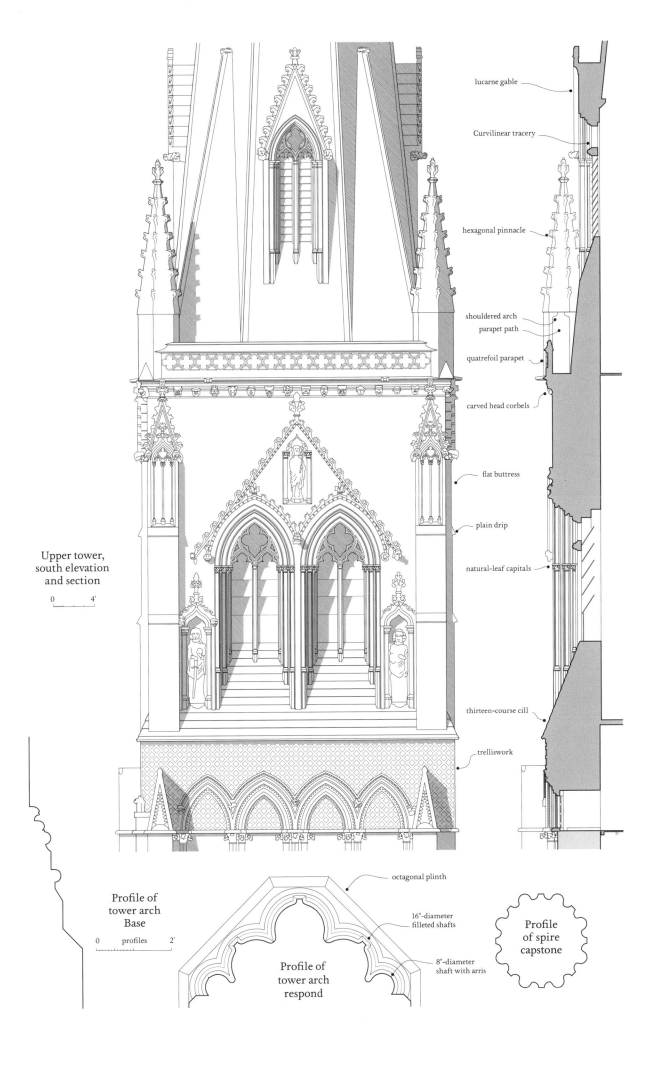

lucarne gable

Curvilinear tracery

hexagonal pinnacle

shouldered arch

parapet path

quatrefoil parapet

carved head corbels

flat buttress

plain drip

natural-leaf capitals

thirteen-course cill

trelliswork

Upper tower,
south elevation
and section

0   4'

Profile of
tower arch
Base

0   profiles   2'

octagonal plinth

16"-diameter
filleted shafts

8"-diameter
shaft with arris

Profile of
tower arch
respond

Profile
of spire
capstone

14

Ketton

KETTON is famous for its fine, creamy oolithic limestone, used locally at Burghley House and Stamford, and exported in great quantity to the Cambridge colleges, Suffolk and Essex. The vast quarries that dominate the northern edge of the village now concentrate on the manufacture of cement from crushed Ketton lime, but choice building stone is still supplied to prestigious projects across the country. Surprisingly, the beautiful parish church of St Mary the Virgin is constructed entirely of Barnack stone, for Ketton's quarries developed only during the fifteenth century, as the great quarry at Barnack, six miles down the River Welland, became exhausted.

A cruciform church was completed at KETTON during the transition from Norman Romanesque to early Gothic, around the year 1190. A superb remnant of this period is the west doorway, its semicircular arch surrounded by pointed niches, zigzag and dogtooth enrichment, and shafts with rings and waterleaf capitals. The two lower stages of the crossing tower are from the same date. Little remains of the first stage, but a skewed bridge over the end of the south aisle is supported by broken zigzag segments from the original Norman tower arch (a).

In 1232 Hugh de Wells, Bishop of Lincoln, granted a release of twenty days' penance to anyone who contributing to the building of St Mary's Church, its condition at the time being described as 'ruinous'.[1] Seven years later, on 7 October 1240, the church was rededicated by his successor, Bishop

Grosseteste. These dates are consistent with the stylistic evidence of a major rebuilding of the nave arcades and the tower around the middle of the thirteenth century.

Nave arcades are broad and high, with double-chamfered arches. Cylindrical piers, rising from water-holding bases, carry circular moulded capitals decorated with nailhead, a popular ornament in the first half of the thirteenth century.[2] Responds are formed against the tower wall with semicircular shafts between quadrants, a pattern followed, with the addition of a central keeled roll, in the tower arches themselves. Extending almost to the full width of the tower, these arches must have been a considerable improvement on the previous late Norman design.

On the second stage shallow setback buttresses, rising from a chamfered string course, frame the corners of the tower, and vertical edges are softened with circular shafts. Gabled roofs originally abutted the tower on every side, for their weathering courses are clearly visible. This weathering is now trapped below the fifteenth-century western clerestory roof (b), and its apex frames the original round-headed doorway to the ringing chamber (c). Another weathering shows the line of a second nave roof predating the clerestory (d). T. G. Jackson's chancel roof of 1863 is only slightly higher than the original weathering course.

So far the work had been good but unexceptional. The bell stage that follows transformed KETTON into the most beautiful tower of its age, for the proportions are exquisite and the geometry is impeccably resolved. This is one of three closely related bell stages in which the early Gothic obsession with the shafted arcade was taken to its ultimate conclusion. ST MARY, STAMFORD, Melton Mowbray (Leics) and KETTON are almost certainly the work of a single lodge of masons. Melton Mowbray and STAMFORD are both broad towers compromised by over-prominent staircases, that at Melton being an unfortunate late medieval addition. By contrast the tower at KETTON has always relied on ladder access, a happy circumstance that allowed the design of the bell stage to be lean, upright and fully symmetrical, with no flabby corners hindering the upward thrust.

The bell stage forms a pure cube divided into three horizontal bands by string courses continuing the profile of the shaft rings and the capital abacus around the corners of the tower. It is encircled by no fewer than eighty-eight shafts separated by lashings of dogtooth. Each elevation is identical, with three lancet-like openings carrying early 'Y' tracery on a free-standing central shaft. Openings are separated by clusters of three detached and two engaged shafts, the central shaft extending up to support the corbel table.

Three varieties of capital are inconsistently arranged. The illustrated south elevation is a typical mix of circular nailhead to the central piers, foliate stiff-leaf capitals to either side and ring capitals to the free-standing shafts. The tower corners are much

tighter than at Melton Mowbray and STAMFORD, and this greatly assists the compact verticality of the composition. Angle shafts continue the lines of the second stage. The delightful corbel table is supported by tiny dogtooth arches bouncing between carved heads that burst with individuality.

The effect of the corbel table is slightly disrupted by the uppermost of three iron bands that, together with tie-rods passing through the structure (h), hold the tower together. This reinforcement was added after the main 1860 restoration, for in 1897 the Bishop of Nottingham found that 'unfortunately the strength of the tower seems to have somewhat collapsed'.[3] This explains why the lowest set of tie-rods is left visible below the soffit of the Victorian ringing chamber floor. One unusual and very effective feature at KETTON is the absence of louvres to the bell chamber. This allows the eye to run straight through the tower to the sky beyond, making the whole structure appear delicate and fragile.

The perennial problem with a central tower over a parish church was arranging a safe means of access, and the route at KETTON, devised in Victorian times, is ingenious. A spiral staircase, squeezed into the corner of the south aisle by George Gilbert Scott (f), leads over the fragments of Norman arch (a), through the wall of the nave and up a precariously cantilevered stair to the ringing chamber door (c). Such awkward arrangements were one of the reasons why central crossing towers fell out of favour in the parish church.

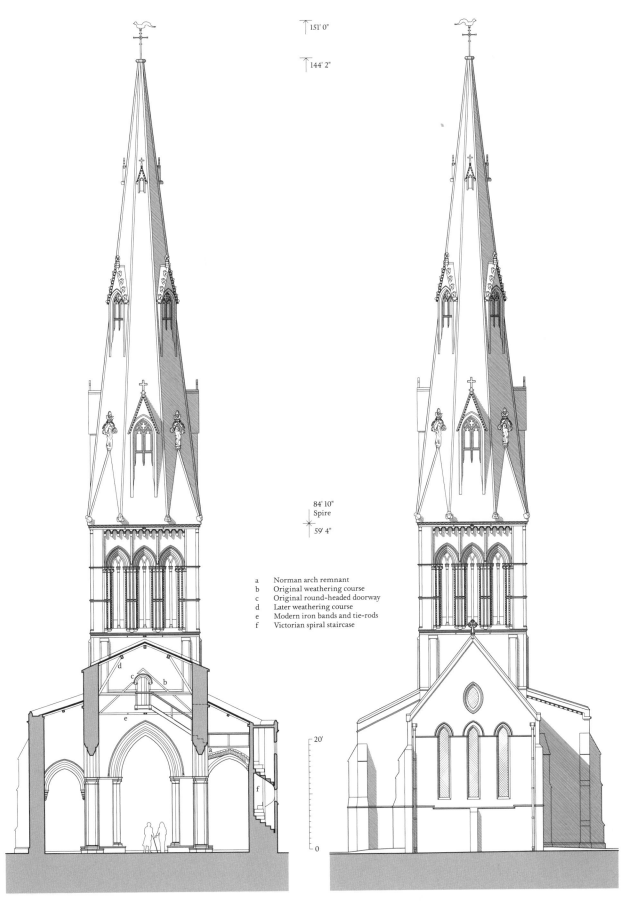

151' 0"

144' 2"

84' 10"
Spire
59' 4"

a   Norman arch remnant
b   Original weathering course
c   Original round-headed doorway
d   Later weathering course
e   Modern iron bands and tie-rods
f   Victorian spiral staircase

d
c
b
e
a
f

20'

0

Elevation and section looking east

East elevation

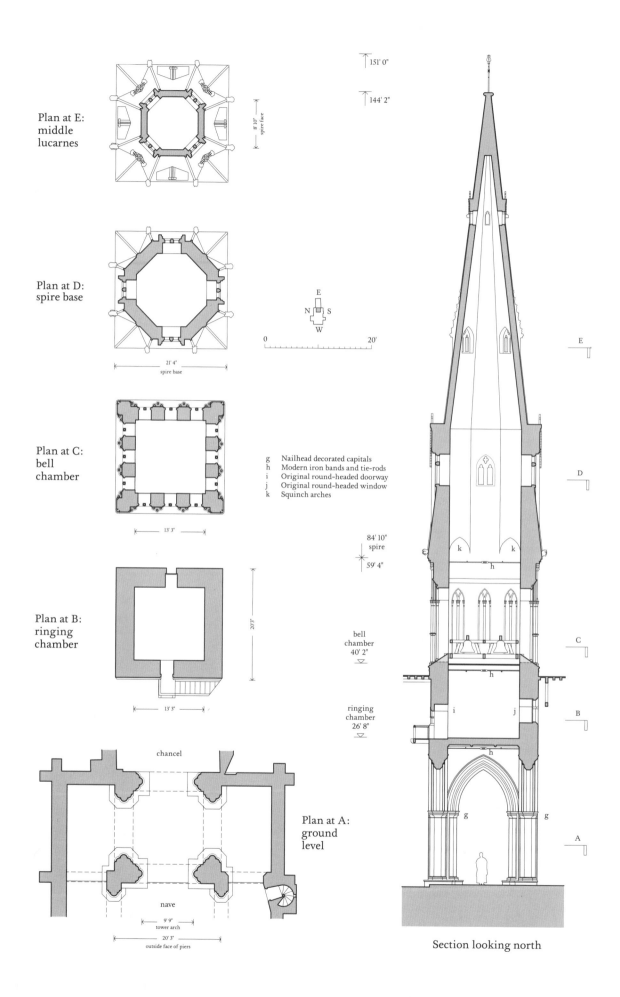

Plan at E:
middle
lucarnes

Plan at D:
spire base

Plan at C:
bell
chamber

Plan at B:
ringing
chamber

Plan at A:
ground
level

151' 0"

144' 2"

E

D

8' 10"
spire face

21' 4"
spire base

g   Nailhead decorated capitals
h   Modern iron bands and tie-rods
i   Original round-headed doorway
j   Original round-headed window
k   Squinch arches

84' 10"
spire

59' 4"

bell
chamber
40' 2"

ringing
chamber
26' 8"

13' 3"

20'3"

13' 3"

chancel

nave

9' 9"
tower arch

20'3"
outside face of piers

E
N   S
W

0   20'

C

B

A

k   k

h

i   j

h

g   g

Section looking north

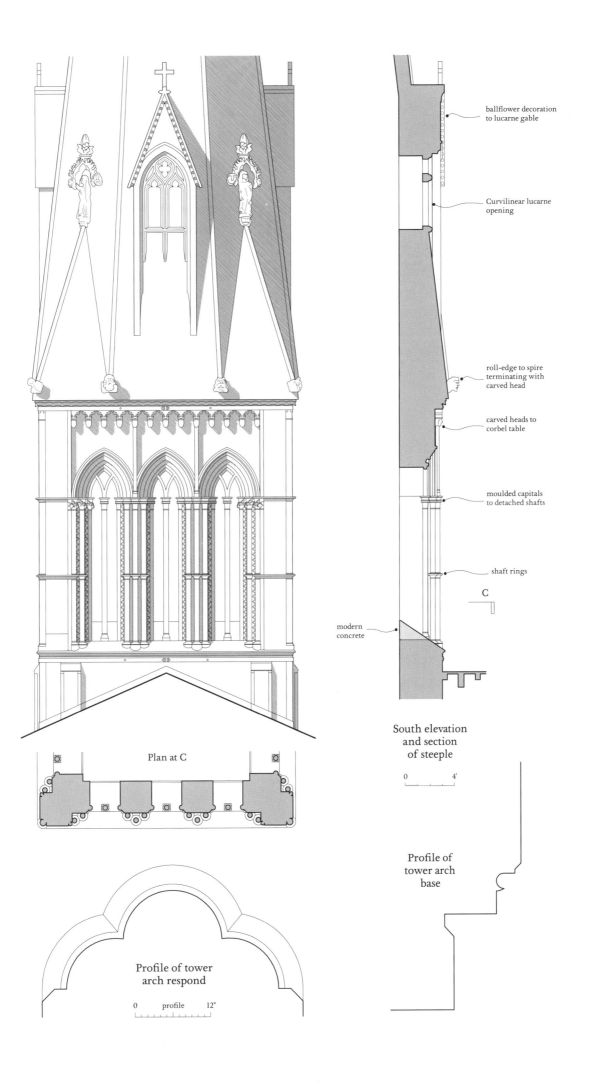

ballflower decoration
to lucarne gable

Curvilinear lucarne
opening

roll-edge to spire
terminating with
carved head

carved heads to
corbel table

moulded capitals
to detached shafts

shaft rings

C

modern
concrete

Plan at C

South elevation
and section
of steeple

0   4'

Profile of
tower arch
base

Profile of tower
arch respond

0   profile   12"

The spires at KETTON and at ST MARY, STAMFORD represent the ultimate development of the ornate English broach spire in the early fourteenth century. STAMFORD is weighty and luxuriant; KETTON is slender and refined. Both are exquisitely beautifully, and both were almost certainly conceived in the mind of one exceptionally gifted mason. The spire at KETTON is tall and follows the excellent proportions of RAUNDS in the previous century. The silhouette is restless yet assured. Ballflower-encrusted lucarnes are of three alternating tiers, and the broaches are modest in height. Roll edges to the spire and to the broaches visually extend the shafted edges of the tower through to the summit of the composition, dramatically accentuating the verticality.

The large first and second tiers of lucarnes display the fashionable twin-light tracery of the day, Curvilinear with a soufflet in the head. The lowest tier carries plain gables and crosses to avoid competition with the statues perched confidently on the tops of the broaches. These figures, set beneath bulbous ogee canopies, represent the Virgin Mary (south-east), the Angel Gabriel (south-west), St Peter (north-east) and St Paul (north-west). Any inhibitions are lost in the second tier of lucarnes, which is ripe with richly carved heads, finials and crockets. The diminutive third tier still finds room for heads, ballflower and a cross, while the flat octagonal finial brings the spire to a somewhat abrupt conclusion.

Like much ornate work from the early fourteenth century, the spire has fallen in and out of favour. Gothic Revivalists were enchanted by its luxurious ornamentation, and KETTON became a place of pilgrimage for architects and students. For straight-laced critics in the twentieth century it was seen as fussy and overblown, and even Alec Clifton-Taylor considered the prominent lucarnes to be mere 'excrescences' that damaged the spire's silhouette.[4] This is unjustified, for KETTON is a timeless, romantic work of art of the highest order, and it is one of the most exquisitely beautiful steeples of any period to be found in England.

NOTES

1   See William Page (ed.), *The Victoria History of the County of Rutland*, vol. 2 (1935).
2   Nailhead ornament originated in Norman work and was widely used to decorate early Gothic capitals but fell into disuse before the end of the thirteenth century. In *The Buildings of England: Leicestershire and Rutland* (1960) Pevsner proposes that the nailhead ornament at KETTON is *c.* 1300, but such a late date would be exceptional.
3   Right Revd Edward Trollope, 'Churches in the Neighbourhood of Stamford, visited May 28th, 1897', *Reports and Papers of the Architectural and Archaeological Societies of the counties of Lincoln and Northampton*, vol. 15 (1897).
4   Alec Clifton-Taylor, *English Parish Churches as Works of Art* (1986), p. 95.

15

St Mary, Stamford

LINCOLNSHIRE

There is no finer stone-built town in England than Stamford, which lies at the convergence of the four most accomplished spire-building counties of Lincolnshire, Rutland, Northamptonshire and Huntingdonshire.[1] The Great North Road brought prosperity, and the River Welland brought stone, from KETTON and Collyweston to the west and BARNACK to the east. Stamford was one of the 'Five Boroughs' during the Danish occupation, and was an early beneficiary of the medieval trade in wool and cloth. What can be seen today is, however, a shadow of the town in its medieval heyday, when there were no fewer than sixteen churches, two monasteries, four friaries and an embryonic university. Considerable destruction was wrought by the Lancastrian army in 1461, and the six churches that remain are surrounded by a predominantly seventeenth- and eighteenth-century townscape following the medieval street plan. ST MARY's spire is the most prominent and venerable architectural ornament of the town.

The situation is magnificent, for the western steeple rises, sentinel-like, to guard the Great North Road as it bridges the Welland and rises steeply into the town. Sir Walter Scott may not have been alone in taking off his hat as his coach passed the church on his way northwards.[2] Such prominence has almost been the undoing of the tower, for the constant traffic at its foot has wrought havoc with the structure. The gradient of St Mary's Hill is passable only

because the ground around the south-west corner of the tower has been dug away, leaving the foundations cruelly exposed. Deep scratches across the base record the passage of lorry drivers who have failed to negotiate the sharp bend at the summit of the hill. Over the centuries the tower has been strapped, tied, stiffened and braced by succeeding generations of masons and architects, but heavy goods vehicles continue to shake its crumbling joints apart.

The elements of the steeple are clearly recognizable from elsewhere. The lower part of the tower is obsessively arcaded like RAUNDS and NEWARK in its earliest form. When the bell stage was reached, around 1240, the design became significantly more refined, in the manner of KETTON and Melton Mowbray (Leics). Finally, the highly sculptural spire, from early the following century, is a sister of KETTON and a cousin of NEWARK.

Four intensive courses of blind arcading, stacked one above the other, and divided by prominent string courses, give a great intensity to the lower part of the composition. Although by later standards the treatment may be naive and overly fussy, there is still plenty of variety to enjoy. On north and south elevations three tiers of pointed arches, each of five bays, are followed by a single tier of trefoiled arches in three bays. Arch profiles are deeply cut, with keeled rolls. Every shaft is detached, for this was the age when the mason took considerable pride in turning smooth stone cylinders on the lathe.

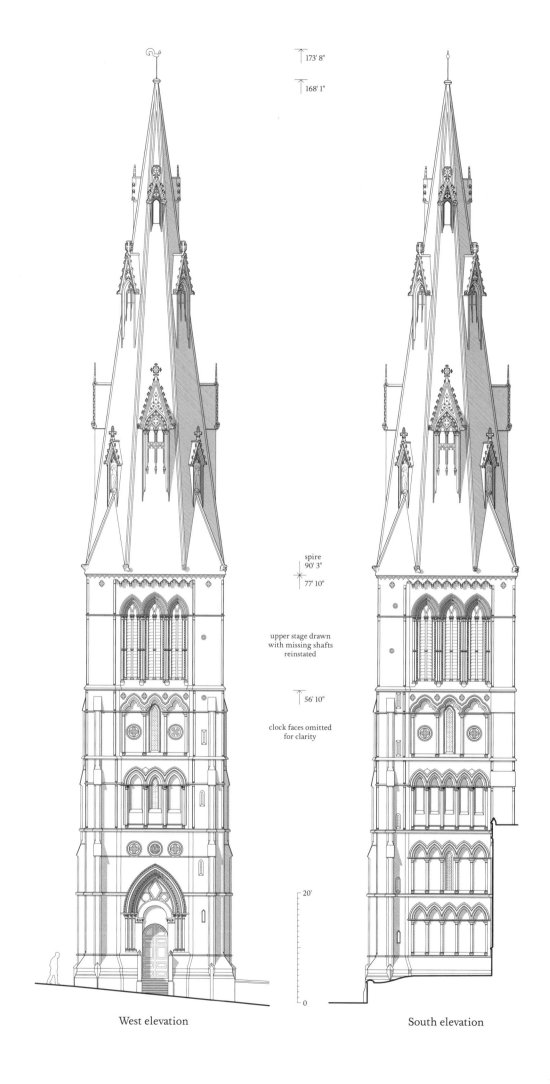

173' 8"

168' 1"

spire
90' 3"

77' 10"

upper stage drawn
with missing shafts
reinstated

56' 10"

clock faces omitted
for clarity

20'

0

West elevation

South elevation

Capitals are also turned, with splendidly wide profiles, except on the third tier of the south elevation, where inferior stiff-leaf makes an appearance. The horizontal line is given considerable emphasis by linking the abaci of the capitals across the blank wall surfaces. The fourth tier, which represents the ringing chamber, rises exuberantly clear of the nave roof, with blind quatrefoil perforations in both spandrels and the outer bays.

The composite buttresses are typical of early Gothic towers, combining clasping and setback types in a rather ambiguous manner. The setback element, with chamfered edges, appears only for show on the prominent western corners of the tower. Structurally these elements are inconsequential, and their visual impact is compromised by their termination before the final stage is reached. These immature and indecisive buttresses fail to counter the strong horizontality of the string courses, and the overwhelming impression is of a stack of independent units set one above the other.

The west elevation differs from north and south in the lower stages. The west door, originally the main entrance to the church, has been badly affected by the lowering of the adjacent street and by some awkward infilling below the arch. The original work here includes the pointed arch carrying two dogtooth bands, the three detached shafts each side, and the stiff-leaf capitals that continue as a dropped frieze on the rounded door jambs. What originally sat on these

jambs is unclear, for a round arch in a yellow stone carries an assortment of rubble and randomly arranged motifs that may be remnants from elsewhere in the church, while the round-headed arch and panelled door below are entirely alien. The original door arch cuts up into the second stage, which is enlivened by three circular openings: two carrying quatrefoils, and the centre one an interlaced knot pattern.

The third stage arcade is of three pointed bays with a small lancet window in the centre. This small western window, together with the lower lights on the side elevations, is the only source of natural light within the base of the tower. Illumination is further decreased by rubble infill, which reduced the original deep internal splays to straight-sided openings (a). This is one of several medieval alterations intended to strengthen the tower before the addition of the heavy masonry spire. All of the upper-level openings were severely reduced (b) or blocked, and the internal corners of the tower were strengthened with rubble infill to their full height (c). A quadripartite vault, with panelled ribs on the diagonal, was added to stiffen the walls above the ground floor (d). This strengthening work also explains the strange infill panels and round arches seen above the west door.

The gloomy interior is rarely visited, for the bells were disabled many years ago in order to safeguard the structure. A modern glazed oak screen separates the vestry within the base of the tower from the body of the church and in doing so considerably reduces the visual impact of the tower arch. The arch profile, of a filleted roll between two chamfers, and the responds of quadrants surrounding a semicircular shaft are all reminiscent of KETTON.

It is typical of the best early steeples to become more self-assured and more accomplished as construction progressed, and ST MARY's is no exception. The arcade of the bell stage is tall, confident and well modelled, with three receding orders of shaft and arch giving considerable depth to the elevation. The three bays of each arcade are supported by beautiful clusters of five shafts separated by vertical dogtooth. Medieval strengthening is visible here, for mean semicircular arches in a yellow stone sit awkwardly beneath the pointed openings.

Originally the similarity to the bell stages of Melton Mowbray and KETTON would have been even stronger, for the openings at ST MARY's were divided by shafts carrying 'Y' tracery. First-hand evidence for this missing tracery is provided by an empty shaft base on the east elevation and by regular gaps in the inner arches where the tracery originally hit. Corroboration is provided by drawings by J. B. F. Cowper from 1911, which note that 'on an old print in the vestry these shafts shown, only the bases now exist.'[3] These shafts have been reinstated on the drawing to striking effect. Dogtooth archlets to the corbel table follow the design of KETTON, but with plain notch heads rather than carving. Angle shafts rise up to prop

the corbel table, and small perforated quatrefoils and circular stair windows repeat the motifs of the previous stage.

Medieval strengthening works were followed in the nineteenth and twentieth centuries with further attempts to prevent the tower from crumbling. The notable architect Sir T. G. Jackson oversaw a major restoration in 1911–13. He concluded: 'There was bad building and scamping then as now ... The lovely Early English tower at S. Mary's at Stamford ... is put together with nothing but dirt scraped off the road containing very little lime, if any.'[4] Numerous metal plates spread around the corners of the building are external evidence of an intricate web of tie-rods inserted at this time to hold the building together. During the course of the restoration fragments of Norman work were discovered within the construction of the tower. Two-inch diameter rods running east–west below the vault (e) are followed by ties in all four directions within the ringing chamber (f) and bell chamber (g), above which a pair of diagonal rods link the north-east and south-west corners (h), passing awkwardly through the spiral stair. Close to these ties are redundant timber beams remaining from an earlier and unsuccessful attempt at strengthening the tower in conjunction with external iron bands.

The spire at ST MARY, STAMFORD took the heavy broach spire to the limit of sculptural exuberance. The proportions are significantly broader than at KETTON,[5] and the lucarnes and niches are even more prominent. The

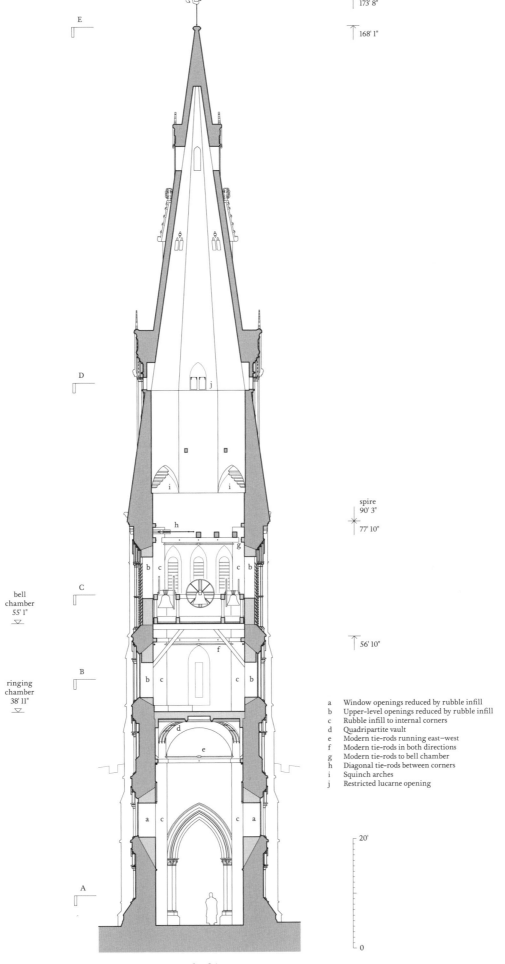

E

173' 8"

168' 1"

D

spire
90' 3"
77' 10"

h

g

C

bell
chamber
55' 1"

56' 10"

f

B

ringing
chamber
38' 11"

b c

c b

d

e

a c

c a

a   Window openings reduced by rubble infill
b   Upper-level openings reduced by rubble infill
c   Rubble infill to internal corners
d   Quadripartite vault
e   Modern tie-rods running east–west
f   Modern tie-rods in both directions
g   Modern tie-rods to bell chamber
h   Diagonal tie-rods between corners
i   Squinch arches
j   Restricted lucarne opening

i   i

j

b   c   c   b

20'

A

0

Section looking east

Reflected
plan of vault

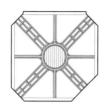

0   20'

Plan at E:
spire

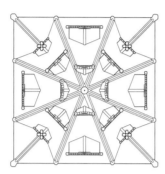

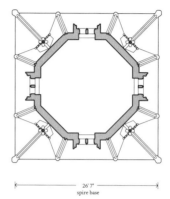

Plan at D:
principal
lucarnes

26' 7"
spire base

Plan at C:
bell
chamber

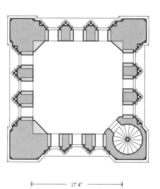

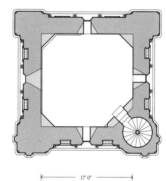

Plan at B:
ringing
chamber

17' 4"

17' 0"

8' 10"
tower arch

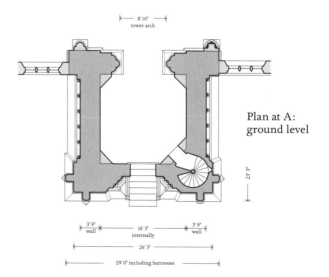

Plan at A:
ground level

23' 3"

3' 9"
wall

16' 3"
internally

3' 9"
wall

26' 3"

29' 0" including buttresses

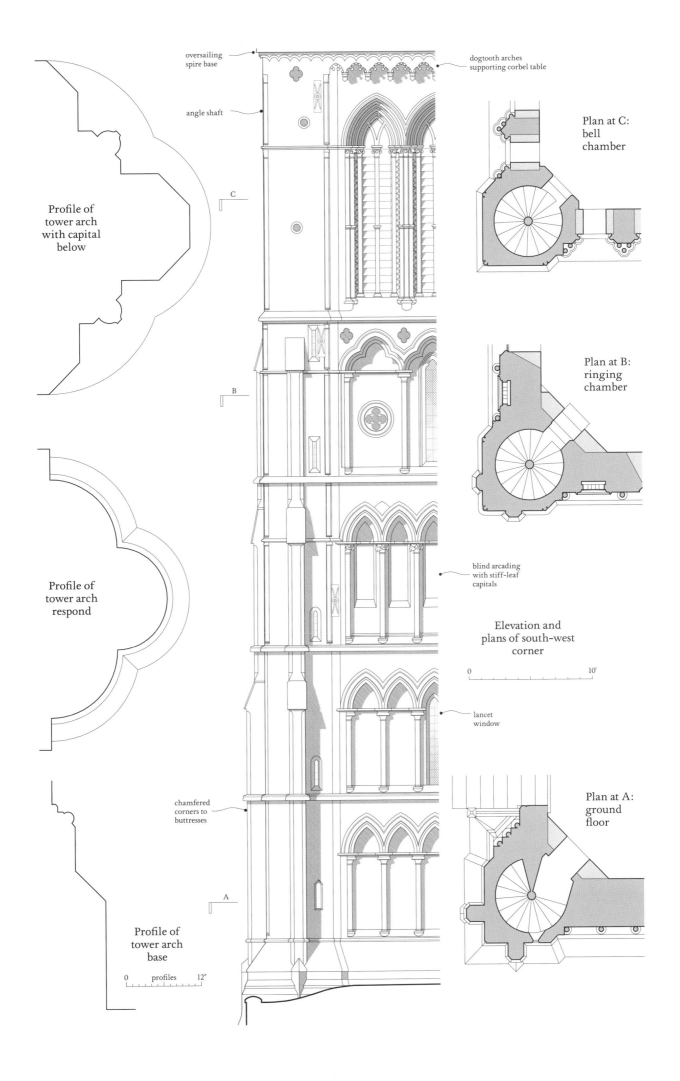

Profile of
tower arch
with capital
below

Profile of
tower arch
respond

Profile of
tower arch
base

0   profiles   12"

oversailing
spire base

angle shaft

C

B

chamfered
corners to
buttresses

A

dogtooth arches
supporting corbel table

Plan at C:
bell
chamber

Plan at B:
ringing
chamber

blind arcading
with stiff-leaf
capitals

Elevation and
plans of south-west
corner

0   10'

lancet
window

Plan at A:
ground
floor

roll edges are exceptionally sophisticated, for here, and at NEWARK, the rolls are set back between quadrant recesses to lie flush with the faces of the spire. Heads support the twelve roll ends around the base of the spire.

The spire is beautifully orchestrated. Not only are the alternating lucarnes exceptionally prominent, but they are set unusually high and are richly decorated with crockets, ballflower and elaborate crosses. The Curvilinear spirit permeates every line. The main lucarnes are impeccably detailed, with ogee-headed openings framed by two orders of engaged shaft. Ogee archlets support a rolled cill and a soufflet in the head. The upper lucarnes are only slightly more restrained. Structurally the design was conservative, with the squinch arches (i) starting five feet above the base, and the lucarne openings kept to a minimum (j). A wavy-edge frieze decorates the underside of the crisp, square spire base. Modest broaches support highly elaborate niches, more developed than at GRANTHAM or KETTON, framing three-quarter life-size statues. Musicians stand on three of the corners, but to the north-west is the figure of St William of Norwich, who gazes across the roofs of Stamford towards the glorious late medieval spire of All Saints' Church.

NOTES

1   The area around Stamford has seen chaotic changes in county boundaries during the twentieth century. Rutland was absorbed by Leicestershire in 1974 but regained her identity in 1997. Stamford south of the Welland was within that part of Northamptonshire known as the Soke of Peterborough, which merged with Huntingdonshire in 1965, and then in 1974 with Cambridgeshire and the Isle of Ely to form modern Cambridgeshire.

2   V. B. Crowther-Beynon, 'Stamford', *Memoirs of Old Lincolnshire* (1911), p. 162.

3   'RIBA Pugin Studentship Prize Drawings, 1911. By J. B. F. Cowper, Ashpitel Prizeman', *The Building News*, 17 February 1911.

4   Sir T. G. Jackson, *Gothic Architecture in France, England and Italy* (1915), p. 259.

5   The apex angle of the spires is 16° 29' at ST MARY, STAMFORD and 13° 46' at KETTON.

16

St Mary Redcliffe

BRISTOL

It is traditional to open an account of ST MARY REDCLIFFE with the famous quotation attributed to Elizabeth I, that it is 'one of the most famous, absolute, fairest and goodliest parish churches in the realm of England'.[1] There may be no documentary evidence to confirm that the queen ever visited the church, but the sentiment cannot be disputed. Along with Beverley Minster, this is indisputably one of the two greatest parish churches in England. ST MARY's chief glories are a cathedral-like cruciform plan; aisled and vaulted throughout; a spectacular early fourteenth-century hexagonal north porch; and a sumptuous steeple asymmetrically positioned on the north-west corner. This unusual location, on the very edge of the red cliff from which the district takes its name, may be explained by the proximity of the church to the medieval centre of Bristol.

Until 1373 Redcliffe was within the county of Somerset, unlike the city of Bristol, which fell within Gloucestershire. Similarly, until the establishment of a separate Bristol diocese in 1540, Redcliffe fell within the diocese of Bath and Wells, and Bristol within the diocese of Worcester. This administrative independence was matched by the spirit of the residents, who considered themselves superior to their more numerous northern neighbours. The huge wealth lavished on ST MARY's, which derived directly from the prosperity of great merchant families such as the Canynges, gave concrete expression to this civic rivalry. It is no coincidence that the

steeple of ST MARY REDCLIFFE dominated the northern approach from Bristol across the Avon and through the Radcliffe Gate. Unfortunately, this critical medieval connection has been all but obliterated by astonishingly insensitive highway engineering.

The commencement date for both church and tower is commonly given as either 1292 or 1294. These dates derive from William Barrett's *History and Antiquities of the City of Bristol* of 1789, in which the old 'chronicles of Bristol' record that Sir Simon de Burton, six times mayor of Bristol, gave money for the building the church in the year 1294. According to Barrett, one manuscript states that 'Simon de Burton, mayor in 1294, had two years before began to build Redcliffe church, but he lived not to finish it, which afterwards William Cannynges did.'[2] Wills and indulgences from 1207, 1229, 1230, 1232, 1246, 1278 and 1287 make no specific mention of the church's construction, but they do not preclude an earlier commencement date suggested by stylistic evidence.

The massive tower buttresses with their filleted angle shafts are reminiscent of TICKHILL at the start of the thirteenth century. Unfortunately the detail of the three-bay north window and four-bay west window can no longer be trusted, for both were unnecessarily remodelled during the Victorian restoration. The steep window cills and deeply profiled arches may follow the original profiles, but the Late Geometrical tracery, in the style of the 1290s, was designed by George Godwin around 1870. To the north are three stepped lancets carrying trilobes and a central quatrefoil circle, while to the west there are trilobes within a 'Y' surmounted by a cinquefoiled circle. Britton's 1818 illustration of the north elevation and a watercolour by T. L. S. Rowbotham from 1826 show the original stepped tracery to be without any elaboration in the head, suggesting that it could have been designed as early as 1260.[3] Britton's 1842 proposal for the restoration of the west elevation is of no help here, for it shows an entirely new three-bay Early Geometrical design that is contradicted by the four-bay plan shown on his 1818 survey of the fabric.[4]

The eccentric position of the steeple results in only one buttress, that of the north-west corner, being fully exposed from the ground. The north-east buttress is concealed behind the magnificence of the north porch, while the south-west buttress is subservient to the symmetry of the west window. Eight of the ten buttress niches are concentrated on this prominent north-western corner, in two connected tiers on each of the four faces. The filleted shafts, foliate capitals and trefoiled heads of these openings appear consistent with the preceding work, but the forward swing of the arch and the unusual crocketed part gables, covering only the centre foil, suggest Victorian embellishment. Two statues in the northernmost niches appear to predate the restoration, for they appear on the 1818 illustration.

Stretching across the two visible faces of the first stage are splendid seven-bay arcades. These are similar to the preceding niches but with free-standing shafts, probably in blue lias, and continuous gabled hood-moulds. The fourteen statues occupying the arcades are the work of William Rice, the directly employed mason who was responsible for supervising the restoration from 1848. A band of filleted roll circles, enclosing subservient quatrefoils, completes the first stage and the earliest campaign of tower construction.

The arrival of the fourteenth century sees increasing elaboration in the following two stages, to the extent that the upper tower wall becomes dematerialized. The effect is not unlike the slightly later crossing tower of Salisbury Cathedral, which may, indeed, have been directly inspired by ST MARY REDCLIFFE. Flowers appear in profusion around every opening and up every gable, first in naturalistic form and then, above the parapet and on the spire edges, as stylized ballflowers. The basic form is of three-bay elevations between angle buttresses terminating with square pyramidal pinnacle caps. Unusually, the projection of the buttresses remains constant, without any set-offs. Their great bulk is softened by the continuation of surface decoration around every available face, reducing the vertical momentum to no more than a gentle stroll. In this respect it is essentially a conservative design, for it is composed as a stack of independent stages separated by continuous

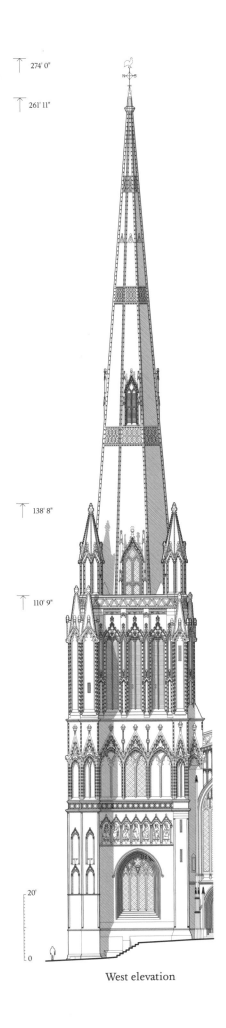

274' 0"

261' 11"

138' 8"

110' 9"

20'

0

West elevation

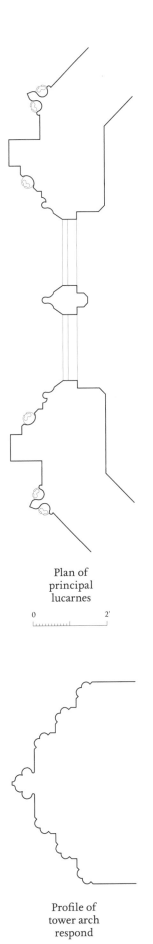

Plan of
principal
lucarnes

0   2'

Profile of
tower arch
respond

274' 0"

261' 11"

138' 8"

110' 9"

20'

0

North elevation

horizontals, following the same principle as EARLS BARTON three centuries earlier. Similarly, the structure is thick-walled throughout, to the extent that the absence of buttressing on the concealed south-east corner has had no adverse structural consequences. The proportions are expansive, and the effect is opulent.

Three bays on the second stage elevations are filled with broad 'Y' tracery under finialled gables, the outer bays blind and the centre bays glazed to the ringing chamber. The same motif carried around the buttresses gains variety from changes in the width and scale of the arches and the consequent steepening of the gables. Inventive Victorian grotesques leer from the base of every gable.

Relaxed articulation is followed on the third stage by an accelerating verticality in the tall, untransomed bell chamber windows and in the thin panelled pilasters that separate them. This articulation becomes so intense that the plane of the tower wall becomes all but invisible – an effect usually encountered only on the most elaborate cathedral crossing towers. The culmination of the design is not at the parapet but several feet below, where an intense line of richly crocketed ogee-headed hood-moulds encircle the building.

A brief interlude of calm is provided by the beautiful parapet, perforated by trefoils set within equilateral triangles.[5] Four huge octagonal corner pinnacles are on the same scale as GRANTHAM, but with greater emphasis on the panelled shafts and the effervescent ogee gables, and less on the crocketed roof. The conflict between large pinnacle and parapet path that badly mars the silhouette of GRANTHAM is resolved here by the simple expedient of providing doors to every penetration. Exceptionally, each of the four pinnacles contains a spiral stair rising from the bell chamber. One subtlety is the varied orientation of the pinnacles, the south-eastern one containing the primary staircase being set square to the tower walls, while the other three are rotated through twenty-two degrees.

Internally, there is much of interest. The fine cusped lierne vault beneath the tower (b) is not unlike that of the adjacent nave, and there are similarities in the bosses to those of the fifteenth-century north aisle. Before the tower was strengthened in the 1870s in preparation for the rebuilding of the spire, the south arch spanned the full width of the tower, and its outline can still be traced on the nave wall. Despite the addition of William Edney's fine wrought-iron chancel screen of 1710, the new south arch is a disappointment, for it robs the west end of much of its drama. Godwin's Perpendicular details reappear in the rebuilt eastern arch leading to the north aisle (a). An 1828 watercolour shows that, prior to the restoration, the inner orders here were cut away at their ends, the original shafts and responds having been removed. The blocked doorway visible in the north-east corner was originally accessed from a twisting staircase leading from the inner porch beneath a plain-ribbed octagonal vault. Another unfortunate consequence of the restoration was that the tower became a repository for every unwanted post-medieval monument in the church.

The upper tower is accessed indirectly from a gallery below the west window of the nave, followed by a short spiral stair finished with a miniature six-bay vault springing from the newel post. Braced oak posts rising from the ringing chamber window cills (d) may have been intended to support an earlier bell frame. A similar arrangement of posts within the bell chamber supports the spire floor, which may have been covered by a flat roof during a pause in the original construction (f). A two-tier steel and cast-iron bell frame is required to accommodate the substantial peal of twelve (e), and the squinches are formed by an impressive array of seven concentric arches (g). Further timber framing within the visible part of the lower spire may have supported the roof of the truncated stump prior to the restoration or it may be later Victorian strengthening work (i).

Only the lowest quarter of the spectacular 155-foot spire is original medieval work. This includes the broaches, visible above the parapet but far less obtrusive than at GRANTHAM, and the main lucarnes. Here for the first time appears Curvilinear tracery, flowing with the same ogee line that animates the crocketed hood-moulds. The ballflower here and either side of the shafted spire edge is consistent with the pinnacles, suggesting that they were part of the same campaign of work. Surprisingly, the

ballflower motif is rarely found on spire edges, appearing elsewhere only at Ashbourne (Derbys) and on the western spires of Lichfield Cathedral. The spire of ST MARY REDCLIFFE is also exceptional in being considerably higher than the tower on which it sits. The question naturally arises as to whether this might be the result of Victorian hubris. Careful examination suggests that the lines of the surviving portion have been extended straight and true in the restoration except for a small exaggeration above the uppermost band. Unless the original spire was convex in shape, such as EWERBY or Caythorpe (Lincs), the original structure must have been close to the current height.

The great medieval spire stood for little more than a century before falling prey to the elements in 1445. Meteorological records do not suggest any abnormal storm activity during this year, but two sources, quoted by the eighteenth-century historian William Barrett, are agreed on this date:

> 1445, at St. Paul's tide was very tempestuous weather by which Redcliffe steeple was overthrown in a thunder clap, doing great harme to the churche by the fall thereof, but by the good devotion of Mr William Canynges it was re-edified to his everlasting prayse.[6]

This is supported by William of Worcester's *Itinerary* of 1480, which states that 'the height of the tower of Redcliffe contains 300

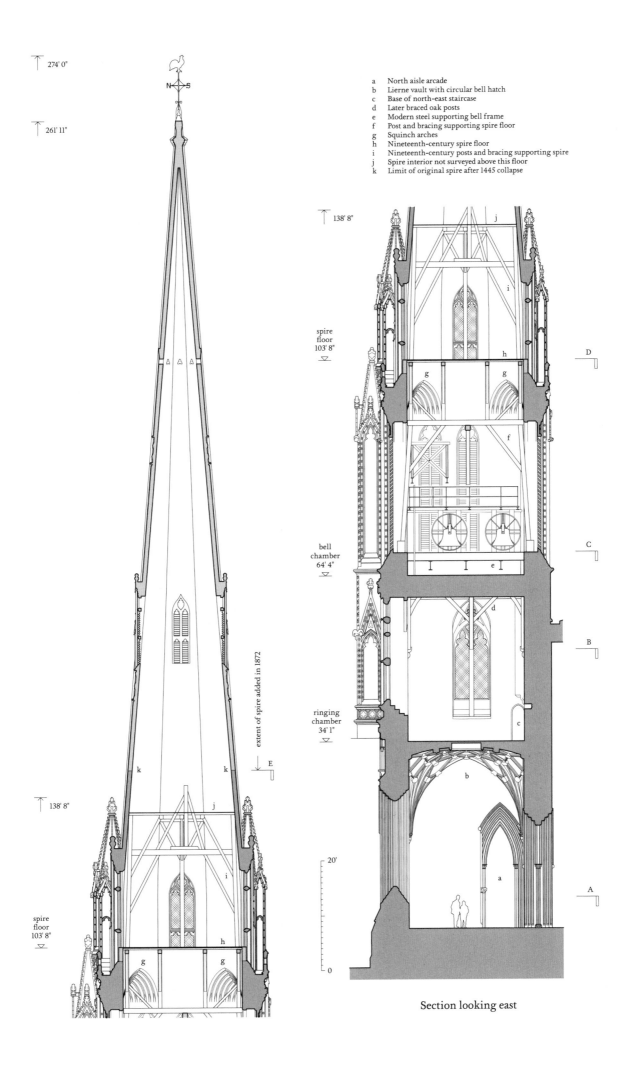

274' 0"

261' 11"

a   North aisle arcade
b   Lierne vault with circular bell hatch
c   Base of north-east staircase
d   Later braced oak posts
e   Modern steel supporting bell frame
f   Post and bracing supporting spire floor
g   Squinch arches
h   Nineteenth-century spire floor
i   Nineteenth-century posts and bracing supporting spire
j   Spire interior not surveyed above this floor
k   Limit of original spire after 1445 collapse

138' 8"

spire
floor
103' 8"

bell
chamber
64' 4"

ringing
chamber
34' 1"

138' 8"

extent of spire added in 1872

spire
floor
103' 8"

20'

0

Section looking east

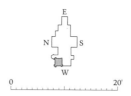

0   20'

Reflected
plan of
tower vault

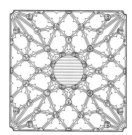

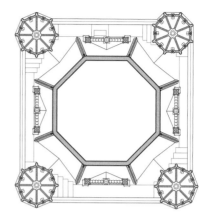

Plan at E:
spire

Plan at D:
spire

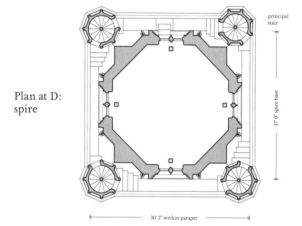

10' 6"
spire face

principal
stair

27' 0" spire base

30' 2" within parapet

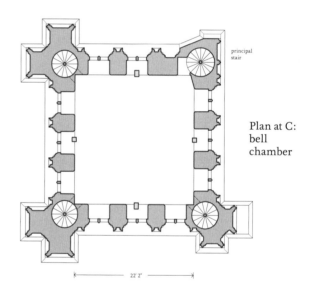

Plan at C:
bell
chamber

principal
stair

22' 2"

Plan at B:
ringing
chamber

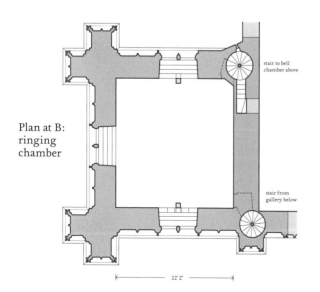

stair to bell
chamber above

stair from
gallery below

22' 2"

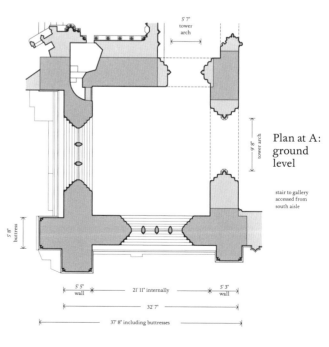

Plan at A:
ground
level

5' 7"
tower arch

9' 8"
tower arch

stair to gallery
accessed from
south aisle

5' 8"
buttress

5' 5"
wall

21' 11" internally

5' 3"
wall

32' 7"

37' 8" including buttresses

feet, of which 100 feet have been thrown down by lightning.' While these dimensions are in themselves hardly credible, it does suggest that the original stump may have been rather higher than the low remnant photographed in the nineteenth century.

In early 1842 a protracted period of restoration was set in motion by the removal of old buildings obscuring the northern elevation. John Britton and Professor Hoskin of King's College London were appointed as joint architects and immediately produced an ambitious scheme for restoring the steeple to its former glory. The proposed spire would have been dominated by four tiers of orthogonal lucarnes separated by three decorative bands. There was no theoretical or archaeological justification for such an extravagant combination, but the temptation to emulate, or even to outdo, the great spire of Salisbury Cathedral was irresistible. In the event Hoskin and Britton had both retired within five years, to be replaced by the architect George Godwin.

Work progressed slowly and methodically around the body of the church for a further twenty-three years, until in 1870 only the steeple remained unrestored. Thankfully Godwin's design was more restrained than that of his predecessors, with only one upper tier of full lucarnes, followed at a distance by tiny triangular windows. The three tiers of Salisbury-inspired banding proposed by Britton were retained but, unlike in the original, the net-like panelling is formed by flowing ogee-form curves. The rebuilding of the spire was finally completed in 1872, bringing to a conclusion thirty years of continual restoration.

The magnificent spire of ST MARY REDCLIFFE is not, as is commonly stated, the second-highest parish church tower in England. In part this anomaly derives from an appendix attached to the 'Notes on the Church of St. Mary Redcliffe' penned in 1878 by the vicar of the church, Revd J. P. Norris.[7] This includes George Godwin's 1870 survey dimensions and an illuminating sketch showing the foundations uncovered immediately prior to the rebuilding of the spire. Above the sandstone bedrock there was found to be 3' 8" of Pennant stone rubble 'with no cement whatever, and with interstices into which the arm might be thrust', followed by 5' 6" of coursed lias, only the final four or five courses of which was bedded in cement. The significance here is not the weakness of the construction, which was, no doubt, rectified by Godwin, but the subsequent inclusion of the foundation depth within the commonly accepted height of 292' 0". The absurdity of including hidden substructure as well as weathervanes within such a calculation is self-evident, and it has resulted in the height of the steeple being overstated by thirty feet for well over a century.

The true height from the lowest point on the north-west buttress to the uppermost stone of the spire determined by theodolite survey is 261' 11". At the time of completion, possibly around 1335, ST MARY's steeple would have been the second-highest on a parish church after GRANTHAM. A few years before the collapse of 1445, ST MICHAEL, COVENTRY relegated it to third position, and had the catastrophe not intervened it would have been further displaced by both LOUTH and BOSTON. Furthermore, if Victorian parish church steeples of all denominations are added into the equation – a not unreasonable premise for a spire designed and fabricated within the late nineteenth century – ST MARY's steeple reaches no higher than eighth position.[8] Such debates should not detract from the primary consideration, and that is one of aesthetic value. In this, the reconstructed steeple of ST MARY REDCLIFFE, despite all its Victorian idiosyncrasies, can be judged only as a spectacular success.

NOTES

1   The wording varies; this version appears in Michael Quinton Smith, *St Mary Redcliffe: An Architectural History* (1995) and is followed by a useful discussion on its origin.
2   William Barrett, *The History and Antiquities of the City of Bristol* (1789), pp. 566–69.
3   Plate VI by John Sherwen in John Britton, *Some Account of Redcliffe Church, Bristol* (1818), and in Quinton Smith, p. 127.
4   Britton, Plate I, and Quinton Smith, p. 136.
5   Contemporary steeples at Ashbourne (Derbys), ADDERBURY and ST MARY, OXFORD have similar trefoil perforated parapets but without the triangular panels.
6   Barrett, pp. 570–78.
7   Revd J. P. Norris, 'Notes on the Church of St. Mary Redcliffe.', *Transactions of the Bristol and Gloucestershire Archaeological Society*, vol. III (1878–79), p. 210.
8   Taller unsurveyed nineteenth-century spires are reputed to exist at St Walbruge, Preston (1854; 308'), St Elphin, Warrington (1867; 282') and St Mary Abbots, Kensington (1872; 279'), which was inspired by, and completed in the same year as, ST MARY REDCLIFFE.

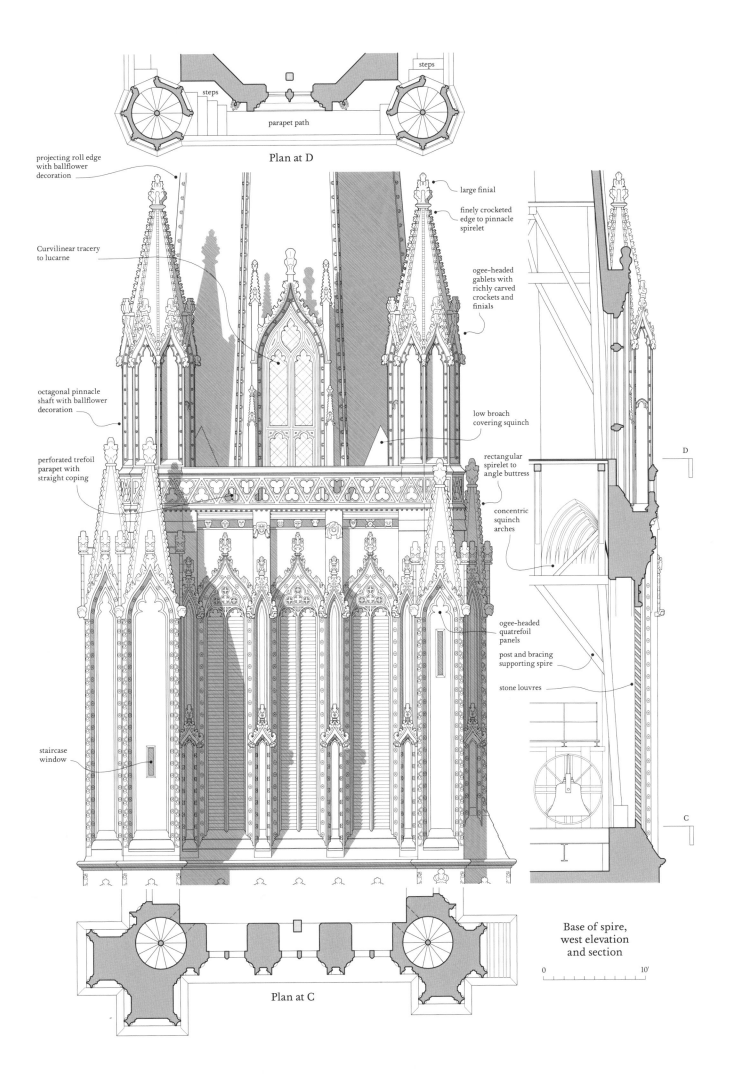

Plan at D

projecting roll edge
with ballflower
decoration

Curvilinear tracery
to lucarne

octagonal pinnacle
shaft with ballflower
decoration

perforated trefoil
parapet with
straight coping

staircase
window

parapet path

large finial

finely crocketed
edge to pinnacle
spirelet

ogee-headed
gablets with
richly carved
crockets and
finials

low broach
covering squinch

rectangular
spirelet to
angle buttress

concentric
squinch
arches

ogee-headed
quatrefoil
panels

post and bracing
supporting spire

stone louvres

D

C

Base of spire,
west elevation
and section

0   10'

Plan at C

17

Ewerby

LINCOLNSHIRE

For the ruling class, the second quarter of the fourteenth century was an age of luxury and pageantry. Edward III's decisive victory at Crécy, in 1346, confirmed that England was becoming the supreme power in Europe. The country's population had rebounded from the terrible famine of 1315–16 to reach a pre-industrial peak of at least four million. Nine out of every ten people worked on the land, and intensively farmed rural districts such as south Lincolnshire were now more prosperous and more densely occupied that at any time in their history. This was the greatest period of Lincolnshire church building.

Across Kesteven, country churches were rebuilt on an unprecedented scale, with soaring spires of crisp Ancaster stone rising across the horizon. The steeples of the previous generation, such as NEWARK and GRANTHAM, had been ambitious but experimental. In the next generation, from around 1325, a consensus evolved among Lincolnshire masons on the principles of tall steeple design. A remarkable consistency appeared in spire height, staircase treatment, fenestration and the principles of decoration.

Every substantial Lincolnshire tower of the period was designed to receive a spire that would reach to 170 feet or thereabouts. The stair was always set in the south-west corner except in free-standing Fenland belfries such as Fleet and Donington. GRANTHAM had shown the folly of projecting the stair shaft too far and too high, and now it was kept under careful

control. The characteristic Lincolnshire stair of the period bulges forward, between the corner angle buttresses, and terminates at the bell chamber floor, comfortably below the parapet. It imparts a well-judged, dynamic asymmetry to the composition of the steeple.

The thirteenth-century obsession with blind arcading and other forms of surface decoration, still evident at GRANTHAM in around 1300, was decisively rejected. Broad expanses of smooth ashlar allowed the vigorous form of the composition to be appreciated to the full. Decoration was of outstanding craftsmanship and individuality, but it was also highly concentrated at the top of the tower and on the buttresses. The middle stage remained austere, with only the most inconspicuous windows to the ringing chamber. The west door was frequently omitted, allowing the west window to be positioned just above the basement course. This is an excellent idea, for a low west window provides a fine termination of the view through the tower arch from the body of the church and, unlike a dark and draughty door, it enlivens the space below the tower.

Within these commonly accepted parameters there was a fascinating variation of treatment by the individual masons. The greatest exuberance was reached in the Sleaford district, in five exceptional towers started in the 1330s and 1340s. The distinguishing feature of this group is the richly decorated buttress gable. This was the period of transition from the broach spire to

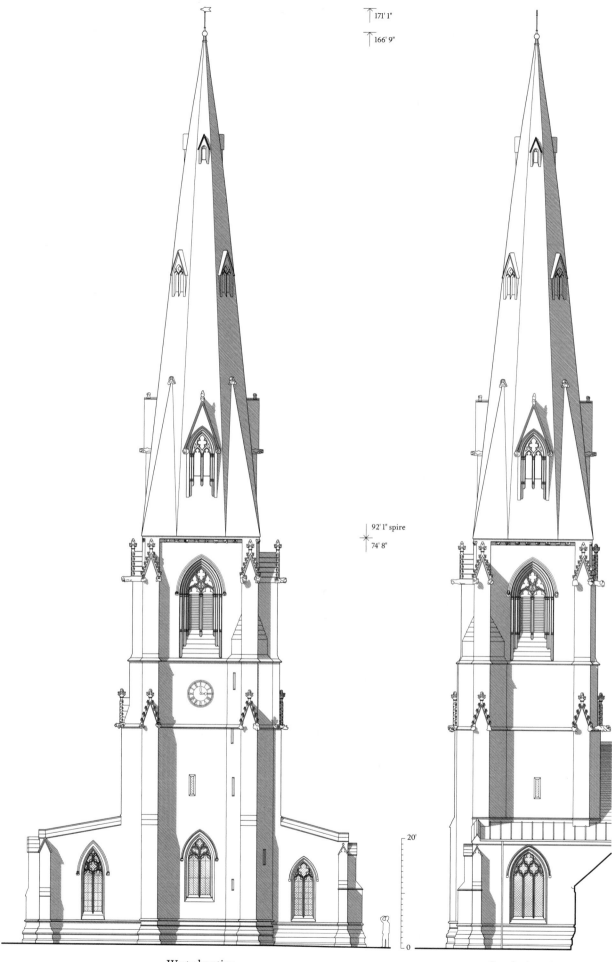

171' 1"

166' 9"

92' 1" spire

74' 8"

20'

0

West elevation

South elevation

the recessed spire. EWERBY and Anwick were completed with broach spires; HECKINGTON and Silk Willoughby with recessed spires; and BRANT BROUGHTON remained incomplete until the following century.

The Domesday Book records that EWERBY was a possession of Godiva, the famous widow of the Earl of Mercia, and that it had a church. The name, sometimes written as Ywarby or Iwardby, was much older, deriving from the Old Danish for 'Ivar's village'. EWERBY prospered, for in 1254 Henry III granted a charter to William de la Lande to hold a market on Thursdays and a fair on the festival of St Andrew (30 November). By the end of the Middle Ages there were fifty families in the village, though no doubt the number had been considerably higher when the rebuilding of the church commenced, before the arrival of the Black Death. In the nineteenth century EWERBY was a country estate of the Earls of Winchelsea, and the church fell into serious disrepair. The architect Raphael Brandon was so horrified when he visited in 1858 that all he could bring himself to say was, 'The shameful and desecrated condition of EWERBY is not to be described.'[1] St Andrew's Church was rescued only by the considerable generosity of the 12th Earl, who funded the 1895 restoration.

The estate was broken up in 1927, but EWERBY still retains the neatly ordered feel of an estate village. It is typical of dozens of unassuming small rural villages and hamlets across the south of Lincolnshire that have inherited a magnificent legacy of extravagant parish churches that they struggle to support. St Andrew's seats 380, and yet the congregation rarely exceeds a dozen.

EWERBY is particularly satisfying because it is entirely of one period and built to a single design. The body of the church, the tower and the spire, all dating from between 1340 and 1360, form part of a unified pyramidal composition, the ideal form for the English parish church of the mid-fourteenth century. Viewed from the east, the steeply pitched nave roof of Collyweston slate, re-created in the 1895 restoration, dominates the composition. The pyramidal west elevation is extended to include the aisles embracing the base of the tower. At large town churches such as TICKHILL, NEWARK and GRANTHAM this feature derived from the internal planning, and the external effect could be unpredictable. Here, however, the aisles were extended in order to give breadth to the external composition, and they extend seamlessly from the side faces of the buttresses.

Externally, the tower is divided by strings into three stages following the unusual proportions of 3:1:2 – divisions that are entirely unrelated to the original floor levels. Ogee curves animate the profile of the satisfyingly rounded basement course, and the angle buttresses are strong and straightforward. The main buttress set-offs are formed by gables rising from the string course marking the top of the first stage. Shallow intermediate set-offs on the western buttresses correspond to the abutments of the aisle roof copings. The third-stage string wraps continuously around the elevations and the buttresses to form another minor set-off, and the buttresses terminate emphatically with a second tier of gables just below the summit of the tower. The buttress set-offs are greatly reduced on the south-west corner so that the staircase, which appears dominant on the floor plans, is successfully masked. As usual, the depth of the eastern buttresses is severely restricted by the proximity of the nave.

Binoculars are essential when visiting EWERBY, for the quality of carving is outstanding. Gloriously vegetative finials and crockets with rippling stalks adorn the edges of the buttress gables. The carved figures projecting from the eaves include men in a boat, a knight carrying a shield, a horse, and a dragon. The tower finishes with a neat corbel table adorned with more fine carving, including foliage, animals and a man immodestly lifting his tunic (the third figure from the left on the south side). One satisfying subtlety is the introduction of small re-entrant angles on the tower corners, giving the appearance of a continuous corbel table running between shallow angle buttresses.

The Curvilinear tower windows are typical of the Sleaford Group. A modest two-light west window, of filleted roll tracery, carries divergent mouchettes over trefoiled archlets, with a soufflet to the head.

Externally the window is framed by a typical Curvilinear wave moulding, and internally there is a deep splay. The adjacent aisle windows are sympathetically designed. Deeply recessed bell-stage openings, with steep cills six courses high, are a development of the NEWARK design. They are framed by three engaged shafts each side, carrying broad ring capitals and rising from octagonal plinths. All of this is typical of the Sleaford Group, but the windows at EWERBY are broader than usual, allowing space for particularly fine roll tracery that flows sinuously between two major trefoils, two minor trefoils and a soufflet. Plain hood-moulds spring from human heads on all the tower windows.

Church clocks are usually an unwelcome addition to a medieval tower; however, at EWERBY the blank middle stage on the west elevation provides the perfect frame for a delicate skeleton face. The copper lightning conductor is more disruptive, for it concentrates the flow of rainwater across weathered stone, creating unsightly streaking across the principal west elevation.

Within the tower the benefits of the engaged aisles and the omission of the west door are abundantly clear. The three tower arches are delightfully modest, with shafts 11' high to the east (a) and 7' 9" high to north and south (b). Nevertheless, the effect on the west end is dramatic, with vistas opening up across the church. Triple-chamfered tower arches, with plain hood-moulds, rise from a flowing cluster of five regular shafts with

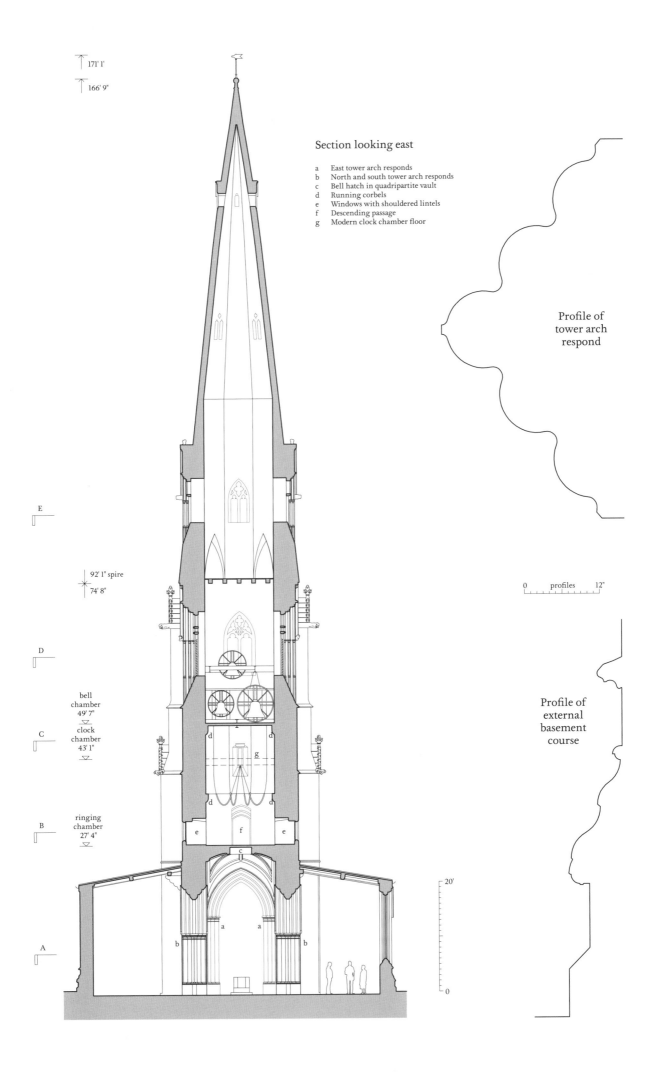

171' 1'
166' 9"

Section looking east

a   East tower arch responds
b   North and south tower arch responds
c   Bell hatch in quadripartite vault
d   Running corbels
e   Windows with shouldered lintels
f   Descending passage
g   Modern clock chamber floor

E

92' 1" spire
74' 8"

D

bell
chamber
49' 7"

clock
chamber
43' 1"

C

ringing
chamber
27' 4"

B

A

a   a
b   b
d   d
g
d   d
e   f   e
c

Profile of
tower arch
respond

0   profiles   12"

Profile of
external
basement
course

20'

0

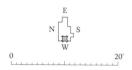

0   20'

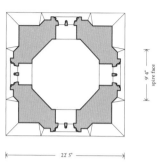

Plan at E:
spire floor

9' 4"
spire face

22' 5"

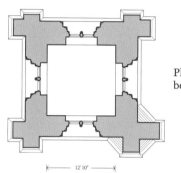

Plan at D:
bell chamber

12' 10"

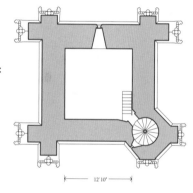

Plan at C:
clock
chamber

12' 10"

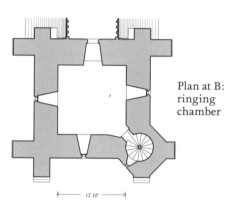

Plan at B:
ringing
chamber

12' 10"

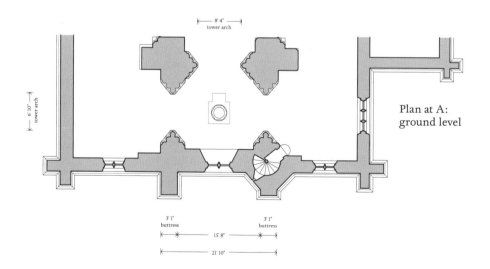

8' 4"
tower arch

6' 10"
tower arch

Plan at A:
ground level

3' 1"
buttress

3' 1"
buttress

15' 8"

21' 10"

central fillet. The quadripartite rib vault with circular bell hatch (c) and the deep west window reveal, with its triple-chamfered arch, complete a superbly intimate space.

The position of the three original upper floors is clear from substantial running corbels on the north and south walls (d). The lowest chamber, finished in smooth masonry, has small, low windows with very deep reveals carrying shouldered lintels to the north and south (e). A stepped passage to the east (f) leads down to a doorway, below a segmental pointed arch that opens into space high above the nave floor but when first constructed may have led to a crawlway through the apex of the roof structure.

Originally the first chamber in the tower would have been too low for bell ringing, which must have taken place on the floor above. This arrangement was reversed in order to provide a chamber for the clock, possibly in 1867, and the modern clock chamber floor now cuts crudely across the east window (g). The bell chamber floor is also a modern replacement but this time at the correct level. Thanks to the benevolence of the 12th Earl of Winchelsea, the four original bells were increased to a peal of ten in 1896, a considerable luxury in a tower of this size. The south-west staircase terminates at the bell chamber, achieving the desired effect externally but limiting access to the spire floor to an ancient ladder balanced precariously on the bell frame.

The spire followed immediately. Tall broaches had been common in early broach spires, but as squinch arch design became increasingly efficient they fell out of fashion. At ST MARY, STAMFORD and KETTON, for example, the broaches are modest and rely upon extravagant ornamentation for their effect. However, by the middle of the fourteenth century masons were pursuing a more sophisticated, even austere, aesthetic in which sculptural massing was of primary importance. At EWERBY the broaches are exceptionally high, the spire edges are entirely plain, and the apex is finished with the simplest of spherical capstones. It is unfortunate that the dates of the Sleaford Group are not confirmed by documentary evidence, for it is unclear what stage they had reached when the Black Death struck in 1348. There is, nevertheless, a strong suspicion that the pronounced austerity of the spire at EWERBY and its contemporaries resulted directly from the shortage of skilled masons after the plague.

EWERBY is one of the earliest spires in the Sleaford district to experiment with convex entasis, predating Walcot, Caythorpe and the gherkin-like spire of Welbourn. Entasis in a spire is a deliberate curve in the profile to impart a sense of plasticity to the form, making it appear as if it were bulging slightly under its own weight. At EWERBY the spire edges run straight to the top of the middle lucarne, gently radius for about forty feet and then straighten for the final six feet to the apex. Unfortunately, the effect has been compromised by uneven rebuilding following a lighting strike in 1810, with

Carvings spring from mid-level gablets on the south-west buttress (left) and the south-east buttress (right).

significant distortion visible on the south-east face.

At EWERBY the proportion of spire to tower is 5:4, and this, rather than the commonly quoted ratio of 1:1, should be regarded as the ideal for a tall broach spire. Three tiers of alternating lucarnes are surprisingly restrained, eschewing the rich crockets of the tower. Reduced versions of the bell-stage windows are employed for the main lucarnes, while the alternating upper tiers are seriously reticent. The effect is

entirely different from the previous generation of sumptuously decorated spires such as KETTON but it is no less beautiful.

St Andrew's steeple was fashioned to a single design in the age of supreme craftsmanship from one of the finest materials known to man. The balance between symmetry and asymmetry, between mass and detail and between restraint and exuberance is exquisite. EWERBY marks the ultimate development of the English broach spire.

NOTE

1   Raphael and J. Arthur Brandon, *Parish Churches*, vol. 2 (1858), p. 20.

18

Brant Broughton

LINCOLNSHIRE

The outstanding beauty of BRANT BROUGHTON church is in no small part due to the wealth and wisdom of the local Sutton family, and in particular Canon Frederick Heathcote Sutton, its rector between 1873 and 1888. When he arrived, 'The whole interior presented an appearance of poverty and squalor.'[1] Canon Sutton poured not only his money but his creativity into an exemplary restoration. The reredos and the chandeliers are to his design, and most of the stained glass was painted by his own hand and fired in a kiln at the rectory. By the greatest good fortune he employed George F. Bodley as his architect, one of the most gifted and sensitive talents of the late Gothic Revival. Where a Butterfield or a Gilbert Scott might have tinkered and scraped, Bodley and his partner, Thomas Garner, conserved and enriched. The work continued under the next rector, Canon Arthur Sutton, until Bodley's death in 1907. In 1897 the spire, which until then terminated abruptly, 'having lost its upper portion and original finial',[2] was restored to its original height, the final seven feet being new work.

BRANT BROUGHTON, along with EWERBY, Silk Willoughby, HECKINGTON and Anwick, is one of five outstanding towers in the Sleaford district started in the second quarter of the fourteenth century. A comparison of the details from BRANT BROUGHTON and from EWERBY, fourteen miles to the east, shows just how closely the group is related. Profiles of the windows, the basement course and the tower arch responds are almost identical. The sumptuous crockets, finials and figure-carving are so similar that they can only be the work of a single lodge of masons. There are, however, some significant differences. The slender proportions and the parapeted spire at BRANT BROUGHTON are decidedly feminine, while EWERBY, with its sturdy broach spire and engaged aisles, is emphatically masculine.

St Helen's Church is essentially of the fourteenth century and, except for the west ends of the aisles, postdates the tower. It is known that the tower was under way in 1338, for the Bishop of Lincoln granted a commission allowing the rector of *Brendebroughton* to reuse the stone from a ruined chapel at Parva Stapleford in its construction.

Simple angle buttresses, divided by three regularly spaced plain set-offs, rise from a basement course of flowing ogee profiles. The south-west stair is more reticent than at EWERBY, for it makes no impact on the re-entrant angles between the buttresses. Slit windows are discreetly hidden on the inconspicuous south-east face of the stair. Externally, the stair shaft terminates well below the parapet, but internally it continues up to the base of the spire. The three-light west window is reputed to be an accurate copy by Bodley of the original, but the Geometrical tracery is decidedly old-school when compared to the openings of the upper tower.

Internally, the triple-chamfered tower arch, with plain hood-mould and filleted five-shaft respond, fills the full width of the tower. The sexpartite tower vault, with decorated ribs, single bays to east and west and paired bays to north and south, is an unusual design re-created by Bodley. The smooth ashlar masonry within the tower might seem an unnecessary extravagance, but such finely jointed stones ensured the strongest possible construction. As at EWERBY, the three upper stages in the tower, with floors resting on running corbels (a), were reorganized in Victorian times to accommodate a clock chamber (b). The clock faces east, towards the main street, leaving the principal faces unencumbered. The original chambers were lit by windows alternately on the side elevations (c) and on the west elevation. A steep stair descends east from the old ringing chamber to a blocked doorway that is visible from the body of the church, just below the apex of the original nave roof weathering.

Externally, the stages are separated by such modest strings that they hardly read at all, and as a result the verticality of the elevation goes almost unchecked. The proximity of a tower to the end of the nave frequently disrupts the positioning of the eastern buttresses. At BRANT BROUGHTON this effect is so pronounced that the north and south elevations appear substantially offset from the centrally positioned spire.

The beautiful bell-stage openings are typical of the Sleaford Group, with a very steep cill of eight courses and three engaged shafts either side rising from octagonal plinths to carry fine natural-leaf capitals. The filleted roll tracery follows the classic Curvilinear arrangement of a broad soufflet above two ogee-headed trefoiled lights. Crocketed buttress gables, tied visually at their apex by fleuron friezes incorporating gargoyles, are a tour de force of the mason's art, as crisp now as the day they were carved. Tall castellated parapets, hexagonal roll-edged pinnacle bases and two courses of a plain edged spire (d) were all completed before work abruptly stopped.

The two most widely reported facts about the spire of BRANT BROUGHTON – that it is 198 feet high and that is contemporary with the tower on which it stands – are both incorrect.[3] The true height of the spire is, by Lincolnshire standards, an almost standard 166' 8", but the tower is so slender and the composition is so effortlessly attenuated that it appears far higher than it actually is.

Silk Willoughby, twelve miles to the east, illustrates how the spire at BRANT BROUGHTON might have looked had work not been interrupted for a century. The effect is entirely different. The glorious spire is tall, but not excessively so. It is finished with plain edges, small lucarnes and delicate flying buttresses. Hexagonal pinnacles of the mid-fourteenth century, for example at Welbourn, terminate modestly and are usually surrounded by gablets, quite unlike the sharp, vertical spikes of BRANT BROUGHTON.

The Black Death arrived through the south-coast ports in June 1348, and within eighteen months at least forty per cent of the English population had perished. In architecture much work, including the

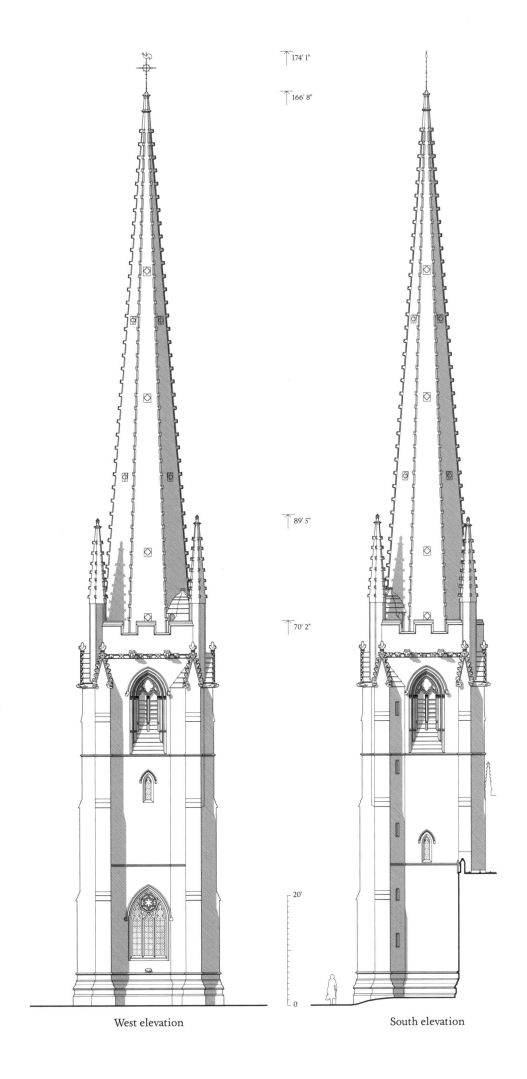

174' 1"

166' 8"

89' 5"

70' 2"

20'

0

West elevation

South elevation

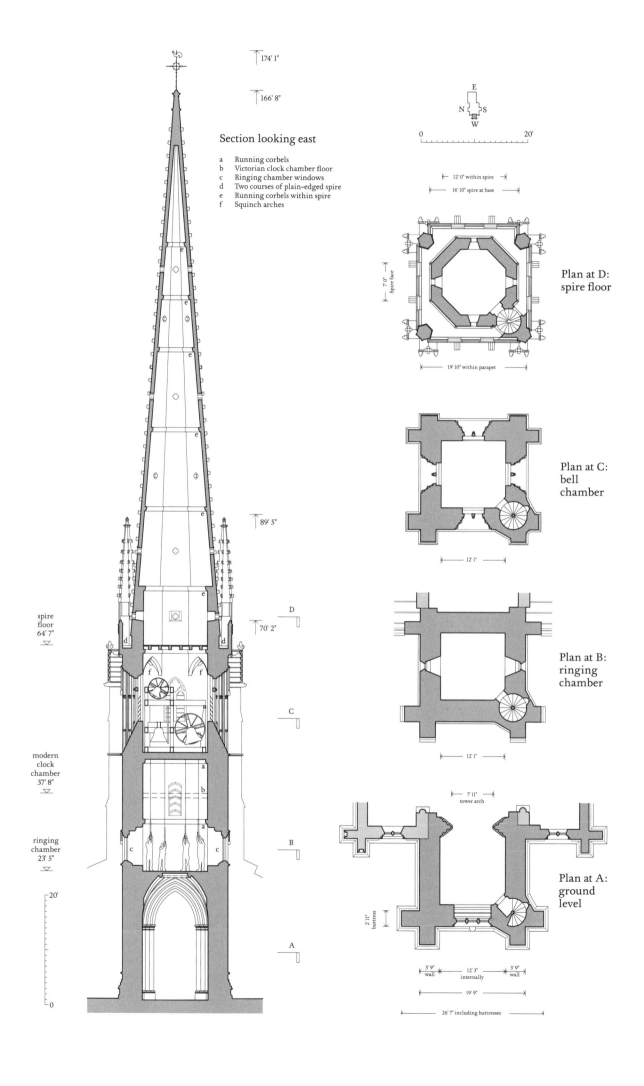

174' 1"

166' 8"

Section looking east

a   Running corbels
b   Victorian clock chamber floor
c   Ringing chamber windows
d   Two courses of plain-edged spire
e   Running corbels within spire
f   Squinch arches

E
N   S
W

0   20'

12' 0" within spire

16' 10" spire at base

7' 0"
Spire face

Plan at D:
spire floor

19' 10" within parapet

Plan at C:
bell
chamber

12' 1"

89' 5"

Plan at B:
ringing
chamber

12' 1"

D

70' 2"

C

spire
floor
64' 7"

modern
clock
chamber
37' 8"

20'

ringing
chamber
23' 5"

B

7' 11"
tower arch

A

2' 11"
buttress

Plan at A:
ground
level

0

3' 9"
wall

12' 3"
internally

3' 9"
wall

19' 9"

26' 7" including buttresses

steeple at St Helen's Church, was abandoned. Construction restarted here only in the mid-fifteenth century, for the razor sharp profiles of the spire and pinnacles speak of a very different age.

Quatrefoil spire lights are a Leicestershire speciality, and it is no coincidence that **BRANT BROUGHTON** and her near neighbour at Caythorpe are just a few miles from the county border. Plain spires with up to three tiers of small quatrefoil perforations appear in Leicestershire from the early fourteenth century. The idea was taken up by the masons at Caythorpe with typical Lincolnshire exuberance, for the bulging spire effervesces with no fewer than six tiers of alternating quatrefoils. These quatrefoils were carved directly into the surface of the completed spire, whereas at **BRANT BROUGHTON** they were pre-cut into square stones in the mason's workshop. Here, twenty-four quatrefoils are set in two orthogonal tiers followed by four alternating tiers. Unlike Caythorpe, the spire at **BRANT BROUGHTON** is as straight as a needle and almost as sharp. Angular ridges carry thirty-seven flat-sided, mass-produced crockets up each of the spire edges. It is may be no coincidence that **LOUTH**, the ultimate needle spire, also carries thirty-seven crockets and shares the same apex angle of nine degrees.

The pinnacles are miniature versions of the spire, with the same soaring proportions and streamlined crockets. The spire is very much higher that the tower (a ratio of around 7:5), but the tall pinnacles create an effective zone of overlap, preventing imbalance and binding the composition together. Inside the spire there are no fewer than six running corbels (e), which may have supported temporary platforms during construction. One delightful extravagance is a miniature ribbed vault with a bearded face for a boss above the spiral staircase.

There are few churches in the whole of England as enchanting as **BRANT BROUGHTON**. Alec Clifton-Taylor considered it to be a treasure.[4] It is like a medieval dream, in which time stands still and the cares of the modern world fall away. The stonework is so crisp and the carving so animated, it is as if the mason had laid down his tools only last week.

NOTES

1   Canon F. H. Sutton, quoted in *A Short Guide to St Helen's Church.*
2   Ven. Edward Trollope, 'The Church of St. Mary Magdalene, Newark, and other Churches visited by the Society on 22nd and 23rd of June, 1871', *Reports and Papers of the Architectural and Archaeological Societies of the counties of Lincoln and Northampton*, vol. 11 (1871).
3   These inaccuracies, which appear in Pevsner and Harris, *The Buildings of England: Lincolnshire* (1964), were repeated three years later in the Statutory Listing. Alec Clifton-Taylor, *English Parish Churches as Works of Art* (1986), also overstates the height but correctly identifies the spire as being from the fifteenth century. The Ven. Edward Trollope had been more accurate in 1871 when he noted the height to be 170 feet.
4   Clifton-Taylor, *English Parish Churches*, p. 27.

19

Heckington

LINCOLNSHIRE

When Sir Banister Fletcher compiled his monumental *History of Architecture on the Comparative Method*, he found room to illustrate just one English parish church. That he should have chosen a medium-sized church serving an obscure parish in rural Lincolnshire, in preference to BOSTON, GRANTHAM or ST MARY REDCLIFFE, is a mark of the high esteem in which HECKINGTON is held by architectural historians. St Andrew's Church is both typical and exceptional. It is typical in its compact cruciform, plan with its western tower, four-bay aisled nave, south porch, north and south transepts, long, square-ended chancel and attached sacristy. It is also typical in its external massing, which steps down from west to east, and in the simplicity of its interior, which is covered by an open timber roof. It is exceptional not just for the quality of its design and workmanship, but because it is all of one period, and that period is regarded by many as being the high point of English architecture.

The rebuilding of an earlier church on this site started modestly with the north transept in the early fourteenth century. In 1345 Abbot Roger of Barrow obtained a royal licence allowing Bardney Abbey, a wealthy Benedictine monastery near Lincoln, to appropriate Heckington Church. This set in motion a comprehensive and expensive rebuilding programme that continued until the completion of the south porch early in the reign of Richard III (1377–99). HECKINGTON represents the final, glorious flourishing of the deeply sculptural Curvilinear architecture of the first half of the fourteenth century. By the of its completion, however, this was becoming an anachronism, for by then the new, crisply efficient Perpendicular style was strongly in the ascendant.

HECKINGTON is at its finest when viewed from the south. Revd Edward Trollope, addressing the Lincoln Diocesan Architectural Society in 1863, captured the essence of its appeal:

> The whole southern elevation of this church is one of the finest examples of Decorated work after it had attained its full perfection, and previous to the period of decadence, which soon followed. The noble base mouldings here, the freely flowing tracery of its aisle windows, the range of the large clerestory lights above, the numerous canopied niches, the beauty of some of the boldly projecting sculptured ornaments, and the strange grotesqueness of others, the crocketed pinnacles, the enriched parapets, and the beautiful porch, together combining to present one of the most triumphant examples of the power of Gothic

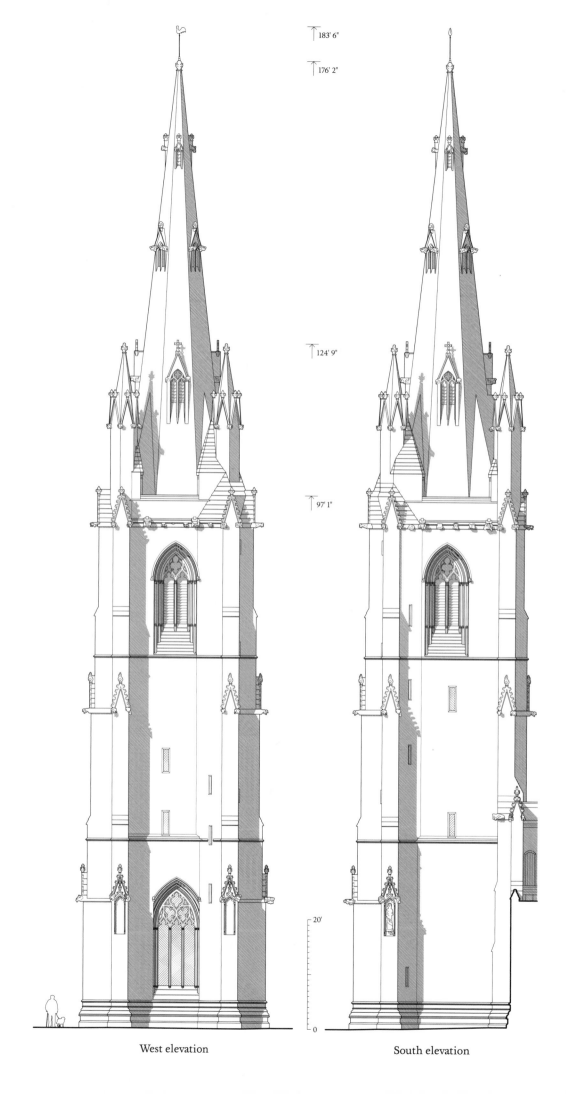

183' 6"

176' 2"

124' 9"

97' 1"

20'

0

West elevation

South elevation

architecture, as applied to the production of a parish church, that we possess.[2]

Rising 97' 1" to the parapet, HECKINGTON is by a considerable margin the largest member of the outstanding group of mid-fourteenth-century towers in the Sleaford district of Lincolnshire. It shares with EWERBY (74' 8"), BRANT BROUGHTON (70' 2"), Silk Willoughby and Anwick a preference for plain, undecorated wall surfaces, deeply recessed openings, richly carved buttress gables, flowing tracery and an asymmetric south-west staircase. This exquisite combination created a sculptural architecture that reached the highest level of artistic achievement. Of these five outstanding towers, only Silk Willoughby and HECKINGTON were immediately crowned with recessed spires. Strong stylistic connections are evident between these churches, set just five miles apart, suggesting the guiding hand of a single mason. One memorable example is in the identical parapet, perforated by a run of wavy trefoils, that appears on Silk Willoughby tower and HECKINGTON chancel.[3]

The base of the tower was constructed after the adjacent aisles, for the eastern buttresses are fitted between existing work until they rise clear of the roofs. A tall basement course rippling with ogee profiles carries pairs of plain-faced angle buttress on each corner. As with Silk Willoughby and BRANT BROUGHTON, the south-east staircase pushes forward on the west and south elevations but does not appear in the re-entrant corner between the buttresses. These three towers may represent a later refinement of the Anwick and EWERBY design in which the stair projects between the buttresses.

Tracery in the west window is a delicious concoction of swinging trefoils and quatrefoils, the only surprise being that the moulded arch dies into flat reveals necessitated by the proximity of the staircase to the right and a desire for symmetry on the left. The first tier of buttress set-offs is placed close to the ground and ornamented with not just fantastically carved gables but niches for statuary, a single figure remaining to the south. These low-level gables, which are unique among the Sleaford Group, are followed by two equally spaced upper tiers.

The second tier of buttress gables follows the pattern of EWERBY rather than Silk Willoughby in being set well below the bell stage and adjacent to wide expanses of plain ashlar walling. This provides a brilliant contrast to the rich profusion of crockets, finials and thrusting figures that decorate the steeply pitched gables. Nothing else disturbs the austere grandeur of the first two stages, the lights to the interior chambers being restricted to small, rectangular chamfered openings. On the third stage the deep-set bell chamber openings are framed by three filleted shafts to either side, rising from nine courses of steeply inclined cill and finished with sweeping Curvilinear tracery. All these features are shared with Silk Willoughby, but at HECKINGTON the

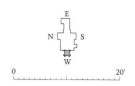

E
N   S
W

0   20'

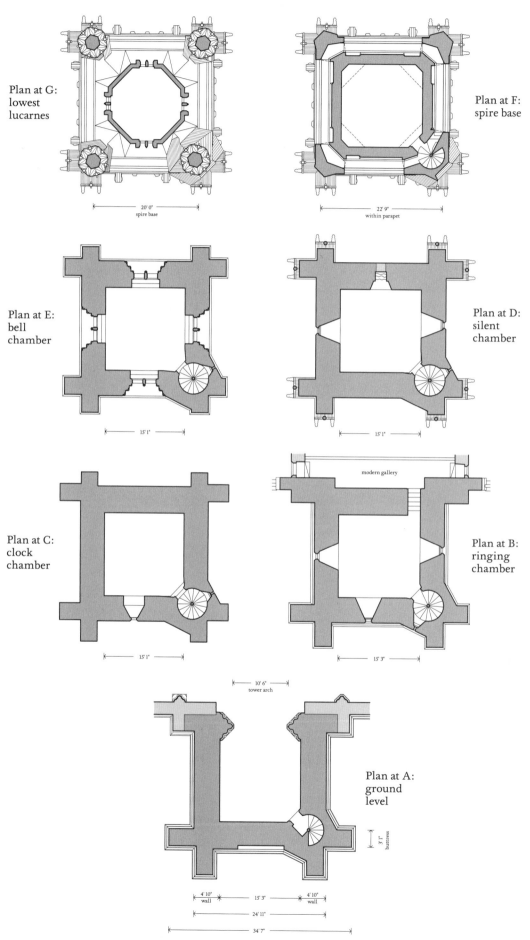

Plan at G:
lowest
lucarnes

20' 0"
spire base

Plan at F:
spire base

22' 9"
within parapet

Plan at E:
bell
chamber

15' 1"

Plan at D:
silent
chamber

15' 1"

Plan at C:
clock
chamber

15' 1"

Plan at B:
ringing
chamber

modern gallery

15' 3"

10' 6"
tower arch

Plan at A:
ground
level

3' 1"
buttress

4' 10"
wall

15' 3"

4' 10"
wall

24' 11"

34' 7"

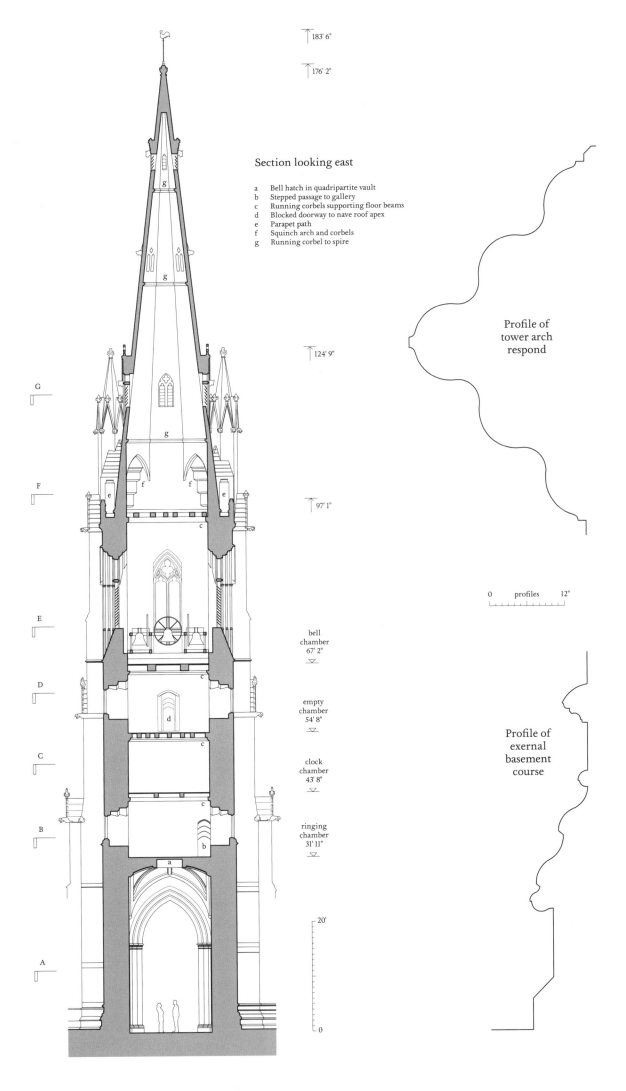

183' 6"

176' 2"

Section looking east

a   Bell hatch in quadripartite vault
b   Stepped passage to gallery
c   Running corbels supporting floor beams
d   Blocked doorway to nave roof apex
e   Parapet path
f   Squinch arch and corbels
g   Running corbel to spire

124' 9"

G

F

97' 1"

Profile of
tower arch
respond

0   profiles   12"

E

bell
chamber
67' 2"

D

empty
chamber
54' 8"

Profile of
exernal
basement
course

C

clock
chamber
43' 8"

B

ringing
chamber
31' 11"

20'

A

0

proportions are more vertical, and circular ring capitals appear in preference to foliage. Carvings below the plain parapet are as good as any in the neighbourhood.

The space beneath the tower, capped by a simple quadripartite stone vault (a), is more intimate than might be anticipated from the scale of the exterior. Ogee curves generate the profile of the responds that support a modest chamfered tower arch. A stepped passage descending to the nave roof (d) is a common feature, but here a similar connection is made to a nave gallery (b). Running corbels support the upper chamber floors (c), but their purpose within the spire (g) is unclear. Tall corbels behind the squinch arches are the internal consequence of high external broaches (f).

It is in the connection between tower and spire that HECKINGTON is at its most inventive, and also at its most conservative. Hexagonal pinnacles, which appear here, at BRANT BROUGHTON (where the terminations are later) and at Caythorpe, look back to NEWARK two decades earlier. Likewise, the

prominent broaches are an immature feature that would soon be consigned to history. The ambiguous masses of masonry that join pinnacles to spire have two clear precedents: GRANTHAM and Oakham (Rutland). At HECKINGTON they achieve the same purpose – to prop the corner of the pinnacle where it is cut by the parapet path (e) – but the effect is one of pure sculpture. The resulting masses may be unfamiliar and difficult to interpret but they impart a vigorous energy to the composition. Pinnacle caps are set high, and their pure, undecorated geometry complements the spire to perfection.

The spire itself is plain-edged, with alternating lucarnes carrying crosses on the first tier and finials above. It has been criticized for being too short and, indeed, the apex angle, of thirteen degrees, is hardly adventurous for the date. At close quarters this has the effect of accentuating the already considerable presence of the tower. Seen from a distance, however, with the base of the tower concealed, the pyramidal composition is superb.

NOTES

1   W. G. Watkins, 'The Church of St. Andrew Heckington', *Memorials of Old Lincolnshire* (1911), p. 114.
2   Revd Edward Trollope, 'Notes on Sleaford and Churches in its Vicinity, visited by the Society in 1863', *Reports and Papers of the Architectural and Archaeological Societies of the counties of Lincoln and Northampton*, vol. 7 (1863).
3   This parapet design also appears on Caythorpe tower.

20

Higham Ferrers

NORTHAMPTONSHIRE

Of all the steeples within this study, HIGHAM FERRERS would benefit most from a thorough archaeological investigation. The broad historical facts are not in doubt. The west-facing tower can be dated to around 1250 by the exceptionally fine carving within the porch. A recessed spire was added ninety years later, collapsed after three centuries, and was promptly rebuilt, along with much of the southern face of the tower. Establishing the precise sequence and extent of building, collapse and rebuilding is, however, extremely difficult without undertaking an exhaustive inspection of the fabric.

The earliest documentary source dates from 1791, when John Bridges recorded that 'Upwards of a hundred years ago, the spire and a considerable part of the tower fell down and were built again by benefactions, to which Archbishop Laud was a contributor.'[1] The Peterborough Diocesan Records confirm the support of Laud, who was Archbishop of Canterbury between 1633 and his execution in 1645.[2] Further embellishment is provided in volume II of John Britton's *Beauties of England and Wales*, published in 1810:

> The re-edification was begun in 1632, by subscription to which Archbishop Laud appears to have been a liberal contributor. In that year articles of agreement were drawn up between the Corporation and Richard Atkins, mason, of HIGHAM FERRERS, by which the later engaged, in consideration of receiving £135 to re-build

> the steeple, then raised as far as the bell stage: so that the said steeple should be from the ground to the battlements, seventy-one feet; and thence to the top of the spire, ninety-nine feet in height.[3]

According to the local historian H. K. Fry, the two engraved panels above the west-facing clock face, now worn smooth by the elements, once recorded that the steeple was 'begun to be builded' on 20 April 1631 and was completed in November of the following year.[4] Historical records do not reveal any unusual seismic or climatic activity in England during 1630 or 1631, so the reason for the collapse remains a mystery.

Nothing is known of the local mason, Richard Atkins. This is unfortunate, for he may have played an important role in a brief but significant resurgence of traditional steeple-building during the Eleven Years' Tyranny that preceded the outbreak of the Civil War. Immediately following the rebuilding at HIGHAM FERRERS there was a flurry of convincingly executed work in the medieval style. Prominent date stones link the steeples of Apethorpe (1633), Oundle (1634) and Nassington (1640) in Northamptonshire with Uffington (1639) just over the Lincolnshire border. Woodnewton (Northants) may also date from 1640, when Thomas Norris of Stamford installed the first bell, as he had done at Nassington and Uffington.[5] Post-medieval 'Gothic survival' is an under-researched area of English architecture, and it is entirely conceivable that other steeples of the 1630s are still waiting to be identified. There is no evidence to support local speculation that the royal military engineer and mathematician Thomas Rudd (c. 1583–1656), who is buried in the north aisle chapel, had any connection with the rebuilding of HIGHAM FERRERS steeple. During the early 1630s Rudd was preoccupied with the king's fortifications in Wales, and the extravagant epitaph that he penned for himself makes no reference to the work.

The tower is a powerful and mature work of the mid-thirteenth century. Rejecting the relentless articulation that prevailed just a few years earlier, the primary forms are confidently expressed in smooth planes of Northamptonshire limestone. The excessive articulation achieved through vertical shafting at ST MARY, STAMFORD and RAUNDS has been replaced by a more considered and expressive mode of composition. Ornamentation is concentrated on four bell chamber windows, a central roundel on the west elevation and the celebrated western portal. The relative proportions of the three stages are a satisfying 2:1:2, the upper and lower stages being pure cubes.

The declining popularity of the trefoiled arcade is evident from the modesty of the single tier that rises from the basement course. This is in a good state of preservation on the north, where the central bay is widened to accommodate a twin-light side window. Shaft rings and circular capitals are crisply moulded, a musician with recorder and drum fills the spandrel panel, and empty brackets indicate that sculpture once occupied the centre of every bay. Unfortunately, on the south elevation all but a few of the shaft bases were lost in the collapse, and insufficient evidence remains to indicate whether or not side illumination was originally provided from this direction.

Confusingly, there are two forms of basement course. The predominant form, which encompasses all of the north and west elevations, runs unbroken across the north-east staircase, suggesting that it is part of the nineteenth-century restoration. The profile is an anachronism, for it incorporates ogee and double-ogee curves that should not have appeared before the end of the thirteenth century. The second profile, which occurs only on the south elevation, is much simpler and most probably original. This is disrupted near to the centre of the elevation by a short protrusion, which has led to speculation that the ground plan was changed at an early stage. Professor Jean Bony developed an elaborate phased construction history for the tower on the basis of this protrusion, inconsistencies in the design of capitals and the history of the de Ferrers family.[6] Without a thorough archaeological survey the evidence is too weak to support a theory of such precision, and in any case inconsistent capitals are commonplace in steeples of this period.

The seventeenth-century collapse and the addition of a nineteenth-century staircase in the north-east corner have left only one original buttressed corner intact. The

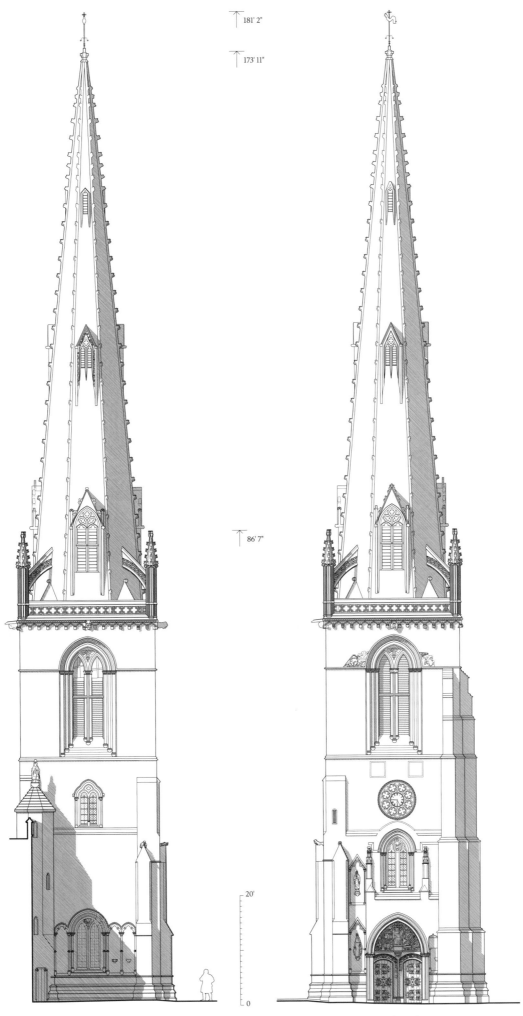

181' 2"

173' 11"

86' 7"

20'

0

North elevation

West elevation

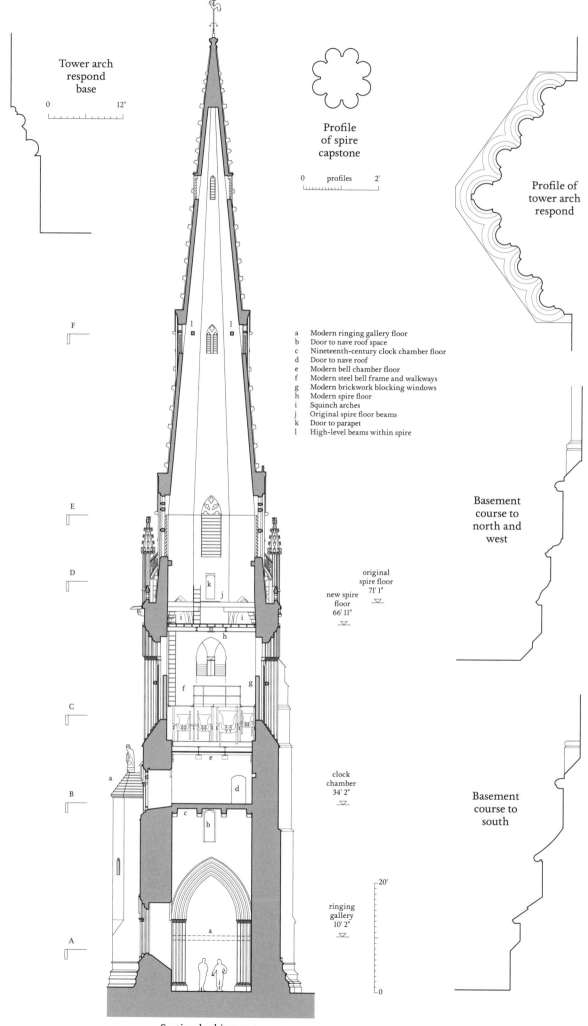

Tower arch
respond
base

0   12"

Profile
of spire
capstone

0   profiles   2'

a   Modern ringing gallery floor
b   Door to nave roof space
c   Nineteenth-century clock chamber floor
d   Door to nave roof
e   Modern bell chamber floor
f   Modern steel bell frame and walkways
g   Modern brickwork blocking windows
h   Modern spire floor
i   Squinch arches
j   Original spire floor beams
k   Door to parapet
l   High-level beams within spire

Profile of
tower arch
respond

Basement
course to
north and
west

original
spire floor
71' 1"

new spire
floor
66' 11"

clock
chamber
34' 2"

Basement
course to
south

20'

ringing
gallery
10' 2"

0

Section looking east

north-west corner is supported by an excellent mid-thirteenth-century setback buttress with chamfered corners, a strong, simple set-off and an emphatic gable termination inhabited by a grotesque. This exemplary design appears within the esteemed pages of Banister Fletcher to illustrate the model 'Early English' corner buttress.[7] There is one very peculiar idiosyncrasy here, for the west-facing buttress exhibits a pronounced clockwise twist on plan away from the face of the wall. Refinement of detail is not matched by physical presence, however, for the buttress pair fails to reach the first major string course.

The tower at HIGHAM FERRERS is famous for its spectacular western porch. Such is the quality and extent of the carving that several authorities have proposed that Henry III's masons from Westminster Abbey must have been responsible.[8] While stylistic similarities to the north transept porch (prior to restoration), roof bosses in the north aisle, and the Jesse Tree doorway in the abbey cloister (all from *c.* 1245–55) are strong, they are insufficient to prove a common authorship. A closer parallel to the ten roundel panels that fill the tympanum at HIGHAM FERRERS is a wall painting illustrating the miracles of St Nicholas at Romsey Abbey, which dates from around 1240.

The portal takes the form of a projecting central bay penetrated by a broad arch supported by shafted responds that project beyond the plane of the tower wall. There is no buttressing of the responds to counter the outward thrust of the arch, and this structural fragility imparts the design with a disconcerting tension. This has caused some historians to jump to the conclusion that the outer arch is not in its original location but has been reset, but there is nothing on plan or section to support such a notion.[9] Within the porch are twin doors beneath flat segmental arches separated by the motif of a rising Jesse Tree and flanked by two-bay arcades on the side walls. Leaf capitals predominate, and floral diaper work covers two soffit bays separated by a chamfered arch. To the north this pattern is disrupted by a musician sitting in the stocks. Carved figures populate the jambs and arches of the doorways.

The pièce de résistance is the broad tympanum that dominates the entrance. Even in 1791, when the first description of the carvings was published by Schnebbelie, there were vestiges of the original colour scheme. He provides a useful interpretation:

Over the doors in the West porch of this church are ten compartments, filled with very rude sculptures of the life of our Saviour ... There are still some tracings to show the figures had been painted, and most of the backgrounds were of a fine light blue; the centre had a much larger figure, as appears by the projecting pedestal.

1. [top panel on the left] represents the Angel appearing to the Virgin Mary, and the Salutation of the Virgin Mary and Elizabeth.

2. The Three Wise Men bringing their offerings.
3. The Angel appearing to St Elizabeth.
4. Christ among the Doctors.
5. The baptism of Christ in Jordan.
6. [to the right] The Angels appearing to the Shepherds.
7. The Crucifixion.
8. The Agony in the Garden.
9. The Angels appearing to the Women at the Sepulchre; about which are four sleeping soldiers, who were intended for its guard.
10. The decent of Christ into Hell.[10]

A sympathetic modern sculpture of the Virgin Mary now occupies the vacant central plinth. Further sculptures have been added in the two stacked niches to the left of the portal that follow the design of the side elevation arcading but with exaggerated gables. The portal volume continues up asymmetrically, for on the south, but not the north, it bridges across to the corner buttress with the help of a small ogee arch. The suspicion must be that this connection was added by seventeenth-century masons, although the tower at RAUNDS does offer a thirteenth-century precedent. Above is a pair of awkwardly set square pinnacles carrying heavy signs of alteration, followed by a restrained twin-light window with a seated figure of Christ in the spandrel. The detailing is simpler here, with ring capitals and plain chamfered arches.

Internally, there are few surprises and several disappointments, in particular the twentieth-century ringing gallery (a) and the partial blocking of the bell chamber openings with brickwork (g). The sole remnants of original floor structure can be found at the base of the spire (j). The chamfered tower arch, which is now impossible to appreciate in its entirety, rises from a respond of one filleted and six plain shafts. The upper tower is now only accessible through the external door to the north-east stair tower which probably dates from Slater's 1857 restoration. No doubt the empty chamber in the south-west corner of the tower represents the original position, for this was the preferred location in Northamptonshire.

Prior to the collapse of the spire the tower would have appeared more solid at the base, exaggerating the height and simplicity of the cubic bell stage with its four great windows. This effect has been compromised by the most prominent legacy of the rebuilding, the setback buttresses which rise as far as the uppermost string on the two southern corners. The resultant asymmetry on the primary west elevation would have been disastrous were it not for the magnificent bell chamber windows which continue to bind the composition together. Although not quite on the cathedral like scale of WEST WALTON these openings follow the same principle of two slender lancets beneath a single broad arch. Here the spandrel panel is not perforated but

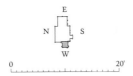

0   20'

Plan at F:
Middle
Lucarnes

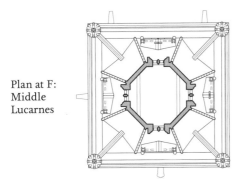

Plan at E:
Lower
Lucarnes

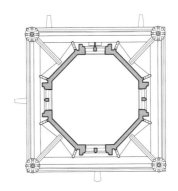

8' 8"
spire face

Plan at D:
spire base

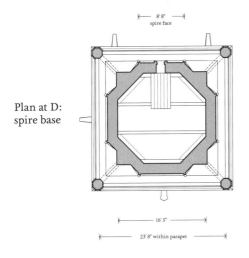

20' 11" spire base

16' 5"

23' 8" within parapet

Plan at C:
bell
chamber

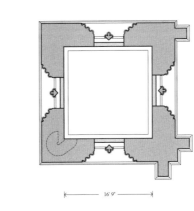

16' 9"

9' 10"
tower arch

Plan at B:
ringing
chamber

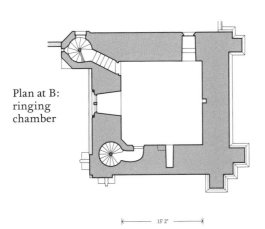

15' 2"

Plan at A:
ground
level

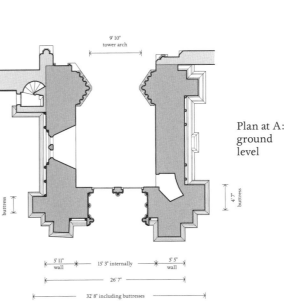

3' 0"
buttress

4' 7"
buttress

5' 11"
wall

15' 3" internally

5' 5"
wall

26' 7"

32' 8" including buttresses

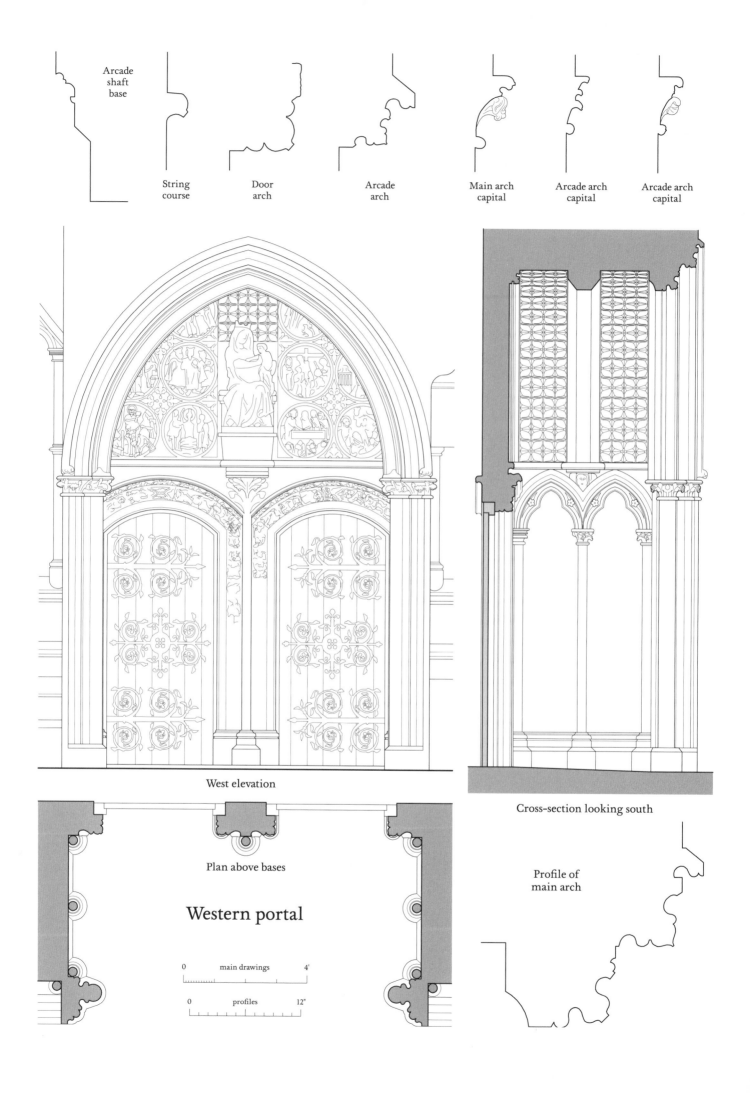

Arcade shaft base

String course

Door arch

Arcade arch

Main arch capital

Arcade arch capital

Arcade arch capital

West elevation

Cross-section looking south

Plan above bases

Profile of main arch

Western portal

0   main drawings   4'

0   profiles   12"

decorated by a flat carving of a tree motif repeated from the porch. The absence of dogtooth between the three orders of shaft is no loss, while the steeply inclined cill emphasizes the generous modelling of the primary opening. This is an important development that would lead to the characteristic deep-set openings of the early fourteenth century such as NEWARK.

The extent of reconstruction here is far from clear. Britton's account suggests that the bell stage was rebuilt, but if this is the case then the evidence, when viewed from the ground, is that much of the original masonry was reused. Finely carved leaf capitals appear on the more prominent south and west elevations, ring capitals elsewhere. Although transoms are not unknown in this period, the awkward intersection with the central mullion suggests that in this instance they are a later addition, probably from 1632. The effect on the noble proportions of the lancet openings is unfortunate. The arch hood-mould continues horizontally to embrace the four corners of the tower.

Either side of the arch on the western elevation are relocated remnants of carving, no doubt salvaged during the 1632 campaign of reconstruction. Most significant is the triangular panel to the left, presumably from a gable, with a seated Christ set within a vesica and flanked by a pair of angelic musicians. Smaller fragments of flat tree carving also appear, suggesting that this motif originally extended more widely across the composition. The splendid corbel table

that follows includes a mixture of original and modern carving united by trefoiled arches and a continuous run of dogtooth. This concludes the thirteenth-century work.

The spire is among the finest in Northamptonshire, and therefore in the whole of England. There are obvious similarities to Rushden, just two miles to the south, but HIGHAM FERRERS is of greater historical significance, for it provides a unique link between the style of the early and late fourteenth century. Two subtle details suggest a date of around 1340. Before this date the perforated parapet, formed of a continuous row of trefoils unbounded by circles, appears at ST MARY, OXFORD, ADDERBURY and Ashbourne (Derbys). The continuous quatrefoil form of perforated parapet appeared around 1338 as the nave of York Minster approached completion, and then on the tower at HIGHAM FERRERS. Where similar parapets appear in Northamptonshire after the Black Death – first at Rushden, then at Easton Maudit and WILBY – the quatrefoil motif is firmly enclosed within a circle. This encircled quatrefoil motif, used in a variety of locations, was to become one of the most familiar features of fine Perpendicular work in the county.

Closely associated with this development is the invention of the Northamptonshire form of flying buttress at HIGHAM FERRERS. It reappears later in six of the finest spires in the region, but there is one subtle difference here, for the quatrefoil perforations follow the curve of the bottom structural member rather than the straight rake of the coping stones. Springing from tall, vertically panelled corner pinnacles, they form an extremely satisfying visual connection between the square tower and the octagonal spire. Smooth roll edges, ornamented by thirty-one curvaceous crockets, provide a perfect silhouette.

Immature visible broaches, finished with curled nodules, conceal squinches that are both arched and corbelled. Three orthogonal tiers of lucarnes reduce in spacing and complexity as they rise. The first tier is noticeable for its Curvilinear tracery, not unlike the contemporary west window of EWERBY, and for its long, wave-like crockets. The transoms here are original, but inconsistencies in detail – for example in the presence of gable crosses to south and east – suggest a degree of restoration and alteration.

The mid-level lucarnes include a second detail that provides significant dating evidence, but only on the inconspicuous northern elevation. On this face alone the standard twin-light opening is richly ornamented by ballflowers linked by thick vegetative stems. The irregularity of the carving suggests that this is original medieval work. Ballflower decoration flourished during the reign of Edward II (1307–27) and appeared rarely after 1340. The implication of this small detail is that the lucarnes on the three more prominent elevations, and potentially on the other two tiers, may be a simplified seventeenth-century version of the original fourteenth-century design. Nevertheless, despite any doubts there may be as to the provenance of the fabric we see today, this remains one of the most original and beautiful of spires to be designed in medieval England.

NOTES

1 John Bridges, *The History and Antiquities of Northamptonshire*, vol, 2 (1791).
2 Northamptonshire Records Office, *Peterborough Diocese Records* Misc. Doc. X650, no. 1.
3 John Britton, *The Beauties of England and Wales*, vol. II (London, 1810), p. 183.
4 William Page (ed.), *The Victoria History of the County of Northampton*, vol. III (1930), pp. 263–79, n. 194.
5 Royal Commission on Historic Monuments, *An Inventory of Architectural Monuments in the County of Northampton*, vol. VI (1984), p. 168.
6 Jean Bony, 'Higham Ferrers Church: Report of the Summer Meeting of the Royal Archaeological Institute at Northampton in 1953', *Archaeological Journal*, vol. 110 (1953), pp. 190–92.
7 Sir Banister Fletcher, *A History of Architecture on the Comparative Method* (1961), p. 497.
8 Bony, 'Higham Ferrers Church', and G. M. Durant, *Landscape with Churches* (1965), p. 111.
9 Bony, 'Higham Ferrers Church'.
10 Jacob Schnebbelie, *An Account of Some Bass Reliefs at Higham Ferrers Church, Northamptonshire* (1791).

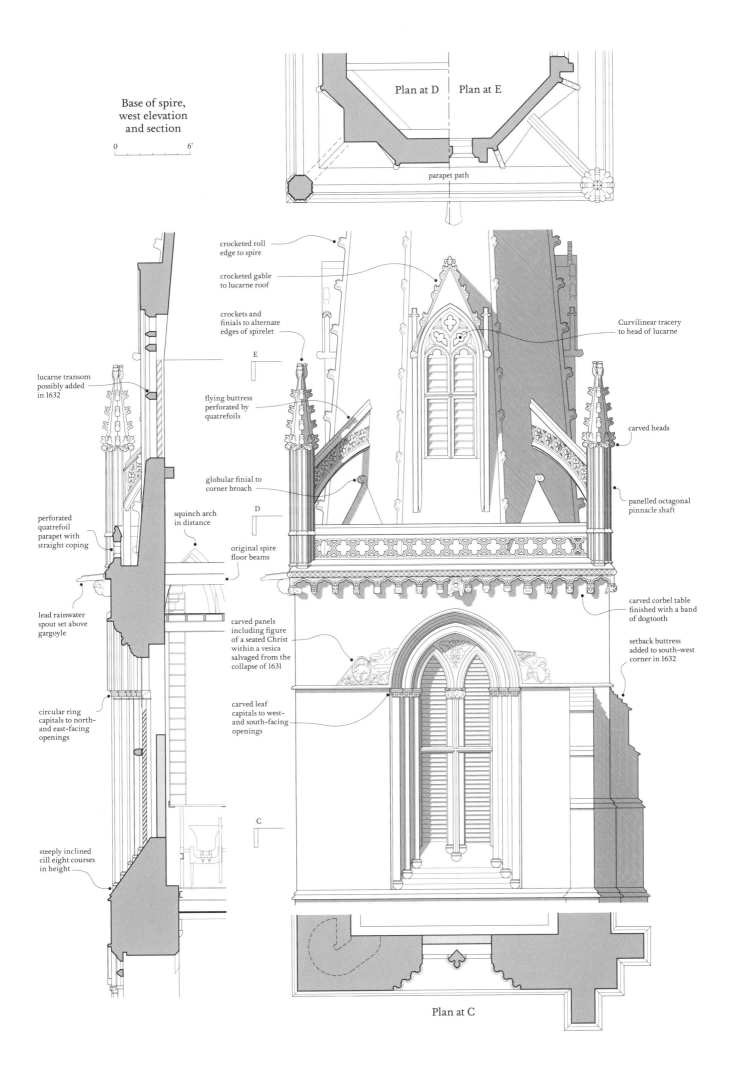

Base of spire,
west elevation
and section

0   6'

Plan at D   Plan at E

parapet path

crocketed roll
edge to spire

crocketed gable
to lucarne roof

crockets and
finials to alternate
edges of spirelet

E

lucarne transom
possibly added
in 1632

flying buttress
perforated by
quatrefoils

globular finial to
corner broach

D

squinch arch
in distance

perforated
quatrefoil
parapet with
straight coping

original spire
floor beams

lead rainwater
spout set above
gargoyle

carved panels
including figure
of a seated Christ
within a vesica
salvaged from the
collapse of 1631

circular ring
capitals to north-
and east-facing
openings

carved leaf
capitals to west-
and south-facing
openings

C

steeply inclined
cill eight courses
in height

Curvilinear tracery
to head of lucarne

carved heads

panelled octagonal
pinnacle shaft

carved corbel table
finished with a band
of dogtooth

setback buttress
added to south-west
corner in 1632

Plan at C

21

Patrington

YORKSHIRE, EAST RIDING

ATRINGTON is without doubt one of the finest half a dozen parish churches in England. This glorious 'Queen of Holderness' is crowned by a steeple that is beautiful and strange in equal measure.

The body of the church is entirely of the first half of the fourteenth century and follows the cruciform plan of an earlier building. Central towers had fallen out of favour since native sensibilities overcame Norman prejudice at the start of the Gothic age, but at PATRINGTON the form made a rare return. The retention of the original steep pitched roofs over all four limbs of the church creates the overwhelming sensation that this is a cathedral in miniature. The classic view from the south-east corner of the churchyard immediately brings to mind the masterpiece of concentrated soaring composition that is Salisbury Cathedral. When completed, PATRINGTON would not have appeared as remarkable as it now does, for centralized pyramidal compositions were commonplace before the widespread introduction of flat lead roofs in the late Middle Ages.

Late Geometrical tracery in the transepts, dating from around 1300, is followed by glorious Curvilinear patterns in the chancel and nave. Buttresses are deep and richly ornamented, and fine carving is in abundance. The base of the tower, at least up to the ridge of the main roofs, must have been built concurrently with the limbs of the church but followed the setting-out of a previous crossing. There is no evidence

to suggest that any earlier work was incorporated in the construction of the tower, as some authorities have suggested; indeed, close inspection reveals the structure to be remarkably consistent.[1] The constraints of the existing foundations resulted in a tower that is set out eighteen inches wider from north to south than it is from east to west. The effect on the tower arches is hard to discern, but above the crossing shallow arcades, supported off corbel heads, have been introduced to bring the north and south walls closer together to form a regular square plan (a).

In earlier cruciform plans the piers supporting the four corners of the tower invariably congest the centre of the church, but here they form the culmination of a beautifully integrated scheme in which both nave and transepts are surrounded by aisles. Even among great churches transepts with east and west aisles are a rarity. It may be no coincidence that three of the finest examples are also to be found in Yorkshire, at Beverley Minster, York Minster and Byland Abbey. The effect of the double aisles is to leave the four magnificent crossing piers exposed on every side.

Clustered filleted shafts are beautifully orchestrated around a rotated square core, and the undulating foliage capitals are among the best in the country. Bases are raised above the pavement on huge square plinths, the effect of which is sadly diminished by a flotilla of cast-iron radiators. Filleted rolls of varying sizes are the main

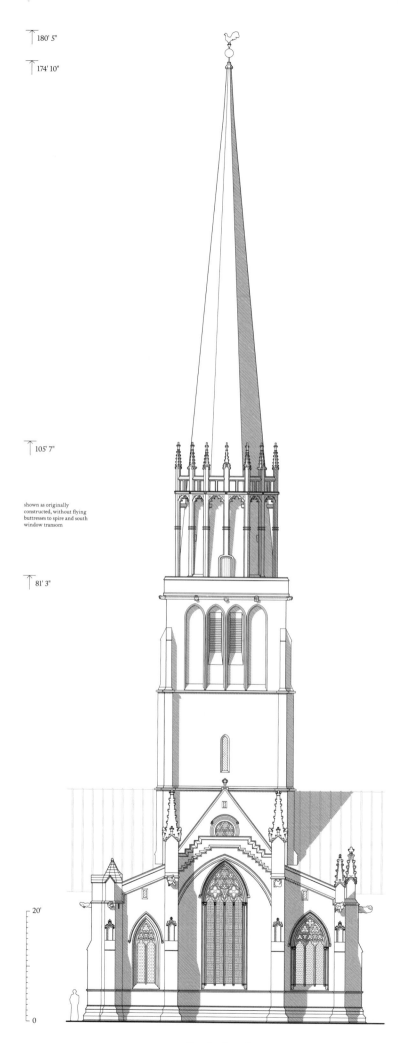

180' 5"

174' 10"

105' 7"

shown as originally
constructed, without flying
buttresses to spire and south
window transom

81' 3"

20'

0

South elevation

constituent of the near-equilateral tower arches. Considered in isolation the details of the crossing are exceptionally fine, but when experienced as a unified ensemble, with noble arcades and vaults radiating in every direction, the effect is spellbinding. Again, there is the feeling that this is a great cathedral reduced to intimate, human proportions. The creamy whiteness of the Magnesian limestone, brought down the Humber and its tributaries, looks even more gorgeous here than it does at TICKHILL or LAUGHTON-EN-LE-MORTHEN.

The aisles may be vaulted throughout, but the tower makes do with a timber soffit. This is a minor criticism, however, for there is much to enjoy in the corbel heads carrying the braces of the ringing chamber floor above. Limited illumination is provided by windows squeezed above the slope of the nave roof. The simple cubic volume of the ringing chamber and the empty sound chamber above form the full extent of the tower as it was originally completed at PATRINGTON, for the work concludes with redundant squinch arches topped by two courses of corbelling (b). What was intended by this is unclear, for if this was to be the base of a spire insufficient room would remain for the bells. In other parts of the church there is similar evidence of incomplete construction, and the suspicion is that this marks the arrival of the Black Death in 1348.

Unused squinches occupy three corners of the tower, for the north-east corner is taken by a spiral stair rising to the bells. This starts at some distance above the floor of the ringing chamber (c) to avoid disruption to the space below. This, however, is nothing compared with the bizarre contortions required to reach the ringing chamber from the floor of the church. The ringers at PATRINGTON require both agility and a good head for heights. The ropes are reached by scaling external stone steps running precariously up the north transept gable before squeezing through a tiny hatch onto a crawlway just two planks wide. This runs through the apex of the transept roof structure, providing a disturbing view of the stone pavement forty feet below and arriving at the ringing chamber through a roughly hewn hole (d). Thankfully, the even more precarious route up stone steps cantilevered over the south transept arch is no longer used.

The level of the ringing chamber relates uneasily to the plain external string courses, but there is nothing to suggest that the arrangement has been altered. Externally, plain chamfered lancets to south and east, and shallow angle buttresses are the only incidents on otherwise plain elevations.[2] Such austerity contrasts dramatically with the sumptuous decoration around the body of the church, but it is entirely consistent with contemporary towers such as EWERBY and BRANT BROUGHTON.

The historian John Harvey has convincingly argued that the spire at St Patrick's Church was constructed by the mason Robert de Patrington between 1368 and 1371.[3] Patrington, who was probably a native of the village, was a notable figure among the first generation of architects to embrace the new Perpendicular style of architecture. It is known that he lived in York from 1353, was appointed master mason at the Minster with responsibility for the presbytery on 5 January 1369, and continued there until 1385. Striking evidence for the theory is provided by the cinquefoiled arcade running along the clerestory at York, a highly idiosyncratic design with obvious precedent in the arcade around PATRINGTON spire.

The final phase of work at PATRINGTON must have included both the bell stage and the spire, for the blind four-bay arcade animating each elevation perfectly complements the open arcade around the spire, even to the extent that the bay widths are identical. Such four-bay arcades are rare on bell stages before the fifteenth century and there is no obvious precedent. The detailing appears almost proto-modern in its restraint, particularly in the mean, flat-headed bell openings. Pevsner mistook the arcade for Early English work. Similar examples of simply moulded openings without hood-mould, capital or base appear on the towers of WITNEY in the thirteenth century and Bloxham (Oxon) in the fourteenth century, but the profiles here are later. Buttresses terminate without ceremony, and even the sixteen gargoyles arrayed beneath the plain parapet appear uncommonly pensive.

PATRINGTON is in many ways a typical Yorkshire spire, for it is tall, plain and built of the best Magnesian limestone. While not achieving the startling imbalance of the famous spire of Hemingbrough, that at PATRINGTON is still rather taller than the tower on which it sits (a ratio of 7:6). The spire wall may be a conservative eight inches thick, but proportions are near-perfect, for this is one of the slenderest spires built before the fifteenth century. In the following century horizontal corbels would dominate squinch design, but here they are still used in combination with traditional arches (e). These squinches are constructed integrally with the parapet, indicating that bell stage, spire and arcade were built to a single design. Two levels of empty corbels may have supported temporary floors during the construction of the spire (f).

Cool restraint is followed by brittle excess. A delicate open arcade of sixteen bays encircles the arcade like a crown. From a distance the screen appears to float quite free, for the occasional through-stones that tie it to the spire are hardly discernible. Slender chamfered piers shoot straight up through the parapet to support tall, crocketed pinnacles, the culmination of the design. Cinquefoil archlets span between the shafts to carry the simplest of open Perpendicular parapets. This protects a precarious ledge reached only by a small hatch set high in the western face of the spire (h). A three-centred arched door leads from the spire floor to the south side of the tower parapet,

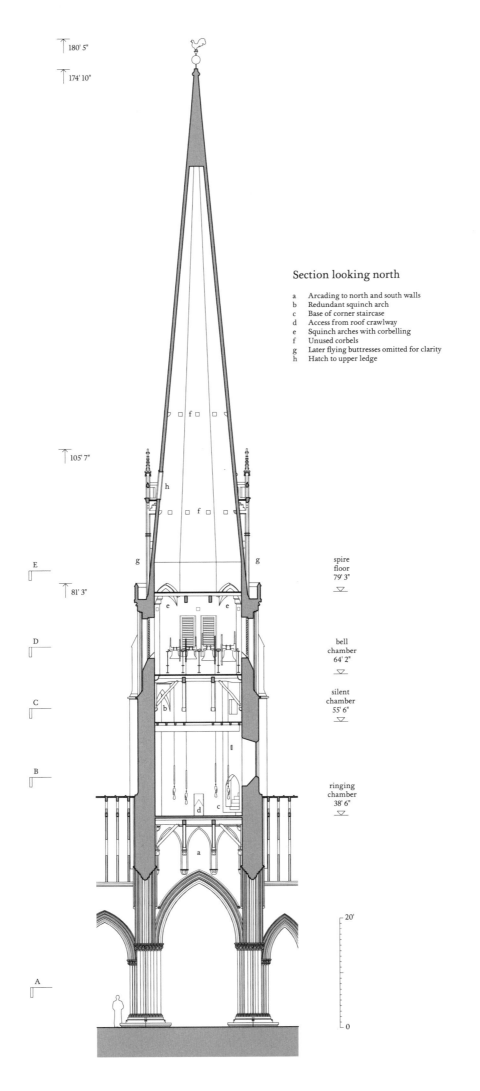

180' 5"

174' 10"

Section looking north

a   Arcading to north and south walls
b   Redundant squinch arch
c   Base of corner staircase
d   Access from roof crawlway
e   Squinch arches with corbelling
f   Unused corbels
g   Later flying buttresses omitted for clarity
h   Hatch to upper ledge

f

105' 7"

h

f

g   g

spire
floor
79' 3"

E

81' 3"

e   e

D

bell
chamber
64' 2"

silent
chamber
55' 6"

C

b

B

d   c

ringing
chamber
38' 6"

a

20'

A

0

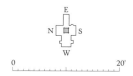

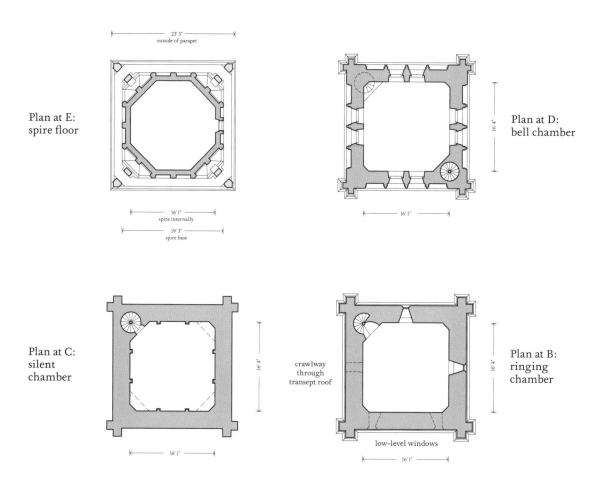

Plan at E:
spire floor

23' 5"
outside of parapet

16' 1"
spire internally

19' 3"
spire base

Plan at D:
bell chamber

16' 1"

16' 4"

Plan at C:
silent
chamber

16' 4"

16' 1"

crawlway
through
transept roof

Plan at B:
ringing
chamber

16' 4"

16' 1"

low-level windows

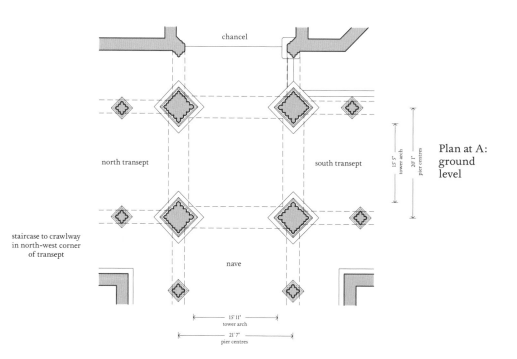

chancel

north transept

south transept

Plan at A:
ground
level

15' 5"
tower arch

20' 1"
pier centres

staircase to crawlway
in north-west corner
of transept

nave

15' 11"
tower arch

21' 7"
pier centres

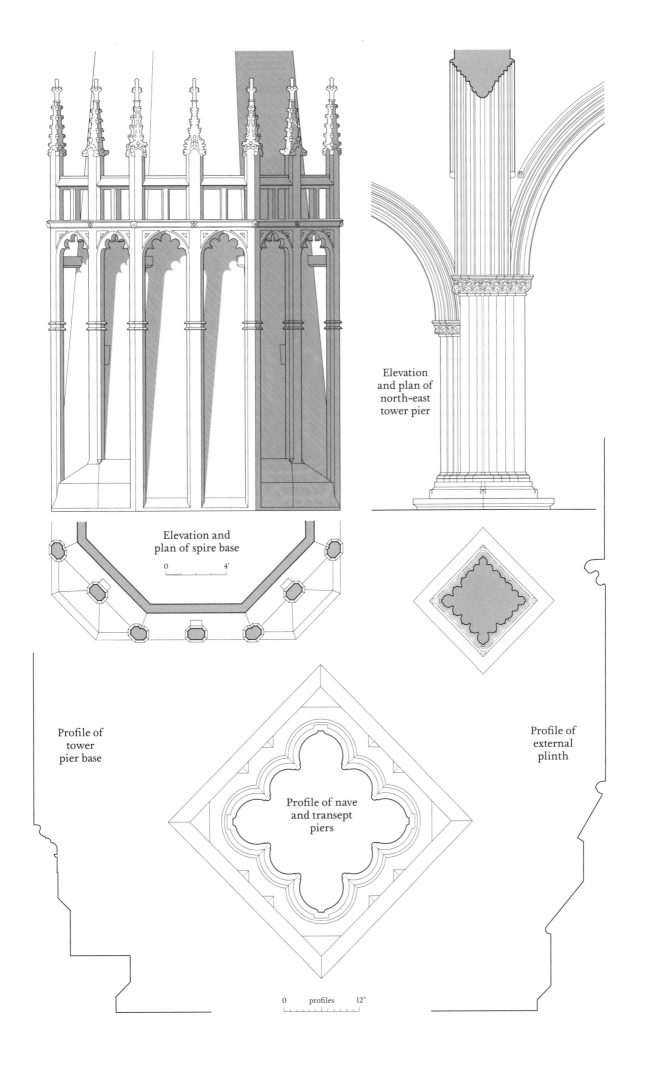

Elevation and
plan of spire base

0   4'

Elevation
and plan of
north-east
tower pier

Profile of
tower
pier base

Profile of nave
and transept
piers

Profile of
external
plinth

0   profiles   12"

with the unfortunate consequence that the central shaft of the arcade is severed at its base.

There is compelling evidence that this arcade was designed to appear in brilliant isolation, and that the prominent flying buttresses are a later and unfortunate addition. These buttresses are entirely separate from the contiguous construction of the parapet and the arcade. Where the mason would normally form a smooth intersection of flying buttress and pier in a single stone, there are crudely abutting members of dissimilar profile. It appears that the buttresses are a medieval afterthought to stiffen the fragile arcade after it started to fall away from the spire. Their design is exceptionally bad, for the parapet path slices the base in two, leaving the outer half staggering drunkenly towards the parapet. It is hard to believe that this could be the work of Robert de Patrington. The elevations are drawn without the flying buttresses and the clarity of the original design is immediately evident.

The splendidly inventive spire at PATRINGTON had no discernible impact on medieval steeple design. The spire of Swineshead (Lincs), with a sixteen-bay ogee-headed arcade of much heavier construction, is the only close relative, although there is some resonance with the miniature three-tier arcade around the spire of Methwold (Norfolk). In part, this lack of influence may have resulted from the dominance of the western tower, for the steeple at PATRINGTON gains much of its power from the centralized plan of which it forms the focus. Equally likely is that then, as now, this glorious church was simply too inaccessible to gain the recognition that it so richly deserved.

NOTES

1   In *Buildings of England: Yorkshire: York and East Riding*, 1st edn (1972), there is an interesting debate on this point. Pevsner originally considered elements of the tower, such as the arcade on the bell stage, to be Early English, but this idea is robustly contradicted by John Hutchinson.

2   The Statutory Listing incorrectly states that the lancets are on the east and west faces.

3   See John H. Harvey, *The Perpendicular Style: 1330–1485* (1978), p. 112, and *English Mediaeval Architects: A Biographical Dictionary Down to 1550*, 2nd edn (1984), p. 229.

22

Moulton

LINCOLNSHIRE

The Black Death slices through the course of English architecture like a hot knife through butter. The destruction wrought by the bubonic plague is hard to comprehend, for even the worst traumas of the modern age pale by comparison. In 1348 and 1349 around half the men, women and children of England perished in the 'Great Pestilence'.

In architecture little was built during the following quarter of a century, and when work resumed in earnest around 1380 it was on a much-reduced scale. The great cathedrals were by this time substantially complete, and owing to the building boom of the early part of the century there were more than enough churches for a vastly reduced congregation. It is commonly asserted that the rich, sculptural architecture and Curvilinear tracery of the first half of the fourteenth century mark the high watermark of English architecture, and that the more efficient and rational Perpendicular style that followed, with its crisp tracery, was debased or even degenerate. This is a false oversimplification, for in quality, quantity and ambition the steeples built in the two centuries following the Black Death surpass those of the previous two hundred years.

MOULTON, the 'Queen of the Fens', is the outstanding steeple of the late fourteenth century in Lincolnshire. It is a satisfying but rare instance of a tower and spire being carried out to a unified design and with an ample budget. The best steeples are invariably those that were designed from the apex of the spire downwards, and at MOULTON this is

demonstrably the case. The learned Victorian architect Edmund Sharpe, who studied the church in great detail, considered that:

> The tower and spire may be taken as the most perfect realization of the Rectilinear form of this noble addition to the English parish church to be found anywhere.[1]

The glory of All Saints' Church dates back to the twelfth century, when great monasteries competed to outdo each other in rebuilding churches within their jurisdiction across the sparsely populated Fens. Crowland Abbey set the standard with Whaplode. The priory of Spalding responded at MOULTON, just one mile to the west, and Castle Acre Priory joined the fray at LONG SUTTON. Crowland followed with Gedney, and – not to be outdone – Spalding concluded with Weston and Pinchbeck. This rivalry was to continue until the dissolution of the monasteries. In the Middle Ages the Fens were damp and inhospitable. Church funds were raised by selling off agricultural land reclaimed from the marsh, but the parishioners were also expected to make significant contributions. The relationship between the priory and the locals could be strained, and several ugly disputes are recorded with the head tenants of Moulton, the Multon family.

The nave of MOULTON church dates from the first competitive rush of church-building, about 1175. The south aisle followed in 1310 and the north aisle a few years later. There is some dispute as to whether the church had a tower at this time. The piers of the western bay of the nave carry tall engaged shafts suggestive of a tower arch on their inner faces and external buttresses on their outer faces. Further evidence that a tower was in existence at this time is provided by church documents. In 1292 the Bishop of Lincoln ordered the men of MOULTON to repair their bell tower. This must have proved ineffective, for at some point the original western tower was either pulled down or fell of its own accord. In around 1380 work started on an ambitious replacement.

The west door of MOULTON directly addresses the picturesque triangular green at the centre of the village. The proportions of the four-centred door arch and the truncated profile of the basement course are disturbing, for the ground level throughout the church is now eighteen inches higher than originally intended. This drastic anomaly dates from William Smith's restoration of 1868 and was, no doubt, an attempt to combat damp rising from the reclaimed marshland.[2] This submerged base is the only blight on an otherwise faultless composition.

The design of the angle buttresses is extraordinary and unique, for they are constructed with a significant and deliberate concave entasis. So unexpected is this device that it has gone unnoticed in all of the existing guidebooks. The buttresses lean in towards each other to the extent that they are two feet closer together at the parapet than they are at the base. A similar device

had been used in the tower at Market Harborough (Leics) half a century earlier, but with straight battered lines. At MOULTON subtle curves are employed, and the effect is far more sophisticated. The tilt is most pronounced at the base and gradually diminishes with height. Edmund Sharpe noticed an irregularity when he visited in 1870 but put this down to corrected settlement caused by poor ground conditions. Such corrected settlement does appear occasionally in medieval structures, most dramatically at the Temple Church in Bristol, but subsidence would not cause the elevation to symmetrically reduce in width. This is an expertly executed design that significantly increases the apparent height of the steeple. One peculiar optical effect can be seen in the re-entrant corner between the buttresses, for the vertical edges appear to diverge as they rise, confounding the normal expectation of perspective.

The detailing of the buttresses is conventional, with crocketed gables dividing the height into unequal thirds, each subdivided by plain set-offs. Below the lowest gable are tall, empty niches. The strings that divide the body of the tower into four stages are entirely independent of the buttresses, and consequently the elevation gains considerable vertical emphasis.

The early Perpendicular tracery of the west window is well proportioned, with four lights and a central mullion diverging to form a 'Y' carrying a castellated supertransom. Semicircular quatrefoiled

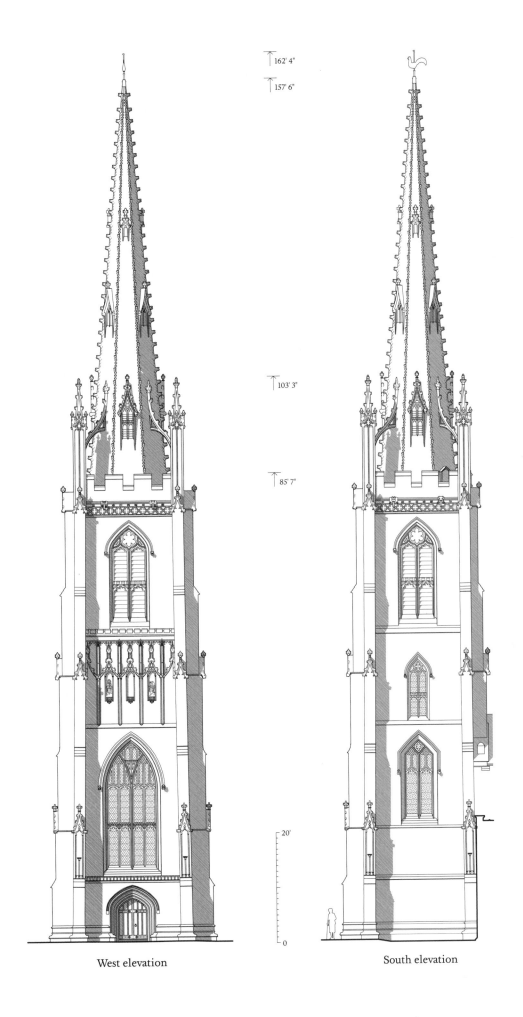

162' 4"

157' 6"

103' 3"

85' 7"

20'

0

West elevation

South elevation

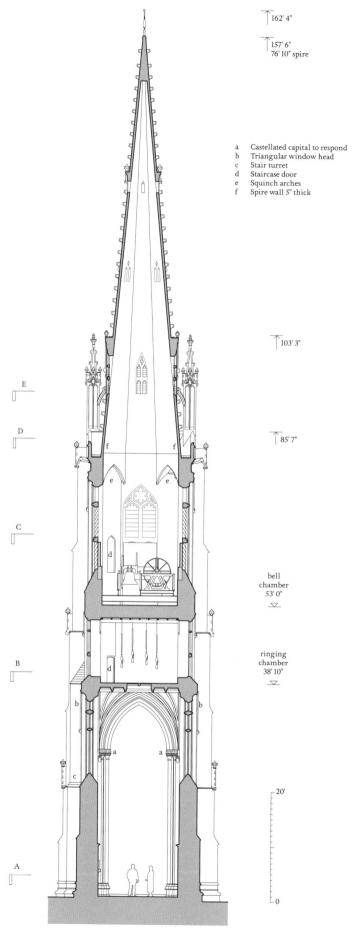

162' 4"

157' 6"
76' 10" spire

a Castellated capital to respond
b Triangular window head
c Stair turret
d Staircase door
e Squinch arches
f Spire wall 5" thick

103' 3"

E

D 85' 7"

f f

e e

C

d

bell
chamber
53' 0"

ringing
chamber
38' 10"

B

d

b b

a a

c

20'

A

0

Section looking east

archlets support a mid-height transom with delicate brattishing, while ogee archlets carry supermullions in the head. The design of the minor arches, the profile of the tracery and the deep casement to the jambs repeat in the upper windows of the tower, confirming that they all form part of one continuous campaign of work.

Some authorities have suggested that the west window and tower vault are later alterations but this is not the case.[3] The authenticity of the west window is confirmed by the unusual position of the stair shaft, which projects from the north-east corner, in contravention of standard Lincolnshire practice. Such a fundamental change would not have been contemplated unless the vault and the broad west window were intended from the first.

The arch of the west window is closely allied to the form of the steeply pointed tower vault within. This painted tierceron vault, with circular bell hatch, is not in itself unusual, but it is transformed by the glorious daylight that floods in from three sides. The important and highly successful innovation of introducing large-scale glazing to both side elevations of the tower appears first at Clifton Campville (Staffs) in the first half of the fourteenth century. The idea resurfaces in the Fens towards the end of the century, at MOULTON, Holbeach and WHITTLESEY, and then on a spectacular scale at the great towers of LOUTH and BOSTON.

The north and south windows are narrow, and the cills are raised. Their triangular heads result from the line of the vault with which they are contiguous (b) and are not, as has sometimes been suggested, the sign of a late date. The eastern tower arch forms the fourth edge of the vault. The profiles of the arch and the responds are much broader and flatter than in earlier towers, and the capitals are delicately castellated (a).

The third stage of the west face carries an ornamental canopied blind arcade decorated with crockets, finials and grotesques. Carving is by no means inferior to the classic work of the Sleaford masons fifty years earlier. The canopies form a continuation of the buttresses gables, providing the only continuity between elevations and buttresses on the entire height of the tower. To the north and south the arcade is replaced by ringing chamber windows, a reduced version of the bell chamber design. The north-east staircase moves inboard immediately as it passes the vault, so that the projecting turret has little external impact (c).

At the fourth stage one of the principal developments in tower design after the Black Death is immediately apparent, for the windows have become significantly shallower. The deep, richly ornamented reveals that contributed so much to the sculptural power of EWERBY, HECKINGTON and BRANT BROUGHTON are gone. In their place is one single shallow casement. Underlying the move from the Curvilinear to the Perpendicular style of window design was the pursuit of efficiency, for in the aftermath of the plague masons were no longer plentiful and cheap. The large bell chamber openings follow the standard Lincolnshire pattern of two lights alternating at the head to leave a symmetrical central figure, but the details have been transformed by the introduction of straight and efficient tracery bars. The most fundamental change, however, is the thinning of the upper tower wall.

A comparison between MOULTON and the similarly sized tower at EWEBY from fifty year earlier is illuminating. Both rise from walls 4' 2" thick at the base, so that two-thirds of the plan area of the tower is occupied by solid masonry. At EWERBY the thick wall rises to the full height of the tower, but at MOULTON the masonry steps back with every string course until it is only 2' 10" thick below the parapet. This reduces the volume of stone required for the construction of the tower by over one-third, and two other important consequences follow. First, the tower visibly tapers as it rises, and second, the upper windows become much flatter than before. If towers of the Curvilinear age appear as sculpture hewn from a solid mass of stone, it is because, essentially, that is what they are. In more straightened circumstances such extravagance was no longer affordable.

Another manifestation of increasing efficiency is the move to prefabrication. The tower is concluded with a band of quatrefoils set in a diagonal lattice. Fifty years earlier these would have been carved in situ, but now they were prefabricated in

the mason's yard. This band is immediately followed by a coved cornice of stylized flowers, animal heads and gargoyles. The battlement is bold and plain-sided. Square pinnacle shafts shoot up from the buttresses, and panelling makes an early appearance. The gabled, finialled and crocketed pinnacle caps are splendidly twiddly.

Reflected plan
of vault

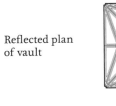

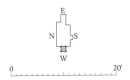

Plan at E:
spire

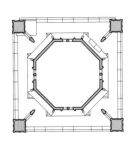

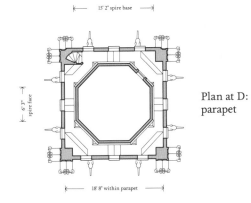

Plan at D:
parapet

15' 2" spire base

6' 3" spire face

18' 8" within parapet

Plan at C:
bell
chamber

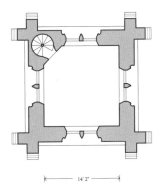

14' 2"

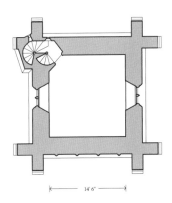

Plan at B:
ringing
chamber

14' 6"

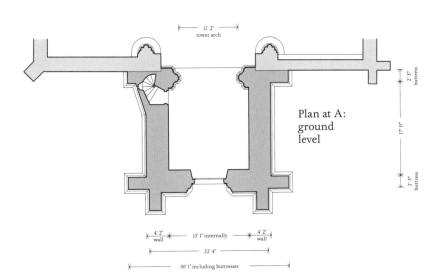

Plan at A:
ground
level

11' 2"
tower arch

2' 3"
buttress

17' 0"

2' 3"
buttress

4' 2"
wall

15' 1" internally

4' 2"
wall

22' 4"

30' 1" including buttresses

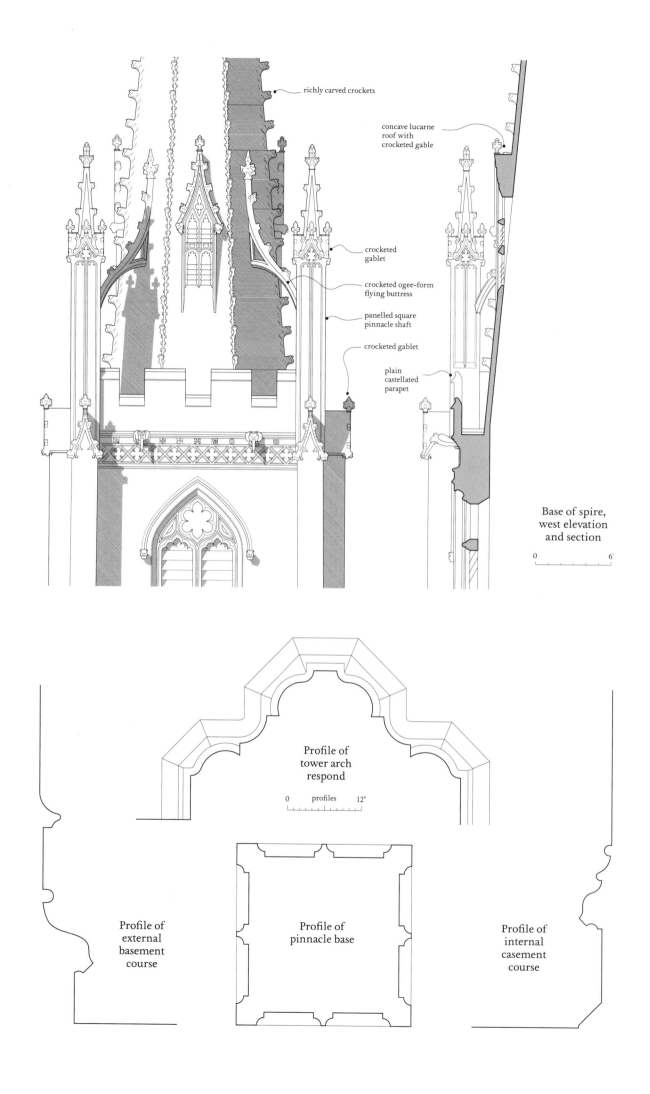

richly carved crockets

concave lucarne
roof with
crocketed gable

crocketed
gablet

crocketed ogee-form
flying buttress

panelled square
pinnacle shaft

crocketed gablet

plain
castellated
parapet

Base of spire,
west elevation
and section

0   6'

Profile of
tower arch
respond

0   profiles   12"

Profile of
external
basement
course

Profile of
pinnacle base

Profile of
internal
casement
course

The spire is a riot of decoration, with 256 crockets trailing rippling tails of vegetation behind them as they dance up the edges of the spire. The crockets are set closer together and their size diminishes as they climb to increase the perspective effect of the soaring spire.[4] Spire walls were also becoming far more efficient in this period, and at MOULTON the shell is a mere five inches thick at the base (f). Delicate crocketed flying buttresses twist one way and then the other, as if to shrug off any semblance of usefulness, and three tiers of alternating, miniature lucarnes are embellished by concave gables. The only criticism that can be raised against the brilliant spire of All Saints' Church is that it is slightly too small for the tower on which it sits.[5]

The crocketed spire had first made an appearance at GRANTHAM but, surprisingly, the idea received little enthusiasm during the following half a century, when English carving was at its most exuberant. However, from the late fourteenth century the idea was embraced with considerable relish. The closely related spires of MOULTON, Spalding and Gosberton (Lincs) represent an initial burst of delirious enthusiasm for full-bodied sculptural crockets that would, a century later, provide direct inspiration for the great spire of LOUTH.

NOTES

1   Edmund Sharpe, quoted in W. E. Foster, 'Notes on the Fabric of All Saints' Church, Moulton', *Reports and Papers read at the Meeting of the Architectural Societies of the Counties of Lincoln and Nottingham ... during the year 1889* (1890), p. 246.
2   Ibid., p. 244.
3   The Statutory Listing states that the tower is mid-fourteenth century with fifteenth-century windows. This confusion stems from the triangular heads of the north and south windows, which result from the proximity of the tower vault; they are not a sign of a late date.
4   Sharpe, p. 247.
5   At 4:5, the ratio of spire to tower falls short of the commonly quoted ideal proportion of 1:1 for a recessed spire.

23

St Cuthbert, Wells

SOMERSET

rchitecturally, ST CUTHBERT, WELLS may be the single most important parish tower in England. It is a revolutionary design of the highest artistic merit that consigned the spire to history and was directly responsible for the pre-eminence of Somerset during the final century of medieval steeple-building. Across the county in around 1400 there was a sudden rejection of the ubiquitous church spire. The spire of Shepton Mallet was abandoned after just eight feet, while at Banwell and Cheddar construction ceased at the squinches. Important though these West Mendip towers are in illustrating a shift in taste, their designs would have suffered no ill effects had spires been added as originally anticipated. It was at WELLS, on the south-west tower of the cathedral and at St Cuthbert's Church, that a fundamental re-examination of the nature of the steeple took place.

ST CUTHBERT's is a work of extraordinary imagination and enormous self-confidence. There is no more vivid illustration of this than the deeply serrated plan of the upper tower (Plan at C). Traditional four-square tower walls are nowhere to be seen, for they have been etched away to reveal a highly articulated pattern combining abstract beauty with irrefutable structural logic. Over three-quarters of the masonry is concentrated in the four corner buttresses, and the connecting wall surface is dissolved into little more than a stiffened membrane. Considered in isolation this plan is impressive, but when extruded vertically for

forty-five feet without a break the impact is extraordinary. Unity of effect and structural efficiency are pursued without compromise, and every line is animated by the youthful Perpendicular spirit. That this is the work of a supremely confident master mason experienced in operating on the largest scale is immediately apparent. Stylistic evidence suggests this is the work of William Wynford, one of England's greatest architects.

Wynford, along with his colleagues the master mason Henry Yeveley and carpenter Hugh Herland, dominated the emergent Perpendicular architecture of the late fourteenth century. His first documented appearance is at Windsor Castle in 1360. His reputation derives from three seminal projects: New College, Oxford (1380–1400), and Winchester College (1387–94), both for William of Wykeham, and his greatest masterpiece, the rebuilding of the nave of Winchester Cathedral (1394–1405). His connection with Wells commenced in February 1365 with his appointment as master of the cathedral, for an annual fee of £2, and lasted until his death on 26 July 1405.

At some point during the decade starting in 1385 Wynford completed the south-west Harewell tower at the cathedral over a pre-existing west front that stretches 147 feet in width. His audacious solution to a near-impossible aesthetic conundrum is not an unqualified success. The magnificent early thirteenth-century west front, celebrated for its unrivalled collection of original sculpture, probably represents only the lower

154' 10"

150' 6"

123' 5"

20'

0

West elevation

South elevation
illustrated with louvres to the bell chamber

half of a much grander composition that was originally intended. This is certainly the implication of the six massive buttresses that project westwards. Wynford's design takes great pains to avoid competition with the sumptuous shafted decoration of the preceding work, but in the process he creates a shocking discontinuity between the new and the old. The main ingredients of his upper tower design are great bulk animated by extreme vertical attenuation. The basic forms of the preceding stage – setback buttresses connected on the diagonal – are continued as simple rising planes of masonry, but with every surface and every external corner articulated by rotated square shafts. The walls are gathered in by steeply rising cills, and the famous long-panel motif makes its first dramatic appearance, with pairs of twin-light openings running undivided through the full height of the upper tower. Just as this huge, surging mass breaks free of its buttresses to soar heavenwards, it stops abruptly with no more than a crenellated parapet to throw off the rain.

Considered in isolation, this is a 200-foot tower cut 50 feet short. Seen in context, however, this is not a tower at all but a visual full stop, holding down the corner of a broadly spreading composition. One can sense Wynford's frustration at working within such constraints and then his delight at the results. His tower for Winchester College, designed around 1387 but constructed only in 1395–96, was finished with a spire in the traditional way, but his

1396 design for New College Tower makes no such provision. John Harvey makes a persuasive argument, on the basis of stylistic evidence, that Wynford was responsible for three spireless Somerset towers between 1385 and the turn of the century: Shepton Mallet, Yeovil and ST CUTHBERT, WELLS.[1] These three towers are very diverse in character, but it is only at ST CUTHBERT's that the lessons learned from the cathedral tower are put directly into effect, and with outstanding results.

There is no documentary evidence to prove Wynford's connection with ST CUTHBERT's, and his involvement may have been limited to the initial design. Bequests suggest that the reconstruction of the church had started before 1401, with funding for the tower coming from Robert Palton before his death in 1400, and from his family at some time between 1435 and 1450. John Harvey has suggested that the master mason responsible for rebuilding the cathedral central tower in 1439–50 may have completed ST CUTHBERT's. If so, the original design was rigidly implemented, for the arcaded parapet at its summit is entirely consistent with Wynford's work on the body of the church, on the Harewell tower and at Yeovil.[2]

At 150' 6" ST CUTHBERT's tower closely matches the height of the cathedral's western towers, but in all other respects it is a considerable improvement.[3] The unity and the power of the design derive primarily from the composite buttresses. An undecorated square core, 5' 3" in width, rises 120 feet from base to parapet. It is divided only once, to acknowledge the joint between the two principal stages of the tower. Simple flat-sided setback buttresses project from the outer faces of this core. Three regular set-offs divide these projections into four unequal parts, taller near the ground and shorter at the top. This imparts visual energy into the zone immediately below the parapet, that erupts into a flurry of panelled buttress pinnacles each composed of a central rotated square surrounded by orthogonal squares on the corners.

At this point the inner clasping cores of the four corner buttress take over. Pinnacles shoot heavenward, dissolving into a wonderfully ambiguous motif that transforms from a recessed panel into a pair of square pinnacles framing a trefoiled gable. The motif, of four minor squares surrounding one major square, repeats in miniature the primary forms of the tower. Octagonal spirelets, crocketed and finialled, provide a satisfying conclusion. This form of pinnacle, albeit with a square termination, was to become a favourite of Somerset masons.[4]

A part-octagonal staircase turret projects from the north-west re-entrant corner, moving inboard as soon as the second stage is reached. This unusual asymmetrical arrangement, which appears in a modified form at Yeovil, is far from unsatisfactory, but it was subsequently rejected in favour of less conspicuous positions away from the principal west elevation.

From ST CUTHBERT's onwards the corner becomes the single most important distinguishing feature of every great Somerset tower. Had the walls between the buttresses at ST CUTHBERT's been finished in a more pedestrian fashion it would still deserve to be classified as a great tower; however, this is far from the case. A single string line crossing the buttress core marks the primary division of the composition into two stages. This line, and the two subdivisions of the lower half of the elevation, are positioned to suit the external proportions and are entirely independent of the internal organization.

The western portal, a six-light west window and five empty niches are neatly spaced across a wide expanse of smooth Doulting ashlar. Six-light west windows are unusual and, despite the simplicity of the trefoiled cusping compared with the ogees and quatrefoils of Shepton Mallet, it provides further evidence of a possible connection between the two towers. In both instances rising mullions divide the window into three equal portions and inverted cusping makes a rare early appearance. Two tiers of delicate shallow niches appear incidental against the soaring expanse of creamy-grey masonry.

The only interruption on the otherwise plain side elevations are pairs of two-centred twin lights illuminating the ringing chamber floor. Within the tower an unnecessary modern floor (a) and screen destroy any connection with the body of the church and rob visitors of the opportunity to enjoy the splendid star-pattern lierne vault decorated by forty gilded bosses (b).

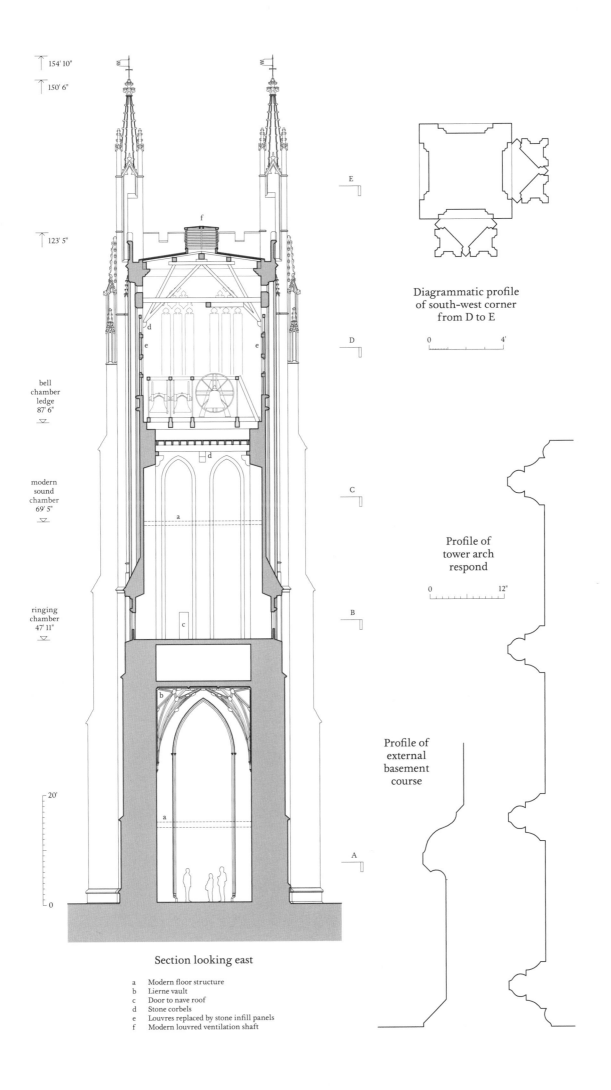

154' 10"

150' 6"

123' 5"

bell
chamber
ledge
87' 6"

modern
sound
chamber
69' 5"

ringing
chamber
47' 11"

20'

0

E

D

C

B

A

Section looking east

a   Modern floor structure
b   Lierne vault
c   Door to nave roof
d   Stone corbels
e   Louvres replaced by stone infill panels
f   Modern louvred ventilation shaft

Diagrammatic profile
of south-west corner
from D to E

0   4'

Profile of
tower arch
respond

0   12"

Profile of
external
basement
course

Reflected
plan of
tower vault

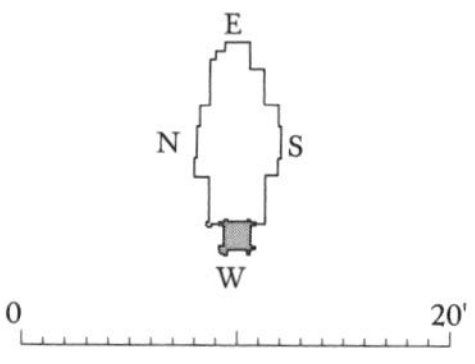

E
N ✦ S
W
0   20'

Plan at E:
roof

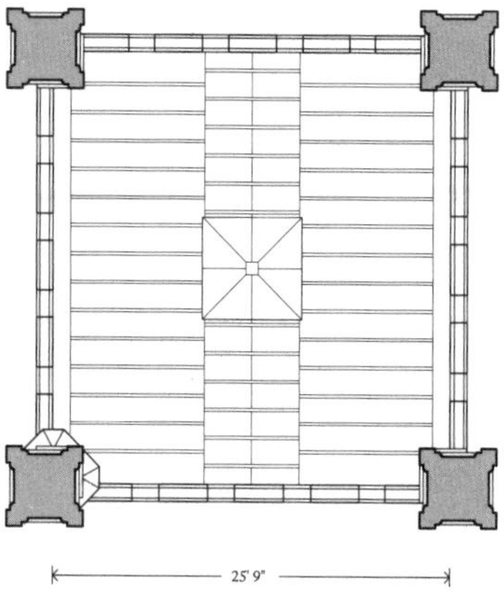

Plan at D:
bell
chamber

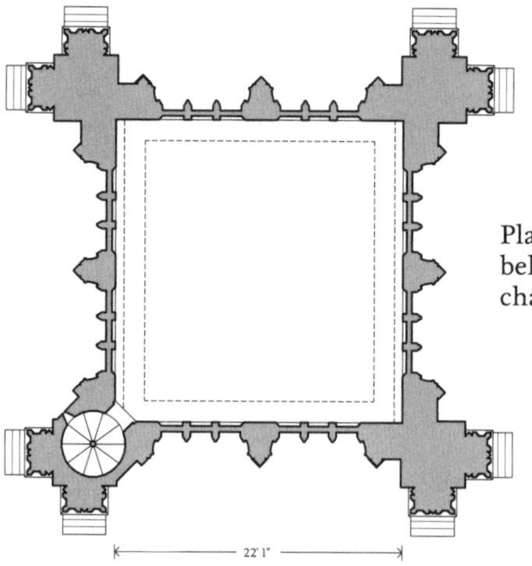

25' 9"

22' 1"

Plan at C:
sound
chamber

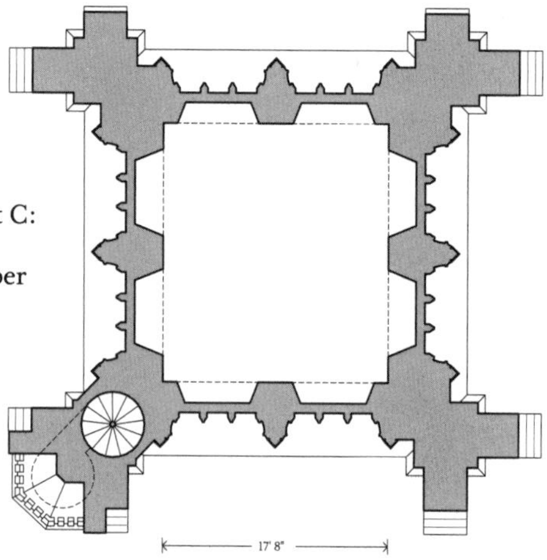

Plan at B:
ringing
chamber

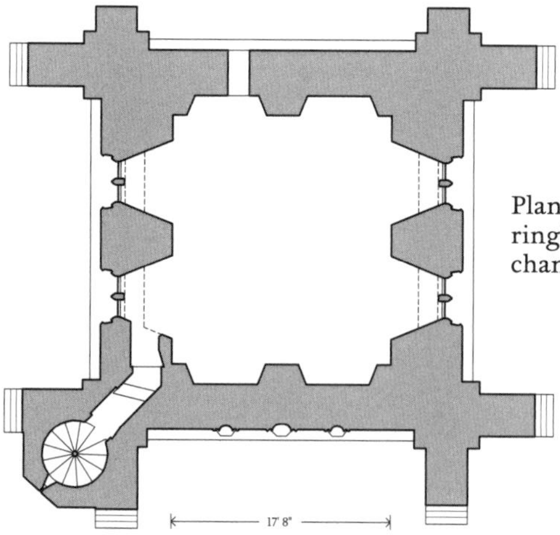

17' 8"

17' 8"

10' 6"
tower arch

Plan at A:
ground
level

3' 4"
buttress

6' 8"
wall

17' 9" internally

6' 8"
wall

31' 1"

43' 6" including buttresses

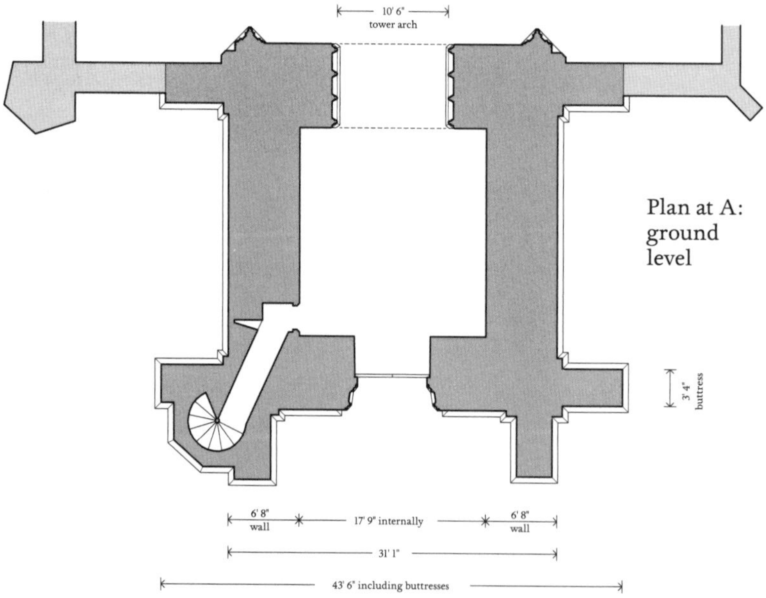

The panelled tower arch, articulated by four slender pear-shaped filleted rolls, rises thirty-six feet above the floor.

The attenuated square shaft set on the diagonal was to become one of the most widespread of Somerset tower motifs. Wynford did not invent the form, which previously appeared around the eastern end of Wells Cathedral, but he did grasp its potential. The motif dominates his cathedral tower, with thirty-two shafts rising the entire height of the upper tower. This is, perhaps, too much of a good thing, and the upper tower at ST CUTHBERT's is far more successful by restricting itself to three shafts on each of the elevations.

The long-panel openings framed by these shafts, with their high cills, trefoil cusping and reticulated head tracery, are directly derived from the cathedral. Except for spatulate cusps, the mouldings are of the utmost simplicity. There are two significant improvements on the cathedral design, for the openings are of three bays rather than two, and the transoms incorporate a quatrefoil band. The only disappointment is that the louvres at ST CUTHBERT's, still visible in Wickes's engraving of 1853, have been replaced by solid, flat slabs of masonry.[5] It is to be hoped that this extremely obvious defect will be rectified in time, as it has been on the south elevation drawing. Trefoiled arcading running along the crenellated parapet has already been noted as evidence of Wynford's involvement. Below this, the cornice is populated by fine array of characterful grotesques and human caricatures.

ST CUTHBERT's revolutionized tower design in the west of England, and yet it stands apart from the majority of work that followed. Few parishes could match the expense lavished on its cathedral-like construction, and most preferred to invest their money on richer surface decoration. Consequently the exquisite architectural purity of ST CUTHBERT's tower was never challenged, and a rather different, though no less beautiful, aesthetic quickly took hold.

NOTES

1   John Harvey, 'The Church Towers of Somerset', *Ancient Monuments Society's Transactions*, vol. 27 (1983), pp. 157–83, and *English Mediaeval Architects* (1984), pp. 352–56.
2   Harvey, 'Church Towers of Somerset', p. 171.
3   Pevsner's 1958 description in *Buildings of England: North Somerset and Bristol* includes several inaccuracies, using Brereton's parapet height of 122' 7" for the height of the entire tower, overlooking two of the niches, and describing diagonal buttresses where none exist.
4   A fifth pinnacle makes a brief, and lethal, appearance at the centre of the north elevation of ST CUTHBERT's tower in the 2007 film *Hot Fuzz*.
5   Charles Wickes, *Illustrations of the Spires and Towers of the Mediaeval Churches of England*, vol. II (1858–59), Plate 4. The solid slabs are present in Plate 1 of Frank J. Allen's *The Great Church Towers of England* (1932).

24

Tickhill

Yorkshire is a county of towers rather than spires, and although they tend to fall short of the superlative craftsmanship of Somerset or the inventiveness of Northamptonshire there is still much to savour. Apart from the three towers of York Minster and the twin towers of Beverley Minster, tall and noble structures are to be found at Great Driffield, Hedon, Holy Trinity, Hull, Howden and Cottingham in the East Riding and at TICKHILL in the West. The best work dates from the fifty years between 1390 and 1440, for beyond this date Hull and the upper stage of Howden suffer from the use of flat Tudor arches. Of all the towers in the East Riding, Hedon is the most satisfying, not only because of the sumptuously arcaded parapet, which carries no fewer than sixteen pinnacles, but also because of the fine proportions and excellent tracery.

The architectural historian Frank Allen identified a strong Somerset influence in the formative years of Yorkshire tower-building through Walter Skirlaw. This former Bishop of Bath and Wells, who had been intimately acquainted with the avant-garde work of the Somerset school, donated a chapel to his native village of Skirlaw in the East Riding in 1401.[1] The tower incorporates many recognizably West Country motifs, including tracery from the West Mendip Group, pinnacles standing on buttress set-offs, a niche to the plain middle stage, large gargoyles, and a crown of eight pinnacles above an openwork parapet. The influence of the Skirlaugh chapel is evident throughout

the upper stages of TICKHILL, which started in around 1390 and was completed around 1429. The earlier date is known from a bequest of 100 shillings left by Richard Raynerson, and the latter date from a bequest of John Sandford of 'a cart with hoss [horse] ... to the making of the stepell [tower]'.[2]

A typical Yorkshire tower has a fine crown above a dull base, and at TICKHILL this sharp distinction reaches comical proportions. For the first fifty-seven feet the tower is ponderous and predictable; from this level upwards it is transformed into the most beautiful parochial tower in Yorkshire. To explain this jarring anomaly it is necessary to return two centuries to the dawn of the Gothic age.

After the Norman Conquest TICKHILL became the site of a major fortification guarding the southern boundary of Yorkshire and the Great North Road. For a time, both castle and town were served by the existing Saxon church of All Hallows, but in around 1200 St Mary's Church was commenced on fresh ground conveniently close to the castle. The impressive scale of this first church is indicated by the remains of the chancel and the lower half of the west tower. TICKHILL is the first major example of an engaged west tower. Very broad pointed arches open the interior of the tower to the north and south aisles, providing dramatic vistas across the west end of the church and creating new routes for ritualistic procession. This idea may have been inspired by the late Norman church of Sherburn-in-Elmet, twenty-five miles to the north, and it was to provide the model for many of the greatest towers of the age, including NEWARK and GRANTHAM.

At TICKHILL the ambition of the early Gothic masons is shown in the extravagance of the detailing, for the three orders of the tower arch are each finished with keeled rolls and nailhead runs around the hood-mould, and the responds are a complex array of keeled and filleted shafts. The square abacus finishing the moulded capitals is a remnant of Norman Romanesque style rarely found after 1190. To north and south the moulded capitals are left plain, but to the east they are carved with naturalistic foliation (a).[3] Originally these would have been at a consistent level, but the eastern arch was substantially raised during the fifteenth-century rebuilding of the nave. Unfortunately, the respond bases are entirely submerged beneath a floor that has been lifted significantly above its original level. Below the tower are the remains of an incomplete tierceron vault (b) added in the fifteenth century and intended to conceal the upper stair shaft that can be seen projecting as a quadrant high up in the south-west corner. Above this, the floor structure of the ringing chamber is concealed by a wilfully patterned twentieth-century ceiling (c). The pantomime baldacchino above the font arrived in 1959.

Externally, the early tower tells a consistent story, but with rather less eloquence. The ground in the churchyard must have risen over the centuries, for the plain basement course is now submerged,

except in a shallow pit in front of the west door. Two colossal but unequal clasping buttresses dominate the west front, that to the south being swollen by the spiral stair. At this early date the integrated stone staircase was a relatively new innovation. The inexperience of the masons is shown both in the expansive width of the stair – at 6' 5" in diameter the largest in the survey – and by the great depth of the surrounding masonry. Even a few years later at NEWARK and RAUNDS a marked improvement in efficiency allowed the stair to be effectively concealed.

The corners of the buttresses are softened by filleted shafts nesting between hollow recesses, at least for the first three stages. The fourth stage shows a slackening enthusiasm, for it remains plain, while the smooth ashlar of the fifth stage reveals it to be part of the remodelling of two centuries later. String courses are plain except where the lowest is enriched with nailhead. One useful innovation is the external door to the stair, which allows ringers access to the tower when the church is locked. It is far from clear how the masons intended to complete these massive buttresses on the upper stages.

It is unfortunate that the base of the west portal has been lost beneath the ground, for this is a fine specimen enriched by lashings of dogtooth ornament. To either side are three detached shafts framed by a tight cluster of engaged shafts separated by running nailhead. Three outer orders of the arch are finished with keeled or filleted rolls. The horizontal string across the head

127' 6"

114' 4"

56' 10"

20'

0

West elevation

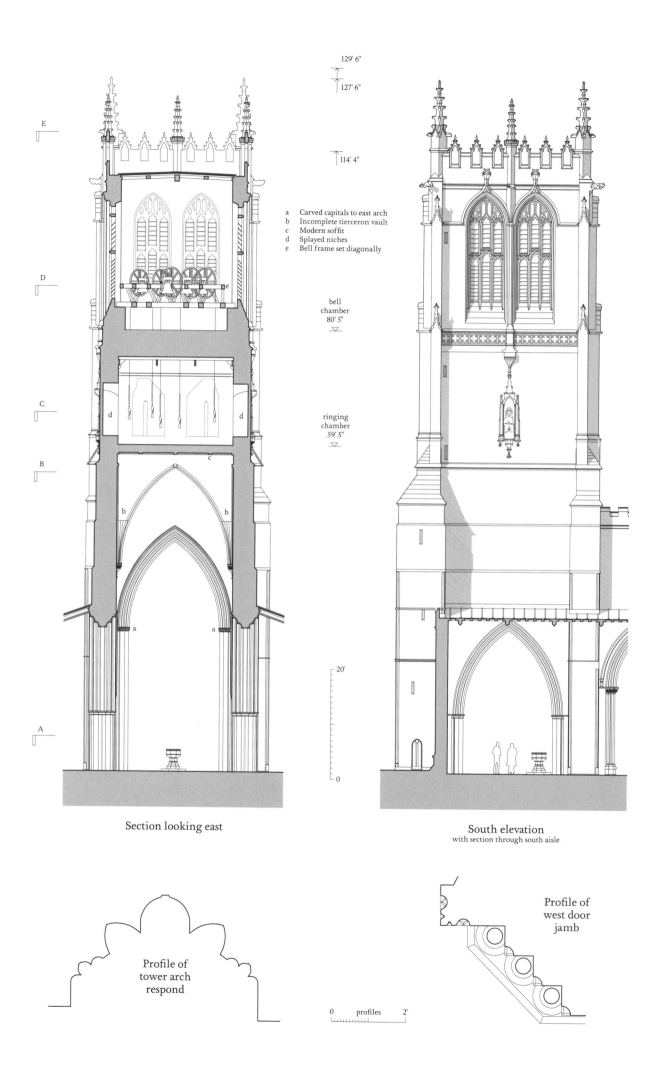

a   Carved capitals to east arch
b   Incomplete tierceron vault
c   Modern soffit
d   Splayed niches
e   Bell frame set diagonally

129' 6"
127' 6"
114' 4"

bell
chamber
80' 5"

ringing
chamber
59' 5"

20'

0

Section looking east

South elevation
with section through south aisle

Profile of
tower arch
respond

Profile of
west door
jamb

0   profiles   2'

of the arch marks the limit of the original elevation between the buttresses.

The great west window is a later insertion that can be dated with some accuracy by heraldic devices set around its perimeter. The arms of Leon and Castile represent John of Gaunt, who held Tickhill Castle between 1373 and 1399. Above the west door are the shields of William Eastfield, who died in 1386, and John Sandford, who is known to have resided in Tickhill in 1394. These dates confirm that the west window and the upper stages of the tower formed one continuous scheme of construction starting around 1390.

The excellent five-bay west window nobly attempts to rescue the ponderous design of the early tower, and it almost succeeds. This is a fine example of subarcuated intersecting tracery, in which minor arches rise from alternate lights and intersect in the centre. Sweeping ogee-headed septafoil archlets confirm this to be early Perpendicular work. The combination of falchions and supertransoms in the head is typical of eastern Yorkshire and derives from the work of Robert de Patrington at York Minster in the 1370s. Immediately above the hood-mould is an expanse of smooth ashlar that marks the effective start of the new upper tower.

Medieval masons frequently showed great ingenuity in sympathetically extending work of earlier styles, but here the difficulty posed by the vast asymmetric buttresses proved insurmountable. Eight steep courses of ungainly battering are required to squeeze the tower into a manageable shape. In the

seventy feet of masonry that follow, the masons of the West Riding seem determined to trump their eastern rivals at their own game. Skirlaugh, Preston-in-Holderness, Beeford, Holm-upon-Spalding-Moor and Great Driffield all have canopied niches on their western faces, but at TICKHILL there is one on every face. Skirlaugh, Beeford, Coxwold and Holm-upon-Spalding-Moor share the same novel form of open gabled parapet, but this is memorably transformed at TICKHILL. Finally, the diagonally set pinnacles, which work so well on the single-windowed towers of the East Riding, are even better when integrated with two windows at TICKHILL. In every respect this is a masterful performance.

Paired angle buttresses, typical of large Yorkshire towers, rise neatly from bases that sweep up the final remnants of the preceding confusion. Concave gablets form set-offs level with the bell chamber drip and with the spring of the bell openings. At parapet level large gargoyles mask the transition to the rotated square shafts of the corner pinnacles. The pronounced angularity of the crockets and the finials confirms that construction has by now extended into the fifteenth century.

The interior of the ringing chamber reveals that, far from being entirely new construction, this is old work refaced and remodelled. Deeply splayed niches (d), two to each wall, suggest that this was originally the bell stage of the early Gothic tower. As the tower was heightened and the bells were raised up a stage, the eight openings were reduced to two slender lancet windows on the inconspicuous east elevation. The smooth ashlar refacing of the four elevations provides the perfect setting for the sumptuously decorated niches. Miniature splayed and pinnacled buttresses frame these openings, and tent-like canopies stretch up to the decorated corbel blocks serving the stage above. Niches are reserved for religious subjects, with decayed medieval figures representing God the Father to the north, Christ in Majesty to the west, the Holy Spirit to the south, and Mary with the infant Jesus to the east. Sculptures of the principal donors – a knight and child to the left, his wife to the right – are left exposed on the face of the west wall. A broad string and a regular band of quatrefoils conclude the penultimate stage.

The paired three-light openings to the bells are among the most generous in the county. Tracery is less exuberant than in the west window, taking the form of conventional cinquefoil archlets throughout and a stepped and crenellated transom. The ogee hood-mould leads the eye smoothly up to the parapet. Ogee hood-moulds would become progressively more attenuated in the north-east of England, at York, Beverley, Bridlington, Hull and particularly Durham, but here the curve is more subtle. The single most successful feature of the upper tower is the centre pilaster, which continues the vertical line of the niches between the windows and through the parapet to a sharp, diagonally set pinnacle. Rotated centre pinnacles appear at Beeford and Holme-upon-Spalding-Moor, but they are less convincing when set centrally over single window openings.

Within the final stage of the tower the late Victorian bell frame is set diagonally for no apparent reason (e). Apart from the stiffening provided by the modern concrete bell chamber floor, the structure remains substantially unchanged. Thankfully there are no clock faces to detract from the superb silvery grey Roche Abbey stone, and no flagpole to compromise the silhouette. The parapet, which derives directly from Skirlaugh, consists of delicate crocketed gables over the dropped embrasures of a conventional battlement. This illogical but delightful conceit completes the most ethereal silhouette of any parish church in Yorkshire.

NOTES

1 See Frank J. Allen, *The Great Church Towers of England* (1932), p. 115.
2 Unattributed quotation in the church guidebook, Tom W. Beastall, *Portrait of an English Parish Church: St Mary's Parish Church, Tickhill.*
3 In *The Buildings of England: Yorkshire: The West Riding* (1959), Pevsner suggests that these foliate capitals are much later 'Perpendicular', but close inspection reveals that the mouldings are consistent with the plain capitals to the north and south arches.

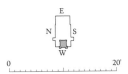

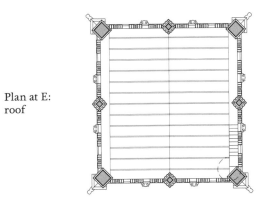

Plan at E:
roof

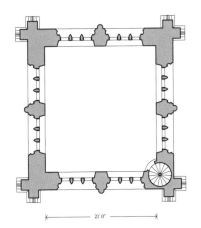

Plan at D:
bell chamber

21' 0"

Plan at C:
ringing
chamber

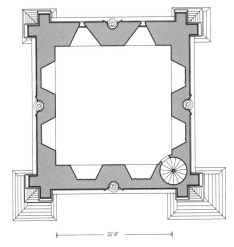

21' 8"

Plan at B:
base for
upper stages

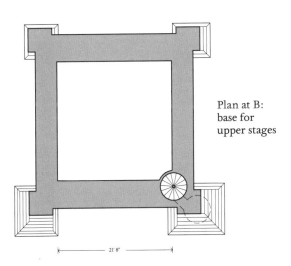

21' 8"

17' 2"
tower arch

16' 9"
tower arch

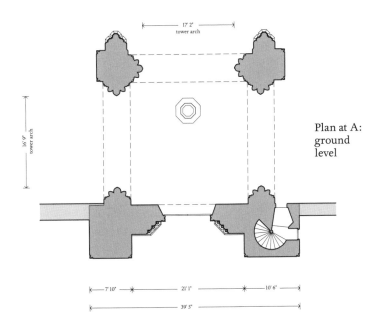

Plan at A:
ground
level

7' 10"   21' 1"   10' 6"

39' 5"

25

Laughton-en-le-Morthen

YORKSHIRE, WEST RIDING

One exceptional group of spires straddling the border between Yorkshire and Nottinghamshire forms such a compact nuclear family that it can only be the work of a single mason or lodge. All four spires share a unique form of octagonal parapet and all are built from creamy white Magnesian limestone. The senior members of the family are LAUGHTON-EN-LE-MORTHEN, tall and muscular, and West Retford (Notts), more delicate and composed. South Anston (Yorks West) is like the adolescent child, and Scrooby (Notts) is the infant, rising only a short distance from the ground. How and when the group evolved and why their innovative design was pursued no further are not documented.

Medieval crocketed spires are rare in Yorkshire, for apart from LAUGHTON-EN-LE-MORTHEN they appear only at Rotherham, Sheffield and Thrybergh.[1] All have small, well-spaced crockets set on a plain spire edge and all date from the early fifteenth century. The tall spire at Rotherham, under construction in 1409, provides the most obvious precedent for the arrangement of multiple pinnacles used at LAUGHTON. For the angular details of the crocketed pinnacle caps, one need look no further than the parapet at TICKHILL, under construction in 1429. In the absence of documentary evidence, it is reasonable to assume a date of around 1430 for the spire at LAUGHTON. The three other steeples in the group must be from the same period, but there is nothing to indicate the order in which they were built.

Like many of the surveyed churches, LAUGHTON-EN-LE-MORTHEN has Saxon roots, was rebuilt by the Normans and was rebuilt for a second time in the Gothic style. The Saxon period is well preserved in a doorway at the east end of the north aisle. Norman work from around 1190 is evident in the chancel and the cushion capitals of the north arcade. In 1322, during the siege of Tickhill Castle, the church was all but demolished by a detachment of Lancastrian soldiers. The rebuilding that commenced in 1377 is commonly associated with William of Wykeham, Bishop of Winchester, Lord Chancellor and the wealthiest self-made man in England. The evidence for this is that Wykeham had been appointed prebend of LAUGHTON-EN-LE-MORTHEN in York Minster in 1363; however, by this stage of his career his responsibilities were so enormous that any suggestion of a meaningful association with the work is pure speculation. Wykeham employed the master mason William Wynford for all his works after 1360, but there is no stylistic evidence to link Wynford's name with LAUGHTON.

There is little to be said about the lower two-thirds of the tower. This is part of the general rebuilding that commenced in 1377 and is of no greater interest than the vast majority of plain church towers in this part of the country. Its greatest asset is the creamy white Anston stone.[2] The three-bay west window follows that of the south aisle except that the four-centred arch is flattened to follow the profile of the

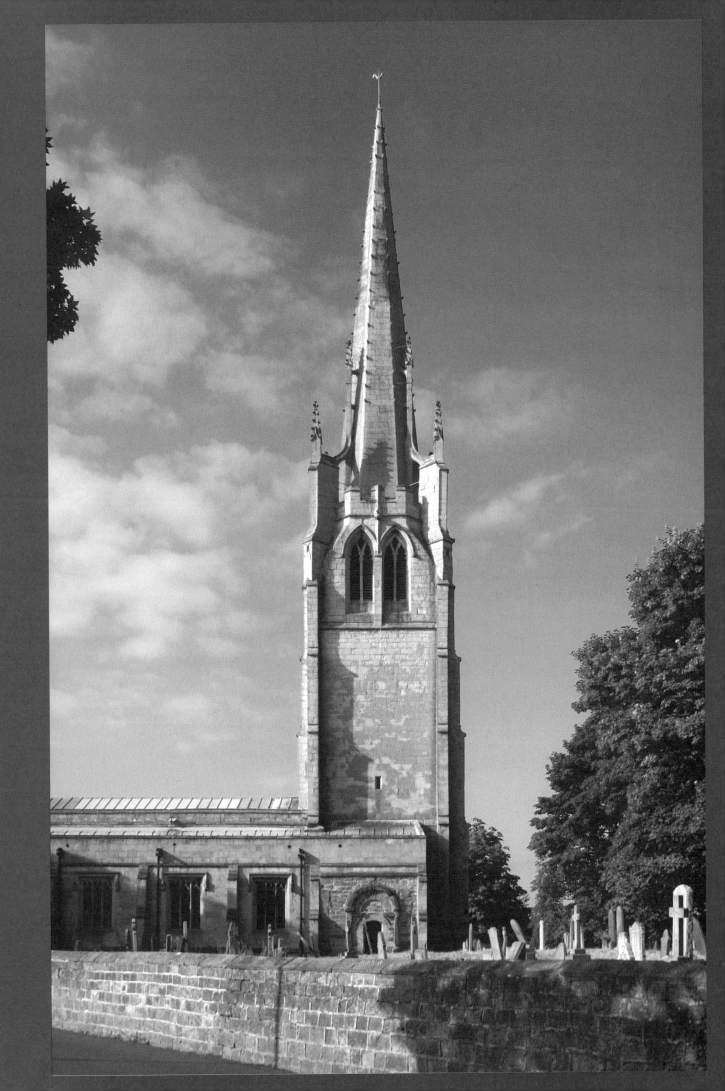

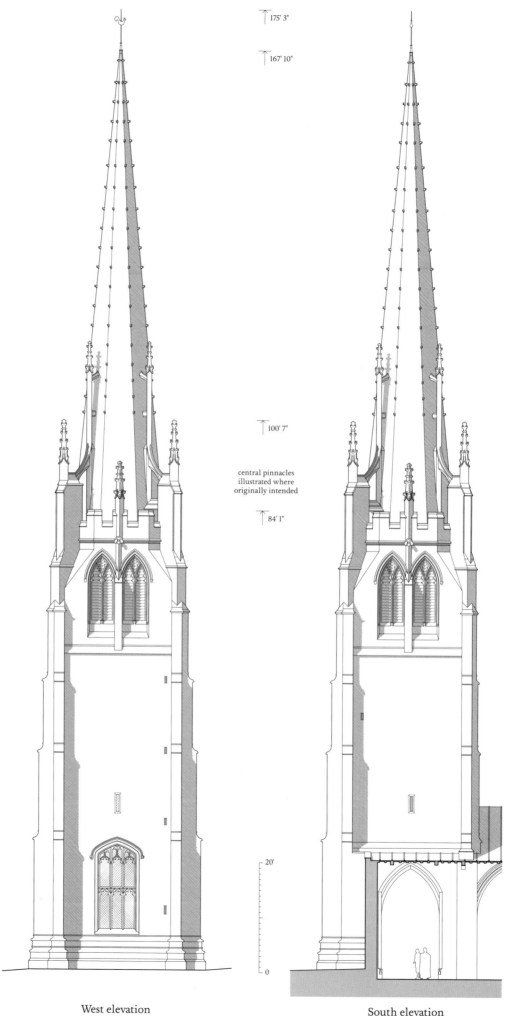

175' 3"

167' 10"

100' 7"

central pinnacles
illustrated where
originally intended

84' 1"

20'

0

West elevation

South elevation
with section through south aisle

vault within. The greatest refinement is in the ogee profile of the basement course, which repeats on each of the buttress set-offs. The flat-sided angle buttresses are of four reducing divisions, but the elevation remains undivided.

Within the tower the treatment is equally straightforward. The inner order of the double-chamfered tower arches dives rudely into the north and south responds (a) and towards the nave is supported by inconsequential brackets (b). Compared with MOULTON or WHITTLESEY, the tierceron vault is crudely detailed and uncomfortably low. The initial ambition was modified as the tower passed above the level of the aisle roof, for the walls visibly reduce to four feet in thickness (c).

Few tower interiors have escaped the heavy hand of restoration as well as LAUGHTON. The cavernous ringing chamber is formed of friable Rotherham red sandstone, the white Anston stone being revealed as a thin outer facing. The difference in durability is startlingly illustrated around the tiny slit windows just above the chamber floor (d). The chamfers of the outer skin are as crisp as the day they were carved, but penetrating wind and rain have eroded great channels through the soft sandstone interior. Apart from these openings, and the narrow slits to the south-west corner stair, the walls are entirely plain, as if the masons' sole intent was to reach the bell stage as fast and as efficiently as possible. Above the clock, which faces east towards the village (e),

the bell chamber floor beams span between continuous running corbels (f).

At this point an unknown mason of outstanding ability took control of the works. A solitary string course across the elevation marks the change from dull predictability to thrilling originality. The single greatest issue that preoccupied spire-builders throughout the Middle Ages was how to link a square tower to an octagonal pyramid. Many inventive and elegant methods of combining broaches, pinnacles, battlements and flying buttresses were explored, and several are illustrated within this volume. One particularly fruitful line of development, starting at BARNACK in the 1230s, was to introduce an octagonal drum between the tower and the spire, and this found its most satisfactory resolution at Bloxham (Oxon), ST MICHAEL, COVENTRY and WILBY. Despite the undoubted success of these rare experiments, a central drum introduces a complexity to the design that can deflect attention away from the spire itself. At LAUGHTON-EN-LE MORTHEN, and at its three close relatives, a fascinating alternative was proposed in which the octagonal form is reserved for the parapet.

At LAUGHTON the corners of the elevations splay back diagonally from just below the springing of the bell openings, so that a pure octagon is achieved immediately below the cornice. The close-set corbels that form the squinches within the tower (g) correspond very closely to the splayed corners on the elevations. The battlement that follows may be straightforward, but this is one design that succeeds entirely through the power of geometry. Angle buttresses are transformed into great diagonal buttresses no less than five feet deep. Their outer faces are set-off twice, transforming into square pinnacles rising fifteen feet above the parapet. Plain concave gables, angular finials and grooved crockets decorating the pinnacle caps are closely related to the fine Yorkshire towers of TICKHILL, Beeford and Holme-upon-Spalding-Moor. On the flat lower face of these buttresses is the sole evidence of modern repair: iron plates terminate diagonal timber and iron tie-bars that prevent the tower from spreading (h).

In an inspired choice, the great immovable buttresses, radiating out from the base of the spire, support the most delicate of flying buttresses, which flow smoothly into exceptionally attenuated pinnacle shafts racing up the diagonal faces of the spire. The spire is beautifully judged, for its austere Yorkshire beauty, in the manner of Hemingbrough and PATRINGTON, is the perfect foil to the geometrical gymnastics around its base. No doubt the masons of Lincolnshire or Northamptonshire would have been unable to finish the task without introducing tiers of decorative lucarnes, but here their absence is entirely appropriate. While the spire falls some way short of the 185 feet claimed by the guidebooks, the proportions are impeccable, for spire and tower are almost identical in height. The angle at the apex is a mere

eleven degrees, the perfect inclination for a slender recessed spire.

At West Retford and the two minor towers in the group, single openings are used to the bell stage, but the greater size of LAUGHTON allows for two twin-light openings. The cusped 'Y' tracery and descending soufflet in the head are elegant, if unexceptional. Of greater significance is the rotated centre pinnacle rising through the parapet, an excellent motif shared by just a handful of outstanding towers outside Somerset including TICKHILL, TITCHMARSH and Great Ponton (Lincs). Unfortunately, at LAUGHTON-EN-LE-MORTHEN the pinnacle shafts terminate abruptly at the parapet line, but the missing terminations have been added on the drawings, using the existing corner pinnacles as a model.

The prominence of the hilltop location is effectively masked by mature trees encircling the churchyard, so the panoramic view from the parapet, which stretches from the Pennines to the Humber Bridge, is entirely unexpected. It is unfortunate that the awkward termination of the stair prevents safe public access, for this must be one of the finest vantage points in the district.

The smaller plain-edged spires at Scrooby and South Anston merit a visit despite the lack of inner pinnacles and flying buttresses. West Retford is an exceptional design, which Pugin considered to be no less than 'a poem in stone'.[3] The summit may not reach the same intensity as LAUGHTON, but the composition is conceptually more

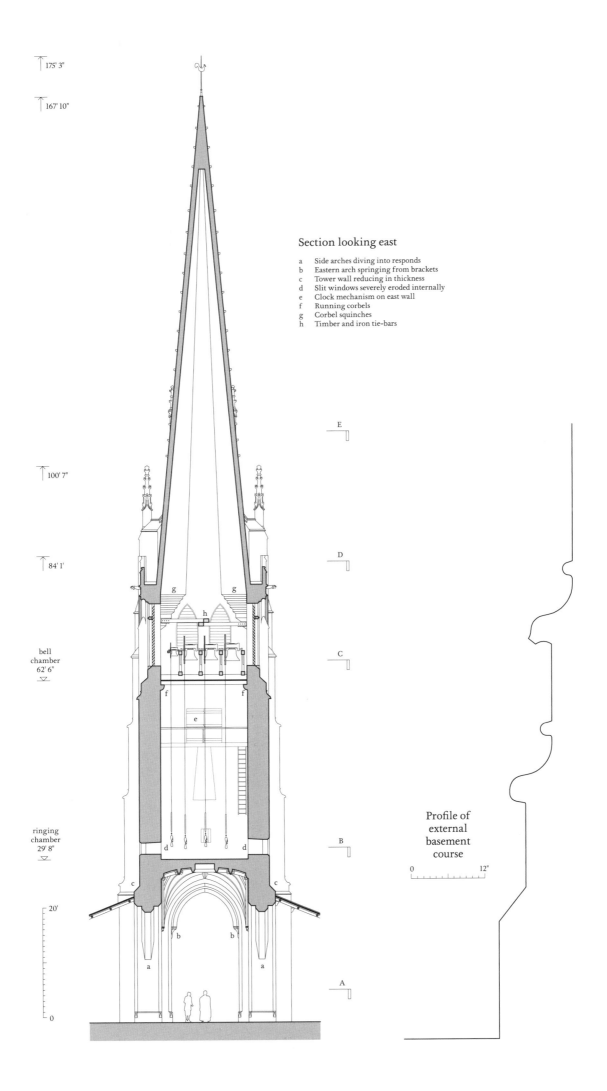

175' 3"

167' 10"

Section looking east

a   Side arches diving into responds
b   Eastern arch springing from brackets
c   Tower wall reducing in thickness
d   Slit windows severely eroded internally
e   Clock mechanism on east wall
f   Running corbels
g   Corbel squinches
h   Timber and iron tie-bars

E

100' 7"

D

84' 1'

g   g

h

C

bell
chamber
62' 6"

f   f

e

Profile of external basement course

0   12"

ringing
chamber
29' 8"

B

d   d

c   c

20'

b   b

A

a   a

0

Reflected plan
of tower vault

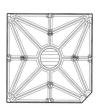

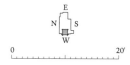

0   20'

Plan at E:
spire

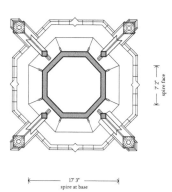

7' 2"
spire face

17' 3"
spire at base

Plan at D:
tower
parapet

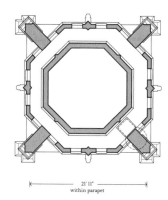

21' 11"
within parapet

Plan at C:
bell
chamber

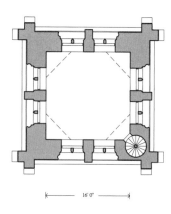

16' 0"

Plan at B:
ringing
chamber

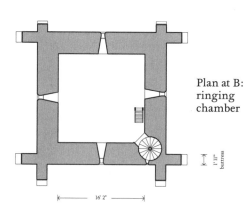

1' 11"
buttress

16' 2"

Plan at A:
ground
level

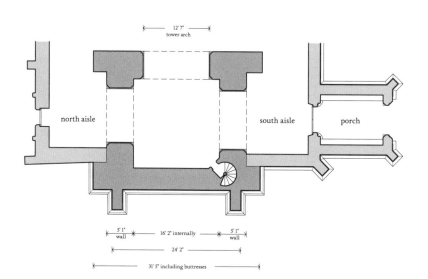

12' 7"
tower arch

north aisle   south aisle   porch

5' 1"
wall   16' 2" internally   5' 1"
wall

24' 2"

31' 5" including buttresses

satisfying, for the diagonal tower buttresses start from the ground. It shares the same slender crocketed spire and inner ring of pinnacles as LAUGHTON, but the flying buttresses spring in the opposite direction. Nevertheless, as a thrilling and highly original spectacle LAUGHTON-EN-LE-MORTHEN takes pride of place among this small but precious group of English steeples.

NOTES

1   Wakefield Cathedral was substantially rebuilt by George Gilbert Scott in 1858, and the details of the spire cannot be trusted.
2   Six centuries later, the same quarries were to supply the stone for Barry and Pugin's Palace of Westminster.
3   Unreferenced quotation in C. Moss, *East Retford and the Dukeries: A handbook for visitors and residents* (1908).

26

St Michael, Coventry

WARWICKSHIRE

'Of all the grand examples of a great church dominating, from a central position, one of our larger towns or cities, the Parish Church of St Michael, Coventry, undoubtedly holds the palm. It lays claim ... to be the finest parochial church in the kingdom.'
(J. Charles Cox, *The English Parish Church*)

When J. Charles Cox recorded these words, ST MICHAEL's steeple was at its most spectacularly brilliant, fresh from a hugely expensive restoration under the direction of John Oldrid Scott. Within four years the church had been elevated to cathedral status, but three great tragedies were to unfold during the course the twentieth century.

On the night of 14 November 1940, the body of the church of ST MICHAEL, along with the city's medieval core, was destroyed by German incendiary bombs. The might have escaped with the loss of the roof and the glass, but cast-iron roof girders, installed by John Oldrid Scott in 1887, buckled and twisted in the heat, pulling down the walls of the nave. In the immediate aftermath, the survival of Coventry's three famous spires of ST MICHAEL's, Holy Trinity and Christ Church – surrounded by a sea of utter devastation – must have appeared as nothing short of miraculous. At ST MICHAEL's, however, the risk to the steeple structure may have been low, for the only combustible

materials were two oak floors protected by a solid stone vault almost a hundred feet above the ground.

Had the fire occurred during peacetime or in Eastern Europe, the church might have been faithfully rebuilt. At Coventry, however, symbolism and modernism dominated the post-war reconstruction. In *Phoenix at Coventry*, the architect Sir Basil Spence explained his conception for a new cathedral:

> I saw the old cathedral as standing clearly for the sacrifice, one side of the Christian Faith, and I knew my task was to design a new one which should stand for the Triumph of the Resurrection.[1]

To maintain this all-powerful symbolism the old cathedral was, therefore, very literally sacrificed, never to be rebuilt. This, then, is the second tragedy of ST MICHAEL's. Despite the merits of Spence's design, and they are considerable, this still ranks as one of greatest losses of medieval architecture since the Dissolution of the Monasteries. Unroofed and unglazed, the hollow, crumbling sandstone walls may be profoundly moving, but this was not why ST MICHAEL's was built.

The third tragedy, which has gone unnoticed, is the rehanging of the bells in 1987. Campanology is a worthy pastime but it should never be allowed to compromise great architecture. Four bells are known to have been hanging in the tower by 1429, and a further two had been added by 1674, when Henry Bagley cast a new peal of eight and change ringing commenced in earnest. A century later, when the bells were recast by the Whitechapel Bell Foundry,[2] concerns were being raised about the structural integrity of the tower. By 1789 a letter in the *Gentleman's Magazine* was commenting on the 'present dangerous state of the steeple' resulting from 'some ignorant person' cutting through the stone tower vault.[3] The writer continued: 'It may be supposed that the bells were not originally fixed so high, which now when at full swing much occasion a stronger vibration ... it is no wonder to see the effects thereof in those large fissures which it has made in the walls.'

Architects Joseph Potter and James Watt ('Watt the Destroyer', as he was to become known) were appointed in 1793 to devise 'a mode of securing the matchless tower and spire and repairing it in the most effectual manner'. The bells were removed, iron bands were added to the structure, cracks were cut out and patched with new stone, and the doors and windows of the lowest stage were filled with solid masonry to improve stability.

All were agreed that the bells had been responsible for the dangerous deterioration, and consequently a separate free-standing bell tower was proposed. When this proved too expensive an eighty-foot-high, structurally independent timber bell frame was constructed within the walls of the tower. Unfortunately, this proved even more unsatisfactory, for the free-standing structure swung so vigorously that it smashed against the walls it was designed to safeguard. Twelve years later the bell frame was reduced in height and the beam ends were again built into the walls of the tower.

George Gilbert Scott's 1851 restoration of the church did not extend to the steeple, which was left for his second son, John Oldrid Scott, to address in 1884. The bells and supporting framework were removed to reveal an interior that was, in Scott's words, 'sadly mutilated and disfigured in every way, its doors and windows blocked up, its walls shattered in every part with hideous cracks, and its once beautiful stone groining poised close on 100 feet above the floor represented by nothing more that broken stumps of its vaulting ribs'. This was the pitiful legacy of two centuries of change ringing.

Photographs taken before the restoration show a severely corroded exterior on which the soft red sandstone had weathered to a mere shadow of its original glory. Enormous cracks ran through the internal masonry, and excavations revealed that the northern edge of the tower was perched precariously close to the edge of a thirty-foot-deep quarry. The problems were so extensive that a full rebuilding was proposed by the eminent church architect John Loughborough Pearson. Thankfully this drastic course of action was rejected, and a risky underpinning operation was carried out to secure the foundations. Internal cracks were repaired, and the magnificent stone vault was

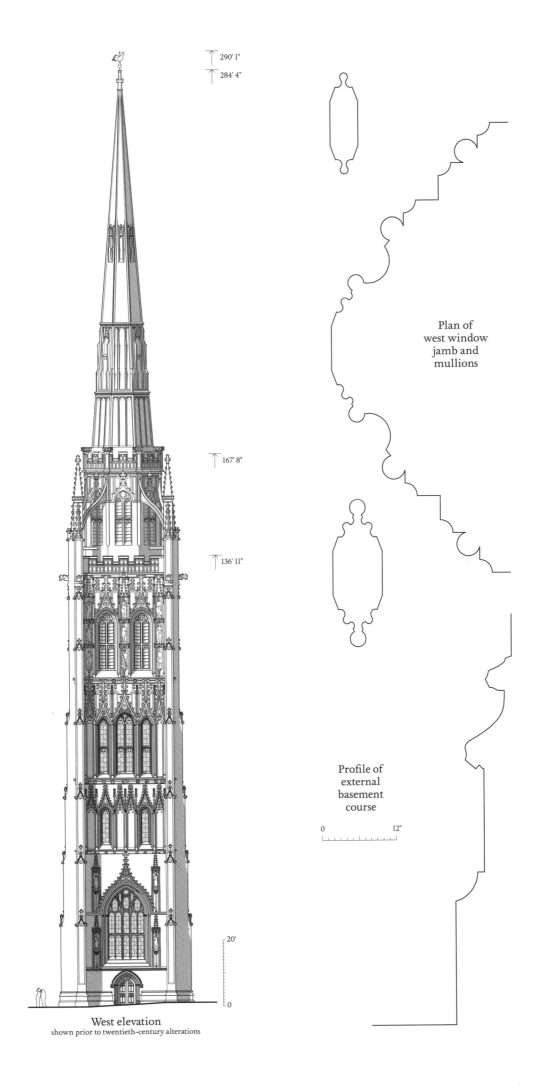

290' 1"

284' 4"

167' 8"

136' 11"

20'

0

Plan of
west window
jamb and
mullions

Profile of
external
basement
course

0   12"

West elevation
shown prior to twentieth-century alterations

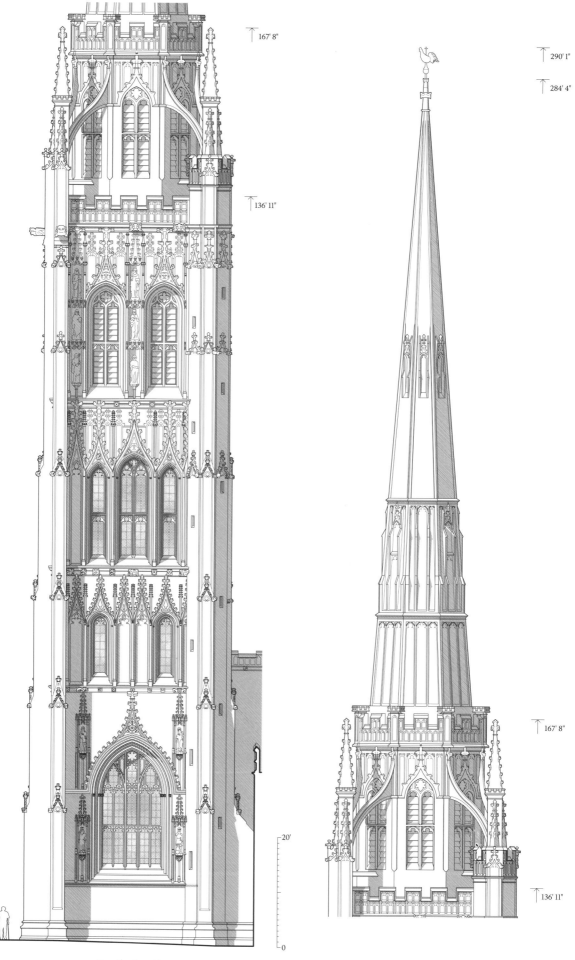

167' 8"

136' 11"

20'

0

290' 1"

284' 4"

167' 8"

136' 11"

South elevation
shown prior to twentieth-century alterations

reinstated to a new design devised by Scott from the evidence of the remaining stones (h). The entire superstructure was refaced in new Runcorn stone, in accordance with measured drawings that had been made by one of George Gilbert Scott's assistants back in 1853. Although the result may be a crisp and faithful reconstruction, the historic outer fabric has been lost forever, and the structural integrity of the building skin has been fundamentally weakened.[4]

In May 1889 a delegation of foremost church architects unanimously rejected the idea of rehanging the bells. George Woodcock, a major industrialist and the primary benefactor of the restoration, offered to pay half the cost of building a free-standing bell tower. One of his objectives was to ensure that 'when the present knowledge of the state of the tower has been lost sight of' the bells would not be rehung to 'once more wreck the beautiful tower and lofty spire'. These fears were to prove well founded.

A splendid belfry design, matching the height of the original tower, was commissioned from Paley and Austen, one of the most progressive practices to emerge from the Gothic Revival. Unfortunately, this laudable scheme was abandoned following the untimely death of Woodcock in 1891. Within four years the bells had been rehung in the octagon to allow chiming but not change ringing.

For the campanologists this compromise was seen as a defeat. Nevertheless, the latent threat to the historic structure remained, and even increased in 1927 when the peal was recast, augmented by an additional four bells and rehung on a three-tier steel frame, part of which remains within the octagon (l). Finally, in 1987, after years of lobbying by the campanology fraternity, a new ringing frame was installed within the tower (e). This is the third tragedy to have been suffered by ST MICHAEL's steeple. Not only did the resumption of change ringing fly in the face of history, but it also destroyed one of the greatest of English tower interiors. Brilliantly lit and rising higher even than LOUTH, this magnificent soaring space is now lost above the ceiling of a humble gift shop (b).

ST MICHAEL's is the slenderest of all medieval English steeples. The ratio of height to width, measured to the outside faces of the buttresses immediately above the base, is 7:1. This is an improvement on the 13:2 ratio at GRANTHAM, and is considerably tighter than the 6:1 ratio later to be employed at LOUTH. The geometrical basis of the design is less readily discernible than at GRANTHAM. The key difference between these two great masterworks is in the role of the tower buttresses, for whereas at GRANTHAM they are inconsistent and unconvincing, at COVENTRY they become the primary generators of one unified Perpendicular composition.

Soaring angle buttresses provide a rigid framework containing four richly articulated elevations. The most audacious element of the entire design is the complete absence of decoration or subdivision on the plain side faces of the buttresses, which rise a sheer 137 feet from base to pinnacle. Their outer faces alone are divided into seven unequal stages commencing with three stages of 19' 6" and two stages of 22' 6". Apart from the fourth and sixth set-offs, the vertical subdivision of the buttresses and the tower are entirely independent. This fourth set-off level is significant, for it divides the tower and octagon (if considered together) into two equal portions: a relatively restrained lower half and an exuberant upper half.

The set-offs are subtle and subservient, for the buttresses reduce by less than six inches at each of the first four divisions and then rise vertically for the final fifty-five feet. They are of an idiosyncratic local form derived from Lichfield Cathedral, Clifton Campville and Tamworth (Staffs), in which the gablet roof rises steeply up towards the tower. The motif may be less pronounced at Coventry, but it still imparts a powerful streamlining effect on the corner of the tower, making it appear almost as if the vertical energy of the buttress were dragging the back of the gablet heavenward. The impeccable logic of the buttress design culminates in square, castellated pinnacles precisely marking the intersection of the two adjacent buttresses.

Richly articulated elevations between these buttresses are divided into four principal stages, the subservient western portal being compressed into the space below the cill of the west window. Small though this four-centred opening may be, John Harvey considered the detailing, of three shafts with capitals, sufficiently close to Robert Skillyngton's work at St Mary, Warwick (1381–96), and John of Gaunt's Great Hall at Kenilworth Castle (Warks; 1391–93) to suggest a common authorship.[5] These dates neatly overlap with ST MICHAEL's tower, which was constructed between 1373 and 1394 with funds provided by the local wool merchants Adam and William Botoner.

The fenestration and decoration of the four stages shows great inventiveness and variety. John Harvey has noted similarities between the expansive five-light windows of the first stage, and Robert Lesyngham's east window at Exeter Cathedral (1390) and his work at Gloucester Cathedral (1368–81), but this is not strong enough to suggest a direct link.[6] One sophisticated detail, which appears in the work of both Henry Yeveley at Durham Cathedral (1372) and William Wynford at Wells Cathedral (c. 1385), is the six-foil cusping in the head of the centre light.

Window profiles are sumptuous, and two pairs of statued niches frame each window. Unfortunately, the brilliant effect of the north, south and west windows within the tower has been lost, for even within the new ringing chamber huge lifeless drapes leave the space in perpetual gloom. The incorporation of substantial glazing on the three outward-facing elevations may derive from Clifton Campville twenty miles to

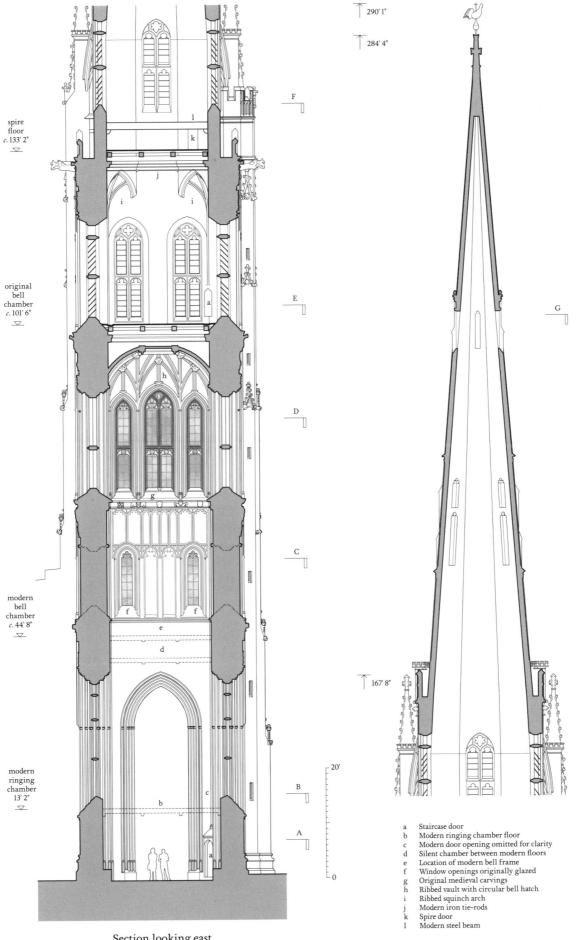

290' 1"

284' 4"

spire
floor
c. 133' 2"

original
bell
chamber
c. 101' 6"

F

E

D

C

G

167' 8"

modern
bell
chamber
c. 44' 8"

modern
ringing
chamber
13' 2"

B

A

20'

0

a Staircase door
b Modern ringing chamber floor
c Modern door opening omitted for clarity
d Silent chamber between modern floors
e Location of modern bell frame
f Window openings originally glazed
g Original medieval carvings
h Ribbed vault with circular bell hatch
i Ribbed squinch arch
j Modern iron tie-rods
k Spire door
l Modern steel beam

Section looking east
shown prior to twentieth-century alterations

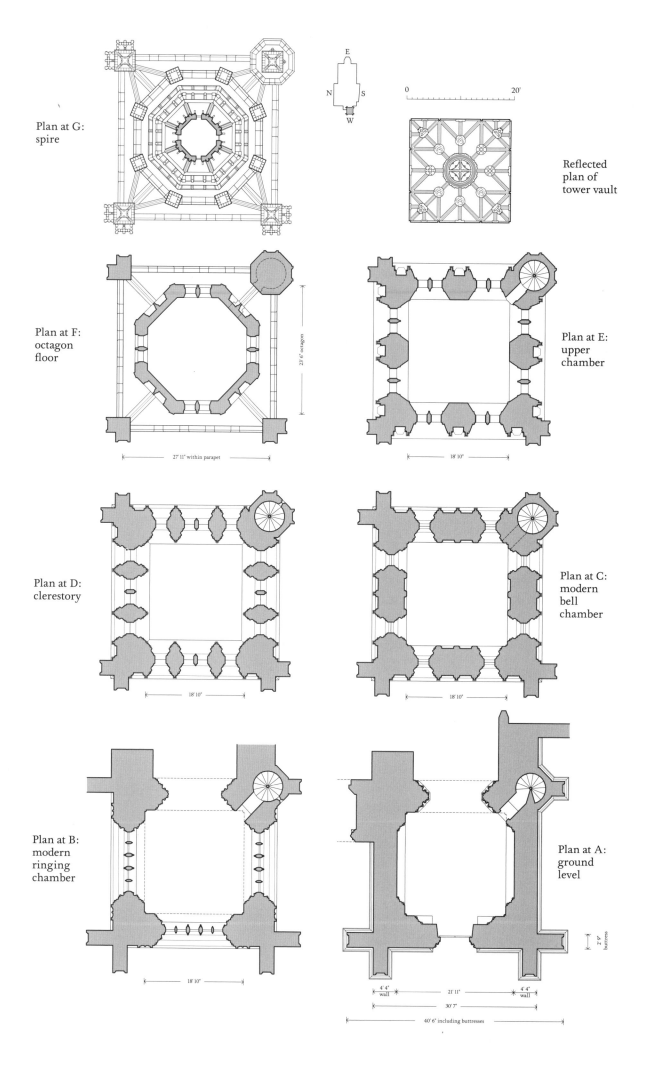

Plan at G:
spire

Reflected
plan of
tower vault

Plan at F:
octagon
floor

23' 6" octagon

27' 11" within parapet

Plan at E:
upper
chamber

18' 10"

Plan at D:
clerestory

18' 10"

Plan at C:
modern
bell
chamber

18' 10"

Plan at B:
modern
ringing
chamber

18' 10"

Plan at A:
ground
level

2' 9"
buttress

4' 4"
wall

21' 1"

4' 4"
wall

30' 7"

40' 6" including buttresses

E

N   S

W

0   20'

north, which also shares with COVENTRY an octagonal south-eastern stair tower. Both the positioning and the handing of this stair are a vast improvement on GRANTHAM, for it is kept away from the principal elevations and is neatly terminated by a standard pinnacle.

The three stages that follow become increasingly luxuriant and complex. On the second stage each half of the elevation contains a glazed bay framed by narrow blind panels. These bays are separated by flat pilasters carrying rotated square pinnacles. The openings are deeply recessed and finished with ogee hood-moulds. Clerestory windows on the third stage are arranged with single lights either side of a central twin-light, all framed by single blind panels. Yet another rhythm animates the original bell stage, which has two twin-light louvred openings framed by nine niches arranged in three columns, housing life-size figures. A general profusion of crocketing, gargoyles, blind panels and blind arcading on the crenellated parapet animates every available surface.

The octagon that follows is an exact contemporary of FOTHERINGHAY but predates BOSTON and the widespread adoption of the form in the Low Countries. It may have been inspired by the splendid early fourteenth-century steeple of Bloxham (Oxon), but the effect is altogether lighter and more confident. This highly original design may not have been intended from the start, for the tower had been over twenty years in the building; nevertheless, it is perfectly integrated into the design. Ogee-form flying buttresses provide a smooth connection with the tower buttresses, and the six-foil cusped figure first seen in the west window makes a reappearance in the head of the twin-light openings.

The castellated terminations of the octagon are consistent with the tower pinnacles and integral with the spire base, suggesting one continuous campaign of work. This is confirmed within the tower, for the inner face of the octagon runs seamlessly into the spire. Internally, the wall surface is articulated in a similar fashion to the exterior up to the level of the splendid reconstructed vault (h). Above the second stage panelling is a cornice of well-preserved carving (g). One exceptional feature is the small ribbed vault filling the void behind the squinch arch (i).

There is an obvious and very strong connection between the spire of ST MICHAEL'S and the adjacent church of Holy Trinity. Ignoring the first stage of Holy Trinity, which effectively replaces the octagonal stage at ST MICHAEL'S, the three-stage design is almost identical. On both churches a stage of three regular trefoiled panels to each face is followed by a second stage of stepped ribs between panels and centre lights on the diagonal faces. Finally, the very tall third stage has roll spire edges and slender single lucarnes to each and every face, those set on the diagonal being blind. Of the two designs Holy Trinity is almost certainly a copy, possibly from the rebuilding of 1665–68.

ST MICHAEL's may have set a regional preference for spires in which all eight faces are given an equal treatment. After GRANTHAM, in the early fourteenth century, this idea was abandoned in the East Midlands. Further west, it is the distinguishing feature of the tall mid-fifteenth-century spires of Coleshill (Warks), Witherley (Leics), Kings Norton (Worcs; 1446–75) and Yardley (Worcs;

c. 1461), albeit not on the same extravagant scale as Coventry.

ST MICHAEL's steeple is a glorious, sophisticated and noble design that confidently surpassed GRANTHAM in height, refinement and beauty. John Harvey considered it to be a work of genius and one of the greatest wonders of the age.[7] It would in turn be surpassed, but only once, and only in the closing decades of the medieval age.

NOTES

1   Sir Basil Spence, *Phoenix at Coventry* (1962).
2   Founded in 1570, the Whitechapel Bell Foundry is Britain's oldest manufacturing company.
3   This and subsequent quotes appear unreferenced in Christopher Pickford's *The Steeple, Bells, and Ringers of Coventry Cathedral* (1987).
4   Original masonry in a tower is subject to considerable loads applied gradually during construction as weight is added to the structure above; new stone inserted later is not subject to the same load.
5   John Harvey, *English Mediaeval Architects* (1984), p. 275.
6   John Harvey, *The Perpendicular Style* (1978), p. 112.
7   Ibid., pp. 112, 130.

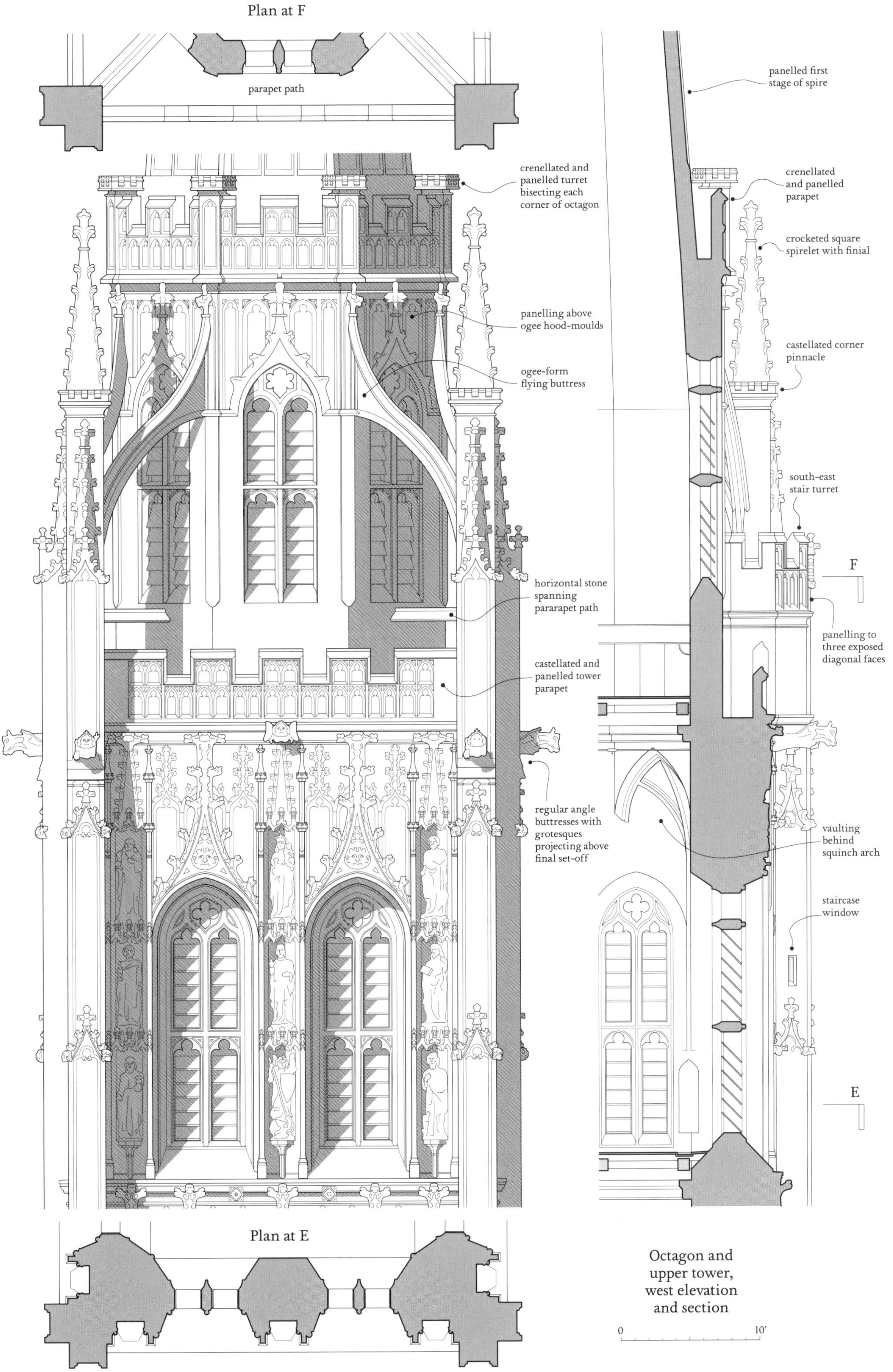

Plan at F

parapet path

crenellated and
panelled turret
bisecting each
corner of octagon

panelling above
ogee hood-moulds

ogee-form
flying buttress

horizontal stone
spanning
pararapet path

castellated and
panelled tower
parapet

regular angle
buttresses with
grotesques
projecting above
final set-off

panelled first
stage of spire

crenellated
and panelled
parapet

crocketed square
spirelet with finial

castellated corner
pinnacle

south-east
stair turret

F

panelling to
three exposed
diagonal faces

vaulting
behind
squinch arch

staircase
window

E

Plan at E

Octagon and
upper tower,
west elevation
and section

0   10'

27

Fotheringhay

NORTHAMPTONSHIRE

FOTHERINGHAY is an enchanting enigma, since it is both a rural parish church and a royal mausoleum. As one approaches through the bucolic landscape of the Nene Valley, it is hard to imagine that this modest village was once the power base of a royal dynasty. The first glimpse of the church is extraordinary, for the magnificent octagon is visible for miles around. This great symbolic crown thrust into the sky is a poignant reminder of the futility of worldly ambition, for this is the spiritual home of the House of York. Seen from across the river, above contentedly grazing sheep, the church is a memorably picturesque composition. At closer quarters the design is disconcerting, for it contains some striking, and hitherto unexplained, discontinuities.[1]

Little remains of the great fortress given by Edward III to his fifth son, Edmund of Langley, later the Duke of York, when he was still a minor. A thriving market town grew up in the shadow of the castle, and, together with LUDLOW, FOTHERINGHAY became one of the great bastions of the most transitory of English dynasties, the House of York. In 1476 Edward IV interred the bodies of his father and his eldest brother here with great ceremony following their deaths at the Battle of Wakefield.[2] His youngest brother, Richard III, was born in the castle, and their mother and great uncle are also buried at the church.

This was far in the future when Edmund of Langley, Duke of York, resolved to found a college at FOTHERINGHAY and rebuilt

the chancel of the parish church on a lavish scale. It was left to his son, Edward, Duke of York, to formally establish the College of the Blessed Virgin and All Saints of Fotheringhay in 1412 on six acres of land between the parish church and the River Nene. The foundation was not philanthropic in the conventional sense, for the sole function of the master, the preceptor, eleven chaplains, eight clerks and thirteen choristers was to pray for the souls of the family of York (and the royal family) in perpetuity. It was effectively one vast chantry chapel. Edward's ambition to rebuild the nave of the church was frustrated by his death at Agincourt in 1415, and almost twenty years elapsed before his successor, Richard, 3rd Duke of York, made arrangements to carry through his uncle's wishes.

On 24 September 1434 a contract was signed between the Duke's commissioners and the local mason William Horwode, who was to receive £300 for building a 'Body and Steeple' for the church. The contract survives, and a copy made by the antiquarian William Dugdale in the seventeenth century has been published on several occasions.[3] Not only does this give a unique insight into the medieval construction industry, but it also provides invaluable documentary evidence that helps to explain the complex history of the steeple.[4]

For such a large building the contract value of £300 appears very low. Detailed accounts exist for ADDERBURY chancel

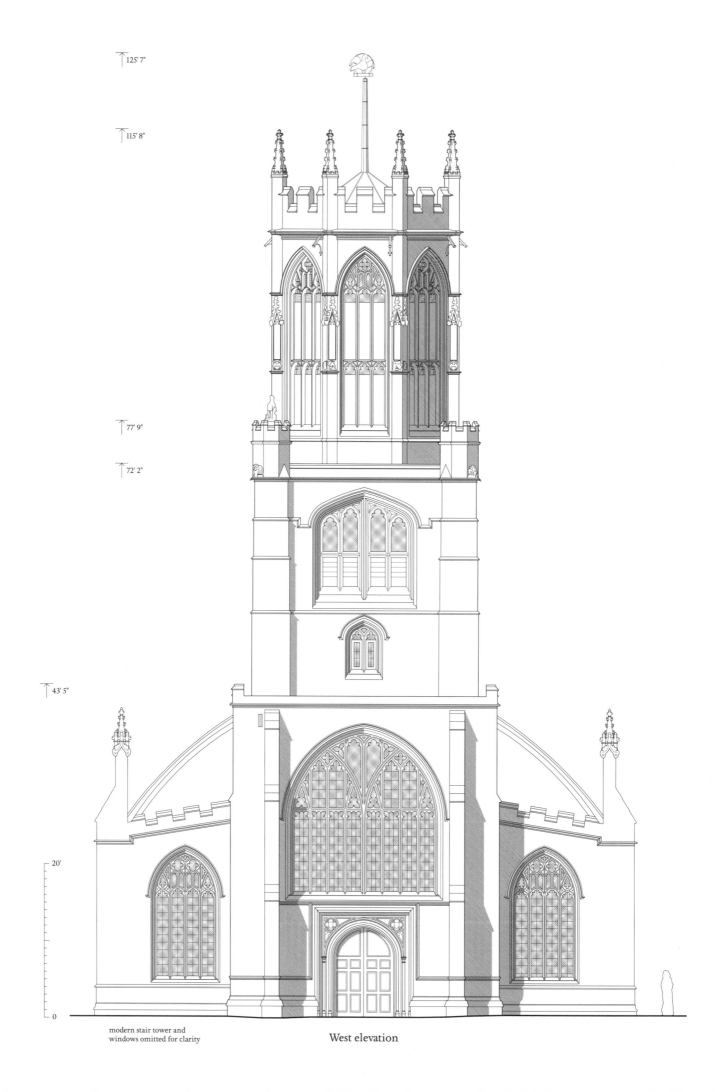

125' 7"

115' 8"

77' 9"

72' 2"

43' 5"

20'

0

modern stair tower and
windows omitted for clarity

West elevation

(1408–18), which cost £399 5s. 4d., despite being a fraction of the size, and for the great spire at LOUTH (1501–15), which cost £305 7s. 5d. The relative economy of FOTHERINGHAY is revealed by the workmanlike quality of much of the detailing.

Many aspects of the contract are familiar to a twenty-first-century architect: dimensions and quality are specified, and there are procedures for stage payments and for arbitration by a professional body. Damages for failing to complete the work are draconian by modern standards, for the contractor is to be imprisoned and surrender all his worldly possessions. The influence of clients is frequently underestimated by architectural historians but here, in one of the earliest written contracts, there is clear evidence of an overbearing client dictating the aesthetics of the design.

William Horwode was to extend the choir with a nave and two aisles, with porches to north and south and a steeple to the west. The steeple was to be octagonal and battlemented, with buttressed corners finished with pinnacles and three-light windows to each elevation. Within, two floors were to be illuminated by clerestory windows. The church was to have three tower arches and a stone vault between, with walls six feet thick at the base. Every detail was to follow the existing choir, except that the buttresses were to be bigger and (in a minor concession to changing taste) bowtells were to be omitted from the window profiles. Significantly, there is

no contractual requirement for a bell chamber, and the octagon was to rise directly from the body of the church.

The original choir was demolished during the Reformation, leaving only the body of the church that William Horwode built, so the composition that originally ran to sixteen bays is now only seven bays long. In most particulars the church follows the contract to the letter. The slavish copying of the details of the choir is anachronistic, and the slender flying buttresses serve no useful purpose when they abut the stable timber roof of the nave or the solid mass of the tower. They do, however, imply that a stone vault spanned the earlier choir from which they were copied (a).

Tower and nave are combined in a highly unorthodox fashion to meet the wording of the specification as economically as possible. The nave occupies the five eastern bays of the composition, while the tower, the two western bays and the aisles run straight through. Embraced towers such as EWERBY are narrower than the nave that they terminate, in order to achieve good vertical proportions, but at FOTHERINGHAY the tower occupies the full width of the nave. Internally, the effect is exceedingly light, for, by a clever slight of hand, the tower arches and their responds appear to be as slender as those of the nave. This is achieved by splitting the tower arches into two parts. The outer parts of the respond (b) follow the detailing of the nave arcade and carry little load. The plain inner responds take most of the weight, and their arches rise up to match the level of the eastern arch (c). The great octagon was originally supported by these plain inner arches and spanned by a simple ribbed vault.

FOTHERINGHAY boasts an exceptionally fine tower vault, of four quarter fans surrounding a circular bell hatch decorated with a falcon and fetterlock, the badge of the House of York, but this is not the original design. The vault of 1434 is represented by four corner corbels, each supporting a small section of plain diagonal rib and decorated with a figure carrying a shield (d). These springers are abruptly terminated by circular rings, the one in the north-west corner bearing an inscription. Archdeacon Bonney deciphered this as 'Anno Domini 1457',[5] Pevsner as 1529, and the Royal Commission on Historic Monuments variously as 1529 or 1539; but a close-up photograph by local historian Michael Lea does not readily support these interpretations.[6]

Stylistic evidence suggests a date of around 1496 for the fan vault, coinciding with the burial of Cecily Neville. The fan vault is in the highly personal style of the great master mason John Wastell, who from 1496 was working at Peterborough Cathedral just eight miles away. Wastell flourished from 1485, built the central tower at Canterbury Cathedral in 1493–97 and died in 1515. His most notable legacy is a series of beautiful fan vaults: to Peterborough retrochoir (c. 1496–1508), Canterbury Cathedral tower (c. 1505), King's College Chapel, Cambridge

(from 1508), and possibly the Red Mount Chapel at King's Lynn (1506). These fans are all compartmented by radiused ribs to form a radiating grid of roll-finished tracery completed with rounded quatrefoil archlets and a cresting of three petal flowers. FOTHERINGHAY follows this design to the letter.

The reflected ceiling plan reveals that the space between the original tower arches is rectangular (20' 2" × 18' 6") and therefore unsuitable for a square fan vault. Consequently ribbed arches had to be inserted against the north and south walls to transform the plan into a pure square before construction of the vault could commence. The measured survey reveals that the second stage of the tower is built directly off these ribbed arches and is therefore contemporary with, or postdates, the late fifteenth-century fan vault. This theory is strongly supported by the external appearance of the middle stages.

Confusingly, the octagon closely follows the setting-out of the earlier rectangular plan form, suggesting that it was originally built in 1434 over the rectangular western bay of the church. This leads to the unexpected conclusion that it was subsequently dismantled to allow the construction of the new plinth-like bell chamber and then rebuilt at a higher level. The relocation of highly valued architectural features, such as Norman doorways, is by no means uncommon in medieval churches, but it is unusual on such a large scale.[7] Such an extravagant

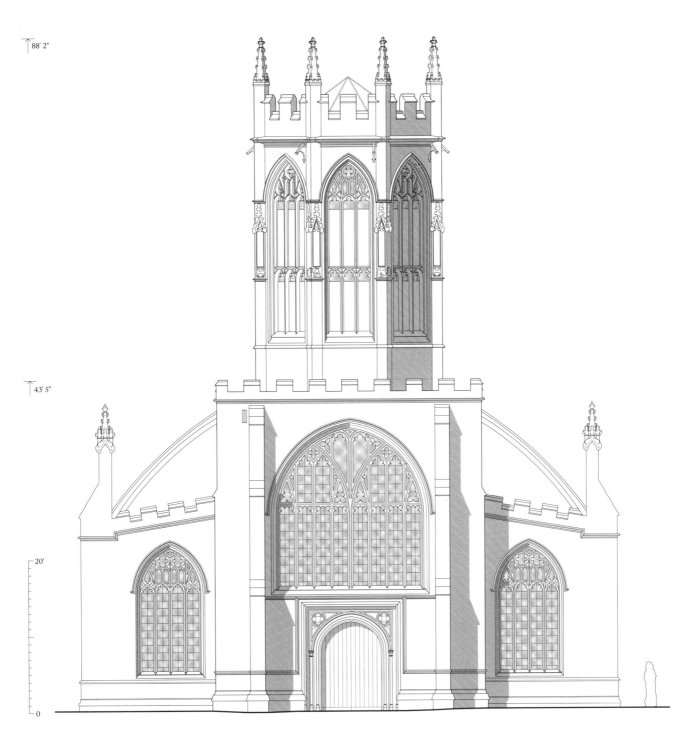

88' 2"

43' 5"

20'

0

West elevation
Hypothetical original design of 1434

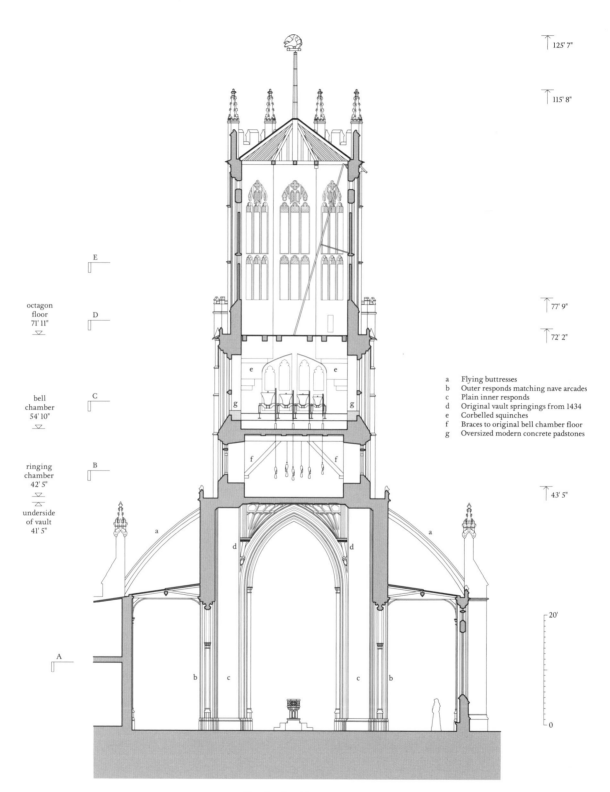

125' 7"

115' 8"

77' 9"

octagon
floor
71' 11"

72' 2"

bell
chamber
54' 10"

a   Flying buttresses
b   Outer responds matching nave arcades
c   Plain inner responds
d   Original vault springings from 1434
e   Corbelled squinches
f   Braces to original bell chamber floor
g   Oversized modern concrete padstones

ringing
chamber
42' 5"

43' 5"

underside
of vault
41' 5"

20'

0

Section looking east

reconstruction is not, however, inconceivable given the particular historical circumstances.

The octagon of 1435 had been built to fulfil the wishes of Richard, 3rd Duke of York, and his father, Edward, 2nd Duke of York, and was the symbolic focus of a college founded to perpetuate their memory. Richard's wife, Cecily Neville, mother and grandmother of three kings of England, spent much of her long widowhood at FOTHERINGHAY before she was laid to rest next to her husband in 1495. Despite the ignominious defeat of the House of York on the field of Bosworth, her granddaughter Elizabeth was by this time Queen of England and owner of FOTHERINGHAY. There would have been ample reason to commemorate the passing of Cecily Neville by raising the octagon heavenward and adding a fine peal of bells.

The drawings lend further support to this hypothesis for, if the massive central stage is removed from the west elevation, the resulting composition is entirely convincing. The original 1435 design, it appears, was not for a conventional steeple at all, but rather for an octagonal lantern terminating the roof of a long horizontal church body. This would explain why there is so little vertical emphasis to the western elevation, which is dominated by a vast eight-bay window beneath a very flat arch.

Externally the effect of this broad window is mechanical, but internally the church is flooded with daylight. Three-stage buttresses to the west front of the tower are set unusually far from the corners, for reasons that become evident only internally. The post-medieval west door is framed by a rectangular hood-mould with bowtells in the jambs and quatrefoils containing shields in the spandrels – a design that may have been copied from the earlier choir. Excavation has confirmed that the basement course is lost beneath a foot of soil that has built up over the centuries.

Although the base of the tower and the octagon were constructed around 1435, the contract required their style to be closer to that of 1400. Between these two original stages is a massive cubic volume that gives every appearance of being built around the year 1500. Like the base on which it sits, the elevation is almost square, and there is little vertical emphasis. Unlike Wastell's fan vault, this design is entirely of the local Stamford school. Late fifteenth-century towers at St John, Stamford, St Martin, Stamford, and Easton-on-the Hill (Northants) all employ square clasping buttresses, broad bell stage windows divided by heavy central mullions, and small two-bay arched windows to the ringing chamber. FOTHERINGHAY is slightly different, both for the excessive number of string courses and for its immensely strong four-light window spanned by a single flat four-centred arch. An arch of similar profile occurs locally at the late fifteenth-century tower of Yaxley (Hunts), and the closest parallel to the clasping buttresses is to be found at the neighbouring village of Elton (Hunts), also from around 1500.

Stubby battlemented corner turrets demonstrate a Cambridgeshire influence and provide plinths for sculptures, although only two now remain. Bonney suggests that these may have represented the Four Evangelists, the remaining figures being an angel and a lion symbolizing St Matthew and St Mark. Two centuries later the evidence is hard to interpret, but another possibility is that they were heraldic symbols representing the House of York. The absence of tall pinnacles and flying buttresses is easy to explain, for originally the octagon was designed to sit on a nave roof that had no significant corner emphasis.

The construction of the second stage is as massive on plan as it appears on elevation, and the corner squinches are formed from the heftiest of flat corbels (e). The ancient timber floor beams are braced below the bell chamber (f), but the bells are hung on a modern steel bell frame supported by oversized concrete padstones (g), masked externally by crude timber slats. The descending spiral stair connects awkwardly with the 1434 work somewhere above the north-west fan vault, while the ascending flight adopts the preferred Northamptonshire position in the south-west corner. The new second stage allowed insufficient room for the original battlement on the west elevation, and it remains crudely cut back on the corners.

The defects in the lower stages of FOTHERINGHAY are easily outweighed by the exceptional beauty of the octagon.

Experiments with octagonal drums started 200 years before at BARNACK, and direct inspiration might have come from the octagon over the Norman west front at Ely Cathedral. The open lantern at All Saints, Pavement, York, built around 1395–1425, provides clear precedent in both scale and composition, but it lacks the refinement of FOTHERINGHAY.

At FOTHERINGHAY the proportions are excellent. Tall three-light windows occupy the full width of each face between rotated square buttresses that press subtly forward. Eloquent Perpendicular tracery – consisting of quatrefoils below a central transom, trefoils above, inverted daggers and a gentle soufflet in the head – is entirely consistent with the aisles of 1434. The buttresses are subtly decorated with lions' heads and flat niches carrying crocketed gables. The falcon and fetterlock rise defiantly above square battlements and square crocketed pinnacles to proclaim the House of York. The octagon is distorted on plan: like the arches on which it was originally supported, it is wider from north to south than it is from east to west.

There is little glass in the openings because solid slabs of masonry fill all but the heads of the arches. This is a puzzle, for if blind panels were intended from the start they would be integral with the mullions. Conservation work has revealed that a glazing groove runs the full height of the mullions, but this is not conclusive proof that glass was ever fitted.[8] The contract is relevant here, for it specifies that the octagon should

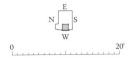

0 |⊦⊦⊦⊦⊦⊦⊦⊦⊦⊦⊦⊦⊦⊦⊦⊦⊦⊦⊦| 20'

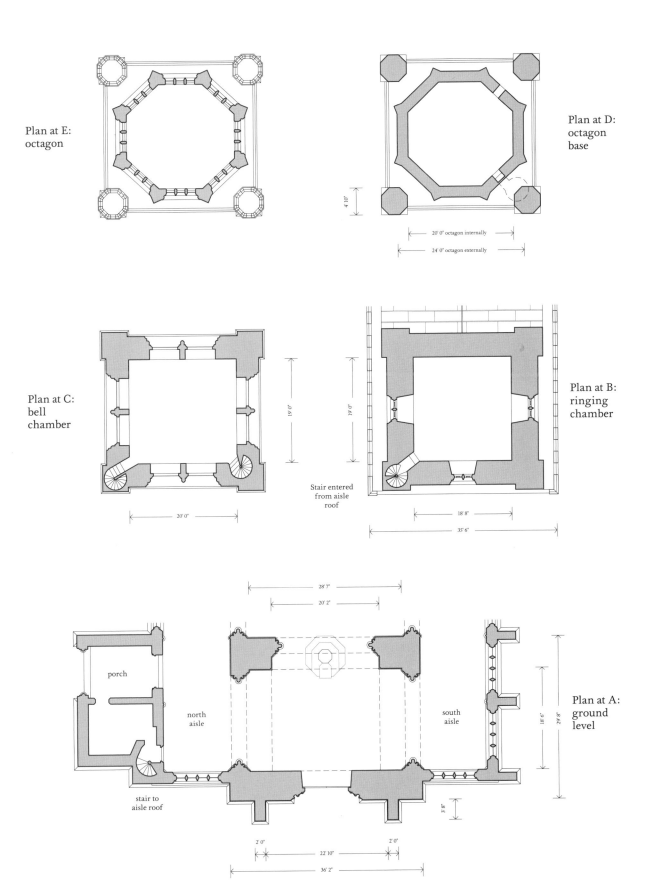

Plan at E: octagon

Plan at D: octagon base

20' 0" octagon internally
24' 0" octagon externally
4' 10"

Plan at C: bell chamber

19' 0"
20' 0"

Plan at B: ringing chamber

19' 0"
Stair entered from aisle roof
18' 8"
35' 6"

Plan at A: ground level

28' 7"
20' 2"
porch
north aisle
south aisle
18' 6"
29' 8"
stair to aisle roof
3' 8"
2' 0"
22' 10"
2' 0"
36' 2"

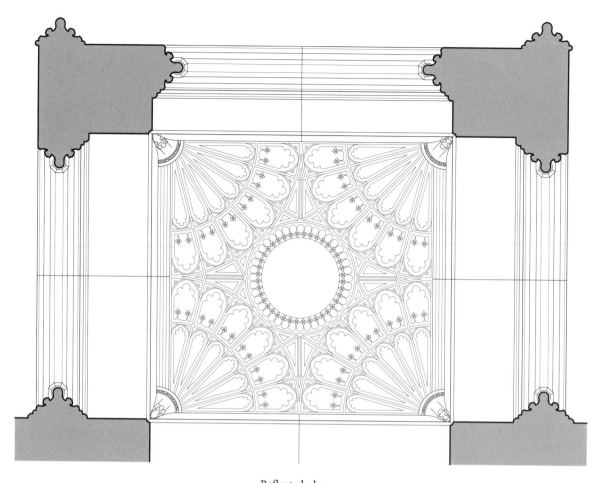

Reflected plan
of tower vault

0   10'

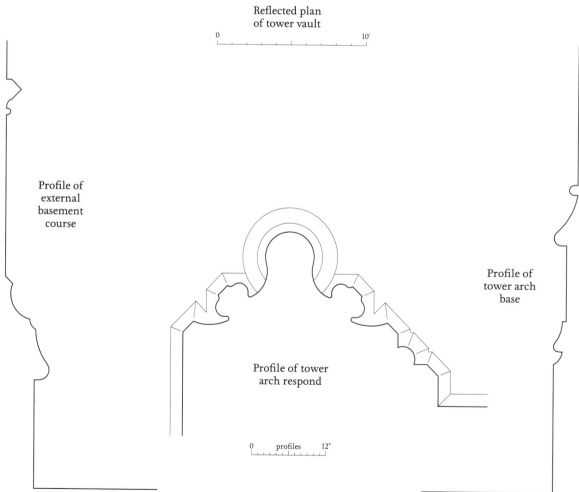

Profile of
external
basement
course

Profile of
tower arch
base

Profile of tower
arch respond

0   profiles   12"

contain two floors, each illuminated by high-level clerestory windows. The internal floors have gone, but the small clerestory lights accurately match this description. An alternative explanation might be that the octagon was fully glazed when first constructed in 1434, and the slabs were added to stiffen the structure when it was rebuilt at a higher level around 1496. As they appear now, the blind openings engender a muted and melancholy atmosphere that is entirely appropriate for a mausoleum.

The contract confirms that the octagon was never intended to admit light into the church and, despite the romantic legends, it is implausible to suggest that it functioned as a lighthouse to guide hunters returning through Rockingham Forest. Octagonal steeple crowns may be known as lanterns, but their purpose was not to provide illumination. Like the church spire, their role was entirely symbolic. They were, quite simply, one of the finest ornaments that the medieval mason could devise.

NOTES

1   There is no reference to the obvious discontinuity between stages in the principal reference sources, the *Inventory of the Historical Monuments in the County of Northampton*, vol. VI (Royal Commission on Historical Monuments, 1984), Pevsner's *The Buildings of England: Northamptonshire* (1961) and the Statutory Listing.
2   Revd H. K. Bonney, *Historic Notes in Reference to Fotheringhay* (1821), gives the date as 29 July 1466, but modern authors favour 29 July 1476.
3   The contract was reproduced with a useful commentary in *Some Remarks Upon the Church of Fotheringhay, Northamptonshire: Read at a Meeting of the Oxford Society for Promoting the Study of Gothic Architecture* (1841).
4   A transcription of the contract appears in Appendix I.
5   Bonney, *Historic Notes*, p. 49.
6   Viewable at www.pennhenry.yolasite.com (accessed 12 May 2016).
7   See Warwick Rodwell, *The Archaeology of Churches* (2012) pp. 241–42.
8   Information provided by the local historian Michael Lea, who has witnessed the slabs being removed.

28

Salle

NORFOLK

SALLE is the most perfectly composed of all late medieval Norfolk towers. Its setting is unforgettable, for it stands in blissful rural isolation with just a handful of estate cottages and a cricket pitch for company. There are many reasons to love this glorious church, but what lingers longest in the mind is the abiding feeling of authenticity. Norfolk escaped the worst ravages of Victorian restoration because there was a sparse population and a huge backlog of disrepair inherited from the Georgians. When an 'exceedingly jovial set of people' visited on an Architectural Association excursion in 1880, they found the church to be 'almost deserted, and given over to the bats and jackdaws', and 'in a most neglected and dilapidated condition'.[1]

When the fabric was finally rescued in 1910, it became a model of sensitive conservation undertaken in strict accordance with the philosophy of William Morris and the Society for the Protection of Ancient Buildings. There is much to savour in this faded masterpiece, from the salvaged pew ends to the spectacular font canopy still hanging from its original crane (a). The bells are the oldest discovered in the course of this survey, and not a trace of modern steel or concrete compromises the fabric of the tower.[2]

The churches of Norfolk exhibit a greater internal consistency than is found in regions of long-lasting prosperity, for most were built or rebuilt in just one or two generations and left untouched when the wool trade fell

into decline. Towers were commonly raised last, after the body of the church, and the unfinished crowns of Cawston, Wymondham and Trunch capture the moment when the finances of the region collapsed. SALLE was more fortunate but still had to wait over fifty years to receive its parapet.

The common characteristics of late medieval East Anglian churches are well known: walls of flint; a rectangular plan with nave and aisles but no chancel arch; continuous clerestories flooding the space with light; fine two-storied porches; open timber roofs; woodwork of the highest quality; large stone fonts with extravagant covers; and tall, plain western towers. The towers of Norfolk are generally taller, plainer and more orthogonal than those of Suffolk. Few churches meet all of these criteria quite as well as SALLE.

The body of the church was built to a single design in thirty years, commencing around 1400, with the abutting west tower starting slightly later. Construction was funded by powerful merchant families – the Uffords, Mautebys, Morleys, Luces, Brewes, Briggs, Kerdistons and Boleyns – in direct competition with the local parish church of Cawston, then being rebuilt by 'old money'. This ostentatious flaunting of new-found wealth was not hindered by the lack of a local population, for the primary purpose of the church was to house guild chapels. After the dismantling of the guilds during the Reformation, the church was left bereft of purpose and parishioners, which explains why it reached the twentieth century so remarkably unchanged.

SALLE was one of the first of the great East Anglian towers, and is a far more assured design than its early contemporaries such as Winterton. The exceptionally slender proportions of the elevations are beautifully balanced by muscular buttresses that project widely at the base but finish abnormally low, at the start of the bell stage. These setback buttresses are crisp and purposeful, with outer faces of smooth ashlar rather than the usual mix of flint and limestone quoins. Four plain set-offs start small and increase geometrically, cutting a vigorous pyramidal silhouette. The buttresses are terminated unexpectedly by massive, undecorated rectangular blocks, almost nine feet high, clasping the four corners of the upper tower. These blocks provide a plinth for clasping panelled buttresses to frame the final stage. The discontinuity introduced by this unorthodox arrangement marks a late change in the design, but the continuity of details and materials suggests that work progressed with only minor breaks until the roof was reached before the middle of the fifteenth century.

As with all flint towers, construction is massive, with walls over six feet thick at ground level reducing but little on the upper strings. Despite the loose coursing of the flint and the sporadic introduction of limestone rubble, brick and geometrically assorted stair windows, there is a surprising uniformity in the appearance of the surface.

When it is viewed from across the fields, the effect is not dissimilar from the grey ashlar of the dressings. This is very different from the rugged, earthy textures of STOKE-BY-NAYLAND, or the hard greys of knapped flint that would appear later. Within the tower, brick appears consistently in areas where precision is necessary but stone would be an extravagance, such as arches and the external corners of reveals. The circular newel stair, rising in the south-west corner, appears to burrow its way through strata of coursed flint.

Above the simple basement course, finely finished Barnack stone is restricted to openings and a modicum of decoration to mark the valued donors around the west door. They are recorded in a row of fourteen shields running directly below the west window – a feature that reappears at Cawston (nine shields), Wymondham west tower (sixteen shields) and a number of other towers across the county. At SALLE the heraldic symbols are in superb condition, allowing the work to be dated accurately to between 1405 and 1413. Below, in the spandrels between the door arch and the rectangular hood, is a pair of censing angels. The three small niches with square-topped canopies framing the arch are now empty. Ancient oak door leaves are of six panels with crossing arches and tracery in the head.

The main features of the shallow door arch are an outer row of tiny quatrefoils and an inner bowtell. Shallowness of openings is a recurring theme, not only here but at all

130' 5"

114' 8"

20'

0

West elevation

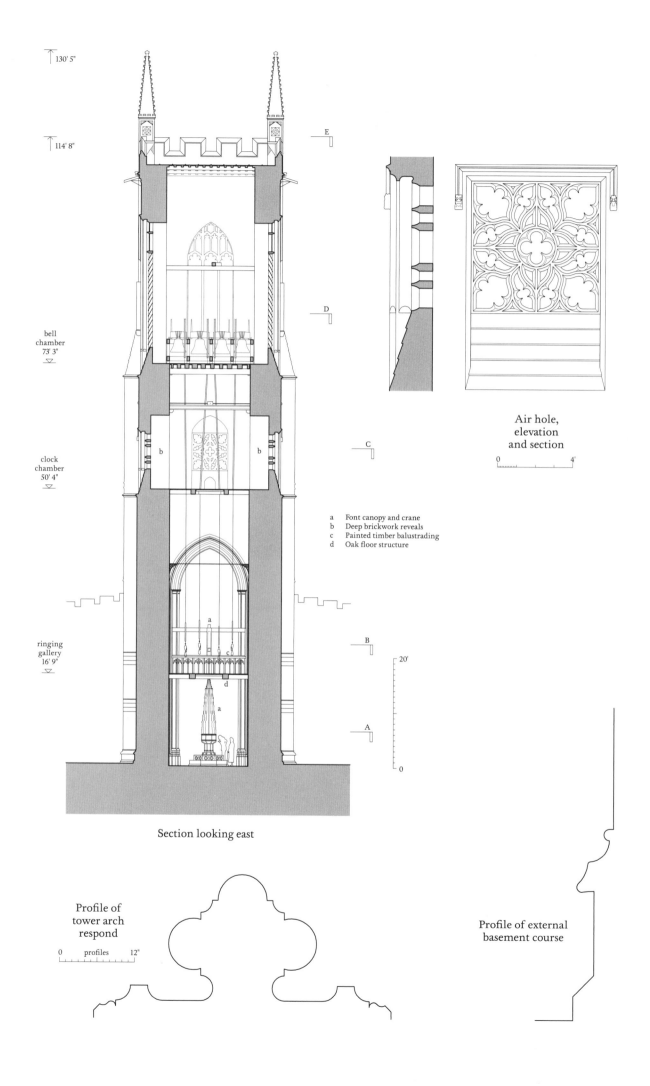

130' 5"

114' 8"

E

D

bell
chamber
73' 3"

clock
chamber
50' 4"

C

a   Font canopy and crane
b   Deep brickwork reveals
c   Painted timber balustrading
d   Oak floor structure

b   b

ringing
gallery
16' 9"

B

20'

a

c

d

a

A

0

Section looking east

Air hole,
elevation
and section

0   4'

Profile of
tower arch
respond

0   profiles   12"

Profile of external
basement course

major towers across the region, with the notable exception of STOKE-BY-NAYLAND. This is frustrating, for the immensely thick walls provided ample opportunity for introducing deep modelling into the centre of the façade. That this opportunity was missed was no doubt due to economy, for it was cheaper to build a deep brick reveal within the tower (b) than a deep stone reveal without. Despite its flatness, the four-light west window at SALLE is a fine design that avoids the dull uniformity of much panel tracery of the period. The most notable features are the tightly packed supermullions both in the head and supporting the transom from ogee archlets.

The clear diamond glazing provides brilliant illumination to the ringing gallery

within, a civilized feature that is not uncommon in East Anglia. The bell ropes may be some of the longest in the country, but the ringers enjoy a fine view towards the altar over the original painted timber balustrade (c). The oak floor structure that forms the soffit to the principal entrance (d) is, however, considerably less distinguished than the vaulting found within the rarely used ceremonial north and south porches. Tower arch responds are some of the most sumptuous recorded in the survey, with a central cluster of three semicircular shafts separated by quadrant recesses, connected to the wall only by a narrow neck, and all rising from tall octagonal bases. These shafts support two inner orders of hollow chamfers rising from moulded capitals, surrounded by one delicate, shallow outer order. The proportions of the tower arch are tall and noble.

The empty middle stage is illuminated by four of the finest air holes in Norfolk. These square openings, commonly known by the misnomer 'sound holes', are decorated with abstract tracery in designs ranging from the reticular at Foulsham and Southrepps to the geometric at Worstead, Cromer, Northrepps and SALLE. When positioned at the centre of the composition they form a wonderful contrast to the rugged severity of the flint walling. The holes at SALLE are among the largest of their type and are recessed to provide some welcome modelling to the centre of the elevation. Single bell openings dominate in East Anglia, and here they are untypically lavish in width and particularly in height. The three-bay design has cinquefoils throughout and conventional panels dividing the head.

Evorard Brigg, a descendant of the original donors, paid for the battlemented parapet and the cornice on which it sits around the year 1511. It is one of the most sumptuously decorated parapets of its date in England and is crammed full of heraldic shields, crowned monograms, flowers of various species and crocketed ogee gablets. More flowers, grimacing faces and cheeky gargoyles run along the hollow cornice line beneath. The panelled square pinnacle bases are decorated with three large, square flowers to each face beneath a flat Tudor arch. Tall, square pinnacle caps, castellated and closely crocketed, form the perfect termination to a memorable composition.

NOTES

1   'Reports on an Excursion of the Architectural Association to Norfolk', *The Building News*, 14 January 1881.

2   Tragically, by the time of the author's second visit in September 2014 the perfection of SALLE had been compromised by the indefensible appearance of a mobile phone mast above the line of the parapet.

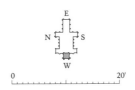

0   20'

Plan at E:
roof

3' 0"

23' 0"

24' 3"

Plan at D:
bell
chamber

16' 9"

Plan at C:
clock
chamber

17' 5"

15' 4"

Plan at B:
ringing
gallery

11' 4"

15' 1"

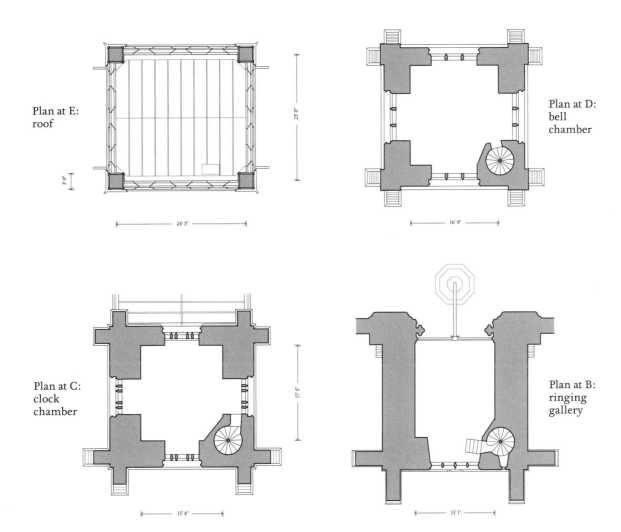

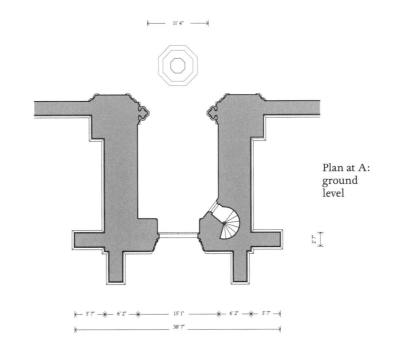

Plan at A:
ground
level

2' 7"

5' 7"   6' 2"   15' 1"   6' 2"   5' 7"

38' 7"

29

Stoke-by-Nayland

SUFFOLK

East Anglian flint and brick towers of the late Middle Ages form a distinct and self-contained group. The region was a late beneficiary of the medieval wool trade, and the church-building boom that gathered momentum after 1415 lasted for little more than a century. Where Norfolk led the way with Cawston, Winterton and SALLE in the early years of the century, Suffolk followed a generation later. STOKE-BY-NAYLAND, which started around 1439, is one of the earliest and certainly the most experimental of the great Suffolk towers. Not only is it the antithesis of the sharp and efficient structures being raised at the time across the Midlands, but it is also a radical development away from the simple orthogonal forms of her northern neighbour. This is an architecture of mass and texture. It marks a provocative return to the heavy, sculpturally rich architecture of the early fourteenth century, and it replaces clean, economical refinement with overwhelming physical presence.

St Mary's Church enjoys a magnificent position high on a ridge above the rivers Stour and Box, and the tower is visible for miles in every direction. This is the heart of Constable country, and the church was a great favourite of the artist. He considered that the tower, which appears in many of his paintings and sketches, was

> its grandest feature, which from its commanding height seems to impress on the surrounding country its own sacred dignity of character.[1]

The tower stands clear of the body of the church, connected only by a neck-like extension of the nave. Great multifaceted buttresses, impossible to justify for reasons of mere stability, dominate the design. On plan, these hulking masses approximate to clasping octagons ten feet across, with diagonal buttresses projecting from the outermost faces. The fortress-like simplicity of these plain masses contrasts beautifully with the slender niches set into their outer faces. Leafy plinths springing from octagonal shafts and covered by delicate, wispish canopies originally housed tier upon tier of saints and sovereigns. Before the arrival of the iconoclasts the effect must have been spectacular, for no fewer than fifty statues populated the four corners of the tower and the parapet. Buttresses are divided into four unequal stages, with two regular niches being supplemented by additional plinths on the second and third stages. The slimming of the octagonal buttresses as they pass each string is constant and unremarkable, but the dramatic raking-back of the diagonal fins cuts the tower into an unforgettable pyramidal silhouette. This design led directly to the diagonal composite buttresses of Brightlingsea (Essex), and indirectly to the octagonal buttresses of EYE, REDENHALL, Laxfield, Woodbridge, Bungay (Suffolk) and DEDHAM, and to the enormous composite forms of LAVENHAM.

The distinguishing feature of East Anglian construction is the lack of good building stone. Flint is the most durable of stones and is

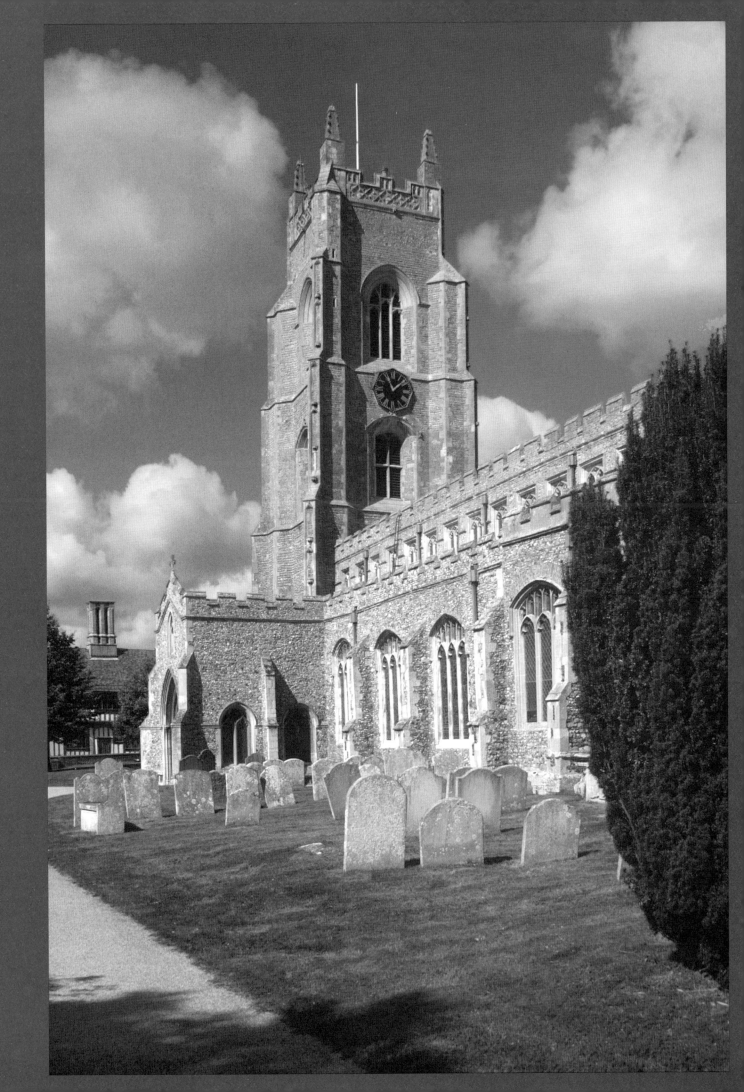

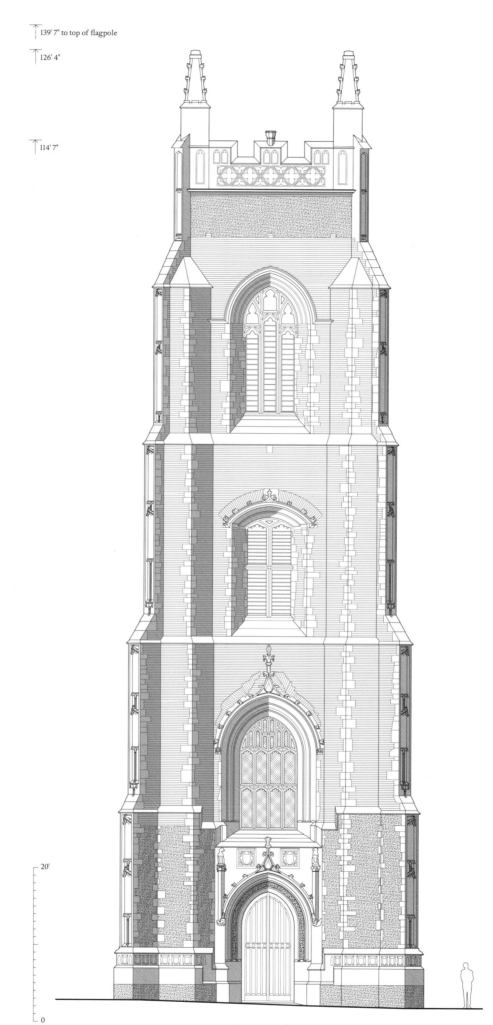

139' 7" to top of flagpole

126' 4"

114' 7"

20'

0

West elevation

in plentiful supply across the region, but it has severe limitations. It is impossible to carve, and when the irregular nodules are used in walling the structure is only as strong as the mortar that holds it together. From the early fourteenth century brickmaking started to reappear in the region as an economical and manageable alternative. In Saxon times the limitations of flint had led to the cornerless round tower, but in the late Middle Ages good freestone to form square corners was available by water from Barnack, Ketton and Caen, at least for those who could afford it. The rising prosperity afforded by the wool trade facilitated a glorious form of composite construction in which cheap local flint or brick provided the bulk of the walling and imported limestone the corners, the openings and the decoration. Eventually this would lead to the celebrated craft of knapped-flint flushwork, but in the first generation of great towers, of which STOKE-BY-NAYLAND is the prime example, rough walling and fine ashlar details work together in rugged sympathy.

The cliff-like elevation of St Mary's tower is an archaeologist's dream. Brick, flint and assorted rubble appear like geological strata mapping the history of construction through the middle years of the fifteenth century. Barely coursed flint is followed by brick and flint randomly intermingled across the second stage, then regular bonded brickwork roughly laid, reverting to random flint below the parapet. Some window arches support radiating voussoirs, others carry horizontal coursing, and around the ogee hood of the great west window bricks are heaped at random. Square brick-filled putlog holes add further to the chaos. So varied is the patterning, and so severe the contrast between materials, that it is hard to believe this is how the work was meant to appear. Without doubt this delirious jumble was originally hidden beneath layers of limewash or render. Be that as it may, the vast, rude patchwork of earthy textures is now one of the greatest attractions of St Mary's Church.

It is usual in English towers for the openings of the different stages to vary considerably in size, with the west window and the bell openings enlarged at the expense of the west door and the ringing chamber. At STOKE-BY-NAYLAND this hierarchy is ignored. The ceremonial west door and the west window are designed as an equal pair, finished with identical crocketed hood mouldings that rise through the same ogee head motif. Both openings are deeply recessed so that their splayed openings read as a continuation of the rippling planes established by the enclosing buttresses. The window profile, of shallow casements either side of a shallow wave, is varied above the door by the introduction of low relief carving in the centre. Decorated panels of stylized lions' heads are surrounded by rippling foliage, a motif that is prominently repeated in the hood stops. These stops support diagonal shafts rising to either side of the portal carrying the proud heraldic devices of a griffin and a lion to represent the families of Tendring and Howard.

A matching pair of Tendring and Howard shields is prominently displayed at the same level within foiled square panels surmounted by miniature brattishing. The two families had been joined in 1398 through the marriage of Sir John Howard to Alice Tendring, and it was their grandson, John Howard, 1st Duke of Norfolk, who provided the principal funding for the tower. Donations recorded from several local merchants allow the work to be accurate dated as starting around 1439 and finishing in 1462. The font that stands adjacent to the tower arch commemorates the completion of the tower, for the shield on the front step is the 'rose en soleil', the Yorkist badge adopted by Edward IV only after the Battle of Mortimer's Cross in 1461.

One of the great treasures of STOKE-BY-NAYLAND is the magnificent south door, described by the architect Raphael Brandon as being 'unsurpassed in richness; tracery, mouldings, saints, and canopies, all of the most costly workmanship, cover the entire surface'.[2] The ceremonial west door may not reach these exalted standards, but nevertheless it is a fine piece of ancient oak, regularly panelled and weathering to a mellow silver-grey. Minor shields, long since robbed of their armorial decoration, run around an understated basement course left overexposed by a modern lowering of the ground. The four-light west window, like the door beneath it, appears to push down through the horizontal strings as if to highlight the immobility of the adjacent buttresses. Unremarkable panel tracery, flat

cinquefoil arches and a transom reduce the glazing to domestic proportions. North and south walls remain massively solid.

In East Anglia, tower interiors fall way below the standard expected in the East Midlands, primarily because the walls are thicker to compensate for the weakness of the material, but also because imported stone was too expensive to waste on inessential vaulting. These failings are abundantly clear at STOKE-BY-NAYLAND. Constable may have approved of the ridiculously slender tower arch, but it leads to an uncomfortably narrow shaft-like volume rising forty-seven feet to a braced timber floor structure (a) enveloped in gloom. The dreadful glass of 1865 adds insult to indifference. The tower arch itself is formed of gentle waves and casements, the central order being carried by a moulded octagonal capital on a three-quarter cylindrical shaft. Mouldings from the tall octagonal base continue around the splayed eastern faces of the buttresses, providing further opportunities for heraldic shields.

Despite differences in tracery, the openings of the upper two stages are united by the use of deeply splayed brick reveals and unmoulded arches that extend the enveloping geometry of the buttresses. This is a radical development, for this eminently practical but unrefined form of construction was usually relegated to the interior of towers. Shallow segmental arches above the four ringing chamber openings emphasize the solidity of the structure, and tracery is reduced to the bare essentials of one mullion, one transom

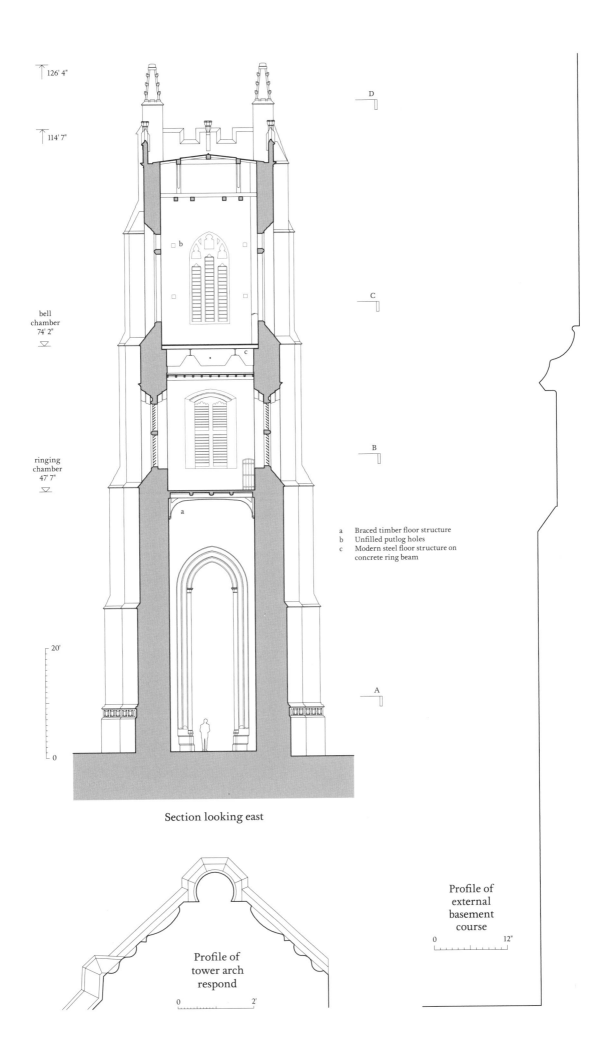

126' 4"

114' 7"

D

bell
chamber
74' 2"

C

b

c

ringing
chamber
47' 7"

B

a

a   Braced timber floor structure
b   Unfilled putlog holes
c   Modern steel floor structure on
    concrete ring beam

20'

A

0

Section looking east

Profile of
external
basement
course

0   12"

Profile of
tower arch
respond

0   2'

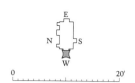

0   20'

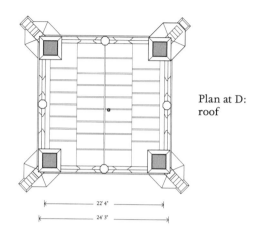

Plan at D:
roof

22' 4"

24' 3"

Plan at C:
bell
chamber

Plan at B:
ringing
chamber

16' 2"

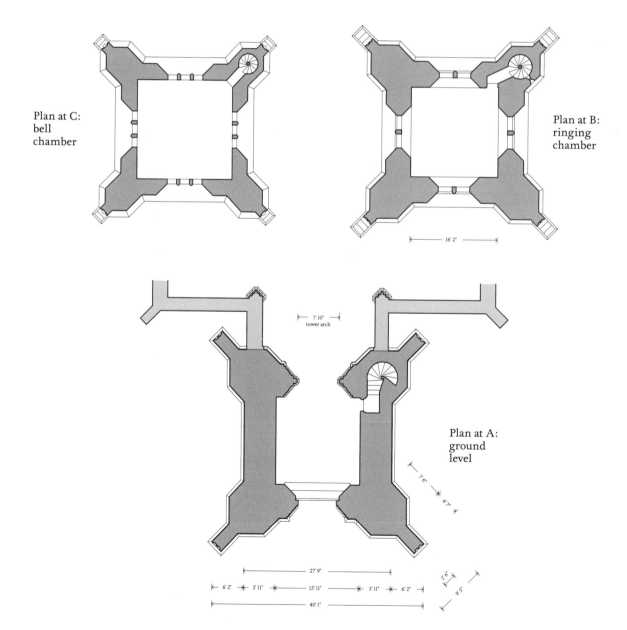

7' 10"
tower arch

Plan at A:
ground
level

7' 6"

4' 7"

27' 9"

6' 2"   5' 11"   15' 11"   5' 11"   6' 2"

2' 6"

9' 5"

40' 1"

and a 'Y' in the head. Decoration is restricted to the crockets of the hood, the quatrefoils of the archlets being simplified almost out of existence. Such elemental 'Y' tracery, which originated in the work of the court masons, was gaining popularity at the time.[3]

Within, the tower the walls are as richly textured as they are externally, except for the putlog holes that remain unfilled (b). Apart from a cast concrete ring beam and steel beams bearing the bell chamber floor (c), the original structure remains substantially intact. The three-light bell chamber openings are more conventional than the preceding stage, with two-centred arches and stepped transoms over trefoiled archlets. Once the apex of the bell chamber openings is reached, the octagonal buttresses die away and the diagonal outriggers rake in one last time, ready to scale the parapet.

The battlemented parapet rises sufficiently clear of the octagonal buttresses for the true scale of the square tower body, submerged within the great pyramidal mass, to be revealed. Stubby square pinnacles have been mistaken for restoration work, but their uncommonly robust profile is like a miniature paraphrasing of the tower itself. Parapets are conventionally decorated with minor panelling and short bands of Midlands-style quatrefoils. Empty statue bases rise from the central merlons on each face. STOKE-BY-NAYLAND started a fashion for hiding the tower stair within one of the octagonal buttresses, in this case on the south-east corner. This works admirably until the parapet is reached, and the continuation of the volume through to the roof adds one small discordant note to an otherwise magisterial composition. This is a heavyweight, masculine building, and yet it is also warm and welcoming. It provided a terrific opening act for the golden age of Suffolk towers.

Few East Anglian towers match the vigour of STOKE-BY-NAYLAND, but Brightlingsea (Essex) comes close. This is only to be expected, for it repeats all of the most idiosyncratic details, including the octagonal composite buttresses with their outward-facing ornamental niches and the stepped string motif over the portal. The soft, random jumble of materials may be replaced by hard, grey flint, but the consistent vocabulary suggests that the two towers, just a dozen miles apart, may well be the work of the same exceptionally gifted mason.[4]

NOTES

1   John Constable writing in 1830, quoted in the church guidebook (2008).
2   Raphael and J. Arthur Brandon, *An Analysis of Gothic Architecture* (1847), vol. I, p. 99, and vol. II, Plate 16.
3   See John Harvey, *The Perpendicular Style: 1330–1485* (1978), p. 187.
4   This would imply that the date of 1490 for Brightlingsea proposed by Pevsner and the Statutory Listing is at least a generation too late.

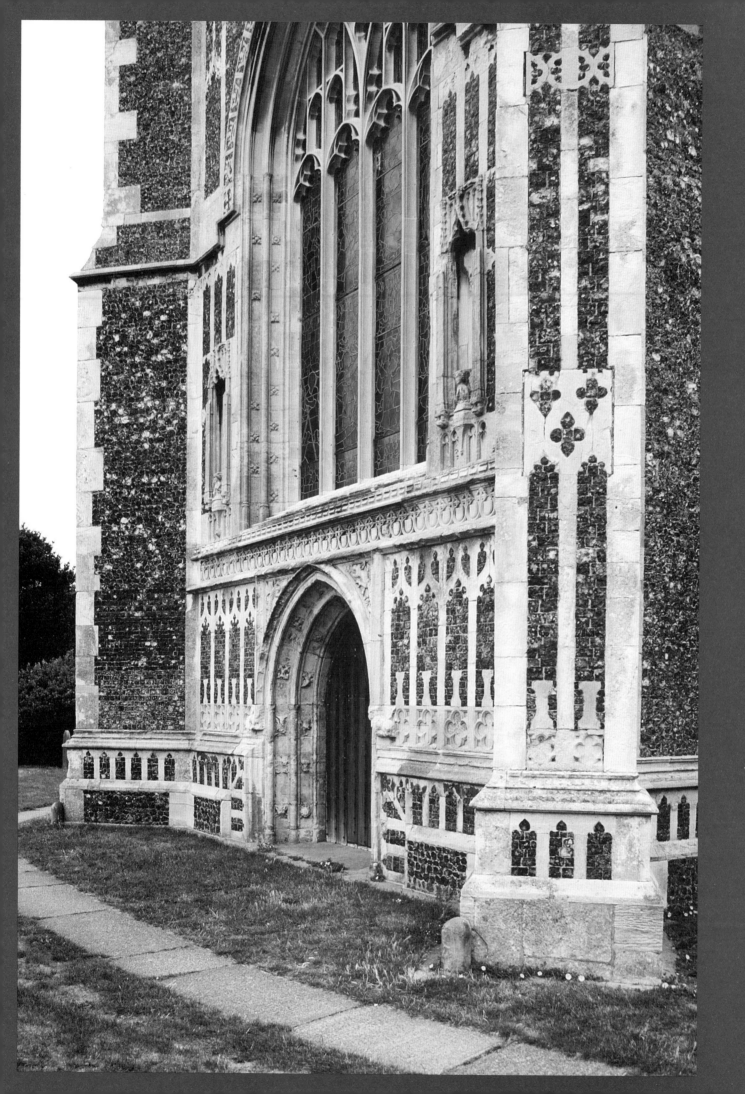

30

Southwold

SUFFOLK

SOUTHWOLD is the most celebrated masterpiece of flushwork decoration in England. Flushwork is the combination of knapped flint and smooth ashlar in flat decorative patterns. Flint nodules are knapped by being split, the fractured silica face forming the exposed surface of the wall. At a time when STOKE-BY-NAYLAND was proposing a sculptural architecture of mass and weight, the masons on the east coast were perfecting an alternative art of flat decorated planes. In the three-quarters of a century of sheep-driven prosperity that remained to Suffolk, flushwork marquetry became the local obsession.

Flushwork was not invented at SOUTHWOLD, for it appears with riotous enthusiasm at the gatehouse of Butley Priory (Suffolk) as early as 1320, but its adoption on church towers was slow. The tower of Walberswick (Suffolk), started in 1426, uses trefoiled arcading to the base and a band of flint quatrefoils above the west door. Ten years later at Kessingland (Suffolk) the arcading is repeated, but the quatrefoils give way to conventional carved stone. These examples are important in demonstrating the radical change that took place at SOUTHWOLD around 1440, for all three projects represent the work of one Richard Russell, mason and Member of Parliament for Dunwich. Russell is named in the contract for Walberswick, which still exists, and his mason's mark can be seen where the western arcade abuts the tower at SOUTHWOLD. It is known that he died in 1441, so it is possible that the final design of the lower stages of SOUTHWOLD may – at least in part – be the work of his successor. The bell stage is certainly by another hand, for it is an idiosyncratic design with no clear precedent.

The unfinished silhouette of SOUTHWOLD is entirely typical of contemporary Suffolk towers. The buttresses are diagonal, and the four principal stages rise to ninety-six feet, a figure that would have increased by fifteen or twenty feet had pinnacles been added. This unremarkable height is deceptive, for the complexity of the decoration suggests to the eye a far grander structure that could hold its own in the company of Cromer or Lavenham.

The plan of the church follows the standard East Anglian model of the time, but the massing is distinguished by a uniform clerestory of nineteen bays running straight from the east wall of the chancel to the embracing buttresses of the tower. This provides a rare degree of continuity between the two volumes, particularly when seen from the east. According to heraldic evidence, construction of the church, which replaced an earlier, fire-damaged structure, started at the east around 1413, ran through to the western tower and finished with the magnificent south porch in 1493. This was a great communal project, for donations to the work have been traced in almost 200 separate legal documents.

Any description of the tower must start with the glorious flushwork of the western elevation, which is without equal in England. The recurring motif is the flint panel finished with cinquefoiled arches at eye level, sub-cusped arches either side of the window head and trefoil arches elsewhere. Over the richer panels, paired mouchettes create the illusion of rising supertransoms, while the bays framing the portal incorporate hourglass-shaped figures suggestive of empty statue plinths. This rising field of pattern-making is contained by one huge chequerboard at the top and by plain flint buttress splays to either side. The pièce de résistance is the run of crowned monograms, fifteen inches high, that encircles the window arch, proclaiming 'SCT EDMUND ORA P NOBIS'.[1] The workmanship is superb.

The masons were intent on achieving the maximum contrast between their materials. Work starts with the whitest of Magnesian limestone from Tadcaster and continues in Caen stone, no less expensive or brilliant. Warmer Ancaster stone is used internally, but where it appears externally, for example in the tracery of the west window, it is a sign of modern restoration. The contrasting knapped flint is predominantly a sharp crystalline black, with square, trimmed edges laid in a tight staggered bond. The deliberate contrast of black and white leads to intriguing figure and ground relationships in which some motifs read as black on white while others read as white on black.

Carved stone provides subtle relief within this strident pattern-making. Plain quatrefoils run below the eye-level niches. Around the west door two broad casements between bowtells and filleted rolls house a fine array of lions, fleurons, five-petal roses and heraldic beasts. Similarities to the portal at Kessingland continue in the hood-mould decoration of square leaf motifs and their supporting pair of winged beasts. Writhing scaly dragons fill the spandrels below the rectangular hood-moulds extending horizontally. Above is a band of brattishing harbouring thirty-one tiny shields, all finished with a castellated drip.

The finest carving is reserved for a pair of tall niches that once housed figures of the Virgin Mary and St Edmund. These introduce a sub-cusped trefoil motif repeated in the archlets of the west window. This noble four-light design is full of incident, with an inverted dagger in the head separating a pair of panelled sub-arches. The dropping of the tracery below the springing of the arch hardly registers. In a variation of the west door jamb, four-petal flowers are strung out between bowtells. The only discordant note in this superb composition is an awkward diversion of the string around a blank square at the springing of the arch.

While the side faces of the buttresses are plain, enlivened only by the random depth of quoining, the outer faces are filled with first-class flushwork that effectively ties the disparate parts of the composition together. Castellated set-offs divide the buttresses into five unequal portions that progressively reduce in height.

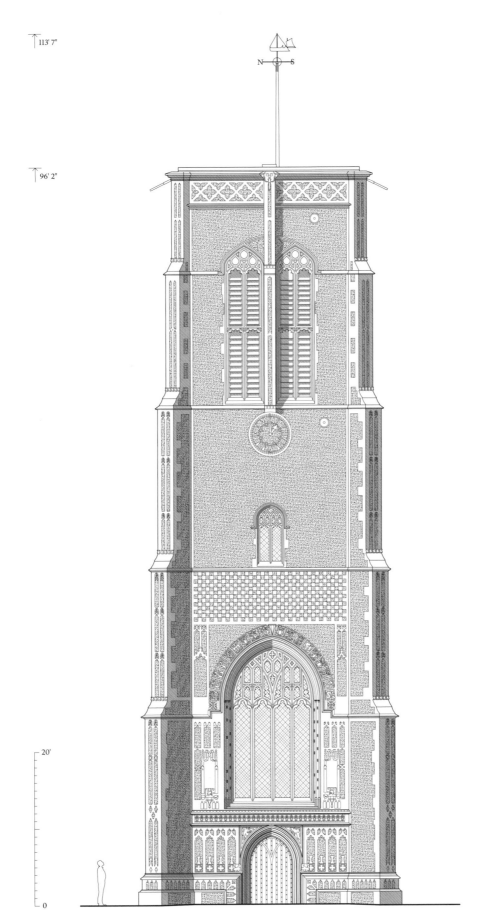

113' 7"

96' 2"

N   S

20'

0

West elevation

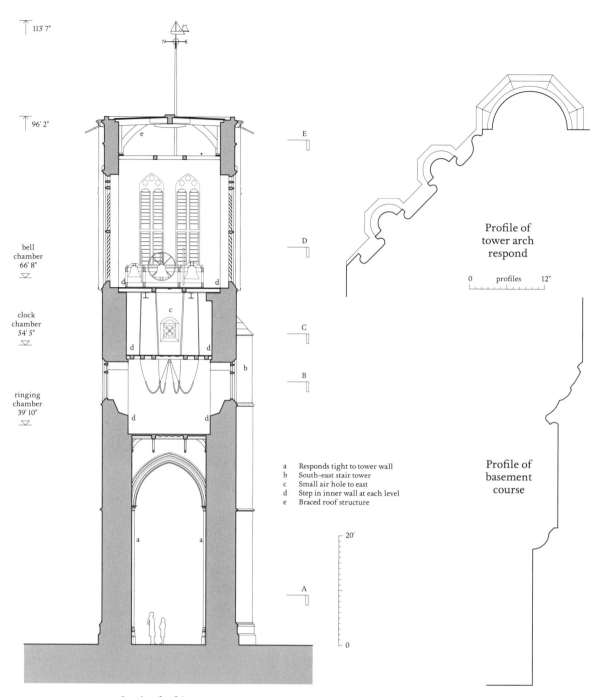

113' 7"

96' 2"

E

D

bell
chamber
66' 8"

C

clock
chamber
54' 5"

B

ringing
chamber
39' 10"

b

a   a

20'

A

0

N   6

Profile of
tower arch
respond

0   profiles   12"

a   Responds tight to tower wall
b   South-east stair tower
c   Small air hole to east
d   Step in inner wall at each level
e   Braced roof structure

Profile of
basement
course

Section looking east

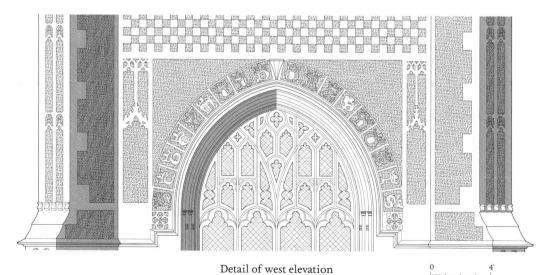

Detail of west elevation

0   4'

Within the church the constricted space beneath the tower is made less evident by pushing the responds as far apart as possible (a). Despite the soaring height of the arch, the proportions are excellent. The profile of the responds is generous but flat, with shallow casements separating three bowtells and a half-round shaft. After the Victorians wisely removed a Georgian tower galley, it is disappointing to find the tower arch compromised again by a modern timber screen. The northern respond is home to Southwold Jack: a helmeted soldier, as old as the church itself, who strikes the hours with his battleaxe. The south-east stair bulges from the external face of the wall until the clock chamber has been reached (b). From here on up it has a mind of its own, hiding first in the north-west corner and then the south-west.

Calm governs the middle stage of the tower, and the modest two-light ringing chamber windows float in a tranquil sea of flint. The only distinguishing feature is the ogee-headed drop tracery developed by Richard Russell at Walberswick and Kessingland. The discontinuity in level between external string and internal floors is not untypical of East Anglia. The east-facing clock room window takes the form of a small Norfolk air hole (c). The skeleton clock faces are sympathetic to the fretted masonry patterns. Lighter grey-pink estuarine flint that appears occasionally on the lower stages now starts to dominate. The tower exhibits a characteristic East Anglian cross section,

with the outer face rising plumb while the inner face steps back at each level (d). Not only is this a pragmatic response to a weak material, but it also provides a convenient ledge to support the floor beams.

Inventiveness returns with a vengeance on the final stage. Paired twin-light bell openings appear in Suffolk, at Woodbridge (1444–56) and Laxfield (1452–60), but neither approaches the height of SOUTHWOLD, and the flat-arched hood that joins the openings into a single entity is employed here on a far more lavish scale. The same motif was favoured at this time

by the Stamford school of masons, and the Midlands pattern of flushwork quatrefoils, which bring the tower to an emphatic conclusion, suggest this as a possible influence.

What makes SOUTHWOLD unique is not only the flat panelled pilaster that rises through the hood, but also the novel tracery of the lights. Clustered above conventional cinquefoiled archlets are three unfoiled pointed arches.[2] It is unclear how this novel design was intended to finish, for the parapet was never built.

There has been much speculation as to whether a spire was intended at SOUTHWOLD and other prominent unfinished towers across the region. The answer has to be a categorical no, for integral squinch arches are conspicuous by their absence, and

without them a recessed spire cannot be supported. Flint-rubble walls are weak in comparison with the solid ashlar walls of the Midlands, and it would require considerable courage, even foolhardiness, to risk the additional weight of a stone spire.

What is missing from SOUTHWOLD is not a spire but four corner pinnacles and a battlement, for the jolly lugger on the flagpole is poor compensation for a bald pate. The splendid view from the roof, or at least from the safety of the roof hatch, is a pleasure denied to the thousands of visitors who throng this charming seaside resort every year. With sensitivity and intelligence it would still be possible to add an appropriate termination to this otherwise splendid composition. SOUTHWOLD's tower is a queen still waiting for her crown.

NOTES

1   'St Edmund pray for us.'
2   A similar motif appears around 1530 at Whiston (Northants).

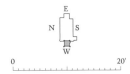

0   20'

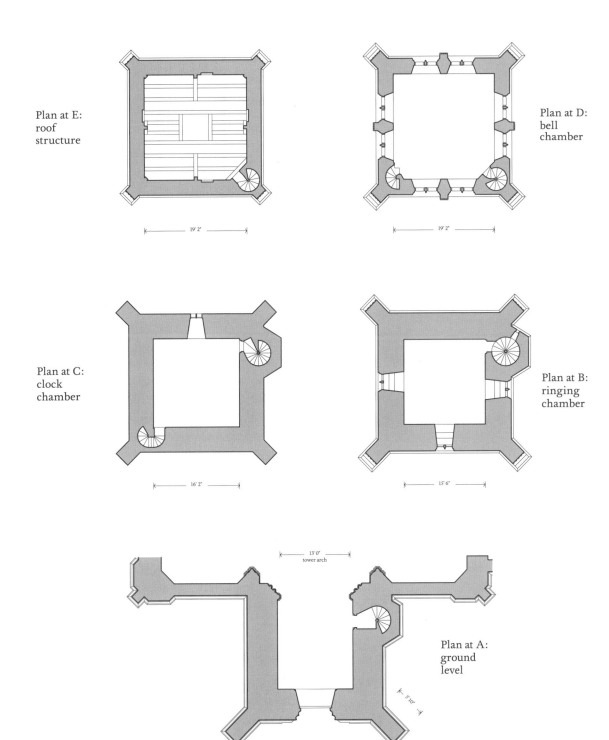

Plan at E:
roof
structure

Plan at D:
bell
chamber

19' 2"

19' 2"

Plan at C:
clock
chamber

Plan at B:
ringing
chamber

16' 2"

15' 6"

13' 0"
tower arch

Plan at A:
ground
level

5' 10"

5' 0"

25' 2"

4' 2"   5' 7"   14' 0"   5' 7"   4' 2"

33' 6"

31

Eye

SUFFOLK

SALLE, STOKE-BY-NAYLAND and SOUTHWOLD all represent the early period of great East Anglian flint towers. In Norfolk the tall plain tower with setback buttresses and square air hole was established early and underwent only limited development in the second half of the fifteenth century. In Suffolk, however, the early towers were more experimental, and it is only after 1450 that a mature style emerges. The prime examples of this phase are strung out along the River Waveney, which marks the county boundary. Laxfield, Bungay and EYE are in Suffolk, while REDENHALL, lying just north of the Norfolk border, is in all essentials a Suffolk tower. The distinguishing features of these towers are octagonal buttresses and sumptuous flushwork decoration.

At Bungay the flushwork is confined to the base and the parapet, the centre stages reverting to unknapped flint. The use of crowned monograms, panelled buttresses and a trefoil arcade around the base form a clear link to SOUTHWOLD. At Laxfield, started around 1452, the entire west front is loaded with flushwork ornament in a style so similar to REDENHALL and EYE that these towers must all be the work of a single mason or lodge. The variety in treatment of the upper levels at these four towers reflects the differing durations of the work. Laxfield was completed within a decade, EYE took considerably longer, and REDENHALL dragged on for over fifty years.

At EYE, bequests record that the tower was commenced around 1458 and was under construction in 1463, 1465 (a cartful of flint) and 1469. In 1470 over £40 was raised for the work, 'partly with the plough, partly in church ales – but chiefly of the frank and devoute hartes of the people'.[1] The principal donor between 1463 and his death in 1491 was John de la Pole, 2nd Duke of Suffolk, whose contribution is recognized by a shield at the centre of the south parapet. The de la Poles were among the greatest patrons of English church-building from the late fourteenth century, at Holy Trinity, Hull, to the late fifteenth century, at Cawston, SALLE, REDENHALL, Wingfield and EYE.

EYE is the perfect model of a mature Suffolk flushwork tower, with an emphasis on texture and line rather than three-dimensional form. Octagonal buttresses telescope upwards in four carefully diminishing stages. Flatness prevails on the elevations, with tracery and glass pushed forward to participate in games of two-dimensional pattern-making. Massive rubble walls adopt the characteristic profile of a flat vertical outer face and a stepped inner face, the beams of the upper floors resting on the steps. In smooth ashlar the design would be unremarkable, even dull, but in its sumptuous flushwork dress EYE is transformed into the most beautiful of all Suffolk towers.

Octagonal clasping buttresses are the ideal form for a flushwork tower, for they minimize sharp shadows, keep the view of the elevation as open as possible, and provide a continuous surface for decoration to wrap

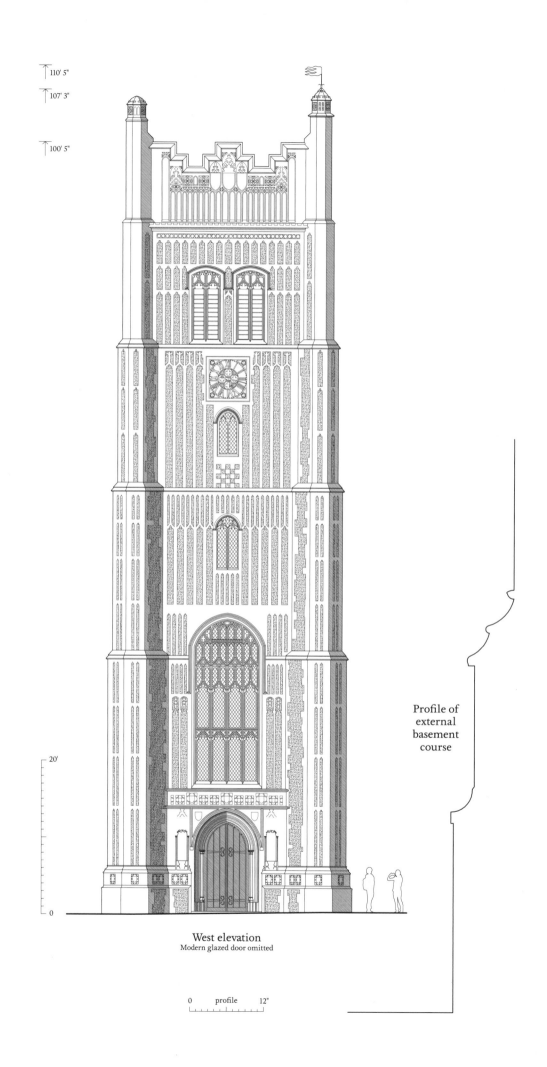

110' 5"

107' 3"

100' 5"

20'

0

Profile of
external
basement
course

West elevation
Modern glazed door omitted

0   profile   12"

smoothly around. In East Anglia and in the south and west of England, for example at LUDLOW, the form reappears more or less simultaneously around 1450.

In the very best flushwork façades – and none are better than the west front at EYE – stone and flint are kept in near perfect balance. Smooth ashlar dominates in the framing of the composition, on the parapet and on the outer faces of the buttresses; knapped flint fills the splayed side faces of the buttresses. Elsewhere, the two materials are evenly matched and the warm, rich, mellow textures are simply gorgeous. The buff limestone is better now than when it left the mason's chisel, for it has gained a silver-grey patina that harmonizes with the rich jumble of grey flints. At SOUTHWOLD the flints are finely trimmed cubes, but here the natural randomness of the nodule shapes and sizes remains unchecked.

EYE follows the ancient tradition of English tower-building, with a stack of independent stages set one above the other, the horizontality of the parts being countered by the verticality of the decoration. At EARLS BARTON the verticality derives from pilaster strips; at ST MARY, STAMFORD from tiers of cylindrical shafts; and at EYE from attenuated flushwork panels.

The western portal, framed with wide casements and a cluster of bowtells, provides the only significant modelling on any of the elevations. Before the addition of unnecessarily assertive modern glazed doors, this opening, and the porch within, would have been open to the elements, adding considerable depth to the base of the composition. Within the porch is a stone fan vault with central bell hatch (a). The engaged corner shafts supporting each of the four quarter fans follow the detail of the door bowtells.

Above, the gallery floor supports an arcaded stone balustrade and the bases of the truncated tower arch (b), an uncomfortable arrangement when seen from the nave. The body of the church suffers from an unfortunate excess of white paint applied indiscriminately across plaster and stone. The spiral stair is accommodated within a slightly enlarged north-east buttress. It is accessed from within the open porch, an inconvenience during services, and so a second stair burrows organically from the nave up to the gallery through the south-east buttress and the deep rubble of the south wall.

The dominant theme around the portal is the display of shields in rounded quatrefoils above the door and in the spandrels, and in rounded sexfoils strung along the basement course. Now their flat faces are featureless and empty, but when they were freshly emblazoned with the donors' heraldry the effect must have been spectacular. Less satisfactory are the empty niches beside the door, which have lost not only their statues but all trace of original detail, for the lower story has been damaged by overzealous cleaning in recent years. The gridded four-bay west window remains subservient to the overriding composition.

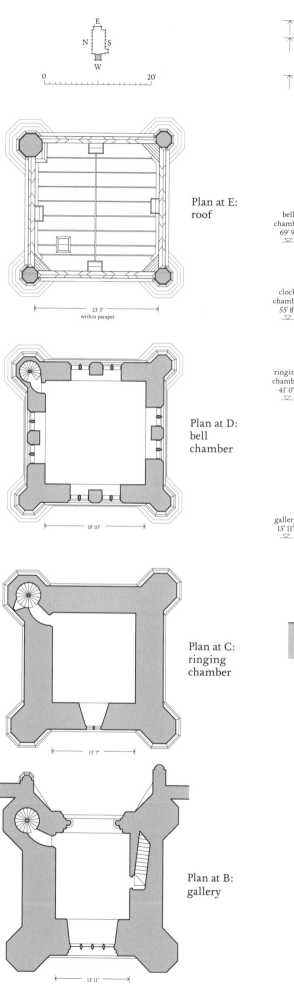

Plan at E:
roof

Plan at D:
bell
chamber

Plan at C:
ringing
chamber

Plan at B:
gallery

23' 3"
within parapet

18' 10"

15' 7"

13' 11"

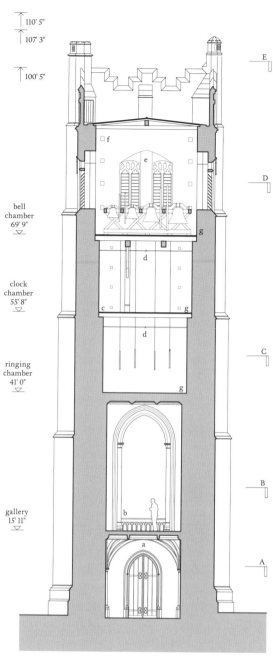

Section looking east

a   Fan vault with circular bell hatch
b   Arcaded stone balustrade
c   Floor level with external string course
d   Wrought-iron tie-rods
e   Brickwork arch and central pier
f   Putlog holes
g   Wall steps in at each level

110' 5"
107' 3"
100' 5"

bell
chamber
69' 9"

clock
chamber
55' 8"

ringing
chamber
41' 0"

gallery
15' 11"

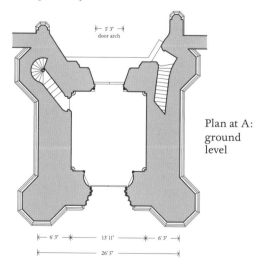

Plan at A:
ground
level

5' 3"
door arch

6' 3"   13' 11"   6' 3"
26' 5"

0   20'

E
N   S
W

Conventional twin-light ogee-headed openings on the following stages are surrounded by a stylized forest of silvery flushwork tree trunks, dividing and doubling in the crown. There is plenty of variety in the development of the pattern so that it never approaches the predictability of a grid. A tiny patch of chequerboard fills the space between the upper window, and cinquefoiled arches make a belated appearance at the top of the third stage. The square clockface panel may not be original, but it fits convincingly into the design. The three other elevations are entirely devoid of incident but not of interest, for there are fascinating variations in the patterns and colours of the flint. The clock chamber floor lines through with the third-stage string (c), but otherwise there is the usual lack of correspondence between internal and external divisions. Pairs of ancient wrought-iron tie-rods, hooked together in the centre, secure the structure (d).

Despite, or perhaps because of, their unassuming size, the two flat-headed, twin-light bell openings of the final stage are a resounding success. Internally these paired openings are spanned by a single flat brick arch, supported on a central brick pier (e) and brick jambs. Neat putlog holes retain a memory of the original scaffold (f). Unlike the preceding stages, all four elevations around the bells are covered in flushwork. The tower finishes with a greater flourish than was perhaps originally intended, for the stone-faced parapet continues high above the flat lead roof. An impressive display of four-petal flowers and shields fills the space between a miniature arcade and the stepped battlement. In both style and chronology, this final stage marks the arrival of Tudor England.

NOTE

1   Details of wills are recorded in Pevsner, *The Buildings of England: Suffolk* (1961). John Harvey, *The Perpendicular Style* (1978), states that the bells were present in 1488. The 1485 end date is taken from the *Historic Manuscripts Commission 10th Report*, vol. IV, p. 529. The quotation regarding the 1470 fundraising is unattributed in the church guidebook, *Eye Church* (1980).

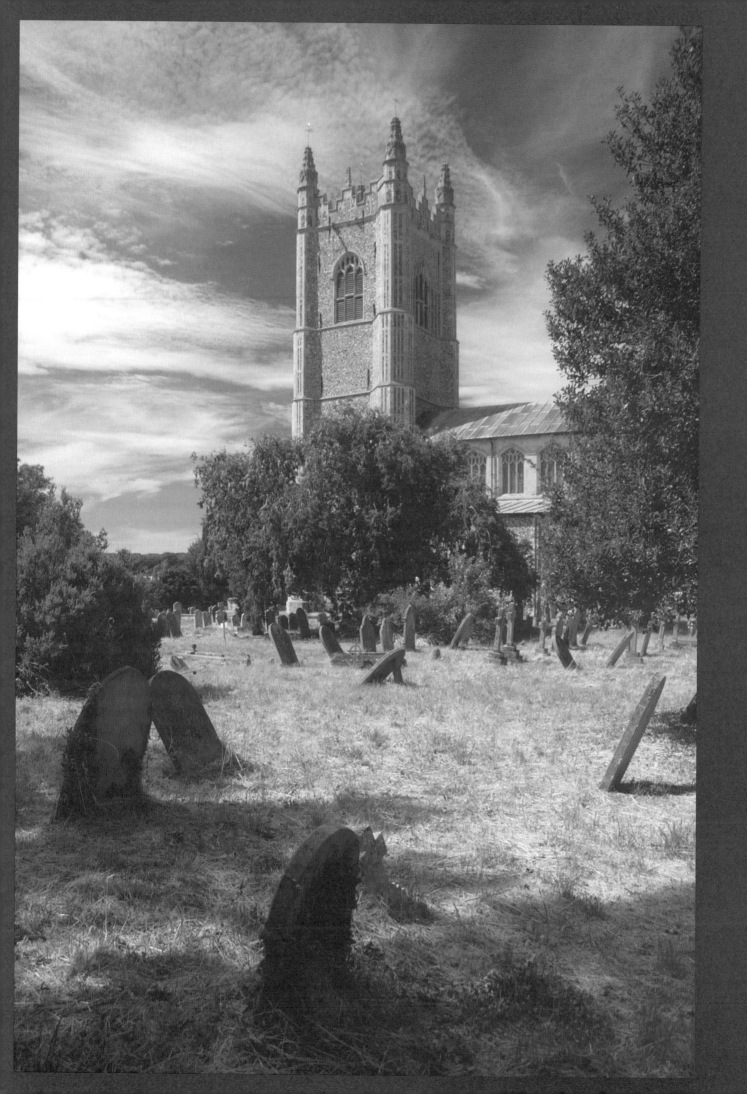

32

Redenhall

NORFOLK

REDENHALL is the last word in flushwork, at least in Norfolk. Without any doubt REDENHALL and its Suffolk rival at EYE were constructed by the same masons at the same time, at least for the first three stages. From then on their paths diverge, for REDENHALL was much slower to complete. It is hard to establish whether one church followed and the other led, or whether both were worked up in parallel. In 1469 the benefactress Joan Bunning, who is buried near the north door, left £3 6s. 8d. towards the building of the tower. Early contributions came from John de la Pole, 2nd Duke of Suffolk, for his shield and leopards' head motifs appear around the basement course. Work continued through 1492 when Thomas Bacon left a legacy, and 1511 when John Bacon followed suit. In 1514 6s. 8d. was donated to the great bell, suggesting that the roof had by then been made watertight. The pinnacles can have risen no earlier than 1518, the year in which Revd Richard Shelton became rector. His rebus, a shell and a tun, appears on the south-east corner.[1]

St Mary's tower is commandingly positioned on high ground overlooking the old road from Bury St Edmunds to Bungay and the coast. Even from the fast modern bypass the first sight of glorious flushwork cliffs rising heavenward is unforgettable. The church is surrounded by a vast, rolling sea of gravestones, for although REDENHALL is little more than a rural hamlet the parish encompasses the neighbouring villages of Harleston and Wortwell. Evidence of a Saxon or Norman round tower and church lies hidden beneath the Victorian flooring of the nave. The nave and aisles gained their present form in the early fifteenth century, the chancel rather earlier, and the two-storeyed porch and the tower rather later.

All the main constituents of EYE are equally present at REDENHALL. This is an architecture of crisply drawn lines and rich texture rather than sculptural form. Octagonal buttress wrap softly around the corners and rise in four unequal stages, each more slender than the last. One of the buttresses swells to hide the staircase, but this time it is on the south-east corner. The prevailing flatness of the surfaces is maintained in the shallow modelling of the openings. The west window is of four lights and carefully matches the width of the portal below. Second and third stage windows are small, with old-fashioned, flowing twin-light tracery. Side and rear elevations remain imperforate and undecorated below the bell stage, and tall trefoil-arched panels, doubled in the head of every stage, are the predominant flushwork motif. Beyond these similarities there are many subtle variations that merit detailed consideration.

The west portal is in far better condition than at EYE, for it retains the lovely mellow patina that only centuries of rain and wind can provide. The empty niches beside the doorway are particularly well preserved. There is much fine carving in the crocketed, ogee-headed canopies, the octagonal statue bases and the miniature splayed buttresses that rise out of the basement course. Heraldic beasts, possibly a lion and a lioness, crouch on the canopy roofs. As at EYE, there are shields in the spandrels beneath the rectangular hood-mould, but here they are clasped by angels still as crisp as the day they were carved. The decoration of the basement course is also richer than at EYE, for the rounded quatrefoils are not only sub-cusped and recessed into square panels, but also finished with heraldic symbols rather than shields. These include flowers and animal heads, including the leopard of the de la Pole family. Above the door are the standard row of donors' shields, this time three large and four small, surrounded by cusps and stars of varying designs. Diverging 'Y' tracery in the supermullioned west window makes a refreshing change from the usual Perpendicular grid, and the absence of a transom assists with the verticality of the composition.

There is no open porch here, and the solid oak door is framed by pairs of bowtells, a roll and a bracket. Within the tower a ringing gallery was added as an afterthought, possibly in the eighteenth century. Whereas Victorian architects usually delighted in removing such intrusions, here the misfortune was merely exacerbated by a timber traceried screen of 1842 (a) and a choir vestry screen and organ of 1897. The noble tower arch is now obscured by ignorance.

The second and third stages are almost identical to the second stage of EYE, except for the chequerboard pattern above the window. Within the tower the two middle floors remain empty apart from vertical wooden troughs used to protect and guide the exceedingly long bell ropes (b). North and south elevations bear the scars of a crude early strengthening exercise, for when the tower was shaken by a lightning strike in 1616 pairs of wrought-iron straps were inserted at five levels. Externally these straps grip the face of the wall with vertical, arrow-headed bars that ought to be painted out in a sympathetic light grey rather than black. Four of the pairs are tied to the ends of the original floor beams (c), and the fifth pair to new timbers spanning the ringing chamber (d). Two more oak ties run from east to west through the bell chamber (e).

The protracted completion of the medieval tower is documented by a coarsening of the details on the fourth stage. Flushwork panels become broader, and stepped transoms awkwardly interrupt the three-light bell openings. Ogee archlets, a distinctive feature of the mid-fifteenth-century work in the region, are notable by their absence. Inexplicably, only three faces of the bell stage are decorated, the south elevation being finished in uncoursed flint. The change of plan is most apparent in the proportions, for no doubt the original mason's intention was to diminish the height of every stage, exactly as at EYE. Up to this point REDENHALL had been raised on a slightly smaller scale than its rival, but the good people of Norfolk were not to be outdone by their southern

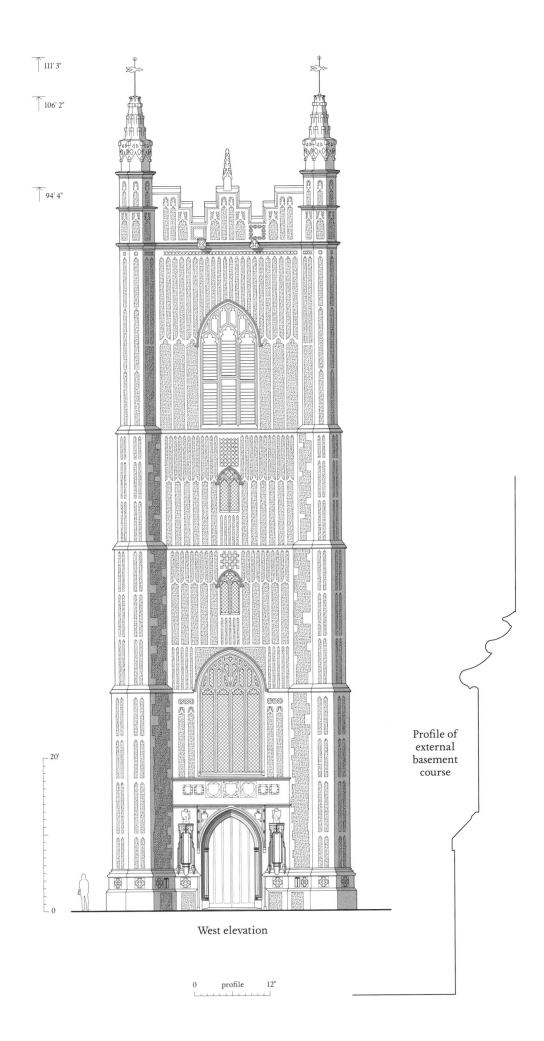

111' 3"

106' 2"

94' 4"

20'

0

West elevation

Profile of
external
basement
course

0   profile   12"

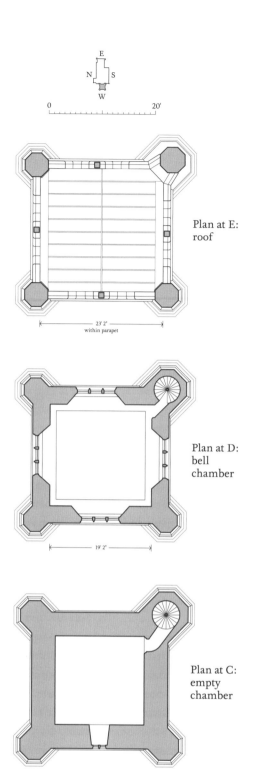

Plan at E:
roof

23' 2"
within parapet

Plan at D:
bell
chamber

19' 2"

Plan at C:
empty
chamber

Plan at B:
empty
chamber

15' 6"

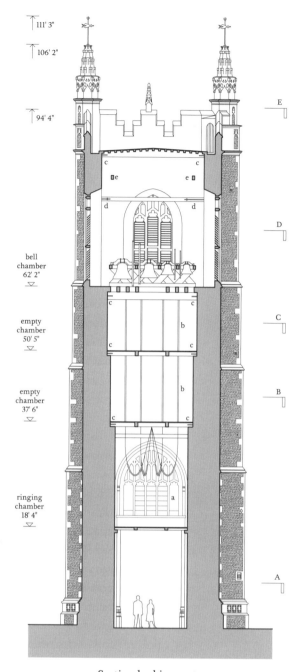

111' 3"

106' 2"

94' 4"

bell
chamber
62' 2"

empty
chamber
50' 5"

empty
chamber
37' 6"

ringing
chamber
18' 4"

E

D

C

B

A

Section looking east

a   Timber screen installed in 1842
b   Bell ropes in wooden troughs
c   Iron ties added to original floors
d   Additional oak tie-beams
e   Oak tie-beams running east−west

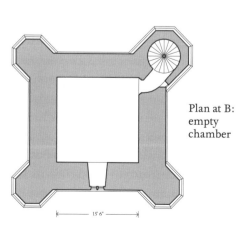

Plan at B:
empty
chamber

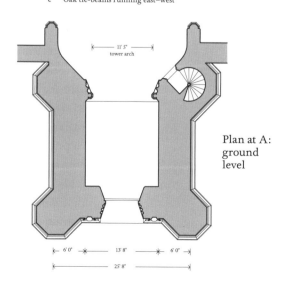

Plan at A:
ground
level

11' 5"
tower arch

6' 0"   13' 8"   6' 0"

25' 8"

0   20'

neighbours. The bell stage stretches up in a final calculated attempt to outdo the parishioners of EYE.

Quality is reasserted on the parapet and the flint changes colour again, suggesting yet another phase of construction. Bungay, Laxfield and EYE all have ashlar parapets, but at REDENHALL the flushwork continues, with excellent results. The battlement is stepped in the conventional pattern, but with a cheeky stub of a secondary pinnacle perched over the centre merlon. Beneath are a mixture of narrow trefoiled panels and wide quatrefoil panels, all finished with the sharp silhouette of crocketed gablets.

Abstract geometrical designs of concentric squares, octagons, wheels and snowflakes are set within squares beneath the embrasures. Beneath all of these motifs are gargoyles of well-intentioned hideousness.

The pinnacle shafts are much broader than at EYE and Laxfield, and as a result the silhouette is much heavier. They rise incongruously from an elegant cornice carrying delicate flower carvings on each corner. By contrast, the pinnacle caps are massive, with hard-edged angular carving, but they serve their purpose well, for the tips of the weathervanes are lifted high enough to outreach those of EYE by a mere ten inches.

NOTE

1   See Francis Blomefield, 'Hundred of Earsham: Redenhall', in *An Essay Towards a Topographical History of the County of Norfolk: Volume 5* (1806), pp. 358–72. A rebus is a representation of a word or name by means of a visual pun.

33

Chipping Campden

GLOUCESTERSHIRE

According to a vernacular rhyme, still circulating in the early nineteenth century, the master mason of St James, Chipping Campden was:

> John Gowere,
> Who built Campden Church
> And Glo'ster towre.[1]

No more is known of John Gower, but stylistic links between the two buildings, along with the tower of Great Malvern Priory (Worcs), lend support to this traditional connection. All three church towers were completed around 1460, and all are within twenty-five miles of each other.[2] They share one highly original feature that may derive from the central tower at Lichfield Cathedral, built a century and a half earlier. On each of the towers, continuous narrow pilasters rise up the full height of the elevations, in three pairs at the great churches and in three individual lines at CHIPPING CAMPDEN. The smaller the tower, the more dominant the motif, for on the larger towers it has to compete with a rich surface articulation of panelling, quatrefoil bands and multiple string courses. At CHIPPING CAMPDEN the pilasters dominate to the extent that panelling and window openings on the upper stages become entirely subservient. This is splendidly self-confident abstract design, consisting of little more than a beautifully balanced grid of lines.

The pilasters are just ten inches wide and between thirteen and ten inches deep,

reducing gradually at each stage. In each tower the articulation is the same, with major strings wrapping fully around the pilaster, and flat-sided drips marking secondary divisions. The vertical force of this simple applied device is far greater than conventional recessed panelling,[3] and it is, therefore, surprising that it did not become an accepted element of the Perpendicular style. This pared-back motif also bears an uncanny, and no doubt unintended, resemblance to the long and short work of Saxon towers such as EARLS BARTON and BARNACK.

Plain diagonal buttresses and glorious golden limestone place CHIPPING CAMPDEN firmly in the Gloucestershire tradition. Gloucestershire towers have a high reputation that is, on the whole, overstated, for good late medieval towers in the county, such as Winchcombe or Northleach, cannot match their counterparts in Northamptonshire, Yorkshire or East Anglia, let alone Somerset. In these great tower-building counties, the diagonal buttress was reserved for less prestigious churches or for the display of flushwork decoration, but the Gloucestershire masons embraced the form wholeheartedly. From Yate, Westerleigh and Thornbury at the southern edge of the county to CHIPPING CAMPDEN in the far north, and even on the upper stages of Cirencester and the middle stages of Gloucester Cathedral, the diagonal buttress was employed without reservation. Usually this has the unfortunate consequence of

124' 4"

119' 4"

20'

0

West elevation

broadening the proportions of the tower elevations, but at CHIPPING CAMPDEN this is hardly an issue, for the plaster strips provide more than enough vertical emphasis.

Church and tower are of one period, funded by the thriving fifteenth-century wool trade. Workmanship is exemplary, and the body of the church is brilliantly lit. The tower arch, hardly pointed at all, rises from beautifully simple responds of three concave faces, a form repeated in the capitals. A simple quadripartite tower vault follows directly from the outer profile of the arch.

Externally, the pilasters commence right from the ground, so that each is served by its own protruding base. Otherwise the side elevations are blank, save for an inconspicuous south-east staircase door for the bell ringers. The potential clash of the centre pilaster and west portal is brilliantly resolved by forming the ogee-headed door arch from a pair of pinnacles joining at the centre. The mason's pleasure in his own audaciousness is evident in the cheeky application of a paper-thin crocketed hood-mould to the face of the square profile, and in the way the pilaster is allowed to fly freely in front of the west window.

The five-bay west window is distinguished by a castellated transom supported on ogee archlets and small rotated quatrefoils. This unusual detail, along with the pattern of two-bay sub-arches either side of rising mullions, forms another connection to Gloucester Cathedral, this time the Lady Chapel of 1457–83. John Harvey suggests

that the mason of that structure might be John Hobbs, but equally it might be the same John Gower who completed the central tower at Gloucester in 1457.[4]

Strings divide the elevation into three stages, the ratio between successive stages approximating the very satisfactory proportion of 5:7. Richly profiled drips on the flat-sided diagonal buttresses, repeated at a smaller scale on the pilasters, imply an equal subdivision of each of the main compartments. The middle of these compartments is finished with nothing but blind panelling, and inconspicuous lancet windows are reluctantly introduced to the side elevations. Crocketed ogee heads join pairs of trefoil-headed panels that fill the space between the pilasters. Originally the two tiers of panels represented the ringing chamber below and an empty sound chamber above. A carillon mechanism was first installed in the sound chamber in 1682, and in the late twentieth century a steel bell frame was added (a). While the decision to retain the original, but obsolete, oak frame in the top stage of the tower (b) is admirable on conservation grounds, the relocated bells are now muffled by their solid enclosure.

The articulation of the original bell stage derives from that of the preceding stage, except that the panels are divided into three bays, the outer two perforated by stone louvres in their upper parts (c). There are clear parallels with the arrangement of bell chamber louvres at the two post-Reformation Gloucestershire towers of

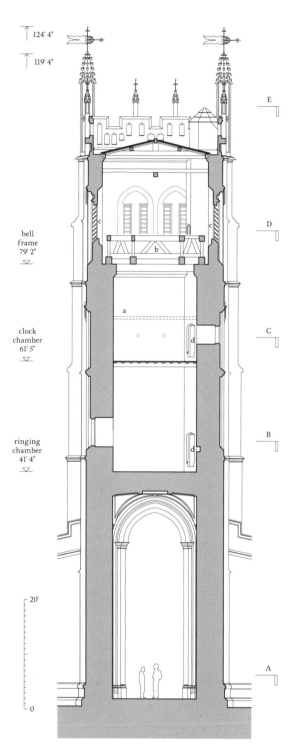

124' 4"

119' 4"

E

bell
frame
79' 2"

D

clock
chamber
61' 5"

C

ringing
chamber
41' 4"

B

20'

A

0

Section looking east

a   Modern bell chamber floor
b   Original bell frame with bells removed
c   Stone louvres
d   Staircase door

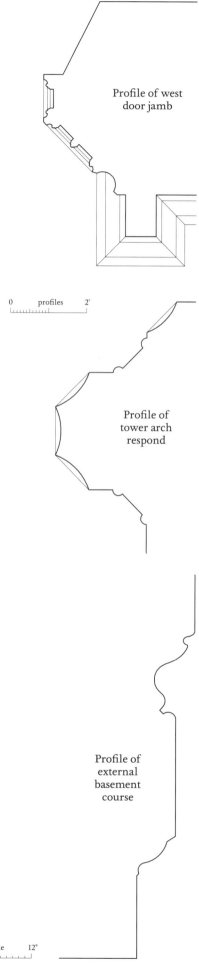

Profile of west
door jamb

0   profiles   2'

Profile of
tower arch
respond

Profile of
external
basement
course

0   profile   12"

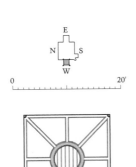

Reflected
plan of
tower vault

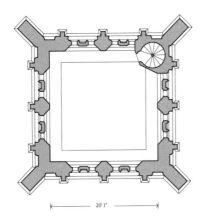

Plan at D:
bell
chamber

20' 1"

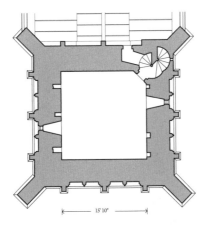

Plan at B:
ringing
chamber

15' 10"

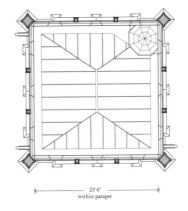

Plan at E:
roof

23' 6"
within parapet

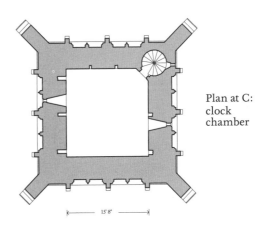

Plan at C:
clock
chamber

15' 8"

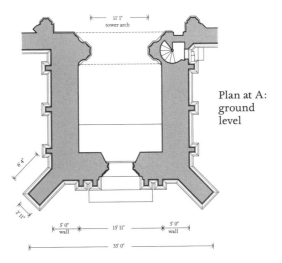

Plan at A:
ground
level

11' 1"
tower arch

6' 4"

2' 11"

5' 0"
wall

15' 11"

5' 0"
wall

35' 0"

Thornbury and Fairford. Blind panels in the outer bays are reminiscent of Gloucester and Malvern, but the flat, emaciated finials rising from the hoods are unworthy of the association. The main criticism that can be levelled against this otherwise fine and memorable design is the unnecessary lack of modelling in and around the upper openings.

Gloucester Cathedral and Great Malvern Priory both conclude with spectacular openwork crowns. The termination at CHIPPING CAMPDEN is much simpler but no less memorable. In front of an open arcaded battlement the three rising pilasters are joined together by pairs of flat ogee arches.

The two resultant pilasters finish above the merlons as square crocketed pinnacles incised with the narrowest of panels. The same principle is followed with greater elaboration at Gloucester, providing further evidence of common authorship. What distinguishes CHIPPING CAMPDEN, however, is the purity of the detailing, for no attempt is made to soften this exceedingly novel motif or to integrate it with the more conventional elements of the design. The whole unfamiliar but exquisitely beautiful composition is neatly concluded by panelled square pinnacles set diagonally on the four corners of the tower.

NOTES

1 Recorded in Revd James Dallaway, *A Series of Discourses upon Architecture in England* (1833), p. 178.

2 In *The Perpendicular Style* (1978) and *English Mediaeval Architects* (1984), John Harvey suggests dates of 1454–57 for the tower of Gloucester Cathedral, and *c.* 1450–60 for both CHIPPING CAMPDEN church and tower, and Great Malvern Priory tower.

3 In *English Parish Churches as Works of Art* (1986), p. 182, Alec Clifton-Taylor mistakenly describes the pilasters as panelling; the effect is entirely different, as can be seen from a comparison with Cirencester.

4 Harvey, *English Mediaeval Architects*, p. 146.

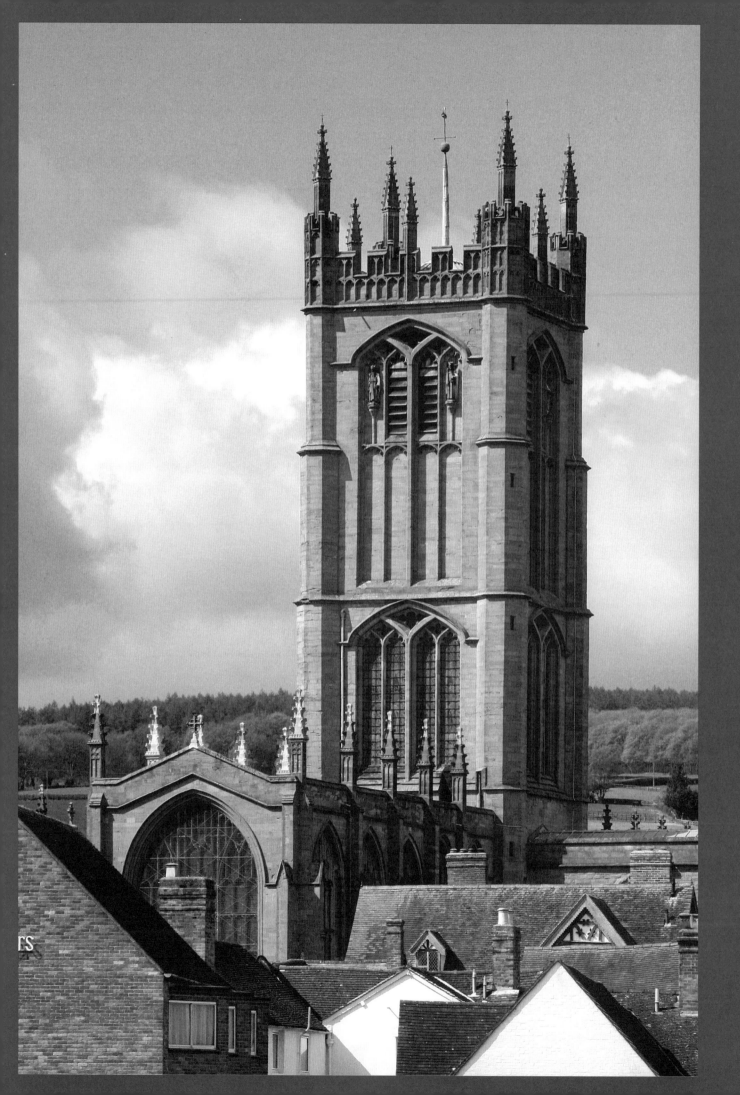

34

Ludlow

SHROPSHIRE

Founded in the eleventh century around a Norman castle, enfolded by hills and forest and blessed with an outstanding heritage of Tudor and Georgian buildings, Ludlow is considered by many to be the finest market town in England. St Laurence's Church, the 'Cathedral of the Marches', dominates every distant view, and yet at close quarters it disappears into the close-knit fabric of the town. The great tower was funded between 1453 and 1471 by contributions from the thriving guilds of carpenters, smiths, butchers, bakers, tailors, dyers and cordwainers. It was both a source of civic pride and a beacon of English power, emphatically asserting political and commercial control over the Welsh border country and the principality beyond. This purpose is admirably achieved by a strong and masculine design that has little time for subtlety. At 157 feet in height, this is one of the half-a-dozen tallest parish towers in the country.[1]

Whenever a late medieval tower appears at the centre of a cruciform plan, the suspicion must be that it represents a rebuilding over Norman foundations. At LUDLOW the magnificent crossing piers are dressed in a sumptuous display of Perpendicular shafting rising thirty-five feet to the capitals, but the core of the structure is twelfth-century work. The helical stair that burrows up the north-east pier is a rare luxury enjoyed by just a handful of large parish churches, including Holy Trinity, Hull and St Mary, Beverly. The

respond profile is the richest part of the entire construction, with no fewer than thirty-six shafts emerging out of a complex mass of waves, rolls and chamfers. Five-foot-high bases (a) leave a powerful impression on the visitor, which is only slightly compromised by the intrusion of the medieval choir screen and the raising of the floor below the crossing.

Few visitors who stand beneath this magnificent crossing are aware of the striking inconsistency between the interior and exterior forms of the tower. The cross section shows that the outer third of the tower arch supports nothing but thin lead roof, while the inner face of the wall steps in by almost twelve inches. A careful comparison of the plans reveals that the octagonal corners of the upper tower project well beyond the faces of the crossing piers and rely upon the slender wall shafts for their support. It is quite evident that the mason responsible for designing the crossing never anticipated the form that the tower would take as it emerged into sunlight. A new master mason must, therefore, have taken control as the tower passed through the roof.

The upper tower exhibits a noble austerity. Its nobility arises from its fine proportions and its silhouette, its austerity from a lack of modelling and a preponderance of plain walling. The smoothness of the surface and the precision of details suggest that Sir Arthur Blomfield's 1891 restoration of the tower included a full refacing. The local

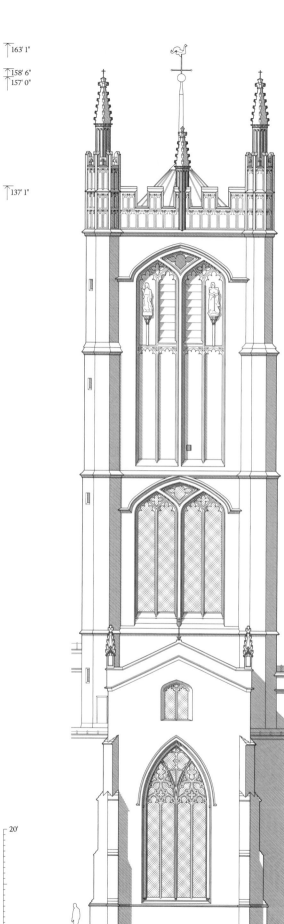

163' 1"

158' 6"
157' 0"

137' 1"

20'

0

North elevation

Profile of
tower arch
respond

0   12"

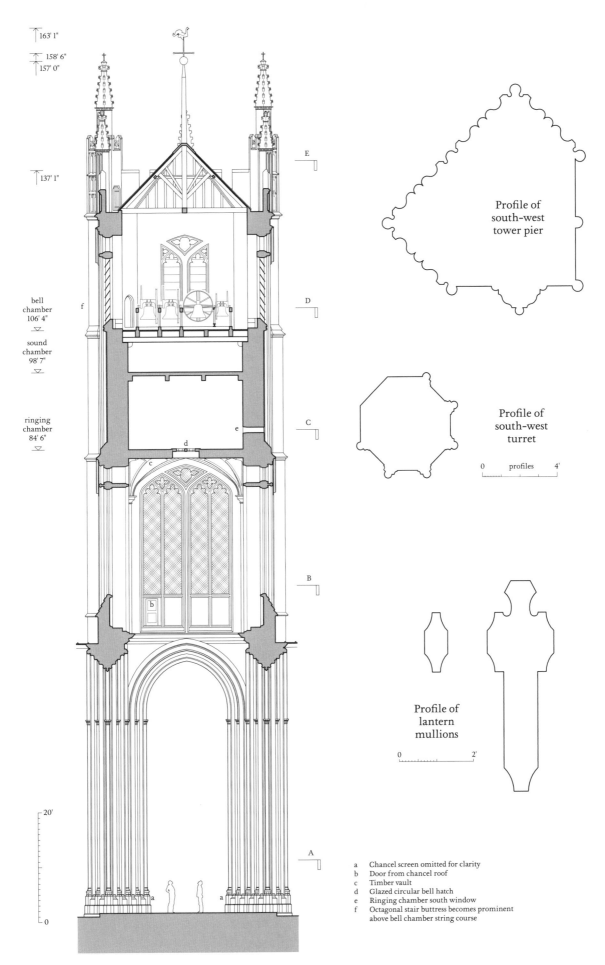

163' 1"

158' 6"
157' 0"

137' 1"

E

D

bell
chamber
106' 4"

sound
chamber
98' 7"

f

ringing
chamber
84' 6"

C

e

d

c

B

b

20'

A

a   a

0

Section looking east
Choir screen omitted for clarity

Profile of
south-west
tower pier

Profile of
south-west
turret

0   profiles   4'

Profile of
lantern
mullions

0   2'

a   Chancel screen omitted for clarity
b   Door from chancel roof
c   Timber vault
d   Glazed circular bell hatch
e   Ringing chamber south window
f   Octagonal stair buttress becomes prominent
      above bell chamber string course

red-brown sandstone may not be quite as friable as elsewhere in the western Midlands, but it still exhibits an unfortunate tendency to soak up sunlight.

Octagonal buttresses, which telescope as they rise, provide a great sense of stability to the tower, but they also soften the corners, replacing strong shadows with gentle modulations of light and shade. Their relationship with the corner of the tower is slightly ambiguous. At top and bottom the faces of the octagon flow smoothly into the plane of the wall, but the two middle segments include narrow return faces that demarcate the elevations with crisp shadow lines. The benefit of this small change, in emphasizing the verticality and autonomy of the buttress, is subtle here only when compared with the slightly later tower at DEDHAM.

The first upper stage sees a welcome return to the concept of the central crossing lantern. Pairs of tall twin-light windows to each elevation send brilliant illumination down into the heart of the church. The flat four-centred arch and hood-mould embracing the windows and those of the following stage are the most problematic element of the composition, for they awkwardly contradict the vertical movement of the tower. Tracery is simple, featuring a hefty central mullion on the plane of the wall splitting in the head to form a low 'Y' motif. Glass is set close to the outer face of the wall, exacerbating the flatness of the elevations but creating deep internal reveals. These plainly arched openings extend down through a level of blind panelling accessible through a perilous door from the eastern roof (b). Below, a broad cornice masks the stepping-in of the inner wall face.

The flat window arches permit only the shallowest of vaults, which consequently is of lightweight timber construction. The delicate design, of four gilded trefoiled panels radiating from each corner (c), makes no pretence of being of structurally significant. Glazed perforated quatrefoils in the bell hatch provide a spectacular view down to the pavement eighty-five feet below.

The shocking austerity of the final stage is broadcast across the town. If this fortress-like solidity was intended as an expression of power and stability, it can certainly be judged a success. Ringing chamber and bell chamber are combined externally in a rare long-panel design that has little in common with ST CUTHBERT, WELLS, EVERCREECH or Wrington. Indeed, there really is no precedent for finishing such a tall blind opening with such an emphatically horizontal arch. John Harvey has observed that this form of simple 'Y' tracery had originated in work for the court and was by this time widely used in buildings for noble patrons.[2]

The floor of the bell chamber is marked by a transom supported by flat four-centred archlets. Bell ringers are permitted no more than a glimmer of daylight from the meanest of rectangular holes (e). Bell openings occupy the central two bays, and

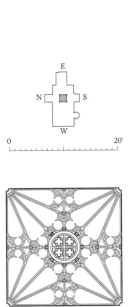

E

N   S

W

0   20'

Reflected
plan of
tower vault

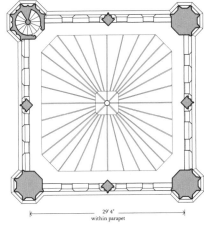

Plan at E:
roof

29' 4"
within parapet

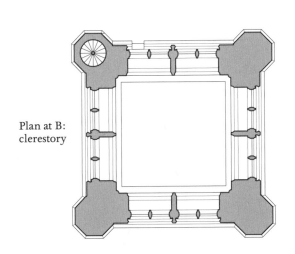

Plan at D:
bell
chamber

23' 5"

Plan at C:
ringing
chamber

21' 5"

Plan at B:
clerestory

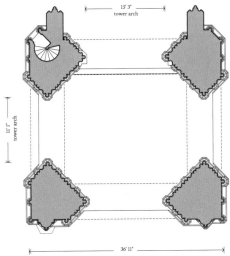

15' 3"
tower arch

11' 1"
tower arch

Plan at A:
ground
level

36' 11"

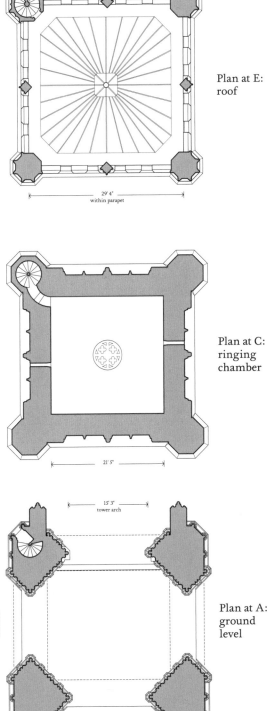

life-size Victorian figures gazing over the bustling marketplace the outer two.

The parapet sees a change of stone and mason, for the design is entirely dissimilar to everything that has gone before. This may mark the arrival of Clement Mason, who was fetched to assist with the work in 1469. Three specialists were called in to advise him: a 'Gloucestre mason', possibly John Hobbs or John Gower;[3] Robert Kerver II, who was paid 4*d* for 'seeing the werk of the stepill'; and 'the mason of Coventry'.[4] It has been suggested that Clement Mason was responsible for the design of the entire tower, but there is no documentary evidence to suggest his involvement prior to 1469, only two years before to the presumed completion date of 1471. It may be no coincidence that the most unusual, if aesthetically questionable, motif in parapet design appears to derive from ST MICHAEL, COVENTRY. There, a generation earlier, a single square-shafted castellated pinnacle had risen from an octagonal staircase turret.[5] At LUDLOW the same device appears on all four octagonal corners, but with the pinnacle rotated and then repeated at the centre of the parapet.

Two tiers of arcading running around the castellated parapet are typical of contemporary towers in the Midlands, including COVENTRY, but the articulation of the turrets is peculiar and very unsatisfactory. Engaged shafts rise up diminutive corner merlons to support the outermost edges of the parapet drip. Fortunately, the great height of LUDLOW ensures that this erroneous detail is hard to distinguish from the general impression of dense but highly regimented panelling around the crown.

LUDLOW tower may fall short of the artistry of Somerset or the ingenuity of Northamptonshire, but judged on its own terms it is extremely successful. Like ST NICHOLAS, NEWCASTLE-UPON-TYNE, LUDLOW was intended to provide a highly visible statement of English technological and economic superiority in a strategically vital location. These frontier towers may lack subtlety, but they are strong, tall and immensely self-assured.

NOTES

1   Excluding towers carrying spires, BOSTON, All Saints, Derby and ST MARY MAGDALENE, TAUNTON are higher than LUDLOW. Cirencester and Cromer are reputed to reach 162' and 159' respectively.
2   John Harvey, *The Perpendicular Style* (1978), p. 187.
3   For John Gower, see CHIPPING CAMPDEN.

4   John Harvey, *English Mediaeval Architects* (1984), pp. 197–98.
5   The same motif appears around 1500, at BOSTON and Holy Trinity, Hull, but without any castellations on the pinnacle.

KETTERING is the one of the few great spires of Northamptonshire to stand apart from the River Nene flowing north or the River Cherwell flowing south. The market town occupies high ground at the junction of several important roads crossing the region. A church may have existed on the site in pre-Conquest times but, with the exception of the chancel, the building that exists today was constructed in its entirety between around 1450 and 1475. Since the nineteenth century the western tower has been framed by an avenue of trees rising up from the main street of the town.

KETTERING is the classic mid-fifteenth-century Perpendicular steeple. It benefits from being entirely of one period, for spire and tower were conceived and realized in one beautifully unified design. While the stone of the spire is lighter than that of the tower, the consistency of the detailing suggests that there was no significant break in construction between the two parts. This stone is believed to be from Weldon, nine miles to the north, although the commissioners who investigated suitable stone for the construction of the Houses of Parliament reported that the church was 'Of a Shelly Oolite, fine grained, the greater portion resembling Barnack Rag. The Tower and Spire in perfect condition. The body of the Church in parts slightly decomposed.'[1]

Quatrefoil bands had been employed singly below parapets or bell stages from early in the previous century; however, from around 1450 a great enthusiasm developed for using multiple bands of quatrefoils and similar repetitive devices. One of the earliest and best examples of this is at KETTERING, where five bands enliven the tower, running across the plinth, beneath the parapet and immediately below the three strings that divide the elevations. By this period such decoration was mass-produced in the mason's yard, as is evidenced by several cuts and gaps at the ends of the upper bands. This is a minor quibble, for the general effect is one of controlled opulence. Every band differs in detail. Rounded quatrefoils within circles on the plinth are followed by the Midlands form of pointed quatrefoils within a diamond grid, then three spiralling mouchettes within a circle, followed by quatrefoils within square bays, and finally, on the parapet, smaller pointed quatrefoils framed by convex arcs within square bays.

The tall basement course is excellent, with prominent drips forming three strong shadow lines. The upper drip and the quatrefoil band are diverted above the doorway to form a rectangular hood-mould containing spandrels filled with regular panelling. Continuous casement and wave mouldings of the door arch are finished with a lightly crocketed hood and finial. To either side, small panelled buttresses rise to exceptionally thin pinnacles rotated diagonally.

The main buttresses are set well back, allowing sufficient room for two full quatrefoils on the exposed corners of the base. These visible corners allow the three

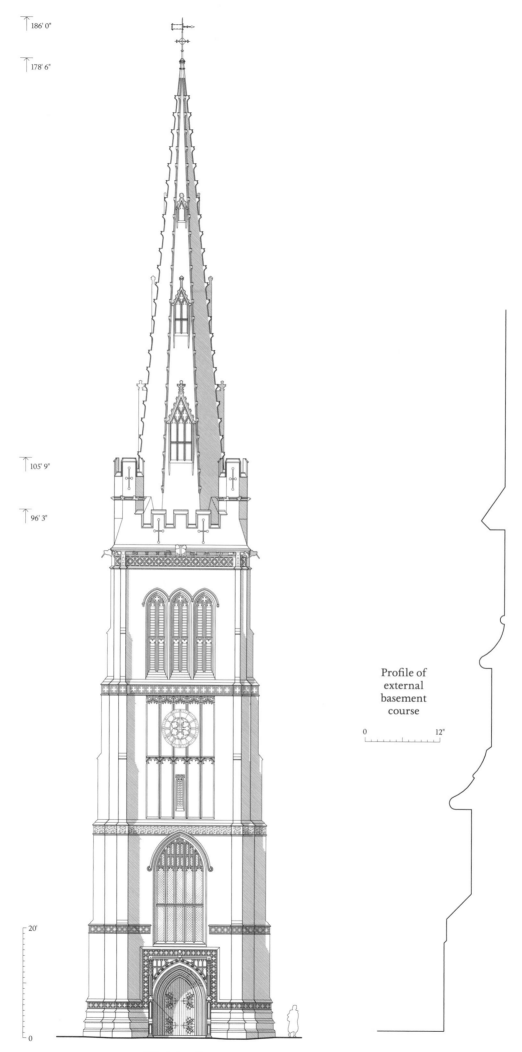

186' 0"

178' 6"

105' 9"

96' 3"

20'

0

West elevation

Profile of
external
basement
course

0   12"

stages of the tower to be read clearly from the ground to the parapet. Tower walls and buttresses step back in unison at the two major string courses. Within each stage the buttresses are further divided into two by plain set-offs, that on the lowest stage running across the elevations with a band of quatrefoil. With this exception, the side elevations remain undecorated on the lowest stage. The five-bay west window is divided by a castellated transom and panel tracery in the head, and the window hood-mould wraps around delicate five-petal flowers.

Internally, illumination from the fifteenth-century west window is compromised by Charles Kempe's dark nineteenth-century glass. The tower arch of four chamfered orders, the inner order supported by moulded capitals on half-round shafts, is appropriately grand in scale (a). Eastern tower buttresses are fully formed within the church, indicating that the end of the nave was rebuilt after the tower had been completed. In typical Northamptonshire fashion the spiral stair is accommodated within the south-west corner of the tower, the external impact being limited to inconspicuous vertical slits rising up the south elevation.

The upper half of the elevation is simple but highly effective. On the second stage the ringing chamber is articulated by five cinquefoiled bays of blind tracery in two equal tiers, the upper tier employing very flat arches. Small arched windows perforate the central bays on both tiers.

The three-bay bell stage is an unusual feature at this date. After KETTON, ST MARY, STAMFORD and Melton Mowbray (Leics), during the thirteenth-century three-bay upper stages are exceptional in eastern England. The tracery is predictable but immaculately proportioned, with pointed foils carrying the transoms and descending quatrefoils over trefoiled archlets in the head. The congregation of grotesques, gargoyles and heads, both animal and human, inhabiting the cornice is in fine condition.

Internally, the upper stages of the tower are a disappointment, for there is a great deal of Victorian patching and modern steelwork, brickwork and joinery. It is unclear how the floors were originally arranged, and the only ancient timbers appear to be those left spanning the base of the spire (b).

The most memorable feature of KETTERING is the fortified battlement. The juxtaposition of full military defences with the ecclesiastical tower beneath must have appeared shocking at the time. Crenellations had been common on church parapets for several generations, and at Leverington (Cambs) ineffectual looking turrets had been added to the base of the spire. At KETTERING the turrets were moved dramatically to the corners of the tower, forming a continuous, and very believable, defensive wall in combination with three substantial merlons on each face of the parapet. Sixteen arrow slits are authentically splayed on their internal faces, and the penetration of the path through the base of the turret is skilfully handled to render it all but invisible from the ground. Turrets are not pure octagons, as might be expected, for the raised merlons on the cardinal faces are wider than the embrasures on the diagonals. Later – possibly much later – this highly original design was to provide the inspiration for the splendid battlemented parapet at Oundle, eleven miles to the north-east.

The precisely detailed spire is a fine example of its date. Crockets and spire edges are sharp and angular and run straight to the apex with no trace of entasis. Squinches are efficiently corbelled (e), and after nine feet the thickness of the spire wall reduces to just six inches.[2] The angle at the apex is an unremarkable twelve degrees, leading to a minor reservation that the spire is slightly underplayed. Nevertheless, at just over 4:5 the ratio of spire to tower is similar to MOULTON and entirely typical of the period.

Lucarnes use crisp diamond tracery in three orthogonally arranged tiers following the sequence of three lights, two lights and one light. This exceptionally satisfying arrangement is found only in the finest mature Perpendicular spires, at Helpringham (Lincs), Easton Maudit (Northants), Thaxted (Essex), St Mary de Castro, Leicester (currently dismantled), Queniborough (Leics) and WHITTLESEY.

NOTES

1   R. W. Billings, *Architectural Illustrations of Kettering Church, Northamptonshire* (1843), p. 6.
2   Francis Bond, *Gothic Architecture in England* (1905), p. 636.

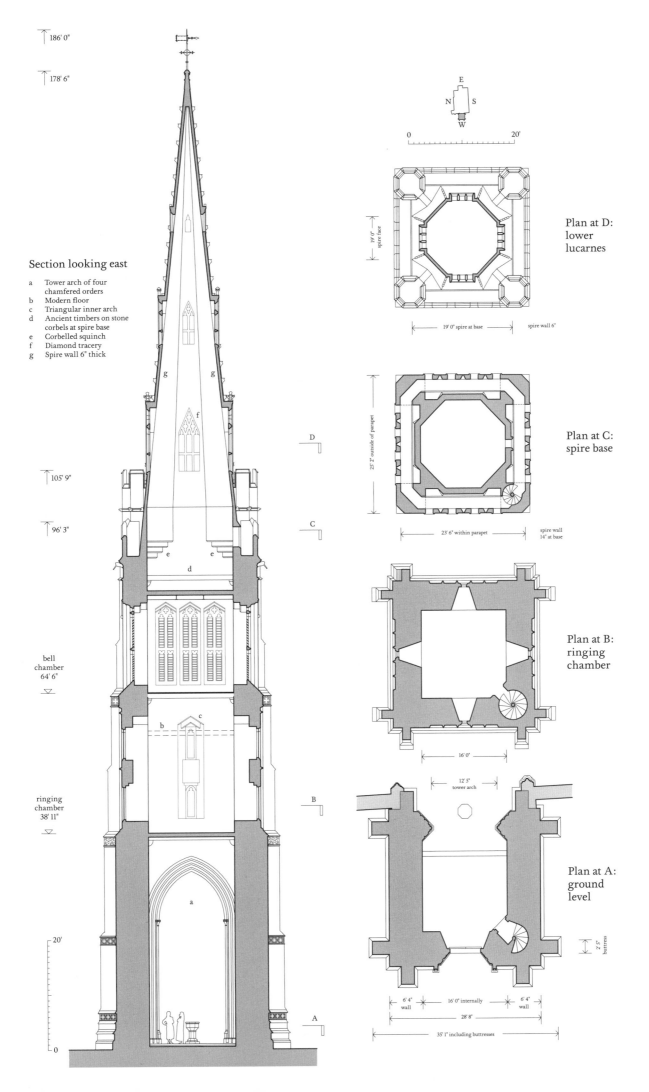

Section looking east

a   Tower arch of four
     chamfered orders
b   Modern floor
c   Triangular inner arch
d   Ancient timbers on stone
     corbels at spire base
e   Corbelled squinch
f   Diamond tracery
g   Spire wall 6" thick

186' 0"

178' 6"

105' 9"

96' 3"

bell
chamber
64' 6"

ringing
chamber
38' 11"

20'

0

D

C

B

A

Plan at D:
lower
lucarnes

19' 0"
spire face

19' 0" spire at base   spire wall 6"

Plan at C:
spire base

25' 2" outside of parapet

23' 6" within parapet   spire wall
14" at base

Plan at B:
ringing
chamber

16' 0"

12' 5"
tower arch

Plan at A:
ground
level

2' 5"
buttress

6' 4"
wall   16' 0" internally   6' 4"
wall

28' 8"

35' 1" including buttresses

E
N   S
W

0   20'

36

Whittlesey

The approach to WHITTLESEY, past the brickworks and wind turbines of Peterborough, may be flat and dreary, but St Mary's Church is a revelation, for it is finished with the most perfect late fifteenth-century spire in England. In medieval times WHITTLESEY was an island surrounded by marsh, accessed only by the Roman Fen Causeway. Whittlesey Mere, to the south-west, was the largest lake in southern England before it was drained in the nineteenth century. Narrow and irregular streets leading from the market square offer welcome relief from the vast horizons of the Fen, but they turn their backs on the churchyard. Regrettably, the Georgian gravestones that Alec Clifton-Taylor so admired in 1974 have been swept away to leave the church standing aloof in a formless expanse of grass.[1]

WHITTLESEY tower, in its early stages, is a contemporary of MOULTON sixteen miles to the north. Similarities extend beyond matters of detail, for both towers are characterized by the immature inventiveness of the early Perpendicular style, with innovative side lighting beneath the vault and highly experimental buttress designs.

The four stages of the tower alternate in character, with profuse decoration of the base and ringing chamber contrasting with the relative restraint of the windowed stages. Buttresses are exceptionally shallow and exceptionally complex. They transform rapidly from clasping to setback, to clasping, to rotated clasping, finishing as square

pinnacle bases above the parapet. The orthogonal clasping sections terminate with pyramidal copings, and the setback sections with delicate concave gablets. These gablets look back to the richly sculptural towers of the early fourteenth century, whereas the plain clasping buttresses look forward to the following century, when they were to become part of the standard repertoire in the Stamford district.

The basement course, now partly submerged below the churchyard turf, is decorated with pointed quatrefoils. This is the first of four bands of repeated motifs, which at this date are still used in isolation but during the following half-century would evolve into one of the dominant motifs of tower design. There follows an intense display of quatrefoiled panelling and empty niches set between shallow pilasters finished with trefoil-arched panels and tiny crocketed gablets. The niche design on the western buttresses is reminiscent of MOULTON, with statue plinths raised high on circular shafts and florid ogee canopies bulging forward below crocketed gables. The ogee form is even more pronounced in the crocketed hood-mould rising above the west door. The door arch is decorated with square flower motifs and framed by massive rotated and crocketed pinnacles. The limit of the first stage is marked by miniature castellations running across all the elevations, an exceedingly rare motif that appears slightly later, in 1401, at Skirlaugh (Yorks East).

Greater restraint is shown on the second stage. Between the arch and the hood of the restored four-bay west window is a band of Perpendicular panelling, five ascending bays on each side. The same motif reappears internally in two bands around the west window and in two bands beneath the tower arch. Tracery was in a state of transition at this time. Perpendicular supermullions, cinquefoil archlets and castellated supertransoms are moderated by smooth, flowing tracery in the head. A similar combination appears in the two-light side windows, which are enlivened by rotated pinnacles rising from the stop-heads of their hoods. Illumination provided by these side windows transforms the space under the tower vault.

The fine tierceron vault, with four large bosses and a circular bell hatch, is almost identical to that of MOULTON, except that it rises from slender corner shafts rather than corbels (a). Like the west door, the windows are set near to the outer face of the wall (b), to the detriment of the elevation but to the benefit of internal space, which feels richly sculpted. The only disappointments are the narrow segmental tower arch (c) and the asymmetric position of the side windows relative to the vault. Externally this disconcerting setting-out, seen clearly on the drawings, is corrected on the symmetrical upper stages. As at MOULTON, the stair was positioned in the north-east corner to make space for the windows, and with access available only from the north aisle the

stair is forced to ascend in an anticlockwise direction (d).

Each elevation of the third stage is divided by gabled pilasters into three shallow bays. Stylized flowers raised on stalks, known as brattishing, are recessed into the base of the pilasters and the buttresses. To north and south the ringing chamber windows are deeply recessed behind an outer arch (e). Originally the three western bays framed statues raised on plinths, though the central plinth, which is emphasized by a minor arch, has been lost. Above runs a band of pointed quatrefoils contained within straight diagonal tracery, a motif that was to become particularly popular in the East Midlands.

The fourth stage is best viewed from the south, for the other elevations are disfigured by three of the most insensitive clock faces to be found on any English church. The paired bell openings are immaculately proportioned. Extravagant sub-cusped trefoils support crenellated transoms to the twin-light openings. Mullions rise vertically into the window arches, indicating a slightly later date of construction, and six encircled quatrefoils fill the blank space under the plain cornice. Below the battlement, decoration varies from full panelling on the west, to a chaotic arrangement that appears as nothing so much as surplus quatrefoils and trefoils from the mason's yard on the east.

The great spire is directly derived from KETTERING, the classic design of the mid-fifteenth century, but with two significant improvements. First, it is

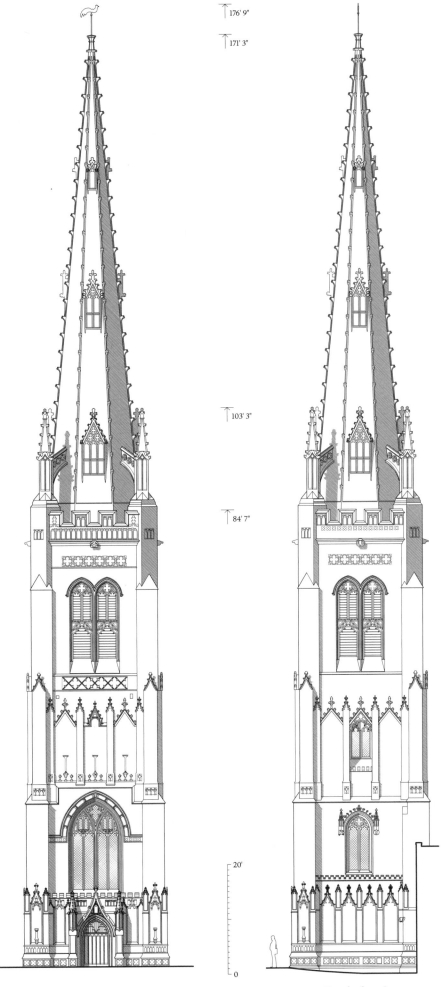

176' 9"

171' 3"

103' 3"

84' 7"

20'

0

West elevation   South elevation

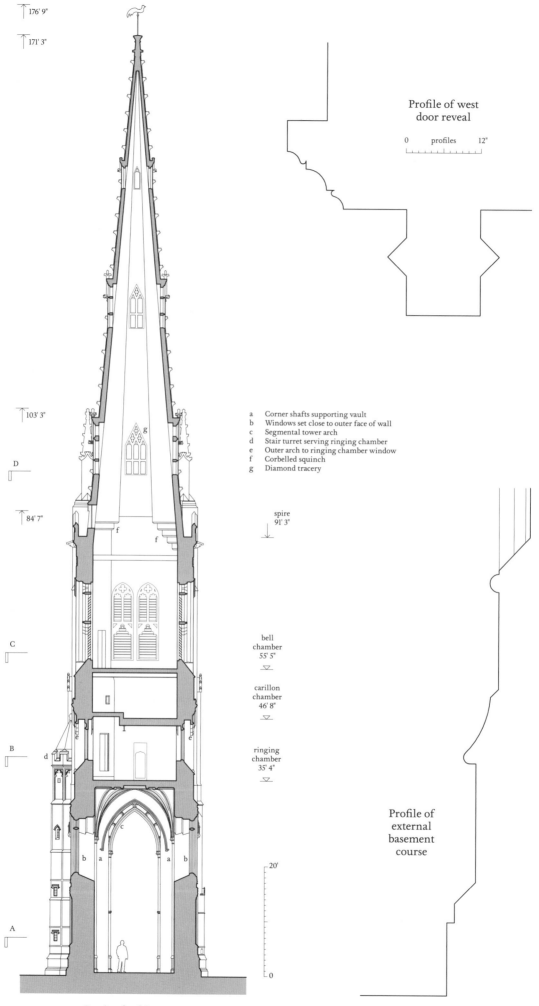

↑ 176' 9"

↑ 171' 3"

Profile of west
door reveal

0   profiles   12"

↑ 103' 3"

g

D

↑ 84' 7"

f   f

a   Corner shafts supporting vault
b   Windows set close to outer face of wall
c   Segmental tower arch
d   Stair turret serving ringing chamber
e   Outer arch to ringing chamber window
f   Corbelled squinch
g   Diamond tracery

spire
91' 3"
↓

C

bell
chamber
55' 5"
▽

carillon
chamber
46' 8"
▽

B

e

d

ringing
chamber
35' 4"
▽

c

Profile of
external
basement
course

b   a   a   b

20'

A

0

Section looking east

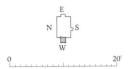

0   20'

Reflected plan of tower vault

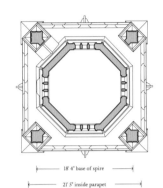

Plan at D: spire base

18' 4" base of spire

21' 5" inside parapet

Plan at C: bell chamber

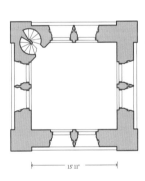

15' 11"

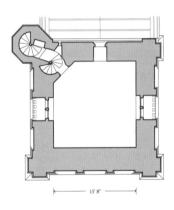

Plan at B: ringing chamber

15' 8"

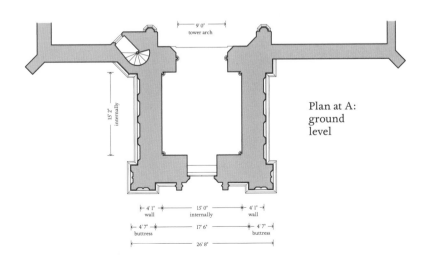

9' 0" tower arch

Plan at A: ground level

15' 2" internally

4' 1" wall

15' 0" internally

4' 1" wall

4' 7" buttress

17' 6"

4' 7" buttress

26' 8"

surrounded by exceptionally powerful flying buttresses, and second, WHITTLESEY is slightly higher and narrower. This has significant benefits, for not only does the extra sharpness impart the composition with increased verticality, but spire and tower are precisely equal in height.[2]

The first six feet of plain-edged spire that conceal the efficiently corbelled squinches (f) are contemporary with the early fifteenth-century parapet. It is reasonable to infer that at least half a century elapsed before work continued, for above this level every detail is assertively Perpendicular.

Angular spire edges are ornamented by the flattest of flat-sided crockets. Lucarnes of diamond tracery are arrayed in three orthogonal tiers of three lights, two lights and one light, and the elegantly drawn-out octagonal capstone is a convincing replacement. Crockets on the lucarnes are austere, and inventiveness is restricted to the heads projecting from the corners of the gables. Other than the sharp proportions, the only noticeable change from KETTERING is an increase from twenty-four crockets to twenty-six.

The flying buttresses, which spring from elegant square panelled pinnacles, derive directly from Northamptonshire. From HIGHAM FERRERS onwards there developed within the county a particular style of flying buttress distinguished by a perforated row of quatrefoils set between a straight coping and a flat arch. At WHITTLESEY, and six miles away at Yaxley (Hunts), this design is realized in an exceptionally robust form that, save for the huge flying buttresses at LOUTH, was never bettered. Stylistically, the spires of WHITTLESEY and Yaxley – sister churches in the possession of the abbey of Thorney – appear to be the work of a single mason. The flying buttresses may be of negligible structural benefit to the thin-walled spire at WHITTLESEY, but as a compositional device for leading the eye smoothly from square tower to octagonal spire they are without fault.

NOTES

1   Alec Clifton-Taylor, *English Parish Churches as Works of Art* (1986), p. 48, illustrated p. 90.
2   The measurement of spire and tower is taken from the top of the parapet. The apex angle of KETTERING is a relaxed 12° 4'. WHITTLESEY is sharper at 11° 8' but still well short of being a true needle spire.

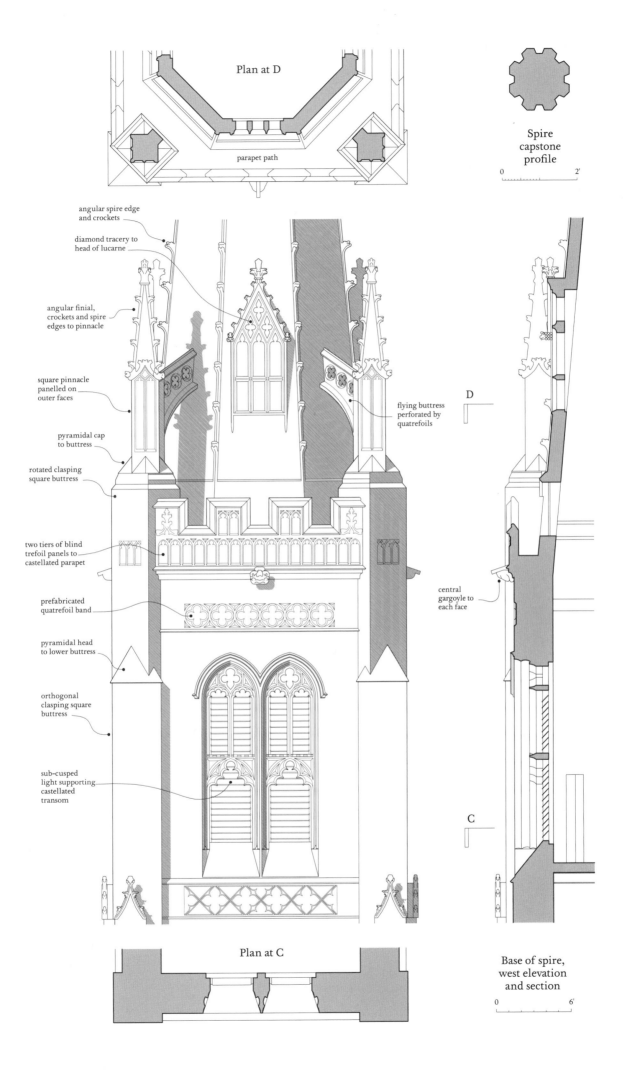

Plan at D

parapet path

Spire
capstone
profile

0   2'

angular spire edge
and crockets

diamond tracery to
head of lucarne

angular finial,
crockets and spire
edges to pinnacle

square pinnacle
panelled on
outer faces

pyramidal cap
to buttress

rotated clasping
square buttress

two tiers of blind
trefoil panels to
castellated parapet

prefabricated
quatrefoil band

pyramidal head
to lower buttress

orthogonal
clasping square
buttress

sub-cusped
light supporting
castellated
transom

flying buttress
perforated by
quatrefoils

D

central
gargoyle to
each face

C

Plan at C

Base of spire,
west elevation
and section

0   6'

37

Wilby

NORTHAMPTONSHIRE

WILBY is one of the most underappreciated and misrepresented small steeples in England. For too long it has been overshadowed by its historically more significant but aesthetically inferior neighbour at EARLS BARTON. That this hidden gem should fail to appear among Simon Jenkins's *England's Thousand Best Churches* (2000) is understandable, for the rest of the structure is unremarkable. More surprising is its exclusion from John Betjeman's extensive *Guide to English Parish Churches* (1958). Even those sources that are available are unreliable, for the Statutory Listing, Pevsner and even the highly dependable *Victoria County History* all consider the steeple to be of the Decorated style, which it clearly is not. This is not unusual, for there are many instances where a solitary ogee arch has been accepted uncritically as evidence of Decorated work. At WILBY the briefest glance at the window tracery, the square panelled pinnacles and the wide casements framing the openings reveal this to be a thoroughly Perpendicular affair. A more detailed examination suggests a date of around 1480.

Approaching from the west, WILBY appears as a rural village nestling in the gentle undulations of the Nene Valley, but to the east it is becoming ensnared by the suburban fringes of Wellingborough town. This district is notable for its rich orange and red ironstones. Towers at Whiston, Irchester and Rushden (Northants) are superb examples of medieval polychromy, in which bands of ironstone alternate with grey Northamptonshire limestone, but at WILBY such banding is confined to the body of the church. The tower is constructed of a light orange ironstone that has mellowed well on the walls but eroded badly on the more exposed details. There is now a good deal of harder grey limestone restoration, particularly to the parapets, the pinnacles and the hood-mould of the west door.

WILBY is unique in combining two fascinating developments in medieval steeple design: the octagonal spired drum and the Northamptonshire style of flying buttress. Superficially, the composition consists of a two-stage square tower, a single-stage octagonal drum and a recessed spire. These stages overlap through pinnacles and flying buttresses to create three approximately equal zones. The extreme intensity of the middle third contrasts with the relative austerity of the upper and lower parts.

The octagonal spired drum rising from a square tower had evolved slowly from the elemental design at BARNACK, completed around 1230. In the East Midlands the oversailing spire at Grafham (Hunts) led to the recessed spire of Houghton (Hunts), but in both cases the octagonal drum is substantially concealed by broaches rising from the square tower. Five steeples of this type constructed in Yorkshire and the north-east from around 1380 are an improvement, for their broaches do not rise far above the base of the drum.[1] The most striking precedent, however, is the grand

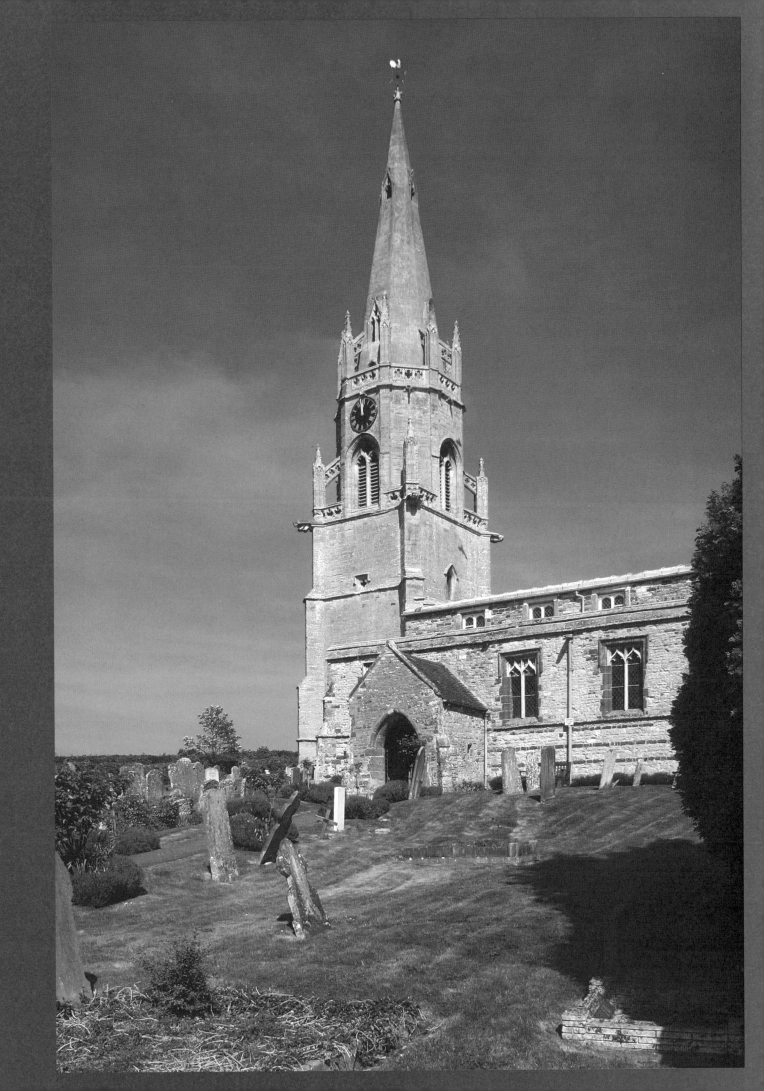

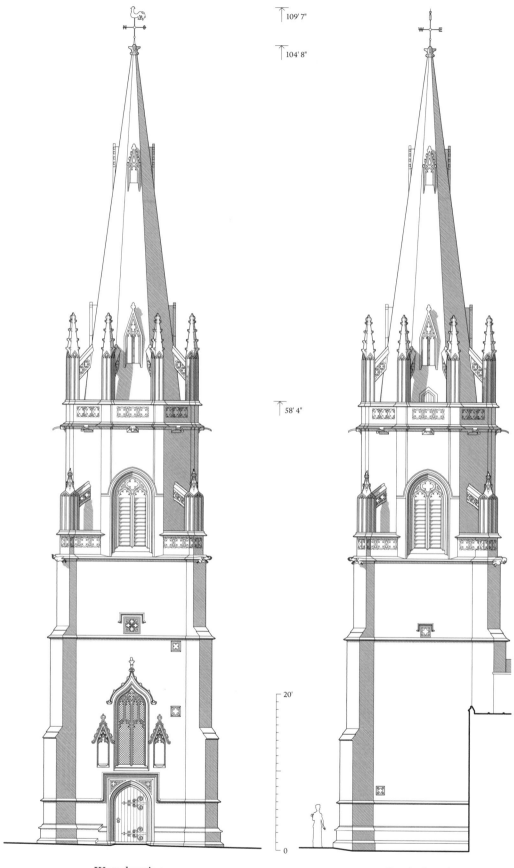

109' 7"

104' 8"

58' 4"

20'

0

West elevation

South elevation

early fourteenth-century steeple of Bloxham (Oxon), thirty-five miles to the south-west. Despite having high broaches, this design includes tall pinnacles rising from diagonal buttresses and embryonic flying buttresses connecting to the octagon.

The Northamptonshire form of flying buttress consists of upper and lower members running close together and connected by a web of stone perforated by quatrefoils. Within the county these flying buttresses are combined with matching perforated parapets. HIGHAM FERRERS, from around 1350, was followed by Rushden and, later, by Easton Maudit and WILBY, between which there are numerous similarities of detail. WILBY is by far the smallest of the four but makes up for its diminutive size by packing in no fewer than twelve flying buttresses.

For a detailed description it is necessary to return to the base. The four-centred door arch and spandrels decorated with quatrefoils are framed by a rectangular hood-mould. The profile of the door arch – two circular rolls between three quadrant recesses – is identical to that of TITCHMARSH, constructed thirteen miles to the north-east around 1474. Some authorities have suggested that the door is a fourteenth-century insertion in an earlier wall, but there is no evidence in the masonry to support this theory. The west window is framed by recessed niches below straight crocketed gables and delicately foiled heads, which are again strongly reminiscent of TITCHMARSH, and the statue brackets and

opening profiles are identical. The west window tracery may well be a nineteenth-century replacement, but the wide casement in the jamb is original Perpendicular work. The one feature that appears to have confounded the critics is the ogee-headed window arch. Such constructional arches are rare and invariably narrow, for the inverted curve of the ogee is a weak structural form. The ogee curve had been a national obsession between 1315 and 1360, but it did not vanish after this date and continued to appear regularly in hood-moulds and archlets within Perpendicular tracery.

Apart from these details the first two stages of the tower are very restrained. Three-stage diagonal buttresses rise from a plain basement course, and a narrow string separates off the second stage. Eastern buttresses are built off the earlier west wall of the church, but the restricted space pushes them significantly off the corner of the tower. Ringing chamber lights are miniature versions of a Norfolk air hole.[2] These small, square openings are filled with an abstract pattern of four-petal tracery on the west and a quatrefoil within a circle to the south (a). To the east, a triangular-headed doorway leads out onto the roof of the nave (b). Quatrefoil lights illuminating the staircase are almost identical to those at TITCHMARSH.

The entire tower is effectively sculpted from one solid mass, the transformation from a square to an octagonal form being achieved very simply by chamfering off the corners. Astonishingly, at 3' 8" thick the walls are more substantial than those of the great tower at BOSTON. Little space remains within for the double-chamfered tower arch, the exceptionally narrow spiral stair in the south-west corner and the double-stacked bell frame. Diagonal spire faces are supported by gradual splays (c) rather than conventional squinch arches or corbels.

Externally the awkward transition between square and octagon is beautifully concealed by a perforated parapet from which panelled pinnacles rise to support miniature flying buttresses. The string course marking the start of the octagonal stage is extended dramatically out into space by four powerful gargoyles that spring from the buttresses. Twin-light bell openings on the cardinal faces are typically Perpendicular, with stiff soufflets above quatrefoil archlets, supermullions rising vertically into the arch, and wide casements in the jambs. The shallow, square buttresses rising up the corners of the octagon are identical to those of LOWICK, constructed around 1479. Parapet, pinnacles and flying buttresses crown the octagon with redoubled intensity. The effect is pure joy. The spire can hardly compete with such fireworks and is left eloquently understated. Spire edges are plain, the proportions comfortable but not strained, and the two orthogonal tiers of lucarnes are straightforward and underplayed. The whole glorious concoction rises just over 100 feet from the ground.

NOTES

1   The five steeples are Chester-le-Street (Durham),
    St Mary Castlegate and All Saints, North Street, York,
    Masham (Yorks North) and Brayton (Yorks West).
2   See the description of SALLE.

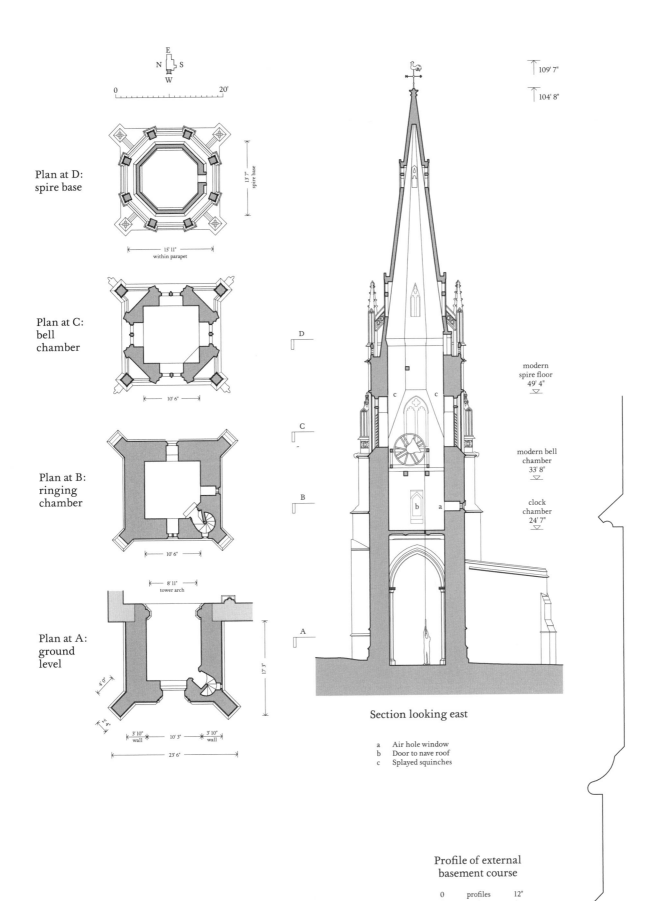

Plan at D:
spire base

Plan at C:
bell
chamber

Plan at B:
ringing
chamber

Plan at A:
ground
level

E
N   S
W

0   20'

13' 7"
spire base

15' 11"
within parapet

10' 6"

10' 6"

8' 11"
tower arch

17' 3"

4' 0"

2' 4"

3' 10"
wall

10' 3"

3' 10"
wall

23' 6"

D

C

B

A

109' 7"

104' 8"

modern
spire floor
49' 4"

modern bell
chamber
33' 8"

clock
chamber
24' 7"

Section looking east

a   Air hole window
b   Door to nave roof
c   Splayed squinches

Profile of external
basement course

0   profiles   12"

38

Lowick

NORTHAMPTONSHIRE

At the Parliament of Salisbury in 1384, Sir Henry Greene and Sir John Holland were given custody of a Carmelite friar accused of denouncing John of Gaunt. Seeking to gain the favour of Gaunt, they tortured the friar to death. Tradition recounts that, in expiation of this terrible act of cruelty, Sir Henry, a 'very covetous, haughty and ambitious' knight, threw himself into the rebuilding of the church of LOWICK.[1] He did not have long to make penance, for in 1399 he was captured and executed by Lancastrians at Bristol. In Shakespeare, this 'Creature to King Richard' departs to his fate with bitter words:

> My comfort is, that heaven will take our
> souls,
> And plague injustice with the pains of hell.[2]

The reconstruction of LOWICK church proceeded through four succeeding generations of the family: the sons Ralph and John Greene, the grandson Henry Greene, his daughter Constance, and finally her son Edward, 2nd Earl of Wiltshire. The second Sir Henry Greene, who inherited the estate in 1432 and died in 1467, was responsible for building the south aisle and Lady Chapel, and for starting work on the tower. It is known that the Greene Chapel was under way in 1468 and that the tower was almost complete by 1479, when the rector, John Martyn, bequeathed money in his will for the 'campanis' and the 'campanili' (the bells and the bell tower).[3]

The entire rebuilding of the church had taken almost a century to achieve. The Greenes' presence is inescapable at St Mary's Church, the recumbent alabaster effigies of Sir Ralph and his wife, Katherine, holding hands being the most poignant reminder.

LOWICK is a jewel of a church. The western tower dominates the approach up a track from the picturesque stone-built village, and though it fails to reach 100 feet it has the self-assurance of many steeples twice its size. The composition is splendidly regal, and the famous octagon resembles nothing so much as a crown guarded by sharpened spears. Built when the War of the Roses was cutting a vicious swathe through the ranks of the English nobility, this is the ideal of chivalry captured for eternity in mellow stone.

The tower is of three principal stages divided by quatrefoil bands, each of the lower stages being further subdivided by strings. It is structurally independent of the church and set slightly forward of the west end of the aisles. The walls reduce progressively at each minor string and at the central quatrefoil band. The immaculately controlled buttresses start with a hefty clasping base, immediately transforming into flat-sided setback pairs, reducing at every string, and finishing at the bell stage string course. Clasping buttresses, relieved with ogee-headed panelling, are then formed by the stepping-back of the bell chamber elevation. Passing through the cornice, the buttresses transform into square-based pinnacles thrusting high into the sky. The vertical emphasis is strong but never excessive.

By this time quatrefoil bands had become a great favourite in Northamptonshire. Three variations are used here: continuous round quatrefoils to the base, pointed quatrefoils set within a diagonal lattice at mid-height, and individual rounded quatrefoils carrying five-petal roses immediately below the parapet. The five-petal rose was a potent symbol of the age, and the quatrefoils may have been decorated and redecorated to express the changing political sympathies of the Greene family, red for Lancaster or white for York.

The first stage is entirely plain on the side elevations save for a sundial to the south. The ceremonial western door is framed by an arch with a gentle profile of casement, bracket, hollow and wave, separated by fillets and rising from a plain plinth. Quatrefoils carry blank shields in the spandrels beneath a rectangular hood. The three-light west window is modest but eminently satisfying, for its three inverted daggers are contained by a perfect example of subarcuated intersecting tracery.

Small ringing chamber windows to south and west are formed of a pair of ogee-headed lights recessed within rectangular chamfered openings. Shallow twin-light openings, beneath ogee hood-moulds, penetrate the bell chamber wall, and large, bog-eyed human gargoyles discharge the gutters from the centre of each face. The castellated parapet is plain-faced but

capped on every edge. All the masonry is as crisp as the day it was carved.

Compared to FOTHERINGHAY, the octagonal lantern at LOWICK is restrained, even plain, for its design remains subservient to the overall composition. The diagonal faces of the octagon are solid, and the stubby flying buttresses that hit their centre points are a structural absurdity. Flat-headed four-centred arches are usually anathema in steeples, but here the horizontality of the openings is entirely convincing. Each is of three transomed lights with the flattest of intersecting tracery filling the head.

The term 'lantern' is something of a misnomer, for light is kept out by solid louvres. Miniature battlements are subtly embellished: the central merlon on the south side is pointed and perforated rather in the manner of TITCHMARSH. The tower comes to a magical conclusion with the shallow corner buttresses springing into a profusion of crocketed pinnacles. Twelve thrusting spikes raise twelve golden weathervanes to swivel in the breeze around a central finial marking the points of the compass.

Internally, the tower is simple but effective. The tall tower arch (a) is of three chamfers facing east to the nave and two facing west. The outer chamfers continue to the ground, but the central order is supported on the responds by semicircular shafts finished with octagonal moulded capitals and bases. The spiral stair, crammed tightly into the north-west corner with

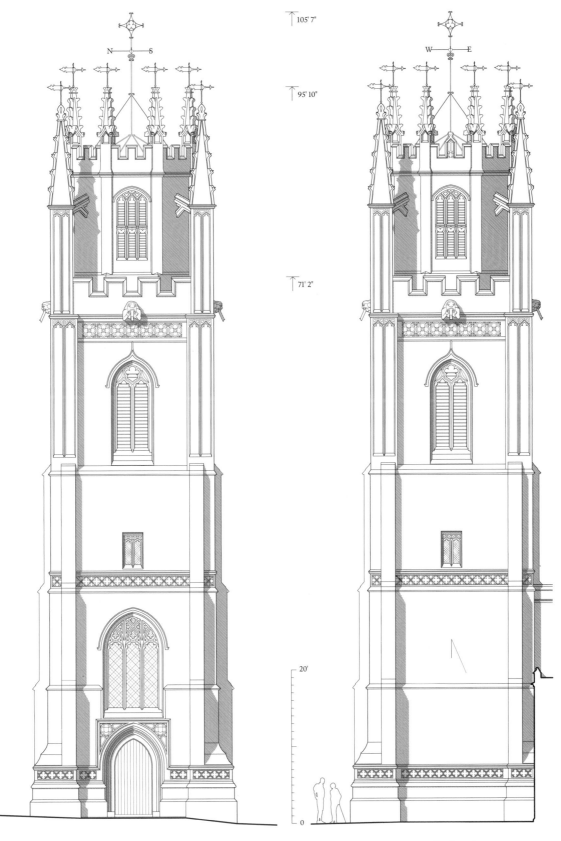

105' 7"

95' 10"

71' 2"

20'

0

West elevation   South elevation

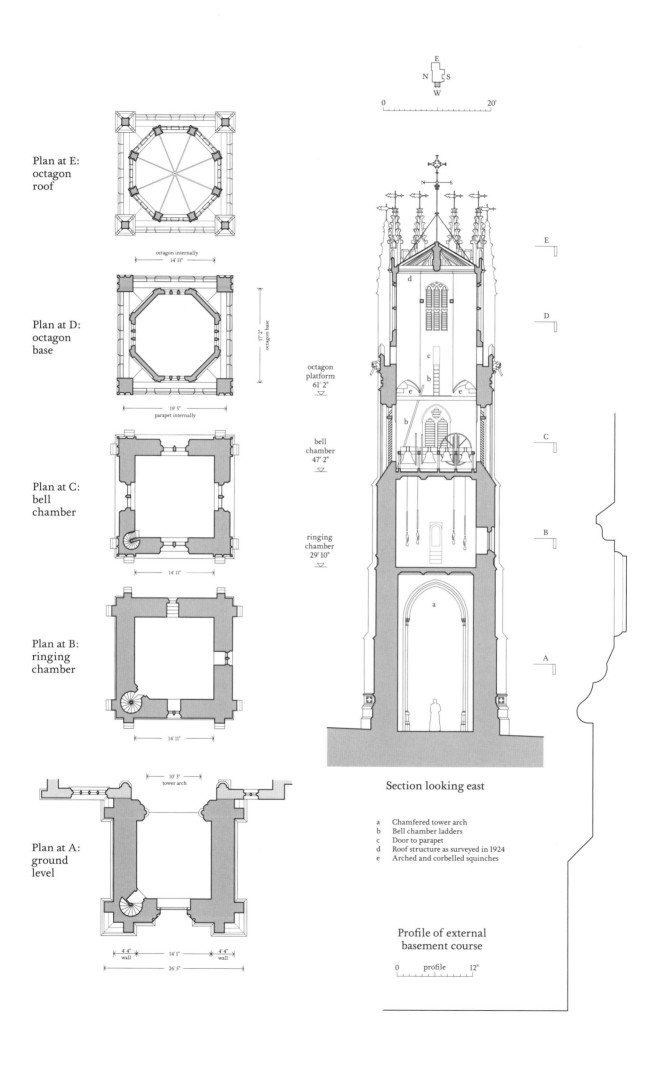

Plan at E:
octagon
roof

octagon internally
14' 11"

Plan at D:
octagon
base

17' 2"
octagon base

19' 5"
parapet internally

Plan at C:
bell
chamber

14' 11"

Plan at B:
ringing
chamber

14' 11"

10' 3"
tower arch

Plan at A:
ground
level

4' 4"
wall

14' 1"

4' 4"
wall

26' 5"

octagon
platform
61' 2"

bell
chamber
47' 2"

ringing
chamber
29' 10"

Section looking east

a   Chamfered tower arch
b   Bell chamber ladders
c   Door to parapet
d   Roof structure as surveyed in 1924
e   Arched and corbelled squinches

Profile of external
basement course

0   profile   12"

minimal illumination, leads to the bell chamber floor, from where ladders snake between precarious platforms (b) leading to the parapet (c) and the hatch to the upper roof. The ancient timber structure is substantially intact save for the pitched roof to the octagon, which was insensitively replaced in the twentieth century by horizontal joists sitting on an intrusive concrete ring beam. On the cross section the roof is shown in its original state, as recorded in a survey of 1924 (d).[4]

LOWICK and FOTHERINGHAY are frequently spoken of together, for their octagonal lanterns are of similar antiquity and they lie just ten miles apart. In truth, they are like chalk and cheese, for they vary in almost every point of substance and detail. LOWICK is controlled and precise, whereas FOTHERINGHAY is inconsistent and mysterious. The histories of both are enmeshed with the turbulent fortunes of the Houses of York and Lancaster. Considered in isolation, the octagon at FOTHERINGHAY is undeniably the better of the two, but as a perfectly unified composition, immaculately detailed and impeccably realized, the steeple at LOWICK takes pride of place.

NOTES

1   Anonymous Lancastrian chroniclers quoted in S. G. Stopford Sackville, 'Notes on Lowick Church ...' (1883).

2   William Shakespeare, *Richard II*, Act III, scene i.

3   See Stopford Sackville, p. 68, for a transcription of the will.

4   Donald Hanks McMorran, measured drawings (1924), RIBA Drawings Collection.

39

Titchmarsh

NORTHAMPTONSHIRE

Titchmarsh is considered by some authorities to be the finest parish tower beyond the borders of Somerset.[1] The resemblance to the great towers of Somerset is both powerful and immediate, but the details reveal that this can only be the work of a highly accomplished Northamptonshire mason. The closest model in the west of England may be found at Isle Abbots, for both towers share the same sturdy proportions, twin bell openings, eight tall pinnacles and three tiers of niches rising up the west elevation. The similarities do not, however, extend far, for TITCHMARSH is a highly original work that defies easy categorization.

St Mary's Church enjoys a commanding position on the brow of a hill, high above the River Nene. It marks the point at which the light industry, vast distribution warehouses and fast roads of the upper Nene give way to a rolling rural landscape of stone-built villages to the north. Few towers are better served by the landscape in which they sit, for a ha-ha provides an invisible boundary between the churchyard and the surrounding meadow sprinkled with ancient horse chestnuts and oaks.

Thomas Gryndall left a bequest for the construction of the tower in 1474, a date that is entirely in accordance with the stylistic evidence. TITCHMARSH was a minor possession of two powerful families in the late fifteenth century: the Lovells, loyal supporters of the House of York, and the Somersets, later the Earls of Worcester, who replaced them in 1486.

St Mary's tower is of four stages emphatically divided by bands of quatrefoils. These are repeated below the parapet and in triplicate around the base. The two upper bands are in the Midlands style of pointed quatrefoils contained within a diamond frieze; the five lower bands are of conventional rounded form but all are subtly different. The quatrefoil motif is repeated in the windows to the staircase concealed within the south-west corner. In late Somerset towers the stair is always expressed as an external turret, usually on the north-east corner, but in the eastern half of England the concealed stair remained the preference. The vertical buttresses remain subservient to the horizontal banding, for quatrefoils, strings and basement profile all wrap continuously around their faces. In Somerset the buttresses would terminate with a tour de force of brilliant pinnacles, but here, in typical Northamptonshire style, they finish abruptly at the top of the third stage.

Decoration reaches a splendid climax at the parapet and at the base, particularly around the ceremonial west door. This doorway is framed by both of the prevalent forms of hood-mould of the age, for a crocketed ogee arch breaks through the centre of a rectangular outer frame. The spandrels, of shields within quatrefoils and mouchetes to either side, are typical of the period. Several of the finest Northamptonshire towers including LOWICK, KETTERING and Whiston, decorate their basement courses with a single band of

364

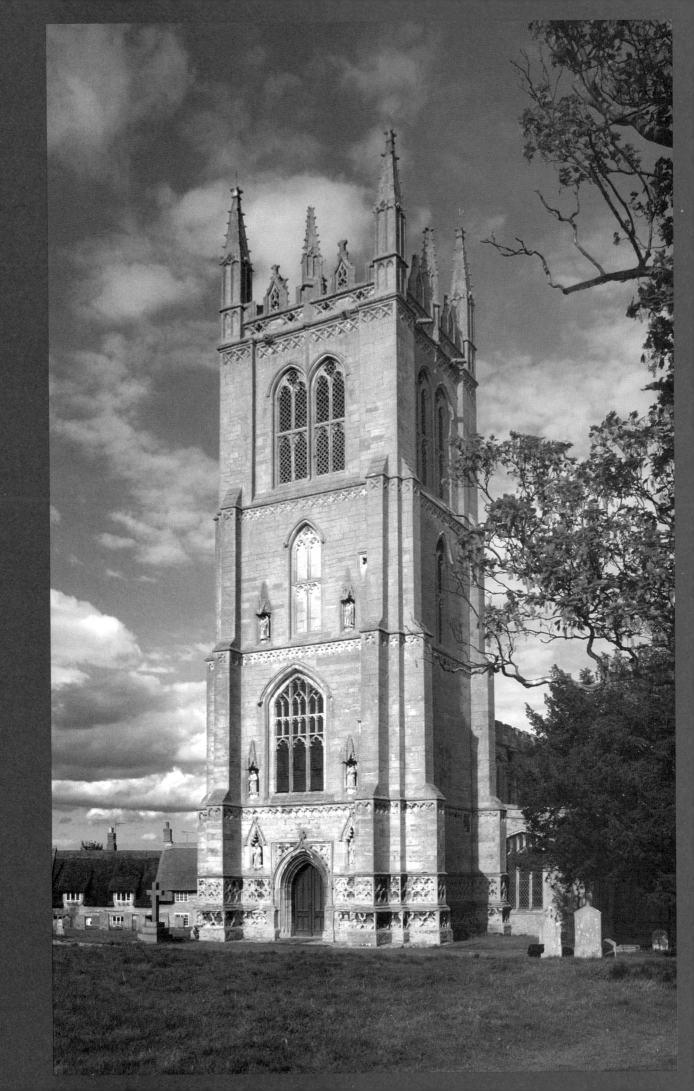

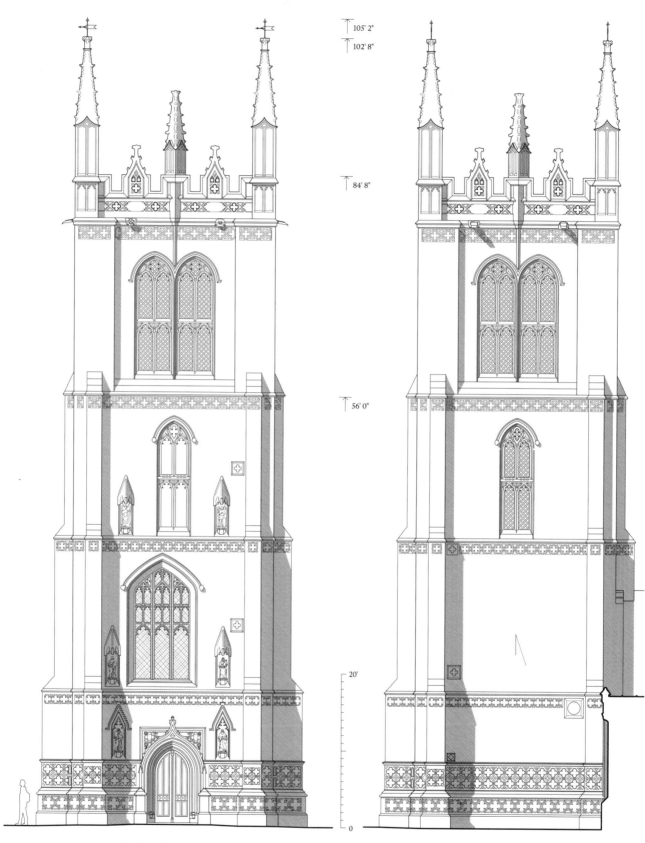

105' 2"
102' 8"

84' 8"

56' 0"

20'

0

West elevation

South elevation

quatrefoils, but the three tiers at TITCHMARSH are an unprecedented luxury. The sumptuous plinth becomes so tall that it occupies fully half the height of the first stage.

The limited space remaining on the first stage is occupied by two septafoil niches recessed beneath straight crocketed gables. These niches are repeated, but with projecting canopies, on the two stages that follow. This is strongly evocative of Somerset, for niches are exceedingly rare in eastern England during this period, except in Yorkshire, where they are used only singly at Holme-on-Spalding-Moor, Beeford, Great Driffield and TICKHILL. The sculptures are from 1901, when the rector's wife raised the necessary funds by breeding black fantail pigeons.[2] Starting at the base, the figures represent Moses and Aaron, the Virgin Mary and St Peter, and the archangels Michael and Gabriel.

The three-light cinquefoiled west window on the second stage is the one significant eccentricity in the design, for it is set decisively off-centre to avoid the staircase, squashing the northern niche tight against the buttress. This window may well be a later insertion, for the panelled drop tracery and triangular four-centred arch are quite unlike anything in the upper stages. Externally the evidence for change is inconclusive, but internally the flat square reveal looks suspiciously like an afterthought. Again, the side elevations are left entirely plain except for a sundial dated 1798 to the south.

On the third stage, elegant twin-light openings with castellated transoms, quatrefoiled arches and head soufflets grace each elevation. To the east and west the openings were always intended to be blind, but to the north and south they appear to be filled with Somerset-style trelliswork louvres. Closer inspection reveals this to be nothing more than a latticework of brick (a) that has weathered sympathetically to resemble the Weldon stone of the tower. Similar louvres reappear on the fourth stage in paired openings that follow the previous pattern. The central dividing shaft continues vertically to the parapet.

Around and above these windows, the tower reverts to the local Stamford school of design, with shallow clasping buttresses and a Midlands-style quatrefoil band. The closest precedents for the fine parapet are Folkingham (Lincs) and St Martin, Stamford (Lincs), from around 1485. Four square corner pinnacles are tall and decorated with two stages of panelling, modest crockets, square finials and copper weathervanes (b) proudly carrying the date 1882. Rotated centre pinnacles – always the hallmark of a fine tower – rise from the bell stage shafts. More satisfying still are the perforated, concave gabled merlons that alternate with the pinnacles, an original invention derived from Yorkshire and shared with St Martin, Stamford. These two towers may indeed be the work of the same mason, for similarities extend throughout the parapet, from the diagonal quatrefoil

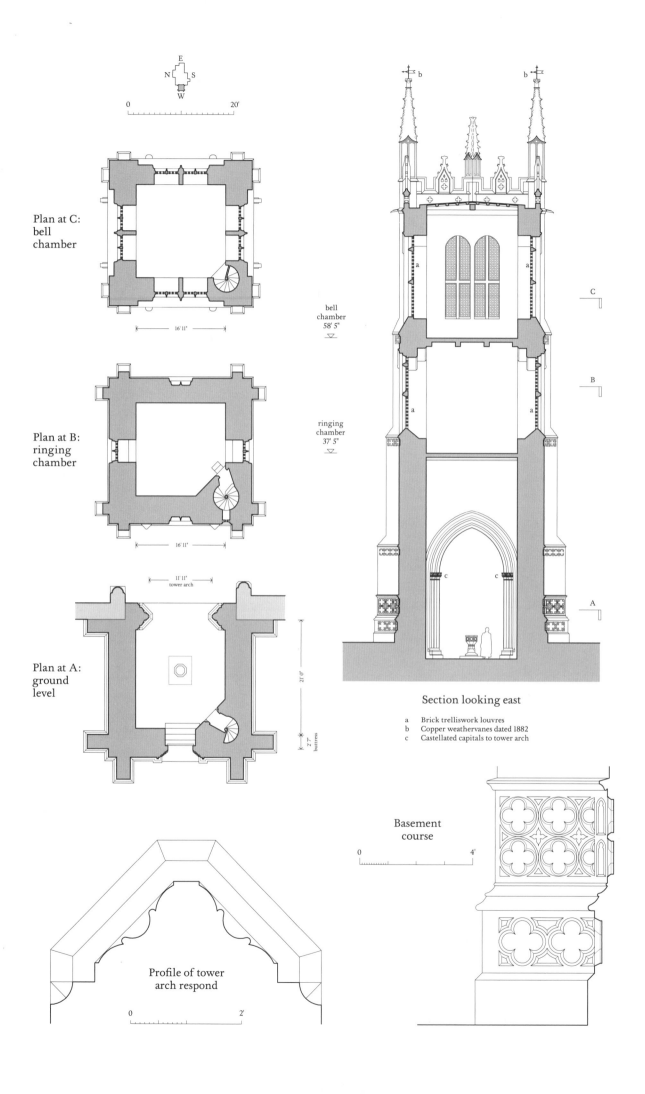

Plan at C:
bell
chamber

16' 11"

Plan at B:
ringing
chamber

16' 11"

Plan at A:
ground
level

11' 11"
tower arch

21' 0"

2' 7"
buttress

bell
chamber
58' 5"

ringing
chamber
37' 5"

C

B

A

Section looking east

a   Brick trelliswork louvres
b   Copper weathervanes dated 1882
c   Castellated capitals to tower arch

Profile of tower
arch respond

0   2'

Basement
course

0   4'

0   20'

frieze to the pairs of gargoyles draining each face of the lead roof.

Internally the tower is sturdy but unremarkable. The floors and roof structure look suspiciously Victorian, as does the florid inscription running above the scraped rubble walling at the base of the tower. By far the best features are the chunky castellated capitals of the tower arch (c). The arch is of three concave chamfered orders, the outer order continuing to the floor, the two central orders being replaced by flat filleted rolls on the responds. Five steps leading up to the west door and damp patches around the walls result from the ground having risen several feet at the west end of the church. The absence of squinch arches confirms that this exceptionally beautiful tower was never intended to carry a spire.

NOTES

1 Frank J. Allen, *The Great Church Towers of England* (1932), p. 128.
2 Reported in the parish magazine, 1901.

40

Evercreech

SOMERSET

Two Somerset towers derive directly from ST CUTHBERT, WELLS: Wrington, twelve miles to the north-west of the city, and EVERCREECH, seven miles in the opposite direction. Both towers date from around 1485, when their source of inspiration was already three generations old, and both share an extreme attenuation that brings to mind nothing so much as the revolutionary work of Charles Rennie Mackintosh four centuries later. With the possible exception of St Stephen, Bristol, these are the most elongated tower designs in England.

In Frank Allen's classification of Somerset towers, EVERCREECH and Wrington are separated according to their geographical locations, EVERCREECH joining the East Mendip Group, despite the design of its buttresses, and Wrington the North Somerset Group. This division is illuminating, for the same basic design is interpreted by masons working in two related but distinguishable local styles. In this work, however, formal consistency is given precedence, and these two outstanding towers are considered as a separate group.

Visiting EVERCREECH for the first time is a disconcerting experience not because of the extraordinary slenderness of the tower, for which one is prepared, but because it appears so unexpectedly small. Photographs that suggest a huge mass soaring heavenward are illusory, for there is an almost toy-like delight in the intimate scale of the tower and of the church within. The head of the west

door is low enough to touch, and there is not even twelve clear feet between the drips of the buttress. The audacity of stretching such a tiny, compact plan skyward for over eighty-three feet is captivating. The cathedral-like authority of ST CUTHBERT, WELLS is replaced by the cheeky impudence of a modest parish church working on a quarter of the budget.

The discrepancy in scale is barley hinted at by the difference in height. At 93' 4" EVERCREECH is slightly less than two-thirds of the height of its noble ancestor. It is, however, far lighter, both in build and in spirit, requiring only around 1,000 tons of Doulting limestone for its construction compared with 4,000 tons for ST CUTHBERT's tower.[1] This dramatic contrast is best appreciated by comparing cross sections that are drawn to the same scale.

As with all late Somerset towers, the description should start with the buttresses. These are entirely untypical of other towers in the East Mendip district such as Bruton, Mells and LEIGH-ON-MENDIP. Two overlapping influences are combined in a novel and entirely convincing way. There is an obvious association with the South Somerset form of buttress, seen best at Norton-under-Hampton and related to several towers in the adjacent county of Dorset. In this form a simple plain-sided buttress of three or four stages terminates at the bell chamber string to support a rotated square shaft that becomes a minor pinnacle above the parapet.

The other, and much earlier, source of ST CUTHBERT, WELLS is demonstrated in two significant details. First, the base of the rotated upper shaft is itself embellished by a pair of small orthogonal pinnacles, which here start lower and rise a great deal further than at WELLS. Second, and more significantly, the upper tower elevation is recessed to reveal clasping square corners terminating above the parapet with minor pinnacles on each of the three external corners. No doubt the mason would have preferred to start this clasping detail from the base, as occurs at ST CUTHBERT's, but was prevented from doing so by the constraints of the narrow plan. The only ambiguity in this otherwise splendid buttress design is the asymmetrically located pinnacle cap, which cowers uncomfortably behind the five encircling minor pinnacles.

The slender elevations remaining between these buttresses follow the principle of ST CUTHBERT's, with a conventional lower half followed by an exceptional upper section. Here the lower portion is subdivided by a continuous string, creating a total of three stages where previously there were only two. The proportions of the tower including the parapet resemble one double cube sitting over two single cubes.

The basement profile steps up to form a square drop label enclosing a flat four-centred west door and spandrel panels filled by quatrefoil roundels. This is typical of the final quarter of the fifteenth century, both in Somerset, at Wrington for example, and

in towers across the country, such as WILBY. At EVERCREECH the double-cusped quatrefoil figures are exceptionally fine. The design of the untransomed four-light west window is equally good, for it includes inverted cusping throughout the head tracery. The crisp, sharp lines of the subarcuated tracery run straight and true. This window pushes up through the string of the second stage and leads the eye to a carved niche occupied by St Peter holding a key. Side elevations are plain apart from tall twin-light blind openings containing incidental slit windows to the ringing chamber.

Paired twin-light long-panel openings on the upper tower are separated by a single rotated shaft rising through the parapet. In size and projection this diagonal shaft is not unlike the parapet string, and so from a distance the two members combine to form a pronounced cross motif that is echoed by minor crosses on the adjacent buttresses. Every inch between the clasping buttresses is utilized for the openings, leaving insufficient room for the hood-moulds. This is by no means detrimental, for the upward surge in energy becomes compressed and amplified.

ST CUTHBERT's tower introduced a quatrefoil motif within the long panel transom, and this is reinterpreted here in a supporting row of ogee trefoil archlets that carry small quatrefoil circles in their spandrels. Rounded trefoiled archlets support a secondary upper transom and typical Somerset head tracery of three rising

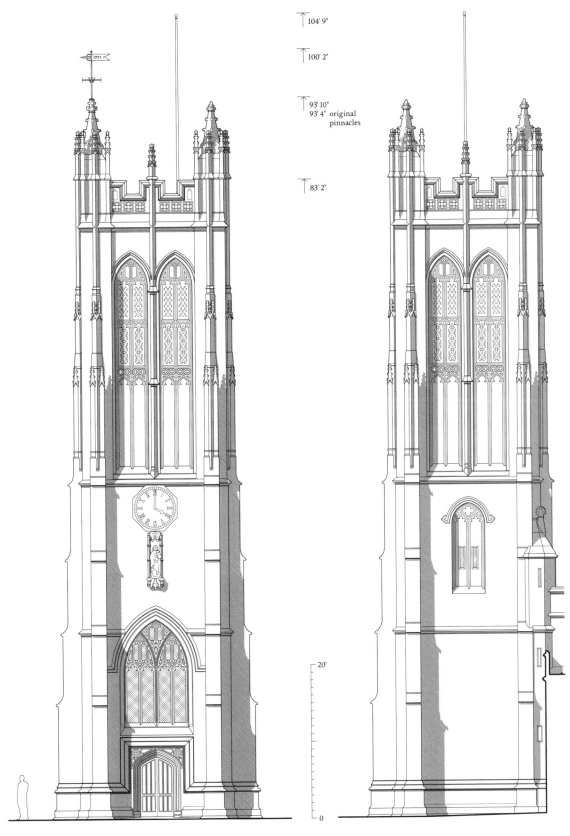

104' 9"

100' 2"

93' 10"
93' 4" original
pinnacles

83' 2"

20'

0

West elevation

South elevation

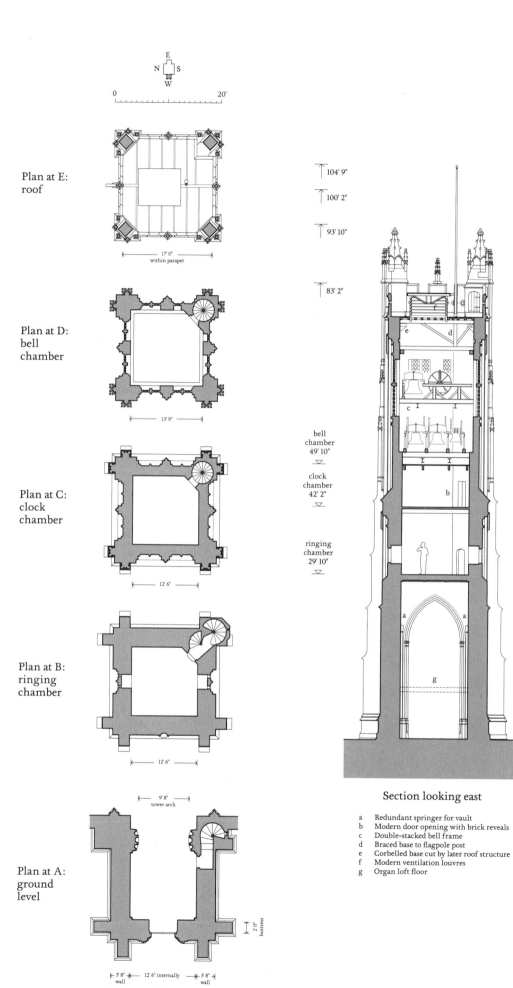

E
N   S
W

0   20'

Plan at E:
roof

17' 0"
within parapet

Plan at D:
bell
chamber

13' 9"

Plan at C:
clock
chamber

12' 6"

Plan at B:
ringing
chamber

12' 6"

9' 8"
tower arch

Plan at A:
ground
level

2' 0"
buttress

3' 8"   12' 6" internally   3' 8"
wall   wall

19' 10"

26' 3" including buttresses

104' 9"

100' 2"

93' 10"

83' 2"

E

D

bell
chamber
49' 10"

clock
chamber
42' 2"

C

ringing
chamber
29' 10"

B

A

Section looking east

a   Redundant springer for vault
b   Modern door opening with brick reveals
c   Double-stacked bell frame
d   Braced base to flagpole post
e   Corbelled base cut by later roof structure
f   Modern ventilation louvres
g   Organ loft floor

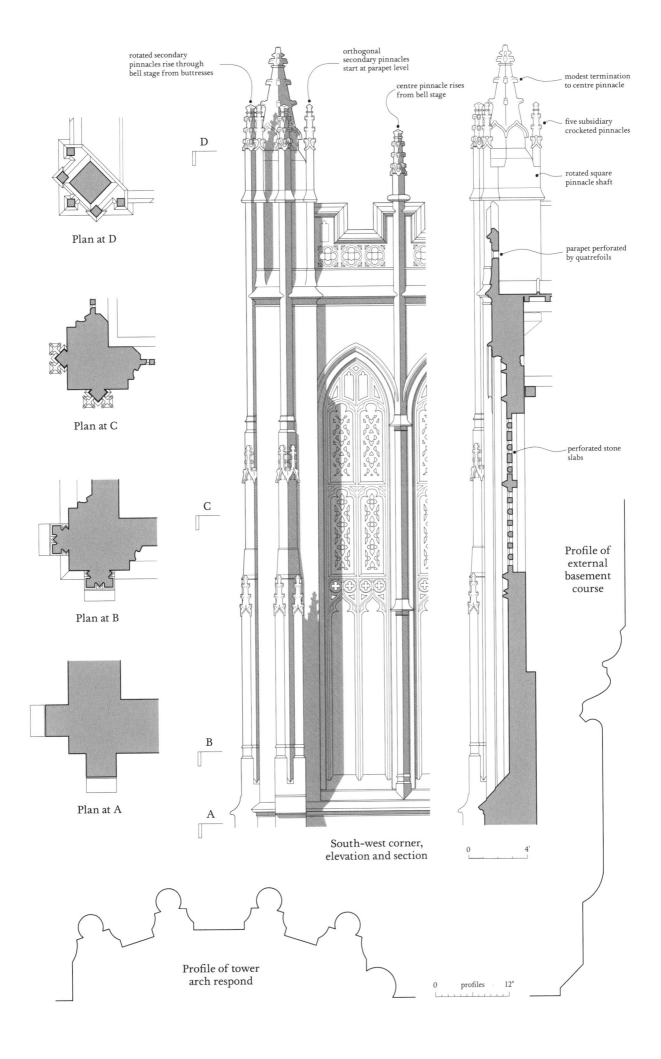

Plan at D

Plan at C

Plan at B

Plan at A

D

C

B

A

rotated secondary
pinnacles rise through
bell stage from buttresses

orthogonal
secondary pinnacles
start at parapet level

centre pinnacle rises
from bell stage

modest termination
to centre pinnacle

five subsidiary
crocketed pinnacles

rotated square
pinnacle shaft

parapet perforated
by quatrefoils

perforated stone
slabs

Profile of
external
basement
course

South-west corner,
elevation and section

0   4'

Profile of tower
arch respond

0   profiles   12"

mullions. One considerable improvement on ST CUTHBERT's, at least in its modern unlouvred form, is the use of perforated slabs to ventilate the bell chamber. Half a century later and three miles to the east, this excellent long-panel design was copied in its entirety across the three bays of Batcombe tower. As at Bruton and LEIGH-ON-MENDIP, the castellated parapet is perforated by quatrefoils set within circles and filled with shields that, when new, would have been painted with the heraldry of Tudor England.

The interior of the tower is so confined that the bell frame has been split between two tiers (c). The splendid tower arch, of three ascending trefoiled panels canted between four filleted shafts, is shared with Wrington and derived from ST CUTHBERT, WELLS. One unusual detail, necessitated by the thinness of the upper walls, is the use of corbels at the top of the tower to support the inner corner of the pinnacles (e). As at

ST CUTHBERT's there is no correspondence between the exterior and interior divisions.

In several respects Wrington sticks more closely to the ST CUTHBERT's model. Crocketed octagonal spirelets, each guarded by four square corner pinnacles, are a direct quotation, and the buttress pinnacles stop below the parapet as they do at WELLS. One minor failing, in comparison with the brilliant design of EVERCREECH, is that the long panels are divided too evenly, reducing the verticality of the composition. Wrington is taller, apparently by 18' 2",and considerably broader, but it is also, unfortunately, more difficult to appreciate, being set uncomfortably close to the churchyard wall. On balance, EVERCREECH is the more beautiful and memorable of these two exceptional towers. Alec Clifton-Taylor considered Evercreech to be an exquisite gem. It was, he believed, the most perfect of all Somerset towers.[2]

NOTES

1 There is approximately 500 m³ of stone above ground at EVERCREECH, and 1,900 m³ at ST CUTHBERT, WELLS. Using a typical density of 2,100 kg/m³ for Doulting limestone, this equates to around 1,050 tonnes and 3,990 tonnes of stone respectively.

2 Alec Clifton-Taylor, *English Parish Churches as Works of Art* (1986), p. 100.

41

Leigh-on-Mendip

SOMERSET

LEIGH-ON-MENDIP is the most perfect of all the mature Perpendicular towers of Somerset. The much-loved architectural historian Alec Clifton-Taylor rated the towers of the county according to their beauty on three separate occasions spanning five decades.[1] The lower ranks fluctuated, but his three favourites remained constant: EVERCREECH, followed by KINGSTON ST MARY and LEIGH-ON-MENDIP. The line drawings within this volume allow the reader to compare these designs in their purest form, removed from any distractions of context. Considered side by side, LEIGH-ON-MENDIP is second to none. EVERCREECH, by comparison, appears rather undernourished, while KINGSTON is slightly too predictable and static as a composition. LEIGH-ON-MENDIP has the advantage of being a three-bay design, and this infuses the composition with a classical sense of balance, harmony and completeness. Alec Clifton-Taylor, who regarded LEIGH-ON-MENDIP as being 'almost faultless', levelled one minor criticism regarding the absence of hood-moulds over the upper windows. This is debatable, for the architecture is purer without such unnecessary distractions.

The defining features of the East Mendip Group, of which LEIGH-ON-MENDIP is a member, are complex buttresses derived from Shepton Mallet, three-bay upper stages ventilated by perforated slabs, a battlemented parapet, and a north-eastern staircase. The earlier West Mendip Group, which employed horizontal parapets, underdeveloped

buttresses and blind outer bays to the upper stage, failed to improve on the basic Shepton Mallet model from around 1385. This formative design, one of the earliest spireless towers in the county, derives from William Wynford's revolutionary work at WELLS, to the extent that he has been proposed by John Harvey as the originator of the design.[2]

The precious East Mendip Group evolved the principles of Shepton Mallet into a highly original and sophisticated aesthetic. With just seven designs spanning over a century there are, not surprisingly, numerous inconsistencies between the members – for example in the form of tower arch and parapet decoration – but this should not obscure the underlying consistency within the group.[3] Chronologically, the East Mendip towers fall into three generations. Bruton and Mells, known to be in progress in 1446, form the first generation. Cranmore, LEIGH-ON-MENDIP, Weston Zoyland and Middlezoy (a two-bay design) follow around 1480, with Batcombe arriving sixty years later. Despite this protracted timescale, strong links are evident across the generations.

Bruton, Mells, LEIGH-ON-MENDIP and Batcombe are all considered to be towers of the first rank. LEIGH-ON-MENDIP is uniquely related to Mells, not only by their shared use of a three-bay middle stage, but also by the shaft-and-wave form of their tower arches, the two-centred west door openings and the concealing of the staircase within the depth of the structure. The plain parapets of Mells and Cranmore predate the perforated

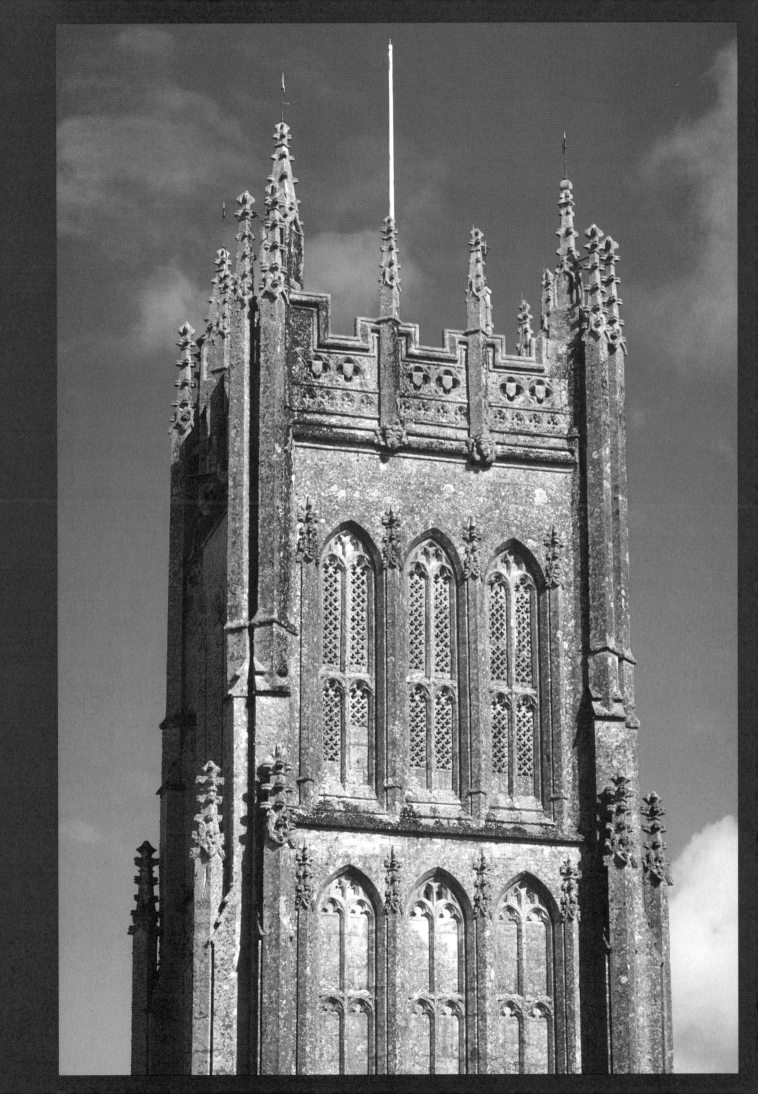

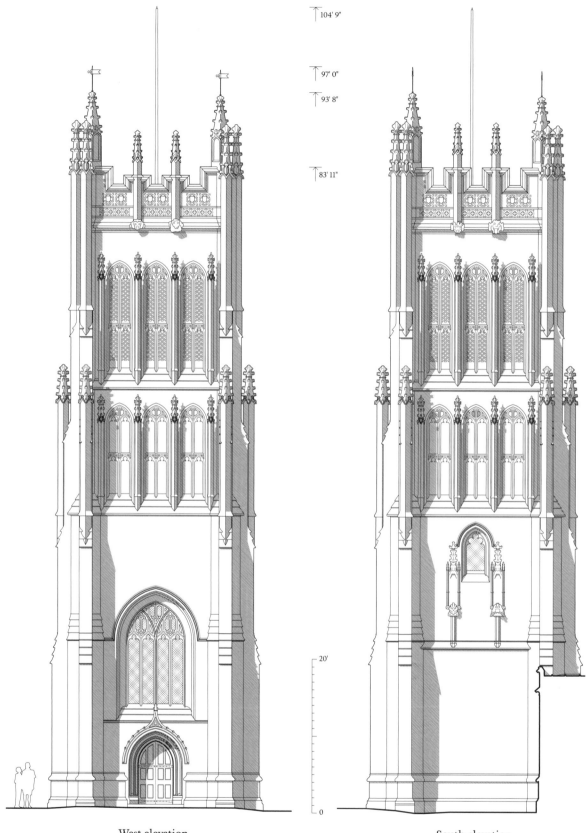

104' 9"

97' 0"
93' 8"

83' 11"

20'

0

West elevation

South elevation

quatrefoils of LEIGH-ON-MENDIP, Bruton, Weston Zoyland and Middlezoy, which are unlikely to have been completed before 1485. Large first-generation west windows, of six bays at Bruton and five bays at Mells, lead to a standardized four-bay design on all subsequent towers. Ogee archlets are universal, and inverted cusping is absent only on the short three-stage towers of Middlezoy and Cranmore. The four-stage tower is the standard type, but in the late design at Batcombe the upper stages are united by a long-panel motif derived from EVERCREECH. Height is not a serious consideration in a group that ranges from 72 feet at Cranmore to just 104 feet at Mells.[4]

The East Mendip form of buttress is less complex than it might at first appear. Its success derives from the beautifully orchestrated overlapping of extruded volumes, which are generated on plan by rotated squares. All the emphasis is placed precisely where it is required, at the base of the final stage and at its summit. The composite base of LEIGH-ON-MENDIP is formed by a rotated square core, 4' 8" in width, superimposed on the intersection of a standard pair of angle buttresses. This square core reduces once, at the level of the west window string, before terminating at the base of the second stage. Prominently serrated set-offs divide the angle buttresses into four segments in accordance with the proportions 4:3:3:3. Tall rotated pinnacle shafts arise from the buttresses at two levels, from the second set-off and from the summit. The crocketed pinnacle caps of the first tier encircle the base of the bell chamber, while the second tier shoots free of the parapet, finishing level with the raised corner merlons. Modest primary pinnacles, set on the chamfered corners of the parapet, appear almost incidental to the preceding fireworks. The glorious silhouette is completed by pairs of secondary pinnacles arising from the inner merlons. Individually none of these components are remarkable, but used in combination, and with a supreme grasp of proportion, the result is exquisite.

Read in ascending order, the plans show sturdy simplicity dissolving into brittle brilliance. Nowhere is this more evident than in the helical stair that all but separates the north-east buttress from the body of the tower. By rejecting the more common form of expressed stair turret, the mason created a fundamental weakness in the structure that may still, in time, require some substantial strengthening. At ground level the bright uncluttered interior allows visitors a clear view of empty springing stones (a) that rise optimistically from corner shafts to support a vault that was never installed. In a delightfully ambiguous gesture, the circular capitals that terminate the three respond shafts supporting the tower arch are repeated over the central swelling of the adjacent wave profiles.

Mells provides the model for the two-centred west door. Subtle vegetative decoration runs up an ogee head rising above the cill of the west window. This window is

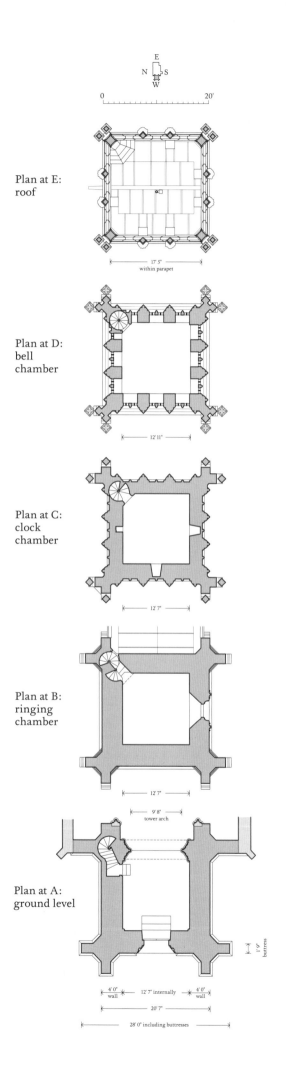

Plan at E:
roof

0   20'

17' 5"
within parapet

Plan at D:
bell
chamber

12' 11"

Plan at C:
clock
chamber

12' 7"

Plan at B:
ringing
chamber

12' 7"

Plan at A:
ground level

9' 8"
tower arch

1' 9"
buttress

4' 0"
wall   12' 7" internally   4' 0"
wall

20' 7"

28' 0" including buttresses

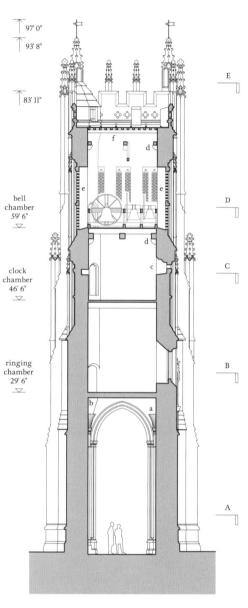

97' 0"

93' 8"

83' 11"

E

f

d

bell
chamber
59' 6"

e   e

D

d

clock
chamber
46' 6"

c

C

B

ringing
chamber
29' 6"

b   a

A

Section looking east

a   Springing stones for unbuilt vault
b   Corner corbelled to support staircase
c   Window in head of blind tracery
d   Stone corbels
e   Perforated stone panels
f   Roof beam dated 1845

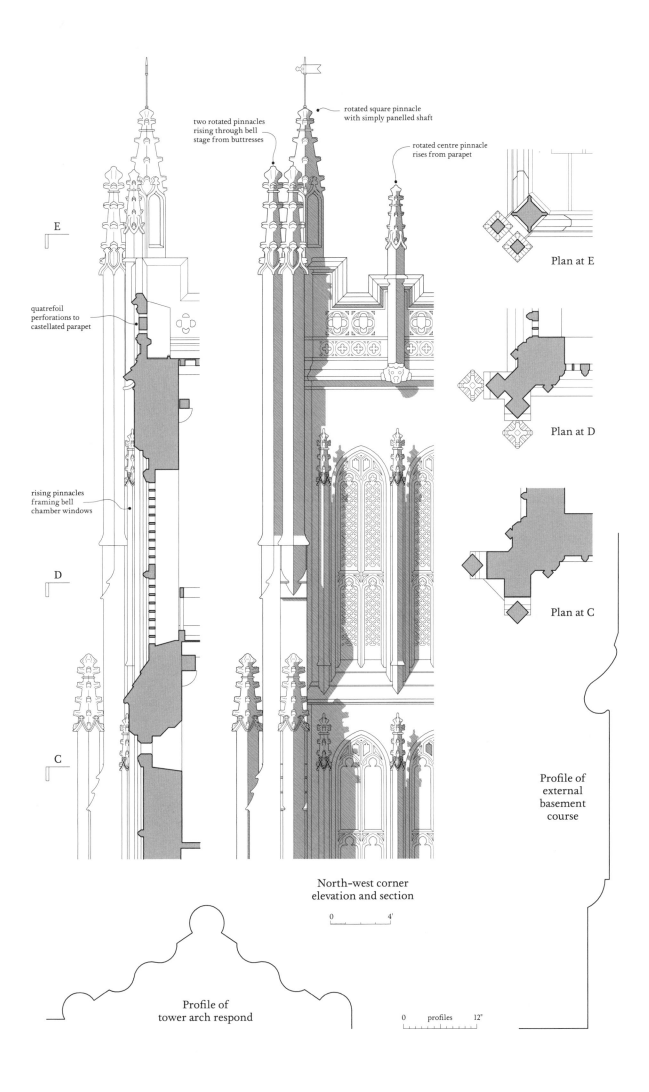

two rotated pinnacles
rising through bell
stage from buttresses

rotated square pinnacle
with simply panelled shaft

rotated centre pinnacle
rises from parapet

E

quatrefoil
perforations to
castellated parapet

rising pinnacles
framing bell
chamber windows

D

C

Plan at E

Plan at D

Plan at C

Profile of
external
basement
course

North-west corner
elevation and section

0   4'

Profile of
tower arch respond

0   profiles   12"

of the near-standard four-bay 'Y' form surrounded by deep, smooth casements shared by all the later East Mendip towers, but the trefoiled lights look back to the earlier example of Bruton. Only the simple hood-mould disrupts the surrounding expanse of smooth limestone ashlar. LEIGH-ON-MENDIP and Mells are unusual in having no niches on their western elevations, a far from unwelcome development that exaggerates the contrast with the sumptuous upper stages. The prominent south elevation, which faces the main street of the village, maintains two second-stage niches flanking a solitary ringing chamber window enclosed by the only cinquefoiled arch in the entire composition.

The fourth stage is splendidly articulated by three twin-light openings perforated by a fine diagonal lattice of ascending trefoils (e) and separated from each other by spear-like pinnacle shafts. With trefoiled archlets supporting the mid-height transom and typical Somerset tracery in the head, these openings are consistent with all the larger East Mendip towers. It is on the preceding third stage that the true genius of LEIGH-ON-MENDIP, and of Mells, resides, for in an inspired move the design of the fourth stage is repeated in full. By compressing the proportions and omitting the perforations the primacy of the final stage is beautifully maintained. The result is architectural perfection.

It would be dangerous for the parapet to compete with such magnificence, but the mason of Mells was too cautious, for he finished his tower with nothing but plain unrelieved masonry. At LEIGH-ON-MENDIP this defect is elegantly rectified by quatrefoil perforations, two below each embrasure, set above a row of miniature quatrefoil circles and pairs of large grotesques on every face.

NOTES

1   In 1946, 1958 and 1982, according to a footnote in his *Buildings of Delight* (1986), p. 136.
2   John Harvey, 'The Church Towers of Somerset', *Ancient Monuments Society's Transactions*, vol. 27 (1983), pp. 181–83.
3   Frank Allen's East Mendip Group also includes EVERCREECH, which in this volume is placed within the separate Long-Panel Group, and Nunney, an inferior single-windowed tower.

4   Apart from LEIGH-ON-MENDIP, surveyed here at 93' 8", Frank J. Allen's *Great Church Towers of England* lists the following (unverified) heights recorded by Brereton: Cranmore 72' 10", Middlezoy 73' 4", Batcombe 87' 0", Weston Zoyland 100' 9", Bruton 102' 6" and Mells 104' 3".

42

Kingston St Mary

SOMERSET

Of the fifteen Somerset towers of the first rank, six are contained within the Quantock Group centred on Taunton. It is, therefore, not unreasonable to assert that this is the finest group of medieval towers in the whole of England. The Battle of Bosworth in 1485 neatly divides the members into two equally splendid sub-groups. The Early Quantock towers are mature Perpendicular in style, with tower arches formed of two waves separated by a casement and parapets perforated by quatrefoils. By contrast, the Late Quantock towers are Tudor through and through, with tower arches articulated by shafts and panels, and multiple bands of quatrefoils dividing the elevations.

As a general rule, Late Quantock towers are better when tall and of four or more stages, whereas the Early Quantock towers become enfeebled if they rise more than ninety feet from the ground. The three masterpieces in this early group – Isle Abbots (80' 11"), Staple Fitzpaine (83' 8") and KINGSTON ST MARY (88' 6"), are all of three stages. At Bishops Lydeard (107' 0") and St James, Taunton (120' 6"), the same constituent parts are stretched to encompass a fourth stage and the design suffers as a result.[1]

Other distinguishing marks are shared by these five pre-Tudor towers. Their west doors are all four-centred beneath drop labels that carry vegetative patterns in their spandrels. Octagonal north-eastern staircase turrets rise above their parapets, those of Staple Fitzpaine, St James, Taunton and

KINGSTON ST MARY terminating with steeply pitched roofs. Somerset 'Y'-form four-bay west windows incorporating ogees are used on the three small towers. Five- and six-bay variants appear respectively on the larger towers of Bishops Lydeard and Taunton. The diamond stop bar, which disappears shortly after 1485, is used consistently to terminate window hood-moulds.

Selecting which one of the three near-identical masterpieces to include within this survey was far from easy. Staple Fitzpaine has the finest stair turret but the middle stage windows are rather too short. Isle Abbots is a good nineteenth-century reproduction in its upper stages, but most of its statues are original and it has six niches on its western face compared with four on its rivals. Its elevations may be considered to be slightly too broad, there may be too much space above the upper windows, and there is no pyramidal roof over the stair turret, but Isle Abbots is alone in having an open interior uncluttered by modern screens or church organs. KINGSTON suffers greatly in this respect, with a garishly painted instrument cantilevering rudely from its gallery (a) above a Gothic Revival screen. Externally, however, the composition is almost without fault, and the site, which nestles onto a gently rolling south-facing slope uncluttered by trees, is idyllic.

These reasons alone would be sufficient for KINGSTON ST MARY to be judged as *primus inter pares*, but its pre-eminence is also assured by the glorious texture and colours of the Keuper new red sandstone, which varies from red to pink, buff, green and grey. Sandstone can be a disastrous choice of material, but here it has survived well and is more characterful than the otherwise excellent blue lias with Ham Hill stone dressings used at Staple Fitzpaine and Isle Abbots.

The decoration of KINGSTON ST MARY is luxurious but never carried to excess. Each area of carving is given room to breathe, with ample unbroken expanses of walling separating niches, windows, door and buttresses. Nothing is cramped, and the proportions and spacing of the individual elements are impeccably defined. The composition can be read as two pure cubes sitting on top of a cuboid, in which the ratio of height to width is 3:2. If the parapet is included within the description the ascending stages follow the numerical ratio 3:2:2:1.

The composite form of buttress plan, which appears outside the Quantock Group only at the very late tower of Batcombe (c. 1539–43), is derived from Shepton Mallet. It differs from the East Mendip Group both in the articulation of the pinnacles and in the use of an external square corner, rather than a diagonal chamfer, in the re-entrant angle between the primary buttresses. The plan at the base can be read in several ways, but is best explained as a pair of setback buttresses set away from the corner of the tower to which they are connected by broad chamfers. The setback element rises in three equal portions to the upper-stage string course, where large rotated-square pinnacle shafts take over. Unlike LEIGH-ON-MENDIP, the pinnacle shafts terminate comfortably below the level of the parapet, their crocketed caps and finials neatly lining through with the uppermost window heads. Set-offs on the square and chamfered infill portions follow after a slight vertical delay to die out completely halfway up the middle stage. Tiny pinnacle shafts, arising from three levels of set-offs, lend the silhouette a continuous but gentle upward momentum.

Apart from the immaculately executed west door and window, both of which follow the standard Quantock format described above, the only lower tower decoration is a pair of empty niches. These frame the portal and rest directly on the basement course, allowing close inspection of the projecting ogee canopy, now softened below an obscuring crust of lichen.

Niches multiply on the second stage, with two to every face, except on the north where the window shuffles sideways to make way for the stair turret. The niches are supported on the wings of angels – not flying, as might be expected, but perching prosaically on panelled shafts. Among Early Quantock towers this delightful detail is absent only at St James, Taunton. Windows on this middle stage are of the near-standard Somerset twin-light design, transomed and quatrefoiled, with ogees and inverted trefoiled cusping in the head. Infill slabs (c) are each ventilated by two columns of small

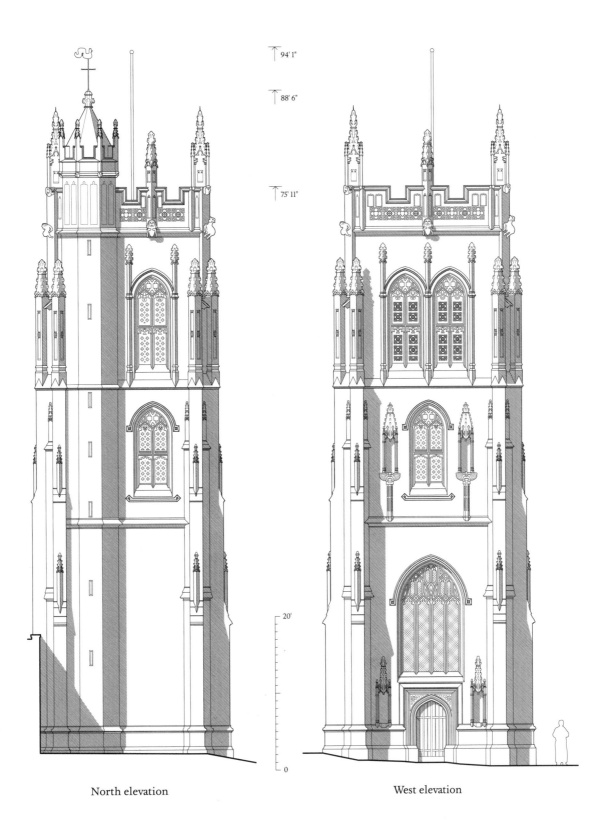

94' 1"

88' 6"

75' 11"

20'

0

North elevation

West elevation

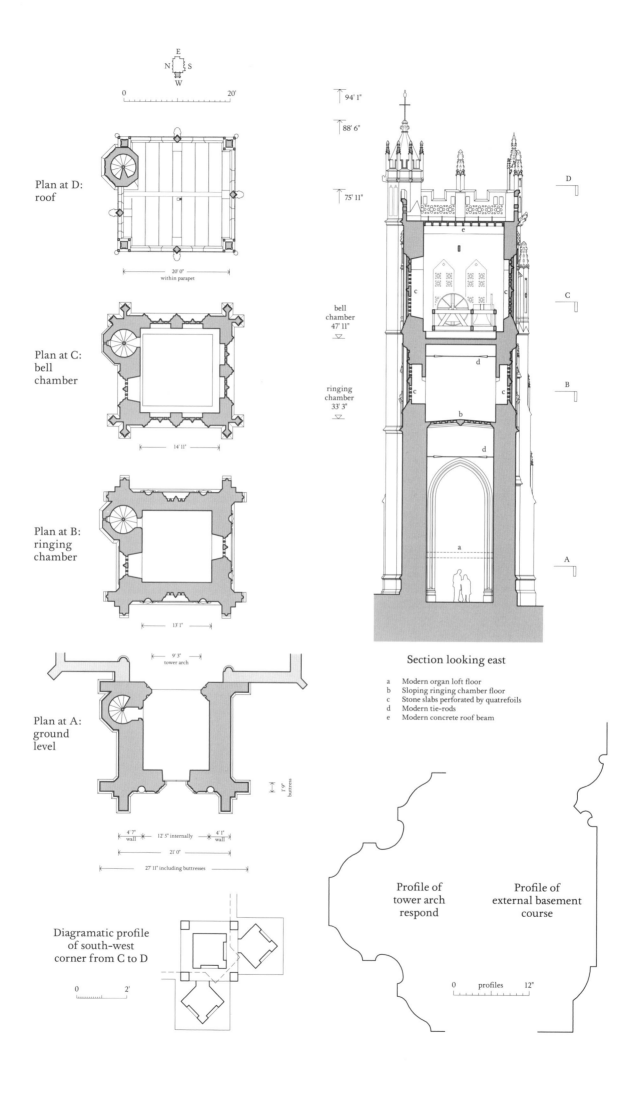

Plan at D:
roof

Plan at C:
bell
chamber

Plan at B:
ringing
chamber

Plan at A:
ground
level

E
N S
W

0   20'

20' 0"
within parapet

14' 11"

13' 1"

9' 3"
tower arch

1' 9"
buttress

4' 7"   12' 5" internally   4' 1"
wall   wall

21' 0"

27' 11" including buttresses

Diagramatic profile
of south-west
corner from C to D

0   2'

94' 1"

88' 6"

75' 11"

bell
chamber
47' 11"

ringing
chamber
33' 3"

D

C

B

A

e

c   c

d

c   c

b

d

a

Section looking east

a   Modern organ loft floor
b   Sloping ringing chamber floor
c   Stone slabs perforated by quatrefoils
d   Modern tie-rods
e   Modern concrete roof beam

Profile of
tower arch
respond

Profile of
external basement
course

0   profiles   12"

quatrefoil roundels with diamond-shaped flowers in the arch above. The only post-medieval intrusions are light grey plates on the north and south elevations terminating the strengthening rods that are visible within the tower (d). The fenestration of the paired upper-stage openings is identical to the preceding stage save for the larger scale of the quatrefoil perforations, which match the parapet above. Hood-moulds bounce between three rotated-square spears that frame the openings.

Each face of the crenellated parapet is perforated by eight quatrefoils carrying flowers, some five-petalled, and each different from its neighbour. Above, each merlon is cut through by a pair of trefoiled flat-arched openings. The placement of the eight 'hunky punk' grotesques – one to each corner and one to the centre of each side – distinguishes the Quantock towers from other groups. In the East and West Mendip groups, for example, pairs of hunky punks are set away from the corners in order to permit the buttresses to run unhindered through the parapet. In the Quantock design, however, the parapet forms an independent crown, and the corner carvings play a prominent role in articulating the junction between two dissimilar systems. KINGSTON ST MARY's grotesques are overflowing with vitality but not with water, for the drainage runs internally.

The only awkwardness in the entire design is that the diagonal face on which the corner hunky punks are set – effectively a very shallow diagonal buttress at the summit of the tower – is geometrically unrelated to what has gone before or what is to follow. The result is a botched corner that is far better viewed without binoculars. The corner pinnacle cluster follows the model of ST CUTHBERT, WELLS, in having four minor square shafts surrounding a major square core. Seen from a distance, and particularly on the diagonal, this fine termination appears to float miraculously close to the edge, the corner shaft balancing on nothing more than an uncomplaining cantilevered head.

NOTE

1   Apart from KINGSTON ST MARY, these heights are taken from R. P. Brereton as recorded in Frank J. Allen, *The Great Church Towers of England* (1932), and have not been verified on site.

The county town of Taunton is dominated by the most elaborate parish tower in England. Rising to 157' 9", the west tower of ST MARY MAGDALENE is easily the tallest parochial tower in Somerset, overtopping St John the Baptist, Glastonbury by more than twenty feet. Along with the unsurveyed towers of Cirencester (Glos) and Cromer (Norfolk), it is one of three contenders for the position of third-highest unspired medieval parish tower in England.[1] One important qualification is required here, however, for TAUNTON is almost entirely a nineteenth-century facsimile of a medieval design.

In 1858–62 the tower was rebuilt from its foundations under the expert supervision of Benjamin Ferrey, who had been working on the church since 1842, and George Gilbert Scott. Eight years later the tower of St James, a quarter of a mile to the north, also underwent a full-scale rebuilding, this time under the local architect J. Houghton Spencer. He recorded that both towers had originally been built of 'a friable grey sandstone' that had weathered beyond repair.[2] Both were reconstructed in red Keuper sandstone with hamstone dressings similar to the authentic fabric of Bishops Lydeard six miles to the north-west. This dramatically changed the appearance of Taunton's twin medieval towers, and not for the better. It is to be hoped that the strident contrast between the red and buff stones will mellow with age, as it has done over the course of five centuries at KINGSTON

ST MARY. The authenticity of St James, Taunton was compromised by the redesign of the dilapidated crown in line with Early Quantock precedent, but no such errors were made at ST MARY MAGDALENE. The enormously expensive reconstruction resulted in what was, by common consent, a true and faithful reproduction of the original design.

Unlike with the majority of Somerset towers, construction at ST MARY MAGDALENE can be accurately dated by documentary evidence. Between 1488 and 1505 twelve wills include bequests for the new tower:[3]

1488 John Beste, one cask of woad
1490 Alexander Tuse, one cask of woad
1492 Walter Dolyng, 40s.
1493 Henry Bysshop, three whole cloths
1494 Joan Wynne, 15s.
1497 Philip Love, 40s.
1499 John Buysshope, a piece of cloth worth 20s.
1502 Richard Best, 40s.
1502 Richard Adams, 26s. 8d.
1503 John Netheway, 10s.
1503 Agnes Burton, half a cask of woad
1505 Symon Fyschare, a hogshead of iron

The full details of these bequests reveal that pinnacles were being fabricated in 1502 and that the work was nearing completion by 1503. That the tower was fully finished around 1505 is evidenced by its absence from four consecutive wills in 1508, 1509 and 1511. In 1514 there follows a bequest from William

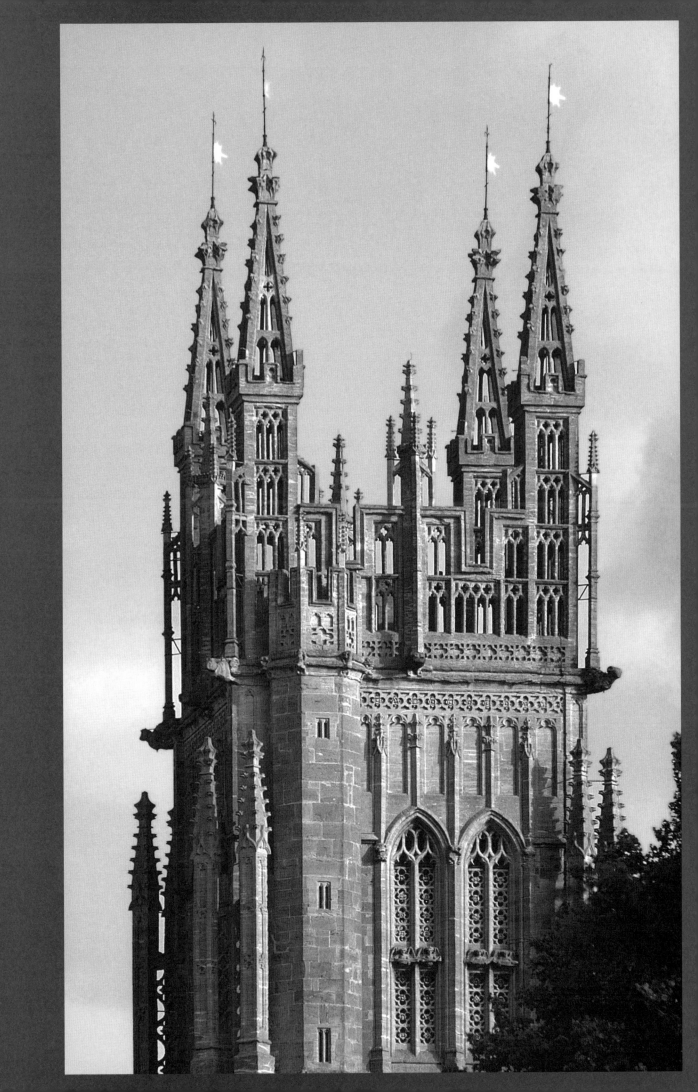

164' 10"

157' 9"

131' 2"

20'

0

North elevation

West elevation

Nethway, 'To the Katerynke of two wyndowis in the tower of the same church 26s. 8d.' This should not be taken to imply that the work was still under way, for 'Katerynke' in this context refers to the cutting of perforated Somerset tracery within the previously completed window openings. These dates confirm ST MARY MAGDALENE's importance as the link between the five Early Quantock towers and the Late Quantock masterpieces of Kingsbury Episcopi, Huish Episcopi and NORTH PETHERTON. Commencing within three years of the Battle of Bosworth it is, along with the tower at LAVENHAM, one of the earliest monuments to celebrate the arrival of the Tudor Age.

The five-stage composition, splendidly framed by the eighteenth-century terraces of Hammet Street, is a complex variation on Early Quantock practice. The major innovation is the introduction of substantial quatrefoil bands to separate the stages of the tower where previously simple string courses had sufficed. This would become one of the defining characteristics of the Late Quantock Group and required careful handling to avoid compromising the verticality of the composition.

The two near-identical middle stages, measured between the framing buttresses, are square on elevation. Pursuing this logic, the lowest two stages, considered together, approximate to a vertical golden rectangle, and the fifth stage, including the parapet, resembles a double cube. These proportions are admirable, but the introduction of a full quatrefoil band to suit the springing of the west window arch, creating two stages below the level of the ringing chamber, is less convincing. The additional elaboration this brings to the side elevations weakens rather than strengthens the design.

Not only is the interior of the tower exceptionally fine, but it also benefits from being the main entrance to the church. As might be expected, the fan vault (b) is one of the best in the county. There are twelve segments to each fan, compared with eight at Kingsbury Episcopi and NORTH PETHERTON, and the supporting corbels are in the form of shield-bearing angels. Shafts and panels on the tower arch are one of the defining characteristics of Late Quantock towers. Here three lines of trefoiled panelling, wide in the centre, narrow and angled to either side, are separated by shafts ornamented by angel capitals.

The internal compartments of the tower correspond more closely to the external divisions than is customary in Somerset, but this may be the result of nineteenth-century rationalization. Even in the most inconspicuous corners the medieval design appears to have been respected, one minor exception being where the ringing chamber openings terminate with a suspiciously Victorian form of chamfer (c). The only disappointment is the crude insertion of a two-tier bell frame, probably in 1922, through a perfectly serviceable running corbel (e).

It is unsurprising to find the Early Quantock form of composite buttress being retained at ST MARY MAGDALENE, the first of the Late Quantock towers. As at KINGSTON ST MARY, this takes the form of a pair of setback buttresses set away from the corner of the tower and connected to the tower walls by diagonal chamfers. Unfortunately, it is here that one of the principal defects in the composition occurs, for the 3' 2" projection of the buttress is entirely inadequate for a tower of this magnitude, being only seven inches longer than at the modest three-stage tower of KINGSTON. The masons must have realized their error, for at NORTH PETHERTON, which immediately followed TAUNTON, the buttresses project by a full 5' 0".

The design of the set-offs, with miniature pinnacles set on top of rotated square shafts, is similar to KINGSTON but with more pronounced mouldings and panelled shafts 9½" square. Following the pattern of the four-stage Early Quantock towers of Bishops Lydeard and St James, Taunton, there are three set-offs dividing the buttresses into four segments, each slightly taller than the last. A large rotated-square pinnacle shaft arises from the head of each buttress to terminate level with the springing of the bell chamber arch. The treatment here is more elaborate than usual, with quatrefoils in squares decorating the base and three tiers of panelling on the shaft faces. Unlike at Early Quantock towers such as KINGSTON, these pinnacles are

in the process of gaining structural independence from the upper tower, an evolutionary step that would reach a natural conclusion at St John, Glastonbury and NORTH PETHERTON.

In scale and elaboration the western portal surpasses all other Quantock towers. The carved spandrels between the four-centred door arch and the square label depict biblical scenes relating to Mary Magdalene. Three angels rest on the upper edge of the hood-mould. There are six occupied niches: two either side of the door head, two squeezed onto the chamfered returns of the buttresses, and two at the springing of the west window arch. Below the outermost niches the basement drip steps up to make way for a further pair of empty recesses. The upper niches continue on the side elevations, with two to the north and three to the south. The five-bay two-centred west window employs alternate sub-reticulation in the head, an unusual choice that works very well with the reticulated patterns of the upper windows.

Pairs of three-bay windows guarded by pinnacled shafts on the third stage are elaborated on the fourth and fifth stages by the addition of angels projecting from the transoms. The fifth stage is further distinguished by its height, with eight tiers of quatrefoils rather than five. The window form is developed from the earlier three-bay openings of Bishops Lydeard, in which ogee archlets support reticulated head tracery. ST MARY MAGDALENE is significantly

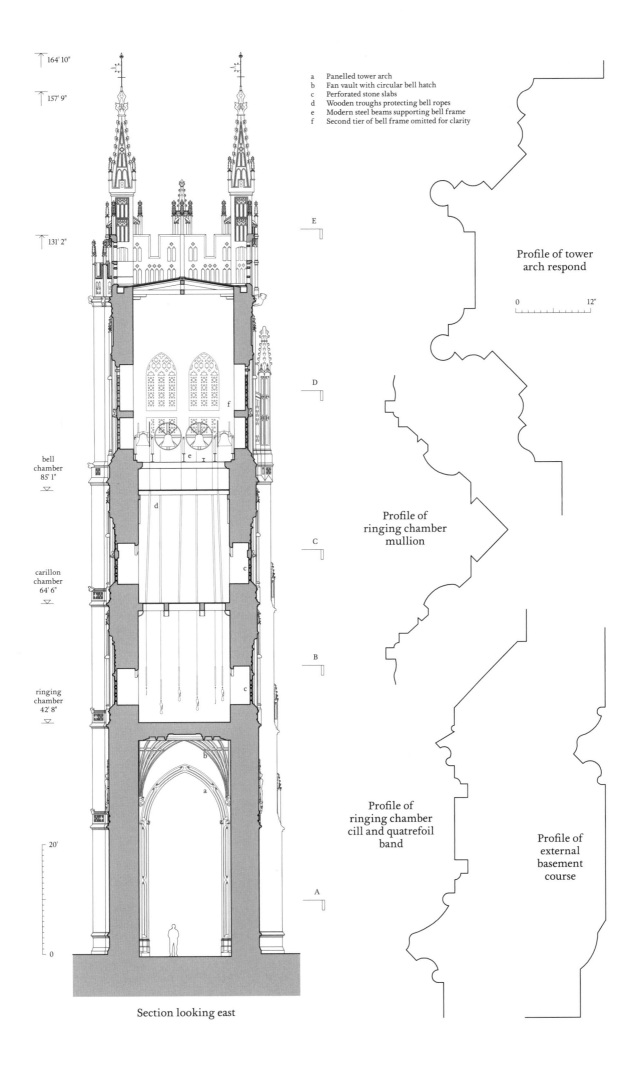

164' 10"

157' 9"

131' 2"

a   Panelled tower arch
b   Fan vault with circular bell hatch
c   Perforated stone slabs
d   Wooden troughs protecting bell ropes
e   Modern steel beams supporting bell frame
f   Second tier of bell frame omitted for clarity

E

D

Profile of tower
arch respond

0   12"

bell
chamber
85' 1"

Profile of
ringing chamber
mullion

C

carillon
chamber
64' 6"

B

ringing
chamber
42' 8"

20'

Profile of
ringing chamber
cill and quatrefoil
band

Profile of
external
basement
course

A

0

Section looking east

Reflected
plan of
tower vault

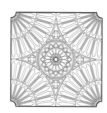

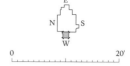

0 ———————————————— 20'

Plan at E:
roof

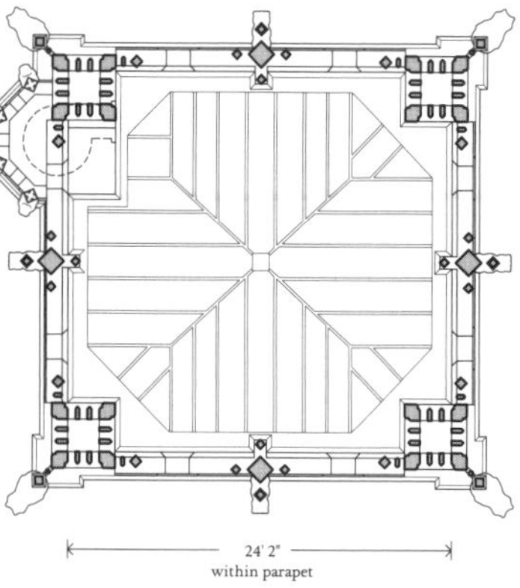

├──— 24' 2" ——┤
within parapet

Plan at D:
bell
chamber

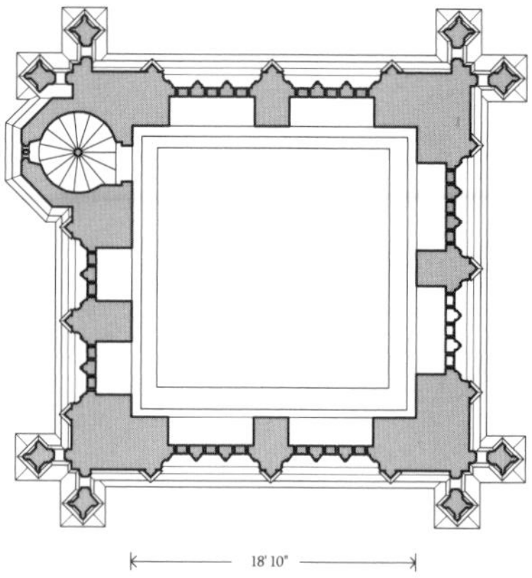

├──— 18' 10" ——┤

Plan at C:
carillon
chamber

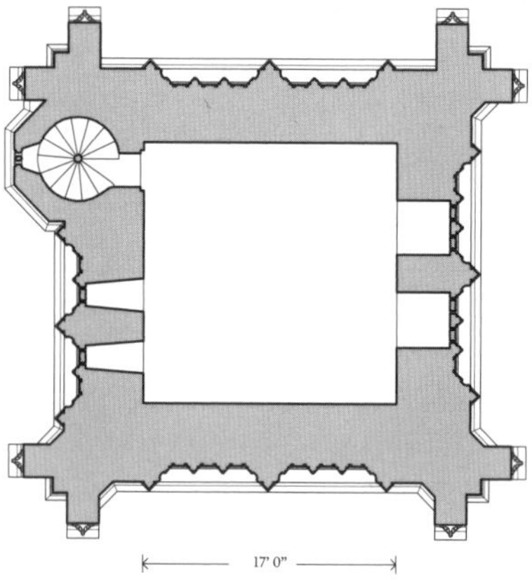

├──— 17' 0" ——┤

Plan at B:
ringing
chamber

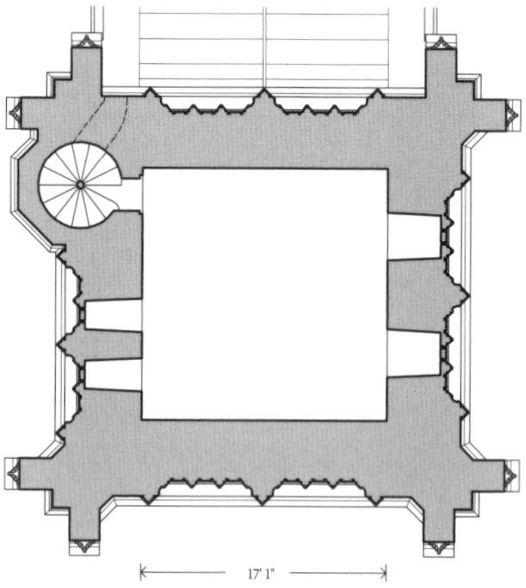

├──— 17' 1" ——┤

├──— 13' 8" ——┤
tower arch

Plan at A:
ground
level

2' 2"
buttress

├ 5' 6" ┤├── 17' 2" internally ──┤├ 5' 6" ┤
wall   wall
├────────── 20' 0" ──────────┤
├──────────— 27' 11" including buttresses ——────────┤

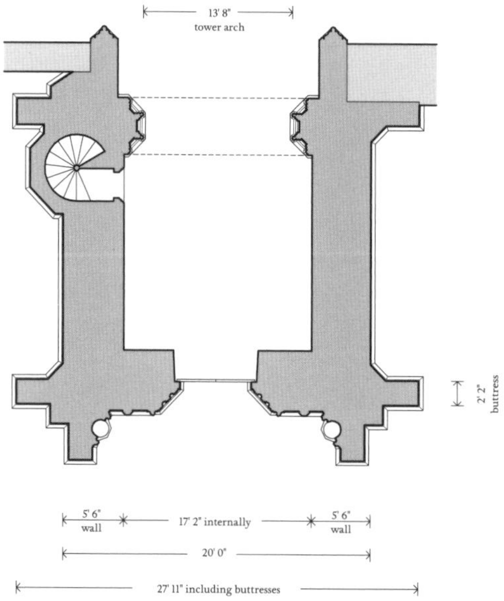

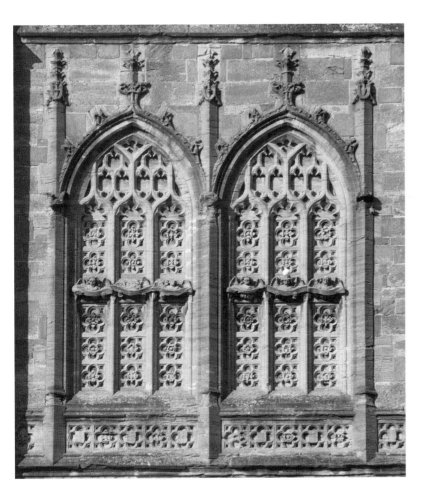

more opulent, with cinquefoiled arches throughout and the addition of a further layer of sub-reticulation. Furthermore, the plain hood-mould of the Early Quantock towers is replaced by an extravagant crocketed ogee hood terminating in a finial. The compressing of pairs of two-bay windows into the narrow space between the north-east stair shaft and the north-west buttress is unique among Quantock towers. All of this elaboration leaves insufficient

room for upper-level niches. One successful embellishment is the trefoiled panelling on the upper tower wall, which may be derived from Temple Church, Bristol (*c.* 1460).

TAUNTON is completed by the finest of all Gloucester crowns, for even the parapet of Gloucester Cathedral, completed to the design of John Hobbs around 1460, cannot match its brittle exuberance. The cathedral provides the theme of four-square corner pinnacles and a parapet etched by the mason's chisel into an unfeasibly delicate filigree screen. Principal Somerset variations are an exaggerated verticality and the addition of centre pinnacles. These take the form of a standard Quantock pinnacle cluster, of four minor shafts surrounding a square core, rotated through forty-five degrees. The silhouette is further embellished by flying shafts on the outermost corners and minor shafts rising from the outer merlons.

There is a prominent contingent of eight hunky punks. Benjamin Ferrey, co-architect of the 1858–62 reconstruction and a pupil of Pugin, commented on this particular Somerset phenomenon:

Monsters both of animal and human shape, are to be seen in most distorted and offensive postures; by some, these oddities are referred to the caprice of the workmen who carved them, but it has also been well observed, that these uncouth devices are meant to represent the vices and depravities of human nature, and placed at the western extremity of the building, to show the distance between holiness and sin.[4]

Unfortunately, elaboration and height are not by themselves guarantors of perfection. TAUNTON may be a splendid spectacle, but it does not merit the same unqualified admiration as LEIGH-ON-MENDIP or KINGSTON ST MARY, both much smaller edifices. Ferrey correctly identified the two principal failings of the design:

It may be questioned whether the tower of St. Mary's is not overcharged with parts tending rather to confusion, and the want of projection in the angular buttresses detracts from the strength of expression which such a large vertical mass should possess.[5]

Both of these defects would be brilliantly resolved eight miles up the Bridgewater Road, at the finest of all Tudor towers, NORTH PETHERTON.

NOTES

1   The highest towers are BOSTON 266' 9" and All Saints, Derby; according to Frank J. Allen's *The Great Church Towers of England* (1932), Derby is 174', Cirencester 162' (Dr Cox), Cromer 159' (W. A. Dutt), and St John the Baptist, Glastonbury 134' 5" (R. P. Brereton). Spired towers at ST MICHAEL, COVENTRY, LOUTH and GRANTHAM are all far higher than TAUNTON.
2   Allen, *Great Church Towers*, pp. 30, 37.
3   Information from Revd F. W. Weaver (ed.), *Somerset Medieval Wills (1388–1500)* and *Somerset Medieval Wills (Second Series: 1501–1530)*, Somerset Record Society (1901, 1903).
4   Benjamin Ferrey, 'Remarks on The Gothic Towers of Somerset', in Revd James Cottle, *Some Account of the Church of St. Mary Magdalene, Taunton, Somerset* (1845), p. 83.
5   Ibid., p. 81.

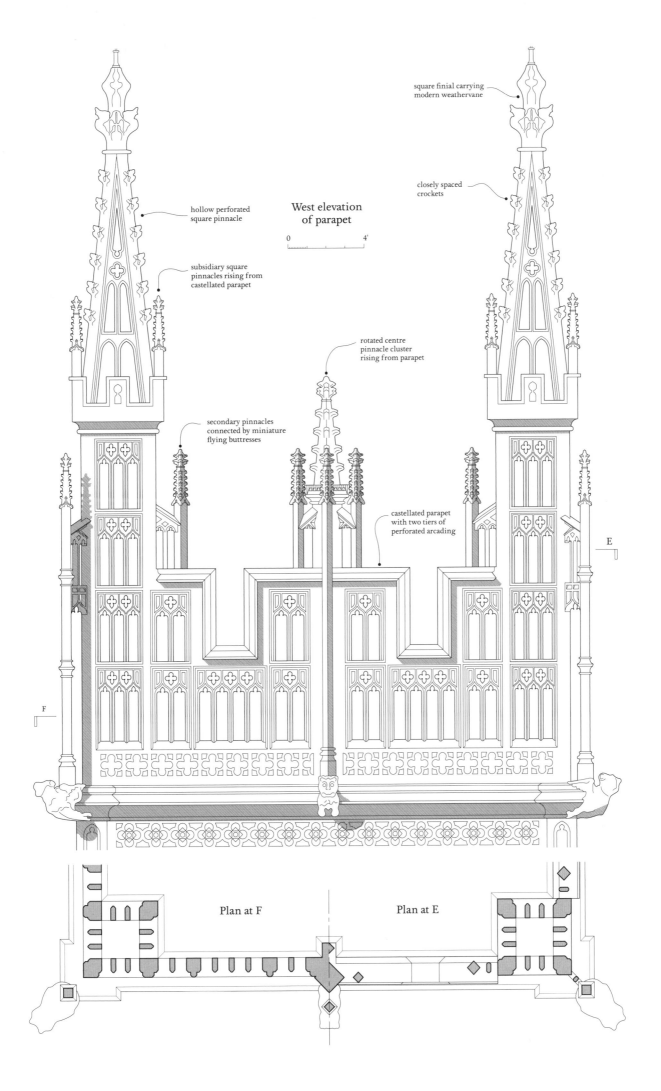

West elevation
of parapet

0   4'

square finial carrying
modern weathervane

closely spaced
crockets

hollow perforated
square pinnacle

subsidiary square
pinnacles rising from
castellated parapet

rotated centre
pinnacle cluster
rising from parapet

secondary pinnacles
connected by miniature
flying buttresses

castellated parapet
with two tiers of
perforated arcading

E

F

Plan at F

Plan at E

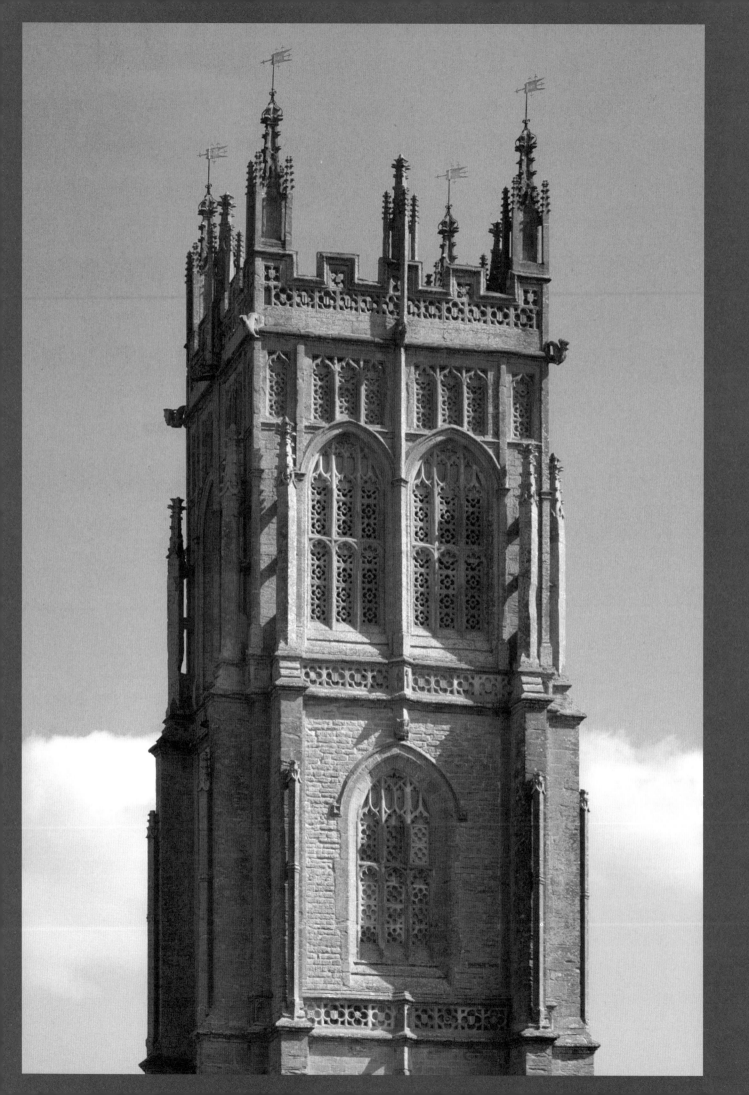

44

North Petherton

SOMERSET

The six towers of the Late Quantock Group divide neatly into three pairs. Kingsbury Episcopi (*c.* 1515) and Huish Episcopi (*c.* 1524) are splendid four-stage towers rising to almost one hundred feet and sharing the same lozenge form of parapet decoration.[1] The superior proportions and details of Huish Episcopi earn it a place within the exalted ranks of the great Somerset towers. NORTH PETHERTON (*c.* 1505–14) and ST MARY MAGDALENE, TAUNTON (1488–1505), both towers of the first rank, are earlier and taller, rising to 111' 5" and 157' 9" respectively. The perforated lozenge parapet of the Episcopi churches may originally have been intended at NORTH PETHERTON, for the quatrefoil design, which imitates the Early Quantock pattern, was only added in 1704. TAUNTON, an exceptional five-stage design, is finished by a magnificent Gloucestershire crown. The third pair of towers, Ruishton (1530–35) and Lyng (*c.* 1535), are smaller and compromised by incompleteness or inferior detailing. There is an obvious association between this group and two excellent towers outside the county – Probus in Cornwall and Chittlehampton in Devon – but it is inconsistent to place these exported designs within the Late Quantock Group itself.[2]

The principal feature that distinguishes Late Quantock from Early Quantock towers is the use of shafts and panels on the tower arch and quatrefoils below the parapet level. Except for at Lyng, where this motif is restricted to the west door spandrels,

quatrefoils are concentrated in strong horizontal bands: two at Ruishton, four at NORTH PETHERTON, Huish Episcopi and Kingsbury Episcopi, and five at TAUNTON. Compared with the pre-Tudor Early Quantock towers, there is a general increase in the density of decoration, but at the same time, except at TAUNTON and Huish Episcopi, there is a move towards a simplified form of setback buttress.

Other features remain entirely consistent with the Early Quantock Group. Apart from at Lyng, the discontinuity between the crown and the body of the tower is masked by a ring of eight hunky punks, one to each corner and one to the centre of each face. The active gargoyle is no longer employed, the rainwater being either collected internally, as at TAUNTON, or discharged through a separate lead spout below the carving, as on the north elevation of NORTH PETHERTON. Four-centred west doors with drop labels appear everywhere except Huish Episcopi, which has a taller, two-centred arch. Similarly, the earlier default design of a four-bay 'Y'-form west window with ogee archlets is retained, the only exceptions being a five-bay split 'Y' at Kingsbury Episcopi and a five-bay reticulated window at TAUNTON.

The distribution of niches varies according to budget and orientation. Prominent north-east stair turrets are universal except at NORTH PETHERTON, where a suppressed south-east tower hides from the primary north elevation and finishes behind the parapet with a flat-roofed box (d). The greatest variety is in the arrangement of openings. Two windows are de rigueur on the upper stage of a Quantock tower. The largest members of the group, TAUNTON and NORTH PETHERTON, are distinguished by three-bay openings, but two bays are the standard. Windows on the middle stage are two-bay at Ruishton and Lyng, three-bay at Huish Episcopi and NORTH PETHERTON, and four-bay at Kingsbury Episcopi. Irrepressible TAUNTON has two three-bay openings, not just once but twice.

NORTH PETHERTON is one-third higher than the classic Early Quantock tower of KINGSTON ST MARY, but the proportions are significantly more vertical. The initial impression that this is a three-stage tower is confounded on the side elevations and above the western portal by the ambiguous presence of a fully developed quatrefoil band seven feet above the basement course.[3] It is entirely logical to classify this division as a separate stage, for similar arrangements can be seen with greater emphasis at Kingsbury Episcopi, with greater height at Huish Episcopi, and with both at TAUNTON, where the transformation into a fully autonomous stage is complete. Considered as a four-stage tower, and including the parapet within the description, the heights of the ascending stages closely follow the numerical ratios of 4:15:15:4.

The arrangement of the interior chambers bears little relation to the external division. There is a splendid stone fan vault beneath the tower, still visible from the nave despite the presence of an intrusive Gothic Revival screen and gallery (a). Perforated Somerset tracery on the middle stage provides the merest glimpse of daylight within the ringing chamber (c).

Deep setback buttresses, projecting five feet from the wall of the tower, are a visual rather than a structural necessity in order to balance the strong horizontality of the quatrefoil bands. They are divided by two set-offs, each carrying tall, rotated square pinnacle shafts before terminating at the bell stage string. Not only are the elongated proportions an improvement on KINGSTON ST MARY, but the shafts are detached from the face of the buttress, allowing a blade of daylight to cut a razor-sharp line down the edge of the silhouette. Detachment is even more pronounced in the eight sentinel pinnacles that stand guard around the spectacular latticework cage of the upper stage. Stability is provided by tiny flying buttresses that are all but invisible from the ground. The parapet of the church conceals a common fault of late Somerset towers, for the eastern buttresses do not fully align with the walls of the nave below and consequently corbel out as they emerge above the lead roof.

The warm limestone of the quatrefoil bands is somewhat deceptive, for originally the shields and flowers at their centres would have blazed with heraldic colour. Individual quatrefoils appear in the spandrels of the four-centred west door. Either side are heavily weathered niches, that to the right

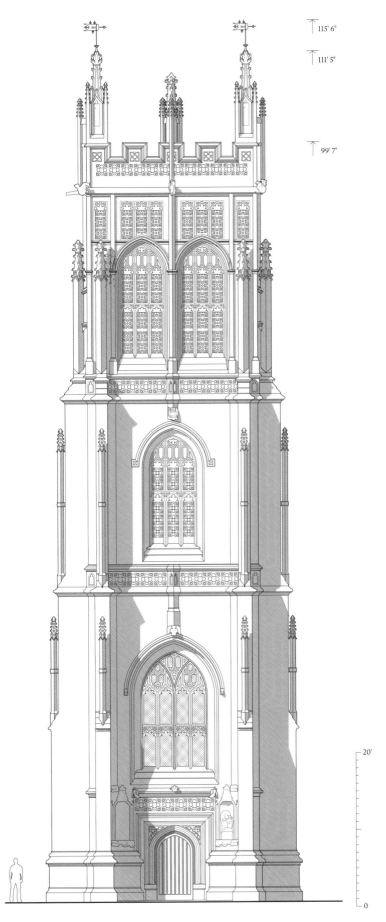

115' 6"

111' 5"

99' 7"

20'

0

West elevation

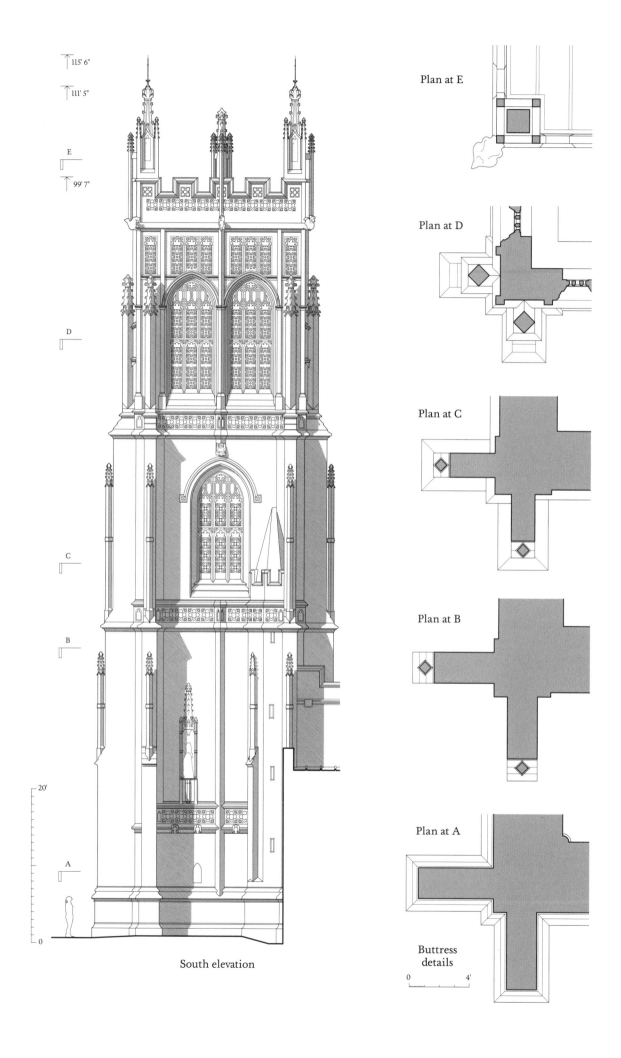

115' 6"

111' 5"

E

99' 7"

D

C

B

20'

A

0

South elevation

Plan at E

Plan at D

Plan at C

Plan at B

Plan at A

Buttress
details

0   4'

containing a decapitated but original sculpture. One note of originality in the otherwise standard west window is the addition of a row of small quatrefoiled circles supported by quatrefoiled arches beneath the transom. This excellent detail appears around 1499 on the north aisle of Langport, and with trefoiled arches on the bell chamber of EVERCREECH (c. 1480–90) and at Batcombe (1539–43). The only disappointment at NORTH PETHERTON is the close proximity to the western boundary of the churchyard, which prevents a full appreciation of the primary west elevation.

From the head of the west window and the basement course on the side faces there arises a unique set of rotated shafts that divide the elevations up their centrelines. These run the full height of the tower, transforming from plain triangular projections at the base into the square outer shaft of the central pinnacle cluster at the parapet. The danger of emphasizing the centreline so emphatically is that a duality might result, splitting the elevations into two. This pitfall is neatly avoided by the presence of a large three-bay window in the centre of the middle stage, effectively the centre of gravity for the entire composition.

Further articulation of the lower tower walls is provided by tall niches occupied by statues, two to the north and one adjacent to the staircase on the south. Unlike at Kingsbury Episcopi, Huish Episcopi and Ruishton, there are no niches on the middle stage, but this is all for the good, for it avoids any competition with the sparkling originality of the upper stage.

On the final stage the predictability of the two three-bay openings is transformed by the articulation of the corners by square pilasters, and of the upper wall surface by semi-perforated panelling. This panelling, which derives from the newly finished tower of ST MARY MAGDALENE, TAUNTON, and indirectly from Temple Church, Bristol, is consistent with the Somerset tracery to the bell chamber except that the perforations are blind. From a distance this is barely noticeable, and the desired effect, of dematerializing the upper tower into a delicate filigree screen, is brilliantly achieved. Surprisingly, only one later tower emulated this highly successful design. Documentary evidence confirms that Probus, 120 miles to the south-west and under construction by 1523, was directly modelled on NORTH PETHERTON.

The crowning parapet is an admirable eighteenth-century invention that differs from the classic Quantock designs of KINGSTON ST MARY, Isle Abbots, Staple Fitzpaine, Huish Episcopi and Kingsbury Episcopi in two significant but beneficial respects. First, where the parapet corner was traditionally chamfered to leave the outermost pinnacle shaft precariously exposed, it is firmly supported by a square shaft on a square corner. Consequently the corner geometry is far better resolved, and there is a greater continuity between tower and parapet. Second, a rotated version of the

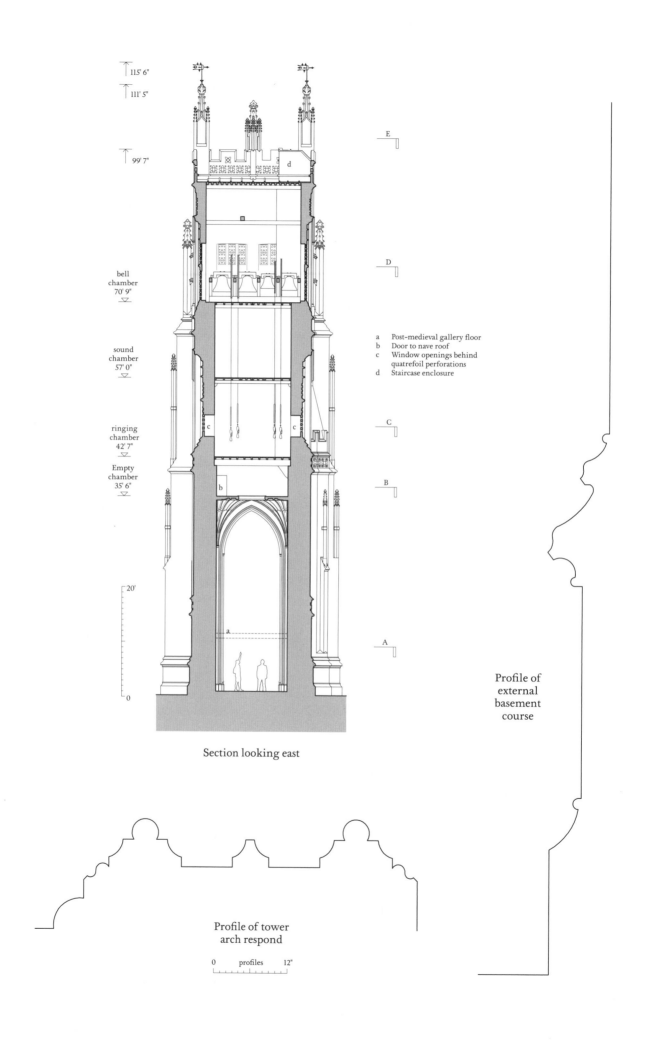

115' 6"

111' 5"

99' 7"

E

bell
chamber
70' 9"

D

a   Post-medieval gallery floor
b   Door to nave roof
c   Window openings behind
    quatrefoil perforations
d   Staircase enclosure

sound
chamber
57' 0"

c   c   C

ringing
chamber
42' 7"

Empty
chamber
35' 6"   b   B

20'

a   A

0

Section looking east

Profile of
external
basement
course

Profile of tower
arch respond

0   profiles   12"

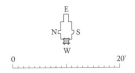

E

N S

W

0   20'

Plan of
fan vault

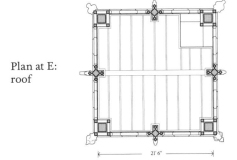

Plan at E:
roof

21' 6"

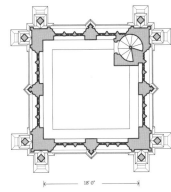

Plan at D:
bell
chamber

18' 0"

Plan at C:
ringing
chamber

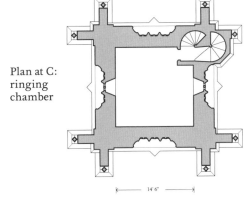

14' 6"

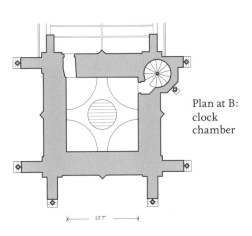

Plan at B:
clock
chamber

13' 7"

Plan at A:
ground
level

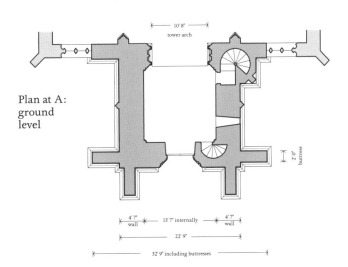

10' 8"
tower arch

2' 0"
buttress

4' 7"
wall

13' 7" internally

4' 7"
wall

22' 9"

32' 9" including buttresses

standard corner pinnacle cluster is repeated in the centre of each elevation.

Alec Clifton-Taylor's four critical aesthetic requirements for a successful tower have never been more harmoniously realized than at NORTH PETHERTON: the horizontal divisions remain subordinate to the vertical lines; the buttresses appear strong and sturdy; decoration is concentrated at the summit of the tower; and the crown leads the eye heavenward.[4] The composition of NORTH PETHERTON is beautifully balanced, the decoration is impeccably orchestrated, and the materials, blue lias with hamstone dressings, are excellent. Along with LEIGH-ON-MENDIP and ST CUTHBERT, WELLS, this is one of the finest towers not just in Somerset, but in the whole of England.

NOTES

1 The heights recorded by R. P. Brereton in Frank J. Allen's *The Great Church Towers of England* (1932) are Kingsbury Episcopi 98' 11" and Huish Episcopi 99' 11".

2 Allen also includes two inferior Somerset towers within his Quantock Group: Chedzoy and the single-windowed Hatch Beauchamp.

3 Both Pevsner and the Statutory Listing describe NORTH PETHERTON as being of three stages.

4 Alec Clifton-Taylor, *Buildings of Delight* (1986), p. 136.

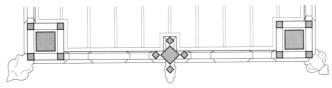

Plan at E

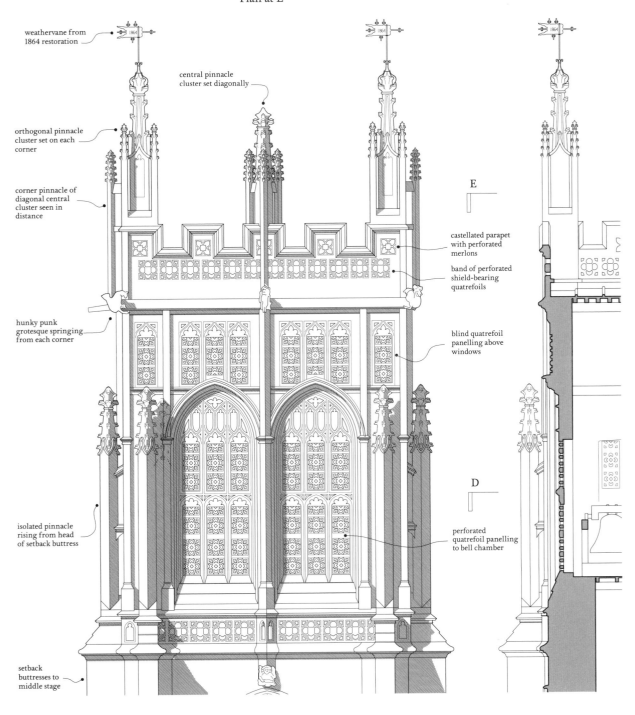

weathervane from
1864 restoration

central pinnacle
cluster set diagonally

orthogonal pinnacle
cluster set on each
corner

corner pinnacle of
diagonal central
cluster seen in
distance

hunky punk
grotesque springing
from each corner

isolated pinnacle
rising from head
of setback buttress

setback
buttresses to
middle stage

E

castellated parapet
with perforated
merlons

band of perforated
shield-bearing
quatrefoils

blind quatrefoil
panelling above
windows

D

perforated
quatrefoil panelling
to bell chamber

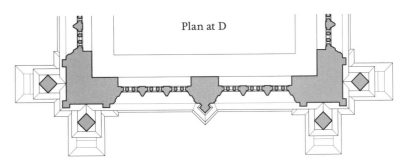

Plan at D

Bell stage,
west elevation
and section

0   6'

45

Lavenham

SUFFOLK

LAVENHAM is a tower of colossal ambition frustrated at the eleventh hour. That this is one of the mightiest of East Anglian towers is widely known, but it is only on drawings that the full extent of its superiority becomes evident. Unfinished, it is lower than tallest Norfolk towers of Cromer (*c.* 160'), North Walsham (as originally completed) or Wymondham, but if the mightiest square pinnacles in England had been added, as was so clearly the intention, the crown would rest with LAVENHAM. It is, however, not for height that LAVENHAM should be remembered, but for bulk. This is construction on a gargantuan scale. The sheer volume of masonry dwarfs the competition. To take an example, DEDHAM, the tallest tower in Essex, contains less than half the quantity of stone, as do EYE and SOUTHWOLD.

This vast extravagance is above all a political gesture, for the tower was raised in celebration of the Tudor victory on the field of Bosworth in 1485. John de Vere, 13th Earl of Oxford, captain-general to Henry Tudor and lord of the manor of Lavenham, resolved, along with the wealthiest cloth merchants of the town, to embark on a wholesale rebuilding of the church to mark the arrival of the new dynasty. As is usual with great cloth churches, the relative status of the benefactors can be judged by the prominence of their heraldic devices. The Spryng family contributed two-thirds of the capital for the tower. Thomas Spryng II gave 300 marks (£200) before he died in

1486, and his merchant marks appear frequently around the base. His son, Thomas Spryng III, left a further £200 to 'the fynysshing of the Stepull' at his death in 1523 and is commemorated by thirty-two coats of arms at the summit of the pinnacles. The de Veres are well represented on the glorious south porch, but also on the tower. in the form of molets (armorial stars) and the motif of a boar, a heraldic pun derived from the Latin word *verres*.

There is general agreement that the master masons were Simon Clerk, then nearing the end of his career, assisted by John Wastell, the leading architects in the region. Wastell's exuberant style is abundantly evident in the nave and aisles, suggesting that Clerk may have taken responsibility for the very dissimilar tower. As a young mason Clerk had worked for John Thirsk, master at Westminster Abbey, and the niche-covered composite buttresses on the west front of the abbey provide the only convincing precedent for LAVENHAM. The effect of the buttresses projecting from the flat façade of Westminster was impressive, but when they were wrapped around the four corners of a 137-foot tower it was thunderous.[1] The composite form here consists of a clasping core, 8' 10" square, from which setback buttresses project up to 8' from the centre of each face. Almost two-thirds of the total width of the tower at its base is taken up by the buttresses – an extraordinary statistic.

Neither Clerk nor Wastell saw the tower rise far above the nave, for they died in 1489

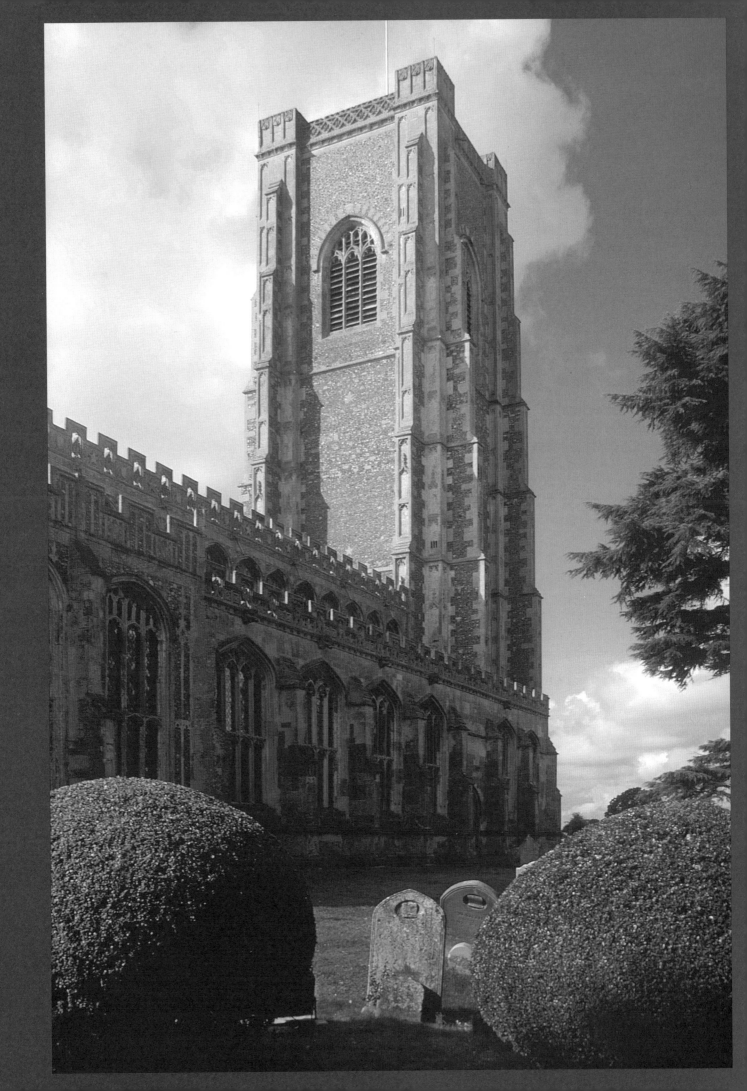

165' 7"

137' 8"

20'

0

West elevation

and 1515 respectively. The work was undertaken in two relatively brief campaigns separated by a lull of twenty years or so. In the first stage and a half, the rectangular cinquefoiled panels on the buttresses are subdivided by crocketed ogee-headed arches stretching up to finials, whereas in the upper stage and a half, the panels remain undecorated. It is reasonable to assume that this marks the break between the first phase of work, completed by 1495, and the second stage, which commenced around 1518. The change is not unduly distracting, for in late medieval work it is not uncommon for details to become simplified as they move further away from the eye.

Conceptually, the tower is of three unequal stages consistently divided by horizontal strings. The lowest stage is further subdivided by a string stopping short of the west window, and the second-stage buttresses are similarly treated. Articulation is principally through the buttress set-offs, which are of regular width but diminishing height, finishing several feet below the parapet string. The square clasping core diminishes subtly at every stage to provide a barely discernible taper. Between one set-off and the next, all the buttresses' faces are divided into two unequal panels. Panelling continues on a reduced scale and with trefoils on the shallow clasping returns. All of this is in the finest Casterton stone, brought by river and sea from Rutland. The huge flint side faces of the projecting fins are enlivened by the random dimensions of the quoins.

Repeated stage after stage, face after face, with only minor syncopation, the buttress design treads an uneasy balance between powerful rhetoric and pompous tedium. The fault lies not with the buttresses but with their lack of purpose, for where the eye should be drawn heavenward by the soaring verticality of a pinnacle it is stopped short by a crude square silhouette. The panelling was intended as the enrichment of a purposeful composition, but with this purpose unfulfilled it takes on undue prominence. The pinnacles of BOSTON, twenty-eight feet high, give some impression of what is missing from the tower at LAVENHAM.

Once the initial shock of the buttresses has been absorbed there is much to enjoy at LAVENHAM. The interiors are palatial, from the cinquefoiled blind arcade running above a continuous stone bench on the ground floor (b) to the recessed helical handrail in the north-east staircase. Most flint towers are disappointing within, for the thick walls press in on the central void, making the proportions uncomfortably vertical. It is here that the great breadth of LAVENHAM is most beneficial. In proportion and in detail the tower arch is among the best in East Anglia (c). The responds have a playful ambiguity in which the smooth brackets and ogees surrounding the central shaft are revealed to be shafts only by the presence of octagonal capitals and bases. The three orders of the arch are complex arrangements of hollow chamfers and fillets.

Internally, the opulence continues between the deep square reveals of the west door, which support a flat-arched vault carved with a grid of diagonal pointed quatrefoils finished with square flowers. The Victorians kindly removed the tower gallery (the blocked doorway is still visible) but unkindly filled the west window with sentimental glass. Internally, the upper stages are entirely of brick, save for a few stone quoins to the window reveals. The cavernous bell chamber, housing a legendary peal of eight, is supported by an impressive braced floor structure (d), but the original roof construction has been lost to an intrusive concrete slab (e).

Externally, the greatest interest lies close to the ground. The west door is easily missed by visitors, for it faces a narrow country lane and was never more than a ceremonial entrance. It is beautifully illustrated in Raphael and J. Arthur Brandon's *An Analysis of Gothic Architecture*, whose description is by no means uncritical:

> A magnificent, though very late specimen. Even in this instance, the two-centred arch is still retained, with the addition of an ogeed dripstone beautifully crocketed ... The mouldings are of very poor character: in the desire for richness of experience ... they produce an effect at once confused and unsatisfactory ... Still the design is so rich and attractive, and the base mouldings and the buttresses to the tower are all in such excellent keeping, that we are

induced to overlook the imperfections of the details, in our admiration of the composition as a whole. The door itself has been a rich and beautiful design, but is now so much decayed, that the mouldings and smaller portions of the tracery are no longer discernible.[2]

The details that were not to the Brandons' taste include a large outer shaft on a tall pedestal supporting a thin, shallow pilaster, and two bowtells (one of an unsatisfactory pear-shaped profile) supporting intensively lined roll mouldings. Between the bowtells runs an array of square animal heads and fleurons. There is no flushwork here, for the basement course is entirely of freestone carved with a variety of armorial motifs. The permutations of shields, cusping, sub-cusping, heraldic symbols, stars, diamonds and snowflakes reward careful study. Workmanship and materials are second to none, and the measured survey revealed an exceptional consistency in the setting out.

The windows are not insignificant in size, but they are made to appear so by the ocean of knapped black flint in which they float. The west window is of four lights, transomed, with sub-arches diverging from the centre and cinquefoiled archlets. Twin-light ringing chamber windows, to north, south and west, incorporate doubled sub-arches and alternating daggers in the head. Large, five-pointed de Vere stars appear above and below. Double sub-arches

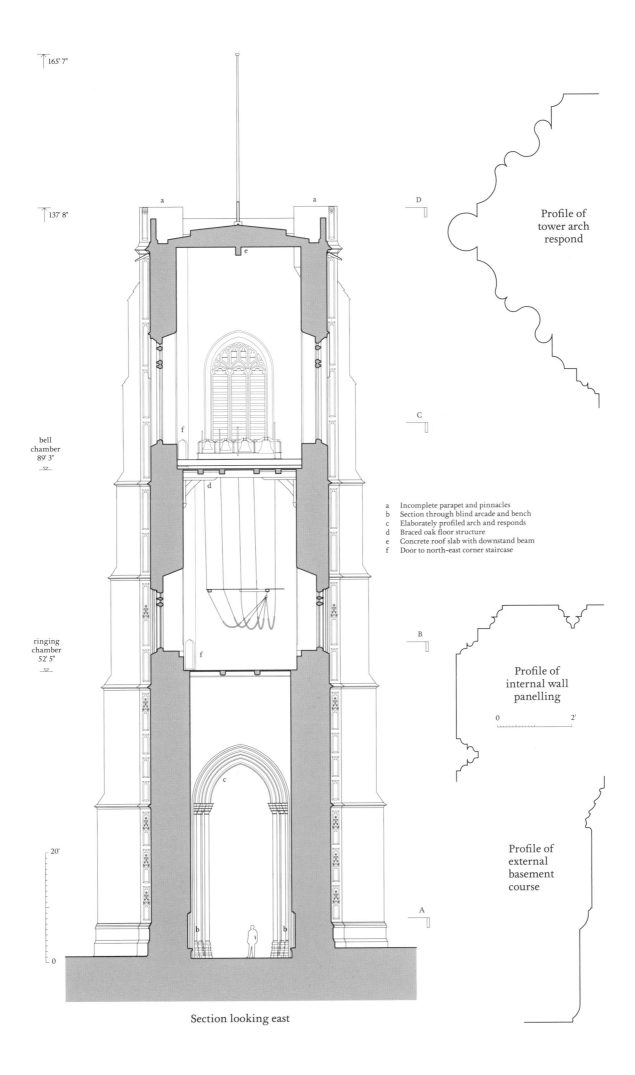

165' 7"

137' 8"

a   a   D   Profile of
                                                                      tower arch
                                                                      respond

                                                                 C

bell
chamber
89' 3"
                                                                 f

a   Incomplete parapet and pinnacles
b   Section through blind arcade and bench
c   Elaborately profiled arch and responds
d   Braced oak floor structure
e   Concrete roof slab with downstand beam
f   Door to north-east corner staircase

d

                                                                 B   Profile of
                                                                            internal wall
                                                                            panelling

ringing
chamber
52' 5"
                                                                      0   2'

                                                                            Profile of
                                                                            external
                                                                            basement
20'   course

                                                                 A

c

b   b

0

Section looking east

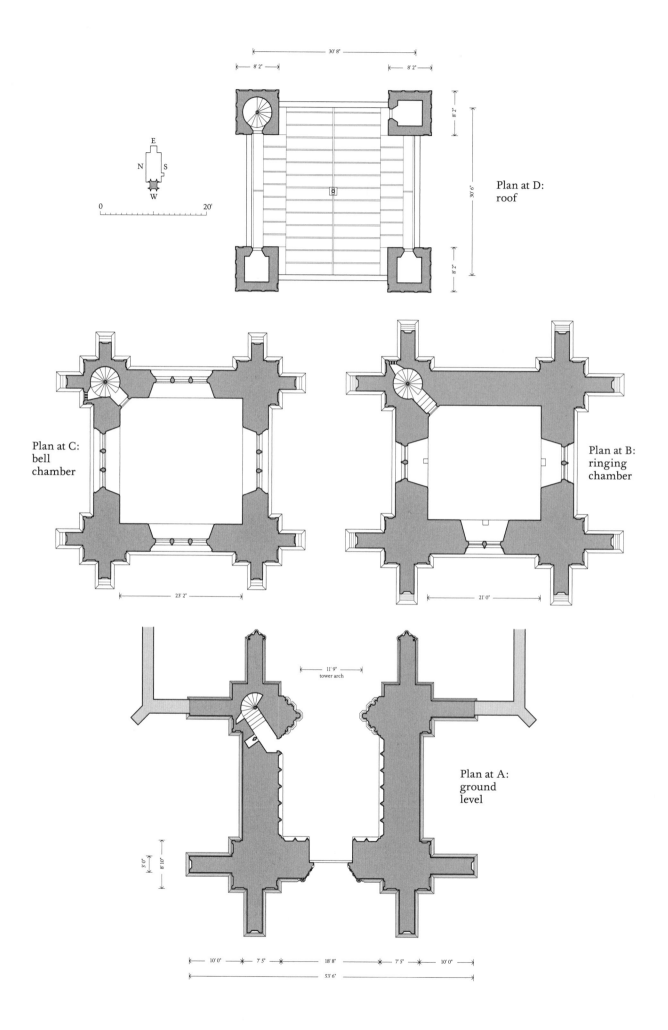

30' 8"

8' 2"

8' 2"

8' 2"

30' 6"

8' 2"

Plan at D:
roof

E

N   S

W

0   20'

Plan at C:
bell
chamber

23' 2"

Plan at B:
ringing
chamber

21' 0"

11' 9"
tower arch

Plan at A:
ground
level

3' 0"

8' 10"

10' 0"   7' 5"   18' 8"   7' 5"   10' 0"

53' 6"

reappear in the otherwise unremarkable supermullioned three-light bell openings.

Raised square corners add interest to the silhouette of the incomplete parapet. The three panels that divide each face of these clasping squares are a continuation of what has gone before, leaving no clues as to how the climax of the design was intended to develop. The shields of Thomas Spryng III terminate every bay, including those on the end returns, but there is no hint of a coping stone. The four hollow corners, each with an arched door opening from the roof, await turret stairs that were never commenced. The straight run remaining between the corners was intended to form a sub-parapet above which there should have been one further tier of decoration before the obligatory battlement. The quatrefoil panelling is heavily moulded and rises from a continuous hollow cornice line decorated with fleurons.

LAVENHAM is awe-inspiring rather than beautiful. Had Thomas Spryng's pockets been just a little deeper, or the prosperity of the cloth trade lasted one decade longer, then LAVENHAM would undoubtedly have been raised to a steeple of the highest rank. How it was to be finished is open to conjecture, but it can be stated with confidence that there was never any intention to add a spire, for there are no squinches in the bell chamber.

Two other questions remain unanswered. First, why does the tower pay so little regard to the scale and character of the body of the church, built at the same time and by the same masons? Second, why was flint still employed when funds were so plentiful? There is no doubt that the parishioners of LAVENHAM could have raised a steeple on the scale of SOUTHWOLD or EYE faced entirely in smooth ashlar had they so desired. The answer must be that flint and stone used together remained the materials of choice in Suffolk throughout the late Middle Ages. We should be thankful for this: despite every reservation, this is still a tremendous building.

NOTES

1 Although the absence of pinnacles makes this a particularly straightforward steeple to measure with a tape, the commonly quoted height of 141' is incorrect.

2 Raphael and J. Arthur Brandon, *An Analysis of Gothic Architecture* (1847), vol. 1, pp. 72–73; vol. II, 'Perpendicular', Plates 6 and 7. Plate 12 also shows details of the south aisle parapet and buttresses.

46

Dedham

ESSEX

Octagonal clasping buttress became a regular feature of towers across the south of England and East Anglia after 1440. LUDLOW, Magdalene College, Oxford, EYE and REDENHALL all employ the octagonal corner, but in every instance the form emerges smoothly from the face of the adjacent walls so that only five faces of the octagon are expressed. An alternative and less common form is where seven faces of the octagon are visible and a crisp perpendicular junction is formed with the tower wall. This subtle difference has significant consequences, for the buttress becomes one continuous, thrusting vertical shaft, distinguished by a hard edge and a crisp shadow. The composition of the tower is transformed from one of stages stacked one above another, to one of four vertical corners framing four vertically proportioned elevations. Consequently the insistent vertical lines of flushwork decoration seen at EYE or REDENHALL are no longer required to counterbalance the horizontality of a stacked composition.

This form of buttress is effective but surprisingly rare. The earliest examples are in Dorset, at Bradford Abbas (around 1436) and at Cerne Abbas. Mere and Marlborough (Wilts) are later, as is Newbury (Berks), built around 1500–32. In East Anglia the form was tried at the colossal unfinished west tower at Wymondham (Norfolk), built in 1445–78, and then at DEDHAM. DEDHAM is the most convincing and refined expression of the form. It is also the finest tower in Essex.

DEDHAM is a picture-postcard village hidden far away from London in the extreme north-east corner of the county. In architectural circles it is well known as a bastion of twentieth-century classicism, for the office of Quinlan Terry, and before him Raymond Erith, is within sight of the church. Evidence of the practice's long-standing relationship with St Mary's Church is visible in the classical furnishings and the excellent state of the fabric. The county boundary and the northern edge of the settlement are marked by the River Stour, along which the creamy-grey Caen limestone was delivered from Normandy for the building of the church. St Mary's is from the final generation of great cloth and wool churches, and was rebuilt in its entirety in less than thirty years. Donations to the tower are recorded in 1494, 1504 and 1505. In 1510 £20 was donated to the tower, and in 1519 Stephen Denton left the substantial sum of £100 for the completion of the battlements.[1]

The church runs parallel with, and to the south of, the main street, with the tower pressing up against the vicarage wall to the west. This awkward boundary condition explains the memorable north–south passage that burrows through the base of the tower, acting as a porch for the concealed west door and allowing processions to circumnavigate the church. The same plan appears at the contemporary tower of East Bergholt (Suffolk), where construction never reached above the first stage. One unfortunate consequence of this peculiarity is that the fine west elevation is hard to appreciate without entering the vicarage garden. The four-stage tower stands quite clear of the west end of the aisles, allowing all four buttresses to rise directly from the ground.

DEDHAM is a Tudor tower through and through: self-confident, balanced and powerful. The external materials of squared, knapped flint and freestone dressings are deceptive, for internally all the indications are that this is a brick tower finished with an expensive outer veneer. The flint is as sharp and as black as at SOUTHWOLD, but decorative flushwork is restricted to the basement course, the parapet and the alternating voussoirs above the arches. Flushwork is used on the deep, moulded plinth in square panels of crowned 'M' monograms alternating with shields set within sub-cusped quatrefoils within circles. 'Maria' monograms are a common motif in churches dedicated to the Virgin Mary – above the west window of St Mary, Bungay, for example. The clarity of these complex designs is sadly obscured by the natural buff colour of the pointing. The superb collection of monograms at Garboldisham (Norfolk) benefits considerably from the application of black-tinted mortar between and around the flint to complete the missing portions of the design.

Understated passageway arches to north and south emphasize the massive solidity of the tower walls (a). Two-centred arches, of two moulded orders, are set beneath rectangular hood-moulds. The inner order is supported by octagonal capitals over engaged circular shafts. Spandrels are filled by cinquefoiled circles with mouchettes running to the corners.

Beyond these arches is an unexpected treasure: a stone wagon vault of thirteen doubled bays of cinquefoiled, ogee-headed panelling (b). The spandrels remaining between the crocketed heads and the ridge are filled with tiny quatrefoiled circles carrying square flowers, replaced on four occasions by human heads and symbols. The nine central panels are filled with conventional vine-leaf brattishing in the base, and portcullises and large five-petal Tudor roses above. Twenty-four tiny shields display a variety of devices to acknowledge the generosity of the principal donors, including the merchants' marks 'I.W.' (for John Webb), 'T.W.' (for Thomas Webb), and 'I.H.' and 'J.H.' for members of the local Hawke family. The west door follows the passageway arch design except for the omission of the shafts (c).

Internally, the west door is framed by a straight internal reveal, repeating the panelled ceiling motif but on a much reduced scale. The effect is somewhat diminished by the proximity of the square south-east stair shaft leading to the ringing chamber gallery. The noble aspirations of the gallery were frustrated even before it was completed, for the corbels and springers of an incomplete fan vault rise redundantly in the four corners of the ringing chamber (d). On the east wall are the remains of a segmental arch of such a flat profile that it makes no structural sense (e). Why such an

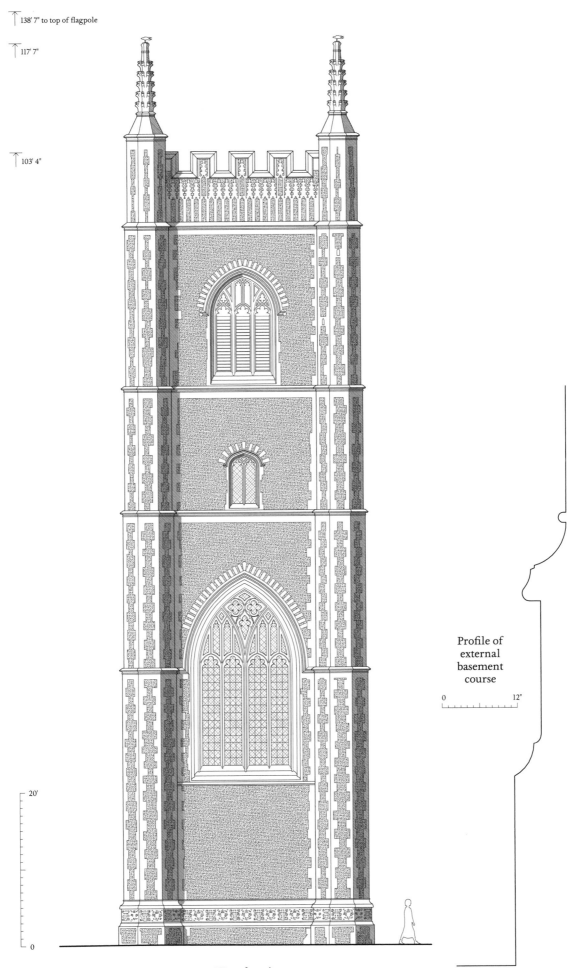

138' 7" to top of flagpole

117' 7"

103' 4"

20'

0

Profile of
external
basement
course

0   12"

West elevation

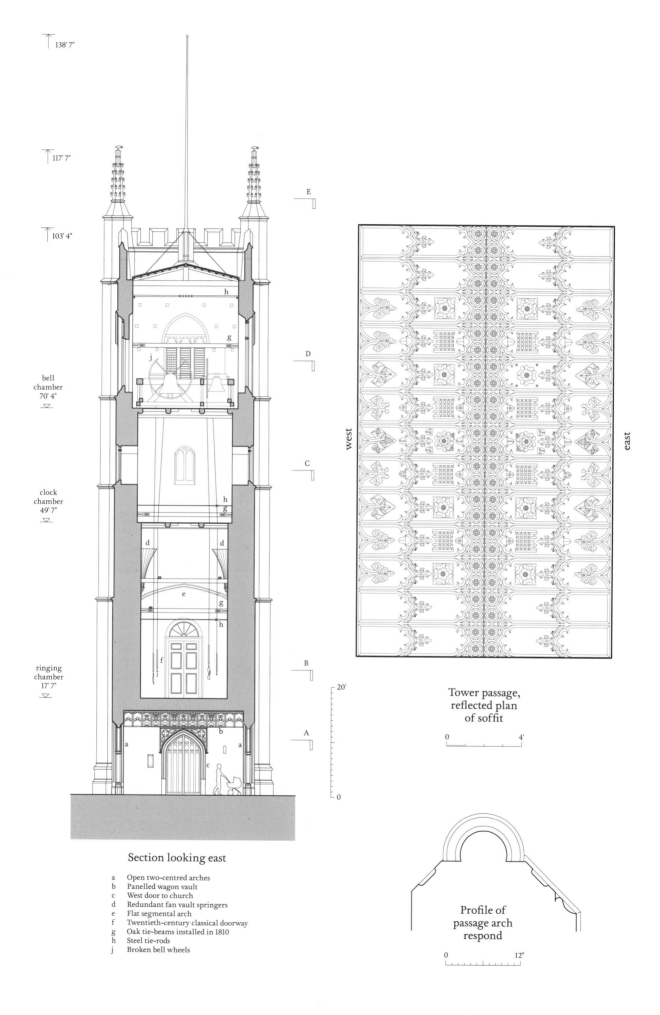

138' 7"

117' 7"

103' 4"

E

D

bell
chamber
70' 4"

C

clock
chamber
49' 7"

B

ringing
chamber
17' 7"

20'

A

0

h

g

j

h
g

d   d

e
g

h

f

a   b   a

c

Section looking east

a   Open two-centred arches
b   Panelled wagon vault
c   West door to church
d   Redundant fan vault springers
e   Flat segmental arch
f   Twentieth-century classical doorway
g   Oak tie-beams installed in 1810
h   Steel tie-rods
j   Broken bell wheels

west   east

Tower passage,
reflected plan
of soffit

0   4'

Profile of
passage arch
respond

0   12"

unstable form was ever contemplated is unclear, but the consequences are very evident. The northern end of the arch, and much of the brickwork above, has sheared and dropped, and the whole structure has been propped by a brick infill wall four feet thick. A twentieth-century classical door and fanlight now fills the original round-headed opening through this masonry (f). On the cross section this amusing incongruity is all the more evident thanks to the proximity of the medieval west door directly below. The tower and its arch are entirely hidden from within the body of the church by a classical organ case of unrelieved boxiness.

Between the ringing chamber and the bell chamber the stair moves into the south-west octagonal buttress. The construction of the stair is unusual, for treads are supported in groups of four by brickwork built off stone lintels spanning from stone newel to brick shaft wall. The plan reveals just how little walling remains around the stair. The masons may have miscalculated here, for there are numerous cracks running through the shaft.

Structural movement has been a long-standing problem at DEDHAM. In 1810 oak tie-beams were strapped between elliptical iron plates that can be seen at three levels on the north and south elevations (g). Even before the great Colchester earthquake of 1884, the tower was so badly cracked that it was deemed unsafe for the ringing of bells. The architect J. T. Mickelthwaite was clear where the blame lay when he reported to the church on the state of the tower in 1891:

'The tower is now seriously shattered above the level of the gallery floor on all its four sides. Most, if indeed not all, of this has been caused by the ringing of the bells. And I am sorry to have to advise you not to allow the bells to be rung again.' He went on to propose the construction of a separate free-standing belfry in the churchyard.

His words were ignored, for in 1907 the respected architect T. G. Jackson was writing to the church in the same vein:

I am of the opinion that the construction of the tower is too slight to allow of the bells being rung, & I should advise their only being chimed, & that the wheels be removed to make ringing impossible.[2]

In truth, the bells are likely only to have exacerbated existing lines of weakness. The foundations appear to be sound, for cracks are not evident below the level of the gallery, and the walls are more substantial than in many sound structures of equal antiquity. The root of the problem undoubtedly lies in poor construction, and quite possibly in inadequate bonding between the inner brickwork and the outer flint and freestone facing. The original strengthening ties have now been doubled by tensioned steel rods (h), the clock room windows have been reinforced with steel and engineering brick, and the bell wheels have been broken in accordance with Jackson's advice (j).

All of this internal complexity is belied by the noble simplicity of the exterior. The soaring buttresses reduce in regular stages from 7' 2" in width at the base to 5' 2" at the roof. Randomly sized ashlar quoins provide texture and scale. Horizontal continuity is provided by the strings, each of which sits on a single levelling course of ashlar. The first string becomes the hood of the underappreciated four-light west window. This is a fine supermullioned design, with a triangle of soufflets held between twin sub-arches. The obsession with flatness seen at EYE has passed, and the single casement on the jambs swings confidently away from the plane of the wall.

Straightforward twin-light flat-arched windows repeat on every face of the clock chamber. The untransomed three-light bell chamber openings are careful not to compromise the solidity of the final stage. Cinquefoiled archlets carry inverted daggers in the head either side of a pair of minor lights.

The battlements are tall and straight, with regimented arcades of trefoiled and crocketed flushwork panels running between the buttresses. There is no visible evidence of the gargoyles recorded in the 1922 survey for the Royal Commission on Historic Monuments, for workmanlike lead waterspouts drain the flat lead roof.[3] The tall, feminine crocketed pinnacles are well judged, for they provide a delicate contrast to the prevailing masculinity of the composition.

The architectural historian John Harvey has identified the great master mason John Wastell from Bury St Edmunds as the designer of DEDHAM tower.[4] To support this theory he sites stylistic evidence connecting the west window and the north–south passage with its panelled vault to Great St Mary's, Cambridge, started by Wastell in 1491. Further corroboration, of which Harvey appears to have been unaware, is provided by the springing of the unfinished fan vault hidden within the tower (d). The details here are consistent with Wastell's personal style seen in the vaults of King's College Chapel, Cambridge, and at the retrochoir of Peterborough Cathedral. This confirmation of authorship, by one of the finest masons of the age, should come as no surprise, for DEDHAM provides a triumphant conclusion to the story of the East Anglian flint tower.

NOTES

1   Dates taken from Sir Nikolaus Pevsner, *The Buildings of England: Essex*, 2nd edn (1965).
2   Taken from copies of the original documents kindly provided by Revd Gerard Moate.
3   A document entitled 'A Survey of Dedham Parish Church, 1922', which included numerous sketches of details, was discovered in the Muniment Room Library above the north porch in 2001 and published by the church in 2006.
4   See John Harvey, *English Mediaeval Architects: A Biographical Dictionary Down to 1550*, 2nd edn (1984), p. 319.

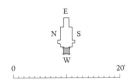

E

N S

W

0   20'

Plan at E:
roof

Plan at D:
bell
chamber

22' 1"

Plan at C:
clock
chamber

Plan at B:
ringing
chamber

17' 9"

16' 2"

external passage

Plan at A:
ground
level

12' 2"

7' 2"
Buttress

2' 2"
wall

2' 2"
wall

22' 6"

3' 0"

3' 0"

26' 10"

32' 9"

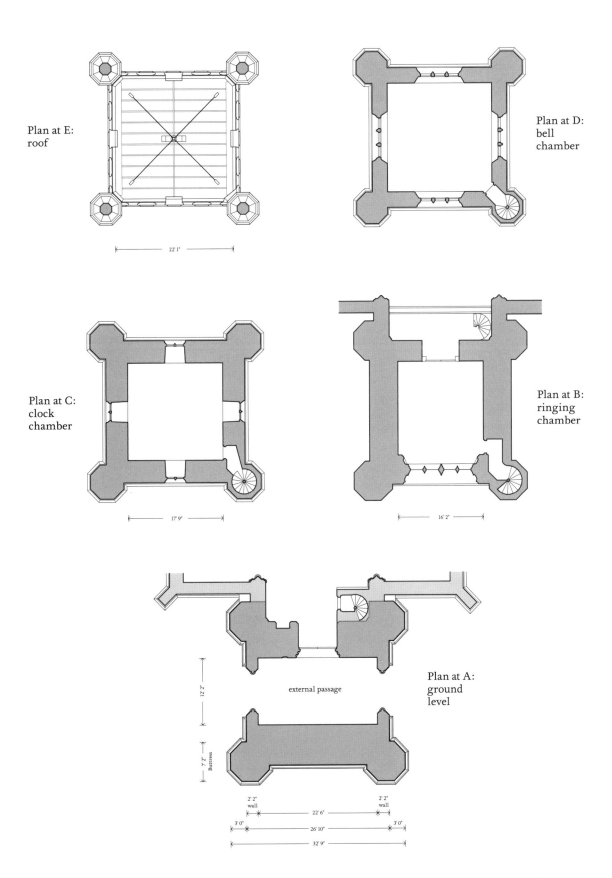

47

Ingatestone

The craft of brickmaking, lost since Roman times, was revived in Essex during the thirteenth century, but for several generations the material was relegated to inconspicuous locations as an economical substitute for stone. In the 1420s brick reveals and structural arches were employed as a matter of routine within the tower at SALLE. At STOKE-BY-NAYLAND twenty years later the material appeared externally, loosely bonded in cliff-like strata that were intended to be hidden beneath a skin of render or limewash. In the following decades the humble material underwent a renaissance in East Anglia and the south of England.

The Tudor age saw a meteoric rise in the popularity of brick from utilitarian obscurity to palatial splendour at the Layer Marney towers (c. 1520), the Great Gate of St John's College, Cambridge (1516), and Hampton Court Palace (1514–21). Essex has an unrivalled collection of thirty brick church towers and fifteen brick porches. The best of the towers, Fryerning and INGATESTONE, are obsessive in their use of brick for, unlike their secular counterparts, they are undiluted by stone or terracotta dressings. In the absence of documentary evidence, it is reasonable to assume that INGATESTONE was built around the year 1500.[1]

Visiting critics have been unanimously impressed by INGATESTONE. Pevsner considered it to be magnificent, and Frank Allen and Simon Jenkins were no less enthusiastic. It is, therefore, surprising to discover that the summit of the turrets is just eighty-two feet from the ground. In stone or flint such a height would be considered unremarkable or even humble, and yet the modern eye is so accustomed to the sight of mean and insubstantial brickwork that INGATESTONE cannot fail to impress. Rather than being a sign of ostentatious wealth, as is sometimes claimed, this modest brick pile is in fact an example of inspired economy. Such qualifications are necessary to place this work in context, but they should not distract from the appreciation of a powerful design distinguished by the distillation of late Gothic forms into the language of brick.

A break in the buildings lining the village high street allows a view to the north-west corner of the tower, an unusual orientation that gives equal prominence to the north and west elevations. This was clearly in the mind of the medieval architect who enriched these two public faces with diaperwork and hid the stair turret in the opposing south-east corner. The diagonal placement creates a powerful first impression, for it exaggerates the width of the tower and the sturdiness of the proportions.

The composition is notable for its solidity and its crisp precision, for the rigours of the brick module govern every line. Deep setback buttresses of four diminishing stages dominate the design. Half-brick modules determine both the set-back distance from corner to buttress and the step in at every cant brick string course. One consequence of this is that the wall thickness reduces from five and a half bricks at the base, to three and

101' 6"

89' 4"

82' 9"

20'

0

South elevation   West elevation

a half bricks at the bell stage and two bricks at the parapet. The relative slenderness of the construction suggests that the English bond brickwork is solid throughout, with no rubble core. On this assumption at least 320,000 bricks would have been required for the construction.

A corbel table of trefoil arches, formed of pairs of profiled bricks laid flat, supports a plain parapet cut into a sharp geometrical silhouette. The stepped battlements are a common feature in this region, hinting at trading associations with Flanders and Holland. Octagonal corner turrets, rigorously organized according to the module of the brick, run smoothly up from chamfered corners. Wisely, no attempt was made to replicate the steep crocketed profile of a stone pinnacle, and the stubby pyramidal caps form an appropriately robust termination. The use of baked clay continues behind the parapet, where tiles make a welcome change from the ubiquitous flat lead roof (a).

The windows are an entertaining exercise in reinventing Perpendicular forms within the discipline of a small, inflexible module. The profile around the western portal is reduced to four recessed orders of brickwork: three of plain chamfers and the outer one an ogee. A rectangular hood frames the depressed four-centred arch. The three-light west window is a remarkably audacious attempt at brick tracery. Chamfered single-brick mullions rise to the window arch in a stack fifty-eight courses high, restrained only by a single tier of two-centred supermullioned archlets. As before, the reveal is of four receding orders of brick, this time a cant nearest the glass, a bulging radiused corner, a cant and a radiused hollow. Complex double-canted bricks incorporating a radiused drip are reserved for the hood.

Ringing chamber windows are of two tall lights to the west, and one smaller light to north and south. The arches, flat and four-centred on the principal face, are composed entirely of cheap, square-edged bricks, specials being restricted to the sloping cills (b). Two-light bell openings follow the same principle, but with a broader centre mullion of three orders. The slit-windowed, semi-octagonal stair turret rising up the east corner of the south elevation (c) limits the adjacent bell opening to just a single light.

Diaperwork is one of the greatest delights of Tudor brickwork. Specially fired headers, turned an almost metallic blue, form patterns of diamond grids and crosses across the lower stages of the tower and down the buttresses on both of the main elevations. Unlike with brash and mechanical Victorian structural polychromy, the difference in hue and tone between the contrasting materials is subtle, so that the eye has to search out the patterns. Charming irregularities provide an endearing record of human indecision and frailty.

Internally, the tower is most impressive on the upper levels, where the raw energy of unplastered brick is experienced to the full. Finest of all is the staircase. Pairs of semicircular bricks, laid in alternate directions, form a sturdy newel from which brick arches spring to the shaft wall, each arch supporting a pair of brick treads. The unusual anticlockwise direction of the stair is due to the proximity of the tower arch at its foot. Tower arch responds are something of an anticlimax, for they consist of little more than two square bricks either side of a wide chamfered shaft, the shaft divided into two by a diagonal rebate at the springing of the arch (d). Overhead an ancient floor structure frames the square bell hatch (e), but there is little mystery in the brightly lit, whitewashed hall.

The tower's severest test came in the great Essex earthquake of 1884, following which cracks opened up, particularly above the west door. In 1908 a major programme of repair and restoration included a thorough overhaul of the roof and the rebuilding of the battlements, the buttress slopes and the window mullions, including those of the west window. Oak louvres were installed to the bell openings, the most dangerous crack was rebuilt with reinforcement, and the tower was 'bound together with two stout steel girders and eight iron rods' concealed within the brickwork.[2] After a century of mellowing there is little evidence of these substantial interventions.

INGATESTONE may be the pick of medieval brick church towers, but its near neighbour Freyerning, which enjoys rural solitude, comes a worthy second. The scale and the detailing are less ambitious, but the parapet is a tour de force of brick corbelling. Brick church towers did not stop with the Reformation, and Castle Hedingham, the largest of the Essex towers, was completed only in 1616. In the straightened circumstances that followed the Break with Rome, these pragmatic and relatively modest structures maintained a currency long after the soaring stone steeple had fallen out of favour.

NOTES

1 Estimates of the tower's date have ranged from later fifteenth century (Buckler) to mid-sixteenth century (Miller Christy). See E. E. Wilde, *Ingatestone and the Essex Great Road with Fryerning* (1913). Medieval brick church towers in Essex with authenticated dates are limited to Gestingthorpe (*c.* 1498) and Theydon Garnon (1520).
2 Wilde, *Ingatestone and the Essex Great Road*, p. 82.

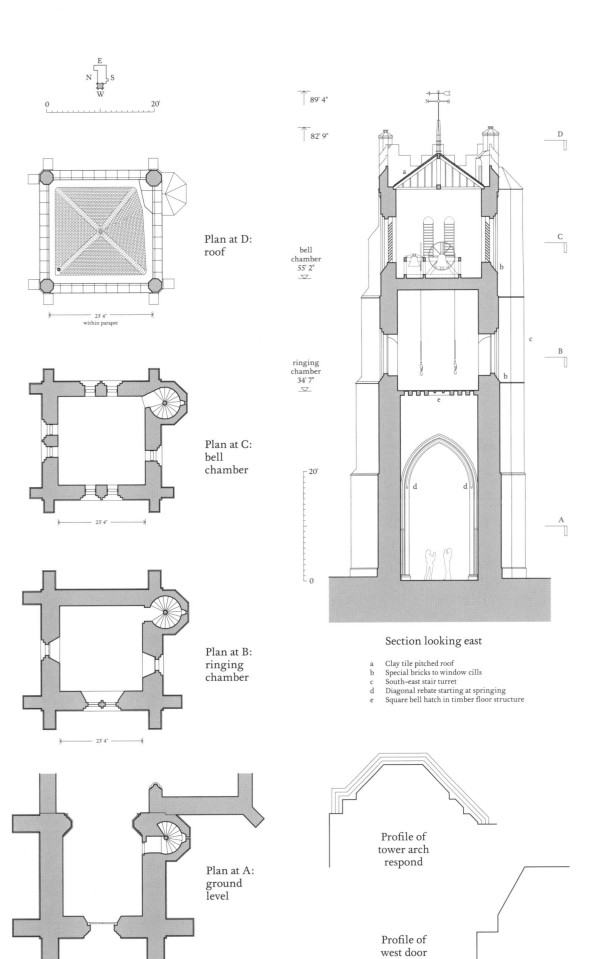

E
N · S
W

0 _____ 20'

Plan at D:
roof

23' 4"
within parapet

Plan at C:
bell
chamber

23' 4"

Plan at B:
ringing
chamber

23' 4"

Plan at A:
ground
level

4' 4"   14' 8"   4' 4"
23' 4"

89' 4"

82' 9"

bell
chamber
55' 2"

ringing
chamber
34' 7"

20'

0

Section looking east

a   Clay tile pitched roof
b   Special bricks to window cills
c   South-east stair turret
d   Diagonal rebate starting at springing
e   Square bell hatch in timber floor structure

Profile of
tower arch
respond

Profile of
west door
reveal

0 _____ 2'

48

St Nicholas, Newcastle-upon-Tyne

NORTHUMBERLAND

In the late Middle Ages openwork stone spires became the height of fashion across continental Europe. From Burgos to Vienna, lacy perforated structures soared heavenward with such dizzying ambition that the spires of Cologne and Ulm, both over 500 feet high, outstretched the resources of the age, to be completed only in the nineteenth century. Such flamboyant excess was too much for the pragmatic English masons who understood and valued the virtue of restraint. Their spires remained universally solid-walled, with one startling exception in the remote north-east of England. The summit of Newcastle Cathedral's[1] west tower is variously described as a steeple crown or a Scottish crown, but the term 'flying spire' best encapsulates the radical dynamism of the form.

There is no precedent for such an extraordinary design in England, but the claim by every guidebook that NEWCASTLE possesses the earliest flying spire in Britain hardly seems credible. In Scotland, at least four steeple crowns were built in the closing years of the fifteenth century. St Giles's Cathedral, Edinburgh (c. 1495, rebuilt in 1648), King's College, Aberdeen (c. 1500), and the lost steeples of Linlithgow (possibly 1484 or 1490) and Haddington (destroyed by the English in 1548) are far less refined designs than NEWCASTLE. At Edinburgh, for example, the flying buttresses are massive in profile and radiate in eight directions rather than four. When English masons adopted this new and alien form in their strategic northern outpost it was, no doubt, intended

as a provocative gesture to demonstrate their technological superiority. These great metaphorical crowns were intended, in part at least, as powerful pieces of political propaganda in an age of rising tension between two old rivals. This symbolic importance is demonstrated both by the fact that it was the corporation of Newcastle, rather than the church wardens, who took responsibility for the maintenance of the crown and by the following story:

In the time of the civil wars, when the Scots had besieged the town for several weeks, and were still as far as at first from taking it, the general sent a messenger to the mayor of the town, and demanded the keys, and the delivering up of the town, or he would immediately demolish the steeple of St. Nicholas. The mayor and aldermen, upon hearing this, immediately ordered a certain number of the chiefest of the Scottish prisoners to be carried up to the top of the old tower, the place below the lanthorn, and there confined. After this they returned the general an answer to this purpose,—that they would upon no terms deliver up the town, but would to the last moment defend it: that the steeple of St. Nicholas was indeed a beautiful and magnificent piece of architecture, and one of the great ornaments of their town; but yet should be blown into atoms before ransomed at such a rate: that, however, if it was to fall, it should not fall alone; that the same moment he destroyed the beautiful structure, he should bathe his hands in the blood of his countrymen, who were placed there on purpose either to preserve it from ruin, or to die along with it. This message had the desired effect. The men were there kept prisoners during the whole time of the siege, and not so much as one gun fired against it.[2]

The Northumbrian merchant Robert Rhodes was a great enthusiast for towers. His crest, a greyhound current above three annulets, appeared with the motto 'Orate pro anima Roberti Rhodes' on tower vaults at three of the four medieval churches of Newcastle: ST NICHOLAS, St John, and All Saints (later destroyed), and also at St Edmund, Sedgefield (Durham). At ST NICHOLAS his shield appears four times around the circular bell hatch and on six faces of the octagonal font beneath. Little is known of the man. He enriched the chantry of St John the Baptist and St John the Evangelist at ST NICHOLAS in 1428. In 1446 he presented a gold cross to Durham Cathedral; in 1486 he is named as one of the bishop's justices; and both he and his wife, Agnes, had died before 1500.[3] ST NICHOLAS's steeple is by far the grandest of the projects he sponsored.

Even in the late Middle Ages Newcastle was at the outer extremity of English civilization and, with the noticeable exception of Durham Cathedral, churches to the north of York rarely rise above the utilitarian. Across the whole of Northumberland and County Durham there is just a handful of unremarkable spires, a fact that makes the extraordinary structural gymnastics at NEWCASTLE seem all the more inexplicable. This is an urban parish church on the scale of GRANTHAM and NEWARK, but longer and lower. The body of the church had been rebuilt in the century preceding the commencement of the great west tower. Some authorities have assumed that an indulgence granted by the Bishop of Durham in 1435, to all those contributing to the fabric of the church, relates directly to the construction of the tower, but this fits uneasily with the dates of the principal donor, Robert Rhodes, and with the style of the work.

The three stages that form the lower part of the tower are reinforced by clasping octagonal buttress, the diagonal faces of which merge with the tower walls. Octagonal buttresses appear in Devon and Suffolk around 1440 and spread slowly across southern England, reaching LUDLOW in 1453, Oxford in 1480 and Gloucestershire ten years later. The style is entirely alien to the northern half of the country, the tower of St Mary, Hull being a seventeenth-century reconstruction of uncertain authenticity. It is unlikely that the form could have reached far-flung Northumberland much before 1460, and it may have been considerably later. This also raises the suspicion that the towers of ST NICHOLAS and St John, where the steeple appears around the same date, may

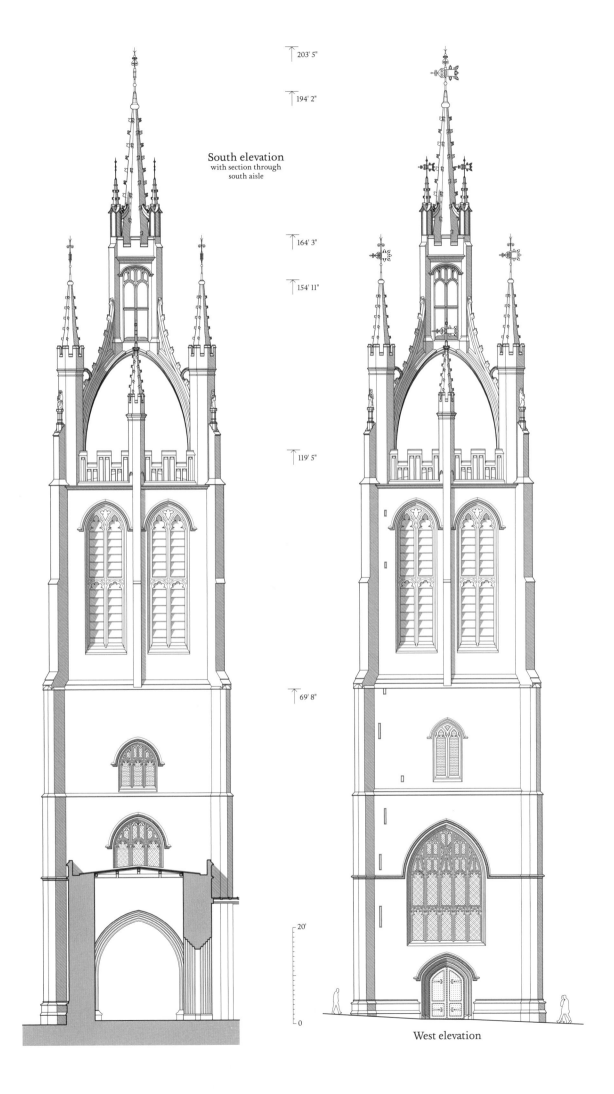

South elevation
with section through
south aisle

203' 5"

194' 2"

164' 3"

154' 11"

119' 5"

69' 8"

20'

0

West elevation

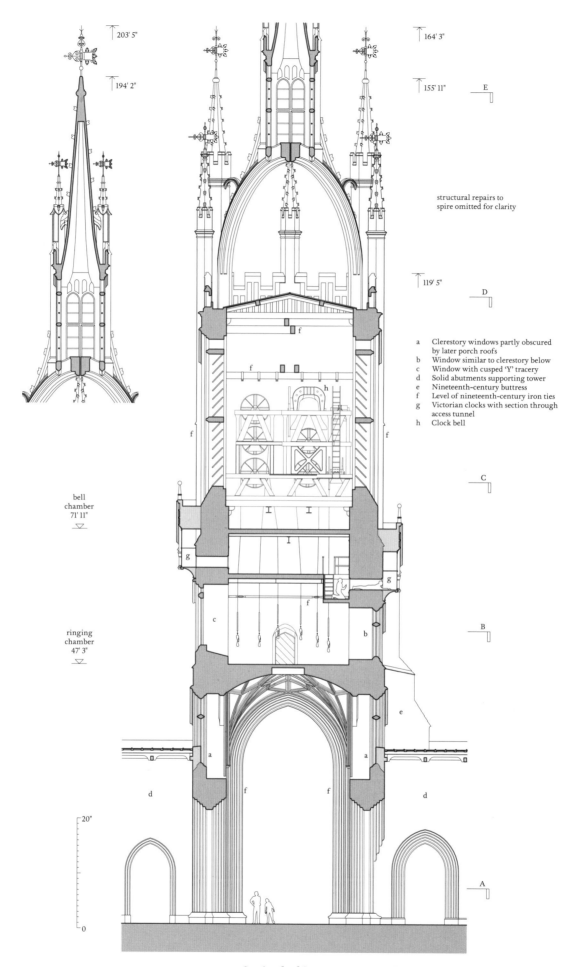

203' 5"

194' 2"

164' 3"

155' 11"   E

structural repairs to
spire omitted for clarity

119' 5"   D

a   Clerestory windows partly obscured
    by later porch roofs
b   Window similar to clerestory below
c   Window with cusped 'Y' tracery
d   Solid abutments supporting tower
e   Nineteenth-century buttress
f   Level of nineteenth-century iron ties
g   Victorian clocks with section through
    access tunnel
h   Clock bell

C

bell
chamber
71' 11"

B

ringing
chamber
47' 3"

20"

A

0

Section looking east

be the work of a visiting southern mason. Octagonal buttresses are most successful on knapped flint towers, where rich flushwork decoration can be displayed to brilliant effect. On smooth ashlar towers they are less successful, for they lack assertiveness, flatten the elevations and broaden the proportions. This is particularly evident in the ponderous lower stages at NEWCASTLE.

The west door and the west window do nothing to improve the lack of modelling, for they are set close to the outer face of the wall. The plain basement course and four-centred west door are unremarkable, while the five-light west window is a direct quotation from the nave of Holy Trinity, Hull (1418), but with the unfortunate addition of a mid-height transom. A similar pattern of tracery reappears to north and south in the three-light clerestory windows, now partly hidden by the porch roofs (a), and in the south ringing chamber window (b). The north and west windows to the ringing chamber (c) are something of a puzzle, for they are narrow and vertical, with cusped 'Y' tracery, though there is no evidence of the masonry having been altered.

Within the tower, the immense thickness of the walls is most impressively displayed by arches of compelling simplicity. The profile, of three chamfered orders each cut by a semicircular hollow, is unrelieved by hood-moulds, capitals or bases. Even more impressive is the high lierne vault, a rare luxury in a parish church. The angular four-petal flower pattern traced out by the liernes is more imaginative and larger than the vault at Louth, but it is let down by inadequate illumination.

Octagonal buttresses reinforce the corners of the tower within the church, but the original clarity has been diluted by subsequent alterations. Massive strengthening works from the nineteenth century are ingeniously concealed at ground level within the fabric of the north and south porches, added in 1832 and 1834 respectively. Where aisles once ran straight through to the west end of the church, solid masses, cut by heavy arches, now abut the base of the tower (d). Externally, the repairs are impossible to miss, for two massive inclined buttresses prevent the south elevation from sliding down the hill towards the Tyne (e).

This proved only partially successful in stabilizing the tower, which was subsequently underpinned on the north side by Sir George Gilbert Scott. No fewer than five tiers of iron ties now prevent the tower from falling apart (f). The drawn elevations omit these unfortunate modern distractions, and the equally unfortunate clocks to north and south, which take the form of great gabled houses, bracketed, crocketed and decorated in High Victorian railway-terminus Gothic (g). Man-sized iron tubes bored straight through the tower walls provide an ingenious route to maintain the clock mechanisms.

Between the third and the fourth stages there is an awkward discontinuity in form.

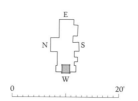

0   20'

Plan at E:
spire
lantern

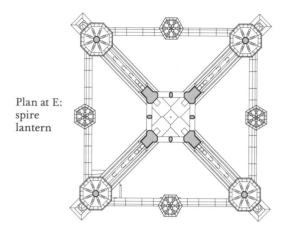

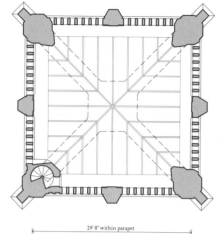

Plan at D:
roof

structural repairs
omitted for clarity

29' 8" within parapet

Plan at C:
bell
chamber

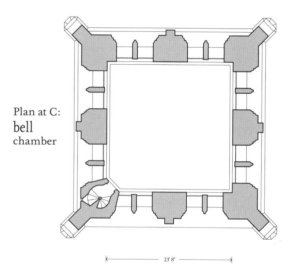

23' 8"

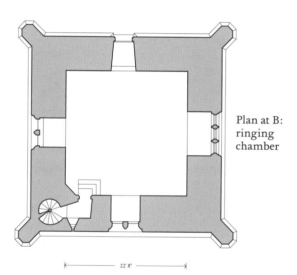

Plan at B:
ringing
chamber

22' 8"

Reflected
plan of
tower vault

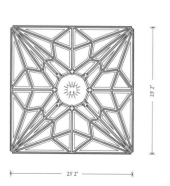

23' 2"

23' 2"

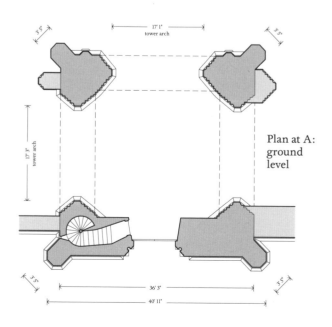

Plan at A:
ground
level

3' 5"

17' 1"
tower arch

3' 5"

17' 3"
tower arch

3' 5"

36' 3"

3' 5"

40' 11"

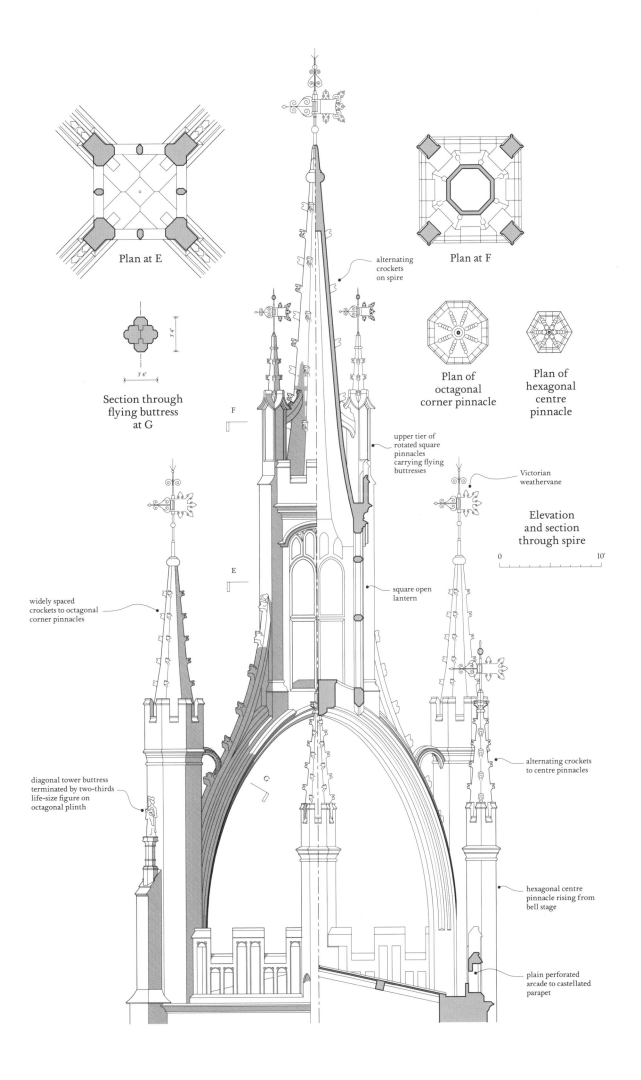

Plan at E

Plan at F

Section through
flying buttress
at G

3' 4"

3' 4"

Plan of
octagonal
corner pinnacle

Plan of
hexagonal
centre
pinnacle

alternating
crockets
on spire

upper tier of
rotated square
pinnacles
carrying flying
buttresses

Victorian
weathervane

Elevation
and section
through spire

0   10'

F

E

square open
lantern

widely spaced
crockets to octagonal
corner pinnacles

alternating crockets
to centre pinnacles

G

diagonal tower buttress
terminated by two-thirds
life-size figure on
octagonal plinth

hexagonal centre
pinnacle rising from
bell stage

plain perforated
arcade to castellated
parapet

This marks the arrival of the anonymous genius responsible for the great crown, for the plan is rudely pushed into a shape determined not by what had gone before, but by what was intended to follow. Diagonal buttresses replace the previous octagonal form, walls step back decisively, central pilasters divide the elevations, and the entire composition gains vertical momentum. The elegant proportions of the pair of transomed twin-light bell openings compensate for the workmanlike details. The cavernous bell chamber, protected by solid stone louvres, comfortably houses a peal of twelve and a colossal clock bell weighing almost six tons (h). Despite the tightening of the plan, the walls are still so thick that the north-west staircase is concealed with ease.

The battlement follows the perforated arcade pattern of Durham Cathedral and many other great towers of the age. Human figures raised on plinths complete the diagonal buttresses of the previous stage midway up the octagonal corner turrets. The distinguishing feature of these castellated and pinnacled turrets is their great attenuation, arising not from the demands of the composition but to counter the huge outward thrusts of the crown. In a novel experiment the edges of the pinnacles are decorated with crockets only on their alternate edges. The hexagonal centre pinnacles stretch up in sympathy with their larger octagonal neighbours.

The crown is one of the masterpieces of late Gothic construction. Great flying buttresses fling the spire high into the sky in a gesture of astonishing audaciousness. In spire design the flying buttress had become little more than a lightweight aesthetic device for leading the eye from one form to another. Suddenly at NEWCASTLE a design appears that is entirely driven by structural logic. Two great obtuse arches are thrown between the four corners of the tower. The chamfered arches, formed of four ingeniously interlocking sections, are remarkable not only for their span of over thirty-five feet, but for the small size of the stones. The uppermost order of the arch, enriched by bold angular crockets, breaks apart and swings upwards in a giant ogee curve that leads the eye smoothly up the thrusting corners of the lantern.

This slender square lantern appears extraordinarily light, for it consists of little more than four corners surrounding fresh air. At such a distance the simplicity of the tracery – a single mullion and transom, uncusped archlets and a flat four-centred arch – is of little consequence. Short battlements tie the rotated square corner buttresses together at the top of the lantern. In a final flurry of enthusiasm, a razor-sharp spirelet reaches to just short of 200 feet. Angular crockets dance up and down the edges of the spirelet, and tiny flying buttresses run to four bristling square pinnacles. Thirteen magnificent Victorian gilded weathervanes provide a triumphant conclusion to an unforgettable composition.

If all of this delirious extravagance appears to be too good to be true, that is because it is. The medieval masons had overreached themselves, and with unreliable foundations it was only a matter of time before the crown would fall. The first recorded rebuilding was as early as 1608 and may have included the addition of two huge diagonal timbers, set just above the apex of the lead roof, that still tie the corners together. The Victorian restorations under Scott, and then under the local architects Oliver & Leeson, left nothing to chance and added metalwork on an industrial scale.

In scale and ambition, the flying spire of NEWCASTLE ranks alongside the two other great swansongs of the medieval steeple-builder: the spire of LOUTH and the octagon of BOSTON. Each in its own way suggests directions that might have been followed in the increasingly prosperous merchant cities had the Reformation not so roughly intervened. Apart from the modest crown of St Mary-le-Bow, built in 1512 but lost in the Great Fire of London, this northern masterpiece led nowhere.[4] NEWCASTLE's flying spire appears now as a concluding statement in the central chapter of English architecture. Had history taken a different turn it could equally well have marked the start of a new adventure in English steeple-building.

NOTES

1   ST NICHOLAS was raised to cathedral status only in 1882.
2   Eneas Mackenzie, 'St Nicholas' church: History and architecture', *A Descriptive and Historical Account of the Town and County of Newcastle-upon-Tyne: Including the Borough of Gateshead* (1827).
3   Dates from Mackenzie, 'St Nicholas' church'. Pevsner in *The Buildings of England: Northumberland* (1957) states that Rhodes died in 1474.
4   In post-medieval times the form reappeared at Tollbooth Steeple, Glasgow (1626–34) and Wren's St Dunstan-in-the-East, London (1698). The form regained popularity during the nineteenth-century Gothic Revival.

The 'Boston Stump', as it is affectionately known, is one of the greatest triumphs of medieval engineering. It is quite as daring at the hammer-beam roof of Westminster Hall, the octagonal lantern of Ely Cathedral or the pendant fan vault of the Henry VII Chapel at Westminster Abbey, and yet is on a greater scale than any of these masterpieces. For sheer spectacle, the 266 feet of masonry soaring straight from the pavement to the sky is unsurpassed by any church or cathedral in England.

St Botolph's is the ultimate wool church. Its tower rises sentinel-like above the River Witham as it meanders through the centre of the town before discharging into the Wash. It was to the Witham that Boston owed its enormous wealth, for along it flowed all the trade from Lincoln and the rich wool and cloth industry of the region. During the thirteenth century Boston was second only to London among English ports, even briefly surpassing the capital during the 1280s. Boston's prosperity was not to last, for during the late fifteenth century, as the great steeple was rising heavenward, the river at its feet was silting up and the wool trade was dwindling. It was reported that by 1570 the town was entirely 'destitute of ships'. There are striking parallels with the great industrial port of Liverpool in the twentieth century, where the crossing tower of the magnificent Anglican Cathedral was rising high above the Mersey as its docks were sinking into terminal decline.

BOSTON's beginnings were humble. The first church was erected in the seventh century by the Anglo-Saxon missionary Botolph, who had been permitted by King Ethelmund to found a monastery in 'some retired and desolate spot'. The remains of a modest Norman church, uncovered during nineteenth-century restorations, show a nave just sixty feet long and a tower nine feet square within the walls. From the Conquest to the Reformation, the church was a possession of St Mary's Abbey, York, the wealthiest abbey in the north of England.

In 1309 work commenced on a wholesale rebuilding of what was eventually to become the most voluminous parish church in England.[1] The day after Palm Sunday, excavation commenced on the foundations of the tower. By Midsummer,

> at a depth five feet below the bed of the haven they found a bed of stone upon sand above the clay subsoil ... on the Monday after the Feast of St John the Baptist the first stone was laid by Dame Margaret Tilney, assisted by Richard Stephenson, a merchant of Boston, and the Rector of Boston, John Truesdale, each of whom placed £5 upon the stone thus laid towards the erection of the proposed tower.[2]

These fine intentions came to nothing, for attention immediately switched to the body of the church. This is a magnificent structure: a nave of seven bays, with aisles to north and south, a chancel of three bays, and

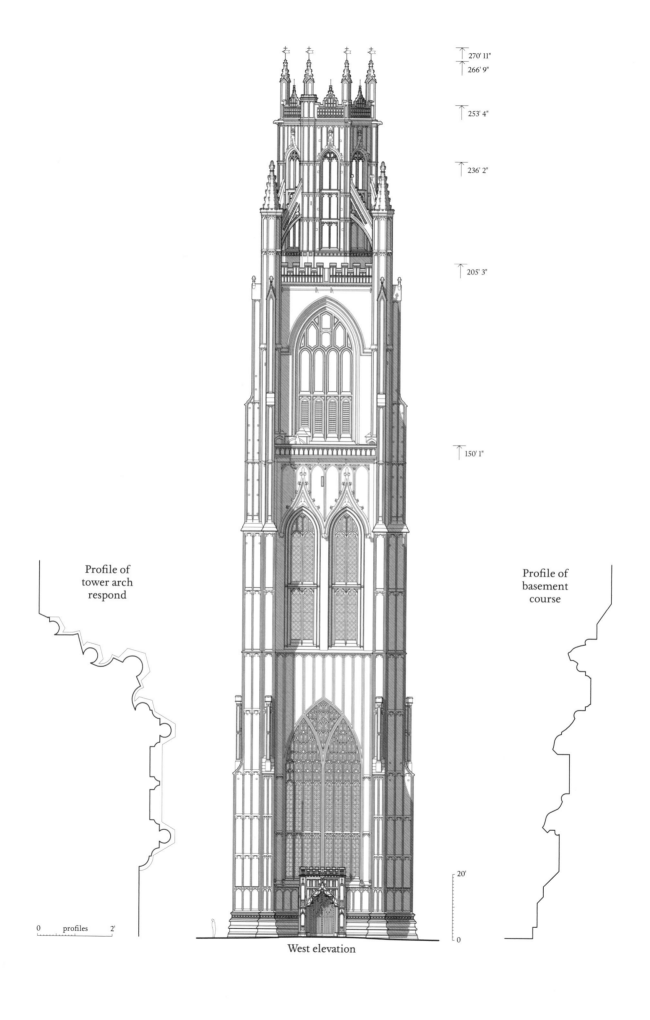

Profile of
tower arch
respond

Profile of
basement
course

270' 11"
266' 9"
253' 4"
236' 2"
205' 3"
150' 1"
20'
0

0   profiles   2'

West elevation

a south porch. During the 1420s the chancel was extended by two further bays; and later a second storey was added to the porch and six chapels were formed, mostly within the body of the church. There is no documentary evidence to confirm the dates of the tower, but it may have been commenced around 1430 and taken the best part of a century to complete, with the four stages representing four consecutive generations of masons.

From the outset the tower was conceived on a magnificent scale, with an internal space 31' 9" square, large enough to accommodate most conventional church towers within its walls. What is even more remarkable is the slenderness of these walls, which at just 3' 1" thick are easily the thinnest post-Saxon walls surveyed. Commentators have observed a general flatness of the elevations, particularly to the first stage, without appreciating the astonishing structural virtuosity of which this is an outcome. At BOSTON, at last, the full potential of the buttress in tower design was realized, so that the wall between the four corners was slimmed down to little more than a thin shell stretched between giant relieving arches.

Another common misconception is that BOSTON was intended to receive a spire, even a spire starting from the top of the second stage.[3] There is no evidence to support this theory, for there are no squinches within the tower other than those that were designed to support the octagon at the top of the third stage. By the middle of the fifteenth century the unspired tower was becoming the norm across the country, even in the supreme spire-building county of Lincolnshire.

There are few obvious precedents for this great work within Lincolnshire. The great steeple of LOUTH was started later than BOSTON, and in many respects can be seen as a smooth refinement of its heavily panelled design. The most direct source of Lincolnshire influence is in the large windows on three elevations of the first stage inspired by the Fenland steeples of MOULTON and Holbeach. The most obvious sources of inspiration are, however, to be found further afield.

In the Low Counties from the mid-fifteenth century, large octagonal crowns were being erected on both ecclesiastical towers and civic buildings including Brussels Town Hall (1449–54) and Bruges Cloth Hall (1482–86). A more direct precedent for the vast ambition of the project is to be found in the magnificent west front of Beverley Minster (Yorks East). In around 1430 Beverley was drawing to a stunning conclusion, with the slenderest of twin towers, a vast panelled west window and huge panelled buttresses leaping straight from the ground. BOSTON takes all of these elements and condenses them into a single tower of even greater ambition.

The main external features are huge angle buttresses transforming into octagonal pinnacles, three tower stages each reducing in height, a beautifully enriched octagon, and a feast of panelling. The divisions of the buttresses are largely independent of the elevations they frame, a sophisticated device used to increase the verticality of the composition. They rise from a sumptuous quatrefoiled basement course and are set out to suit the standard module of the blind panelling. There is a significant simplification with height. To the side faces of the buttresses, one tier of cinquefoiled panels is followed by seven tiers with trefoils then three tiers with plain uncusped arches. Similarly, the grid of shafts that divide each panel from the next start circular, become octagonal on the second stage and are omitted altogether on the third. In part, this reduction is the result of changing fashion during the extended construction process, but it is also an effective form of economy that is surprisingly hard to distinguish from ground level.

The slender projecting faces of the buttresses start with four accelerating tiers of paired cinquefoiled panels beneath a sweeping set-off supporting an almost free-standing shaft, castellated around its square head. Above this eccentric feature are three standard tiers of cinquefoiled panels before the buttresses slim to spear-like proportions and slice through the air with razor-sharp gables. The octagonal pinnacles that gradually emerge provide reassuring solidity and a return to convention with trefoiled panels, mini-castellations and the hard, angular crockets typical of late medieval steeples. The solidity is an illusion, for each octagonal shaft is hollow and carries a spiral stair to the upper parapet.

Returning to ground, the first stage of the elevations is entirely subsumed by panelling. In the same way that flatness rules the flushwork-panelled towers of East Anglia, modelling is reduced to a minimum here. The mullions and transoms of the huge windows are strictly regimented to follow the module of the wall panelling, and even the divergent 'Y' tracery in the window heads is set out to respect the grid. Considered in isolation, the eight-light west window and the four-light north and south windows, crowded with small-scale drop tracery, are predictable and repetitive, but within their context they work admirably. Internally, the effect is spectacular, for this is one of the most brilliantly illuminated of all English church interiors. The logic of the design is immediately apparent here, for the deep internal reveal of the west window repeats on the other three faces to form huge relieving arches to north, south and east (a).

The tower is set tight to the pre-existing west elevation of the fourteenth-century church. On the cross section this is most evident in the lower tower arch formed by the original west window of the church being extended down to the floor (b). On the side elevations the setting-out has unfortunate consequences, for the west end of the church originally terminated with two octagonal stair turrets, much as the chapel of King's College, Cambridge, still does. These stairs were retained to link into the new work before the second stage gallery was reached. Unfortunately these turrets

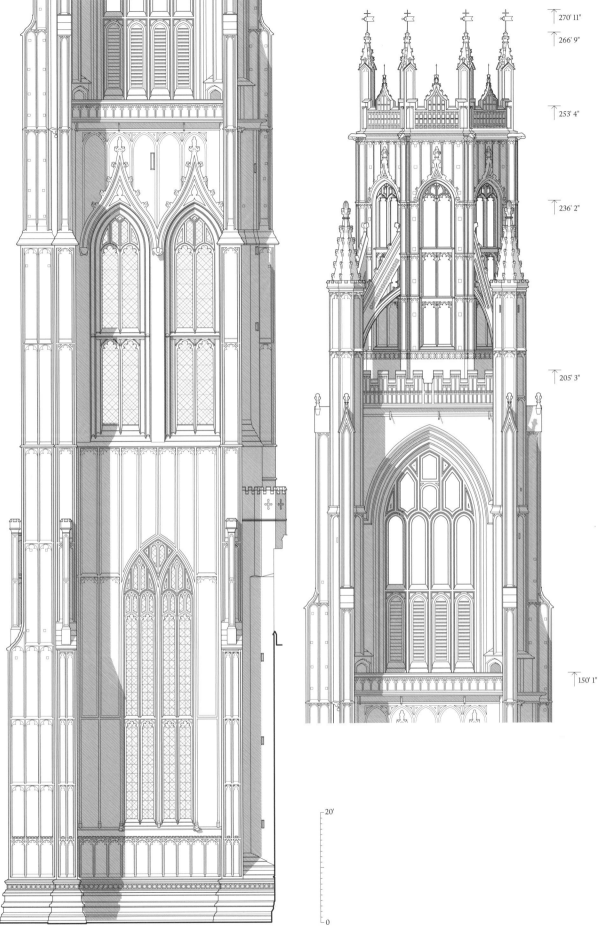

270' 11"

266' 9"

253' 4"

236' 2"

205' 3"

150' 1"

20'

0

South elevation

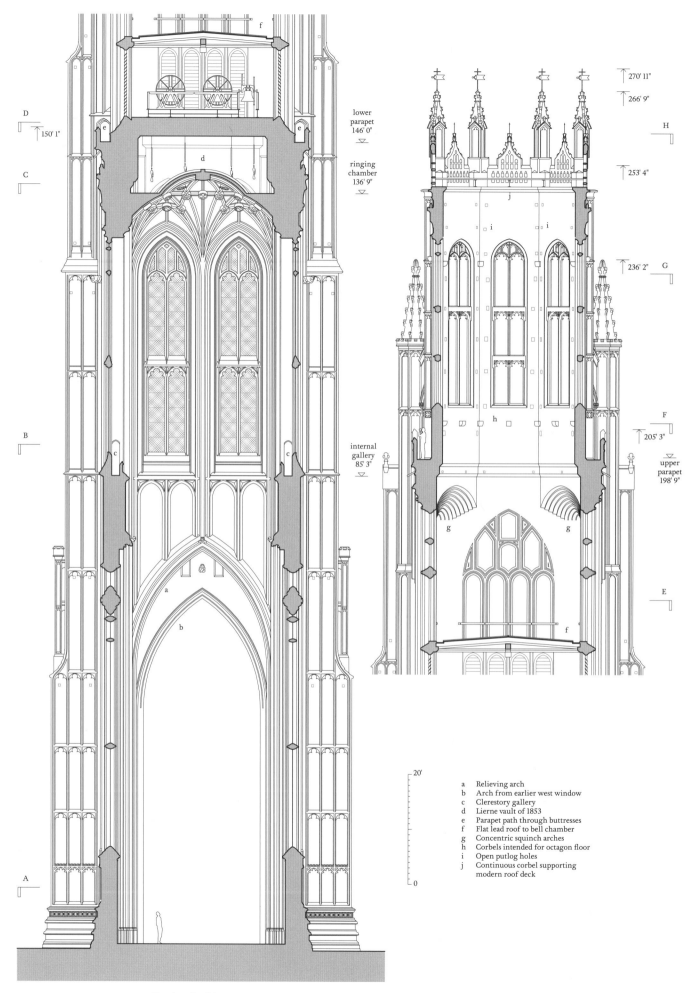

D
150' 1"

C

B

A

lower parapet
146' 0"

ringing
chamber
136' 9"

internal
gallery
85' 3"

f

e

d

c

a

b

e

c

270' 11"

266' 9"

H

253' 4"

236' 2"   G

205' 3"   F

upper
parapet
198' 9"

E

j

i   i

h

g   g

f

20'

a   Relieving arch
b   Arch from earlier west window
c   Clerestory gallery
d   Lierne vault of 1853
e   Parapet path through buttresses
f   Flat lead roof to bell chamber
g   Concentric squinch arches
h   Corbels intended for octagon floor
i   Open putlog holes
j   Continuous corbel supporting
     modern roof deck

0

Section looking east

displace the eastern buttresses of the tower four feet towards the centre of the north and south elevations, so that the first- and second-stage windows appear to be awkwardly off-centre. This is frustrating, for had the masons set the tower just four feet further west it could have been fully symmetrical on every face.

The grand western portal may have been reused from the previous west elevation of the church, which would account for the crude abutment of the basement course externally and the truncated reveals internally. This is not Decorated in style, as is sometimes claimed,[4] but early Perpendicular work of a particularly florid variety. There is indeed a superfluity of ogee curves, and the cinquefoil main arch is sub-cusped and sub-cusped again. There are, however, tell-tale signs of the second half of the fourteenth century, from the vertical mullions that rise straight to the archlets of the spandrel arcading to the exceptionally slender, flat-sided buttresses that frame the piers to either side. The door reveals are shallow and unimaginative, but they are framed by stacked canopied niches rising into octagonal corner turrets, all magnificently battlemented, arcaded and filled with vegetative carving.

It has been suggested that Reginald Ely, the first master at King's College Chapel, was responsible for the design of the Boston Stump on the basis of an insubstantial bequest of 6s 8d he made to the Guild of Our Lady of Boston, but this is unconvincing.[5]

The architect for the second stage at BOSTON is no less anonymous, but stylistic evidence suggests that he was also the master mason of the magnificent tower then under way at LOUTH. In both designs there are tall paired windows, each of two cinquefoiled lights, with identical supermullioned tracery in the head. The profiles of casements, ogees and fillets have some similarities, although the glass at BOSTON is set unusually far forward. The windows at BOSTON receive elegant ogee hood-moulds that do not appear at LOUTH until the following stage. More significantly, both designs include the same form of internal gallery that burrows neatly through the centre of the deep internal reveals (c). This is a brilliant variation of the established twin-wall construction of great crossing towers, and the spectacular results make the late medieval towers of York Minster and Canterbury Cathedral appear pedestrian by comparison.

Unfortunately the masons responsible for this technical marvel never lived to appreciate their work, for the intended tower vault was abandoned and a temporary floor remained at the level of the gallery. It was only in 1853 that the architect George Place installed a magnificent vault using the medieval springings and opened the space into one colossal, soaring volume, 137 feet high. Place could be guilty of the blatant fudging of history, for example by replacing the original east window to the chancel by one copied from Carlisle Cathedral, but there can be no doubting that the opening-up of

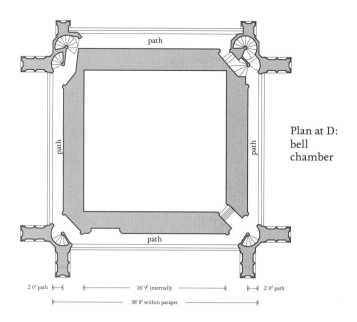

Plan at D:
bell
chamber

path

path

path

path

2' 0" path   26' 9" internally   2' 0" path

38' 8" within parapet

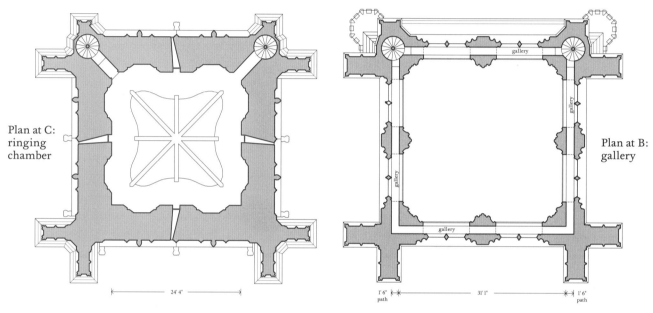

Plan at C:
ringing
chamber

24' 4"

gallery

gallery

gallery

gallery

Plan at B:
gallery

1' 6"
path   31' 1"   1' 6"
path

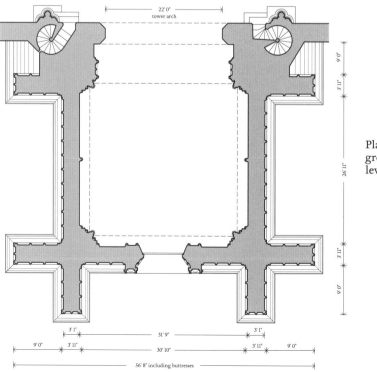

22' 0"
tower arch

9' 0"

3' 11"

26' 11"

Plan at A:
ground
level

3' 11"

9' 0"

3' 1"   31' 9"   3' 1"

9' 0"   3' 11"   30' 10"   3' 11"   9' 0"

56' 8" including buttresses

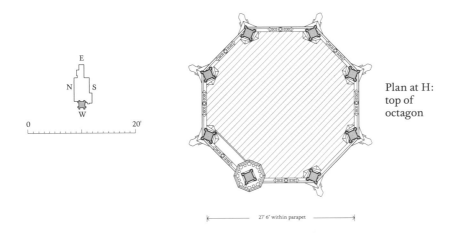

E

N S

W

0   20'

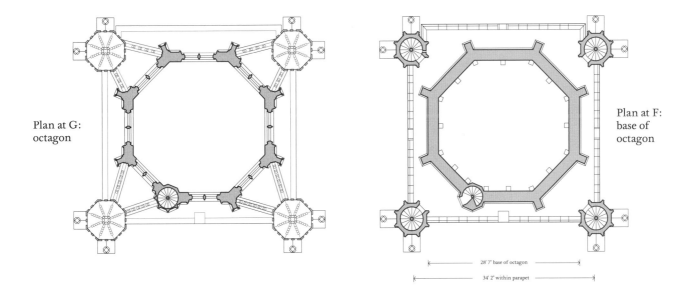

Plan at H:
top of
octagon

27' 6" within parapet

Plan at G:
octagon

Plan at F:
base of
octagon

28' 7" base of octagon

34' 2" within parapet

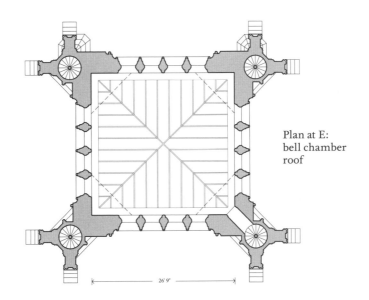

Plan at E:
bell chamber
roof

26' 9"

the tower was entirely merited. The star lierne vault, formed of octagons repeated in each of the four quadrants, is superb, even if the forty-one bosses are rather overdone and there is no traditional central bell hatch.

It is unclear how the medieval masons had intended to subdivide the upper levels, but the tallest parish tower in the land now has one of the lowest and most bizarre ringing chambers in the country, for the centre of the room is filled by the domed upper surface of the Victorian vault (d). Not all of Place's work was so successful. The iron glazing bars in the windows continue to cause problems and, as Sir George Gilbert Scott had warned, the introduction of the vault necessitated some strengthening of the tower. A number of iron tie-rods had been inconspicuously added to the structure in the nineteenth century, but in 1929 Sir Charles Nicholson installed a continuous concrete slab above the ringing chamber. The vault conceals the base of eight corbelled arches, two to each face, which move the tower walls inboard by one foot.

At the third level, and slightly lower on the buttresses, a third master must have taken charge. One possible candidate is John Cowper, a mason employed by the Bishop of Winchester to build the collegiate church of Tattershall (Lincs), eleven miles north-west of BOSTON, from around 1478. Cowper is known to have served his apprenticeship at Eton College, and he built Kirkby Muxloe Castle in Leicestershire until 1484, when the work was abandoned. In his two major works

there is the same highly distinctive use of plain, uncusped arches that distinguishes the huge, austere four-light windows of the bell stage at BOSTON. The alternate tracery, in which the supermullions in the head are offset from the mullions below, also suggests a mason trained outside the region, for this feature is alien to the east of England. The third stage is pulled back behind an arcaded parapet and path (e), allowing the diagonal faces of the octagonal buttresses to return against the elevations.

The treatment of the bell chamber is peculiar, for the plain transoms of the great windows conceal the edge of its flat roof (f). Below the transom the openings are louvered, but above they are left entirely open. Together with the open lights of the octagon, this creates a stunning perforated silhouette that dominates the slow, flat approach to BOSTON from the west. This third stage is easily the least successful in the composition, not only because of the severity of the openings, but also because the large expanses of plain ashlar walling are inconsistent with the panelling above and below. Worse still is the setting-out of the north and south side elevations, for the asymmetry of the two proceeding stages is disregarded and the openings are set centrally between the buttresses. The castellated battlement that follows, decorated with two miniature tiers of arcading, is standard for the period. Pinnacles or statues were clearly intended for the square centre shafts. Within the tower no fewer than ten

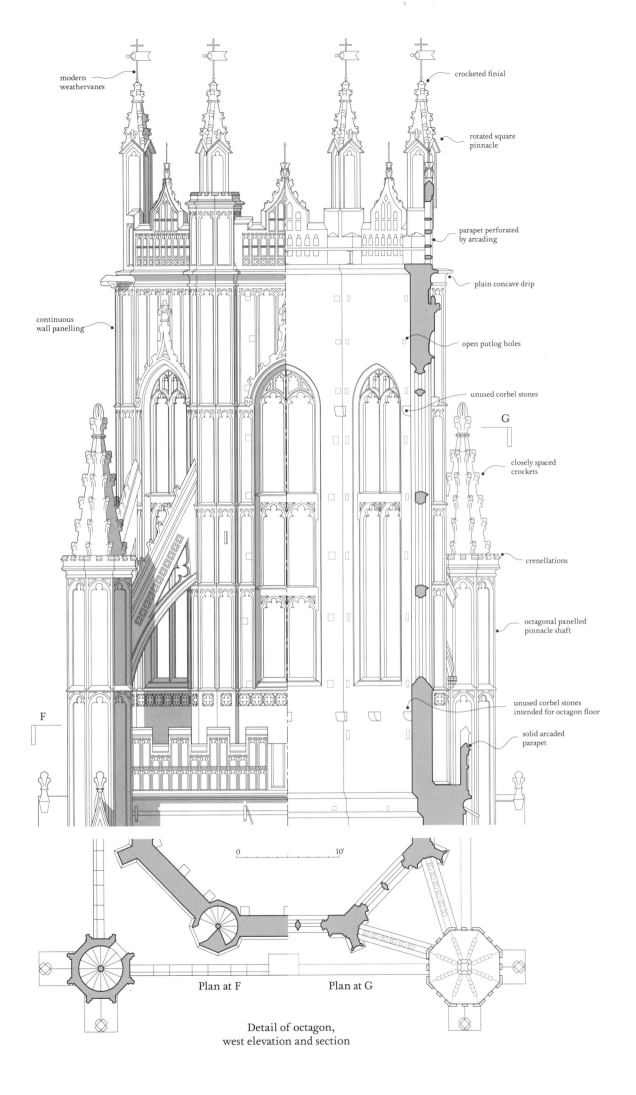

modern
weathervanes

crocketed finial

rotated square
pinnacle

parapet perforated
by arcading

plain concave drip

continuous
wall panelling

open putlog holes

unused corbel stones

closely spaced
crockets

G

crenellations

octagonal panelled
pinnacle shaft

F

unused corbel stones
intended for octagon floor

solid arcaded
parapet

0   10'

Plan at F   Plan at G

Detail of octagon,
west elevation and section

concentric semicircular squinch arches span each corner in preparation for the octagon (g).

The octagon is entirely hollow, lacking either a floor, though corbels are provided for it (h), or a roof, though there is a modern open timber deck on steelwork. The view from the summit is spectacular, but it is the sheer audacity of the medieval imagination that takes the breath away. It is commonly suggested that the octagon was an afterthought, but it is equally likely that it was intended from the outset. That William Horwode's octagon at FOTHERINGHAY, built in 1434, provided the model is indisputable, and it is not inconceivable that Horwode may have played some role in the earliest designs for BOSTON. In its final form, the lantern may be the work of the master mason John Cole, who was recruited from BOSTON in the summer of 1515 to complete the spire of LOUTH.[6]

The design is symmetrical except for an exceptionally tight stair shaft on the north-west corner. Each elevation is divided into four tiers of panelling in five bays, all set above a quatrefoil band. Two-light windows are subservient to the grid and employ the same tracery as the gallery windows but on a smaller scale. Each of the eight corners is stiffened by a square buttress restrained by magnificent flying buttresses springing from the pinnacles. These are of the Northamptonshire type, with a straight upper member perforated by quatrefoils. Although there is no sign of economy in the construction, the putlog holes here and on many of the lower buttresses are left unfilled, suggesting that the finances had become exhausted and the scaffold was dropped in a rush. The parapet is battlemented, gabled, crocketed and perforated in one final flurry of enthusiasm. Eight corner pinnacles, rotated diagonally and topped by Victorian weathervanes, bring the gargantuan construction to the most delicate of conclusions.

NOTES

1   BOSTON is reputed to be the largest parish church by volume of space enclosed. In terms of floor area, BOSTON (20,270 or 20,070 square feet, according to different sources) was surpassed by only ST MICHAEL, COVENTRY (24,015 or 22,000 square feet), Great Yarmouth (23,265 or 23,000 square feet) and possibly ST NICHOLAS, NEWCASTLE (20,110 square feet).

2   Ven. Edward Trollope, 'Boston and other Churches visited by the Society, June 16th and 17th June 1870', *Reports and Papers of the Architectural and Archaeological Societies of the counties of Lincoln and Northampton*, vol. 10 (1867), p. 177.

3   Alec Clifton-Taylor, *English Parish Churches as Works of Art* (1986) p. 110, and Sir Nikolaus Pevsner and John Harris, *The Buildings of England: Lincolnshire* (London, 1964), for example.

4   See e.g. Pevsner and Harris, *The Buildings of England: Lincolnshire* (1964).

5   See John H. Harvey, *English Mediaeval Architects: A Biographical Dictionary Down to 1550* (1984).

6   See Appendix 2: The First Churchwardens' Book of Louth, 1500–24.

50

Louth

The great steeple of LOUTH stands quite apart from the mainstream of Lincolnshire spires, both geographically and chronologically. The fine market town of Louth lies in the far north-east of the county, where the Wolds meet the Marshland, some twenty-five miles from the spire-building district of Sleaford. The first church was built in around 1190 and substantially reconstructed sixty years later. By 1430 St James's Church was failing to meet the aspirations of a town grown rich on the wool trade, and a comprehensive programme of rebuilding commenced, of which the steeple was the penultimate phase. GRANTHAM provided the model both for the church and for the steeple. The two churches share a simple rectangular plan almost 200 feet long and 80 feet wide embracing the base of the spire. Both have a nave of six bays, a chancel of four bays and porches projecting to the north and south.

While the building of the spire at LOUTH is documented in unparalleled detail, the early history of the tower is not so well served. One indirect piece of evidence comes from the document known as 'The First Churchwardens' Book of Louth',[1] which records that, during the celebrations marking the completion of the spire in September 1515,

> Thomas Bradley, mercer [textile merchant], said that he might mean well, and saw the first stone set upon the said steeple [tower], and also the last stone set

upon the said broach [spire]. And also Agnes, the wife of Robert English Barker, said the same with many more.

Since a number of the townspeople witnessed and remembered both the start and completion of the steeple within their lifetime, when one bears in mind the lower life expectancy of the period it is unreasonable to propose a construction span of much more than sixty years. This suggests that a commencement date of around 1440 put forward by several twentieth-century historians is probably too early.[2] A date nearer to 1455 appears more realistic, and this is supported by other evidence in the fabric.

Externally, the tower is of three principal stages, the third of which is exceptionally attenuated. Decoration is sumptuous and beautifully executed, but it is also carefully controlled, reaching a crescendo around the base of the spire. The typical late medieval flat-sided crockets and mass-produced quatrefoil bands find no place here. The design, if not necessarily the execution, must have been by a single unknown mason, for the composition is meticulously organized and the detail rigorously consistent.

Vast and magnificent buttresses dominate the composition, imparting a soaring verticality and a sublime silhouette. Deep and slender angle buttresses on the first two stages are augmented by octagonal clasping buttresses that transform into octagonal pinnacles above the parapet. The deeply projecting lower stages not only stabilize the tower, but also support giant relieving arches (c) that allow the interior to be opened up to an unprecedented extent. The staircase is discernible by the regular slit windows perforating the south-west re-entrant angle between the buttresses.

Buttresses set-offs are entirely independent of the elevation – an effective device developed in sophisticated designs of the previous century, such as MOULTON, to increase the verticality of the composition. MOULTON may also have provided the inspiration for the gloriously rich crocketed gables, which divide the buttresses into three unequal parts. Each part is in turn subdivided into approximately equal divisions, effectively concentrating the energy of the composition at the top of the tower. This intensification continues in the division of the octagonal pinnacle shafts into two unequal stages of panelling. The scale of the crocketed pinnacles, which reach to fifty feet around the base of the spire, is perfect.

English west doors are remarkable for their modesty, and LOUTH is no exception, for it is incidental to the composition and designed to be appreciated best at close quarters. The deeply moulded portal sits between small pinnacled buttresses, and the ogee hood-mould is richly crocketed, with the finial rising above the cill of the west window. The outer edge of the arch carries delicately perforated compound cusping finished with six-petal roses, and in the head is a quatrefoil surrounded by three round-headed daggers.

The three tiers of windows above are consistently detailed, although, surprisingly, not in a single material. Construction up to the cill of the west window is in white Yorkshire Magnesian limestone, which then changes to Ancaster stone, a light buff weathering to a light grey. It has been suggested that the original supplies were disrupted during the intermittent conflict of the Wars of the Roses, possibly by the campaigns of 1459–60.

The two-centred window arches become more acutely pointed with each stage. Openings are framed by broad casements surrounded by filleted rolls. Internally, the casements are widened to accommodate passageways serving the triforium gallery (b). Five bays of predictable grid tracery in the west window are the only dull note in the entire composition. To the north and south pairs of steeply arched clerestory lights sit between the aisle roofs and the internal relieving arches (c). The motif of two cinquefoiled bays, with supermullions and a regular pointed quatrefoil in the head, reappears in both upper stages. The tower becomes fully symmetrical from the second stage as it rises clear of the body of the church. The paired twin-light windows are hard to see internally, but the effect is spectacular, for the tower is flooded with daylight from every direction.

Within the tower is one of the most stupendous volumes found in any English church, for the glorious lierne vault soars eighty-six feet above the pavement (g). At

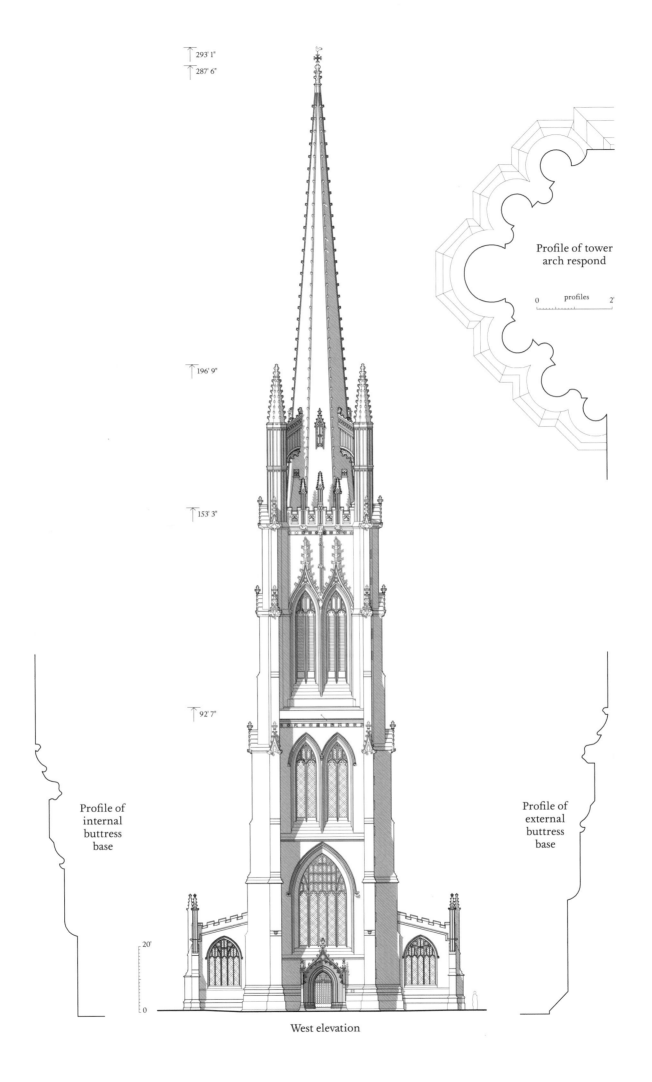

293' 1"
287' 6"

196' 9"

153' 3"

92' 7"

Profile of tower
arch respond

0   profiles   2'

Profile of
internal
buttress
base

Profile of
external
buttress
base

20'

0

West elevation

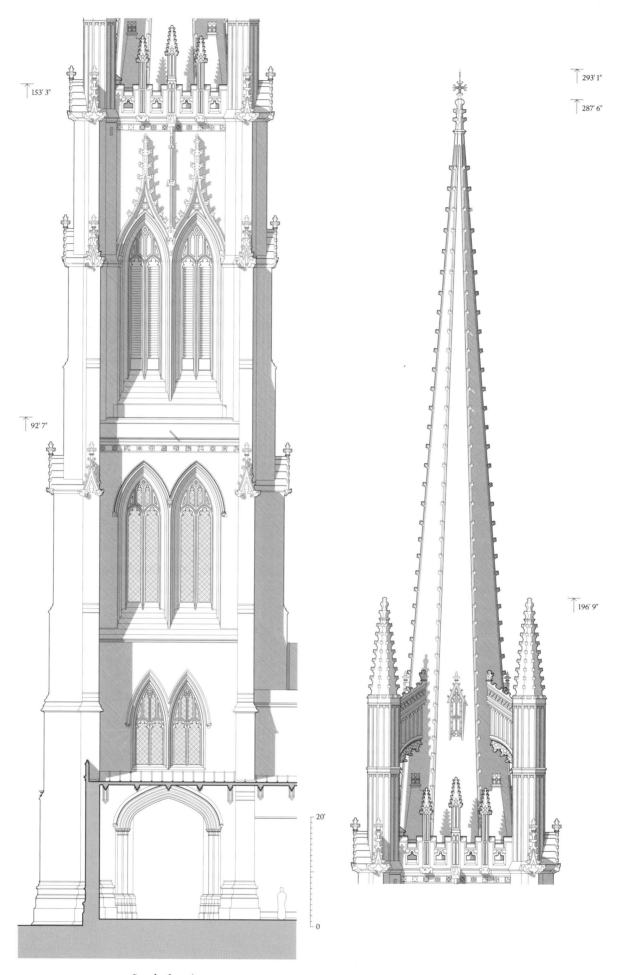

153' 3"

92' 7"

20'

0

293' 1"

287' 6"

196' 9"

South elevation
with section through south aisle

fifty-three feet a continuous galley runs around the base of the eight windows of the second stage (b). This is supported by the tower arch to the east and giant relieving arches on the other three faces. The similarities to the contemporary tower at BOSTON are striking. According to James Fowler, architect of the nineteenth-century restoration, the self-weight of the tower caused subsidence of seven inches relative to the church, and this is most evident around the northern tower arch. The responds, of five clustered shafts separated by semicircular recesses, are almost thirty feet high, with the single corner shafts shooting straight up to the springing of the vault. Flat four-centred arches opening to the north and south aisles are the only pedestrian element of the whole composition, but they are set discreetly behind the main respond shafts (h).

Nave walls fit neatly between the eastern tower buttresses, which rise magnificently through the body of the church.

The lower half of the tower is brought to an emphatic conclusion by a straight parapet above a cornice decorated by square panels of foliate decoration (d). The third stage steps back so that the walls sit entirely over the giant relieving arches below. The proportions of the elevations become increasingly vertical, for they are constrained between the side faces of the emerging octagonal buttresses. Openings are extraordinarily attenuated, with spectacular ogee hood-moulds stretching fourteen feet above the window heads. These hoods show a clear northern influence, not only from Yorkshire towers such as TICKHILL, Great Driffield and York Minster, but more particularly from Durham Cathedral, where the central tower was rebuilt by Thomas Barton between 1465 and 1475. Not only are the window proportions, tracery and hood-moulds at Durham remarkably similar to those at LOUTH, but so are the deep, narrow buttresses. LOUTH is far better proportioned and more refined in execution than Durham, but there are obvious stylistic connections between the two buildings.

The louvres of these tall openings conceal an awkward arrangement of ringing chamber, empty sound chamber and bell chamber, which is all too clear on the sections. A modern bell frame carries the eighth-heaviest peal in the country. The ancient floor structure above the ringing chamber is propped off triangular steel wall shafts added in the twentieth century (e). Squinches of three concentric arches (f) are set well down into the tower, providing a substantial base for the spire but leaving a large expanse of masonry above the windows.

At the top of the tower, more original structure supports the 'Wild Mare' (a), installed according to the accounts in 1501–02 and one of only three medieval treadmill hoists remaining in England. The richly castellated parapet, perforated by delicate sub-cusped trefoil arches, has three panelled pinnacles to each elevation. Central pinnacles rise between the window hood-moulds, and grotesques spring from the pinnacle bases. Workmanship is consistently of the very finest quality.

The construction of the great spire is recorded in meticulous detail, for the churchwardens' accounts provide a comprehensive record of thousands of individual transactions with masons, apprentices, labourers, quarry-owners and suppliers of lead, lime, timber and sand. The spire cost £305 7s. 5d., and it represents the work of twenty-nine individual masons and apprentices employed sporadically by the church as and when funds and supplies of stone permitted.

William Nettleton, a local stonemason, was employed in 1500–01 to complete the gallery and carry out some preliminary works. Construction commenced in earnest after Trinity Sunday 1501 under the control of the master mason John Cole. The main scaffold was erected immediately before Easter 1502, with timber centering for the flying buttresses following in early 1504. The striking of scaffold after a concerted period of activity in December 1506 probably represents the completion of the four great pinnacles.

Two or three masons were constantly employed on the works until 1503 but, as funds were exhausted and the stockpile of stone depleted, activity on the site became intermittent. The replacement of Cole by master mason Christopher Scune around Easter 1505 only made matters worse, and work was suspended for months at a time. No masons were employed in 1506–07, and in 1509–10 Scune worked for just six days, leaving his apprentice unsupervised for eleven weeks. After his first year Christopher Scune rarely visited site despite, receiving his annual fee of 13s. 4d.

Unsurprisingly, the accounts record an increasingly acrimonious relationship between the master mason and the wardens. Contemporary sources shed some light upon this, for Scune was appointed as master at Ripon Cathedral some time between 1503 and 1514, and at Durham Cathedral some time between 1508 and 1515.[3] Several letters were sent to him in 1514, including one to Ripon, and a final ultimatum in 1515, following which he was replaced by John Tempas from BOSTON. The new master's responsibilities were limited to an intensive three-month summer campaign to finish the

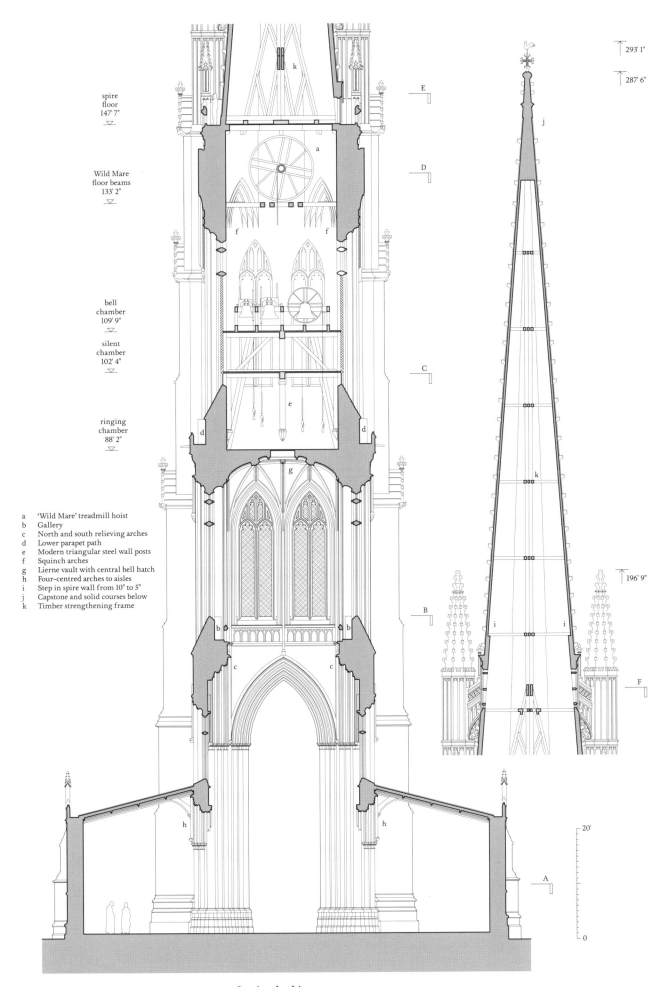

spire
floor
147' 7"

Wild Mare
floor beams
133' 2"

bell
chamber
109' 9"

silent
chamber
102' 4"

ringing
chamber
88' 2"

a   'Wild Mare' treadmill hoist
b   Gallery
c   North and south relieving arches
d   Lower parapet path
e   Modern triangular steel wall posts
f   Squinch arches
g   Lierne vault with central bell hatch
h   Four-centred arches to aisles
i   Step in spire wall from 10" to 5"
j   Capstone and solid courses below
k   Timber strengthening frame

E

D

C

B

A

293' 1"

287' 6"

196' 9"

F

20'

0

Section looking east

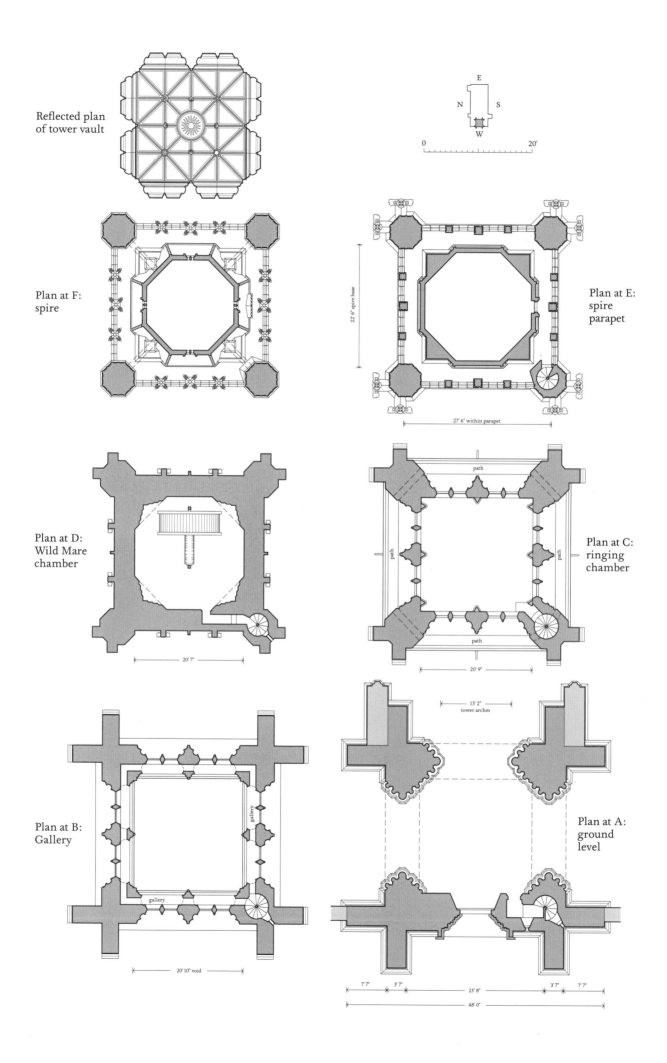

Reflected plan
of tower vault

Plan at F:
spire

Plan at E:
spire
parapet

22' 6" spire base

27' 6" within parapet

Plan at D:
Wild Mare
chamber

20' 7"

Plan at C:
ringing
chamber

path

path

path

path

20' 9"

13' 2"
tower arches

Plan at B:
Gallery

gallery

gallery

20' 10" void

Plan at A:
ground
level

7' 7"   3' 7"   25' 8"   3' 7"   7' 7"

48' 0"

E

N   S

W

0   20'

spire, which was recognized by his modest reward of 6s. 8d., compared with 20s. given to long-serving mason Laurence Lemyng.

On Holy Rood Eve (13 September) 1515 the weathercock was raised amid great celebrations. The churchwardens' accounts record that,

> William Ayleby, parish priest, with many of his brethren priests, there present, hallowed the said weathercock and the stone that it stands upon, and so conveyed upon the said broach [spire]; and then the said priests singing Te Deum Laudamus with organs, and the kirk-wardens garred ring all the bells, and caused all the people there being to have bread and ale, and all the loving of God, our Lady, and all saints.

Neither Tempas nor Scune before him were in any meaningful sense the architects of the LOUTH spire, for the design had been established by John Cole at the base in all but a few particulars. Reginald Dudding's suggestion that John Spencer, steward of the Bishop of Lincoln, was responsible for the design on the basis of his supplying parchment for a drawing in 1503–04 is patently absurd. The only caveat to John Cole's position as designer of England's greatest spire is the extent to which the scheme may have been inherited from the architect of the original tower, and this can only be a matter of conjecture.

Funds to pay for the work were either raised from the congregation in the normal manner or borrowed. John Chapman, churchwarden and merchant, donated 8s. 9d. when the first stones were laid, spent four days inspecting the quarries with the mason and bequeathed £20 in gold to the work when he died in 1505. Much later Thomas Taylor, a draper, donated the weathercock, which was made in Lincoln using the copper from a great basin lost by the Scots at Flodden Field. Despite such generosity, the wardens were forced to borrow large sums of money: £59 2s. 9d. from the Guild of Our Lady, £7 12s. 1d. from the Guild of St Peter, and £7 9s. 5d. from the Trinity Guild.

LOUTH's remoteness from the Great Limestone Belt is reflected in the disproportionate cost of stone transport. Almost one-quarter of the total budget was spent on carriage from the quarries at Wilsford Heath, near Ancaster, by land and water up the Slea and Witham to Dogdyke, and then by cart to LOUTH. Wages throughout the fifteen-year duration remained remarkably constant, with only a modest differential between the master mason, on 8d. per day, his masons on $6^2/_3d.$, and the apprentices on 6d.

The churchwardens' accounts record that the spire reached 360 feet, but this is a huge exaggeration. The first accurate measurement, derived from a 'Quadrite Theodolite', was recorded in Thomas William Wallis's 1884 autobiography. His dimension of 287' 6" to the top of the stone finial has been confirmed by the current survey.[4] With height came risk. In 1558 a grete tempeste threw down the cope stone, which was sixteen inches in diameter, and the iron cross, nine feet high ... and shattered eighteen feet more of the spiral work which cost in repairs £34 13s. 7d.[5]

Lightning strikes and storms destroyed the apex of the spire in 1587, 1634, 1828 and 1843. On each occasion the parishioners dutifully raised the funds necessary for rebuilding.

The spire at LOUTH is a thin shell right from its base. James Fowler recorded that the spire walls start at ten inches thick and step back to five inches thick after about thirty-six feet (i), and that the top twenty feet or so are solid (j). So efficient is the structure that it contains only around 200 tons of Ancaster stone, compared with 290 tons used in the four corner pinnacles.[6] The substantial timber frame rising from a triangulated base that stiffens the spire walls at regular intervals (k) predates Fowler's restoration and was most probably installed following a lightning strike in 1843. Externally, the spire is exceptionally sophisticated in the Yorkshire rather than the Lincolnshire manner, for there is just a single tier of tiny lucarnes. This is one of the slenderest needle spires in England, with an apex angle of only 9° 5'. One potential problem with needle spires is that they can appear too narrow at the base, but the four great pinnacles effectively mask this weakness. The broaches around the base of the spire, which carry cubic crowns decorated with stacks of tiny quatrefoils, are entirely ornamental.

For Francis Bond, the flying buttresses around the spire at LOUTH are equalled only by those of the Henry VII Chapel at Westminster Abbey. There is, however, one fundamental difference between these two sumptuous designs, for whereas the vault at Westminster would collapse without the support of flying buttresses, the spire at LOUTH would suffer no ill effects. Nevertheless, as an aesthetic device for clasping the spire firmly between the corner pinnacles they are without fault. These flying buttresses are formed of two parallel upper members separated by a trefoil band, in the Northamptonshire fashion, supported by a closely spaced arcade rising from an arched bottom member. There are crockets above and a lacy foliation carrying diamond points below.

Thirty-seven crockets embellishing each spire edge are as rich as any carved in

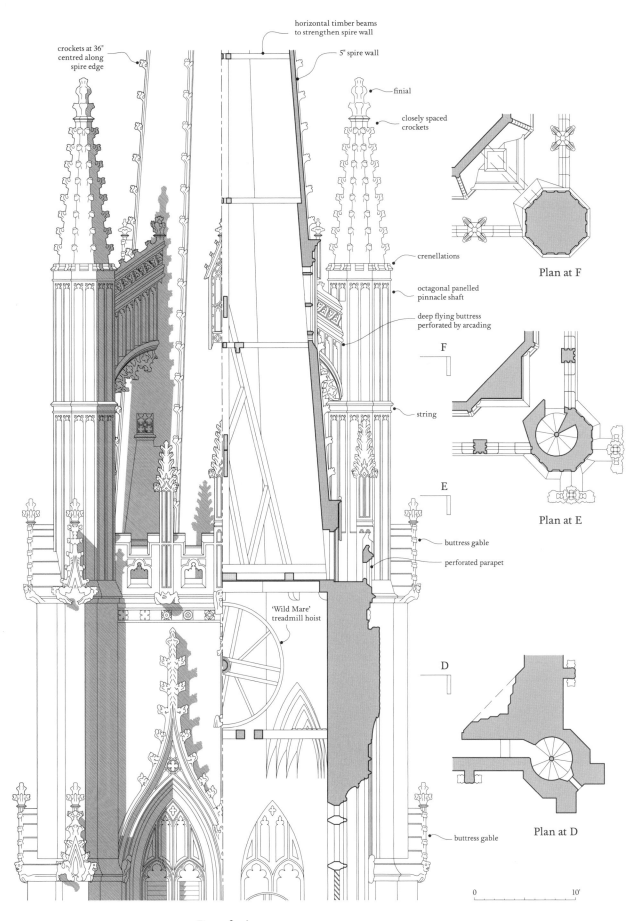

crockets at 36"
centred along
spire edge

horizontal timber beams
to strengthen spire wall

5" spire wall

finial

closely spaced
crockets

crenellations

octagonal panelled
pinnacle shaft

deep flying buttress
perforated by arcading

string

buttress gable

perforated parapet

'Wild Mare'
treadmill hoist

buttress gable

Plan at F

F

E

D

Plan at E

Plan at D

0   10'

Base of spire,
west elevation and section

Lincolnshire a century and a half earlier. There is no trace of entasis, but the crockets are spaced more closely as they approach the summit; according to James Fowler, they also project further around the middle third of the spire. The hard, dark capstone and the gilded weathercock form a perfect termination to this most beautiful of English steeples.

There are just two faults that distract from the perfection of LOUTH. The low aisles, which awkwardly overlap the tower buttresses, appear uncomfortably humble, but this is a common fault in late medieval steeples. More disappointing is the inadequacy of the setting, for whereas the steeples of GRANTHAM and BOSTON address spaces that are commensurate with their scale, LOUTH faces the blank corner of a Georgian house across a tarmac chicane.

These are, however, minor defects, for LOUTH remains a seamless distillation of all that had been learned in the art of steeple-building during the preceding two centuries of evolution. Faultless in conception and faultless in execution, the tower and spire of St James's Church form one of the most sublime achievements of English architecture.

NOTES

1   In 1790 Sir Joseph Banks presented extracts of the churchwarden's accounts to the Society of Antiquaries, and a record of this lecture appears in John Britton, *The Architectural Antiquities of Great Britain*, vol. IV (1814). The original book was lost and rediscovered in the library of Sir Charles Anderson in 1891. The painstaking task of transcribing the work was undertaken by Revd Reginald C. Dudding and published posthumously in 1941. A detailed synopsis of *The First Churchwardens' Book of Louth*, with particular reference to the construction of the spire, appears in Appendix 2.

2   Francis Bond suggests construction of the tower occurred *c.* 1445–1500. John Harvey's proposed start date of *c.* 1440–45 is repeated in Pevsner and Harris, *The Buildings of England: Lincolnshire* (1964). In *The Perpendicular Style* (1978), Harvey suggests on stylistic evidence that John Porter was master for the LOUTH tower; however, if work started only around 1455–60, as suggested here, Porter could not have been involved, for he was fully occupied at York Minster from 1454 until his death in 1466.

3   John Harvey, *Cathedrals of England and Wales* (1950), p. 225, and *English Mediaeval Architects: A Biographical Dictionary Down to 1550* (1984), p. 270.

4   Reginald C. Dudding, *The First Churchwardens' Book of Louth*, Introduction, p. xix. In all other sources Thomas William Wallis's accurate measurement recorded in 1884 has been overlooked.

5   Robert Slater Bayley, *Notitae Lundae; or, Notices of Louth* (1834), p. 147.

6   Calculations based on a density of 2200 kg/m³ for stone quarried at the Wilsford Glebe Quarry, Ancaster. The calculation also makes the assumption that the pinnacles are solid.

Supplementary Information

ADDERBURY, ST MARY
OXFORDSHIRE
Date of tower: *c.* 1315–50
Date of spire: after 1450
Position: west tower
Material: Oxfordshire limestone and marlstone
Steeple height: 148' 0", to vane 152' 9"
Tower width: 36' 2" to outer corners of buttresses
Spire dims: 74' 2" high, 19' 8" wide
Spire angle: 15° 29'
Squinches: single arch
Stairs: clockwise-up helical stair in south-west corner, 5' 9" to 3' 8" dia. stair, 6" dia. newel; 117 steps to parapet
Bells: peal of eight in D: John Briant 1789 (6), G. Mears & Co. 1863, John Taylor & Co. 1927; overhauled and rehung in cast-iron frame by John Taylor & Co. in 1927
Restorations and alterations:
1766: spire repointed by White of Witney
1777: part of spire fell
1815: John Cheshire of Over Whitacre rebuilt 17' of spire
1866–70: restoration, architect George Gilbert Scott
1927: tower restored
1922: spire partly rebuilt
1952: spire repaired by Souwestone Restoration Co.
1956: pinnacles restored by Souwestone, architect John Surman
Survey date: May 2013
Ground datum: north-west buttress

BARNACK, ST JOHN THE BAPTIST
HUNTINGDONSHIRE
Date of tower: *c.* 1020–50
Date of spire: *c.* 1230, including stair and tower vault
Position: west tower
Material: Barnack ragstone
Steeple height: 113' 11", to vane 117' 7"
Tower width: 26' 2" at base
Spire dims: 42' 8" high, 25' 11" wide
Spire angle: 33° 51'
Squinches: single arch
Stairs: clockwise-up helical stair in south-west corner, 6' 1" dia. stair, 6" dia. newel; 46 steps up to bell chamber, modern ladders above
Bells: peal of six in G sharp: John Seliok of Nottingham *c.* 1500, Tobias

Norris I of Stamford 1608 and 1609, Henry Penn of Peterborough 1715, John Taylor & Co. of Loughborough 1897 and 1998; steel frame by Haywood Mills Associates of Nottingham 1999
Clock: mechanism by Smiths of Clerkenwell 1870, skeleton face on south elevation, bell by John Taylor & Co. of Loughborough 1936
Restorations and alterations:
1853–55: restoration of church, tower strengthened
1935–37: major restoration under Canon Henry Fry, cost £2,000
Survey date: January 2011, July 2014
Ground datum: south-west corner

BOSTON, ST BOTOLPH
LINCOLNSHIRE
Date of steeple: started *c.* 1425–50, completed *c.* 1500–20
Architect/mason: third stage possibly John Cowper, octagon possibly John Cole
Position: west tower
Material: Barnack ragstone; restorations in Ketton stone (1840s–50s), Ancaster stone (1929–33) and Clipsham stone (ongoing)
Steeple height: 266' 9", to finial 270' 11"
Tower width: 56' 8" above base
Lantern dims: 67' 2" high, 31' 5" wide
Squinches: ten concentric arches
Stairs: clockwise-up helical stairs in north-east and south-east turrets to main parapet, 5' 4" to 4' 6" dia. stair, 6½" dia. newel; four clockwise-up helical stairs in corner butresses to octagon parapet, 4' 4" dia. stair, 6" newel; one clockwise-up helical stair in north-west corner of octagon to roof, 3' 10" stair, 5½" newel; 209 steps to main parapet, 354 steps to octagon roof
Bells: peal of ten in E flat, all 1932; chiming bells 1932 (4) and 1949 (11); steel and cast-iron frame; all by John Taylor & Co. of Loughborough
Restorations and alterations:
1840: George Gilbert Scott advised brother-in-law and vicar John Henry Oldrid
1843–47: church restoration, architect George Gilbert Scott, cost £3,831

1853: tower vault added, architect George G. Place of Nottingham, consultant George Gilbert Scott, cost £13,421
1873: further restoration, architect Sir George Gilbert Scott
1928–33: tower repairs, architect Sir Charles Nicholson of London
Ongoing repairs: architects Buttress Fuller Alsop Williams of Manchester
Survey date: February and July 2011, July 2014
Ground datum: centre of west elevation

BRANT BROUGHTON, ST HELEN
LINCOLNSHIRE
Date of tower: *c.* 1338–48
Date of spire: *c.* 1450
Position: west tower
Material: Ancaster limestone
Steeple height: 166' 8", to vane 174' 1"
Tower width: 26' 7" above base
Spire dims: 101' 8" high, 16' 10" wide
Spire angle: 9° 19'
Squinches: two concentric arches
Stairs: clockwise-up helical stair in south-west corner, 5' 2" dia. stair, 7' dia. newel; from ground 99 steps to parapet
Bells: peal of six in E: Thomas Osborn of Downham 1792 (3), John Taylor & Co. of Loughborough 1881 (3); two-tier oak frame, possibly 1881, overhauled 1957
Clock: mechanism by William Potts & Sons of Leeds 1881, modernized John Smith of Derby 1983, octagonal face to east
Restorations and alterations:
1860: work on lightning conductor
1871: recorded that top of spire missing
1873–76 and later: restoration, architect George F. Bodley, Bodley & Garner of London
1897: spire restored, raised 7', new weathervane, architect George F. Bodley
1925–27: tower repairs, architect Wilfred Bond
Survey date: January 2011, July 2014
Ground datum: south-west buttress

CASTOR, ST KYNEBURGHA
HUNTINGDONSHIRE
Date of tower: *c.* 1114–24, dedicated in 1124

Date of spire and parapet: 15th century
Position: central crossing tower
Material: Barnack ragstone
Steeple height: 115' 3", to vane 118' 3"
Tower width: 23' 9" outside of piers above base
Spire dims: 48' 10" high, 19' 1" wide
Spire angle: 21° 51'
Squinches: single arch
Stairs: clockwise-up helical stair in north transept, 4' 1" dia. stair, 4" dia. newel; 30 steps to ringing chamber, modern ladders above
Bells: peal of eight in G: Henry Bagley II of Ecton 1700 (6), John Taylor Ltd. 1999 (2); steel frame by John Taylor Ltd. of Loughborough 1999
Clock: modern mechanism, solid face to south
Restorations and alterations:
1848–51: general restoration, architect Edward Blore, London
Survey date: March 2011, September 2014
Ground datum: south-west buttress of south transept

CHIPPING CAMPDEN, ST JAMES
GLOUCESTERSHIRE
Date of tower: *c.* 1450–60, by John Gower
Position: west tower
Material: Gloucestershire limestone
Steeple height: 119' 4", to vane 124' 4"
Tower width: 35' 0" to buttress corners
Stairs: clockwise-up helical stair in south-east corner, 5' 8" dia. stair, 4" to 5" dia. newel; 136 steps to roof
Bells: peal of eight in E flat: Richard Keene 1678 and 1683, Abel Rudhall 1737, Charles & George Mears 1851 and 1857, John Taylor & Co. 1912, Whitechapel Bell Foundry 1986 and 2004; oak bell frame
Clock: original mechanism 1675; now at base of tower, replaced by electronic mechanism 1962
Carillon mechanism: mechanisms installed 1682, 1718 and 1816 by Richard Huls of Campden
Glass: west window, memorial to Revd Canon Kennaway, 1876
Restorations and alterations:
1875–76: exterior restoration, architects Habershon & Pite, cost over £4,000

1884: interior restoration, architects
Waller & Wood of Gloucester,
cost over £1,000
Survey date: March 2013
Ground datum: west elevation

DEDHAM, ST MARY THE VIRGIN
ESSEX
Date of tower: *c.* 1494–1519
Architect/mason: John Wastell
of Bury St Edmunds
Position: west tower
Material: flushwork; knapped flint
with dressings of Caen stone, brick
internally
Tower height: 117' 7", to flagpole 138' 7"
Tower width: 33' 9" above base
Stairs: clockwise-up helical stairs
in south-east corner to gallery,
in south-west corner from gallery
to roof, 4' 8" to 3' 8" dia. stair,
5½" dia. newel; 132 steps to roof
Bells: peal of eight in E, disabled:
Robert Burford of London *c.* 1400,
John Darbie of Ipswich 1675, John
Thornton of Sudbury 1717, Thomas
Gardiner of Sudbury 1754 (5); oak
frame 1830, ringing stopped 1891
Clock: skeleton face to north
Restorations and alterations:
1629: gallery built
1810: oak and iron tie-rods installed
1859–63: church repairs, architect
James Roberts of London
1884: damaged in Colchester
earthquake, 22 April
1891: report on tower, architect
J. T. Micklethwaite
1907: report on poor state, architect
T. G. Jackson
1977: organ moved back to tower
gallery
1980–90: general church repairs
including tower
Survey date: August 2010, September
2014
Ground datum: south-west buttress

EARLS BARTON, ALL SAINTS
NORTHAMPTONSHIRE
Date of tower: *c.* 970, 15th-century
battlements
Position: west tower
Material: Barnack ragstone with
local limestone-rubble infill
and render
Tower height: 68' 7", to flagpole 86' 3"
Tower width: 24' 0" at base
Stairs: ancient split-log ladders;
53 rungs to bell chamber, modern
ladders above
Bells: peal of eight in F sharp: Henry
Penn of Peterborough 1720 (3),
Thomas Eayre of Kettering 1761,
Edward Arnold of St Neots 1775,
John Taylor & Co. 1934 (3); oak
frame by John Taylor & Co. of
Loughborough 1934–35
Restorations and alterations:
1868–70: church restoration, architect
E. F. Law
1884–85: restoration of tower,
architect William Slater of Slater &
Carpenter
1935–36: repairs to tower, architect
William Wier of Letchworth
1989: battlements replaced
Survey date: October 2010, June 2014
Ground datum: south-west corner

EVERCREECH, ST PETER
SOMERSET
Date of tower: *c.* 1480–90
Position: west tower
Material: Doulting limestone
Steeple height: 93' 10", to flagpole
104' 9"
Tower width: 26' 6" to outside of
buttresses
Stairs: clockwise-up helical stair in
south-east corner, 4' 1" to 4' 9" dia.
stair, 4½" dia. newel; 146 steps to
roof
Bells: peal of ten in E flat: all by John
Taylor & Co. 1948; cast-iron and
oak frame
Clock: 1897
Restorations and alterations:
1825: church restoration, architect
Jesse Gane of Evercreech
1843: further church restoration
1986: South Petherton organ rebuilt,
west gallery
Survey date: April 2013
Ground datum: north-west buttress

EWERBY, ST ANDREW
LINCOLNSHIRE
Date of steeple: *c.* 1340–60
Position: engaged west tower
Material: Ancaster limestone
Height of steeple: 166' 9", to vane
171' 1"
Width of tower: 30' 2" above aisle
parapets
Spire dims: 92' 1" high, 22' 5" wide
Spire angle: 13° 47'
Squinches: single arch
Stairs: clockwise-up helical stair in
south-west corner, 2' 2" dia. stair,
7" dia. newel; 74 steps to bell
chamber
Bells: peal of ten in D: Henry Dand
of Nottingham *c.* 1590, Henry
Oldfield II of Nottingham 1616,
Henry Penn of Peterborough 1710,
Thomas Osborn of Downham
1783, John Taylor & Co. (6) 1896;
two-tier cast-iron and steel
frame John Taylor & Co. of
Loughborough 1896, overhauled
1947, 2009
Clock: Tucker of London 1867, west
skeleton face
Weathervane: 1897 by F. Coldron &
Son of Brant Broughton
Glass: west window, W. F. Dixon of
London, 1883
Restorations and alterations:
1810: spire struck by lightning and
repaired
1890–95: restored and scraped,
architect Charles Hodgson Fowler
of Durham
1908–10: spire struck by lightning
and repaired
1961–64: repairs, architect Lawrence
Bond of Grantham
Survey date: January 2011, July 2014
Ground datum: south-west buttress

EYE, ST PETER AND ST PAUL
SUFFOLK
Date of tower: *c.* 1458–85, bells hung
1488
Position: west tower
Material: flushwork: knapped flint
with ashlar stone dressings
Tower height: 107' 3", to vane 110' 5"

Tower width: 32' 3" above base
Stairs: clockwise-up helical stair
in north-east corner, 4' 7" to 3' 11"
dia. stair, 5" dia. newel; 188 steps
to roof
Bells: peal of eight in D: Richard
Brasyer II of Norwich *c.* 1499,
Miles Graye I of Colchester 1640,
John Stephens of Norwich 1721,
Pack & Chapman of Whitechapel
1779, Thomas Osborn of Downham
Market 1789 (2), Mears & Stainbank
of Whitechapel 1905 (2) and 1961,
rehung in oak frame 1962
Clock: F. Day of Eye, skeleton face
to west
Restorations and alterations:
1868–69: church restoration, architect
James K. Colling
1937–39: tower repairs, architect
Arthur B. Whittingham,
Survey date: July 2010, September
2014
Ground datum: west face of
north-west buttress

FORNCETT ST PETER, ST PETER
NORFOLK
Date of tower: *c.* 1000, 15th-century
battlements
Position: west tower
Material: coursed flint laid
in herringbone pattern
Tower height: 60' 10"
Tower width: 18' 8" diameter at base
Stairs: ancient timber flight; 26 steps
up to first platform, modern
ladders above
Bells: peal of six in F: William Brend
of Norwich 1602 (2), Thomas
Newman of Norwich 1737, John
Warner & Sons of Cripplegate
1875, John Taylor & Co. 1937 and
1982; two-tier oak frame set
diagonally by John Taylor & Co.
of Loughborough 1937
Restorations and alterations:
1832: restoration, louvres added to bell
openings
1851: render stripped from flint, under
Revd William Greive Wilson
19th century: west door surround
replaced
2005–07: tower restoration, architect
Ruth Blackman of Norwich
Survey date: September 2010
Ground datum: west door threshold

FOTHERINGHAY,
ST MARY AND ALL SAINTS
NORTHAMPTONSHIRE
Date of steeple: lower stage and
octagon *c.* 1435–45, fan vault and
middle stages *c.* 1496
Architect/mason: William Horwode,
freemason of Fotheringhay; tower
vault probably John Wastell
Contract: dated 24 September 1435,
for £300
Position: engaged west tower
Material: Stanion stone for walls and
buttresses, Weldon stone for
windows, King's Cliffe stone in
parapet, Lincolnshire limestone
rubble (British Geological Survey)
Steeple height: 115' 8" to finial 125' 7"
Tower width: 36' 2" above base
Lantern dims: 44' 9" high, 25' 1" wide
Squinches: five corbels

Stairs: access across north aisle roof,
clockwise-up helical stair in
north-west corner to bell chamber,
anticlockwise-up to octagon floor,
ladder to octagon roof, 4' 10" to 4' 2"
dia. stairs, 5" dia. newels; from aisle
roof 56 steps to octagon floor
Bells: peal of six in F sharp: Edward
Newcombe of Leicester 1595,
Tobias Norris I of Stamford 1614,
Thomas Norris of Stamford 1634,
Mears & Co. of Whitechapel 1860,
Whitechapel Bell Foundry Ltd.
1989 (2); Sanctus bell Thomas
Mears II of Stamford 1817; steel
frame 1989
Weathervane: 1819, designed by Miss
Linton
Restorations and alterations:
1882: restoration, architect Henry
Milnes Townsend
1911–13: repairs to buttresses, architect
Temple Moore
1967: repairs, architect Lawrence
Bond of Grantham
1981–90: restoration of bell and
ringing chambers
Survey date: July 2010, August 2014
Ground datum: centre of west
elevation

GRANTHAM, ST WULFRAM
LINCOLNSHIRE
Date of steeple: *c.* 1280–1320
Position: engaged west tower
Material: Lincolnshire limestone
Steeple height: 274' 0", to vane 283' 7"
Tower width: 42' 2" to outside of
buttresses at aisle roof level
Spire dims: 138' 2" high, 25' 1" wide
Spire angle: 10° 17'
Squinches: two concentric arches
Stairs: anticlockwise-up helical stair
in south-west corner, 6' 4" to 6' 1"
dia. stair, 7" dia. newel; 210 steps to
parapet
Bells: peal of ten in D flat: all by John
Taylor & Co. of Loughborough
1946, two additional trebles by
John Taylor Bellfounders Ltd.
2004, iron and steel frame possibly
1946
Clock: mechanism by Gillett & Bland
of Croydon 1876
Glass: west window commemorating
Revd Charles Bradley of Elton,
1852
Restorations and alterations:
1640: repairs to bell frame, stair built
to a ringing gallery below the
tower
1652: lightning strike
1664: lightning damage repaired
1752: ringing gallery removed
1797: lightning strike, first conductor
fitted, spire capped with a
millstone
1818: weathervane installed
1865–69, 1877: church restoration,
spire restored, architect Sir George
Gilbert Scott, cost £21,428
1883: lightning strike
1884: top of spire rebuilt, architect
John Oldrid Scott of London
1921: four lowest statues added to
tower west front
1945–47: spire restored, 20' rebuilt
1956: eight upper statues added to
tower west front

2014–15: top 40' of spire rebuilt,
architect Graham Cook
Survey date: March and August 2011,
July 2015
Ground datum: west door threshold

HECKINGTON, ST ANDREW
LINCOLNSHIRE
Date of steeple: c. 1345–60
Position: west tower
Material: Ancaster limestone
Steeple height: 176' 2", to vane 183' 6"
Tower width: 34' 7" to outside of
buttresses
Spire dims: 82' 4" high, 20' 0" wide
Spire angle: 13° 23'
Squinches: five corbels within a
single arch
Stairs: clockwise-up helical stair in
south-east corner, 5' 8" dia. stair,
6" dia. newel; 139 steps to parapet,
140 steps to spire base
Bells: peal of eight in D: George I
Oldfield 1633 and 1651, Henry II
Hanson 1773, Thomas II Mears
1824, John Warner & Sons 1859 (2),
Mears & Stainbank 1880 (2)
Clock: B. Cooke of Hull 1872
Restorations and alterations:
1867: church restoration, architects
Kirk and Parry
1887–88: restoration, architect
J. Fowler of Louth
1952–77: repairs, architects Bond
& Read
Survey date: June 2013
Ground datum: west face of
south-west buttress

HIGHAM FERRERS, ST MARY
NORTHAMPTONSHIRE
Date of tower: c. 1250–70
Date of spire: c. 1340
Position: west tower
Material: Northamptonshire
limestone
Steeple height: 173' 11", to vane 181' 2"
Tower width: 32' 8" to outside of
buttresses
Spire dims: 103' 0" high, 20' 11" wide
Spire angle: 11° 48'
Squinches: six corbels within two
arches
Stairs: clockwise-up helical stair in
north-east corner, 4' 7" dia. stair,
5½" dia. newel; 50 steps to clock
chamber; clockwise-up helical
stair in north-west coner, 4' 6" dia.
stair, 5½" dia. newel; 68 steps to
bell chamber
Bells: peal of ten in E flat: Hugh I
Watts 1611, Hugh II Watts 1633
and 1636, Robert Taylor 1820,
John Taylor & Co. 1892 (4) and
2014 (2); cast-iron and steel frame
by John Taylor & Co. 2014
Clock: John Smith & Sons of Derby
1895, replaced 1969
Restorations and alterations:
1631: spire collapse
1631–32: reconstruction of steeple,
mason Richard Atkins, cost £135
c. 1857: restoration, architect William
Slater
Survey date: August, September
2015
Ground datum: west face of
south-west buttress

INGATESTONE,
ST EDMUND AND ST MARY
ESSEX
Date of tower: c. 1500
Position: west tower
Material: red brick
Tower height: 82' 9", to vane 89' 4",
to flagpole 101' 6"
Tower width: 33' 6" above base
Stairs: anticlockwise-up helical stair
in south-east turret, 6' 0" to 5' 4" dia.
stair, 9" dia. newel; 112 steps to roof
Bells: peal of six in G: Peter Hawkes
of Essex 1610, Miles Graye III 1660,
Lester & Pack of Whitechapel 1758,
John Warner & Sons of Cripplegate,
London 1875, Mears & Stainbank
of Whitechapel 1923 and 1963, oak
frame 1875; bells rehung 1876 and
by Alfred Bowell of Ipswich 1900
Clock: electric mechanism 1970,
skeleton face to west
Restorations and alterations:
1884: damaged by Colchester
earthquake 22 April
1866–67: general restoration, bell
chamber floor and gallery
removed, architect Frederic
Chancellor of Chelmsford &
London, cost £1,600
1905: interior scraped and cleaned
1908: restoration of tower by Messrs
Brown of Braintree, cost £470,
scaffold £80
1966: Victorian lobby removed from
tower
Survey date: September 2010,
September 2014
Ground datum: west door threshold

KETTERING, ST PETER AND ST PAUL
NORTHAMPTONSHIRE
Date of steeple: c. 1440–75
Position: west tower
Material: Barnack or Weldon stone
Steeple height: 178' 6", to vane 186' 0"
Tower width: 34' 3" above base
Spire dims: 88' 7" high, 19' 4" wide
Spire angle: 12° 4'
Squinches: five corbels
Stairs: clockwise-up helical stair in
south-west corner, 5' 4" to 3' 9" dia.
stair, 8" dia. newel; 118 steps to
parapet
Bells: peal of twelve in E flat: all
bells and steel bell frame by
Whitechapel Bell Foundry Ltd.
2004; service bell by Thomas
Eayre I of Kettering 1722
Clock: skeleton clock faces to all
elevations
Restorations and alterations:
1887: spire restored, 31' rebuilt, height
increased by 2'
1889–93: general restoration, bell
chamber floor raised, galleries
removed, architects Arthur
Blomfield & Sons of London
Survey date: June 2010, September
2014
Ground datum: south-west buttress

KETTON, ST MARY THE VIRGIN
RUTLAND
Date of tower: lower part c. 1175–90,
tower arches and bell stage
c. 1232–40, church consecrated
1240

Date of spire: c. 1320
Position: central crossing tower
Material: Barnack stone
Steeple height: 144' 2", to vane 151' 0"
Tower width: 20' 3" to outside of piers
Spire dims: 84' 10" high, 21' 4" wide
Spire angle: 13° 46'
Squinches: single arch
Stairs: clockwise-up helical stair in
south wall of south aisle; 29 steps
leading to cantilevered timber
stair, 13 steps to ringing chamber,
probably all by George Gilbert
Scott 1862; modern ladder to bell
chamber
Bells: peal of six, restricted to
chiming only: unknown 1598,
Hugh Watts of Leicester 1601,
Newcombe of Leicester 1606,
Henry Oldfield of Nottingham
1609, Henry Penn of Peterborough
1713, unknown 1748; oak frame
with carillon mechanism
Restorations and alterations:
1860–62: church restoration, architect
George Gilbert Scott
1863: restoration of chancel, architect
T. G. Jackson of Stamford and
London
Survey date: May 2010, August 2014
Ground datum: corner between north
transept and chancel

KINGSTON ST MARY, ST MARY
SOMERSET
Date of tower: c. 1470–90
Position: west tower
Material: Keuper new red sandstone
Steeple height: 88' 6", to vane 94' 1"
Tower width: 27' 11"
Stairs: clockwise-up helical stair in
north-east corner, 5' 3" to 4' 8" dia.
stair, 6" dia. newel; 91 steps to roof
Bells: peal of six in E: Bristol foundry
c. 1400 and c. 1450, George Purdue
1622, William Wiseman 1634,
Thomas II Wroth 1730, Llewellins
& James 1876; oak frame,
overhauled and rehung by Mears
& Stainbank 1968
Restorations and alterations:
Mid-19th century: west gallery
removed
1867: organ chamber added
1952: tower reroofed
1976–78: tower restored
Survey date: May 2013
Ground datum: south-east buttress

LAUGHTON-EN-LE-MORTHEN,
ALL SAINTS
YORKSHIRE, WEST RIDING
Date of tower: started c. 1377, upper
stage c. 1430
Date of spire: c. 1430
Position: semi-engaged west tower
Material: Anston Magnesian
limestone, Rotherham red
sandstone internally within upper
levels of tower, Slade Hooton stone
to top of spire
Steeple height: 167' 10", to vane 175' 3"
Tower width: 31' 5" to outside
of piers
Spire dims: 89' 0" high, 17' 3" wide
Spire angle: 10° 57'
Squinches: seven corbels
Stairs: clockwise-up helical stair in
south-west corner, 4' 4" to 4' 0"

dia. stair, 6" dia. newel; 94 steps
to parapet
Bells: peal of three in F sharp,
chiming only: Chesterfield
foundry c. 1500, Daniel Hedderly
of Lincoln c. 1704, William
Oldfield I of Doncaster c. 1621, one
additional 18-inch bell; oak frame,
bells rehung by John Taylor & Co.
2002
Clock: possibly by William Potts
& Sons of Leeds, plain face to east
Restorations and alterations:
Mid-19th century: gallery below
tower removed
Late 19th century: possible restoration
by George Gilbert Scott recorded
in *The Builder*
1895: spire restored, 14' replaced, ties
replaced with copper
1948–51: repairs to spire and
pinnacles, architect George Pace
1956: west window reglazed
1974: tower slate louvres replaced with
timber, architect George Pace of
York
1989: steeple restored, architect Peter
Pace, R. G. Sims of York
Survey date: August 2011, July 2014
Ground datum: south-west buttress

LAVENHAM, ST PETER AND ST PAUL
SUFFOLK
Date of steeple: lower part c. 1486–95,
upper part c. 1518–25
Architect/mason: Simon Clark with
John Wastell
Position: west tower
Material: flushwork: knapped flint
with Casterton stone dressings
from Rutland
Tower height: 137' 8", to flagpole
165' 7"
Tower width: 53' 6" above base
Stairs: clockwise-up helical stair in
north-east corner, 7' 7" dia. stair,
5½" dia. newel; 198 steps to roof
Bells: peal of eight in D flat: Richard
Bowler of Colchester 1603 (2),
Miles Graye I of Colchester 1625,
Henry Pleasant of Sudbury
1702 and 1703, William Dobson
of Downham Market 1811 (2),
Charles & George Mears of
Whitechapel 1846, steel and
cast-iron frame by John Taylor
& Co. of Loughborough 1965
Clock: mechanism by Thomas Watt
1775, electronic winding 1968,
no external face
Glass: west window, life and death
of St Peter, 1862
Restorations and alterations:
1861–67: restoration, tower gallery
removed, architect Francis C.
Penrose of London
1908–11: general repairs, architect
William Caroe
1932–33: tower repairs, architect
Frank Howard
1957: tower roof repairs
1980–81: tower repairs, architects
Whitworth & Hall of Bury
St Edmunds
Survey date: August 2010, September
2014
Ground datum: south-west buttress

LEIGH-ON-MENDIP, ST GILES
SOMERSET
Date of tower: *c.* 1475–90
Position: west tower
Material: Doulting limestone
Steeple height: 93' 8", to flagpole
104' 9"
Tower width: 28' 0"
Stairs: clockwise-up helical stair in
north-east corner, 4' 3" to 3' 6" dia.
stair, 5" to 4" dia. newel; 110 steps
to roof
Bells: peal of six in F sharp: Thomas
I. Bilbie 1757 (4), John Warner &
Sons 1858, Llewellins & James 1910;
oak bell frame, overhauled by
Llewellins & James 1910
Clock: late 18th-century faceless clock
restored in 2004–05
Restorations and alterations:
not known
Survey date: April 2013
Ground datum: west end of south
elevation

LONG SUTTON, ST MARY
LINCOLNSHIRE
Date of tower: lower stages *c.* 1200,
third stage *c.* 1260
Date of spire: slightly later
Position: detached tower
Material: Barnack stone
Steeple height: 148' 11", to vane 157' 11"
Tower width: 31' 2" above base
Spire dims: 85' 8" high, 25' 1" wide
Spire angle: 16' 10'
Squinches: single arch
Stairs: clockwise-up helical stair in
south-west corner, 4' 6" to 4' 1" dia.
stair, 7" dia. newel; 106 steps to
spire floor
Bells: peal of eight in F sharp, bells
and steel and cast-iron frame by
John Taylor & Co. of
Loughborough 1934
Clock: plain diamond face to east
and west of spire
Restorations and alterations:
1865–67: church restored, architects
Slater & Carpenter
1873: tower and porches restored,
architect William (Bassett) Smith
of London
1895: restorations by
W. & C. A. Bassett Smith
1972: spire restored, cost £40,000,
27 tons of lead
Survey date: February 2011, June 2014
Ground datum: centre of south
elevation

LOUTH, ST JAMES
LINCOLNSHIRE
Date of tower: *c.* 1455–1501
Date of spire: 1501 to 13 September
1515
Cost of spire: £305 7s. 5d.
Architect/mason: John Cole
(1501–05), Christopher Scune
(1505–15), John Tempas (1515)
Material: lower tower Yorkshire
Magnesian limestone, upper tower
and spire Ancaster limestone
from several quarries
Position: engaged west tower
Steeple height: 287' 6", to vane 293' 1"
Tower width: 48' 1" at base
Spire dims: 138' 11" high, 22' 6" wide
Spire angle: 9' 5'

Squinches: four concentric arches
Stairs: clockwise-up helical stair in
south-west corner, 5' 1" to 4' 2" dia.
stair, 6" to 5" dia. newel; 199 steps
to parapet
Bells: peal of eight in D: Daniel
& John Hedderly of Lincoln
1726 (5), John Taylor & Co. of
Loughborough 1909 (1) and 1953
(2); rehung by John Taylor & Co.
1953 in oak frame by James
Copland 1819
Clock: mechanism by Leonard Hall
of Louth 1901, no external face
Glass: west window, 'Te Deum',
Hardman, 1874
Restorations and alterations:
1558: 'grete tempeste' shattered
capstone and 18' of spire, repairs
cost £34 13s. 7d.
1587: spire struck by lightning
1588: spire restored for £39 3s. 4d.
1627–28: spire repaired by Thomas
Egglefield
1634: upper spire blown down,
repaired by Thomas Turner for
£81 7s.
1805: restoration of belfry windows,
architect Thoms Espin
1824: new weathercock
1843: spire struck by lightning
1844: spire rebuilt and raised by 7',
architect Lewis N. Cottingham
of London
1860 and 1868–69: church restoration,
architect James Fowler of Louth
1936–38: restoration of the spire,
architect Robert Godfrey of
Lincoln
2008: west window restored
Survey date: February 2011, July 2014
Ground datum: south-west buttress

LOWICK, ST PETER
NORTHAMPTONSHIRE
Date of steeple: *c.* 1466–79
Position: west tower
Material: Lincolnshire limestone
Steeple height: 95' 10", to vane 105' 7"
Tower width: 26' 5" above base
Lantern dims: 28' 9" high, 17' 2" wide
Squinches: two corbels within a flat
single arch
Stairs: clockwise-up helical stair
in north-west corner, 4' 4" to
4' 0" dia. stair, 6" dia. newel;
67 steps to bell chamber, ladders
to parapet and roof
Bells: peal of six in F: possibly
Richard Wood of Newcombe or
Leicester *c.* 1540, Hugh Watts of
Leicester 1595 (2), Hugh Watts II
of Leicester 1619, John Taylor & Co.
of Loughborough 1884 and 1896;
oak frame probably 1884 replacing
one of 1682
Clock: mechanism 1891, skeleton face
to south
Restorations and alterations:
1868–72: church restoration,
architects Slater & Carpenter
of London
1880–87: church restoration, architects
Thompson & Ruddle
1973–75: repairs, architect Eric
Roberts, Brown Panter & Pts
Survey date: June 2010, June 2014
Ground datum: south-west buttress

LUDLOW, ST LAURENCE
SHROPSHIRE
Date of tower *c.* 1453–71, master
mason from 1469 Clement Mason,
bells hung in 1469
Position: central tower
Material: reddish-brown medium-
grained local sandstone (British
Geological Survey)
Steeple height: 157' 0", to vane 163' 1"
Tower width: 36' 11" to outside of
western piers
Stairs: anticlockwise-up helical stair
in north-east corner, 4' 9" dia. stair,
5½" dia. newel; 201 steps to roof
Bells: peal of ten in E: Abraham II
Rudhall of Gloucester 1732 (5),
Gillett & Johnston of Croydon 1935
(2), Whitechapel Bell Foundry
2008 (3); three carillion bells,
Abraham II Rudhall 1732,
unknown 1824, Whitechapel Bell
Foundry 2008; overhauled and
rehung in oak and cast-iron frame
by Whitechapel Bell Foundry 2008
Clock and carillion: 1638, replaced by
modern computerized mechanism
Restorations and alterations:
1859–69: church restoration, architect
George Gilbert Scott
1889–91: tower restoration, architect
Sir A. Blomfield
Survey date: March and May 2013
Ground datum: north-west buttress

MOULTON, ALL SAINTS
LINCOLNSHIRE
Date of steeple: *c.* 1380 onwards
Position: west tower
Material: Barnack stone
Steeple height: 157' 6", to vane 162' 4"
Tower width: 30' 1" above base
Spire dims: 76' 10" high, 15' 2" wide
Spire angle: 10' 55'
Squinches: two corbels within a
single arch
Stairs: clockwise-up helical stair in
north-east corner, 4' 5" dia. stair,
5" dia. newel; 104 steps to parapet
Bells: peal of six in E: Tobias Norris I
of Stamford 1620, Joseph Eayre of
St Neots 1769, John Briant of
Hertford 1805, John Taylor & Co.
of Loughborough 1911, 1911 and
1923; cast-iron and steel frame by
John Taylor & Co. 1850, overhauled
1951
Clock: skeleton clock face to west
Restorations and alterations:
1867: restoration, west gallery
removed, ground floor raised,
architect William Smith of
London
1904: restoration of steeple
Survey date: June 2011, June 2014
Ground datum: centre of south
elevation

NEWARK-ON-TRENT,
ST MARY MAGDALENE
NOTTINGHAMSHIRE
Date of steeple: lower stage
c. 1220–45, upper stage and
spire *c.* 1315–38
Architect/mason: possibly
Alexander II, master of Lincoln
Cathedral, for the original bell
stage
Position: engaged west tower

Material: Ancaster limestone
Steeple height: 231' 11", to vane 237' 6"
Tower width: 35' 4" above base
Spire dims: 120' 3" high, 25' 7" wide
Spire angle: 12' 1'
Squinches: seven corbels within a
single arch
Stairs: clockwise-up helical stair
in north-west corner, 5' 4" to 4' 0"
dia. stair, 6" dia. newel; 189 steps
to parapet, 192 to spire floor
threshold
Bells: peal of ten in C: first complete
peal of ten installed by John Taylor
& Co. of Loughborough 1842 (9)
and 1846; cast-iron and steel
frame by Mears & Stainbank
(Whitechapel Foundry) 1913,
rehung by John Taylor & Co. 1954
Clock: mechanism by Joyce of
Whitchurch 1898, electrical
conversion by John Smith & Sons
of Derby 1971; skeleton clock faces:
9' 0" dia. to south, 7' 0" dia. to north,
east and west
Glass: west window, 'Perfect
Priesthood on Earth', 1887
Restorations and alterations:
1570: spire repointed
1763: weathercock installed
1793: finial renewed
1852–56: church restoration, architect
George Gilbert Scott, cost £6,000
1869: tower restoration, architect
George Gilbert Scott
1913: spire refurbished
1961–65, 1976: church restorations
2011–14: weathercock removed,
restored and refixed
Survey date: March 2011, April
2015
Ground datum: north-west buttress

NORTH PETHERTON, ST MARY
SOMERSET
Date of tower: *c.* 1505–14, parapet
1704
Position: west tower
Material: blue lias with hamstone
dressings
Steeple height: 111' 5", to vane 115' 6"
Tower width: 32' 9" to outside of
buttresses
Stairs: clockwise-up helical stair in
south-east corner, 5' 8" to 4' 9" dia.
stair, 5½" dia. newel; 101 steps to
roof
Bells: peal of six in E flat: all Mears
& Stainbank 1895; retuned at
Whitechapel Bell Foundry and
rehung in 18th-century oak frame
by Nicholson Engineering Ltd.
2006
Clock: Pyke of Bridgewater 1809
Glass: west window, Sir Henry
Holiday, 1913
Restorations:
1838–39: tower arch reopened,
architect Richard Carver of
Taunton
1878–84: repairs, architects Champion
& Spencer
1909: tower restoration, architect
Charles King
1989: tower restoration
2008–09: tower pinnacle restoration
Survey date: April 2013
Ground datum: south-east buttress

NORTH RAUCEBY, ST PETER
LINCOLNSHIRE
Date of tower: lower part *c.* 1180,
    upper part *c.* 1220
Date of spire: *c.* 1220 (vicarage
    established 1229)
Position: west tower
Material: Ancaster stone
Steeple height: 107′ 3″, to vane 111′ 3″
Tower width: 24′ 3″ outside of
    buttresses
Spire dims: 56′ 7″ high, 21′ 8″ wide
Spire angle: 21° 2′
Squinches: single small arch and splay
Stairs: clockwise-up helical stair in
    south-west corner, 4′ 10″ dia. stair,
    6″ dia. newel; 100 steps to spire floor
Bells: peal of five in F: Henry II
    Oldfield of Nottingham 1619,
    Paul Hutton (Doves) or Henry II
    Oldfield of Nottingham (bell
    chamber listing) 1621, Tobias III
    Norris of Stamford 1684, Mears
    & Stainbank 1935 (2); bells retuned
    and rehung 1909, oak frame
    overhauled by Mears & Stainbank
    1935
Restorations and alterations:
1853, 1865: restorations, architect
    S. S. Teulon
1860: lightning conductor by Lewis
    of Manchester
1907–09: tower restored, floor added
    in spire
1981–82: tower restoration, architect
    Bond & Read of Grantham, cost
    £8,000
Survey date: September 2011, July 2014
Ground datum: centre of north
    elevation

PATRINGTON, ST PATRICK
YORKSHIRE, EAST RIDING
Date of tower: *c.* 1325–50, top stage
    c. 1368–71
Date of spire: *c.* 1368–71, flying
    buttresses later
Architect/mason: possibly Robert
    Patrington for upper tower and
    spire
Position: central crossing tower
Material: Yorkshire Magnesian
    limestone
Steeple height: 174′ 10″, to vane 180′ 5″
Tower width: 25′ 10″ to outside of piers
Spire dims: 96′ 8″ high, 19′ 3″ wide
Spire angle: 11° 2′
Squinches: three corbels within two
    arches, redundant single squinch
    arches at lower level
Stairs: access to ringing chamber
    from crawlway through north
    transept roof, clockwise-up helical
    stair in north-east corner of
    ringing chamber, 3′ 10″ dia. stair, 6″
    dia. newel
Bells: peal of eight in F sharp:
    Nottingham foundry *c.* 1570,
    George Oldfield I of Nottingham
    c. 1674, John Taylor & Co. of
    Loughborough 1906 (3), 1948 (2)
    and 1887; cast-iron and steel frame
    by John Taylor 1906 and 1948
Clock: William Potts of Leeds 1893,
    cost £100, skeleton clock face to
    north, east and west
Restorations and alterations:
1715: spire repointed by John Burdas,
    bricklayer

1810: top 17′ 6″ of spire rebuilt,
    cost £199 19*s.* 6*d.*
1833: north-east pinnacle blown
    down, 21 August
1866, 1885: church restorations
1884: lightning strike, 26′ rebuilt,
    cost £130
1892–94: tower repairs, architects
    Smith & Brodrick of Hull
c. 1946: spire repointed
2004: spire repointed, Stone Technical
    Services of Darlington
2008: repairs to spire and pinnacles
    by Stone Technical Services
    following earthquake damage
Survey date: April 2011, July 2014
Ground datum: centre of south
    elevation

RAUNDS, ST PETER
NORTHAMPTONSHIRE
Date of tower: *c.* 1230, 15th-century
    vault
Date of spire: started *c.* 1250
Position: west tower
Material: Raunds limestone (British
    Geological Survey)
Steeple height: 175′ 8″, to vane 184′ 1″
Tower width: 26′ 10″ above base
Spire dims: 105′ 9″ high, 27′ 0″ wide
Spire angle: 13° 44′
Squinches: four corbels within a
    single arch
Stairs: clockwise-up helical stair in
    south-west corner, 4′ 9″ to 4′ 2″ dia.
    stair, 7″ dia. newel; 99 steps to spire
    floor
Bells: peal of eight in E flat: Henry
    Penn of Peterborough 1723, Thomas
    Eayre of Kettering 1732 (2), John
    Warner & Sons of Cripplegate 1879,
    John Taylor & Co. of Loughborough
    1898 (3) and 1949; cast-iron bell
    frame by John Taylor & Co. 1898
Clock: 15th-century 24-hour clock,
    internal, with painted clock face
    to nave
Restorations and alterations:
1826: lightning strike 31 July, 30′ fell,
    rebuilt by Charles Squirhill
1873–74: church restoration, west
    gallery removed, tower arch
    opened up, paintings revealed,
    architect Sir George Gilbert Scott
1895: storm damage, 11′ of spire rebuilt
1923: spire restored
Survey date: December 2010, June
    2014
Ground datum: south-west buttress

REDENHALL, ST MARY
NORFOLK
Date of tower: *c.* 1460–1520
Position: west tower
Material: flushwork: knapped flint
    with limestone ashlar dressings
Tower height: 106′ 2″, to vane 111′ 3″
Tower width: 31′ 9″ above base
Stairs: clockwise-up helical stair in
    south-east corner, 6′ 3″ to 4′ 11″ dia.
    stair, 5″ dia. newel; 120 steps to
    roof
Bells: peal of eight in D: Bury
    St Edmunds foundry 1514, Thomas
    Draper of Thetford 1588, John
    Draper of Thetford 1621, Richard
    Phelps of Whitechapel 1736 (3),
    Alfred Bowell of Ipswich 1924 (2);
    oak bell frame, restored since 1980

Restorations and alterations:
1616: struck by lightening, iron ties
    installed
1680: north-west pinnacle struck
    by lightning
1681: pinnacle rebuilt by masons John
    Fenton and Edmund Knights
1834: pinnacle struck by lightning
    and rebuilt
1842–43: upper tower screen and
    organ installed, architect John
    Brown of Norwich
1858: church restoration, architect
    Richard M. Phipson of Ipswich
1897: organ gallery modified, new
    tower screen, architect J. Arthur
    Reeve of London
1980: tower restoration
Survey date: July 2010, September
    2014
Ground datum: centre of south
    elevation

ST CUTHBERT, WELLS
SOMERSET
Date of tower: *c.* 1385–1430, probably
    by William Wynford
Position: west tower
Material: Doulting limestone
Steeple height: 150′ 6″, to vane 154′ 10″
Tower width: 43′ 6″ to outside of
    buttresses
Stairs: clockwise-up helical stair in
    noth-east corner, 5′ 7″ to 4′ 11″ dia.
    stair, 5″ dia. newel; 168 steps to
    roof
Bells: peal of eight in D flat: Thomas
    Purdue 1683, William Bilbie
    1785 and 1787, John Taylor & Co.
    1887 (3) and 1888, Eijsbouts 1992;
    overhauled by Eayre & Smith 1992,
    oak and cast-iron frame
Restorations and alterations:
1561: original central tower collapsed
1960: tower restored
Survey date: April 2013
Ground datum: west face of
    south-west buttress

ST MARY, OXFORD
OXFORDSHIRE
Date of tower: *c.* 1275–1300
    by Richard de Abingdon
Date of spire: *c.* 1315–25
Position: north tower
Material: Oxfordshire limestone,
    possibly Tainton, 1896 repairs in
    Clipsham stone from Rutland with
    Purbeck stone to apex of spire
Steeple height: 191′ 4″, to vane 200′ 5″
Tower width: 43′ 4″ outside of
    buttresses
Spire dims: 105′ 8″ high, 26′ 7″ wide
Spire angle: 14° 28″
Squinches: three concentric arches
Stairs: clockwise-up helical stair in
    north-west corner from ringing
    chamber to parapet, 5′ 2″ to 4′ 7″ dia.
    stair, 6″ dia. newel; 60 steps from
    ground to ringing chamber,
    127 steps to parapet
Bells: peal of six in D: William Yare
    1611, Robert III, Thomas III and
    William Newcombe 1612 (2), Ellis I
    Knight 1639 and 1641, Abraham II
    Rudhall 1731, John Taylor & Co.
    1894; oak & cast-iron frame,
    overhauled by Whites of Appleton
    2012

Restorations and alterations:
Before 1586: spire pinnacles severely
    damaged
c. 1607–10: steeple repaired and 'thick
    set with pinnacles'
1666–69: steeple repairs, university
    donated £20
1675–66: major repairs to church,
    mason Robinson
1692–93: university gave £20 for
    steeple repairs
1734: weathercock fell
1791: tower damaged by wind
1808: top of spire rebuilt, weathercock
    repaired and conductor added,
    mason Hudson, cost over £300
1848–52: tower repaired, architects
    J. C. & C. Buckler
1856: tower considered unsafe
1861–62: repairs, architect George
    Gilbert Scott
1892–96: top 48′ of spire rebuilt,
    statues repaired or replaced,
    pinnacles replaced, architect
    T. G. Jackson
Survey date: July 2013
Ground datum: east end of north-east
    buttress

ST MARY, STAMFORD
LINCOLNSHIRE
Date of tower: *c.* 1240, vault after
    1461
Date of spire: *c.* 1320
Position: west tower
Material: Barnack stone
Steeple height: 168′ 1″, to vane 173′ 8″
Tower width: 29′ 0″ above base
Spire dims: 90′ 3″ high, 26′ 7″ wide
Spire angle: 16° 29′
Squinches: six corbels within a single
    arch
Stairs: clockwise-up helical stair in
    south-west corner, 5′ 10″ to 5′ 6″ dia.
    stair, 8″ dia. newel; 120 steps to
    spire base
Bells: peal of eight in E, disabled:
    Tobias Norris I of Nottingham
    1625–26 (3), Thomas Norris of
    Stamford 1638, Henry Penn of
    Peterborough 1727, Thomas Mears I
    of Whitechapel 1802 (3); oak bell
    frame 1635 and 1802
Clock: skeleton clock face to south
    and west
Restorations and alterations:
1842: spire struck by lightening,
    top rebuilt
1865: lightning conductor installed
1870–73: structural repairs to tower,
    architect T. G. Jackson
1911–13: tower restoration, architect
    Henry F. Traylen of Leicester
    and Stamford, consultant Sir
    T. G. Jackson of London
Survey date: February 2011,
    September 2014
Ground datum: south-west buttress

ST MARY MAGDALENE, TAUNTON
SOMERSET
Date of tower: 1488–1505, Somerset
    tracery added 1514
Position: west tower
Material: 19th-century reconstruction
    in Keuper red sandstone with
    hamstone dressings, originally in
    friable grey sandstone
Steeple height: 157′ 9″, to vane 164′ 10″

Tower width: 27' 11" to outside of
buttresses
Stairs: clockwise-up helical stair in
north-east corner, 5' 11" to 5' 3" dia.
stair, 6" dia. newel; 160 steps to roof
Bells: peal of twelve in D flat: Thomas
I Bilbie 1748, Thomas II Mears 1816
and 1840 (2), George Mears 1861
and 1865, John Taylor & Co. 1885
(3), Mears & Stainbank 1922 (2) and
1955; oak and cast-iron frame by
Mears & Stainbank
Glass: west window, 'Last Judgement',
Alexander Gibb, 1862
Restorations:
1745: parapet rebuilt
1843–44: church restoration,
Benjamin Ferry and Mr R. Carver
1856–62: rebuilt, architects George
Gilbert Scott and Benjamin
Ferrey
Survey date: May 2013
Ground datum: west door

ST MARY REDCLIFFE, BRISTOL
SOMERSET (until 1373)
Date of steeple: *c.* 1270 to *c.* 1335
Date of tower vault: 15th century
Position: north-west tower
Material: Dundry limestone (British
Geological Survey)
Steeple height: 261' 11", to vane 274' 0"
Tower width: 37' 8" on west elevation
Spire dims: 155' 8" high, 27' 0" wide
Spire angle: 9° 23'
Squinches: seven concentric arches
Stairs: from gallery clockwise-up
helical stair in south-west corner
to ringing chamber, then in
south-east corner to parapet, stairs
in three other corners starting
from bell chamber; 5' 3" to 5' 0"
dia. stairs, 6" dia. newels; 53 steps
from ground to ringing chamber,
161 to parapet
Bells: peal of twelve in B, with sharp
treble and flat sixth: Roger I
Purdue 1622, Thomas I Bilbie 1763,
John Taylor & Co. 1903 (9), 1951,
1970 and 2012; steel and cast-iron
frame
Restorations and alterations:
1445: spire struck by lightning
leaving stump
15th-century: stump finished with
Bath stone parpet
1846–72: church restoration, architect
George Godwin
1870–72: upper spire rebuilt
Survey date: July and September 2013
Ground datum: north face of
north-west buttress

ST MICHAEL, COVENTRY
WARWICKSHIRE
Date of tower: 1373–94, possibly by
Robert Skillyngton, bells hung
before 1429
Date of spire: *c.* 1433
Position: west tower
Material: Red Warwickshire
sandstone, refaced in 1883–90 with
Runcorn stone
Steeple height: 284' 4", to vane 290' 1"
Tower width: 40' 6" including
buttresses
Spire dims: 152' 9" high, 23' 6"
including octagon
Spire angle: 9° 21'

Squinches: ribbed vault within a
single arch
Stairs: clockwise-up helical stair in
south-east corner, 5' 7" dia. stair,
5½" dia. newel; 180 steps to parapet
Bells: peal of twelve in D flat: Gillett
& Johnston 1927, steel frame John
Taylor & Co. of Loughborough 1987
Restorations and alterations:
1793: tower strengthened, bells
rehung
1818: condition poor, bell ringing
suspended
1849: galleries removed, architect
George Gilbert Scott
1851: condition poor, bell ringing
suspended
1883–90: steeple restoration, architect
John Oldrid Scott
1895: bells rehung following
restoration
1918: raised to cathedral status
1940: body of church bombed,
14 November
Survey date: September 2013
Ground datum: east end of north
elevation

ST NICHOLAS, NEWCASTLE-UPON-TYNE
NORTHUMBERLAND
Date of steeple: *c.* 1460–1515
Position: engaged west tower
Material: Northumberland sandstone
Steeple height: 194' 2", to vane 203' 5"
Tower width: 40' 11" above base
Crown dimensions: 81' 4" high, 35' 5"
wide to outside of buttresses
Stairs: clockwise-up helical stair in
north-west corner, 5' 6" to 4' 3" dia.
stair, 6" dia. newel; 163 steps to roof
Bells: peal of twelve in D flat: John
Taylor & Co. 1892 (9), 1914 (2), 1928,
with extra bells 1914 and 1999,
and clock bell 1891; unused bells
William Dawe of London *c.* 1385
(3), York foundry *c.* 1425 (2);
three-tier iron and oak frame
Clock: mechanism 1761, rebuilt by
William Potts & Sons of Leeds
1895; gabled clock face to north
and south, probably by Sir George
Gilbert Scott
Restorations and alterations:
1608: spire rebuilt
1645: siege damage by Scots repaired
1723: Newcastle Corporation fund
steeple repairs
1777: lighting conductor fixed,
pinnacle rebuilt, architect
Mr Wooler
1790: one weathervane blown down
and refixed
1795: steeple repaired, copper vane
fixed, architect Mr Stephenson
1823: two weathervanes blown down
and refixed
1838: south buttresses and north and
south porches added, architects
John and Benjamin Green of
Newcastle
1867–76: tower repaired, north piers
underpinned, architect Sir George
Gilbert Scott
1882: church raised to cathedral status
1895–98: spire restored, architects
Oliver & Leeson of Newcastle
Survey date: April 2011
Ground datum: lowest corner of
south-west tower buttress

SALLE, ST PETER AND ST PAUL
NORFOLK
Date of tower: *c.* 1413–49, parapet
c. 1511
Position: west tower
Material: flint with Barnack stone
dressings
Tower height: 130' 5"
Tower width: 38' 7" above base
Stairs: clockwise-up helical stair in
south-west corner, 5' 11" to 5' 1" dia.
stair, 5" dia. newel; 129 steps to roof
Bells: peal of eight in F: Edmund
de Lynn of Kings Lynn *c.* 1353,
Richard Baxter of Norwich *c.* 1420,
Charles Newman of Norwich 1698,
Thomas Mears II of Whitechapel
1836 (2), Charles & George Mears
of Whitechapel 1852, Mears &
Stainbank of Whitechapel 1912 (2),
oak frame
Clock: solid faces to east and west
Restorations and alterations:
1910–12: general restoration funded
by Sir Alfred Jodrell, Sir Woolmer
White and Duleep Singh
1957: south-east pinnacle on tower
replaced
1962–63: repairs, architect Francis
Swindells of Edward Boardman
& Sons of Norwich
Survey date: September 2010,
September 2014
Ground datum: west door threshold

SOUTHWOLD, ST EDMUND
SUFFOLK
Date of tower: *c.* 1440–61
Position: west tower
Architect/mason: Richard Russell of
Dunwich (d. 1441) in lower stages
Material: flushwork: knapped flint,
Magnesian limestone dressings
from Tadcaster, Yorkshire and
Caen; also Ketton stone, King's
Cliffe stone and modern
restorations in Ancaster stone
Tower height: 96' 2", to flagpole 113' 7"
Tower width: 33' 6" above base
Stairs: clockwise-up helical stairs in
south-east turret to clock chamber,
north-west corner to bell chamber,
and south-west corner to top
platform; 5' 3" to 4' 2" dia. stairs
5" dia. newels; 110 steps to top
platform, modern ladder to roof
Bells: peal of eight in F: Brasyers of
Norwich *c.* 1513, William Barker
of Norwich *c.* 1538, John Darbie
of Ipswich 1668 (2), William
Dobson of Downham Market 1820,
William Dobson 1828, Moore,
Holmes & Mackenzie of Redenhall
1881 (2); rehung on oak frame by
Day 1897, overhauled by
Whitechapel Bell Foundry 1990
Clock: mechanism by John Smith of
Derby 1892, electrified 1975,
skeleton faces to north, south and
west
Glass: west window, Lavers, Barraud
and Westlake, 1880
Restorations and alterations:
1836–37: new gallery added below
tower
1847–51: repairs, architect William
Bardwell of London
1867: church restoration, gallery
removed, architect Richard M.

Phipson of Ipswich
20th-century: restoration following
damage in WWII
Survey date: July 2010, September
2014
Ground datum: south-west buttress

STOKE-BY-NAYLAND, ST MARY
SUFFOLK
Date of tower: *c.* 1439–62
Position: west tower
Material: flint, brick, rubble,
limestone dressings
Tower height: 126' 4", to flagpole 139' 7"
Tower width: 40' 1" above base
Stairs: clockwise-up helical stair in
south-east corner, 5' 9" to 3' 10" dia.
stair, 6" dia. newel; 144 steps to roof
Bells: peal of eight in D: *c.* 1380, John
Sturdy of London *c.* 1458, Henry
Pleasant of Sudbury 1699, Thomas
Gardiner of Sudbury 1725, Thomas
Mears II of Whitechapel 1811, John
Taylor & Co. of Loughborough
1956 (3) and cast-iron frame
Clock: electric mechanism, octagonal
face to east
Glass: west window, Messrs
O'Connor, 1865
Restorations and alterations:
1864: north-west pinnacle destroyed
by lightning
1865: general restoration, architect
John Gibson
1963–66: tower repairs, architect
Donald Insall of London
Survey date: September 2010,
September 2014
Ground datum: south-east buttress

TICKHILL, ST MARY
YORKSHIRE, WEST RIDING
Date of tower: lower stages *c.* 1200,
upper stages and west window
c. 1390–1429
Position: engaged west tower
Material: Roche Abbey Magnesian
limestone (British Geological
Survey)
Tower height: 127' 6"
Tower width: 39' 5" above base
Stairs: clockwise-up helical stair in
south-west corner, lower stages
6' 5" dia. stair, 6½" dia. newel,
upper stages 5' 1" dia. stair, 5½" dia.
newel; 161 steps to roof
Bells: peal of eight in E flat: Daniel
Hedderly of Lincoln & Bawtry
1725–26 (4), James Harrison III of
Barrow & Barton 1796 & 1815, John
Taylor & Co. of Loughborough
1896 (2); timber frame set
diagonally by John Taylor & Co.
of Loughborough 1897; carillon
mechanism by John Smith & Son
of Derby 1896
Restorations and alterations:
1842–50: repairs, architect Joseph
Mitchell of Sheffield
1880–82: tower repairs, architect John
Webster of Sheffield
1959: baldacchino over font, architect
George Pace
1982: ceiling beneath ringing
chamber, architect R. G. Simms
Survey date: April 2011, July 2014
Ground datum: reduced level at west
door

TITCHMARSH, ST MARY
NORTHAMPTONSHIRE
Date of tower: *c.* 1474–85
Material: Weldon stone
Position: west tower
Tower height: 102' 8", to vane 105' 2"
Tower width: 35' 0" above base
Stairs: clockwise-up helical stair in
    south-west corner, 4' 11" dia. stair,
    6" dia. newel; 80 steps to bell
    chamber, ladder to roof
Bells: peal of eight in E: all bells
    and cast-iron and steel frame
    by Gillett & Johnston of Croydon
    1913
Clocks: clock of 1745 replaced but
    face visible low on south elevation;
    clock mechanism of 1886 but no
    external face; sundial to south
    elevation 1798
Restorations and alterations:
1836–43: general restoration,
    architects Browning & Browning
    of Stamford
1866: further restoration
1882: pinnacle weathervanes installed
1901: sculptures added to niches
1920s: tower restored
1969–71: repairs, architects Blackwell,
    Storry & Scott of Kettering
Survey date: May 2010, August 2014
Ground datum: north-west buttress

WEST WALTON, ST MARY THE VIRGIN
NORFOLK
Date of tower: *c.* 1240–50, parapet
    and pinnacles *c.* 1380
Position: detached tower
Material: Barnack ragstone
Tower height: 90' 3", to vane 96' 8"
Tower width: 35' 9" above base
Squinches: single arch
Stairs: clockwise-up helical stair in
    south-east corner, 6' 1" to 4' 8" dia.
    stair, 4½" dia. newel; 104 steps to
    roof
Bells: peal of five, disabled: John
    Draper of Thetford 1620, Thomas
    Norris of Stamford 1629, Tobias
    Norris III of Stamford 1693,
    unknown 1699, Henry Penn of
    Peterborough 1708; oak frame
Restorations and alterations:
1885: possible restoration,
    weathervanes replaced
1907–14: tower restoration, architect
    William Wier of Letchworth
1985: tower restoration, architect
    Feilden & Mawson of Norwich
1987: passed to the Redundant
    Churches Fund (later renamed the
    Churches Conservation Trust)
Survey date: March 2011, June 2014
Ground datum: south-east corner

WHITTLESEY, ST MARY
CAMBRIDGESHIRE
Date of tower: *c.* 1380 onwards
Date of spire: *c.* 1475
Position: west tower
Material: Barnack stone
Steeple height: 171' 3", to vane 176' 9"
Tower width: 26' 8" above base
Spire dims: 91' 3" high, 18' 4" wide
Spire angle: 11° 8'
Squinches: five corbels
Stairs: anticlockwise-up helical stair
    in north-east corner, access from
    north aisle; moves and changes to

clockwise from ringing chamber,
    4' 11" dia. stair, 5½" dia. newel;
    108 steps to parapet
Bells: peal of eight in E: Joseph Eayre
    of St Neots 1758 (4), Osborn &
    Dobson 1803 (4); cast-iron frame
    by John Warner & Sons, Cripplegate
    1902, overhauled 1954; carillon
    mechanism
Clock: mechanism by John Smith
    & Sons of Derby; large domed
    faces to north, east and west
Restorations and alterations:
1860–63: church restoration,
    including reopening of tower arch,
    architect George Gilbert Scott
1926–27: restoration
1976–80: repairs, architect Ronald
    Sims of York
Survey date: October 2010, June
    2014
Ground datum: south-east buttress

WILBY, ST MARY
NORTHAMPTONSHIRE
Date of steeple: *c.* 1480
Position: west tower
Material: Mears Ashby ironstone
    (British Geological Survey)
Tower height: 104' 8", to vane 109' 7"
Tower width: 23' 3" to outside corners
    of buttresses
Spire angle: 15° 13'
Squinches: long splay
Stairs: clockwise-up helical stair in
    south-west corner, 3' 10" dia. stair,
    6" dia. newel; 33 steps to clock
    chamber, ladders above
Bells: peal of six in B flat: Matthew I
    Bagley of Chacomb 1682, Henry
    Penn of Peterborough 1705, John
    Taylor & Co. of Loughborough
    1878 (2), 1893 and 1947; steel frame
    possibly 1947
Clock: face to south elevation of
    octagon
Restorations and alterations:
1879: general restoration
c. 1912: tower screen incorporating
    old work from Yaxley (Hunts),
    architect Temple Moore
Survey date: May 2010, June 2014
Ground datum: south-west buttress

WITNEY, ST MARY THE VIRGIN
OXFORDSHIRE
Date of steeple: mid-13th century,
    rededication 1243
Position: central tower
Material: Oxfordshire limestone
Steeple height: 153' 9", to vane 158' 5"
Tower width: 27' 2"
Spire dims: 84' 9" high, 26' 7" wide
Spire angle: 16° 20'
Squinches: long splay
Stairs: clockwise-up helical stair to
    ringing chamber in south-east
    corner, 5' 2" dia. stair, 5½" dia.
    newel; 48 steps from ground to
    ringing chamber, 65 steps to bell
    chamber
Bells: peal of eight in E: Richard
    Keene 1660, Henry III Baguley
    1731, Abel Rudhall 1755, Thomas
    Rudhall 1765, Thomas II Mears
    1815, John Taylor & Co. 1938 (3);
    rehung in cast-iron frame by John
    Taylor & Co. in 1938
Clock and carillon: 1876

Restorations and alterations:
1636: top of spire blown down,
    rebuilt by Humphrey Smith
1797: possible addition of ringing
    chamber floor
1865–69: church restoration,
    G. E. Street architect, Alfred
    Groves of Milton-under-
    Wychwood contractor, cost £4,500
1901: spire repairs and weathercock
    replaced
1925–26: spire repaired
1942: tip of spire destroyed
    by crashing RAF plane
1944: spire rebuilt
1963: spire gablets replaced
1966: further spire repairs
Survey date: March 2013
Ground datum: north-east corner

Appendix I

THE CONTRACT FOR FOTHERINGHAY CHURCH

This Endenture made between William Wolston squire, Thomas Peckham clerk, commissioners for the high and mighty prince, and my right redoubtable lord, The Duke of York on one part; and William Horwod free-mason dwelling in Fotheringhay on the other part; witness, that the same William Horwod has granted and undertaken, and by this same has indented, grants and undertakes to make a new body of a Church joining to the Choir of the College of Fotheringhay; of the same height and breadth of the said Choir; and in height 24 feet from the said Choir downward within the walls, a metre-yard of England accounting always for three feet. And in this Covenant the said William Horwod shall also prepare all the ground work of the said body, and take it and empty it at his own cost, as quickly and sufficiently as it ought to be by oversight of Masters of the same Craft, with materials sufficiently provided for him at my said Lord's cost, as required for the work. And to the same body he shall make two Aisles, and take the ground ... ... border in the aforesaid manner, both the Aisles according to height and breadth of the Aisles of the said Choir, and in height to the aforesaid body; the ground of the same body and Aisles to be made within the end under the ground-table-stones [basement course] ... ; and all the remnant of the said body and Aisles unto the full height of the said Choir; and all the inside of rough stone except the bench-table-stones, the sills of the Window, the Pillars and Capitals that the Arches and Pendants

[roof structure] shall rest upon, which shall be altogether of Freestone, wrought true and neat as it ought to be.

And in each Aisle shall be Windows of Freestone, according in all points to the Windows of the Choir, save they shall have no bowtells at all. And in the West end of either of the said Aisles, he shall make a window of four lights, according altogether to the Windows of the said Aisles. And to either Aisle shall project a square battlement of freestone, and both the embattled ends butting against the Steeple. And either of the said Aisles shall have six mighty Buttresses of clean hewn Freestone; and every Buttress finished with a finial, according in all points with the finials of the said Choir, save only that the buttresses of the body shall be larger, stronger and more mighty than the buttresses of the said Choir.

And the Clerestory, both within and without, shall be made in clean Ashlar, grounded upon ten mighty Pillars, with four responds; that is to say, two above jointing to the Choir, and two beneath joining to the end of the said body. And to the two responds of the said Choir shall be perpendicular connecting walls of Freestone, clean wrought; that is to say, on either side of the middle Choir door; and in either wall three lights and lavatories [hand basins] in either side of the wall, which shall serve for four Alters, that is to say on either side of the middle door of the said Choir, and on either side of the said Aisles.

And in each of the said Aisles shall be five Arches above the Steeple, and above every arch a window, and every window

of four lights, according in points to the windows of the clerestory of the said Choir. And either side of the said Aisles shall have six mighty arches [flying buttresses] butting on either side to the clerestory, and two mighty Arches butting on either side of the said Steeple, according to the arches of the said Choir, both in table-stones and crests, with a square battlement thereupon.

And in the North side of the Church the said William Horwode shall make a Porch; the outer side of clean Ashlar, the inner side of rough stone, twelve feet in length, and in breadth as the said buttresses of the said body will allow; and in height to accord with the Aisle of the same side, with reasonable lights in either side, and with a square battlement above.

And in the South side to the Cloister [of the College] another Porch joining the Door of the said Cloister, being as wide as the buttresses will allow, and in height between the Church and the said ..., with a Door in the west side of the said Porch facing the Town; and in either side as many lights as will suffice; and a square battlement above, and in height according to the place where it is set.

And in the West end of the said body shall be a Steeple standing ... the Church upon three strong and mighty Arches vaulted with stone; to which the Steeple shall be in length [height?] 24 feet after the metre-yard, three feet to the yard, above the ground table stones, and twenty foot square within the walls, the walls being six foot thick above the said ground table stones. And to the height of the said body it shall be square with two mighty buttresses joining thereto, on either side of a large Door which shall be in the West end of the same Steeple.

And when the said Steeple comes to the height of the said body then it shall be changed and turned into eight panes, and at every Angle a buttress finishing with a finial, according to the finials of the said Choir and Body; the said Steeple embattled with a large square battlement; and above the Door of the said Steeple a window rising in height as high as the great Arch of the Steeple, and in breadth as the body will allow. And in the said steeple shall be two floors, and above either floor eight clerestory windows set in the middle of the walls, each window of three lights, and all the outer side of the Steeple of clean wrought Freestone, and the inner of rough stone. And in the said steeple shall be a turning Vice [a spiral stair], reaching the said Body, Aisles and Choir, both below and above, with all manner of other works necessary for the size of such a Body, Aisles, Steeple and Porches, also will nothing comprehended in this Endenture as comprehended and expressed.

And of all the work that in this same Endenture is described and rehearsed, my said Lord of York shall fund the carriage and the materials, that is to say, Stone, Lime, Sand, Ropes, Bolts, Ladders, Timber, Scaffold, Gins [lifting tackle], and all manner of materials required for the work, for which work, well, truly and duly to be made and finished in the way previously devised and declared, the said Will Horwode shall receive from my said Lord £300 Sterling; the sum of which he shall be paid in the way described hereafter;

that is to say, when he has made the foundations of the said Church, Aisles, Buttresses, Porches and Steeple, cut and laid his ground table stones, and his ligaments [strings], and the wall thereto within and without, as well and duly made as it ought to be, then he shall have £6 8s. 4d. And when the said William Horwode has set oo [?] foot above the ground table stone, also good throughout, the outer side as the inner side of all the said work, then he shall have payment of £100 Sterling; and so for every foot of the said work, after it is fully wrought and set as it ought to be, and as previously described, until it comes to the full height of the highest of the finials and battlement of the said body, forming, setting and rising ... of the Steeple, after it has passed the highest battlement of the said body he shall receive all but £30 sterling until it be fully ended and performed in the ways previously described.

And when all the work written, described and rehearsed above is fully finished, as it ought to be, and as it is accorded and described above between the said Commissioners and the said William: then the said William Horwode shall have full payment of the said £300 sterling, if any be due or left unpaid to him: And during all the said work William Horwode shall neither set no fewer Free Masons, Rough Setters, not Leyes thereupon, but as such as shall be ordained to have the governance and oversight of the said work under my Lord of York who will appoint him and assign him.

And if it be that the said William Horwode does not make full payment to all or any of his Workmen, then the Clerke of Works shall pay him in his

presence and stop all mykyll in the said William Horwode hand, as the payment due to the Workmen comes to.

And during all the said Work, the Setters shall be chosen and taken by those who have the governance and oversight of the said Works by my said Lord; they are to be paid by the hand of the said William Horwode, in form and manner written and described above. And if it be that the said William Horwode complains and say at any time, that the two Setters, or any of them, be neither profitable nor sufficient Workmen for my Lords work, then they shall be judged by the oversight of the Master-Masons of the Country; and if they be found faulty or unable, then they shall be changed, and others taken and chosen, by those who have the governance of the said Work by my said lord's ordnance and commandment.

And if it should be that the said William Horwode fails to complete the said Work within a reasonable term, which shall be determined by my said Lord, or by his Council, in form and manner previously written and described in these same Endentures, then he shall yield himself to prison at my Lords will, and all his moveable goods and possessions will be at my said Lords disposition and ordnance. In witness the said Commissioners, as the said William Horwode to these present Endentures have set their seals interchangeably, the 24th day of September, the 13th year of the Reign of our Sovereign Lord King Henry the Sixth, after the conquest of England.[1]

NOTE

1 Transcribed from *Some Remarks Upon the Church of Fotheringhay, Northamptonshire: Read at a Meeting of the Oxford Society for Promoting the Study of Gothic Architecture* (1841).

Appendix 2

THE FIRST CHURCHWARDEN'S BOOK OF LOUTH, 1500–24

The accounts form a comprehensive record of all receipts and expenses at the church of St James from 1500 to 1524. John Caywod (d. 1529), priest, scribe, organist and composer, was paid 3s. 4d. each year for writing the accounts, in addition to his basic salary of 8s. 4d. (rising to 13s. 4d. by the end of the account). The body of the accounts is in English, with preambles and titles for each year in Latin, and each financial year runs from Easter. This summary has been compiled from the full transcription published by Revd Reginald C. Dudding, F.S.A. (Oxford, 1941).

The synopsis that follows covers only those expenses directly related to the building of the spire, with the weekly payments recorded to individual masons and workmen totalled for each year. The church income derived mainly from Sunday collections, legacies, gifts, and fees for burials and for the ringing of the great bells to commemorate the dead. A few legacies were specifically intended for the work on the spire, particularly during the initial burst of enthusiasm, but otherwise most of the cost was met from general church income and substantial borrowing from three local guilds. The direct payment for materials and workmen by the church, as and when funds became available, makes an interesting contrast with the formal contract for Fotheringhay (Appendix 1). Had initial progress and fundraising been maintained, the spire might have taken only six years to construct rather than fifteen.

26 APRIL 1500 TO APRIL 1501

Local mason William Nettleton, assisted by his son and two labourers, undertook preparatory works during the year, including repairs around the bell chamber and to the west porch. He was paid the modest sum of 2s. for producing moulds (profiles) for the spire and, together with

leading parishioners John Chapman and William Joneson, he spent three days visiting the quarry to select the stone for the spire. Large quantities of stone were procured, in particular from the quarry of Will Bonett at Kelby near Ancaster, and moved by land and water to Dogdyke on the River Witham, some twenty-one miles south of Louth. These preliminary expenses were not included within the final cost of the spire.

APRIL 1501 TO 18 APRIL 1502

William Nettleton continued his preparatory work, at the rate of 6d. per day, in the 'galile' or western porch of the tower. He undertook a second trip to buy stone and to find a master mason to take charge of the works. This took four days, suggesting that the mason, John Cole, was found within the local region. Cole duly received 'God's penny' as a token confirming his appointment to take charge of the works. He was to be paid at 8d. per day and led a team of five masons and two apprentices. Initially he spent four days preparing the design, for which he received 2s. 8d. Over seventy loads of stone were dragged by cart from Dogdyke to a newly built storehouse at Louth, and labourers spent thirty-four days lifting stone up the tower on a new windlass. Warden William Joneson rode to the quarries twice, on one occasion with Cole, to place large orders for stone with Bonett and several other quarry-owners. The records include payments for lime and lead, and to carpenters for the building of scaffolding. The total expenditure of almost £54 during the year was made possible only by substantial borrowing from the Trinity Guild and the Guild of Our Lady.

APRIL 1502 TO APRIL 1503

John Cole and William Nettleton continued to be fully employed on the spire for most

of the year, assisted by a changing pool of jobbing masons and apprentices. Revesby Abbey lent 15 cwt of stone to St James's Church, and more was purchased from William Bonett and John Lefle. Payments were recorded to a large numbers of mason's servants and suppliers. Over half of the year's expenditure of £46 11d. was borrowed from the guilds.

23 APRIL 1503 TO 14 APRIL 1504

The third year of construction saw a reduction in impetus, with John Cole working for only sixty-one days and William Nettleton's replacement, John Stobard, responsible for more than half the work carried out during the year. Forty-one loads of stone were hauled from Dogdyke to Louth, and more visits were made to the quarries. Further scaffolding was erected as the spire slowly rose, and eight weeks before Easter the carpenters erected centring to support the four flying buttresses. John Spencer, steward of the Bishop of Lincoln's manor, was paid 6d. for a skin to draw the spire on, possibly to allow Cole to design the flying buttresses.

14 APRIL 1504 TO 30 MARCH 1505

Mason John Wilkinson and apprentice John Stobard undertook the majority of work this year, assisted by William Nettleton. John Cole received an annual fee for the first time, which, at 26s. 8d., almost equalled his pay for forty-one days' work. Among the thirty-four loads of stone supplied by quarries at Wilsford were 54 feet of crockets at 3d. per foot, 230 feet of ashlar at 2d. per foot, and 100 feet of ashlar and squinches, 16" to 18" high, for 25s. More ashlar crockets and squinches were supplied by a quarry at a place called Hessilbrugh. For no obvious reason, the total cost for the year of £33 12s. 4d. excluded all the unskilled labour.

30 MARCH 1505 TO 19 APRIL 1506

The year 1505 saw the replacement of Cole by master mason Christopher ('Xpoforo') Scune and his apprentice Ralfe Hudchynson, with William Nettleton making on occasional appearance. Some design work was required at this stage, for Scune was paid 2 days for making moulds in addition to the 109 days he spent working on site. Included in the purchases from quarry-owners John Lefle and William Bonett are a further 26 feet of crockets and squinches, and thirteen great pieces containing 4 tons of stone, which may have included the capping stones for the pinnacles. On the thirteenth Sunday after Trinity (13 August) carpenter Thomas Cooper, with five assistants, was paid 4s. 8d. to erect scaffold, and several labourers were employed to wind stone up the tower. Cooper was paid a further 5s. for striking scaffold in the week prior to the second Sunday in Advent, following which the masons stopped work for the remainder of the year, suggesting that the pinnacles may have been completed by Christmas 1505.

19 APRIL 1506 TO 4 APRIL 1507

No further work too place during 1506–07, the only payment to a mason being 10s. annual fee and the reward of a gown to Christopher Scune. Quarry-owners' debts from the previous year were paid off, and stone remaining at Dogdyke was moved by cart to Louth.

11 APRIL 1507 TO 30 APRIL 1508

Churchwarden John Okeland visited Lefle and Bonett at their quarry and placed a further order for ten tons of stone. Christopher Scune was notable by his absence and for borrowing 6 tons of stone from Louth. Work finally resumed on site on the twelfth Sunday after Trinity, with Scune's assistant Ralfe Hudchynson and William Medylton working together for the remainder of the year.

30 APRIL 1508 TO 15 APRIL 1509

Hudchynson and Medylton continued to work throughout the year, with regular supplies of stone being delivered from the Wilsford quarries. Christopher Scune drew his annual fee of 13s. 4d. despite taking no active part in the proceedings.

15 APRIL 1509 TO APRIL 1510

Christopher Scune made a rare appearance for six days in the week after Trinity, leaving apprentice John Tours to continue alone for a further eleven weeks. Such lamentable progress required no further supplies from the quarry, and the most notable entry in the accounts is for the repair of the windlass, followed by the purchase of a new cable 384 feet long (3 score 4 fathoms) from Kings Lynn for 16s. 4d.

12 APRIL 1510 TO APRIL 1511

In 1510 Laurence Lemyng, who was to see the project through to completion, made his first appearance, working with a mason William, who may be the previously mentioned William Medylton. Christopher Scune was responsible for sawing and hewing stone, and his apprentice was also at work. Activity remained at a pitifully low level, but preparations were made for a renewed campaign of work, with 60 tons of stone being ordered from quarry-owners Rob Stefnett and Rob Taylor of Kelby.

APRIL 1511 TO APRIL 1512

Lawrence Lemyng and William continued to work throughout the year. Scune appeared on site for the five weeks following the tenth Sunday after Trinity, departing as soon as he received his annual fee. Several labourers were engaged on the sawing of stone, both at Louth and at a workshop in Coningsby near Dogdyke, and carpenter Thomas Cooper erected more scaffolding around the slowly rising spire.

18 APRIL 1512 TO 3 APRIL 1513

The mason Laurence Lemyng continued to work from Easter, with William joining two weeks later. Christopher Scune arrived in the eighth week after Trinity (1 August), leaving after just two weeks, his assistant Gilbard remaining behind. In the week before the nineteenth Sunday after Trinity (17 October), the three masons stopped work and received rewards, and two weeks later the great rope was taken down. This may signal the achievement of an important

milestone, or it may simply have been that the supply of stone had been exhausted.

10 APRIL 1513 TO 10 APRIL 1514

Work became infrequent during 1513–14, with Christopher Scune failing to make an appearance despite receiving his annual fee. With the wardens becoming increasingly frustrated at the lack of progress, a man named Pole was paid 12d. to take a letter to the master mason and 16d. to bring back a reply before Easter. These sums suggest that Scune was working a great distance away. A further 30 tons of stone was bought from quarries, this time at Ewerby and Hather, and 32 tons of stone was sawn by labourers ready for the masons.

10 APRIL 1514 TO 14 APRIL 1515

Progress came to a halt during 1514 owing to absence of Christopher Scune, Laurence Lemyng completing just three weeks' work. Thomas Richardson was paid 8d. to ride to Ripon to ask the master mason to return to work. This was followed by a 'pore scolare' bearing a letter to him for 8d., and Will Gossauk delivering a further letter for 3d. All of this correspondence proved fruitless.

APRIL 1515 TO APRIL 1516

After Easter 1515 Lawrence Lemyng rode north to make one final attempt to persuade Scune to return. When this failed, Lemyng visited Boston with churchwarden William Walker to find a replacement master mason. The final concerted campaign of work started on Monday 16 June, with the new mason, John Tempas, arriving three weeks later and being present for ten of the remaining twelve weeks. His limited involvement was reflected in the modesty of his reward on completion: just 6s. 8d. compared with the 20s3 presented to the long-serving Laurence Lemyng. On Holy Rood Eve (13 September) 1515, the weathercock was finally raised on top of the spire amid great rejoicing. Following the celebrations the masons departed, except for Laurence Lemyng, who remained to fill the putlog holes as the labourers dropped the scaffold. Subsequent accounts note that Lemyng briefly returned to work on the church walls in 1517–18 and with an apprentice in 1520–21.

NOTES

1   It is assumed that the windlass installed in 1501–02 is the 'Wild Mare', which still remains at the top of the tower.

2   Other sources confirm that Scune had been appointed as master at Ripon some time between 1503 and 1514, and at Durham some time between 1508 and 1515.

DAYS WORKED BY MASONS

	1501–02	1502–03	1503–04	1504–05	1505–06	1506–07	1507–08	1508–09	1509–10	1510–11***	1511–12	1512–13	1513–14	1514–15	1515–16	Total
Master masons																
John Cole	149	142	61	41												**393**
Christopher Scune					109	0	0	0	6	25	30	12				**182**
John Tempas															57	**57**
Masons																
William Nettleton*	195	196		33	4											**428**
Thomas Busche	93															**93**
Ranald Curtas	70															**70**
John Symson	73	46														**119**
Thomas Symson		21														**21**
John Sainton	41	12														**53**
Giles Charleton		35														**35**
Edmund Shaw			50													**50**
William Wilkinson		2														**2**
John Wilkinson			148													**148**
Rob Lyn					56											**56**
John Copelay					31											**31**
William Medylton							216	193								**409**
Laurence Lemyng										13	238	153	97	18	81	**600**
William										13	148	122	23			**306**
Gilbard												66				**66**
Nicholas													21			**21**
Will Wode															22	**22**
Nicholas Upton															6	**6**
Apprentices																
to John Symson	6															**6**
master apprentice	132															**132**
Nicholas Hutton	42	150														**192**
John Stobard***		206	250	209												**665**
John Tours***		7	18						71	13						**109**
Ralfe Hudchynson					161		213	185								**559**
to John Tempas															66	**66**
Total days	**801**	**815**	**381**	**431**	**361**	**0**	**429**	**378**	**77**	**64**	**416**	**353**	**141**	**18**	**232**	**4897**

* William Nettleton worked for twenty-nine days on preparatory works in 1500–01, but these are excluded from the costs of the spire within the accounts and are therefore omitted here.

** Apprentices John Tours and John Stobard became masons in 1503.

*** Insufficient information in 1509–10 regarding individual masons, so subtotals have been spit pro rata.

NOTES

1 Totals have been rounded down to the nearest day.

2 Throughout the accounts master masons are paid 8*d*., masons 6–7*d*., apprentices 5–6*d*. and labourers 3–4*d*.

	Masons	Masons' servers*	Stone etc., incl. carriage to Dogdyke**	Stone carriage Dogdyke to Louth	Total stated in accounts
1501–02	£21 18s. 5d.	£3 5s. 1d.	£22 5d.	£6 15s. 2d.	£53 19s. 1d.
1502–03	£23 8s. 8d.	£5 8s. 7d.	£11 4s. 8d.	£5 15s. 4d.	£46 11d.
1503–04	£10 10s. 10d.	£1 2s. 2d.	£6 10s. 11d.	£3 15s. 4d.	£21 19s. 3d.
1504–05	£12 10s. 11d.	[not included]	£15 19s. 9d.	£5 1s. 7d.	£33 12s. 4d.
1505–06	£10 8s. 9d.	£2 9s. 4d.	£5 6s. 1d.	£1 19s. 9d.	£20 3s. 11d.
1506–07	£1	nil	£5 3s. 4d.	£1 4s. 7d.	£7 7s. 11d.
1507–08	£9 18s.	[not included]	£7 18s.	£4 8s. 7d.	£22 4s. 7d.
1508–09	£3 15s. 1d.	18s. 5d.	£2 4s. 11d.	10s.	£7 8s. 5d.
1509–10	£3 1s. 10d.	£7 11s. 11d.	nil	nil	£10 13s. 9d.
1510–11	£3 3s. 10d.	[not included]	£5 5s. 10d.	£2 3d.	£10 9s. 11d.
1511–12	£10 4s. 10d.	£3 15s. 5d.	£8 16s. 9d.	£3 12d.	£25 18s.
1512–13	£10 10s. 10d.	£3 5s.	£6 1s. 5d.	£1 8s. 10d.	£14 8s. 9d.
1513–14	£4 7s.	14s.	£5 16s. 8d.	13s. 6d.	£11 11s. 2d.
1514–15	10s.	13s. 10d.	nil	2s. 2d.	26s.
1515–16	£9 8s. 1d.	£6 10d.	£1 15s. 4d.	nil	£17 4s. 5d.
Total	**£134 17s. 1d.**	**£35 3s. 9d.**	**£104 4s. 1d.**	**£36 16s. 1d.**	**£305 7s. 5d.**

* Including scaffolding, sawing of stone, general site labour, lifting equipment
** Including carriage of stone to Dogdyke, and small sums for lime, sand, etc.

NOTE

1 No attempt has been made to reconcile several minor discrepancies, and a few major discrepancies, in the original calculation of the accounts.

LOANS FROM GUILDS

	Our Lady's Guild	St Peter's Guild	Trinity Guild
1501–02	£14 12s.		21s. 8d.
1502–03	£21 16s. 8d.	£6 12s.	
1503–04	£4 4s. 1d.		
1504–05	£2 8s. 8d.		16s. 7d.
1508–09	20s.		
1509–10	69s.		16s. 8d.
1511–12	£4 1s. 8d.		£2 5s.
1512–13	£7 10s. 8d.	20s. 1d.	9s. 6d.
1515–16			40s.
Total	**£59 2s. 9d.**	**£7 12s. 1d.**	**£7 9s. 5d.**

Total loans: £74 4s. 3d.

Appendix 3

THE DISTRIBUTION OF SPIRES AND LANTERNS

TABLE 1
DISTRIBUTION OF OVERSAILING SPIRES

	Lincs	Rutland	Northants	Leics	Cambs & Hunts	Bucks, Beds, Sussex	Derbys & Notts	Yorks & NE	Oxon & Warks	Gloucestershire	West Country	Welsh Borders	Total
Lucarnes													
no lucarnes					1B	1			1	3	4	2	**12**
orthogonal													
1 tier +	2	1		5		1	4	2	7	9	8	4	**43**
2 tiers ++	4	3	21	8	10	5	13			5			**69**
3 tiers +++	1	3	10	2	8					1			**25**
4 tiers ++++						1							**1**
alternating													
1 tier ×										1			**1**
2 tiers +×	4		2	5	5		1			1			**18**
3 tiers +×+	10	4	3	1	3	1							**22**
3 tiers ++×	1		1										**2**
4 tiers ++×+	1												**1**
4 tiers +×+×				1									**1**
quatrefoils					1R								**1**
Spire type													
broach	21	9	34	23	22	7	17	1	1	14	12	6	**167**
splay-footed	2	2	2		2	2	1	1	1	1	1		**15**
octagonal drum					3						1		**4**
octagonal tower			1S										**1**
Oxfordshire									6	3			**9**
Total	23	11	37	23	27	9	18	2	8	18	14	6	**196**

+ Spire lights set square to the tower
× Spire lights set diagonally
B Barnack
R Ravenstone
S Stanwick

TABLE 2
DISTRIBUTION OF RECESSED SPIRES AND LANTERNS

	Lincs	Rutland	Northants	Leics	Cambs & Hunts	East Anglia, Bucks & Beds	Derbys & Notts	Yorks & NE	Oxon & Glos	South & West ***	West Midlands	Heref & Shrops	Total
Lucarnes													
no lucarnes	1			3		1	21	30	8	32	3	5	**104**
orthogonal													
1 tier +	13	1	2	13	6	2	12	3	21	5	6	8	**92**
2 tiers ++	7	6	14	19	14	5	11	2	4	2	8	1	**93**
3 tiers +++		2	9	1	2	4					5	1	**24**
4 tiers ++++											1		**1**
5 tiers +++++											1L		**1**
alternating													
2 tiers +×	14		9	10	2	1	1	1	1		1		**40**
2 tiers -I				1**	1**								**2**
2 tiers ×+	1W												**1**
3 tiers +×+	12*	1		3	1	3	2	1			4	1	**28**
3 tiers ***				1							3		**4**
4 tiers +×+×	1H						1N						**2**
5 tiers +×+×+							1A						**1**
quatrefoils	4			10							1		**15**
Spire type													
recessed spire	53	10	34	61	26	16	49	35	33	39	33	16	**405**
flying spire								1					**1**
octagonal lantern	1B		2		1			2			1		**7**
Total	54	10	36	61	27	16	49	38	33	39	34	16	**413**

+ Spire lights set square to the tower
× Spire lights set diagonally
* Spire lights on all eight faces

A Ashbourne   B Boston
H Holbeach   N Newark
W Wilsford   L Lichfield Cathedral

* Includes Grantham if blind lucarnes are ignored
** Stoney Stanton (Leics), Conington (Cambs): only two lights on each tier, EW then NS
*** South & West includes Wiltshire, Somerset, Devon, Dorset, Cornwall, Hampshire and Sussex

Glossary

abutment: Masonry resisting outward thrust from a vault or arch, in Gothic work reinforced by a buttress.

air hole: A square wall opening containing abstract tracery, particularly in Norfolk flushwork towers.

alternate tracery: Perpendicular tracery, typical of the west of England, with mullions offset by half a bay in the window head.

angle buttresses: A pair of perpendicular buttresses supporting and concealing an external corner.

angle shaft: Vertical shaft set on the external corner of a wall or buttress.

annulet: A circular ring connecting two sections of detached stone shaft; used until *c.* 1240.

arcade: A continuous run of arched openings supported by regularly spaced piers or columns.

archlet: A secondary arch spanning one bay of a subdivided opening.

arris: A sharp edge between two surfaces.

arrow slit: Narrow vertical or crossed slit in a wall or battlement, splayed internally.

ashlar: Smoothly finished stone with narrow joints.

ballflower: Running decoration, of small globular balls enclosed by petals, used in Late Geometrical tracery.

bar tracery: Tracery formed from linear members; invented in France *c.* 1210, introduced to England in 1245.

basement course: Profiled masonry courses running around the base of a wall to shed rain, form strong shadow lines and spread the load onto the foundations.

battlement: A parapet of military character employed on all medieval building types, formed of alternating merlons and embrasures.

bay: Vertical division of a building or building element, such as a window, into a series of regular compartments.

beakhead: Norman decoration of repeated bird, animal or human heads with beak-like projections wrapping around a roll.

belfry: A free-standing tower, not necessarily carrying bells; from the Old French *belfrei*, meaning a safe hiding place.

bell chamber: Room in the upper part of a tower holding the bells, surrounded by openings to allow the sound out.

bell frame: A substantial oak, iron or steel frame spanning between tower walls for the hanging of bells.

bell hatch: Removable hatch in a vault or floor, allowing bells to be lifted to the bell chamber; usually central and circular.

bell stage: The stage of a tower containing the bells.

blind arcade: A decorative arcade placed immediately in front of a solid wall.

blind tracery: Tracery applied to the face of a solid wall rather than a window opening.

boss: A carved panel covering the intersection of members in a vault or ceiling.

bowtell: A slender engaged shaft, usually with an individual base and capital.

brace: A structural member set diagonally to strengthen an internal corner.

bracket: A mirrored pair of ogee curves employed in Perpendicular profiles.

brattishing: Decorative cresting running along a horizontal member, often with Tudor flowers.

broach: A small, hipped roof concealing a squinch arch and covering the space between a square tower and an octagonal spire or drum; originally meaning any type of spire.

broach spire: An octagonal oversailing spire with broaches rising from a square base.

buttress: A significant projection from the face of a masonry wall to resist outward thrust, set perpendicular to a straight wall, of several different forms on a corner.

capital: The head of a column, shaft or pilaster, often decoratively carved.

capstone: Large apex stone on a spire or pinnacle.

cardinal face: The four principal faces of a church, nominally north, south, east and west.

casement: A wide, shallow hollow occupying the centre of a Perpendicular reveal.

castellated: Finished with battlements.

chamfer: A diagonal cut across a surface, usually at 45 degrees.

chamfer-plane: The first diagonal cut made across a stone to be profiled, the mouldings of the profile then being cut back into the surface of the chamfer-plane.

chevron: Norman Romanesque 'V'-shaped moulding around doors and windows.

cinquefoil: A regular geometrical figure of five foils between five cusps, used in tracery and surface decoration, frequently set within a circle.

clasping buttress: A buttresses fully enclosing an external corner of a building, usually square or octagonal.

clerestory: High-level windows set above the aisle roofs; also the stage in which the clerestory windows sit.

column: An upright structural or decorative member, broader than a shaft but more slender than a pier.

compound buttress: A buttress combining two or more primary forms of buttress.

compound cusping: Cusping subdivided by minor cusping, developed in the fourteenth century.

compound pier: A pier made from a central mass surrounded by shafts or columns.

coping: Top course of masonry protecting a wall, usually with a sloping top surface and an overhang.

corbel: Masonry projecting from the face of a wall to support a load.

corbel table: A regular series of corbels supporting a projecting course of masonry or the edge of a parapet, roof or spire.

crenellation: *see* **battlement**

crocket: Carved decoration of abstract vegetative form running up the prominent edge of a gable, flying buttress, hood-mould, canopy, pinnacle or spire.

crossing: The central space in a cruciform church where nave, transepts and chancel meet, usually square.

cruciform: Cross-shaped; in architecture, the cross-shaped church plan favoured by the Normans.

Curvilinear tracery: Flowing tracery incorporating ogee curves, popular from 1315 to 1360.

cushion capital: Romanesque capital formed of a large square block, the lower part rounded to provide a transition to a circular column.

cusp: Projecting point separating two foils.

dagger: Small tracery motif of two unequal parts; in Curvilinear tracery pointed at both ends, in Perpendicular tracery often inverted, with only the blade pointed.

detached shaft: A shaft structurally separate from any adjacent wall or pier.

diagonal buttress: A single buttress projecting diagonally from a corner.

diamond tracery: Perpendicular lucarne tracery of straight intersecting bars running parallel to the slopes of the gable.

diaper: Low relief or painted surface decoration of regular motifs set in squares or diamonds.

dogtooth or **tooth:** Closely spaced running ornament, each tooth of four leaves forming a small square pyramid, used profusely in the thirteenth century.

dormer: Window projecting from the sloping face of a roof, with solid cheeks and an individual roof.

dressed stone: Stone with at least one finished face.

dripstone or **drip:** An external string course with a lip to throw rainwater clear of the wall below.

drop-arch: An obtuse two-centred arch with the centre points set inside the opening.

drop-tracery: Tracery that starts below the spring of the main arch of a window.

Early Geometrical tracery: Style of bar tracery based on foliated and nested circles, from 1245 to 1290.

embattled: Finished with battlements.

embrasure: *see* **crenel**

engaged shaft: A shaft profile integral with the masonry of an adjacent wall, typically three-quarters exposed, used from 1240.

engaged tower: A tower at least partly enclosed by the continuation of the aisles.

entasis: The application of a subtle curve to the profile of a building element such as a column or spire, creating the illusion of greater solidity, height or strength.

equilateral arch: Two-centred arch with arc radii the same as the width of the opening.

falchion: Small tracery motif similar to a dagger but asymmetrically curved.

fan vault: A vault formed of inverted half or quarter conoids with arched radial ribs rising to a radiused ridge.

fenestration: Windows, or the arrangement and proportion of windows in a building.

fillet: A continuous flat band running the length of a shaft or roll, used throughout the Gothic period.

finial: Prominent carved stone finishing the apex of a spire, pinnacle or gable.

Flamboyant tracery: Flame-shaped late Curvilinear tracery.

fleuron: A decorative carved stylized flower.

flushwork: Knapped-flint walling combined with dressed stone to produce richly textured decoration, popular in East Anglia from 1320.

flying buttress: Stone strut spanning a void to take the load of a high vault or other structure to a perimeter buttress, sometimes used for decorative effect.

flying spire: Small spire or lantern raised above the roof of a tower by four or more flying buttresses.

foil: Small arc spanning between cusps, arranged in groups of three (trefoil), four (quatrefoil), five (cinquefoil), six (sexfoil), seven (septafoil), eight (octafoil) or more.

foiled or **foliated:** The addition of small arcs within a circle, arch or similar geometric form.

four-centred arch: A late form of Gothic arch with two pairs of centres giving a tight radius at the springing and a wide radius at the head.

four-leaf flower: A decorative motif of four leaves forming a square, widely spaced and common in cornices; popular in late medieval work.

freestone: Homogeneous stone with a fine grain that can be cut smoothly in any direction.

fully engaged tower: A tower completely enclosed on either side by extended aisles.

gable: The triangular termination of a pitched roof.

gablet: A small gable, for example on a lucarne or at the head of a buttress.

gallery: A raised balcony overlooking the main space of a building.

gargoyle: A spout discharging rainwater from a parapet gutter, often in the form of a carved grotesque.

glazing bar: Metal or wooden member reinforcing the glazing in a window, not to be confused with masonry tracery bars.

great church: A large cruciform medieval church of three internal stages; a cathedral, minster or abbey.

helical stair: Geometrically correct term for a circular stair that rotates around a central newel post as it rises.

herringbone: Masonry laid in alternating diagonal courses; typical of early Norman work.

hood-mould or **hood:** Continuous moulding projecting from the plane of the wall above an opening to frame the extrados of an arch and throw rainwater clear.

hunky punk: Late medieval form of grotesque carving in Somerset.

impost: A block, capital or bracket supporting the end of an arch.

intersecting tracery: Simple Geometrical tracery, of three or more bays, in which each mullion splits and rises with the same radius as the main arch.

jamb: A vertical edge to an opening such as a door, window or niche.

keeled: Shaft or moulding profile shaped like the keel of a ship, popular in the Lancet period.

keystone: A central voussoir.

knapped flint: Flint split down the centre to expose the dark core, sometimes with the edges cut back to form square or rectangular blocks.

label: A rectangular hood-mould.

label stop: A carved bracket or head from which a label or hood-mould springs.

lancet arch: An acute two-centred arch with a pronounced point, common in England *c.* 1170 to 1270.

lantern: Originally the upper stage of a tower perforated by clerestory windows illuminating the crossing, later used purely for external effect.

Late Geometrical tracery: Style of bar tracery employing complex figures such as pointed trefoils, lozenges and spherical triangles, from *c.* 1290 to *c.* 1315.

lattice transom: A rare form of transom supported by a row of quatrefoils over trefoiled archlets.

lesene: *see* **pilaster strip**

lierne vault: A vault containing tertiary ribs that do not run from either the centre or the spring of the main vault, used from 1350.

lintel: A horizontal beam across an opening.

long and short work: Saxon pilasters or quoins formed of long vertical stones alternating with square stones, both of similar square cross-section.

loophole: *see* **arrow slit**

louvre: Overlapping slats of wood, metal, stone or glass protecting an opening while allowing ventilation.

lucarne: A gabled dormer on a spire, usually unglazed and left open for ventilation.

mason: A builder in stone, from the Old French *maisoner*, 'to build'.

masonry: Stonework and brickwork.

master mason: Senior mason in overall charge of the design and construction of buildings, equivalent to an architect but with wider responsibilities.

merlon: The raised part of a battlement originally provided to conceal defending soldiers.

mitre: An angled cut applied to sections of a profile so that it appears to run continuously around a corner.

mouchette: Curvilinear tracery motif similar to a dagger but curved.

moulding: The profile of stone or woodwork, sometimes of considerable complexity and depth; alternatively a member having a continuous moulding.

mullion: Vertical structural member between the bays of a window or other opening.

nailhead: Running ornament of small, square pyramids, used predominantly in the first half of the thirteenth century.

natural-leaf: Naturalistic foliage decoration on capitals, in use from *c.* 1280 to 1315.

needle spire: Very slender recessed spire, with an apex angle of no more than ten degrees.

newel: The principal post in a staircase, especially the circular post around which a helical stair winds.

newel stair: Helical stair in which the step and the adjacent section of newel post are formed from a single stone.

niche: A recess in a wall or buttress provided to house a statue or other carving.

nook shaft: Shaft set within a re-entrant angle.

octagonal buttress: A clasping buttress that is octagonal or part octagonal in plan.

octagonal oversailing spire: An octagonal spire overhanging the octagonal tower or stage on which it sits.

oculus: A circular opening or tracery motif, larger than an eyelet but smaller than a wheel or rose window.

ogee: A smooth-flowing curve that swings first in one direction and then more or less equally in the opposite direction, appearing in England around 1290.

ogee arch: An arch in the form of a mirrored pair of ogee curves; a structurally weak form more commonly used in archlets than main arches.

order: A general term for the hierarchy of readily distinguishable parts forming an architectural element, e.g. concentric sub-arches forming an arch.

orthogonal: Using only right angles; in particular the setting-out of a plan using lines that are parallel or perpendicular only to each other.

orthogonal lucarnes: Lucarnes following the orientation of the cardinal faces of a tower.

oversailing spire: A spire that is wider than the tower on which it sits to ensure that rainwater is thrown clear of the tower walls.

panel tracery: Late Perpendicular tracery of close-set mullions and transoms in the head, often beneath a four-centred arch.

panelling: A regular grid of window tracery or blind tracery applied to a wall, used in late medieval work.

parapet: A wall screening the edge of a roof and protected by a coping.

parish church: A church serving a parish, as opposed to a cathedral, abbey or monastery.

perforated parapet: A decorative form of parapet perforated by geometrical motifs such as quatrefoils.

pier: A broad, free-standing masonry support, wider than a shaft or column.

pilaster: A shallow engaged vertical column or pier projecting slightly from the face of a wall.

pilaster strip: A Saxon form of flat pilaster of sufficient depth to reinforce the adjacent rubble wall.

pinnacle: The slender pyramidal termination of a buttress or corner of a building, providing weight that aids the stability of the structure below.

plate tracery: The simplest and earliest form of tracery, in which geometrical figures are cut through the spandrel between lancet windows; from 1160 to c.1260.

pointed arch: An arch struck from two, four or more centres, with intersecting arcs at the apex.

polygonal: Many-sided; an imprecise term.

portal: A major ornamented doorway.

principal elevation: The most important face of a building.

profile: The geometrical outline of a section through a masonry or timber moulding.

putlog holes: Holes left in masonry during construction to support scaffolding, sometimes left unfilled or filled with noticeably different material.

quatrefoil: A regular geometrical figure of four foils between four cusps, used in tracery and surface decoration, frequently set within a circle.

quatrefoil light: A small quatrefoil window used mainly for staircases and on spires in Leicestershire.

quoin: Large stones reinforcing the corner of a building, as in Saxon upright and flat work and flushwork corners.

recessed spire: A spire set back behind a parapet, with a wide gutter forming a path around its base.

re-entrant corner: An inward-pointing corner.

relieving arch: A broad arch carrying an upper wall to reduce the load on a lower arch, lintel or wall.

respond: The part of an engaged pier that forms the springing of an arch, such as the tower arch.

reticulated tracery: Net-like Curvilinear tracery formed by alternating tiers of ogee archlets.

reveal: The face of a jamb to the side of a door or window opening.

rib: Originally a thin, linear structural member forming and supporting a vault in combination with other ribs, the primary ribs being arched; later also used as non-structural surface decoration.

rib vault: A vault formed from a framework of ribs with non-structural infilling between.

ridge rib: A rib running along the highest line of a vault, usually straight but circular around a bell hatch or fan vault.

ring capital: A circular moulded stone capital, common in the early Gothic period.

ringing chamber: The room in a tower where the bells are rung, usually on an upper floor.

roll: Thin, cylindrical edge moulding.

round tower: In England, a Saxon or Norman circular flint bell tower.

rubble walling: A wall constructed from uncut stones laid randomly or in courses.

running corbel: Continuous horizontal course of masonry projecting from a wall to support a load.

segmental arch: An arch formed of a single segment of a circle where the diameter is greater than the width of the opening.

segmental pointed arch: A segment of a pointed arch in which the radii of the arches extend beyond the width of the opening.

setback buttress: A perpendicular pair of buttresses supporting an external corner but set back so that the corner remains visible.

set-off: The stepping-back of masonry, particularly a buttress, protected by a sloping weathering stone.

shaft: A continuous, slender vertical member of circular, octagonal or hexagonal section providing support and adding vertical emphasis to a composition.

shaft ring: *see* **annulet**

soffit: The underside of an architectural element, such a ceiling, vault, beam or arch.

soufflet: Tracery motif of a quatrefoil with two opposing ends that are pointed, the other two rounded; from the French for 'bellows'.

sound hole: *see* **air hole**

spandrel: A panel of wall enclosed between an arch and rectangular framing members.

spiral stair: *see* **helical stair**

spire: A tall, steeply pitched pyramidal roof terminating a church tower, usually octagonal on plan.

spire light: *see* **lucarne**

spire path: A path running between the base of a recessed spire and the parapet.

spirelet: A small spire.

splay: A wide, chamfered surface of masonry around an opening such as a door, window or loophole.

splay-footed spire: An octagonal spire rising from a square base, the lower part resembling a square pyramid with chamfered corners.

springer: The first voussoir immediately above the springing of an arch.

springing or **spring**: The horizontal level from which an arch starts to rise.

squash tracery: Tracery compressed into the space beneath a four-centred arch.

squinch: Masonry arches, corbels or other structure spanning the internal corner of a square tower to support the diagonal face of an octagonal spire or lantern.

stage: A principal vertical division of an elevation.

steeple: All-embracing term for a tower and any spire or lantern that it may support.

stiff-leaf: Conventionalized upright foliage decoration with prominent stalks and rounded lobes, typical of Gothic capitals c. 1170–1280.

stilted arch: An arch in which the window head defined by the capitals, imposts or head tracery starts below the spring of the arch.

string or **string course**: Projecting horizontal course of masonry dividing a wall into vertical sections, sometimes acting as a drip or joined to a hood-mould.

subarcuated: A window having secondary arches beneath the main arch.

sub-reticulated: Tracery in which a smaller reticulation occurs within a main reticulation.

supermullion: An intermediate secondary mullion springing from the head of an archlet.

supertransom: A transom in a window head above the springing of the arch.

three-centred arch: An arch struck from three centres, the central arc being much wider than the outer arcs, approximating half an ellipse.

tie-beam: Horizontal roof beam that ties the feet of the principal rafters.

tierceron rib: Secondary rib rising directly from the springing of a vault to the ridge.

tower arch: An arch supporting a tower wall at ground level, opening the tower to the body of the church.

tracery: The pattern of intersecting or abutting stone bars concentrated in the head of a window of two or more bays springing from the mullions and jambs.

transennae: Saxon mid-wall decorative slabs.

transept: The transverse arm of the main body of a church, projecting north or south from a crossing.

transom: Horizontal structural member in the body of a window.

trefoil: A regular geometrical figure of three foils between three cusps, used in tracery and surface decoration, frequently set within a circle.

triforium: A high-level arcade within the body of a church set below the clerestory, in England forming the middle of three stories in a great church.

Tudor arch: An exceptionally shallow form of four-centred arch.

Tudor flower: Stylized upright leaf-like decoration used particularly in brattishing.

Tudor rose: Stylized five-petal rose decoration, symbolic of the Tudor dynasty, combining the roses of York and Lancaster.

turret: A small, slender tower capable of occupation, or at least appearing as such; frequently battlemented and often accommodating a spiral stair.

two-centred arch: An arch struck from two centres level with the springing of the arch

tympanum: The area of wall between a horizontal lintel and an enclosing arch, usually decorated with sculpture; common over Norman doorways.

upright and flat work: Saxon quoins formed of long vertical stones alternating with square horizontal slabs.

vault: An arched masonry ceiling, occasionally imitated in other materials.

vaulting shaft: A shaft supporting the springing a vault.

vesica: A pointed vertical figure of two mirrored segments of an arc, often in the form of a shallow niche containing a statue.

voussoir: A wedge-shaped stone forming the segment of an arch.

wall post: Upright timber post tight to a perimeter wall and supported on a corbel.

'Y' tracery: Simple divergent tracery in a two-light window, with the mullion branching into two arches of the same radius as the main arch.

Bibliography

GENERAL SOURCES

Allen, Frank J., *The Great Church Towers of England* (Cambridge: Cambridge University Press, 1932).

Baldwin, John, et al., *Dove's Guide for Church Bell Ringers to the Rings of Bells of the World* (n.p.: Central Council of Church Bell Ringers, 2012).

Betjeman, Sir John (ed.), *Collins Guide to English Parish Churches* (London: Collins, 1958).

Bond, Francis, *Gothic Architecture in England* (London: Batsford, 1905).

Bond, Francis, *An Introduction to English Church Architecture*, 2 vols (Oxford: Oxford University Press, 1913).

Brandon, Raphael and J. Arthur, *An Analysis of Gothic Architecture*, 2 vols (London: Pelham Richardson, 1847).

Brown, G. Baldwin, *The Arts in Early England*, 6 vols (London: John Murray, 1903–37).

Clifton-Taylor, Alec, *English Parish Churches as Works of Art* (London: Batsford, 1986).

Cox, J. Charles, *The English Parish Church* (London: Batsford, 1914).

Fisher, E. A., *Anglo-Saxon Towers: An Architectural and Historic Study* (Newton Abbot: David & Charles, 1969).

Freeman, E. A., *An Essay on the Origin and Development of Window Tracery in England* (Oxford: John Henry Parker, 1851).

Hart, Stephen, *The Round Church Towers of England* (Thorndon: Lucas Books, 2003).

Hart, Stephen, *Flint Flushwork: A Medieval Masonry Art* (Woodbridge: Boydell Press, 2008).

Hart, Stephen, *Medieval Church Window Tracery in England* (Woodbridge: Boydell Press, 2012).

Harvey, John H., *Gothic England: A Survey of National Culture 1300–1550* (London: Batsford, 1947).

Harvey, John H., *The Master Builders: Architecture in the Middle Ages* (London: Thames & Hudson, 1971).

Harvey, John H., *The Perpendicular Style: 1330–1485* (London: Batsford, 1978).

Harvey, John H., 'Somerset Perpendicular: The Dating Evidence', *Ancient Monuments Society's Transactions*, vol. 26 (1982), pp. 49–60.

Harvey, John H., 'The Church Towers of Somerset', *Ancient Monuments Society's Transactions*, vol. 27 (1983), pp. 157–83.

Harvey, John H., *English Mediaeval Architects: A Biographical Dictionary Down to 1550*, 2nd edn (London: Allan Sutton, 1984).

Haward, Birkin, *Suffolk Medieval Church Arcades, 1150–1550* (Hitcham: Suffolk Institute of Archaeology and History, 1993).

Historic England, *The National Heritage List for England* (c. 1947–70) [containing the Statutory Listing for all listed Buildings].

Hutton, Graham, and Olive Cook, photographs by Edwin Smith, *English Parish Churches* (London: Thames & Hudson, 1976).

Jackson, Sir T. G., *Gothic Architecture in France, England and Italy* (Cambridge: Cambridge University Press, 1915).

Jenkins, Simon, *England's Thousand Best Churches* (London: Penguin Books, 2000).

Lee, L. G. H., *The Church Spires of Northamptonshire* (Rushden: Northamptonshire Printing and Publishing Co., 1946).

Paley, F. A., with Fawcett, *A Manual of Gothic Mouldings*, 5th edn (London: Gurney & Jackson, 1891).

Pevsner, Sir Nikolaus, with John Harris (Lincs), Ian A. Richmond (Northumberland), et al., *The Buildings of England* (London: Penguin, 1951–74; Yale University Press, 2002).

Prior, E. S., *History of Gothic Art in England* (n.p.: London, 1900).

Rickman, Thomas, *An Attempt to Discriminate the Styles of Architecture in England*, 5th edn (London: John Henry Parker, 1848).

Rodwell, Warwick, *The Archaeology of Churches* (Stroud: Amberley Publishing, 2012).

Sharpe, Edmund, *A Treatise on the Rise and Progress of Decorated Window Tracery of England* (London: John van Voorst, 1849).

Sharpe, Edmund, *The Seven Periods of English Architecture*, 3rd edn (London: E. & F. N. Spon, 1888).

Sharpe, Edmund, J. Johnson and A. H. Kersey, *Churches of the Nene Valley* (London: Batsford, 1880).

Taylor, H. M. and J., *Anglo-Saxon Architecture* (Cambridge: Cambridge University Press, 1964).

Wickes, Charles, *Illustrations of the Spires and Towers of the Mediaeval Churches of England*, 3 vols (London: Thompson & Co., 1853–59).

SOURCES FOR INDIVIDUAL CHURCHES

Adderbury

Allen, Nicholas, 'The Medieval Stone Carvings of the Church of St. Mary's Adderbury', *Cake and Cockhorse*, Banbury Historical Society, vol. 15, no. 4 (2001).

Allen, Nicholas, *An English Parish Church: Its Story. St Mary the Virgin, Adderbury Oxfordshire* (Wykeham Press, 2011).

Lobel, Mary D. and Crossley, Alan (eds), *A History of the County of Oxford*, vol. IX: *Bloxham Hundred*, Victoria County History (London: Oxford University Press, 1969).

Barnack

Dickinson, Philip, revised J. Martin Goodwin, *A Guide to the Historic Parish Church of St John the Baptist, Barnack* (Stamford: Chadwick Associates, 1990).

Boston

Jebb, G. S. W., 'Boston Church', *Memorials of Old Lincolnshire*, ed. E. Mansel Sympson (London: George Allen, 1911).

Spurrell, Revd Mark, revised Michael Haynes et al., *The Stump: Boston Parish Church, St Botolph's* (Much Wenlock: R. L. J. Smith, 2001).

Trollope, Ven. Edward, 'Boston and other Churches visited by the Society, June 16th and 17th June 1870', *Reports and Papers of the Architectural and Archaeological Societies of the counties of Lincoln and Northampton*, vol. 10 (1867).

Brant Broughton

Trollope, Ven. Edward, 'The Church of St. Mary Magdalene, Newark, and other Churches visited by the Society, June 22nd & 23rd June 1871', *Reports and Papers of the Architectural and Archaeological Societies of the counties of Lincoln and Northampton*, vol. 11 (1871).

Castor

Tovey, Helen (ed.), *St Kyneburgha's Castor* (St Kyneburgha Building Preservation Trust: 2006).

Dedham

Cooper, Janet (ed.), *A History of the County of Essex*, vol. X: *Lexden Hundred (Part)*, Victoria County History (Oxford: Oxford University Press, 2001).

Moate, Revd Gerard (ed.), *Royal Commission on Ancient Monuments: A Survey of Dedham Parish Church, 1922* (2006).

Earls Barton

Audouy, Michael, B. Dix and D. Parsons, 'The tower of All Saints' Church, Earls Barton, Northamptonshire: Its construction and context', *Archaeological Journal*, vol. 152 (1995), pp. 73–94.

Baker, M. R. H., *The Anglo-Saxon Tower at Earls Barton, Northamptonshire: Its history, structure and form*, unpublished MA thesis (Keele University, 1988).

Hart, Andrew, *Earls Barton, All Saints Church* (Earls Barton, 1997).

Salzman, L. F. (ed.), *The Victoria History of the County of Northampton*, vol. IV, Victoria County History (London: Oxford University Press, 1937).

Ewerby
Brandon, Raphael and J. Arthur, *Parish Churches*, vol. 2 (London: W. Kent & Co., 1848).

Trollope, Revd Edward, 'Notes on Sleaford and Churches in its Vicinity, visited by the Society in 1863', *Reports and Papers of the Architectural and Archaeological Societies of the counties of Lincoln and Northampton*, vol. 7 (1863).

Eye
Jones, David, and Salmon, John, *Eye Church* (Norwich: Jarrold, 1980).

Forncett St Peter
Izat, Rosemary, revised John Webster, *The Parish Church of Forncett St Peter, Norfolk: An Historical Guide* (Norfolk, 2009).

Fotheringhay
Anon., *Some Remarks Upon the Church of Fotheringhay, Northamptonshire: Read at a Meeting of the Oxford Society for Promoting the Study of Gothic Architecture* (1841).

Bonney, Revd H. K., *Historic Notices in Reference to Fotheringhay* (Oundle: T. Bell, 1821).

Brandon, Raphael and J. Arthur, *An Analysis of Gothic Architecture* (London: Pelham Richardson, 1847).

Royal Commission on Historic Monuments, *An Inventory of the Architectural Monuments in the County of Northampton*, vol. VI (London, 1984).

Grantham
Bonney, Revd H. K., *Bonney's Church Notes* (Lincoln: Keyworth, 1937).

Maddison, George, 'St. Wolfran's Parish Church, Grantham', *Grantham Red Book* (Grantham: Ridge, 1878).

Pointer, Michael, *Glory of Grantham: Story of St Wulfram's Church* (Grantham: Bygone Grantham, 1978).

Scott, Sir George Gilbert, 'The Architectural History of St Wolfran's Church, Grantham', *Reports and Papers of the Architectural and Archaeological Societies of the counties of Lincoln and Northampton*, vol. 13 (1875).

Street, Revd Benjamin, *Historical Notes on Grantham and Grantham Church* (Grantham: S. Ridge & Son, 1857).

Sympson, E. Mansel (ed.), *Memorials of Old Lincolnshire* (London: George Allen, 1911).

Trollope, Ven. Edward, 'Notes on the Churches visited by the Society, June 19th & 20th 1867', *Reports and Papers of the Architectural and*

Archaeological Societies of the counties of Lincoln and Northampton, vol. 9 (1867).

Heckington
Fletcher, Sir Banister, *A History of Architecture on the Comparative Method*, 17th edn (London: Athlone Press, University of London, 1961), pp. 430–31.

Trollope, Revd Edward, 'Notes on Sleaford and other Churches in its vicinity, visited by the Society in 1863', *Architectural Society of the Diocese of Lincoln Associated Architectural Societies Reports and Papers*, vol. 7, pt. 1 (1863).

Watkins, W. G., 'The Church of St. Andrew Heckington', *Memorials of Old Lincolnshire* (London: George Allen, 1911).

Higham Ferrers
Bony, Jean, 'Higham Ferrers Church: Report of the Summer Meeting of the Royal Archaeological Institute at Northampton in 1953', *Archaeological Journal*, vol. 110 (1953), pp. 190–92.

Bridges, John, *The History and Antiquities of Northamptonshire, Compiled from the Manuscript Collections of the Late Learned Antiquary John Bridges, Esq. by the Revd. Peter Whalley*, vol. 2 (London: T. Payne, 1791).

Britton, J. and Evans, Revd J., *The Beauties of England and Wales*, vol. XI (London: Vernor, Hood & Sharpe, 1810), pp. 182–84.

Fry, H. K., *Higham Ferrers Church* (London: SPCK, 1927).

Page, William (ed.), *The Victoria History of the County of Northampton*, vol. III, Victoria County History (London: St Catherine Press, 1930).

Schnebbelie, Jacob, *An Account of Some Bass Reliefs at Higham Ferrers Church, Northamptonshire* (London: J. Nichols, 1791).

Ingatestone
Wilde, E. E., *Ingatestone and the Essex Great Road with Fryerning* (London: Oxford University Press, 1913).

Kettering
Billings, R. W., *Architectural Illustrations of Kettering Church, Northamptonshire* (London: Thomas & William Boone, 1843).

Page, William (ed.), *The Victoria History of the County of Northampton*, vol. III, Victoria County History (London: St Catherine Press, 1930).

Ketton
Trollope, Right Revd Edward, 'Churches in the Neighbourhood of Stamford, visited May 28th, 1897', *Reports and Papers of the Architectural and Archaeological Societies of the counties of Lincoln and Northampton*, vol. 15 (1897).

Page, William (ed.), *The Victoria History of the County of Rutland*, vol. II, Victoria County History (London: St Catherine Press, 1935).

Parsons, David, 'St Mary, Ketton and some other Rutland churches', *Archaeological Journal*, vol. 136 (1979), pp. 118–24.

Lavenham
Anon., *Lavenham Church, Suffolk*, church guide (n.d.).

Brandon, Raphael and J. Arthur, *An Analysis of Gothic Architecture* (London: W. Kent & Co., 1847).

Caroe, W. D., *Lavenham: The Church and its Builders* (London: William Clowes & Sons, 1910).

Leigh-on-Mendip
Clifton-Taylor, Alec, *Buildings of Delight* (London: Victor Gollancz, 1986), pp. 133–37.

Long Sutton
Trollope, Ven. Edward, 'The Churches of Holbeach and other parishes in Lincolnshire visited by members of the Architectural Society, June 5th 1872', *Reports and Papers of the Architectural and Archaeological Societies of the counties of Lincoln and Northampton*, vol. 11 (1872).

Wills, Norman T., *History of the Parish and Church of Long Sutton, Lincolnshire*, 5th edn (Boston: L. J. Ruskin, 1986).

Louth
Bayley, Robert Slater, *Notitiae Lundae; or, Notices of Louth* (London: Simpkin & Marshall, 1834).

Britton, John, *The Architectural Antiquities of Great Britain*, vol. IV (London: Longman, Hurst, Rees and Orme, 1814).

Dudding, Revd Reginald C., *The First Churchwardens' Book of Louth, 1500–24* (Oxford: Oxford University Press, 1941).

Fowler, James, 'The Church of St James, Louth, and other churches visited by the Society on the 26th and 27th of June, 1873', *Transactions of Lincoln Archaeological Society, 1873, Reports and Papers of the Architectural and Archaeological Societies of the counties of Lincoln and Northampton*, vol. 12 (1873).

Lowick
McMorran, Donald Hanks, measured drawings (1924), RIBA Drawings Collection.

Page, William (ed.), *The Victoria History of the County of Northampton*, vol. III, Victoria County History (London: St Catherine Press, 1930).

Rouse, E. C., 'Lowick Church: Report of the Summer Meeting of the Royal Archaeological Institute at Northampton in 1953', *Archaeological Journal*, vol. 110 (1953), p. 190.

Sackville, S. G. Stopford, 'Notes on Lowick Church, with especial reference to its Monuments and Heraldic Glass: A Paper read at the Annual Meeting of the Architectural Society of the Archdeanery of Northampton, December 10th, 1883', *Reports and Papers Read at the Meetings of the Architectural Societies of the Diocese of Lincoln, County of York, Archdeaconries of Northampton and Oakham, County of Bedford, Diocese of Worcester and County of Leicester during the year 1883*.

Ludlow
Irvine, J. T., *Historical sketches of church of St Lawrence in Ludlow; and its restoration in 1859–60 by G. G. Scott Esq., architect ARA* (Ludlow: J. Evans, 1860).

Woolley, George, *The Parish Church of St Lawrence Ludlow: A Monograph of the Tower Restoration 1889–91* (Ludlow: George Woolley, Bull Ring, 1873).

Moulton
Foster, W. E., 'Notes on the Fabric of All Saints' Church, Moulton, Read to Members of the Lincoln and Nottingham Architectural Society at the Annual Meeting of 1890', *Reports and Papers read at the Meeting of the Architectural Societies of the Counties of Lincoln and Nottingham ... during the year 1889* (1890).

Newark-on-Trent
Dimock, Revd J. F., 'Newark Church, its Documented History', *Lincoln Diocesan Architectural Society, Reports and Papers of the Architectural and Archaeological Societies of the counties of Lincoln and Northampton*, 1856.

Pask, Brenda M., *The Parish Church of St Mary Magdalene, Newark-on-Trent, Nottinghamshire* (Newark: St Mary Magdalene PCC, 1995).

Scott, George Gilbert, 'Newark Church, its Architectural History', *Reports and Papers of the Architectural and Archaeological Societies of the counties of Lincoln and Northampton*, 1856.

Trollope, Ven. Edward, 'The Church of St Mary Magdalene, Newark, and other Churches visited by the Society on the 22nd and 23rd of June, 1871', *Lincoln Diocesan Architectural Society, Reports and Papers of the Architectural and Archaeological Societies of the counties of Lincoln and Northampton*, vol. 11 (1871).

North Petherton
Dunning, R. W., *A History of the County of Somerset*, vol. VI: *Andersfield, Cannington and North Petherton Hundreds*, Victoria County History (Oxford: Oxford University Press, 1992).

North Rauceby

Clarke, Basil V. F., *St Peter's Church, North Rauceby: A Brief History* (South Rauceby: n.d.).

Trollope, Revd Edward, 'Notes on Sleaford and Churches in its Vicinity, visited by the Society in 1863', *Reports and Papers of the Architectural and Archaeological Societies of the counties of Lincoln and Northampton*, vol. 7 (1863).

Patrington

Allison, K. J. (ed.), *A History of the County of York: East Riding*, vol. V: *Holderness Southern Part*, Victoria County History (London: Oxford University Press, 1984).

Fawcett, Joshua, *Churches of Yorkshire*, vol. 2 (Leeds: T. W. Green, 1844).

Poulson, George, *The History and Antiquities of the Seigniory of Holderness* (Hull: Thomas Topping, 1841).

Raunds

Brandon, Raphael and J. Arthur, *Parish Churches*, vol. 2 (London: W. Kent & Co., 1858).

Salzman, L. F. (ed.), *The Victoria History of the County of Northampton*, vol. IV, Victoria County History (London: Oxford University Press, 1937).

Redenhall

Tricker, Roy, *St Mary's Church: Guide* (Redenhall, 2010).

Salle

Parsons, W. L. E., *Salle* (Norwich: Jarrold & Son, 1937).

Pink, R. C., et al., drawings by T. C. Yates, 'The Architectural Association's Excursion in Norfolk', *The Building News*, 14 January 1881.

St Cuthbert, Wells

Serel, Thomas, *Historical Notes on the Church of Saint Cuthbert in Wells: The Priory of St. John, College of La Mountery, and Chapels Formerly at Southover, Southway, Polsham, and Chilcote* (Wells: J. M. Atkins, 1875).

St Mary, Oxford

Case, Thomas, *St Mary's Clusters: An Historical Enquiry Concerning the Pinnacled Steeple of the University Church, Oxford* (Oxford: James Parker, 1893).

Crossley, Alan (ed.), *A History of the County of Oxford*, vol. IV: *The City of Oxford*, Victoria County History (Oxford: Oxford University Press, 1979).

Jackson, Sir Thomas G., *The Church of St Mary the Virgin, Oxford* (Oxford: Clarendon Press, 1897).

Jackson, Sir Thomas G., 'The Church of St Mary the Virgin in Oxford', 3 parts, *Architectural Review*, vol. 4 (1898).

Pugin, A. C., *Specimens of Gothic Architecture; Selected from Various Antient Edifices in England*, vol. II (London: J. Taylor, 1823).

R. H. [Revd Richard Harington], 'Remarks on the Church of St. Mary the Virgin, Oxford', *Archaeological Journal*, June 1851, pp. 126–42.

St Mary, Stamford

Crowther-Beynon, V. B., 'Stamford', *Memorials of Old Lincolnshire*, ed. E. Mansel Sympson (London: George Allen, 1911).

'RIBA Pugin Studentship Prize Drawings, 1911. By J. B. F. Cowper, Ashpitel Prizeman', *The Building News*, 17 February 1911.

St Mary Magdalene, Taunton

Askwith, W. H. et al., *The Church of St Mary Magdalene Taunton 1508–1908* (Taunton: Alfred E. Goodman, 1908).

Cottle, Revd James, *Some Account of the Restoration of the Church of St. Mary Magdalene, Taunton, Somerset* (London: Vizetelly Brothers, 1845).

Weaver, Revd F. W. (ed.), *Somerset Medieval Wills (1388–1500)*; *Somerset Medieval Wills (Second Series: 1501–1530)*, Somerset Record Society (London: Harrison & Sons, 1901 and 1903).

St Mary Redcliffe

Aughton, Peter, *St Mary Redcliffe: The Church and Its People* (Bristol: Redcliffe Press Ltd., 2008).

Barrett, William, *The History and Antiquities of the City of Bristol* (Bristol: William Pine, 1789), pp. 566–99.

Britton, John, *Some Account of Redcliffe Church, Bristol* (London: M. Taylor, 1818).

Norris, Revd J. P., 'Notes on the Church of St. Mary Redcliffe', *Transactions of the Bristol and Gloucestershire Archaeological Society*, vol. III (1878–79), pp. 193–210.

St Mary Redcliffe Church Restoration Committee, *Sixteen years' doings in the restoration of St. Mary Redcliffe Church* (Bristol: C. T. Jefferies, 1858).

Smith, Dr Michael Quinton, *St Mary Redcliffe: An Architectural History* (Bristol: Redcliffe Press Ltd., 1994).

St Michael, Coventry

Anon, 'St Michael Coventry to be restored by J. O. Scott', *The Building News*, vol. 47, 31 October 1884, pp. 800–801, and 14 November 1884, pp. 790–91.

Pickford, Christopher J., *The Steeple, Bells, and Ringers of Coventry Cathedral* (Bedford: C. J. Pickford, 1987).

Reader, William, *Description of St. Michael's Church, Coventry; With the Inscriptions &c* (Coventry, 1830).

Sharp, Thomas, *Illustrations of the history and antiquities of St. Michael's Church, Coventry, from Original Documents* (Coventry, 1818).

Stephens, W. B. (ed.), *A History of the County of Warwick*, vol. VIII: *The City of Coventry and Borough of Warwick*, Victoria County History (London: Oxford University Press, 1969).

St Nicholas, Newcastle-upon-Tyne

Johnson, R. J., drawings and description of Newcastle Cathedral spire, *The Building News*, 7 June 1878.

Longstaffe, W. Hylton Dyer, 'St Nicholas' Church, Newcastle-upon-Tyne', *Architectural and Archaeological Society of Durham and Northumberland, Transactions*, vol. 2, pt. 1, 1869/1875, pp. 134–39.

Lovie, David, *The Cathedral Church of St Nicholas, Newcastle upon Tyne* (Norwich: Jarrold, 2005).

Mackenzie, Eneas, 'St Nicholas' church: History and architecture', *A Descriptive and Historical Account of the Town and County of Newcastle-upon-Tyne: Including the Borough of Gateshead*, vol. 1 (Newcastle: Mackenzie & Dent, 1827).

Oliver & Leeson, drawings and description of Newcastle Cathedral spire, *The Builder*, 8 October 1898.

Southwold

Bottomley, Alan, *The Church of St Edmund, King and Martyr, Southwold* (Norwich: Jarrold, 1991).

Dowding, A. T. W., *History of Southwold Church* (1930).

Stoke-by-Nayland

Brandon, Raphael and J. Arthur, *An Analysis of Gothic Architecture* (London: Pelham Richardson, 1847).

Engleheart, Francis, revised Henry Engleheart et al., *Church of St Mary, Stoke by Nayland* (Stoke-by-Nayland: Friends of St Mary's Church, 2000).

Torlesse, Revd Charles Morton, *Some Account of Stoke by Nayland, Suffolk,* (London: Harrison & Son, 1877).

Tickhill

Beastall, Tom W., *Portrait of an English Parish Church: St Mary's Parish Church, Tickhill* (Tickhill: St Mary's PCC, n.d.).

Titchmarsh

Page, William (ed.), *The Victoria History of the County of Northampton*, vol. III, Victoria County History (London: St Catherine Press, 1930).

West Walton

Follett, S. G., 'RIBA Pugin Studentship Drawings', *The Building News*, 30 October 1908.

Wilson, A. N., 'RIBA Silver Medal Drawings', *The Building News*, 20 June 1884.

Whittlesey

Pugh, R. B. (ed.), *The Victoria History of the County of Cambridge and the Isle of Ely*, vol. IV, Victoria County History (London: Oxford University Press, 1953).

Wilby

Brandon, Raphael and J. Arthur, *Parish Churches*, vol. 2 (London: W. Kent & Co., 1848).

Salzman, L. F. (ed.), *The Victoria History of the County of Northampton*, vol. IV, Victoria County History (London: Oxford University Press, 1937).

Witney

Townley, Simon (ed.), *A History of the County of Oxford*, vol. XIV: *Witney and its Townships: Bampton Hundred (Part Two)*, Victoria County History (Woodbridge: Boydell Press, 2004).

Index

Index of Places

Historic county names are used throughout.

Ab Kettleby (Leics) 47
Aberdeen, Kings College 48, 435
Adderbury (Oxon) 10, 21, 24, 33, 89, **124–29**, 472
Agincourt, Battle of 274
Aldwinkle (Northants) 25
　All Saints 23, 25
　St Peter 37
Ancaster stone 78, 182
Anston stone 254
Anwick (Lincs) 185, 193
Apethorpe (Northants) 207
Asgarby (Lincs) 45, 47
Ashbourne (Derbys) 24, 40, 46, 127, 176

Bampton (Oxon) 85, 89, 127
Banwell (Som) 238
Bardney Abbey (Lincs) 198
Barkby (Leics) 37
Barkston (Lincs) 47
Barnack (Hunts) 10, 27, 35, 36, 38, 48, 53, **64–69**, 160, 257, 282, 352, 472
Barnack stone, ragstone 90, 153, 288, 297
Barrowden (Rutland) 37
Barton-on-Humber (Lincs) 16, 53, 57
Batcombe (Som) 27, 377, 378, 388, 407
Bath Abbey (Som) 18, 23
Bath and Wells, diocese 247
Beeford (Yorks East) 25, 251, 258, 367
Bernières 85
Beverley (Yorks East)
　Minster 171, 218, 447
　St Mary 331
Billingborough (Lincs) 45, 46
Bingham (Notts) 40
Binham Abbey (Norfolk)
Bishops Lydeard (Som) 25, 387, 392
Blakeney (Norfolk) 24
Bloxham (Oxon) 89, 222, 257, 271, 355
Blyth (Notts) 25
Bolsover (Derbys) 37
Boston (Lincs) 23, 31, 33, 35, 45, 46, 64, 150, 180, 415, **444–57**, 472
Bosworth, Battle of 395, 412
Bradford Abbas (Dorset) 421
Brant Broughton (Lincs) 12, 13, 19, 21, 25, 27, 33, 34, 35, 40, 47, 78, 127, 149, 185, **192–97**, 221, 472
Brayton (Yorks West) 47
Bretteville 85
Bridlington (Yorks East) 252

Brigstock (Northants) 37
Bristol
　Cathedral 26
　St Mary Redcliffe 5, 12, 13, 21, 27, 33, 40, 46, **170–81**, 477
　St Stephen 25, 371
　Temple Church 230, 399
Brixworth (Northants) 31
Broadwell (Oxon) 89
Broughton Astley (Leics) 47
Broughton-by-Brigg (Lincs) 31, 57
Bruton (Som) 24, 371, 378, 381
Buckminster (Leics) 44
Buckworth (Hunts) 37
Bungay (Suffolk) 23, 310, 422
Burton-le-Coggles (Lincs) 36, 78
Bury St Edmunds (Suffolk) 317, 426
Butley Priory (Suffolk) 303
Byfield (Northants) 41
Byland Abbey (Yorks North) 218
Bythorn (Hunts) 34

Caen 297, 421
Cambridge
　colleges 15, 153
　Great St Mary 426
　King's College Chapel 9, 278, 426, 448
　St John's College 428
Cambridgeshire 282
Canterbury Cathedral 16, 278
Carlisle Cathedral 451
Casterton stone 415
Castle Acre Priory (Norfolk) 99, 229
Castle Hedingham (Essex) 432
Castor (Hunts) 16, 27, 33, 36, **70–77**, 106
Cawston (Norfolk) 287, 294
Caythorpe (Lincs) 24, 25, 45, 47, 189, 197
Cerne Abbas (Dorset) 421
Chartres Cathedral 35
Cheddar (Som) 238
Chedzoy (Som) 26, 410
Cherwell, River 338
Chester-le-Street (Durham) 47
Chesterfield (Derbys) 474
Chichester Cathedral 90
Chipping Campden (Glos) 12, 23, 27, 34, **322–329**, 472
Chittlehampton (Devon) 403
Church Honeybourne (Worcs) 89
Cirencester (Glos) 392
Claypole (Lincs) 47
Clifton Campville (Staffs) 27, 45, 229, 268
Clipsham (Rutland) 36
Colchester earthquake 425, 432

Coleby (Lincs) 45, 47
Coleshill (Warks) 47, 272
Collyweston slate 72, 185
Colne Engaine (Essex) 25
Cologne Cathedral 435
Conington (Cambs) 41, 485
Cotswolds 10
Cottingham (Yorks East) 37, 247
Coventry (Warks) 27, 48, 115
　Christ Church 263
　Holy Trinity 271
　St Michael 10, 13, 21, 31, 45, 46, 68, 132, 138, 180, 257, **262–73**, 477
Coxwold (Yorks North) 18, 251
Cranmore (Som) 24, 378
Crécy, Battle of 182
Cromer (Norfolk) 34, 35, 392, 412
Crowland Abbey (Lincs) 99, 229

Dedham (Essex) 12, 13, 19, 23, 24, 31, 294, 334, 412, **420–27**, 473
Deene (Northants) 46
Denford (Northants) 40, 46
Deopham (Norfolk) 25
Derbyshire 24, 37, 41
Desborough (Northants) 37
Digby (Lincs) 47
Doddington (Cambs) 37
Dogdyke (Lincs) 467, 481
Donington (Lincs) 18, 46, 90, 182
Dorset 371
Doulting stone 242, 371
Driffield *see* Great Driffield
Durham Cathedral 436, 463, 464
Durham, county 436

Earls Barton (Northants) 10, 16, 24, 31, 35, **52–57**, 64, 67, 71, 106, 175, 313, 322, 473
East Anglia 12, 18, 19, 24, 287, 294, 412
East Bergholt (Suffolk) 421
East Harling (Norfolk) 24
East Lexham (Norfolk) 67
Eastdean (East Sussex) 57
Easton (Hunts) 23
Easton Maudit (Northants) 24, 45, 46, 47, 342, 355
Easton-on-the-Hill (Northants) 25, 281
Edinburgh, St Giles Cathedral 47, 435
Ellington (Hunts) 37, 38
Elm (Cambs) 25
Elton (Hunts) 281
Ely Cathedral 18, 25, 38, 48, 444
Ely, Isle of 169
Empingham (Rutland) 24, 41, 46

Ermine Street 71
Essex 36, 428
Eton College (Berks) 454
Etton (Hunts) 36, 68, 78
Evercreech (Som) 12, 24, 27, 334, **370–77**, 407, 473
Ewerby (Lincs) 12, 18, 21, 27, 33, 34, 35, 38, 124–127, **182–191**, 193, 221, 234, 277, 473
Exeter Cathedral 71
Exton (Rutland) 46
Eye (Suffolk) 12, 23, 24, 33, 34, 53, 63, 294, **310–15**, 317, 318, 421, 473

Fen Causeway 345
Fenny Drayton (Leics) 47
Fens, The 90, 99, 229, 345
Fenton (Lincs) 47
Flanders 24, 431
Fleet (Lincs) 18, 45, 47, 90, 182
Flodden Field, Battle of 467
Folkingham (Lincs) 367
Forncett St Peter (Norfolk) 10, 24, 31, 33, 35, **58–63**, 473
Fosse Way 142
Fotheringhay (Northants) 12, 13, 18, 19, 23, 25, 27, 35, 48, 271, **274–85**, 360, 363, 457, 473, 479–80
Foulsham (Norfolk) 34, 292
Frampton (Lincs) 36, 81
France 16, 33, 45
Freyerning (Essex) 24

Garboldisham (Norfolk) 25, 422
Gedling (Notts) 46
Gedney (Lincs) 229
Gestingthorpe (Essex) 432
Glasgow, Tollbooth Steeple 443
Glastonbury, St John the Baptist (Som) 400
Glinton (Hunts) 41
Gloucester
　Cathedral 25, 322, 329, 399
　crown 25, 26, 329
Gosberton (Lincs) 45, 47
Grafham (Hunts) 40, 68, 352
Grafton Underwood (Northants) 46
Grantham (Lincs) 10, 12, 21, 27, 33, 34, 40, 45, 46, 47, 96, 115, **130–41**, 175, 182, 267, 459, 473
Great Bromley (Essex) 24
Great Driffield (Yorks North) 34, 367, 463
Great Malvern Priory (Worcs) 322
Great North Road 160
Great Ponton (Lincs) 19, 25, 258
Great Tey (Essex) 33
Great Yarmouth (Norfolk) 457

Haddington (Scotland) 435
Haddiscoe (Norfolk) 59
Hadleigh (Suffolk) 99
Ham Hill stone 388
Hampton Court Palace 428
Hanslope (Bucks) 46, 47
Harrold (Beds) 41
Haslingfield (Cambs) 25
Hatch Beauchamp (Som) 26, 410
Heckington (Lincs) 12, 25, 33, 45, 46, 124–127, 138, 149, 185, 193, **198–205**, 474
Hedon (Yorks East) 25, 247
Helpringham (Lincs) 45, 47, 342
Hemel Hempstead (Herts) 99
Hemingbrough (Yorks East) 222, 258
Hemingford Abbots (Hunts) 41
Herefordshire 90
Higham Ferrers (Northants) 12, 24, 46, 47, 106, **206–17**, 350, 355, 474
Holbeach (Lincs) 27, 233, 447
Holderness (Yorks East) 218, 251
Holland 431
Holme-on-Spalding-Moor (Yorks East) 25, 45, 251, 258, 367
Hough-on-the-Hill (Lincs) 31
Houghton (Hunts) 47, 352
Howden (Yorks East) 34, 247
Huish Episcopi (Som) 24, 25, 27, 395, 403, 407
Hull (Yorks East)
  Holy Trinity 25, 34, 247, 331, 439
  St Mary 436
Humber, River 142, 258
Humberstone (Leics) 47
Huntingdonshire 24, 64, 68, 71, 160

Ibstock (Leics) 47
Ingatestone (Essex) 12, 21, 24, 33, 34, **428–33**, 474
Irchester (Northants) 352
Isle Abbots (Som) 25, 27, 364, 387, 407
Italy 16

Kensington, St Mary Abbots 180
Kessingland (Suffolk) 303
Kesteven (Lincs) 182
Kenilworth Castle (Warks) 268
Kettering (Northants) 12, 45, 46, **338–43**, 346, 364, 474
Ketton (Rutland) 12, 16, 31, 33, 38, 40, 104, 146, **152–59**, 160, 164, 189, 341, 474
Ketton stone 153, 297
Keyston (Hunts) 38
Kimboulton (Hunts) 38
Kingsbury Episcopi (Som) 395, 403, 407
Kings Lynn (Norfolk)
  Red Mount Chapel 278
Kings Norton (Worcs) 47, 272
Kings Sutton (Northants) 46
Kingston St Mary (Som) 12, 19, 21, 24, 25, 27, 33, 34, 378, **386–91**, 396, 400, 404, 474
Kirkby Muxloe Castle (Leics) 454

Langford (Oxon) 67
Langport (Som) 407
Laughton-en-le-Morthen (Yorks West) 12, 18, 21, 27, 35, 46, 47, 221, **254–61**, 474
Lavenham (Suffolk) 12, 13, 19, 23, 24, 33, 34, 35, 294, 395, **412–19**, 474
Laxfield (Suffolk) 23, 24, 294, 307, 310
Layer Marney (Essex) 428
Leadenham (Lincs) 47

Leicester
  St Mary de Castro 45, 342
Leicestershire 44
Leigh-on-Mendip (Som) 12, 21, 24, 25, 27, 33, 371, **378–85**, 400, 474
Leire (Leics) 47
Leverington (Cambs) 90, 341
Lichfield Cathedral 40, 138, 176, 268, 322
Lincoln
  Cathedral 9, 35, 90, 93, 99, 131
  Priory of St Katherine 142
Lincolnshire
  county 10, 44, 45, 46, 53, 182, 447, 459
  limestone 78
  Wolds 459
Linlithgow (Scotland) 435
Liverpool Cathedral 444
London
  Old St Paul's Cathedral 34, 36, 99
  St Dunstan-in-the-East 443
  St Mary Abbots, Kensington 180
  St Mary-le-Bow 442
Long Sutton (Lincs) 10, 18, 23, 33, 90, **98–105**, 475
Longstanton (Cambs)
Louth (Lincs) 8, 9, 13, 18, 19, 23, 27, 34, 40, 44, 45, 46, 47, 115, 138, 150, 180, 451, **458–71**, 475, 481–84
Lowick (Northants) 12, 18, 23, 31, 48, 356, **358–63**, 364, 475
Ludlow (Shrops) 12, 13, 23, 27, 33, 34, 313, **330–37**, 421, 475
Lyng (Som) 403

Maldon (Essex) 18, 35
Malvern see Great Malvern
Market Harborough (Leics) 38, 40, 230
Markfield (Leics) 47
Marlborough (Wilts) 23, 421
Masham (Yorks North) 47, 68
Mears Ashby ironstone 478
Mells (Som) 24, 371, 378
Melrose Abbey 100
Melton Mowbray (Leics) 18, 154, 160, 341
Mendip
  East Mendip Group 25, 27, 28–29, 371, 378, 385, 391
  West Mendip Group 24, 247, 378, 91
Mere (Wilts) 421
Methwold (Norfolk) 47
Mickleton (Glos) 89
Middleton Cheney (Northants) 46, 127
Middlezoy (Som) 378
Mortimer's Cross, Battle of 298
Moulton (Lincs) 19, 21, 27, 31, 34, 40, 45, **228–37**, 257, 345, 346, 447, 475

Nassington (Northants) 47, 207
Nene, River 53, 90, 106, 274, 338, 364
Newark-on-Trent (Notts) 12, 13, 18, 21, 24, 25, 31, 34, 40, 44, 46, 106, 131, **142–51**, 160, 182, 215, 475
Newbury (Berks) 23, 421
Newcastle-upon-Tyne (Northumb) 13, 18, 34, 45, 48, 475
  All Saints 436
  St John 436
  St Nicholas 12, 23, 337, **434–43**, 475, 477
Newton Linford (Leics) 47
Norfolk 287, 310
Normandy 85
North Petherton (Som) 12, 24, 25, 27, 34, 396, **402–11**, 475

North Rauceby (Lincs) 10, 21, 33, 35, 36–37, 38, 68, **78–83**, 89, 104, 475
North Repps (Norfolk) 34, 292
North Walsham (Norfolk) 41221
Northamptonshire 10, 12, 24, 44, 45, 46, 350
Northleach (Glos) 322
Northumberland sandstone 477
Norton-under-Hampton (Som) 371
Norwich Cathedral 38, 71
Nottinghamshire 142, 254

Oakham (Rutland) 21, 45, 46, 138
Old Weston (Hunts) 40, 68
Olney (Bucks) 44
Oundle (Northants)
  St Peter 27, 106, 207
Oxford
  Magdalen College Chapel 421
  New College 238
  Radcliffe Square 115
  St Frideswide (Cathedral) 35, 78, 116
  St Mary 12, 13, 24, 40, 46, 89, **114–23**, 127, 476
Oxfordshire 35, 85, 89

Paston (Hunts) 37
Patrington (Yorks East) 12, 16, 19, 31, 47, **218–27**, 258, 476
Pennant stone 179
Pennines 142, 258
Pertenhall (Beds) 38
Peterborough (Hunts) 72, 278, 345
  Cathedral (Abbey) 426
  Soke of 169
Piddington (Northants) 36
Pinchbeck (Lincs) 229
Polebrook (Northants) 37, 124
Pontefract (Yorks West) 48
Preston, St Walbruge (Lancs) 180
Preston-in-Holderness (Yorks East) 251
Probus (Corn) 403, 407
Purbeck marble 90

Quantock Group 25, 27, 28–29, 387–88, 395, 399, 403
Quarrington (Lincs) 41
Queniborough (Leics) 44, 45, 342

Radcliffe Culey (Leics) 47
Raunds (Northants) 12, 21, 24, 27, 35, 38, 40, 86, 89, 96, 104, **106–13**, 115, 142, 146, 159, 160, 208, 212, 476
Redenhall (Norfolk) 2, 12, 19, 23, 25, 33, 63, 294, 310, **316–21**, 421, 476
Redcliffe see Bristol
Roche Abbey stone 252
Rockingham Forest 285
Romsey Abbey (Hants) 211
Rotherham (Yorks West)
  All Saints 46, 254
Rotherham stone 257
Ruishton (Som) 24, 407
Runcorn stone 267
Rushden (Northants) 24, 46, 47, 106, 215, 352, 355
Rutland 21, 24, 31, 41,152

St Albans Abbey (Herts) 71
St Neots (Hunts) 473, 475
Salisbury Cathedral (Wilts) 40, 44, 46, 90, 131, 138, 172, 179, 218
Salle (Norfolk) 12, 19, 21, 24, 31, 34, **286–93**, 294, 428, 476
Sancton (Yorks East) 18
Scrooby (Notts) 47, 254
Sedgefield (Durham) 436
Sheffield (York West) 254

Shepton Mallet (Som) 24, 238, 241–242, 378, 388
Sherburn-in-Elmet (York West) 247
Shipton-under-Wychwood (Oxon) 85, 127
Silk Willoughby (Lincs) 24, 45, 46, 78, 193, 201
Skirlaugh (Yorks East) 25, 247, 251, 252, 345
Slade Hooton stone 474
Sleaford (Lincs) 27, 36, 44, 78, 81, 182, 186
Snettisham (Norfolk) 46
Soham (Cambs) 25
Somerset 10, 12, 24, 25, 27, 28–29, 238, 364, 378, 392
South Anston (Yorks West) 47, 254
South Luffenham (Rutland) 47
South Repps (Norfolk) 34, 292
Southwell Minster (Notts) 33, 71
Southwold (Suffolk) 12, 21, 23, 24, **302–09**, 422, 477
Spalding (Lincs) 47
  Abbey 99, 229
  Spaldwick (Hunts) 38
Stamford (Lincs) 308
  All Saints 46
  St John 23
  St Martin 23, 367
  St Mary 12, 13, 19, 21, 27, 31, 38, 40, 53, 104, 150, 154, 159, **160–69**, 189, 208, 341, 476
Stanion stone
Stanwick (Northants) 40
Staple Fitzpaine (Som) 25, 27, 387, 407
Stoke-by-Nayland (Suffolk) 12, 13, 18, 23, 35, 288, 291, **294–301**, 428, 477
Stoke Golding (Leics) 47
Stour, River 421
Stowe-Nine-Churches (Northants) 53
Suffolk 36, 287, 303, 310
Sutton-in-the-Isle (Cambs) 48
Sutton St Mary see Long Sutton
Swineshead (Lincs) 47, 227

Tadcaster stone 304
Tainton stone 119
Tamworth (Staffs) 268
Tattershall (Lincs) 454
Taunton (Som)
  St James 25, 387, 392
  St Mary Magdalene 12, 13, 24, 25, 27, **392–401**, 403, 404, 476–77
Terrington St Clement (Norfolk) 18, 90
Thaxted (Essex) 44, 45, 47, 342
Theydon Garnon (Essex) 432
Thornbury (Glos) 23, 322, 329
Thorney Abbey (Cambs) 350
Thrybergh (Yorks West) 254
Tickhill (Yorks West)
  All Hallows 247
  Castle 254
  St Mary 12, 13, 18, 19, 23, 24, 25, 33, 34, 131, 145, 171, 221, **246–53**, 463, 477
Titchmarsh (Northants) 12, 23, 25, 31, 34, 355, 360, **364–69**, 477
Todenham (Glos) 89
Trunch (Norfolk) 24, 287

Uffington (Lincs) 47, 207
Ulceby (Lincs) 47
Ulm 435
Uppingham (Rutland) 41

Walberswick (Suffolk) 303
Walcot (Lincs) 128, 189

Walsoken (Norfolk) 90
Warboys (Hunts) 33, 36
Warmington (Northants) 35, 38, 82
Warrington, St Elphin (Ches) 180
Warwick
  St Mary 268
Warwickshire 37, 41, 477
Waveney, River 11, 310
Welbourn (Lincs) 45, 47, 189, 194
Weldon stone 338, 367
Welland, River 153, 160
Wellingborough (Northants) 352
Wells (Som)
  Cathedral 27, 238, 241, 245
  St Cuthbert 12, 23, 25, 27, 31,
  238–45, 334, 371–372, 476
West Deeping (Lincs) 47
West Mendip district (Som) 24, 238,
  378, 391
West Retford (Notts) 23, 46, 47, 254,
  258
West Walton (Norfolk) 10, 18, 19, 23,
  24, 31, 33, 86, **90–97**, 478
Westerleigh (Glos) 322
Westminster
  Abbey 211, 412, 444, 468
  Great Hall 444
  Palace 9
Weston (Lincs) 229
Weston Zoyland (Som) 378, 381
Whaplode (Lincs) 18, 90, 229
Whiston (Northants) 352, 364
Whittlesey (Cambs)
  Mere 345
  St Mary 12, 19, 23, 24, 27, 31, 33, 45,
    46, 47, 257, 342, **344–51**, 478
Wickham Market (Suffolk) 36
Wilby (Northants) 12, 23, 33, 34, 35,
  46, 47, 68, 257, **352–57**, 372, 478
Wilsford Heath Quarry (Lincs) 467
Windsor
  Castle 238
  Chapel 9
Winchcombe (Glos) 124, 322
Winchester (Hants)
  Cathedral 16, 238
  College 238, 241
Wingfield (Suffolk) 310
Winterton (Norfolk) 288, 294
Wisbech (Cambs) 18, 25, 90
Witham, River 444, 481
Witherley (Leics) 47, 272
Witney (Oxon) 10, 36, **84–89**, 115,
  127, 222, 478
Woodbridge (Suffolk) 307
Woodford (Northants) 46
Woodnewton (Northants)
  207
Worcester
  Cathedral 90
  diocese 171
Worcestershire 37
Worstead (Norfolk) 292
Wrington (Somerset) 27, 334, 371, 372
Wymondham (Norfolk) 287, 412, 421

Yardley (Worcs) 47, 272
Yate (Glos) 322
Yaxley (Hunts) 45, 46, 47, 281, 350
Yeovil (Som) 241
York
  All Saints, North Street 47
  All Saints, Pavement 48, 282
  Minster 218, 222, 463
  St Mary Castlegate 47
  St Mary's Abbey 444
Yorkshire 25, 247, 468
  Magnesian limestone 221, 254

Index of People

Alexander, Master, mason 90, 146
Allen, Frank J. 27, 247, 428
Allen, Nicholas 124
Atkins, Richard, mason 207

Bacon, John 317
Bacon, Thomas 317
Barrett, William 171, 176
Barton, Thomas, mason 463
Betjeman, Sir John 352
Bigot, Roger 59
Blomfield, Sir Arthur, architect 331
Blore, Edward, architect 119
Bodley, George F., architect 12, 193
Bodley & Garner, architects 193
Bond, Francis 9, 85, 86, 131, 468
Bony, Professor Jean 208
Bonney, Archdeacon Henry Kaye 278
Botolph, Saint 444
Botoner, Adam & William 268, 493
Brandon, J. Arthur, architect 185, 416
Brandon, Raphael, architect 298, 416
Britton, John, architect 207
Brown, G. Baldwin 54
Buckler, J. C. & C., architects 119
Bunning, Joan 317
Burton, Sir Simon de 171
Butterfield, William, architect 193

Canynges, William 176
Case, Thomas, Professor 120
Caywod, John 481
Chapman, John 467, 481
Clerk, Simon, mason 412
Clifton-Taylor, Alec 159, 197, 345,
  377, 378, 410
Cole, John, mason 457, 464, 467, 481
Constable, John 298
Cowper, J. B. F., architect 164
Cowper, John, mason 454

Denton, Stephen 421
Dudding, Revd Reginald C. 467, 481
Dugdale, Sir William 274

Eastfield, William 251
Edney, William 175
Edward III, King of England 182, 274
Edward IV, King of England 274
Elizabeth I, Queen of England 171,
  281
Ely, Reginald, mason 451
Erith, Raymond, architect 421
Ethelmund, King 444

Ferrier, Captain, surveyor 118, 123
Ferrey, Benjamin, architect 392, 399
Fletcher, Sir Banister 198, 211
Fowler, James, architect 463, 468, 471
Fry, Canon Henry 67

Garner, Thomas, architect 193
Gaunt, John of, 1st Duke of Lancaster
  251, 359
Godiva, Lady 185
Godwin, George, architect 172, 179
Gower, John, mason 322, 325, 337
Greene, Sir Henry 359
Greene, John 359
Greene Ralph 359
Grosseteste, Robert, Bishop of Lincoln
  153
Gryndall, Thomas 364

Harvey, John, architect 221, 241, 272,
  325, 334, 426

Houghton Spencer, J., architect 392
Henry III, King of England 185
Herland, Hugh 238
Hobbs, John, mason 337, 399
Holland, Sir John 359
Horwode, William, mason 274, 277,
  457, 479–480
Hoskin, Professor, architect 179
Howard family 297298
Howard, John, 1st Duke of Norfolk 298

Jackson, Sir T. G., architect 115–116,
  153, 425
Jenkins, Simon 352, 428
Jewitt, Orlando, architect 109, 119

Kempe, Charles E., glassmaker 341
Kerver, Robert II, mason 337
King, Vice-Chancellor 119
Kyneburgha, Saint 71
Kyneswitha, Saint 71

Lande, William de la 185
Laud, Archbishop of Canterbury 207
Lemyng, Laurence, mason 467, 482
Lesyngham, Robert, mason 268
Lexington, Revd William de 78
Lincoln, Bishop of 193, 230
Lovell family 364

Mackintosh, Charles Rennie, architect
  371
Martyn, Revd John   359
Mason, Clement, mason 337
Micklethwaite, J. T., architect 425
Morris, William 120, 287
Multon, family 229

Nethway, William 392, 395
Nettleton, William, mason 464, 481
Neville, Cecily 278, 281
Nicholson, Sir Charles, architect 454
Norfolk see Howard
Norris, Thomas, bellfounder 207
Nottingham, Edward, Bishop of 154

Oliver & Leeson, architects 442

Paley & Austin, architects 267
Palton, Robert 241
Patrington, Robert de, mason 221
Pearson, John Loughborough,
  architect 264
Pevsner, Sir Nikolaus 25, 222, 278,
  428
Place, George, architect 451
Pole, John de la, 2nd Duke of Suffolk
  310, 317
Potter, Joseph, architect 264
Pugin, A. C., architect 118, 123
Pugin, A. W. N., architect 78, 258

Rhodes, Robert 436
Rice, William, mason 172
Richard III, King of England 274
Rickman, Thomas, architect 10, 109,
  124
Rudd, Thomas, engineer 208
Ruskin, John 131
Russell, Richard, mason 303, 307

Sandford, John 247, 251
Scott, Sir George Gilbert, architect
  120, 131, 141, 142, 149, 154, 264, 392,
  439, 454
Scott, John Oldrid, architect 141, 263,
  264
Scott, Sir Walter 160
Scune, Christopher, mason 464, 482

Shakespeare, William 359
Sharpe, Edmund, architect 10, 229
Shelton, Revd Richard 317
Simms, Ronald George, architect 477
Skillyngton, Robert, mason 268
Skirlaw, Walter, Bishop of Bath and
  Wells 247
Slater, William, architect 212
Smith, William, architect 105, 230
Somerset family, Earls of Worcester
  364
Spence, Sir Basil, architect 263
Spencer, John, steward of the Bishop
  of Lincoln 467, 481
Spryng, Thomas II and III 412, 419
Squirhill, Charles, architect 112, 476
Street, George Edmund, architect 478
Sutton, Canon Fredrick Heathcote
  193

Taylor, Thomas 467
Tempas, John, mason 464, 467
Tendring family 297, 298
Terry, Quinlan, architect 421

Vere, John de, 13th Earl of Oxford 412

Wallis, Thomas William 13, 467
Wastell, John, mason 278, 426
Watt, James, architect 264
Webb, John 422
Webb, Thomas 422
Welby, Adlard 78
Wells, Hugh de, Bishop of Lincoln
  138, 153
Wickes, Charles 105
Wiltshire, Edward, 2nd Earl of 359
Winchcombe, Richard of, mason 124
Winchelsea, 12th Earl of 189
Woodcock, George 267
Wulfhere, King of Mercia 64
Wykeham, William of, Bishop of
  Winchester 238, 254
Wynford, William, mason 238, 254

Yeveley, Henry, mason 238
York
  Edward, Duke of 274, 281
  House of 274, 278, 282
  Richard, Duke of 274, 281

General Index

abacus 85, 154
air hole 34
aisles
  embracing 78, 185, 303, 334, 459
Anglo-Saxon 16, 33, 35, 53–57, 59
annulet *see* shaft rings
arcade 47, 109, 146, 154, 164, 172, 208, 222,
  blind 132, 160, 182
arch
  acute 45
  four-centred 230, 254, 281, 334, 360
  lancet 33, 81, 96
  ogee 34, 124, 252, 317–18
  relieving 23, 447
  segmental 93
  tower 67, 81, 153, 186, 29
  Tudor 247, 292, 387
  two-centred 32, 242, 322, 378
Architectural Association 287
ashlar 112, 182, 297, 303, 321

ballflower 159, 176, 216
basement course 115, 142, 208
base 331
  water-holding 100, 106
battlement *see* parapet
belfry 90
bell chamber 54, 60, 96, 109, 116, 189, 221
bell frame 31, 63, 96, 137
bell hatch 19, 27　, 67
bells 27, 31, 33, 263–264
Black Death 146, 185, 194, 229, 233
blue lias stone 172, 388, 410, 474,
boss 27, 175, 197, 211
brace 19
bracket 208, 257
brattishing 233, 298, 304, 346, 422
brickwork 12, 428
buttresses 20, 21–25, 22
  angle 21, 23, 100, 115, 138, 146, 230, 459
  composite 23–24, 388, 412
  diagonal 21, 124, 127, 322
  entasis 38
  flying 12, 20–25, 44, 45, 48, 49, 350, 435, 442
  gabled 24, 201
  octagonal clasping 23, 33, 90, 93, 310, 421, 436, 459
  setback 21, 142, 153, 163, 345
  square clasping 33, 85, 345, 372

capitals
  circular ring 154
  cushion 60, 72, 254
  foliate 75, 146, 172
  natural-leaf 106, 194
  scalloped 54
  stiff-leaf 154, 163
  waterleaf 153
casement 145, 233
change ringing 31, 264
Churches Conservation Trust 97
churchwardens' accounts 467
corbel
  running 19, 194
  table 106, 124
court mason 301
crenellation *see* parapet
crocket 38, 45, 46, 186, 237
cruciform plan 16, 198, 218, 331

dagger 145
Decorated style 352
diaper 431

dogtooth 142, 145, 154, 163
Domesday Book 53, 59, 115, 185

Early English style 10, 211, 224
East Mendip Group 25, 27, 28–29, 371, 378, 385, 391
embrasure 252, 321, 342, 385
entasis 21, 38, 189, 230

finial 146, 186
flint 18, 33, 60, 287, 294–297, 303–04, 415
flushwork 303–04, 310, 317
freestone 297, 416, 422, 479

gallery 19, 109
gargoyle 40, 124, 341
Gothic Revival 387, 439
Great Famine 182
Great Limestone Belt 10, 467
guild chapel 131, 287

herringbone masonry 60
hexagon 35, 46, 47
hood-mould 35, 297
hunky punk 391, 403

ironstone 54, 57, 128, 352, 478

Keuper sandstone 388, 392
knapped flint 303, 304, 439

label 372, 387
Lancet period 35
lantern 12, 45, 281, 334, 360
lesenes 54
licence to crenellate 24
limestone 40, 53
long and short work 54, 64
loophole 46
louvre 154, 245
lucarnes 44, 46, 82, 86, 112, 150
  alternating 38, 82, 112, 150, 159, 169, 191, 205, 237
  orthogonal 44, 47, 75, 179, 216, 342, 350, 356

Magnesian limestone 304
mason 483
mason's mark 303
merlon 25
Monasteries, Dissolution of the 9
monogram 292, 304
mouchette 32, 45
mullion 33, 34, 137

nailhead 81
nave 16, 18, 24
newel stair 31, 425, 431–32
niche 116, 134, 367
Norman
  architecture 16, 54, 63, 71
  construction 16, 31, 71, 76
  invasion 16
North Somerset Group 281–91, 371

oculi 59
octagon 35, 36, 38, 40, 45, 48, 49, 100, 257, 271, 278, 285, 359, 447, 457
octagonal drum 12, 47, 257, 282, 352
ogee curve 34, 45, 46

parapet 24–25, 40, 47
  crenellated 24, 341
  perforated 47, 75, 215
  stepped 24–25
  straight 25
Perpendicular style 34, 46, 229, 338, 345

pinnacle 119, 128
  hexagonal 25, 149, 194
  octagonal 25, 68, 175, 459
  square 24, 25, 132, 212, 258, 412
porch 211
putlog holes 297, 305, 315, 457

quatrefoil 45, 47, 109, 197, 338, 367

Redundant Churches Fund 478
Reformation 277, 287
Romanesque 68, 78, 100, 247
Rome, Break with 9
Roses, Wars of the 160, 359, 460
Round Tower Churches Society 59
Royal Commission on Historic Monuments 278, 426

shaft 54
  angle 171
  detached 81, 142, 160, 163
  engaged 71, 93, 131, 132
  nook 100
shaft rings 93, 154, 208
Society for the Protection of Ancient Building 287
sound chamber 221
sound hole *see* air hole
spire
  broach 9, 10, 36, 44, 68, 78, 81–82, 89, 104, 150, 164, 189
  flying 49, 215, 435–43
  hexagonal 35
  needle 12, 487
  oversailing 35, 37, 38, 39
  recessed 35, 40, 41–43, 44, 46, 207
  splay-footed 36
  timber 10, 35, 36, 99, 104–05
spire light *see* lucarne
squinch 68, 104, 112, 127, 369
stairs 30, 31–33, 182
  anticlockwise 33
  helical 31, 331
  spiral 31, 67, 109, 120
steeple 10–12, 11, 33, 50–51,
  definition of 10
string course 19, 115, 124, 145, 153, 160
supermullion 346
supertransom 32

Taylor, John & Co., bellfounder 149
tierceron vault 17, 27, 109, 233, 248, 257, 346
tower 18, 31
  central 16, 18, 78
  freestanding 99
  octagonal 18, 36
  rectangular 18, 25
  round 35, 59
  triangular 18
  west 18, 78, 247
tracery 32
  alternate 486
  blind 486
  Curvilinear 34, 38, 44, 46, 149, 159, 176, 186, 198, 229
  diamond 44, 47, 75, 112
  dropped 307
  Geometrical 46, 131, 171, 218
  intersecting 115
  Lancet 33
  panel 175, 179, 241
  plate 33
  squash 488
  subarcuated 34
  sub-reticulated 488
  'Y' 36, 112, 154, 164, 175, 318, 334
transennae 54
transept 16

transitional period 78, 153
transom 32, 34
trefoil 109, 134, 160, 208, 245
triforium 460
Tudor
  arch *see* arches
  flower 486, 488
  period 315, 377, 428
  rose 422
turret 364
turriform church 16, 57
tympanum 211

upright and flat work 54, 57, 64

vault 17, 27
  fan 278, 395
  lierne 27, 175, 454, 460
  pendant 444, 479
  quadripartite 27, 67, 163, 189, 205, 325
  sexpartite 27, 194
  tierceron 27, 109, 233
  wagon 422
vesica 215

weathervane 360, 457
West Mendip Group 24, 247, 378, 391
Whitechapel Bell Foundry Ltd 264
Wild Mare 464ff., 469, 482
wool church 294, 297, 325, 412, 444

Acknowledgments

This volume owes its existence entirely to the generosity of the wardens, clergy, architects, local historians and parishioners who allowed me unhindered access to their churches.

For facilitating my surveys during 2010 I wish to thank the Revd Jim Mynors and Jean Bussens at St Mary, Titchmarsh; the Revd Christopher Pearson, Jo Pearson and John Murphy at St Mary, Wilby; Mr and Mrs Nicholas Hart at St Mary the Virgin, Ketton; the Revd Dominic Barrington, Pat Edkins and Bruce Lamfort at St Peter and St Paul, Kettering; Mrs E. M. Halifax and her colleague David at St Peter, Lowick; Ann Gould and Michael Lee at St Mary and All Saints, Fotheringhay; Anne Willoughby at St Peter and St Paul, Eye; Lindy and Gordon Ellis at St Mary the Virgin, Redenhall; Alan Greening at St Edmund, Southwold; the Revd Gerard Moate at St Mary the Virgin, Dedham; Samantha Chrystal and Martin Weaver at St Peter and St Paul, Lavenham; Andrew Norman-Butler and Richard Channon at St Mary, Stoke-by-Nayland; Allen Matthews at St Edmund and St Mary, Ingatestone; Jolyon Booth at St Peter and St Paul, Salle; Bev Poole and John Webster at St Peter, Forncett St Peter; the Revd Nigel Whitehouse at St Mary, Whittlesey; the Revd Miranda Hayes at All Saints, Earls Barton; and Revd Sheena Bell, Rita Chantrell and Ted Buckby at St Peter, Raunds. I would also like to thank Brian Norris for arranging my visit to survey the steeple of St Peter, Oundle and to apologize for its absence from the current work.

I hope this omission will be rectified in a future volume.

My surveys during 2011 would not have been possible without the help of John Ward at St John the Baptist, Barnack; Jennifer Harvey and Will Thornton at St Helen, Brant Broughton; the Revd John Patrick at St Andrew, Ewerby; Tom Leyland and the masons and visitor assistants at St Botolph, Boston; Canon Stephen Holdaway, Shirley Keyes and Michael Day at St James, Louth; Father Jonathan Sibley at St Mary, Long Sutton; Morris Felton at St Mary, Stamford; Rita McCall and Debby Smith at St Mary Magdalene, Newark-on-Trent; Val York and Lynda Basford at St Wulfram, Grantham; Canon William Burke, William Baxter, and Parish Assistant, Jo Morris at St Kyneburgha, Castor; Brian Clarke, Conservation Manager at the Churches Conservation Trust responsible for St Mary's bell tower, West Walton; Julian Haynes at St Nicholas's Cathedral, Newcastle-upon-Tyne; Canon Stephen Cope, Phil Beavers, John Horrigan and John Marsden at St Mary, Tickhill; Richard Babington at St Patrick, Patrington; the Revd Rosamund Seal at All Saints, Moulton; Simon Johnson at All Saints, Laughton-en-le-Morthen; and Jenny and Peter Coombs at St Peter, North Rauceby.

For assisting with my surveys in 2013 I would like to thank James Mills of St Mary the Virgin, Witney; Dawn Keitley, Stephen Nixon and David Hallett at St James, Chipping Campden; Paul Harris and Shaun Ward of St Laurence, Ludlow; John Dunford and Carol Searle of St Peter, Evercreech; Revd Alistair Wheeler, Sheila Jenkins and Ruth Harris of St Cuthbert, Wells; Revd Jane Haslam, Sue Sayer and Dora Hinkley of St Mary, North Petherton; Alistair Weston and Anthea Brooks of St Giles, Leigh-on-Mendip; Margaret Laver and Nick at St Mary Magdalene, Taunton; Revd Ann Fulton and Richard Flood at St Mary, Kingston St Mary; Jonathan White and Trevor Trivett of St Mary, Adderbury; Revd Chris Harrington of St Andrew, Heckington; Ruth Rundle of St Mary, Oxford; Mike King and Caroline Pausch of the Bodleian Library, Oxford; Pat Terry of St Mary Redcliffe, Bristol; Tony Auty and Ges Clarke of Coventry Cathedral; and Michael Clews of Acanthus Clews Architects. I would also like to thank David Rockley and Bob Dennis for facilitating my survey at St Mary, Higham Ferrers in 2015.

I would like to thank Julian Honer of Thames & Hudson for his guidance and support, and particularly for his enthusiastic response to the first draft of this book, which had a significant influence on its final form. It has also been an enormous pleasure to work with Susanna Ingram and Sam Wythe of Thames & Hudson, and the graphic designers Peter Dawson and Namkwan Cho of Grade Design.

Final thanks are due to my family for their support throughout the past five years. In particular I would like to thank my wife, Julia, for her constant encouragement and advice, without which this book would never have been completed.